MAINE
A GUIDE 'DOWN EAST'

AMERICAN GUIDE SERIES

MAINE

A GUIDE 'DOWN EAST'

Written by Workers of the Federal Writers' Project of the Works Progress Administration for the State of Maine

---

SPONSORED BY THE MAINE DEVELOPMENT COMMISSION

Illustrated

917.41044
F293m
1972

HOUGHTON MIFFLIN COMPANY · BOSTON
The Riverside Press Cambridge

Republished 1972
SOMERSET PUBLISHERS — a Division of Scholarly Press, Inc.
22929 Industrial Drive East, St. Clair Shores, Michigan 48080

148006

COPYRIGHT, 1937, BY EVERETT F. GREATON
EXECUTIVE SECRETARY, MAINE DEVELOPMENT COMMISSION

ALL RIGHTS RESERVED INCLUDING THE RIGHT TO REPRODUCE
THIS BOOK OR PARTS THEREOF IN ANY FORM

```
Library of Congress Cataloging in Publication Data

Federal Writers' Project.  Maine.
   Maine, a guide 'Down East.'

   (American guide series)
   Bibliography:  p.
   1. Maine--Description and travel--Guide-books.
I. Series.
F17.3.F42  1972         917.41'04'4        72-884478
ISBN 0-403-02170-7
```

MAY 1 72

DEC 6 '73

𝔗𝔥𝔢 𝔑𝔦𝔳𝔢𝔯𝔰𝔦𝔡𝔢 𝔓𝔯𝔢𝔰𝔰
CAMBRIDGE · MASSACHUSETTS
PRINTED IN THE U.S.A.

PREFACE

AS THE perspective broadens on the picture of the American scene, past and present, being portrayed by the Federal Writers' Project of the Works Progress Administration in the American Guide Series, the State by State development of this vast panorama now brings into focus the Nation's northeast corner. How strong a light Maine's contribution can stand depends to a great extent upon one's point of view.

Whatever the point of view, it should be remembered that the presentation of the many diverse elements embodied in a State the size of Maine in a single volume is necessarily of a general nature, under the rather rigid requirements of a guidebook; therefore certain phases may not seem to be treated in this book as thoroughly as they merit. An attempt has been made, however, to capture the spirit of Maine life and to highlight the Maine scene for the visitor, without being either romantic or encyclopedic.

The Maine staff of the Writers' Project, like those of other States, has had its own particular trials and tribulations in preparing a Guide. In presenting facts about Maine, the staff's supreme effort at accuracy often bogged down before several accepted authorities who were at variance on a given point. Items accepted as fact were occasionally found to be legendary. A single word at any moment might creep up and baffle the most intrepid research worker. Verification and re-verification through the turbulent days of production had members of the personnel in various emotional states, from rank pessimism to apoplectic rage, with the State Director prepared momentarily to emulate Rumpelstiltskin of the folk tale.

Now, as the tumult and the shouting die, the things that stand out are the united elements that brought the book to completion. Among these were steadfast sincerity of purpose and seriousness of effort on the part of staff members, which elements stood by and overcame many seemingly insurmountable difficulties. Perhaps most important of all was the interest and sympathy, within and without the State, of persons who gave invaluable aid to the Project in many ways. Our gratitude and appreciation of their kindness are only exceeded by the regret that space forbids personal acknowledgment in every instance here.

Of the many persons, including officials of various public and private institutions, who have given valuable assistance, a word of especial appreciation is due to Albert A. Abrahamson, associate professor of Economics at Bowdoin College, whose sympathetic support while he was Maine Works Progress Administrator was a source of continual encouragement. Henry E. Dunnack and Mrs. Marion C. Fuller of the State Library, the librarian of the Portland Library, and the director of the Maine Historical Society at Portland were especially helpful in matters of reference and in giving the Writers' Project access to their collections. Josiah T. Tubby aided materially in connection with the architectural detail. The Gannett Publishing Company and the Maine Development Commission supplied many of the photographs used as illustrative material. The wholehearted co-operation of Everett F. Greaton, executive secretary of the Development Commission, has been a major factor in the entire production of the Guide.

Thanks are also due the following for expert advice and assistance in their special fields: H. L. Baldwin, of the Boston and Maine Railroad; Alexander M. Bower, Director of the L. D. M. Sweat Museum, Portland; Philip J. Brockway, Placement Director at the University of Maine; Freeman F. Burr, State Geologist; Judge Benjamin F. Cleaves, Secretary of Associated Industry; Harry B. Coe, of the Maine Publicity Bureau; Cressey and Allen Music Company, Portland; William S. Crowell, Maine W.P.A. Director of the Division of Operations, Portland; Mrs. Fanny Hardy Eckstorm, Brewer; Judge Edward K. Gould, State Historian; Professor Orren C. Hormell, of Bowdoin College; Captain Alfred E. Mulliken, of the State Planning Board; Dorothy Hay, of the Maine W.P.A. Art Project; Arthur H. Norton, Curator of the Portland Society of Natural History; Colonel Henry W. Owen, Bath; the late Professor Edward H. Perkins, of Colby College; John Calvin Stevens, Portland; George J. Stobie, State Fish and Game Commissioner; Professor William J. Wilkinson, of Colby College.

This volume was prepared under the supervision of Joseph Gaer, Editor-in-Chief of the New England Guides and Chief Field Supervisor of the Federal Writers' Project.

DORRIS A. WESTALL, *State Director*

CONTENTS

PREFACE	vii
By State Director, Federal Writers' Project	
ON USING THE GUIDE	xix
GENERAL INFORMATION	xxi
CALENDAR OF EVENTS	xxv

I. MAINE: THE GENERAL BACKGROUND

THE NATION'S NORTHEAST CORNER	3

    State Name   Soil
    Geography and   Water Resources
      Topography   Mineral Resources
    Climate   Flora
    Geology   Fauna

EARLIEST INHABITANTS: THE RED PAINT PEOPLE	20
THE ABNAKI INDIANS	24
HISTORY	28
The State Government	48
PINE, PAPER, AND POWER	50
THE MAINE FARM	63
FROM WATERWAYS TO AIRWAYS	68
RACIAL ELEMENTS	74
FOLKLORE AND FOLKWAYS	76
EDUCATION AND RELIGION	80
ARCHITECTURE	86
THE ARTS	94
HANDICRAFTS	108

II. SEAPORTS AND RIVER TOWNS
(City and Town Descriptions and City Tours)

Augusta	117
Bangor	129
Brunswick	139
Houlton	149
Lewiston-Auburn	155
Portland	163
Waterville	190

III. HIGH ROADS AND LOW ROADS (TOURS)
(Mile-by-Mile Description of the State's Highways)

Tour	1	From New Hampshire Line (Portsmouth) to Canadian Line (Clair, N.B.). US 1	201
		Sec. a. Portsmouth to Brunswick	204
		Sec. b. Brunswick to Belfast	215
		Sec. c. Belfast to Ellsworth	226
		Sec. d. Ellsworth to Calais	230
		Sec. e. Calais to Fort Kent	240
	1A	From Junction with US 1 (Kittery) to Cape Neddick. Unnumbered road and State 1A	249
	1B	From Junction with US 1 (Wells) to Biddeford. State 9	253
	1C	From Saco to Dunstan. State 9	255
	1D	From Brunswick to Bailey Island. State 24	257
	1E	From Bath to Fort Popham. State 209	259
	1F	From Woolwich to Five Islands. State 127	261
	1G	From Junction with US 1 (Wiscasset) to Southport. Local road and State 27	264
	1H	From Damariscotta to Pemaquid Point. State 129 and State 130	267

Contents

1J	From Junction with US 1 (Thomaston) to Port Clyde. State 131	271
1K	From Stockton Springs to Ellsworth. State 3	273
1L	From Junction with US 1 (West Gouldsboro) to Junction with US 1 (Gouldsboro). State 186	275
1M	From Whiting to Lubec (Treat's and Campobello Islands). State 189	276
1N	From Perry to Eastport. State 190	278
2	Mount Desert Island: From Ellsworth to Tremont. State 3, State 198, and State 102	281
3	From Ellsworth to Orland. State 15 and State 175	286
4	From Houlton to New Hampshire Line (Shelburne). US 2	292
4A	From Junction with US 2 (Rumford Center) to South Arm. State 5	303
5	From Brewer to Junction with US 1 (Calais). State 9, The Air Line	304
6	From Fort Kent to Mattawamkeag. State 11	308
7	From Medway to Greenville. State 157 and unnumbered road	311
8	From West Enfield to Bingham. State 11, State 155, and State 16	315
8A	From Milo to Katahdin Iron Works. State 221 and unnumbered road	319
9	From Waterville to Canadian Line (St. Zacharie, P.Q.). State 11, State 7, and State 15	320
10	From Brunswick to Canadian Line (Quebec, P.Q.). US 201	325
11	From New Hampshire Line (Dover) to Canadian Boundary (Quebec, P.Q.). State 4	336
11A	From Rangeley to Haines Landing. State 16	348
12	From Wiscasset to Stratton. State 27	349
13	From Hampden to Naples. US 202 (State 9, State 3) and State 11	353
14	From Portland to New Hampshire Line (Errol). State 26	360
15	From Saco to Bethel. State 5	366
16	From Belfast to South China. State 3	371

17	From Augusta to Rockland. State 17	372
18	From Portland to New Hampshire Line (Center Conway). US 302, The Roosevelt Trail	375
19	From Portland to New Hampshire Line (Freedom). State 25	382

ISLAND TOURS

1	Portland to the Islands of Casco Bay	386
	A. To Orr's Island	387
	B. To Gurnet	392
	C. To Birch Island	392
2	Boothbay Harbor to Squirrel Island	395
3	Boothbay Harbor to Monhegan Island	396
4	Rockland to Vinalhaven Island	398
5	Rockland to Swan Island	399
6	Belfast to Islesboro Island	401

IV. SPORTS AND RECREATION

INTRODUCTION	405
FISHING IN INLAND WATERS	407
Dennys River Fishing Trip	410
Moosehead Lake Fishing Trip	411
SALT-WATER FISHING	412
Tuna Fishing off Ogunquit	413
HUNTING	414
Animals	414
Birds	416
Game Areas	417
CANOEING	418
Allagash River Canoe Trip	419
East Branch Canoe Trip	422
Dead River and Moosehead Waters Canoe Trip	424
Rangeley Lakes Canoe Trip	426
Other Selected Canoe Trips	426

HIKING AND MOUNTAIN CLIMBING	427
Hunt Trail	429
Saddleback Mountain Trail	430
Squaw Mountain Trail	430
Mount Blue Trail	430
Other Selected Mountain Trails	431
RIDING	432
Saddle Trip out of Bangor	433
Saddle Trip out of Augusta	435
Other Selected Saddle Trails	436
YACHTING	437
WINTER SPORTS	438
CHRONOLOGY	443
SELECTED READING LIST	454
INDEX	459

ILLUSTRATIONS AND MAPS

GLIMPSES OF HISTORY *between 20 and 21*

'Red Paint' (Indian) vault at the Forks
Avanzato
Fort McClary, Kittery Point
Avanzato & Hubbard
Fort Halifax, Winslow
Avanzato & Hubbard
Old Oxford County Jail, Paris Hill
Avanzato & Hubbard
Fort Knox, Prospect
Avanzato & Hubbard
Casco Castle, Freeport
Avanzato
Fort Edgecomb, North Edgecomb
Avanzato
Fort Popham, Popham Beach
Avanzato
First pile bridge in North America, Sewall bridge at York
Maine Development Commission
Old covered bridge, Stillwater
Avanzato & Hubbard
Old powder house at Wiscasset
Avanzato & Hubbard

INDUSTRY, COASTAL AND INLAND *between 50 and 51*

The Falls, Veazie
Avanzato & Hubbard
Hayfield near Palermo
H. G. Hawes
Air view of the State Pier, Portland
Portland Maine Pub. Co.
Shipbuilding, Thomaston
Avanzato
On the Portland waterfront
Avanzato
Fish weirs, Bucksport
Avanzato
Old hull, Boothbay Harbor
Avanzato
Grounded schooners in Boothbay Harbor
Avanzato
Maine Seaboard Paper Company, Bucksport
Avanzato
Logging
Maine Development Commission
Large-scale potato digging, Aroostook County
Maine Development Commission
Blueberry pickers, Jonesboro
Avanzato
Packing lobster bait, Sebasco
Avanzato & Hubbard
Lobster pots
Maine Development Commission

OF ARCHITECTURAL INTEREST *between 96 and 97*

From the Old Stone Jail, Paris Hill
Avanzato & Hubbard
The hearth in the Means House, Portland
Avanzato & Pratt
Doorway, Major Reuben Colburn House, Pittston
W. Lincoln Highton
A farm cottage near Bar Harbor
W. Lincoln Highton
Carved door case, Means House, Portland
Avanzato & Pratt
St. John's Church, Brunswick
Avanzato
Nickels-Sortwell House, Wiscasset
W. Lincoln Highton
Ruggles House, Columbia Falls
Avanzato
Doorway of the Ruggles House
Avanzato
Stairway of the Black Mansion, Ellsworth
Avanzato
'Wedding Cake' House, Kennebunk
Avanzato & Pratt

IN TOWN AND CITY

between 190 and 191

Wiscasset Courthouse
 W. Lincoln Highton
Swans at Deering's Oaks, Portland
 Avanzato
Canal, Androscoggin Mills, Lewiston
 Avanzato & Hubbard
Jed Prouty Tavern, Bucksport
 Avanzato & Hubbard
Androscoggin River at Rumford
 Avanzato
East Machias, 1855, Photograph of painting
 Winfred C. Tracy
Heart of Bangor
 Portland Maine Pub. Co.
Portland business area
 Avanzato
Old cemetery at Waldoboro
 Avanzato
Blaine House (Governor's Mansion) Augusta
 Avanzato
The Capitol at Augusta
 Avanzato

CULTURAL LANDMARKS

between 252 and 253

Wadsworth-Longfellow House, Portland
 Portland Maine Pub. Co.
Longfellow's birthplace, Portland
 Avanzato & Hubbard
L. D. M. Sweat Museum, Portland
 Avanzato & Hubbard
Fryeburg Academy
 Maxcy
Administration Building, University of Maine, Orono
 Maxcy
Coburn Hall, Colby College, Waterville
 Avanzato & Hubbard
Rear wing of Bowdoin College Library, Brunswick
 W. Lincoln Highton
Madame Nordica's Homestead, Farmington
 Avanzato
Emma Eames House, Bath
 Avanzato & Hubbard
Quillcote, home of Kate Douglas Wiggin, Hollis
 Avanzato & Hubbard
Redington Museum, Waterville
 Avanzato & Hubbard
Home of Jacob Abbott, Farmington
 Avanzato & Hubbard
Sarah Orne Jewett Memorial, Berwick
 Avanzato

OLD HOUSES AND OLD CHURCHES

between 330 and 331

Second Parish Unitarian Church, Saco
 Avanzato & Pratt
Congregational Church, Kennebunkport
 Avanzato
Lady Pepperell Mansion at Kittery Point
 Portland Maine Pub. Co.
Church at Phippsburg
 Avanzato
McIntire Garrison House, York
 Avanzato & Hubbard
Swinging sign of Burnham Tavern, Machias
 Avanzato
Burnham Tavern, Machias
 Avanzato
Andrew Homestead, South Windham
 Avanzato & Hubbard
First Parish Unitarian Church, Kennebunk
 W. Lincoln Highton
A white church near Surry
 W. Lincoln Highton
Montpelier, Thomaston
 W. Lincoln Highton

Illustrations and Maps   xvii

LANDSCAPE AND SEASCAPE *between 392 and 393*
  Screw Auger Falls, Grafton   West Quoddy Head Light at sunset
    Maine Development Commission   *Maxcy*
  Tranquillity   Thunder Hole, Mount Desert Island
    Maine Development Commission   *W. Lincoln Highton*
  Off for a canoe trip, Megunticook Lake   Bar Harbor and Frenchman's Bay, from Cadillac Mountain
    Maine Development Commission   *W. Lincoln Highton*
  As shadows deepen   Riding the tide, Boothbay Harbor
    Maine Development Commission   *W. Lincoln Highton*
  Mount Desert Island as seen from Sullivan   Portland Head Light
    Avanzato   *New England Council*
  Parlin Pond, Somerset County   Snow scene
    Avanzato   *Maine Development Commission*

VACATIONLAND *between 422 and 423*
  Dreaming of a duck hunt   Almost in the net, Pleasant River, Gray
    Maine Development Commission   *Maxcy*
  On the bank of Sourdnahunk   Ice fishing, Sebago Lake
    Maxcy   *Avanzato*
  Trotting race on the ice at Camden   Autumn trail
    Maine Development Commission   *Maine Development Commission*
  Winter scene, near Fryeburg   Hunting party at camp, Kokadjo
    Maine Development Commission   *Maxcy*
  Morning paddle on Moosehead, Mount Kineo in the background   Camp site near Mount Katahdin
    Maine Development Commission   *Maine Development Commission*
  Sails in the sun   Popham Beach
    Maine Development Commission   *Avanzato*

MAPS
Augusta	124–125
Bangor	134–135
Brunswick	143
Houlton	153
Lewiston and Auburn	160–161
Portland	174–175
Waterville	193
Portland to Rockland Section of Maine Coast	200
Key to Maine Tours	202–203

ON USING THE GUIDE

General Information on the State contains practical information for the State as a whole; the introduction to each city and tour description also contains specific information of a practical nature.

The *Essay Section* of the Guide is designed to give a reasonably comprehensive survey of the State's natural setting, history, and social, economic, and cultural development. Limitations of space forbid elaborately detailed treatments of these subjects, but a classified bibliography is included in the book. A great many persons, places, events, and so forth, mentioned in the essays are treated at some length in the city and tour descriptions; these are found by reference to the index. 'Maine: A Guide Down East' is not only a practical travel book; it will also serve as a valuable reference work.

The nineteen Tour Descriptions are written, with a few exceptions, to follow the principal highways from south to north or from east to west. This orientation will not, of course, always coincide with the direction in which the tourist travels through the State. Since most visitors plan their trips as loop tours, it is clearly impossible to accommodate a standard pattern to individual desires, and, for the sake of uniformity, some more or less arbitrary procedure must be adopted. The descriptions are, however, written and printed in such a style that they may be followed in the reverse direction. In many cases the highway descriptions are useful to travelers on railroads. For such travelers the Transportation map on the back of the general State map will be convenient.

As a matter of convenience, lengthy *Descriptions of Cities and Towns* are removed from the tour sections of the book and separately grouped in alphabetical order. Maps indicate in numerical order the points of interest to be visited.

Each tour description contains cross-references to other tours crossing or branching from the route described; cross-references to all descriptions of cities and towns given special treatment; and cross-references to recreational activities and island trips.

Readers can find the descriptions of important routes by examining *Index to Tours* or the tour key map. As far as possible, each tour description follows a single main route; descriptions of minor routes branching from, or crossing, the main routes are in smaller type. The long route descriptions are divided into sections at important junctions.

Cumulative mileage is used on main and side tours, the mileage being counted from the beginning of each section or, on side tours, from the junction with the main route. The mileage notations are at best relative, since totals depend to some extent on the manner in which cars are driven — whether they cut around other cars, round curves on the inside or outside of the road, and so forth. Then, too, the totals will in the future vary from those in this book because of road-building in which curves will be eliminated and routes will be carried around cities and villages formerly on the routes.

Inter-State routes are described from and to the State Lines; in the *Index to Tours* and in the tour headings the names of the nearest out-of-State cities of importance on the routes are listed in parentheses to enable travelers readily to identify the routes.

Descriptions of points of interest in the larger towns and cities are numbered and arranged in the order in which they can conveniently be visited.

Points of interest in cities, towns, and villages have been indexed separately rather than under the names of such communities, because many persons know the name of a point of interest, but are doubtful as to the name of the community in which it is situated.

The *Sports and Recreation Section* of the Guide gives brief topical descriptions of the major recreational activities to be found in Maine. Two or more detailed trips are given under each topic, supplemented by a selected list. Condensed as it is, this section is a handy reference for those interested in the types of sports this State has to offer. A special Recreation map locates the activities treated in this section.

The *Island Tours* give the most convenient points of departure for a sail with stops among a number of the coastal islands.

GENERAL INFORMATION

Railroads. Interstate: Boston & Maine (B. & M.), Maine Central, Bangor & Aroostook (B.&A.), Canadian Pacific, Canadian National Rys. (Grand Trunk). Intrastate: Belfast & Moosehead Lake, Bridgton & Harrison.

Highways. 128 State highways. Four Federal highways as follows: US 1, Fort Kent to Florida; US 2, Woodstock, N.B., via Houlton; US 201, Quebec, Canada; US 202, Wilmington, Del.; US 302, Montpelier, Vt., via Conway, N.H. (See folding map.) State police patrol the highways.

Bus Lines. Intrastate: 218 lines connecting all principal cities and towns. Interstate: Boston & Maine Transportation Co. (Portland and Boston), Liberty Motor Tours, Inc. (Portland and Boston), Eastern Greyhound Lines, Inc., of New England (Portland and Boston, Portland and St. John, and St. Stephen, N.B., via Lewiston and Bangor), Maine & New Hampshire Stages (Portland and Berlin, N.H., via Lewiston and Rumford), Checker Cab Co. (Portland and Manchester, N.H., via Portsmouth, N.H., and Lawrence and Haverhill, Mass.), Vermont Transit (Portland and Montreal, via Fryeburg), Coast to Coast Stages (Greyhound Lines, national coverage).

Air Lines. Interstate and intrastate: Boston & Maine Airways, Inc. (airports at Bangor, Waterville, Augusta, Portland, and Boston); summer service between Bangor and Bar Harbor. Portland Municipal Airport for Portland Flying Service, charter service to all points in Maine and scheduled summer service between Rangeley Lakes and Portland. Northeast Airways, charter service and flying school.

Waterways. No regular interstate passenger service. Intrastate steamer and motorboat service; inquire at coastal points. Boat service also available on the larger lakes in the State.

Traffic Regulations. All passenger vehicles owned by non-residents and properly registered in their home States may be operated on a reciprocal basis for an unlimited period on the highways of the State.

Speed: On State highways motorists are required to drive at a careful and prudent speed, not to exceed 25 miles per hour in residential or built-up sections or 15 miles per hour when approaching within 50 feet and when crossing an intersection of ways, when the driver's view is obstructed, and when passing a school during school recess or at opening and closing hours. Speed limit varies in different cities and towns.

Lights: Every vehicle, whether stationary or in motion, must have a light attached to be visible from front and rear, and every vehicle having objects which project more than 5 feet from the rear must have a light on the rear of such objects.

Accidents: Every person operating a motor vehicle in any manner involved in an accident in which a person is killed or injured, or in which it appears that $50 or more property damage has been done, must report to local police and the Secretary of State.

Accommodations. The State is adequately provided with year-round hotels in larger communities and summer hotels at resorts; numerous tourist homes and overnight cabins and a few trailer camps along the main highways; sporting camps at lakes. Infrequent gas stations and accommodations in delimited areas only.

Climate. Variable, with temperatures ranging from the nineties in summer to below zero in winter. Cool evenings may be expected in summer, particularly along the coast. Clothing should be provided according to season.

Recreational Areas. All forms of outdoor sport are found in Maine's widely diversified recreational areas (*see Sports and Recreation*), with accommodations as a whole good throughout the State.

Amateur sports enthusiasts should inquire as to conditions and facilities as well as local laws, if any, for their particular sport in a specific locality.

For sea bathing, cove and inlet waters are comfortable, exposed points cold. Life guards posted and warning signs set where there is dangerous undertow. Fresh waters inland always warmer.

Occasional interstate and intrastate 'snow trains' operate during the winter to sports resorts, destinations depending upon snow and ice conditions in various sections.

Hunting and Fishing. Opportunities abound in most sections of the State. License required for hunting and for fishing inland waters. *Fishing:* non-resident, 3 days $1.65, 30 days $3.15, season $5.15; resident, season $1.15. *Hunting:* non-resident, season, small game $5.15, big game $15.15; resident, season $1.15, combination hunting and fishing $2.15. No license required for salt-water fishing; boats and equipment available at most coastal resorts. (For detailed information consult Maine State Fish and Game Commission or local game warden.)

Fires: The forest fire hazard in Maine cannot be too strongly emphasized, since nearly three-fourths of the State's entire area, or 15,000,000 acres, is woodland. The State law on this subject is as follows: 'Non-residents shall not kindle fires upon any unorganized township, while engaged in camping, fishing, or hunting from May first to December first, without being in charge of a registered guide, except at public camp sites maintained by the forestry department. No person shall kindle a fire on private property within a township without the consent of the owner. No person shall within a municipality or township set a bonfire or any kind of a fire which is not enclosed with a metal or a non-inflammable material without a written consent of the fire department.'

Wild Animals, Poisonous Plants. The only dangerous animals found in Maine are bears, bobcats, moose, and occasionally lynxes and wolves, which appear only in the northern part of the State in thickly wooded areas; they seldom attack unless they are wounded or cornered. Poison-ivy grows near stone walls, in pasture and woodland, and occasionally along the seashore.

Information Bureaus. The Maine Publicity Bureau, Danforth and St. John Sts., Portland, and branch offices at York Corner, Bangor House in Bangor, Fryeburg, and Damariscotta; the Maine Development Commission, State House, Augusta, which is establishing (1937) other information service units in various recreational centers in the State. Railroad stations and hotels are equipped to give information on travel, resorts, accommodations, recreational opportunities, and road conditions.

CALENDAR OF EVENTS

ANNUAL

Jan.	nfd*	Fryeburg	Winter Sports Carnival.
Jan.	nfd	Portland	Portland Automobile Exhibit (6 days).
Feb.	1st wk	Fort Fairfield	Winter Carnival (3 days).
Feb.	nfd	Rumford	Rumford Winter Carnival.
Feb.	nfd	Camden	Camden Winter Carnival.
Feb.	nfd	Bangor	Bangor–Caribou Ski Race.
March	1st wk	Presque Isle	Winter Carnival and Sportsmen's Show (5 days).
April	19	Brunswick	Maine Open Handicap Golf Tournament.
May	nfd	East Eddington	Bird-Dog Field Trials.
May	nfd	variable: Brunswick, Lewiston, Waterville, or Orono	State Intercollegiate Track Meet.
June	1st Sun.	Frenchville, St. Agatha, Van Buren, Fort Kent	Corpus Christi Procession.
June	1st part	Augusta	Boy Scout Camporee.
June	nfd	Old Orchard	Grand Circuit Horse Races (several days).
July	30–31	South Berwick	Dramatization of Gladys Hasty Carroll's 'As the Earth Turns.'
July	last half	variable	Maine Resident Amateur Golf Championship.
July	nfd	Boothbay Harbor	Yacht Regatta.
July	nfd	variable	State Championship Trap Shoot.
July	nfd odd years	Portland	Portland–Halifax Yacht Race.
July	nfd	Chebeague Island	Casco Bay Regatta.
July	nfd	Kennebunkport	Yacht Regatta.
Aug.	1st part	variable	Maine Summer Visitors' Day.
Aug.	latter part	Buxton	Dramatization of Kate Douglas Wiggin's 'Old Peabody Pew.'
Aug.	latter part	Portland	Portland–Monhegan Island Yacht Race.
Aug.	latter part	variable	Maine Open Amateur Golf Championship.

*no fixed date.

Calendar of Events

Aug.	latter part	Etna	Spiritualist Camp Meeting.
Aug.	nfd	variable	State of Maine Tennis Championship.
Aug.	nfd	Bar Harbor	Maritime Tennis Tournament.
Aug.	nfd	Bar Harbor	Floral Exhibit.
Aug.	nfd	Wiscasset	Open House Day.
Aug.	nfd	Old Orchard	Horse Racing (several days).
Aug.	nfd	variable	State Championship Skeet Shoot.
Aug.	nfd	variable	Three-Quarter Century Club.
Sept.	1	Lewiston	Maine State Fair (6 days).
Sept.	nfd	Damariscotta	Bird-Dog Field Trials.
Oct.	nfd	Portland	Maine State Dog Show.
Nov.	nfd	variable	Maine Pomological Seed Exhibit and Flower Show.
Nov.	nfd	Portland	Maine Poultry Show.
Spring Summer Fall months	nfd	Yarmouth Bridgton Waterville Winthrop Bowdoinham	Coon Hound Field Trials.

I. MAINE: THE GENERAL BACKGROUND

THE NATION'S NORTHEAST CORNER

STATE NAME

THE name of Maine, it is supposed by some historians, was bestowed as a tribute to England's Queen Henrietta Marie, feudal ruler of the French province of Meyne or Maine; some think the name was brought directly from France by early French colonists; others hold that it was a term used to distinguish the mainland from the coastal islands on which early fishermen dried their catch. The 'mainland' theory seems especially apt in view of the facts that the serrated coastline of the State measures some 2500 miles, and that there are more than 400 offshore islands, ranging in area from 1100 to 16,000 acres, with a host of lesser ones. Islanders to this day speak of 'the main.' Variously spelled Main, Mayn, and Mayne, the name was in use as early as 1622. Under the jurisdiction of Massachusetts, the region was known as 'The Province of Maine'; and when it was admitted to the Union in 1820, 'The State of Maine' became its official title. The inclusion of the word 'State' was probably inspired by the resounding title of the mother State, 'The Commonwealth of Massachusetts.'

GEOGRAPHY AND TOPOGRAPHY

Maine, the extreme northeastern State in the Union, is the only one adjoined by but a single sister State. Its comparatively isolated position may be accountable for an aloofness sometimes said to be characteristic of its people. The southern boundary of the State is the Atlantic Ocean; the eastern boundary follows the St. Croix River to its source, thence due north to the St. John River; the northern boundary extends roughly from the St. John Grand Falls along the river to Crown Monument; the western boundary extends from Crown Monument to the sea at the mouth of the Piscataqua River near Kittery Point. The State is thus

bordered only by the ocean, by Canada, and by New Hampshire. Early
charters defined none but the northern and southern boundaries, so that
Maine once theoretically extended, like other eastern colonies, to the
Pacific Ocean. Many bitter quarrels arose before the boundaries were
established by the Webster-Ashburton Treaty in 1842, when all disputed
territory on the Maine border was granted to England in return for concessions in other matters.

Maine is much the largest of the New England States, its total area
greatly exceeding that of New Hampshire, Vermont, Rhode Island, and
Connecticut combined. Approximately one-tenth of its area of 33,040
square miles consists of water. Large sections of the State are still unpopulated and have been only partially explored.

The terrain might be best described as a broad plateau running from
the western boundary to the northeast across the Rangeley and Moosehead Lake districts, gradually sloping eastward toward the Penobscot
River Basin and northward to the St. John. Toward the southeast, the
plateau gradually inclines to sea level. Occasional mountains rise from
the plateau to relatively high elevations, particularly in the central and
western parts of the State. Spread over the land surface is a remarkable
system of *eskers* or *kames*, known variously as 'horse-backs' or 'hog-
backs.' These are long ridges of gravel deposited by the receding glacier
of the Ice Age, extending from one mile to a hundred and fifty miles in
length. From these deposits come most of the State's road material, and
in many cases the roads follow their course.

Contrary to popular impression in other sections of the country, Maine
is a mountainous State. Cadillac Mountain, with an almost sheer rise of
1532 feet, has the highest elevation of any point on the Atlantic coast
north of Rio de Janeiro in Brazil. Mount Katahdin, 5267 feet, is Maine's
highest peak; from its base on the shores of the Penobscot, about 800 feet
above sea level, it appears to be as high as some of the Rockies, which rise
from a plateau 5000 to 7000 feet above sea level. According to Maine
State Planning Board figures, Hamlin Peak on Katahdin, 4751 feet, is the
second highest mountain; 'Old Spec' in Grafton Township, 4250 feet, and
Sugarloaf in Crockertown, 4237 feet, are the third and fourth highest
respectively; and there are five other mountains in the State more than
4000 feet and 97 more than 3000 feet in height. Most of these are more or
less conical in form, their sloping sides being heavily wooded and always
green. Outstanding mountains are Bigelow, Saddleback, Abraham,
Russell, Haystack, and Whitecap (in Franklin County). Often, as in the
case of Mount Kineo, the best known are not the highest mountains.

Maine has well over 2200 lakes and ponds. Moosehead Lake, about forty miles long and from two to ten miles wide, is one of the country's largest bodies of fresh water lying wholly within the boundaries of a single State. More than 5100 rivers and streams appear on the State map; of these, four are navigable for considerable distances into the interior. Augusta, on the Kennebec, and Bangor, on the Penobscot, are accessible to seagoing vessels. Only six of Maine's sixteen counties are not open to water traffic. The longest rivers are the St. John, 211 miles from its source in St. John Pond to the point where it leaves the Maine boundary; the St. Croix, 75 miles; the Penobscot, 350 miles; the Kennebec, 150 miles; the Androscoggin, 175 miles; and the Saco, 104 miles. The streams of Maine, marked by narrow and rapid currents, and fed by springs and the melting snows of the forest regions, are perhaps the most important natural resource of the State.

CLIMATE

Maine's climate is invigorating and healthful. The mean annual temperature is 44° or 45° F. in the southern part and 39° in the extreme northern part of the State. The summer heat is less than that of Massachusetts, New York, Wisconsin, Iowa, and the Dakotas by about 32 per cent; and the Maine winter, proverbial for harshness, is actually not so severe as that experienced in many places of corresponding latitude. The lowest temperatures on record range from about − 16° on the coast to − 36° at Greenville in the Moosehead region. The longest periods of extreme cold occur near Van Buren, where freezing temperature is recorded on an average of 208 days a year; whereas at Portland, the average is only 132 days a year. Freezing temperatures at night are common throughout the State in October and November, continuing to mid-April or early May. The average temperature from June to October is 60° or higher in most parts of the State. July, the warmest month, has an average temperature ranging from 60° at Eastport to 69° in the interior. Daily maximum temperatures run as high as 80° in central sections. The highest recorded temperature, 105°, occurred at Bridgton in July, 1911. On the coast, and during the summer in particular, the temperature is modified considerably by the sea winds. An Arctic current surging in from the east, sometimes bearing icebergs, prevents the climate of this region from being ameliorated by the Gulf Stream.

Days of sunshine in Maine average close to sixty per cent for the year, and monthly averages vary little during the change of seasons, though frequently the winter has more sunny days than the summer. Fog is common on the coast during the summer, especially in July and August, but dense night fogs usually burn off during the day.

Maine's growing season ranges from about 150 to 170 days along the coast, while thirty miles inland it is about thirty days shorter. The shortest season is found near Farmington, where the average is only 103 days.

Precipitation is well distributed over the State throughout the year, with a range of from forty to forty-six inches annually. The average annual snowfall varies from about seventy inches on the coast to about one hundred inches in the northern part of the State. Near the coast the snow is often completely melted in midwinter. Destructive storms are rare in Maine — in nearly sixty years the State has had only six severe blizzards and one hurricane. There are commonly from six to twelve heavy rainfalls each year, usually accompanied by northeast winds. The State is relatively free from serious floods and droughts; the 1936 flood was exceptionally serious.

GEOLOGY

The bed-rock of Maine, with little exception, was formed during the Pre-Cambrian and Paleozoic Eras. The Pre-Cambrian rocks occur principally in the western and southern parts of the State, and consist for the most part of sandstones, shales, and limestones greatly altered by weathering and erosion. No fossils have been found in them. Where they were compacted to a crystalline rock by the intrusion of molten granite, valuable mineral deposits resulted, particularly pegmatite, coarse-grained masses of feldspar and quartz crystallized under special conditions. Where these deposits are quarried for feldspar, many gems and rare minerals are found. The pegmatite area extends northwest across the State from Popham, at the mouth of the Kennebec River, to the wilderness of northern Oxford County. Famous mineral localities in this belt are Topsham, Mount Apatite, Mount Mica, Paris, Buckfield, and Newry.

In Maine, the Paleozoic rocks differ from the Pre-Cambrian in being less altered by metamorphism and in the fact that they contain fossils. Covering the central and northern parts of the State, they represent most of the periods into which the Paleozoic era is divided. The first of these periods, the Cambrian, is represented by beds of quartzite and slate. Cambrian fossils have been found only on the east branch of the Penobscot River. Ordovician beds have not been clearly distinguished from earlier Cambrian and the later Silurian. Most sedimentary rocks in central and northern Maine are Silurian, principally shales, slates, and impure limestones. Silurian fossils have been found in central Maine, along the coast at Eastport, and in Aroostook. Good exposures of these rocks are common along the State highways of central and northern Maine.

Rock of the Devonian period is represented by a belt of sandstone, the Moose River formation, extending from west of Moosehead Lake to northern Aroostook. This is probably the most fossiliferous formation in the State, including those glacial boulders containing 'clam shells' which attract attention in central and southern Maine. In the Devonian period an earth movement took place that resulted in the intrusion of great bodies of granite called 'batholiths'; and most of Maine's granite seems to have come into position at this time. Volcanoes left beds of lava and ash, erupting first in the Silurian period. Deposits are found along the coast from Penobscot Bay to Eastport. Of these, Mount Kineo is the most famous; others are East Kennebago, Big and Little Spencers, the Coburn Hills in northeastern Aroostook, Haystack, and the Quoggy Joe Mountains near Presque Isle.

The youngest Paleozoic rocks in Maine are the quartzite slates bordering the coast from Kittery to Casco Bay. The Paleozoic Era ended in the Appalachian Revolution, when mountains once more rose across New England.

The Mesozoic Era is almost without record in Maine. From studies made elsewhere, it is believed that this part of New England was then an upland undergoing erosion. The Cenozoic Era was also a time of erosion. Weaker rocks were worn away, and the more resistant were left standing as mountains on a plain that extended over the State. Later uplifts of the land followed; hills and valleys were carved from the plain. The even skyline formed by the merging of the hilltops represents today the level of the old plain. Katahdin, the Blue Mountains in the western part of the State, and the Mount Desert Mountains on the coast are examples of the more resistant rock.

During the Ice Age that ended the Cenozoic Era, Maine was covered by a continental glacier similar to those of Greenland and Antarctica today. Moving southward, the glacier smoothed off the irregularities of the hills. It left large deposits of gravel, sand, and clay; and these, damming the pre-glacial valleys, brought about the formation of lakes and waterfalls.

Rivers were thrown from their former courses to flow over bed-rock ridges and through narrow gorges, creating today's resources of water-power. During the thousands of years of the Ice Age, the weight of the glacier depressed New England below its former level. As water from the melting ice poured into the ocean, the latter's level rose, and it flooded the coastal lowland up into the larger valleys. The receding flood left a layer of sand over the clays along the coast, creating sand plains. In some places, notably Freeport and Leeds, this sand, freed of vegetation and blown by the wind, has formed so-called deserts.

Finally the land rose to about the present level and the sea retreated. The coastline has not receded to its pre-glacial position; the lower valleys are still flooded, and the highlands form the projecting headlands and islands of the present Maine coast.

SOIL

It is believed that at the time of the first settlements, nearly the entire land area of Maine was occupied by forests. More than three-fourths of this area is still tree-covered; and of the cleared land, about one-third is devoted to agricultural use. The number of acres under cultivation has decreased considerably in the last fifty years, due chiefly to the competition arising from intensive specialization on various crops in other parts of the country. The soil types are exceedingly varied, the most productive being the famous potato-growing district in Aroostook County, one of the richest in the country.

Soil erosion presents a more serious problem than is commonly realized, though the continuous vegetative cover and the rolling topography generally prevailing in most parts of the State keep the spread of barren lands to a minimum. The most significant damage from this cause may be seen along the sloping banks of the St. John River and its tributaries, where brush and grass were thoroughly removed in the cultivation of the land and nothing was left to prevent the top-soil from being washed from the hillsides during heavy rains. Much has been done in recent years, in the way of proper scientific planting and reforestation in many parts of Maine, toward controlling this problem. The same may also be said in regard to the control and eradication of insect pests and plant diseases.

Despite adverse soil conditions, the comparatively short growing period, and competition from more productive areas, Maine has been in the past and continues to be primarily an agricultural State. Its temperate climate during the growing season, with a minimum of natural hazards, and its well-distributed and unfailing rainfall, offset some of the disadvantages noted above.

WATER RESOURCES

Maine's coast is indented by many safe harbors and pierced by many navigable rivers upon which the tidewater sometimes reaches as far as sixty miles inland. The water-power of the rivers is the State's greatest natural resource. The rainfall is sufficient to insure the maintenance of a constant flow of water, and the sources of the rivers are high enough above sea level so that there are many natural falls or favorable opportunities for the development of power plants. At the present time, less than half the potential power of the State has been developed. Conservative estimates put the possible water-power production at 1,200,000 horse-power.

Approximately ninety-five per cent of the hydro-electric power produced in Maine is controlled by three companies, which by means of interconnecting lines form a super-power system nearly blanketing the State. Numerous storage dams and steam generators enable these companies to supply a nearly constant output of power, regardless of natural hazards. The greater part of the industrial water-power is used by the paper manufacturing companies, while several power developments formerly used by lumber and pulp mills are now idle. A comprehensive program of watershed forestation and damming for flood control is being carried on both by the State and by private companies. There have been created on several of the rivers in the State, mainly by raising and controlling the flow from several of the larger lakes, fifty reservoirs with a capacity of more than two hundred billion cubic feet. State and Federal commissions have made studies of the most important rivers and lakes in regard to potential power, drainage, and storage.

A new and unusual development of Maine's water-power is the projected dam at Passamaquoddy Bay, where the presence of unique coastal pools and a twenty-foot average tidal fall make this one of the very few sites in the world that are feasible for the development of tidal power.

MINERAL RESOURCES

In Maine are found ores of most metals, as well as useful non-metallic minerals such as quartz, feldspar, mica, graphite, asbestos, and gem stones such as tourmalines, beryl, amethyst, garnet, and topaz. At least one mineral, beryllonite, has been found nowhere outside Maine, and this State has yielded the finest emerald beryl ever found in the United States. In mineral production, Maine stands about midway among the States, the average annual yield being valued at about $6,000,000. One-third of the State is still unexplored in respect to mineral resources, and only limited areas have received adequate investigation.

Granite has always been one of the State's important products. In 1934 there were as many as ninety scattered quarries — not all, however, being worked regularly. Their products range from rubble, concrete aggregate, and paving stones, to great blocks from which may be cut monolithic columns. Maine granites show great variation in color, grain, and texture, and have been used in the construction of many buildings and monuments throughout the country.

Limestone deposits are found in many parts of the State, and are used particularly in the manufacture of cement; outstanding for this product is the Penobscot Bay region. In Monson and Brownville, slate quarrying has been carried on for many years. Feldspar is mined in Oxford, Androscoggin, Cumberland, Sagadahoc, and Lincoln Counties. The raw 'spar' is ground in mills at Topsham and West Paris, and shipped away for use in the manufacture of porcelains, scouring powders, and soap. Great reserves of it exist, many deposits being still unexplored. The rock known as pegmatite, or 'giant granite,' from which commercial feldspar is obtained, also yields mica, quartz, beryl, most gems, and many rare and interesting minerals. The clays that form enormous deposits around Passamaquoddy and Penobscot Bays and elsewhere are particularly rich and promising sources of bauxite, the only ore of aluminum now in commercial use. The existence of cheap power, which the completed tide-harnessing project at Quoddy would supply, should make the development of this important resource economically possible.

Of other metals, platinum and iridium are reported, although the possibility of obtaining them for commercial use is not yet clear. Gold is present in small quantities in a number of places; in at least fifty localities, placer or stream gold is plentiful enough to offer fair returns to the prospector who is willing to pan persistently. Gold quartz of promising content has been found in sufficient quantity to warrant at least small-scale mining. Silver is found in most of the lead and zinc localities, and in the copper ores at Bluehill. Some pure silver has been mined at Sullivan and elsewhere. That there are considerable bodies of lead and zinc of definite value has been known since they were first mined in 1860. The most successful copper mine is at Bluehill, last worked in 1917-18, where more than two million pounds of copper have been obtained. Other valuable copper deposits are known to exist in northern Franklin County. Iron ore has been worked on a small scale for local use for a great many years, notably at Clinton. At the Katahdin Iron Works, extensive operations were carried on for a long time; but since the opening of the great deposits in Michigan and Minnesota, small-scale iron operations have been impracticable. It is now thought that Maine bodies of iron ore may be developed successfully in conjunction with some other metal, such as molybdenum, for the production of alloys in demand by the steel industry. Deposits of bog iron ore are numerous, and there are other types of promising quality, particularly in Aroostook County. A large company at the present time (1937) is engaged near Cooper in the production of molybdenum.

Cassiterite, the usual ore of tin, has been found at a number of the feldspar localities, and a definite attempt to mine it has been made at Winslow. This is the only source of tin known to exist in the United States. Antimony ore, pyrite, marcasite, and pyrrhotite (the three latter being valuable sources for sulphite) are widely distributed throughout the State, as are ores of manganese.

Deposits of diatomaceous earth occur at Bluehill, Beddington, Phillips, Houlton, and generally throughout the lake country. This material, consisting of the shells of microscopic plants, is nearly pure silica. It is a plastic white powder deposited in bogs and ponds, and much in demand for filtering, scouring, and wall insulation. The Phillips deposit is now under operation.

The probability that coal or oil will ever be found in Maine in commercial quantities is slight, but the State contains a large and practically untapped fuel reserve in its deposits of peat. Bogs containing peat suitable for fuel purposes, from a few acres to several square miles in size, are found all over the State. The bogs also provide a moss that has considerable commercial importance to florists and nurserymen.

Asbestos of commercial grade is known to exist in large quantities in Maine, particularly in the Spencer Lake region, near Eustis on the Arnold Trail, and in northern Penobscot County.

FLORA

Maine's flora falls into two classifications: Canadian in the cooler sections, and Transition in the warmer. Isolated areas of one type of flora are sometimes found well within the confines of the other.

Alpine flora occurs on the upper reaches of Mount Katahdin and other high peaks. A blue-leaf birch is known to occur in these regions; and mountain white birch and mountain alder are found on Katahdin. Among the more hardy plants in Alpine areas are Lapland diapensia, Alpine bearberry, Greenland starwort, lance-leaved painted-cup, Alpine trailing azalea, Alpine holy-grass, narrow-leaved Labrador tea, blue spear-grass, Lapland rose-bay, and fir club-moss.

The Transition flora grows below Cape Elizabeth on the coast, in all of York County, and in the southern sections of counties west of the Penobscot River, a great wooded area of pine and oak. The Canadian flora is found along the coast north of Scarboro, and inland above an imaginary line running from Umbagog Lake in the Rangeley section to Mars Hill in lower Aroostook County.

The white pine, sometimes called the 'masting pine' because in Colonial times the larger trees were reserved for masts for the Royal Navy, is displayed on the State seal and gives Maine its name of 'the Pine Tree State.' These pines are known to reach a height of two hundred and forty feet, and a diameter of six feet at the butt. Once abundant in groves throughout the State, they now exist for the most part only in second growth.

Hemlock, its bark valuable for tanning, is plentiful. Balsam fir, sometimes grown commercially for the Christmas-tree trade, runs wild all over the State; the wood, imparting no flavor, is commonly used in making butter-tubs. Red oak occurs in all parts of Maine except the extreme north. The burr oak is common in the central part of Maine. White or paper birch is prevalent throughout all but southern Maine, often appearing in nearly pure stands of considerable area. The yellow birch is the largest native birch, though often not so tall as the white.

There is an abundance of sugar or rock maple. Mountain maple is seen all over Maine; and box elder (also a maple), planted as an ornamental tree in southern sections, grows wild in Aroostook County. Tupelo, or black gum, is not found north of Waterville.

Pitch pine is the principal tree appearing on large tracts of the Brunswick district. On the shore of Bauneg Beg Lake in North Berwick there is a large stand of pitch pine, many of the old trees of great size. Coast white cedar is found only in York County, as is butternut, an introduced tree and the only species of walnut growing in Maine. Shagbark is found occasionally in southern sections and as far east as Woolwich, and the nuts are sold in market.

Maine's oldest and most valuable trees are the white oaks, some of them well over five hundred years old. The bark is used for tanning. Black or yellow oak is confined to the southerly coastal regions, and the swamp white oak and the chestnut oak are found locally in southern Maine. Chestnuts are not common, most of them having been destroyed by the chestnut-bark disease. The slippery elm, so named because of its mucilaginous inner bark, and the sassafras are little known. The sycamore or buttonwood is found along streams in southern Maine. Poison sumach is found as a shrub in the Transition area.

Trees common throughout the State are tamarack, locally called by its Indian name of hackmatack; red spruce, most abundant of Maine's conifers, growing as high as eighty feet, and valued as the principal wood used for paper pulp (it also supplies spruce gum, which is gathered from September to June); white spruce, called 'skunk spruce' by lumbermen because of the odor of its foliage; white cedar or arborvitae, growing in dense stands on swampy ground; and black willow, the largest and most conspicuous American willow.

The rapid-growing aspen poplar, used for book-paper pulp, is abundant, being often found in nearly pure stands. The large-tooth aspen and the balsam poplar are common throughout the State. Ironwood, or hornbeam, is widely distributed, though not abundant. Common beech is plentiful.

The white or American elm, one of Maine's largest and most graceful trees, is common throughout this State, as it is through all of New England. It is generally planted near houses, many persons believing that it diverts lightning. Fully as beautiful is the mountain ash. Wild cherry, found in every section, is of little value except as cover for burned-over areas. But the wild black cherry, widely distributed though not abundant, provides one of the State's most valuable furniture woods. The red plum is occasionally grafted and often used as an ornamental tree. Striped maple or moosewood is a lovely tree found all over Maine. The silver maple grows near the coast, its sap being used to make an inferior maple syrup. Red maple is the most abundant, growing in swamp lands. The basswood, a species of linden, is attractive for its flowers, which are popular with honey bees. The black ash and white ash, the latter a valuable timber tree, are prominent all over the State.

A rare shrub called the prostrate savin or trailing yew is found on Monhegan Island, and other islands east of Casco Bay; on Mount Desert Island it is called the Bar Harbor juniper.

Among the common shrubs of Maine are the speckled alder, in swamp and pasture lands; witch hazel, bordering most forest areas; several nearly indistinguishable varieties of shad-bush, whose white sweet-scented flowers are the first harbingers of spring and whose wood is used in making fishing rods; the hawthorn or thorn apple; the chokecherry, found along farm fence-rows; and the staghorn sumach.

Trees introduced into Maine with marked success include the Norway spruce, the Colorado or blue spruce, and three poplars — the white poplar, the cottonwood or Carolina poplar, and the Lombardy poplar. The European beech, the copper beech, and the English elm have been introduced largely as ornamental trees, as has the European mountain ash or rowan tree, superior to the native mountain ash in brilliancy of coloring, its bright red berries remaining well into the winter. The black locust and the honey locust were brought into the southern part of Maine, and the latter is now common in the vicinity of Paris and elsewhere. The horse-chestnut was introduced from Asia by way of southern Europe.

In Washington and Hancock Counties low-bush blueberries have developed considerable commercial importance. Mountain cranberries grow abundantly in the Mount Desert region, having long since given their name to the Cranberry Isles, and the large bog cranberry is widely distributed in marshlands over the State. Most flowers and blossoming shrubs common to the north temperate zone can be found, generally more brilliantly colored along the shore than in the interior. Among the more widely distributed species of the Mount Desert region are American wood anemone, New England aster (introduced), seaside aster, swamp aster, wild bergamot, American bittersweet, black-eyed Susan, bluet, tall meadow-cup, clover, sweet clover, white ox-eye daisy, and dandelion. Others are blueflag, Canada goldenrod, salt marsh goldenrod, fragrant goldenrod, goldthread, blue-eyed grass, harebell, orange hawkweed, false heather, hepatica, and Indian pipe.

Familiar are Jack-in-the-pulpit, Joe-pye, seaside knotgrass, sea lavender, and wild lily-of-the-valley or Canada mayflower. The most common wayside lilies are the Canada lily and American turk's cap (introduced). Mayflower, the trailing arbutus, ushers in the spring. Of the many orchids native to Maine, the best known are arethusa, common and yellow lady-slippers, rose pogonia, and the small purple and white orchids. Devil's paintbrush grows in profusion, spreading through the fields to the grief of the farmer and the joy of the passer-by. Other bright flowers are the scarlet pimpernel, the sea or marsh pink, the swamp pink, pitcherplant, and pokeweed (rare). Maine's two rhododendrons are not common, but the well-known rhodora, immortalized by Emerson, is no less beautiful. Best known of the wild roses are the swamp rose, meadow rose, and wild brier rose. Purple trillium and painted trillium, yellow violet, common purple violet, blue marsh violet, and sweet white violet, the giant sunflower (escaped from gardens), eglantine or sweetbrier, woodbine, and yellow wood-sorrel are all commonly found.[1]

FAUNA

In wide areas still untouched by urban civilization, Maine is today rich in many of the species of birds, mammals, and fish that attracted the early explorers. On the other hand, man's continual slaughter of wild life has caused extinction of the great auk, the passenger pigeon, the heath hen, and the Eskimo curlew, and has driven the timber wolf, the panther, the wild turkey, and the swan out of the State. Northern white-tailed deer, first noticed in numbers about 1900, have increased in the State. Some believe that the migration of the caribou, not seen south of the Canadian border for nearly thirty years, is due to the close cropping of forest vegetation by the deer. The Maine State Planning Board reports that even with an annual kill of more than sixteen thousand, deer are more plentiful now than they were a hundred years ago. American elk, commonly called moose from the Indian *musu*, are found in all the northern counties. Since they have been protected by law, they have even been seen along the coast, particularly in the marshy woodlands of Waldo County. Black or cinnamon bear, sometimes of large size, are numerous along the beech ridges of northern Aroostook. Bay lynx or bobcat are known in every county, especially in Aroostook. But panther and catamount are no more; and the gray wolf, once known all over Maine, was last seen in 1930 in Bluehill. The Canada lynx, the so-called loup-cervier, is not uncommon in the Magalloway region.

[1] The Portland Society of Natural History, 22 Elm St., has on exhibition in its Herbarium well-authenticated specimens of practically all plants known to occur in Maine. The State Park in Augusta also has a fine collection of plants, shrubs, and trees of the State.

Except in the extreme southwestern part, Canadian beaver are increasing throughout the State. There are more than two thousand of them in the Penobscot east country alone. It is now considered that the damage done by beavers to streams and woods is more than offset by the value of their dammed-up pools in aiding fire-fighters. Muskrat, American otter, American mink, fisher, and marten (known as American sable) are all to be found in Maine. The Maine weasel is the only animal to which the State has given its name. Raccoon are increasing. Skunk are common, as are red foxes in all their color variations — cross, silver, and black. The hare (commonly called snowshoe rabbit), gray rabbit, confined principally to York and Cumberland Counties, northern red squirrel, northern gray squirrel, and chipmunk are plentiful. Woodchucks abound; but hedgehogs, generally known as American porcupine, have been nearly exterminated since a bounty was placed on them. The common shrew and the mole or short-tailed shrew are known generally, and a rare species of shrew, Sorex thompsoni, has been found in Brunswick, Norway, and Waterville. Maine has the brown bat, the little brown bat, hoary bat, and silver-haired bat; as well as the wood mouse, field mouse, and house mouse. In the Alpine areas are found the chickaree, northern flying squirrel, Canada porcupine, Labrador jumping mouse, and Canadian white-footed mouse.

Pickering's tree frog sounds the first note of spring; there are also the bullfrog, yellow-throated green frog, marsh or pickerel frog, woodfrog, common or leopard frog, and tree frog — the latter often erroneously called tree toad. Maine has several varieties of turtle — the snapping turtle, mud turtle or painted terrapin, yellow-spotted or speckled tortoise, wood tortoise, and box tortoise — the latter very rare this far north. According to Dr. Ditmars, of the New York Zoological Park, there are no poisonous snakes in Maine, but there are, of course, the small garter snake, striped snake, ribbon snake, green snake, water snake, and an occasional milk adder.

Seals abound along the coast above Casco Bay, and there is a bounty on them in the Passamaquoddy Bay region. Finback whales are increasing along the lower Maine coast; in 1936 as many as twenty or thirty at a time were seen off Wells and Kennebunk early in March. Maine has a wide variety of game fish (*see Sports and Recreation*). There is an abundance of lobster and clams along the coast, the small white Scarboro clam being particularly succulent. Shore or rock crabs, scallops, shrimps, and mussels are all plentiful.

Of the three hundred and twenty-one known species of birds within the

State, twenty-six are permanent residents. In Maine's Canadian areas are the Acadian chickadee and the eastern snow bunting, while Bicknell's thrush is known to breed on the upper reaches of the mountains. From Labrador to the Everglades, the nests of only twenty northern bald-headed eagles have ever been discovered, and of these two are at Georgetown and one at Newcastle; they are occupied each year. There are known to be at least twenty-five giant eagles in the hills near Cherryfield. A great golden eagle was reported as seen on Eagle Cliff at Carrying Place near Bingham in 1933, and others have been seen in the past at Penobscot. The Canada ruffed grouse, erroneously called partridge, is Maine's most highly prized game bird. The Fish and Game Commissioner annually liberates thousands of ring-necked pheasants along the coastal range from North Berwick to Cherryfield, and this species is increasing rapidly. The common mallard or wild duck and the common black duck breed here, and are the most popular game birds among the waterfowl.

The more common birds of Maine's Canadian fauna are the brown creeper, American golden-eye, eastern goshawk, rusty grackle, Holboell's grebe, Canada jay (known otherwise as moosebird and whisky jay), slate-colored junco, eastern golden-crowned kinglet, common loon, red-breasted nuthatch, old-squaw, snowy owl, spruce partridge, northern raven, red-poll, red-backed sandpiper, white-winged scoter, pine siskin, Acadian sharp-tailed sparrow, Lincoln's sparrow, white-throated sparrow, olive-backed thrush, water thrush, black-poll warbler, myrtle warbler, yellow palm warbler, eastern winter wren, and lesser yellow-legs.

A partial list of the birds of Maine's Transition fauna includes the eastern least bittern (rare), red-winged blackbird, eastern bluebird, bobolink, eastern bob-white, black-capped chickadee, American crossbill, eastern crow, yellow-billed cuckoo (very rare), eastern mourning dove, alder flycatcher, olive-sided flycatcher, bronzed grackle, ruffed grouse, bluejay, eastern belted kingfisher, eastern meadowlark, white-breasted nuthatch, Baltimore oriole, orchard oriole (very rare), barred or hoot owl, screech owl, short-eared owl, saw-whet owl, domestic pigeon, eastern or American robin, spotted sandpiper, eastern field sparrow (uncommon), Savannah sparrow, sharp-tailed sparrow, starling, bank swallow, barn swallow, cliff swallow, tree swallow, scarlet tanager, brown thrasher or song thrush, wood thrush (rare), and hermit thrush, towhee, Philadelphia vireo, black-throated blue warbler, black and yellow or magnolia warbler, whippoorwill, northern downy woodpecker, northern hairy woodpecker, northern pileated woodpecker (uncommon), and eastern house wren.

The domestic pigeon, the pheasant, the English sparrow, and the starling have been introduced into the State.

The islands off the Maine coast constitute the great nursery of the North Atlantic sea birds. Green Island, six or seven miles out from Cliff Island in Casco Bay, is a favorite breeding place for gulls. Of one hundred and eleven offshore islands visited in 1931, seventy-seven had nesting colonies of American herring gulls, which are so common in Washington County as to be an annoyance to blueberry growers. In 1934, herring gulls decimated a colony of double-crested cormorants on a Penobscot Bay island, and have wiped out other colonies. Great numbers of them breed inland on Gull Island in Moosehead Lake, and many others on Rangeley waters. The black guillemot was found breeding on twenty-four islands. The American merganser stays close to fresh water, and is a coast resident in winter only. The red-breasted merganser or sea robin, common in coastal areas of Canadian fauna, is found inland in summer. Leach's petrel is the only representative of its order known to breed along the Maine coast. The northern raven is common along the upper coast, but is rarely seen inland. The great black-backed gulls are just returning to Maine after an absence of many years. Double-crested cormorants breed regularly on Penobscot Bay islands.

American eider ducks, the largest of Maine sea ducks, now breed here and are seen frequently near the outer islands in January. Canada goose, commonly called wild goose, was once known to breed as far south as Mere Point, instead of entirely in northern Quebec, and the Arctic as at present. Merrymeeting Bay is one of the most important way stations on the coast for them in the spring. From early March until the middle of May, they gather there in great numbers.

Terns are often blamed for the mischief done by herring gulls, but this is a mistake since they eat live gamey food only. The common tern breeds on most of Maine's grassy islands. On Upper Sugar Loaf Island, not far from Popham Beach, there are colonies of common tern and roseate tern, the latter now increasing from a distinct rarity. Puffins, also called sea parrots, are likewise increasing; the best place south of the Gulf of St. Lawrence to see these interesting birds is on Machias Seal Island, where there is a colony of several hundred. On the same island are many razor-billed auks, which apparently do not breed there. Although the island belongs to the United States, the light there is operated by the Canadian Government, and permission to visit the island must be obtained from the Canadian Department of Marine, at St. John, New Brunswick.

The laughing gull is rare, but there is a colony of this species in Penobscot Bay. The common loon breeds in inland ponds. The great blue herons are increasing rapidly on the coast; one of their large breeding grounds, Bartlett's Island near Bar Harbor, is protected by the Federal Government. Black-crowned night herons are also more frequently seen than formerly. And the osprey is no longer uncommon on the Maine coast.[1]

[1] The Portland Society of Natural History, 22 Elm St., Portland, maintains an exhibition room with a complete collection of representative birds of the State. Information and suggestions about bird colonies may be obtained from the director.

EARLIEST INHABITANTS: THE RED PAINT PEOPLE

SCATTERED all along the Maine coast and through southern New England are great shell-heaps, said to have been accumulated from one thousand to five thousand years ago. Allowing a century for a certain number of inches of mold upon the mounds, archeologists have been able in some degree to estimate their great age. They were made, it is supposed, by the Indians who in summer migrated to the coast and reaped mighty harvests from the sea. The heaps are so large that it must have required centuries of clam-feasts for their accumulation. They are valuable because of the many interesting relics found buried in them.

But these are not the earliest archeological remains. Throughout the central and eastern part of the State, along the coast and in stream valleys, Maine inhabitants have been discovering since the time of the first settlers the graves of a prehistoric people who had either become extinct or had evolved a new civilization by the time the shell-heaps began to take form. While these graves occur most thickly in Maine, the area in which they are found extends throughout New England and into Canada. Because the shell-heaps contain remains of mollusks now found only in southern waters and the surface of the land along the shore seems to have suffered some change, we know that this early people existed in a time when geologic evolution was still going on and the climate of New England was much warmer than it is now. That this people antedated those who made the shell-heaps is ascertained by the difference in the quality and workmanship of the weapons found in the shell-heaps and in the graves.

Very little actually is known about these earliest inhabitants. They are called the Red Paint People because each of the discovered graves contains a quantity (varying from less than two quarts to a bushel) of a brilliant red ocher (powdered hematite). Sometimes, though rarely, this pigment is shaded to yellow or brown, the yellow coloration often found in the graves having been created by iron corrosion. The fact of 'ocher burial' is not particularly distinctive, however, because it is a characteristic of certain early peoples the world over. Paleolithic graves in France and Australia show evidences of ocher; later races in New England

GLIMPSES OF HISTORY

ARCHEOLOGICAL discoveries casting greater light on our earliest inhabitants are still being made. Tombs such as that pictured here add new facts to old history, help round out the mysterious story of Maine's paleolithic people, the so-called 'Red Paint' Indians.

Visible monuments to the early struggles of the pioneers to establish themselves on the first frontiers of America are the old forts with their stockades and blockhouses, many of which remain standing today. Scattered along the coastline for protection of harbors and port towns there are many more substantial, but long since abandoned, fortifications dating back to the Civil War and the War of 1812. Good examples of these are Fort Knox and Fort Popham, pictured here.

More useful and more beautiful landmarks appear in many of the State's old bridges, for they record development and progress in times of peace. The Old Covered Bridge at Stillwater is of a type fast disappearing from the New England scene.

Casco Castle is another significant landmark, all that is left of a great amusement resort which knew considerable popularity in the heyday of the streetcar.

RED PAINT (INDIAN) VAULT AT THE FORKS

FORT McCLARY.

FORT HALIFAX, WINSLOW

OLD OXFORD COUNTY JAIL, PARIS HILL

FORT KNOX

CASCO CASTLE, FREEPORT

FORT EDGECOMB, NORTH EDGECOMB

FORT POPHAM, POPHAM BEACH

FIRST PILE BRIDGE IN NORTH AMERICA, SEWALL BRIDGE AT YORK

OLD COVERED BRIDGE, STILLWATER

OLD POWDER HOUSE AT WISCASSET

occasionally painted their bodies with it, and sometimes it is found in their graves. The now extinct Beothuks of Newfoundland had a particular predilection for red ocher, smearing not only their bodies with it but their huts, their canoes, and all their possessions; and for this they were called Red Indians by early explorers. The Beothuks were a comparatively modern race, however, and there are no evidences of paleolithic man in this section of the New World. Maine's Red Paint People, apparently very early in the development of neolithic culture, may be regarded then as a cultural unit. Many of their stone artifacts are unlike those of the Indians who later occupied the same territory; certain of their implements, indeed, were made of different materials from any used by later Stone Age people. The similarity of their culture, as manifested by the stone implements, to that of the Eskimo has led some writers to suggest that they were not red Indians at all; others, influenced by their common use of ocher, see in them early relatives to the Beothuks of Newfoundland.

At any rate, they were a somewhat widely scattered and highly developed people. Although not agriculturalists like later Indians who occupied the same territory, they had developed a high degree of craftsmanship. They used fire-making tools of a sort superior to those of the later Indians; their implements imply skill in woodworking, and they made boats, possibly log dug-outs, in which they seem to have traveled considerable distances.

Since the time of the earliest white settlements, red ocher graves have been found. Early New Englanders regarded them with extreme suspicion; to find one was considered an evil omen. Hardy adventurers, however, unearthing the paint, put it to good advantage when they saw that it gave a satisfactory finish to their furniture and other woodwork. At first the ocher deposits, always accompanied as they were by strange stone weapons, were not imagined to be associated with burials. Only more recently have bone dust and even tiny fragments of undecayed human bone been discovered in them. A startling find was turned up not long ago when city employees of Waterville, in excavating a public road, uncovered two skeletons preserved in red ocher; when the air struck them, they visibly turned to dust, all but a few fragments that are now preserved in Portland's Museum of Natural History.

In the late nineteenth century, Dr. Augustus C. Hamlin of Bangor interested archeologists at Harvard University's Peabody Museum in investigating the Maine Red Paint cemeteries. The first extensive exploration was carried on by the Peabody Museum, and later work was done by expeditions from Phillips Academy of Andover, Massachusetts.

Some of the best collections of Red Paint artifacts are at the Peabody Museum and at Phillips Andover Academy — the largest at the latter. The findings in about thirty Red Paint cemeteries have been recorded; the best reference is C. C. Willoughby's 'Antiquities of the New England Indians' (Peabody Museum Publications, 1935). Of course, many other cemeteries have been found of which there is no record, the relics having been dug out and lost or scattered. All the recorded cemeteries in Maine are near water navigable for small boats. All but two are on stream banks or near the coast; the two exceptions, although on high ground, lie beside what may once have been the course of a stream now deflected in another direction. The recorded cemeteries are as follows: on Penobscot waters, one each in Howland, Eddington, Hampden, Milford, and Swanville; two each in Bucksport, Bradley, Old Town, and Passadumkeag; five in Orland. On the Kennebec, one each at Kineo, Oakland, Waterville, and Winslow. Three have been found on the Georges River in the townships of Warren and Union; and two in Ellsworth on the Union River. One was discovered at Pemaquid Pond in Bristol, one in Bluehill on Bluehill Bay, and one at Sullivan Falls on Frenchman's Bay. These are among the oldest archeological remains of North America, and are therefore of great importance.

Most of the graves contain knives and spear-points, but not arrowheads — apparently the bow and arrow were not known to these people. Red Paint or, more properly, pre-Algonquian, implements consist mainly of adze blades, pear-shaped sinkers, fire-making sets, chipped-flint knives, long slender lance-heads and projectile points, sharpening stones, a few slate pendants in the form of a whale's tail, and several perforated slate ceremonials commonly called 'bannerstones.' These types are found to a rather less extent throughout New England and portions of the adjacent territory. Instruments are found in varying numbers and of uneven workmanship, though of a fairly consistent high-grade quality. Some of them are covered with what seem to be inscriptions or designs, which no doubt are meant to tell some story. In at least one case, inscriptions were made on a thin tablet intended for no other use.

But notwithstanding the discoveries made, no one has yet been able to say where these people came from, how long they were here, or whence and why they departed. Of them we really know nothing — what they looked like, how they lived, even how they talked. The sources of certain types of minerals and rocks which they used have never been discovered. Their uses of certain specialized artifacts are unknown to us. No one has ever found the sites of any of their villages. A theory which would ac-

Earliest Inhabitants: The Red Paint People 23

count for their disappearance may be that they inhabited regions of the coast now sunk below the sea, and that they themselves or their villages were borne away in a tidal wave. Certain geological discoveries in regard to the sinking of the Maine coastal level seem to bear out this hypothesis. Furthermore, some archeologists believe that many of the cemeteries are not on their original sites, having apparently been hastily moved *en masse*, as if it were that the sacred objects contained in the graves had to be carried to higher ground to escape the ravages of floods. This explanation does not, however, account for the disappearance of those pre-Algonquian people who lived further inland in what are now other states than Maine. The supposition that they were an early branch of the Beothuks of Newfoundland, whom they seem to resemble in many ways, is not proved. Some scientists continue to believe that the Red Paint People were driven into the North, and are now represented there by the Eskimos, many of whose ceremonial instruments closely resemble artifacts which have been unearthed in Maine.

There are collections of Red Paint artifacts in the State Museum at Augusta, the Bangor Historical Society exhibit at the Bangor Public Library, the Maine Historical Society at Portland, Dr. J. Howard Wilson's Museum at Castine, the Knox County Historical Society at Thomaston, and the Robert Abbe Memorial Museum at Bar Harbor. Many other extensive and interesting collections are in the possession of individual persons or families throughout the State.

THE ABNAKI INDIANS

OF THE many tribes of Indians that inhabited Maine at the time of the white man's coming in the early seventeenth century, only two remain, the Penobscots and the Passamaquoddies. They are all that is left of the Abnaki or Wabenaki, 'people of the dawn,' a once powerful nation of more than twenty tribes inhabiting parts of Canada, Maine, New Hampshire, and northern Massachusetts. The Passamaquoddies and the Indians of the St. John River are descendants of the ancient Etchimins, a seafaring people who were originally a branch of the Abnaki. However much they differ in customs and in dialect, both of these tribes derive their language and principal characteristics from a common Algonquian stock. They are the least disintegrated racially of all the present-day descendants of New England's aborigines; many families among them have a heritage unmixed with white or African blood. But their tribal distinctions have long since become blurred by inter-association with the remnants of other vanishing tribes, and by the effacing of many of their traditions under the stress of modern industrial life. Also, to please the tourist trade, they have been tempted into adopting manners and costumes entirely foreign to them.

The Penobscots live mainly on a reservation at Indian or Panawamske Island in Old Town; the Passamaquoddies or Pestumokadyik ('people who spear pollock') have reservations at Pleasant Point near Eastport, and at Peter Dana Point near Princeton. There are probably not many more than one thousand Indians of fairly unadulterated stock in Maine today, the majority of whom live at Old Town; but that is a considerably larger number than was estimated to be living in the State one hundred years ago.

The Indians of Maine have always been a peaceful and friendly people, living chiefly by agricultural activities. It was they who kept the early settlers of Massachusetts alive by sending presents of food to the settlements. They were ultimately aroused to violent action only by the prolonged aggression of the settlers and by being forced to take sides in the English-French struggles. And when they did rise up, whole tribes were remorselessly exterminated. It is a significant fact that the custom of taking scalps was not known among them until instituted by English officers. Today they live harmoniously among themselves and with their white neighbors, and in general maintain high standards of conduct. The Indian villages are autonomous in government, each electing its own officers. The tribes may send representatives to the State legislature, although the people are not citizens. Most of them are deeply religious, the majority being communicants of the Roman Catholic Church. They have their own convents and schools, the latter supported largely by the State. Each summer the Old Town Indians present an historical pageant. They commonly dress in conventional costume and speak English, own their homes and radios, drive automobiles, and indeed are indistinguishable from their white neighbors. They are, however, taught to speak their native language at an early age, and much is being done among them to preserve their native traditions and arts.

For most of them, no great effort is required to make a living, since each family has an inherited income from funds held in trust for them. In 1786, a treaty confirmed to the Indians certain lands as well as liberal gifts. These lands were sold at various times to Massachusetts and to Maine for considerable sums, to be held for the Indians and their descendants. In 1818, Massachusetts agreed to pay the Penobscots the following: one six-pounder cannon, one swivel, fifty good knives, two hundred yards of calico, two drums, four rifles, one box of pipes, three hundred yards of ribbon; and in October of each year, 'as long as the Penobscots shall remain a nation,' to give them five hundred bushels of corn, fifteen barrels of wheat, seven barrels of clear pork, one hogshead of molasses, one hundred yards of double-width broadcloth (red one year and blue the next), fifty good blankets, one hundred pounds of gunpowder, six boxes of chocolate, one hundred and fifty pounds of tobacco, and fifty dollars in silver — or their equivalents. Since for many years certain families did not draw upon the sums due them, among the Indians today there must be persons of considerable wealth. The average Indian takes up his income in trade at the agency store. The Penobscot tribe receives further compensation from corporations which make use of the Indian shore on the river above Old Town; the tribe owns all of the one hundred and forty-six islands above Old Town, with a total area of forty-five hundred acres. The Indians work as river-drivers and as guides to hunting and fishing parties, or they make baskets which they sell to tourists.

The Penobscots are sometimes erroneously called Tarantines, a name for an earlier tribe or group of tribes. The Puritans called the Abnaki 'Tarrateens.' Among the Penobscots today live descendants of Baron de Castin, who married the daughter of Chief Madockowando 'of the

Tarantines,' but the latter was an Etchimin and not a Penobscot. It may be that the Pentagoets of Castine, the remnants of the so-called Tarantines of de Castin, have moved to Old Town and joined with the Penobscots. There was once a clan or totem system among the tribes, but it is now largely obliterated. The Bear Clan, one of the largest groups, still has its representatives among both Passamaquoddies and Penobscots, who say the clan originated with a lost child who was brought up by a mother bear. Joseph Polis, the Penobscot Indian who served as Thoreau's guide in the Maine woods, used a drawing of a bear on his canoe as a personal emblem. Old Governor Neptune, the Penobscot descendant of a long line of chiefs and governors, used the sign of the snake, signifying mental prowess.

The office of chief or governor (president, sachem, or sagamore) was formerly held for life, but in 1862 it became annually elective. Even so, the same man often held the position through life, and from him it might pass to his son — as in the Attean family. Dissension at the elections gave rise to the 'Old Party' and 'New Party,' which now take turns in electing officers each year. One of the most famous governors was Joseph Orono, for whom the town of Orono was named — a blue-eyed Indian believed to be a natural son of the Baron de Castin. He is said to have saved Maine for the Union by rallying his men to the aid of the whites in the wars with the Mohawks. He died in 1801, at the reputed age of one hundred and thirteen. Another Indian equally revered was the saintly Aspinquid, one of John Eliot's converts who did much toward spreading Christianity and peace among the New England tribes. It was the Abnaki, indeed, who of the North American Indians first embraced Christianity. In the past, Saint Aspinquid's grave-marker could be found, high on Mount Agamenticus; it bore this inscription:

> Present Useful: Absent Wanted:
> Lived Desired: Died Lamented.

The Indians no longer practice the old crafts of making fish-nets, spears, bows and arrows, wampum, carved pipes, and pottery; and such things as canoes, snowshoes, and moccasins, formerly produced by them, are now more efficiently turned out in large factories. But the Penobscots still excel in basket-making. The Passamaquoddies also make baskets, but are more expert as fishermen and hunters. Baskets are usually made from the flexible wood of the brown ash, although basswood and sweetgrass are also used. With the Penobscot women, sewing is a fine art; but weaving seems always to have been unknown to them. Lovely designs are made by threading dyed quills upon cloth or leather. Some striking examples of Indian carving and painting are occasionally seen.

The Abnaki Indians

Before their movements were restricted by white settlers, the Indians used to wander with the seasons, according to the location of food supplies. In the spring they went to the rivers for alewives, shad, and salmon; on the banks they planted corn, squash, beans, and other vegetables. In June they went to the sea for porpoise and seal in order to get oil and skins, and for the eggs and nestlings of sea birds; they dried clams and lobsters, and stored them for winter use. In September they returned to the river valleys to harvest their crops, and in October they went into the big woods to hunt. Before Christmas they held their annual thanksgiving feast for not less than two weeks. Our national Thanksgiving Day is a direct imitation of the Indian festival, even to the kinds of food served — turkey, cranberries, Indian pudding. When snow came they went into the deep woods hunting for moose and setting traps. Before the ice broke up in March or April they had made their spring catch of otter and beaver. When the ice broke and the river was clear they were ready for the catching of muskrat; they could start out in their canoes to fish and to go to the lower valleys for the planting.

Throughout Maine, the scene has actually changed but little since the time of the Indians' supremacy. Today, in the great woods or by the lonely shore, one can see them in the mind's eye, a people historically great neither in numbers nor in deeds, but industrious, loyal, and generous.

HISTORY

THE ancient Norse sagas tell of the voyages of Eric the Red and those of his son, Leif the Lucky, and how Eric, banished from Norway in A.D. 981, sailed westward and came to a fabulous 'green' land across the sea. Eric got no farther than Greenland; but Leif, in A.D. 1000, reached the mainland, the coast of which he followed southward to a place he called Vinland, from the abundance of grapes he found there. This, it is believed, was Mount Hope Bay in Rhode Island. In 1003, 1006, 1007, and 1011, it is believed, other Norse navigators reached the shores of what is now called New England. These early rovers must have been the first Europeans to explore the coast of that region, and, therefore, they would have been the first to sail along the coast of Maine.

Nearly five hundred years passed before white men again came to the New World. In 1496, the Cabots — John and his sons, Lewis, Sebastian, and Sancius — were named in letters patent granted to them by King Henry VII of England 'to discover and occupy isles or countries of the heathen or infidels before unknown to Christians, accounting to the king for a fifth part of the profit upon their return to the port of Bristol.' In 1497-99, the Cabots made a number of voyages, the reports of which, excepting the later testimony of Sebastian (which has been challenged by authorities of the period), are very meager. However, the records established beyond question that the Cabots did reach and explore the Atlantic coastline of the North American continent. One old Bristol record reads: 'In the year 1497, June 24, on St. John's Day, was Newfoundland found by Bristol men, in a ship called the "Matthew."' Again, one entry from the privy purse expenses of Henry VII reads: '£10 to hym that found the new isle.' A map, drawn by Sebastian Cabot, of the Atlantic coastline from 60° to 40° N. lat., is preserved. It is obvious, therefore, that the Cabot expeditions explored southward along the Maine coast, and if the reports of Sebastian Cabot's conversation with Butringarius, the Pope's legate, be true, he went as far as the Carolinas. At all events, it was upon the Cabot discoveries that England in the seventeenth century based its claim to North America.

But England did not follow up the Cabot discoveries immediately, and for many years the land was left open to the subsequent exploration of the

French. Giovanni da Verrazzano, an Italian navigator in the service of France, reached the Maine coast in 1524. He was followed a year later by the Spaniard, Gomez. But these two, like other early explorers, were looking for the gold and rich tropical lands of the Indies, and therefore took no interest in what they found here. About 1527, Jean Allefonsce, a French master pilot, explored and described the cape and river of Norumbega (probably the Penobscot). Thevet, a French geographer, on a return voyage from Brazil to France in 1556, followed the North American coast from Florida to Newfoundland. But perhaps the first white men actually to tread Maine soil for any distance were three English sailors, survivors in 1568 of an unsuccessful expedition to Mexico led by the freebooter, Sir John Hawkins. Put ashore from their ship in the Gulf of Mexico, they made their way north and east, eventually reaching Maine. Traveling up the coast to the St. John River, they encountered a French trading vessel, on which they returned to Europe. One of these men, David Ingram, wrote a highly colored account of his adventures, in which he tells of visiting the fabulous city of Norumbega.

In 1580, Captain John Walker, sailing in the employ of Sir Humphrey Gilbert, dropped anchor in Penobscot Bay. In 1602, Bartholomew Gosnold, in command of the English vessel 'Concord,' reached Maine's southern shores. In 1603, Captain Martin Pring, with the vessels 'Speedwell' and 'Discoverer,' entered Penobscot Bay, and thence sailed southward.

After considerable French exploration in America, Pierre du Guast, the Sieur de Monts, accompanied by Samuel de Champlain and the Baron de Poutrincourt, in 1604 established a settlement on an island at the mouth of the river that Champlain called the St. Croix. In the fall of that year, Champlain set forth to explore the coast westward, going by the great island to which he gave the name of Mount Desert ('Isle des Monts Deserts'), up the Penobscot River to the site of present-day Bangor, and then up the Kennebec the following summer. In 1606, de Monts and Champlain sailed down the coast as far as Cape Cod, looking for a more satisfactory site for colonization than the St. Croix island. They found nothing, however, that pleased them more than a place across the Bay of Fundy which they had ceded to de Poutrincourt and called Port Royal. De Monts accordingly moved his colony there and returned to France.

In 1605, Captain George Waymouth visited Monhegan and explored the coast. He secured valuable information about the country and assistance for future colonization by kidnaping five Indians, whom he took back to England. To this crime, subsequent Indian hostility to white men on the Maine coast may be attributed. In 1606, James I granted a charter to the Plymouth Company for the lands lying between the 41st and 45th parallels; and in 1607, the Popham Colony, called St. George, was set up on Sagadahoc Peninsula at the mouth of the Kennebec, where the village of Popham now stands. Although unsuccessful, this was the beginning of British colonization in New England. Before very long, many English settlers had established themselves along these rugged shores. The first Dutch came to Maine in 1609, when Henry Hudson, commissioned by the Netherlands to search for a northwest passage to the Indies, hove to in Casco Bay, to repair his storm-battered vessel, the 'Half-Moon.' The Maine Indians received him kindly, but Hudson requited their hospitality by robbing them of much of their supplies. So fierce was their resentment that Hudson was forced to put from shore. He sailed southward and eventually came into New York waters, ascending the North (Hudson) River until he was sure it was not an 'arm of the sea.'

Soon the French were sending missionaries to the new world. In 1611, Father Pierre Biard founded an Indian Mission on the Penobscot, ancestor of the present Indian church at Oldtown. In 1613, a Jesuit colony was established on Mount Desert Island, only to be dispersed shortly by the crew of an English vessel commanded by Captain Samuel Argall, who had come from Virginia ostensibly for a supply of fish. At the mission on Mount Desert, Fathers Biard and Masse had established the first monastery east of California in what is now the United States. In spite of active English hostility, the French continued to set up scattered settlements, notably on the Penobscot and St. Croix Rivers and at Machias. But these settlements did not prosper. Most of the immigrants of this period were unenterprising and ignorant, or they were French gentlemen in search of gold or glory and with no desire to build homes in a new world. The chief interest in America on the part of the French was always the opportunity for trade in furs with the savages.

Captain John Smith arrived at Monhegan from England in 1614. Exploring the coast from the Penobscot to Cape Cod, he made a map of the territory, which he called New England. On November 3, 1620, a new charter, known as the 'Great Patent,' was granted to the Plymouth Company under a changed corporate name, 'The Council for Plymouth,' otherwise called 'The Council for New England.' It made the company 'absolute owners of a domain containing more than a million square miles,' between 40° and 48° N. lat., which was to be called New England. From this company the Pilgrims derived their patent to the Plymouth Colony.

The Pilgrims, arriving in America in 1620, reported a thriving fishing and trading post at Pemaquid. There were probably trading settlements at both Pemaquid and Monhegan from the beginning of the century, but Father Biard wrote that the Indians had driven the English out of Pemaquid in 1608–09. In 1622, the Council for New England gave to Sir Ferdinando Gorges and Captain John Mason the land between the Merrimac and the Kennebec, which, the indenture stated, 'they intend to call *The Province of Maine.*' Permanent settlements were established — Monhegan in 1622, Saco in 1623, and York (as Agamenticus) about 1624. All the early settlements were easily accessible to shipping, and they grew rapidly.

In 1629, Mason and Gorges divided their province between them, with the Piscataqua River as middle boundary. Mason's land was called New Hampshire, Gorges's New Somersetshire. Mason died in London in 1635, and Gorges, who had become governor-general of all New England in the same year, when the Plymouth (England) Council surrendered its patent, was in 1639 granted from King Charles I a charter to the territory between the Piscataqua and Kennebec Rivers, extending one hundred and twenty miles north and south. The charter specified that the tract should 'forever be called the Province and Countie of Maine and not by any other name whatsoever.' The political status of the 'Province' was that of a palatinate, of which Gorges was lord palatine, a vassal enjoying royal privileges. Thus Maine was for a time under purely feudal tenure. Gorges appointed a council of seven colonists to administer the province and act as court. This body superseded the judicial court established March 28, 1636, by William Gorges, Sir Ferdinando's nephew, for a short time governor of New Somersetshire. In 1640, under Thomas Gorges, Sir Ferdinando's son, sent over to Maine as his deputy, the first recorded body representative of the people in a permanent Maine settlement met at Saco, in a court having both legislative and judicial functions for the 1400 whites west of the Penobscot River.

In 1630, the Plymouth Council, among other dispensations of New England lands, granted a large tract of territory in Maine to John Beauchamp of London and Thomas Leverett, a Boston merchant. This grant, comprising about a million acres, was called the Muscongus Patent. Eighty-nine years later, Samuel Waldo was given half the grant 'for services rendered.' Eventually he bought the other half, and the grant became known as the Waldo Patent. In 1753, Waldo imported a party of immigrants from Germany, who founded a large and prosperous settlement, the present Waldoboro. The initials 'N.W.P.,' occasionally found in modern deeds and titles, signify 'North of Waldo Patent.'

French trading continued in the land east of the Penobscot, and the English trading posts at Machias and Penobscot were seized by the French in 1634 and 1635. But the region from Penobscot to Port Royal was finally subdued in 1654 by the English under Major Sedgwick; and in 1635 the whole of the Acadian province was confirmed to the English, who held it for thirteen years. Nevertheless, French missionary activities among the Indians were continued in Maine, chiefly by the Jesuits, but also by the Franciscans and Dominicans. In 1646, Father Gabriel Druillettes, accompanied by Indian converts, entered the Norridgewock territory — the first white man to travel down the Kennebec to the ocean from the north. The trail he blazed was followed by Fathers Aubry and Loyard, the Bigots, and Father Rasle, who in turn succeeded him at his post, the most important seat of missionary work in Maine.

In the meantime, the settlement originally called Agamenticus was endowed with a city charter in 1642 under the name of Gorgeana. In 1652, it was reorganized as a town, and its name changed to York. The first town in Maine was Kittery, organized in 1647. From the beginning, each settlement ordered its own affairs, local government being far more important than central. The courts were informal, deriving their authority from the general consent of the colonists.

In 1643, the four New England Colonies had formed an alliance for mutual defense, excluding therefrom the Gorges settlements. After the death of Gorges in 1647, the inhabitants of Kittery, Gorgeana (later York), Wells, Cape Porpoise (now Kennebunkport), Saco, Casco (now Portland), and Scarborough formed themselves into a body politic, experimenting with self-rule; but, soon realizing the importance of a strong and settled government, they became freemen of Massachusetts in 1652 on liberal terms. They sent representatives to the Massachusetts General Court (1653), suffered no requirement of church membership or tithe, and paid only town and county taxes (the southern section of the Province of Maine became in 1658 the separate and autonomous County of Yorkshire). By this time the democratic form of government based on the town meeting was already assured and strong throughout New England.

Upon the restoration of Charles II to the English throne in 1660, Ferdinando Gorges, a grandson of Sir Ferdinando, claimed Maine as his property. Four years later, a royal order bade Massachusetts restore the Province to him. The investigating commissioners set up a government in the Province, but they were shortly recalled; and in 1668, Massachusetts assumed control. A clear title was finally secured when the Gorges rights were sold to an agent for Massachusetts, May 6, 1677.

The territory (known variously as Sagadahoc and New Castle) from Pemaquid to the St. Croix was granted to the Duke of York in 1664, together with the New Netherland. As the County of Cornwall it retained a slight connection with New York; in 1674, both Colonies were united under the rule of Sir Edmund Andros. Yet a supplementary article added to the Treaty of Breda, by which in 1667 Charles II ceded Nova Scotia to France, surrendered the whole of Acadia to France and especially mentioned 'Pentogoet' or Penobscot. On this basis, France laid claim to all of the Province of Maine east of the Penobscot. The Baron de St. Castin soon established himself in this region, and for more than thirty years protected French (and his own) interests and traded with both Indians and English. In 1673, the Dutch captured and held the French fortifications at Penobscot, the Dutch West Indies Company in 1676 appointing a governor for the conquered territory; but they were shortly driven out by the English. In 1688, Governor Andros seized Penobscot again, and sacked the house of Baron de Castin. This event marked the beginning of the rapid decline of French influence in Maine. The Governor of Canada, it is true, continued in large measure to control the Indians through the agency of the Jesuit missionaries, of whom Father Sebastian Rasle came to be the best known. The latter's interest in the temporal welfare of his Indian flock led to his death at the hands of the English in 1724, during the sack of Norridgewock, where he had taught since 1691.

After 1730, the Indians had no regular priests; and when in 1763 France finally surrendered Canada, the Catholic missions were badly hurt, for, while the English Government guaranteed religious freedom, it was taking quiet steps to rid Maine and Canada of the Jesuit influence. The last mission in Maine had disappeared by the time of the Revolutionary War. After the work of Father Cheverus and Father Romagne (1797-1818), however, the Roman Catholic Church gained strength in Maine, and has not ceased to prosper since.

The French were consistently successful in their dealings with most of the eastern Indians. The Iroquois nation, always hostile to them, was an important exception, but that federation had little influence in Maine. The French sought trade rather than settlement, and unlike the English they made no attempt to dispossess the natives of their ancestral lands; while the French Catholic missionaries worked continually with great self-sacrifice and altruism in behalf of the Indians, many of whom became Christian converts. The natives naturally responded to the better treatment the French offered them.

In 1672, a new survey of the northern boundary of Massachusetts had extended the Colony beyond the Kennebec to Penobscot Bay, and after two years this region was organized as the County of Devonshire. At this time there were nearly six thousand inhabitants between the Piscataqua and the Penobscot, and at least one hundred and fifty families east of the Kennebec.

In 1675, King Philip's War burst upon the startled colonists. It was seventy years from the time that Waymouth kidnaped his Indians before active warfare resulted from the almost continual aggression and treaty-breaking on the part of the whites. Yet in the following eighty-five years of sudden savage raids and skirmishes there were few inhuman barbarities aside from the custom of scalping which was practiced by both sides. Most of the Maine Indians had become Christians, and were influenced by the Church.

Saco was attacked on September 18, 1675. Two days later, Scarborough was burned and the inhabitants of Casco driven out or cut down, the survivors taking refuge on the outer islands of Casco Bay. The settlements at Arrowsic and Pemaquid were burned, and during the next summer the Indians even penetrated to Jewell Island, the farthest outpost of the bay, where the beleaguered colonists had barricaded themselves. The burning and sacking continued ruthlessly, until a commission from the Massachusetts Government negotiated peace with the Indians of the Androscoggin and the Kennebec at Casco on April 12, 1678.

When peace was attained, Massachusetts provided a government for the Province, the Council in 1680 appointing Thomas Danforth 'President of Maine' to serve for one year and councilors to serve until removed; Maine towns were annually to elect a House of Deputies. After the Massachusetts charter was revoked in 1685, the Colonies were governed directly by the Crown until 1688, when New England, together with New York and New Jersey, came under the single administration of Andros. James II in 1686 appointed Joseph Dudley royal deputy; later in the same year, Dudley was superseded by Andros. In April, 1688, Andros attacked Penobscot and sacked the stronghold of Baron de Castin, thus precipitating the French and Indian conflict with the English of Maine and Massachusetts that is known as King William's War. The first outbreak occurred in August, 1688, when Indians attacked the North Yarmouth settlement. The fighting continued sporadically throughout the following winter; but the Maine colonists, aroused by the unwise measures taken by Governor Andros against the Indians and chafing under his arrogant rule, joined with the people of Massachusetts in taking independent control of the government, news having reached New England of the landing of William of Orange in England and of the flight of King James. Massachusetts appointed Simon Bradstreet as its Governor, and Maine restored Danforth as Provincial President on April 18, 1689. The French and their Indian allies actively continued the war with the English. The garrison at Pemaquid surrendered on August 2, 1689. In 1690, Newichawannock (now Salmon Falls) was destroyed, and Fort Loyal at Falmouth (formerly Casco) was razed by Baron de Castin with five hundred French and Indians from Canada, who took many of the inhabitants, most of them women and children, back to Quebec as prisoners. Sir William Phips in 1690 carried the war to the French in Nova Scotia, captured Port Royal, and took possession of the entire coast to Penobscot. But a campaign against Quebec failed; and the capture by the French of Fort William Henry at Pemaquid, 'the most expensive and the strongest fortification that had ever been built by the English on American soil,' still further increased French prestige with the Maine Indians. By the autumn of 1691, only four towns, Wells, York, Kittery, and Appledore, remained inhabited, Falmouth and other leading settlements having been almost totally destroyed. The fighting continued intermittently until 1697; then, under the Treaty of Ryswick, the French claimed all of eastern Sagadahoc as part of Nova Scotia.

Massachusetts' second charter, that of 1691, conferred fewer powers than had been granted by the old charter. The first royal governor was Sir William Phips, a native of Maine and perhaps the first of America's prominent self-made men. Until this time, Maine had been constantly beset by political changes and internal revolutions, owing to the succession of claimants and the zeal of the competitors for its land. The districts east of the Kennebec had suffered particularly in vicissitudes of ownership and government. With each part separated from and giving no aid to the others, the Province offered few inducements to settlers. The territory remained a sort of buffer province, subject to continual attack from Indians and French. But under the administration of Phips, the contention of royalist and republican partisans for proprietorship and government ceased. Town government in Maine now took the same form as that in the rest of New England, the county continuing to be useful as an intermediate organization for judicial purposes. Each county had a court consisting of a resident magistrate or a commissioner and four associates chosen by the freemen of the county and approved by the General Court.

During the contest over acceptance of the Massachusetts charter in

1691, there had originated the political parties of Republicans and Loyalists. Though they eventually assumed new names, their general policies continued to the Revolution, the Republicans or 'liberty men' adhering to the democratic principles in the old charter, and the Loyalists or 'prerogative men' professing to be more loyal subjects of the King and accordingly enjoying more of his favor.

For a long time the Province of Maine had been poor and weak, suffering greatly in the wars with the French and Indians. Obedience to the laws of Massachusetts was rendered unwillingly until the resettlement of the Colonies after King Philip's War, and the Province was early a resort for those with but small regard for creed or church. The settlers continued to aggravate the ill-will of the Indians; and the latter, greatly reduced in numbers by continual epidemics dating from the first coming of the white men, now began to see that they must fight for their very existence as well as for their lands. The colonists generally failed to discriminate between members of different tribes; an Indian was an Indian, and a good Indian was a dead one. The innocent were constantly being killed. Many were sold into slavery for the crimes of others, their women ravished, their homes destroyed. Queen Anne's War, beginning in Maine in 1703 with attacks on Casco Bay colonies and lasting to 1713, caused great damage, but it broke forever the main force of Indian strength and importance.

Although English advance into the interior of Maine was slow, since the French claimed all land east of the Penobscot, by 1722 it had made considerable headway. The British were sometimes aided by Indians of the forest lands, who joined them to fight their hereditary enemies of the coast and the east. In 1729, David Dunbar was granted royal sanction to settle and govern the 'Province of Sagadahoc.' His arbitrary acts, however, resulted in his removal from office in 1733, Massachusetts thereupon resuming jurisdiction.

In 1739, the King in council fixed the line between Maine and New Hampshire to 'pass through the entrance of Piscataqua Harbor and the middle of the river to the farthermost head of Salmon Falls River, thence north 2°; west, true course, 120 miles.' York and Falmouth (Portland) were now the principal towns in Maine, the former the political center, the latter the commercial center. Economic prosperity was growing; by 1743 there were 12,000 people in the Province. The Reverend George Whitefield, the famous Calvinist preacher, came to Maine with his wife in 1741 and again in 1744, where he preached at York, Wells, and Biddeford.

War between England and France broke out again in 1744, bringing the fifth Indian war to Maine, with attacks on Fort St. George and Damariscotta in the summer of 1745. A Massachusetts army aided by an English fleet won the most conspicuous success of the war, the capture of Louisburg at Cape Breton in 1745. Edward Tyng of Falmouth commanded the squadron co-operating with the English fleet, while William Pepperell of Kittery, for years New England's most important landowner, headed the land forces. Maine, with but one-fourteenth of the total population of the Bay Colony, was providing one-third of its troops. Nearly one-third of Maine's citizen soldiers participated in the siege of Louisburg, the 'Gibraltar of the West,' the capture of which resulted in Pepperell's being made a baronet.

Newcastle, the first of the towns in the territory of Sagadahoc and the twelfth town in Maine, was incorporated in June, 1753. In 1755, the Acadians of Nova Scotia, refusing to take the oath of allegiance to an English sovereign, were exiled and dispersed among the American Colonies. Many of them settled in Maine along the St. John River.

With the capture of Quebec by the British in 1759 and the subsequent surrender of all Canada, peace was finally secured with France and with the Indians, and Indian warfare in Maine ceased forever.

Possession of the Penobscot country was taken in July, 1759, when Fort Pownal was built and garrisoned. Peace was formally made with the remnants of the Indian tribes in the vicinity of Fort Pownal on April 29, 1760. The creation, on June 19, 1760, of two new counties — Cumberland, embracing that part of Maine between the Saco and the Androscoggin, and Lincoln, whose jurisdiction extended over that part east of the Androscoggin — was evidence that Maine was rapidly increasing in population. Pittston, the fortieth and last town established by the General Court under the royal charter, was incorporated on February 4, 1779.

The first indication of resistance in Maine to the taxes laid on the American Colonies by Parliament was the seizure of a quantity of tax stamps in Falmouth by a mob in 1765. In 1774, the people of Falmouth in town meeting declared that no power had a right to tax them without their consent or that of their representatives. Nine towns in Cumberland County sent delegates to a county convention held at Falmouth in September, 1774. The delegates advised 'a firm and persevering opposition to every design, dark or open, framed to abridge our English liberties.' Sheriff William Tyng declared his intention to obey the law of the Province, but not that of Parliament.

In the Revolution that followed, Maine suffered more than any other part of New England. The services of the Indians were enlisted on both sides, and bounties were paid for white scalps. In 1775, Falmouth was almost completely destroyed by an English fleet, and the country east of the Penobscot was constantly subjected to harassing raids by enemy warships after the British occupation of the Castine Peninsula in 1779. Communication with Boston was difficult, and at times impossible. Food was scarce, and illicit trade with Nova Scotia subsequently sprang up. Many of Maine's citizens were ready to accept neutrality or even submit to the enemy.

But the majority of the colonists were of fighting stock — pioneers, hunters, and trappers, veterans of Indian wars and foreign sea battles. In the first naval engagement of the war, the citizenry of Machias, with no cannon, few small arms, and little powder, attacked a British armed cutter, the 'Margaretta,' and forced it to surrender. Had England been able to withdraw her troops and ships engaged in the hopeless task of subjugating Maine, and to use them in an offensive against the Continentals in Massachusetts and Connecticut, the outcome of the war might well have been different. As it was, Maine not only staved off attack but served as a highway for the invasion of Canadian provinces — a highway which Benedict Arnold used in September, 1775, on his ill-starred march through the wilderness to the Chaudière and on to Quebec. Maine bled itself white in providing soldiers for the Continental army; more than one thousand of them were at Valley Forge.

In 1775, the Continental Congress divided Massachusetts into three admiralty districts, of which the northerly, made up of York, Cumberland, and Lincoln Counties, was to be known as the District of Maine. At the declaration of peace in 1783, the St. Croix River became the eastern boundary of this District, and the Indian tribes became wards of the State, no longer possessing any control over the land. Immigration increased, and towns were rapidly incorporated. The first town established by the new government was Bath, incorporated in 1781. In 1784, a land office was opened at the seat of government, and State lands on the navigable rivers in the District of Maine were sold to soldiers and immigrants at one dollar an acre. In 1786, more than a million acres of land between the Penobscot and the St. Croix Rivers were disposed of by lottery, the largest purchaser being William Bingham of Philadelphia.

In 1793, a new political alignment resulted from a split in the old parties over the French Revolution and basic principles of government. The Federalists opposed democracy, desiring the rule of the few and conservative rich; the Republicans (or Democrats), adhering to democracy and

the town meeting method of government, consisted of the poorer and more
radical elements. The District of Maine was a Federalist stronghold until
1805, when the party had become greatly diminished. The land policy
of Massachusetts was highly unsatisfactory, tracts already settled by
pioneers having been sold or granted to wealthy men or companies. Some
owners expelled the squatters; some would neither sell nor lease; in other
cases the ownership of the land remained in dispute and no one could give
a clear title. Feeling that the Massachusetts legislature favored the
absentee landlords, a majority of voters in the District went Republican
during a general democratic movement in 1805.

The growth of population in Maine after the Revolution was rapid —
from 96,540 in 1790 to 151,719 in 1800, and 228,705 in 1810. Hancock and
Washington Counties in 1789 and Kennebec in 1799 were formed from
Lincoln County; Oxford was assembled from parts of York and Cumberland in 1805, and Somerset formed from Kennebec in 1809. During this
period many towns were incorporated, including Portland in 1786, built
on the site of Falmouth, which had been destroyed in 1775; Bangor in
1791; Augusta in 1797. Plantations were organized as governmental
units for taxing groups outside the regular incorporated areas.

The Embargo Law of 1807, forbidding commercial intercourse between
the United States and foreign countries, checked the rising tide of Republicanism. Various methods were used to evade the law, and Eastport
became notorious as a center for goods smuggled across the Canadian
line. When in 1812 the United States declared war on Great Britain, a
strong anti-war sentiment existed in Maine, yet the Embargo Laws had
so hurt the shipbuilding and fishing industries that there were many
enlistments for military service from among Maine's unemployed.

The attempt on England's part to cripple or destroy American commerce without striking a decisive blow at Maine would have been hopeless, and British men-of-war soon appeared along the coast. But they
found it no less difficult to prevent her shipyards from launching vessels
and to paralyze her commerce than it had been to break the spirit of her
patriots during the Revolution. Since the District of Maine, according to
American interpretation of the Treaty of 1783, so separated the British
provinces that there was no direct trade route between Halifax and Quebec, the English sailed down and occupied the land as far as the Penobscot,
made Castine a port of entry, and proclaimed a provincial government
between the Penobscot and New Brunswick. But the peace treaty of
1814 left the boundaries between the United States and Canada as they
had been before the war. Ownership of the islands in Passamaquoddy

Bay was settled in 1817 by a joint commission, the United States receiving Moose, Dudley, and Frederick Islands. Foreign occupation ended in 1815, when the last British troops left Maine soil. In 1817, President Monroe visited Maine and inspected her fortifications, but never since have fortifications been considered necessary on the Canadian border. It seemed, too, at this time that the United States had little need of warships; the United States vessel 'Alabama,' of eighty-four guns, which was laid down at Kittery, was left unfinished on the stocks in 1818.

At the close of the Revolutionary War, the question of separation of Maine from Massachusetts came up repeatedly. Maine's first newspaper, *The Falmouth Gazette*, was devoted to the separation cause. The interests of Maine and Massachusetts were widely divergent; the seat of government was distant, and the expense of justice great; trade regulations were unjust to Maine; many residents in unorganized districts were denied representation in the legislature; the tax system was unbalanced; the District was separated from Massachusetts by New Hampshire; there was a different viewpoint toward national politics, and a desire on the part of Maine to avoid the burden of the State debt. But public opinion was not ready for separation; and the adoption of the United States Constitution in 1787 turned people's thoughts in another direction. Furthermore, the Massachusetts legislature quickly passed acts benefiting Maine's residents. The War of 1812, however, and the Hartford Convention stimulated anew the separation movement. Massachusetts' failure to aid in defending the District during the war had aroused great bitterness, and the State was accused of partiality in educational matters. A separate government would be cheaper. The old objection that statehood would place a heavy burden on the coastal trade was removed in 1819, when Congress passed a law permitting coasters to trade from the St. Croix to Florida without entering and clearing. Party prejudice was less active; the era of good feeling had arrived. Maine separated from Massachusetts in 1819 (at which time she possessed 236 incorporated towns), and was admitted as a State into the Union on March 15, 1820, the seat of government being placed at Portland.

In Maine's early years, the conversion of forest trees into marketable lumber and of woodlands into fields for cultivation was the chief end of labor. Wampum, corn, fish, and other products were mediums of exchange, for real money was scarce. Fishing and the fur trade were the principal early industries. As the fur trade suffered a gradual decline, commerce with the West Indies increased. Lumber was exported there in exchange for molasses, most of which was made into rum, then a popular beverage. Rum, lumber, fish, and furs were exchanged in southern Colonies and abroad for the great number of commodities which Maine did not produce. There was very little manufacturing until the embargo of 1807, when necessity proved to be the father of industry. Maine has, of course, continued to be a predominantly rural State; but even in the early nineteenth century, farming was often combined with fishing, lumbering, boat-building, and other occupations. The Betterment Act finally ended the turmoil over land titles; since it required that the defeated litigants be reimbursed for all improvements, there were few lawsuits over property rights. Timber continued from earliest days to be Maine's most important raw material. The first sawmill in the United States was built at York in 1623; the first timberland grant of any importance was the Muscongus Grant of 1630, later known as the Waldo Patent; Brunswick, on the Androscoggin, was one of the earliest centers for the lumber business. The forest regions of the Kennebec and the Penobscot soon began to be exploited, but individual and private operations were not displaced by river driving and co-operative enterprise until after the Revolution. With the rise of lumbering, shipbuilding became an important industry. The first ship to be built in the New World was launched at the Popham Colony in 1607-08, and by the middle of the eighteenth century the industry was flourishing.

In the early days, travel in Maine was accomplished by boat or on foot. Roads were only gradually developed, for horse-drawn vehicles were not numerous until the Embargo stimulated the use of stagecoaches. There was little traveling in those days; Maine's people, a sturdy middle class, stayed at home and worked. When not attending to their crops, they were shaving shingles to exchange for goods at the store, working on highways or in the woods, fishing or trapping; the boys did the chores, and the women spun and wove cloth and made the clothing. There were few distinctions of rank or wealth. Settlers, both French and English, wished to be allowed to live and work as they chose, to raise their large families in peace.

There was little law or respect for law. Rum was the common beverage, and spirits were consumed on all occasions; the tavern or public house and the church were among the first buildings to be erected in every community. Maine's settlers were at first wholly liberal in their viewpoint, tolerating and even welcoming newcomers of any creed. Under Gorges, the Church of England was dominant; then, with an increased population, Congregationalism and a Puritan movement spread over the land, imposing a rigorous New England code of limited suffrage (only freemen, that is, men of property, could vote), compulsory enlistment in the militia, hidebound conventional morality, prosecution of heresy (Baptists, Quakers, and Jews were to be persecuted and driven from the Colonies), prohibition of games and dancing, and strict regulations for public houses. But the people of Maine were not zealous in enforcing these laws, holding that the keys of Church and State need not necessarily be committed exclusively to the hands of ministers and magistrates. In general, a spirit of religious toleration prevailed, although the church continued always to be the principal center of intellectual and social life. Resentment against support of the church by public taxation resulted in the rise of a variety of Protestant denominations, notably the Baptist and Methodist. The State Constitution of 1820 provided that no public funds raised by taxation could be used for denominational purposes.

Common schools and orthodox ministry went hand in hand, since the Puritans considered a proper education next in importance to godliness. The Bible was the first textbook. Since 1788, the State has followed a policy of using land and timber wealth as a basis for school aid. Bowdoin College was chartered in 1794, and Waterville (Colby) College in 1820. Until 1820, Maine's public-school system was essentially that of Massachusetts, and since then it has developed gradually along its original lines.

With William King as its first Governor, Maine entered the Union as an anti-Federalist State in 1820. With its agricultural and seafaring population, it was naturally a democratic State. Its growth was rapid; the population increased from 228,705 in 1810 to 501,793 in 1840. The seat of government was removed from Portland to Augusta in 1832. Penobscot County had been formed in 1816. Waldo County was established in 1827, Androscoggin and Sagadahoc Counties in 1854, and Knox County in 1860.

Meanwhile, the northeastern boundary remained unsettled and in dispute. In 1831, Maine refused to accept the compromise solution offered to Great Britain and the United States by the King of the Netherlands. Repeated minor incidents led finally to the danger of open combat at the boundary; and the State militia in 1839 marched two hundred miles through wilderness and deep snow to repel a threatened attack from New Brunswick. The mediation of General Winfield Scott prevented armed conflict, however, in this 'Aroostook War.' He arranged for a truce and joint occupation by both parties. In 1842, the Webster-Ashburton Treaty settled the fifty-nine-year-old dispute, and lost for Maine about 5500 miles of claimed territory.

Of reform movements influencing the political scene, the least important but the first to take shape was anti-masonry. A temporary triumph of this movement nearly brought about the total disappearance of freemasonry in Maine. In 1831, 1832, and 1833, anti-masonic candidates entered the elections for Governor. There was a revival of the movement in the 1840's, but the anti-slavery agitation soon took its place in the public mind.

Very few Negroes were kept as slaves in Maine even in Colonial days, most of the early Negroes being paid servants. There is no record of any slavery legislation in Maine, either as Province or as State. However, an anti-slavery society was formed as early as 1833, and a year later a State body was organized. Political fireworks were touched off as the Abolitionists and their opponents began to appeal to public opinion. Feeling against the Abolitionists was very strong in the coastal towns, much of whose prosperity depended upon the Southern trade; but in the interior of the State the anti-slavery movement, headed by the clergy, was backed by most persons. Every county had an anti-slavery society, and in 1841 an anti-slavery candidate entered the election for Governor. Since the new movement worked largely through church groups, there was violent protest from both Whigs and Democrats against its entry into politics, since they felt that the Church should keep itself above partisanship. The result was that, although the Whigs were more anti-slavery than the Democrats, anti-slavery men made up a third party, called at first the Liberty Party and later the Free-Soil Party. Between 1850 and 1855, party lines disintegrated over the prohibition and slavery questions. In 1854, the Free-Soilers and the anti-slavery Whigs united to form the Republican Party, which soon swept into power. The Kansas question in all its ramifications proved disastrous to the Democrats. Their failure to take a stand against the extension of slavery further diminished what was left of the Whigs, and the Abolitionists increased rapidly in strength. The Democrats declared that the prosperity of the State depended upon commerce which would certainly suffer if the South were alienated by a Republican triumph; they declared also that if Hannibal Hamlin, the Republican candidate for Governor, were elected, the fishing bounties would be withdrawn. Nevertheless, the Republicans acquired the seat of power in 1856, and they held it continuously thereafter until 1879. Hamlin, after serving a year as Governor, was elected to the U.S. Senate; and in 1861, Vice-President.

Closely connected with the anti-slavery issue was the prohibition movement. At the time of separation, almost everyone drank liquor, which was sold by the most respectable citizens; but soon regulations against abuses were inaugurated. As early as 1815, a total abstinence society had been formed in Portland, and in 1834, the first convention of temperance societies was held and a State organization formed. A split occurred on whether prohibition should be brought about by legal action or moral influence, and a militant minority for legal action won. In 1846, a law was passed forbidding the sale of spirits except for medicinal and industrial purposes.

The law, however, did not prove effective, or at least it was not well enforced, for illegal traffic in liquors at once made its appearance in all parts of the State. A stricter law of 1851 offended many temperate citizens, who felt that private rights were being invaded by the granting of warrants to searching parties. A split in the Democratic Party over this issue allowed a Whig Governor to be elected in 1853. The limited sale of liquor for beverage use was allowed in an act passed in 1856 under Democratic sponsorship, but this was attacked by the Republicans as discriminating against the poor. Another prohibitory law was therefore enacted in 1858.

In the 1850's, the rise of the so-called American or 'Know-Nothing' Party was attended by anti-Catholic and anti-foreign agitation, directed chiefly against the Irish. In 1853, the Roman Catholic See of Maine and New Hampshire was constituted, with the Reverend Daniel Bacon as Bishop. At this time there were only eight priests in the two States. A hostile mob first desecrated and then burned the church at Bath. The Reverend John Bapst, refusing to obey the town meeting's order to leave Ellsworth, was tarred and feathered and ridden out of town on a rail. Bath in 1855, and Bangor in 1856, refused to allow construction on new Catholic church buildings; and the old Baptist church used by the Catholics in Lewiston was burned during a riot there. At Bishop Bacon's death in 1874, however, Catholics residing in Maine numbered over 80,000.

President Lincoln's first call for Civil War volunteers met with a quick response in Maine; great public meetings were held, at which support of the National Government was pledged. Yet the outbreak of the war found Maine totally unprepared. The old musters had been abandoned as burdensome and useless occasions for drunkenness and dissipation. The enrolled and unarmed militia comprised about 60,000 men, and in addition there were a few volunteer companies. Nevertheless, Maine contributed thirty-two infantry regiments, three of cavalry, and one heavy artillery regiment, seven batteries of field artillery, seven sharpshooter companies, thirty other companies of infantry, seven companies of coast artillery, and six companies for coast fortifications. In all, 72,945 Maine residents served in the military and naval forces of the Union; and of these, 7322 died in the service. The State's war expenditures were about $7,000,000; while those of towns and individuals were more than $11,000,000. Many towns, feeling they would be shamed if they could not fill their quotas without a draft, bid wildly for recruits and accumulated large debts thereby. The State's commerce suffered greatly from the activities of Confederate cruisers, and companies of home guards were formed to protect the coastal districts from depredations. Two prominent generals of the Civil War were citizens of Maine — General O. O. Howard, who distinguished himself at Gettysburg, and General Joshua L. Chamberlain, later president of Bowdoin College and Governor of Maine.

After the war, the prohibition question continued to be a factor in State politics. The statutes forbidding the sale of intoxicating liquors were extended in 1871 so as to apply to wine and cider. Since the farmers were accustomed to make these lighter beverages from native fruits and berries, the Democrats hoped to use the law to turn rural districts against the Republicans. But the prohibition and total abstinence movement was continually growing, and the Democrats failed once more. It is significant, however, that the constitutional amendment passed in 1884 forbidding the manufacture of intoxicating liquors exempts cider from its list.

The growing tide of emigration from the State assumed sufficiently serious proportions in the late 1860's to arouse concern as to Maine's future on the part of some of her leading citizens. Determined to make a serious venture in home colonization, the State legislature commissioned the Honorable William W. Thomas, Jr., a former United States Consul in Sweden, to go to that country and bring back a party of settlers. Thomas returned from Sweden in 1870 with fifty-one persons, who immediately set about the development of a tract set aside for them by the State and given the name of New Sweden. In less than a year, the population of the district was doubled by other Swedes who came of their own accord to join the group; and by the end of three years, the original population of New Sweden had increased twelve-fold.

During the 1870's, many Maine cities and towns suffered financially from an enthusiasm for internal improvements which had been sweeping the nation since 1830. The result was a constitutional amendment severely limiting the total debt which any municipality might incur. A State organization of the national Greenback Party was formed, and nominated a candidate for Governor in 1876 and 1877. So quickly did the new party win popular favor with its stand against the resumption of specie payments and its plea for a cheap currency that the gubernatorial campaign of 1878 was fought on this issue. The Greenbackers were especially strong in the eastern counties, the majority of independent Democrats and many Republicans being drawn into the party. By a great oratorical display, many of the farmers were persuaded that they were being abused and plundered by the moneyed interests; and with their aid the Democrats, having temporarily formed an alliance with the Greenbackers, carried the State for the first time in many years.

The next year, 1879, there was no election by popular vote. Governor Garcelon and his council, accused of manipulating election returns so as to secure a fusion majority in the legislature, were declared in error by the State Supreme Court, and the Republicans seized the legislature chambers and chose a governor from their own ranks. Although its candidate won the governorship in the next election, the fusion tide had ebbed; and the State returned almost completely to the Republican fold.

Maine suffered greatly in the severe depression of the 1890's. The Spanish War drew one infantry regiment, four batteries of field artillery, and a signal corps, besides many individual enlistments in the regular army and navy, from Maine; and volunteer naval reserve associations were mustered for national service. A Republican victory in 1908 on the prohibition issue resulted in strict enforcement; but in 1910 the Democrats won for the first time in thirty-two years. Yet in 1911, a proposed amendment to repeal the prohibitory laws was defeated, though only by a very close margin. The adoption in 1911 of a direct primary law was due mainly to a new progressive movement which also placed on the statute books the initiative and referendum and a corrupt practices act; no longer were 'ring' and 'anti-ring' to struggle for party control, nominating conventions and picking political plums. In 1911 also, much valuable social welfare legislation was enacted.

Another Democratic victory came in 1914, when there was a division in the Republican Party between regulars and progressives — a phenomenon to occur again in 1932. A consolidation of Maine's leading newspapers in 1921 left the State with virtually no Democratic press. Political contests have become largely confined to the Republican primaries.

Following the United States' entry into the World War, more than 35,000 Maine men joined the fighting services. A considerable, though unknown number had already entered the war as members of Canadian

units. Nearly $116,000,000 in war loans and other contributions was
raised in the State. National Guard units were quickly recruited to full
strength, and the naval militia was mobilized. Sheriffs were authorized
to appoint special deputies; the Governor was empowered to take over
in the State's name any land desirable for military use; municipalities
were required to raise money to aid in the support of families of men in
military service, the State providing for reimbursement of all money
thus spent; and the organization of a Home Guard was provided for.
Maine's casualties in the war were 2094; 228 men were killed in action,
and the deaths from all sources numbered 1073.

Toward the end of the nineteenth century, a political awareness of the
importance of Maine's water-power resources had come into being. The
'power fight' started in 1909 with a law prohibiting the export of hydro-
electricity on the theory that, if kept within the State, the power would
attract industries which otherwise might settle elsewhere. An effort to
strengthen this law in 1917 divided the Republican Party into two oppos-
ing camps, a split which resulted in the fight for and against the direct
primary. In the 1920's, the 'Insull-ization' of public utilities was constantly attacked by politicians. The controversy finally ceased in 1929,
when by popular vote Maine decided to remain the only State in which
chartered companies are forbidden to export hydro-electric power.

Though they won the election of 1932, when Louis J. Brann became
Maine's first Democratic Governor in twenty years, and though they
were again successful in 1934, the Democrats have never gained greatly
in strength. The Republican Party returned to power in the 1936 elections. The great nation-wide financial collapse in 1929 affected Maine
disastrously, particularly in the rural districts. By a large majority vote
in 1934, the State repealed its historic prohibition amendment.

Today Maine is a conservative, but not necessarily a reactionary,
State. Her people are slow to change; they learned their political faith
in the Civil War, and have found no reason to abandon it. Few of her
citizens are millionaires, few are miserably poor. Although the number of
her people of native stock has remained virtually stationary for four
decades, she has contributed to the country at large many prominent
citizens who were born and raised here. Perhaps, indeed, one of Maine's
greatest glories lies in the number of her gifted sons and daughters who,
throughout the country's history, have left their home State to find
elsewhere greater opportunities for their native abilities.

THE STATE GOVERNMENT

Maine's government has not changed materially since 1820. The original constitution grants wide powers to the legislature, definitely curtails those of the Governor by creation of a council of seven members which must approve nearly all executive actions, and limits the terms of the judiciary to seven years. The government is unusual in several respects. The Governor is the only executive official elected by popular vote (Maine has the shortest ballot of any State); organized plantations are retained; and Maine Indians govern themselves as an incorporated republic, sending non-voting representatives to the State legislature.

Maine's 16 counties are important chiefly as judiciary units. They are divided into 20 cities and 435 towns, 63 organized plantations, 40 second-class plantations, 376 unorganized townships, and two government reservations for Indians.

State elections are held biennially, on the second Monday in September of even-number years. Since this is nearly two months earlier than other election dates throughout the country, the result usually attracts nation-wide attention, and Maine formerly was considered the nation's political barometer. A plurality vote is necessary for election, although a majority was formerly required. Maine has no lieutenant governor, the President of the Senate succeeding to the governorship in case of vacancy. Maine, like Massachusetts, has a strong Executive Council which severely limits the powers of the Governor, who is nominated by direct primary and elected for a two-year term. The Council, with all other State officials, is elected biennially by a joint ballot of both houses of the legislature, and its members are not necessarily of the same political party as the Governor. Under the Maine Administration Code of 1931, twenty-five departments and agencies were consolidated in five main departments, each headed by a commissioner appointed by the Governor and confirmed by the Council for a term of three years or more. These departments are: Finance, Health and Welfare, Education, Audit, and Sea and Shore Fisheries. The constitutional offices of Secretary of State, State Treasurer, and Attorney General were not affected by the Code. The system of initiative and referendum, but not of recall, is in force.

The State's judiciary system consists of a supreme court of eight justices; superior courts, with jurisdiction only within the respective counties; probate and municipal courts; notaries and justices of the peace.

All members of the judiciary are appointed by the Governor and Council, with the exception of the probate judges and the registers, who are elected by popular vote in each county.

The central government, according to New England tradition, exercises little power over local governmental units, and home rule is jealously guarded by the municipalities. The town in New England (known elsewhere as township) is the important political unit. Since no minimum population requirement for the incorporation of cities exists in Maine, many of the towns are larger than some of the cities. The government of the town, through the medium of the town meeting, is the only existing type of pure democracy. In recent years, owing largely to the efforts of Dr. Orren C. Hormell, authority on municipal government at Bowdoin College, about twenty of Maine's cities and towns (more than in all the rest of New England) have adopted the council-manager form of government. Elected on a non-partisan basis, the city or town council is the general authority (except for an independent school committee), with a specially trained executive as manager or administrative head.

In thinly settled and undeveloped areas, local districts have been created as governing and taxing units, chief of which is the plantation, Maine being the only State in which the organized plantation is an important element in the governmental system. All unorganized townships are governed by the Maine Forestry District, which is divided into twenty-eight sub-districts, each in charge of a chief warden; seventy-one watchmen and sixty-five patrolmen are employed from May to September, and seventy-one lookout stations and ninety camps are maintained within the district.

PINE, PAPER, AND POWER

THE story of industry in Maine antedates that of actual settlement by an indeterminate number of years. One Maine industry in particular, the fisheries, had its beginnings in that vague age of adventure and exploration along the Atlantic seaboard prior to the seventeenth century. Searching though they were for the wealth of the Indies, the early voyagers were not unaware of the commercial possibilities of the fisheries.

Maine's fisheries supplied some of the State's earliest and most important exports, and greatly influenced its later commmercial development. Almost without exception, the problems of fisheries and fishing rights have entered into the State's international and interstate negotiations during its history. Captain John Smith, who carefully noted the variety of fish found here, established fisheries at Monhegan in 1614; and eight years later, Governor Winslow of Plymouth reported that there were thirty ships of different nationalities at Monhegan and Damariscove, most of them engaged in taking on cargoes of fish. Even before the Revolution, Maine was exporting thousands of tons of fish to Europe and the West Indies; and between 1820 and 1826, the State produced approximately one-fifth of the total fish tonnage of the United States. With minor economic fluctuations, the fisheries consistently stimulated Maine commerce throughout the nineteenth century. During the years from 1905 to 1930, Maine's coastal fisheries produced between 116,000,000 and 173,000,000 pounds of fish and shellfish annually. Seven per cent of the State's population derives a livelihood from the fishing industries.

Maine has been, and still is, famous for the quality of its lobsters. In 1936, Knox County and its principal fishing port, Rockland, led the rest of the State in the landing of lobsters, the retail value of which exceeded $1,750,000. The Penobscot Bay scallop fisheries supply a widespread market, and the 1936 sardine (herring) pack of nearly 2,000,000 cases was the largest since 1929. Other commercially important Maine fish are alewives, cod, cusk, haddock, hake, mackerel, halibut, pollock, crabs, and clams. Portland is the State's chief fishing port, while other towns in Cumberland, Knox, and Washington Counties hold important places in the industry. Experiments are being made with shrimp fisheries in

INDUSTRY, COASTAL AND INLAND

INDUSTRY in Maine follows closely the power and port resources of the waters of the State. Maine has grown chiefly around its harbors and along its rivers. About Maine waters today are evident the signs of economic history: old industries decaying and disappearing, seen especially in the picturesque hulls tied up in most of the harbors, and new industries, such as the manufacture of paper, rising up and prospering. Continuing from earliest days with little change in method and product are the important businesses of harvesting the natural resources in which the State is rich — fish and lobsters from the sea, hay and potatoes grown on the inland farms, and wood products and blueberries from the forests and the plains.

THE FALLS, VEAZIE

HAYFIELD NEAR PALERMO

AIR VIEW OF THE STATE PIER, PORTLAND

SHIPBUILDING, THOMAS

FISH WEIRS, BUCKSPORT

ON THE PORTLAND WATERFRONT

OLD HULL, BOOTHBAY HARBOR

GROUNDED SCHOONERS IN BOOTHBAY HARBOR

MAINE SEABOARD PAPER COMPANY, BUCKSPORT

LOGGING

LARGE-SCALE POTATO DIGGING, AROOSTOOK COUNTY

BLUEBERRY PICKERS

PACKING LOBSTER BAIT, SEBASCO

LOBSTER PO

Maine waters. Important work in fish propagation and conservation is conducted in the State's Sea and Shore Fisheries Department.

The State's fisheries reached their production peak in 1902, when 242,390,000 pounds were landed. Since then, the industry has been gradually declining in Maine, though increasing in other North Atlantic States. The Maine fisheries were especially injured by the decline of the salted fish business several years ago, and Maine fishermen have been slow to develop new methods of handling and merchandising fish products. Although situated near the chief fishing banks of the North Atlantic, the State's fisheries are at a disadvantage in the matter of transportation costs; while the prevalent tariff rates, in combination with improved methods of packaging and refrigeration utilized by competitor States and Canada, still further increase their difficulties. The years of scarcity for certain kinds of fish have left their mark on the industry; a few seasons when there is a dearth of herring, for example, bring disaster to the State's sardine-packing plants. River dams and the pollution of waters by manufacturing plants have affected the supply of such migratory fish as the Atlantic salmon and alewives, which seek fresh water for spawning purposes. The supply of lobsters, scallops, and clams has been seriously depleted by reckless harvesting methods and natural causes.

Although the State's fisheries production has declined to but little more than 90,000,000 pounds annually, the industry shows signs of recovering some of its lost ground. The modernization of fishing equipment and packaging, and the introduction of filleting, have been beneficial. A recently enacted measure bars non-resident fishermen from Maine waters for seven months each year; this is designed to protect the State's fisheries from the encroachments of many out-of-State fishermen who have hitherto reaped large harvests during the height of the season. Fishermen and canning factories rest their hopes for capacity production, and the allied industries (glue, oil, fish meal, and pearl essence) their plans for expansion, largely on the possibility of increase in the nation's fish consumption and greater attention paid to modern methods of handling, packaging, and selling.

SHIPBUILDING

Maine shipbuilding, closely allied with fishing, lumbering, and some other industries, has had a long and distinguished history. Since the State relied chiefly on its shipping to maintain its commercial position through several centuries, it was inevitable that its people should early engage in shipbuilding and should develop a high degree of skill in that work. The 'Virginia,' launched from the banks of the Kennebec by the Popham colonists in 1608, was the first ship built by Englishmen on the North American continent. Twenty-four years later, John Winter established a shipyard on Richmond Island. Winter may well be considered the pioneer in American shipbuilding for the export trade, since his vessels engaged in carrying lumber, fish, oil, and other products to England. Wherever warranted by a sufficiently large settlement along the coast and rivers, shipbuilding became a necessary means of livelihood well before the eighteenth century. Maine was 'sea-minded' for generations before the 'Ranger,' a Kittery-built ship under the command of John Paul Jones, received in 1778 the first formal salute given to the American flag by a foreign fleet.

Contract shipbuilding in Maine was inaugurated in 1762 by Captain William Swanton of Bath, and has been identified with that city ever since. Swanton and other shipbuilders received contracts from Spain, France, and the West Indies. By 1790, ships were being built all along the coast and up the principal rivers. The city of Hallowell, situated more than thirty miles from the open sea, entered upon an era of shipbuilding that lasted beyond the middle of the nineteenth century. Although shipbuilding had been checked by the effect of embargoes, one-third of the total tonnage in the United States in 1812 was Maine-built. For nearly half a century after the War of 1812, the State led all others in the shipbuilding industry. In the 1830's, Maine built more tonnage than any other State; and from 1841 to 1857, the period when Bath became America's leading shipbuilding city, this was its most important industry. Of the four hundred and twenty-eight ships, barks, and brigs built in America in 1848, Maine supplied more than half. In approximately fifty coast towns, this was the chief industry, supporting about 200,000 persons.

Maine shipyards have turned out practically every kind of craft known along the Atlantic seaboard, from fishing smacks and dredges to million-dollar yachts, six-masters, submarines, and the most modern type of destroyer. The expansion of certain industries, such as lumbering and lime production, gave new impetus to shipbuilding. The demand for wood to be burned in lime kilns led to the construction of such curious vessels as the 'St. John wood-boats,' probably the most inexpensive type ever built on this side of the Atlantic. Squat and broad, with no bowsprit or overhanging stern, and having a single deckhouse and an exposed rudder, these craft used to skim into port with their decks piled so high with lumber that they were often several inches awash. This kind of woodboat was so unusual that one was exhibited in Boston, complete with its Yankee skipper.

Not all vessels were built in the ordered efficiency of the shipyards. Many were constructed far inland in the midst of the timber supply. One thirty-ton vessel (almost as large as Columbus's 'Pinta') was built in 1830 on the north end of Megunticook Mountain in Camden, and then hauled more than six miles over the ice of Megunticook Lake and River to Penobscot Bay, there to be placed in the fishing and lime coasting-trade. The lumber industry, too, was responsible for odd departures in marine architecture. A raft constructed of squared timber in the form of a ship's hull, and equipped with sails, set forth from the Kennebec in 1792. Its crew intended to cross the Atlantic, but abandoned their craft off the Labrador coast. Two other rafts of the same design very nearly completed the crossing, but foundered off England.

The increasing use of steel in ship construction after the Civil War seriously crippled the industry in this State, although half the nation's ships afloat in 1900 had been built in Maine, and there was a tremendous boom in the industry all along the coast during the World War. The population of the six leading shipbuilding counties — Hancock, Knox, Sagadahoc, Lincoln, Waldo, and Washington — was much smaller in 1910 than in 1870. Yet there are many persons along the coast who still recall the time when Maine yards were working to capacity, and who can remember the names of between three hundred and four hundred vessels that were built, owned, or sailed from a single Maine port. The passing of the wooden ship era, the falling off of maritime commerce, and Maine's distance from cheap and adequate raw materials have contributed to the industry's decline. In one year (1922) of the immediate post-war period, when the country was overstocked with vessels, Bath failed to launch a single ship, for the first time in one hundred and forty years.

Maine-built ships have won distinction of one sort or another for more than three centuries. The clipper 'Red Jacket,' launched from a Rockland shipyard in 1854, made the crossing from New York to England in thirteen days, one hour, and twenty-five minutes, establishing a record that has never been broken by a sailing vessel. The six-masted freighter 'Wyoming,' built in the present century and the largest wooden ship afloat in its time; the 'William P. Frye,' the first American ship sunk by the Germans during the World War; the destroyer 'Lamson,' the fastest ship of its type in the United States Navy in 1936 — these were all Bath-built vessels. Scores of other Maine ships, heavy with cargoes of lumber, rum, wheat, slaves, molasses, or tea, have sailed the seven seas in their day, and left their wreckage and nameboards from twoscore Maine coastal towns upon the far shores of the world.

Several of the famous old Maine shipyards are experiencing a revival — the caulking mallets are again busy, and the pungent odors of resin and tar once more fill the air. An increasing interest in yachting has created a demand for small and medium-sized pleasure-craft. There are few second-hand boats on the market, and these command high prices. The fishing industry requires new vessels, while Government and private contracts for new shipping pour into Maine shipyards. The fitting out of a four-masted schooner at Portland for the molasses trade, in April, 1937, is strongly reminiscent of the nineteenth century, and indicates that the day of the wooden ship is by no means over.

LUMBERING AND ALLIED INDUSTRIES

Furnishing the materials for shipbuilding and long the foundation of Maine industry in general, lumbering has had a varied history in the Pine Tree State. Despite the facts that the forests have been cut back from the coast and that Maine contributed a large share of the nation's lumber for decades, more than 15,000,000 acres of forest land still remain, and improved conservation methods seem to assure an adequate supply of timber in the future. The lumber industry has passed through three economic phases of development: the phase of operations undertaken by individuals and partners, lasting until about 1820; the phase of co-operation, lumbering associations, and the river-drives, between 1820 and 1880; and the present mass-production phase, largely influenced by the growth of the paper industry, with the bankers, promoters, and large corporations in control. Lumbering and its allied industries remain leaders in the State's industrial field.

Climate and topography, an extensive system of waterways, quantities of raw material, and cheap transportation all played their part in the development of Maine lumbering. Many of the State's industrial centers and transportation systems were established to meet the needs of this industry. Lumber and lumbering have also figured prominently in Maine's history. Resentment against the policy of reserving the best timber for the British Navy prior to the Revolution provoked ill-feeling, aroused agitation, and resulted in open disputes in such towns as Bath and Portland. Speculation in timber lands brought on the State's financial panic in 1835, anticipating the nation-wide panic by two years, and doing much to determine Maine's subsequent land policies. The international controversy that resulted in the Aroostook War was fundamentally a dispute regarding lumbering rights along the northeastern boundary.

The early explorers were impressed by both the size and the extent of the Maine timberlands. Later, the Popham colonists reported that there were 'fish in the season in great plenty all along the coast, mastidge for ships; goodly oaks, and cedars with infinite other sorts of trees.' Lumbering and sawmill operations were active at Berwick and York before 1640, and the export of timber began almost immediately. Cutting trees for shipbuilding and masts, particularly for the Royal Navy, became a distinct industry in itself. 'Mast ways,' or lanes carefully prepared and cleared of obstructions to prevent injury to the forest giants, were cut through the woods; and a special type of vessel, capable of carrying as many as five hundred masts at a time, was constructed for their transportation. Pine, which remained king of the forests and the lumber industry until it began to be replaced in importance by spruce after the Civil War, was abundant and greatly in demand.

Early lumbering, like all other Colonial industries, was affected by a population rendered unstable as a result of Indian warfare. By the eighteenth century, however, the lumber and mast trade in northern New England had gradually become centered about Portland and the Saco River basin. In Colonial times, lumber was often used as currency, and as late as 1840 shingles were used as a medium of exchange by the Aroostook settlers. The industry spread from river to river, north and northeast. Operations along the Androscoggin, which declined because of the difficulty of the 'drive' in that region, caused Brunswick to become the center of the industry by the first quarter of the nineteenth century. Lumbermen moved on to the Kennebec and then to the Penobscot basin, the latter becoming the State's greatest timber reservoir during those decades when the industry was at its height. Concurrently with the growth of the State, lumbering followed wherever settlements were made along the smaller rivers that had outlets to the sea. If Maine was New England's last frontier, the Maine pine lands were a special frontier in themselves. Thoreau wrote in 1846 of Maine lumbering that 'It is a war against the pines, the only real Aroostook or Penobscot war.'

In the production value of lumber, Maine ranked second in the United

States during the early nineteenth century. Her decline from this status after 1840 was later accelerated by the exploitation of the forests of the Lake States in the post-Civil War period. The actual value of timber rose consistently, however, between 1840 and 1900, when Penobscot County became pre-eminent in the industry. The peak year of lumber production was not reached until 1909. Despite the fact that Maine lumber found extensive markets in the West Indies, abroad, and on the West Coast (California used 5,000,000 board feet from Bangor alone in 1849), Maine imported lumber in considerable quantities during the middle period of the nineteenth century. Timber, particularly for shipbuilding purposes, was brought in from the South, New York, New Hampshire, Canada, Michigan, and Ohio. At the same time, Maine lumbermen and river-drivers were following the course of the lumber empires westward, attacking the forests from the Atlantic to the Pacific, taking with them the skill, songs, and legends learned on drives along the Penobscot, Kennebec, Androscoggin, and other Maine waterways.

Although the demand from many of Maine's former lumber markets is nearly non-existent today, the development of the pulp and other wood-using industries towards the end of the nineteenth century created a network of new enterprises entirely dependent upon the lumber industry. Softwood lumbering on any great scale practically disappeared after 1910, but new uses were found for spruce, fir, and hemlock. Tens of thousands of board feet of long lumber and pulpwood were cut along the tributary waters of the Kennebec alone in 1926–27. In 1935, in the Maine woods, 91,185,120 feet of lumber were cut, in addition to more than half a million cords of pulp, firewood, and timber for other purposes. Although threatened by adverse tariff rates, competition, a drop in the value of lumber, and lack of an adequate market, the industry is nevertheless still vigorous.

Pulp and paper now hold the foremost place in Maine's list of manufactures. Pulp for commercial purposes was first produced in 1868 at Topsham; and by 1914, Maine had assumed a national lead in this field. Such towns as Winslow, Millinocket, Rumford, and Woodland owe their growth almost wholly to the pulp industry. One Maine concern today is the country's largest manufacturer of newsprint; while a plant at Bucksport, operated entirely by electricity, is capable of turning out 1280 feet of newsprint, 18 feet wide, per minute.

The paper manufactories, reaching a production-value peak of $106,000,000 in 1926, were producing less than half of this volume in the following six-year period. Chief among the causes of this decline were European competition (as evidenced by the cargoes of Baltic baled pulp shipped into the port of Portland), the free entry of newsprint and pulp from Canada, and the Canadian mills' competitive advantage of low property, wood, power, and labor costs. Yet Maine pulp and paper manufactories still contribute more than half the tonnage carried by Maine transportation systems, and continue to dominate the State's industries.

Of lesser importance commercially are numerous products allied with the lumber and the pulp and paper industries. Planing mill and fiber products, wooden boxes, toys, and novelties of Maine manufacture have an annual value of several million dollars. Other allied industries include the manufacture of such diverse items as toothpicks and the famous Old Town canoes.

MISCELLANEOUS INDUSTRIES

The making of boots and shoes ranks second in Maine's manufacturing. The first recorded shoe factory in the State began operating at West Auburn in 1835. The center of the industry shortly became established at Auburn, and other factories sprang up elsewhere within the next decade. The industry has grown steadily, and even during the depression period of 1929–33 the number of shoe factories increased from thirty-six to fifty. Every kind of moccasin, boot, and shoe is made in Maine, the total production now being nearly $40,000,000 annually. Factories are distributed throughout Androscoggin, York, Kennebec, and Cumberland Counties, with the city of Auburn employing nearly one-half of the shoe workers in the State. More than a century ago, Maine had two hundred tanneries in active operation; but, owing to new methods of tanning, the industry relapsed swiftly after reaching its production peak of $2,500,000 in 1879.

Maine's textile manufactures are comparative newcomers in the industrial field. When machinery began to be substituted for hand labor in the textile industries, capital was attracted to the State because of its water-power resources. Much of the national supply of wool in the early nineteenth century was grown in New England, southern cotton had not yet become important, and Maine had an easily accessible supply of raw materials. Pioneer cotton mills were established in 1809–11 at Brunswick, Wilton, and Gardiner, and by 1820 there were nine cotton and woolen mills in the State.

For several decades, the manufacture of cotton-goods was among the most important of Maine's industries, in some years being exceeded in production value only by the lumber industry. Many small woolen mills were scattered throughout the State in the early nineteenth century, but the expansion of this phase of the textile industry was not rapid. The making of hand-loomed woolen goods was continued in many homes until after the middle of the century, and in 1860 there were only twenty-eight woolen mills in the State. By 1900 the number of textile mills had increased to seventy-nine, a number which by 1935 had decreased to forty-nine. In 1935 there were twelve cotton manufactories in Maine, with a total annual production value of $25,000,000; several mills produce between 30,000,000 and 40,000,000 yards of cloth a year.

As the textile industries have expanded, Maine mills have kept pace with innovations in the types of materials produced. Maine cotton twill, introduced into India by missionaries about fifty years ago, is still considered of superior quality for tropical wear. A Brunswick concern was a pioneer in the manufacture of rayon goods. Many of the textile mills in such centers as Augusta, Waterville, Lewiston, Biddeford-Saco, and Sanford have become noted for their particular products — clothing fabrics, sheets, blankets, bedspreads, and plush for automobile and railway car upholstery. More than 23,000 workers now derive their living from the textile industry, the annual production value of which is approximately $60,000,000. As a whole, Maine textiles have shown a marked increase in production and sales within the past two years.

The many other manufactories include one of the country's largest textile machinery factories, situated at Biddeford. More than a score of Maine companies manufacture textile machinery, machine tools, and related products, for sale all over the world. Nearly one hundred plants are engaged in the canning of fruits, vegetables, and fish. A cement company at Thomaston, the only concern of its kind in New England, manufactures more than a quarter million tons of its product annually.

With a few exceptions, Maine's mineral resources have scarcely been touched. Some twenty-four quarries, extracting granite, lime, slate, and feldspar, are in operation today. The granite industry, which once made famous the stone from such Maine quarries as those at Hallowell and Vinalhaven, declined after the general adoption of other materials in building and as a result of excessive transportation costs. However, more than a dozen granite quarries are still in operation, and the quarries at North Jay are among the country's largest producers of ornamental granite. The lime industry, inaugurated at Thomaston in 1734, centered about Rockland and adjacent Knox County towns. Rockland became the nation's greatest lime-producing center during the nineteenth century, but did not reach the height of its production until about 1900-01. The city's lime markets were impaired principally because of the increasing use of steel and domestic Portland cement in construction work, as well as the tapping of hitherto unworked limestone deposits elsewhere. The industry is now reviving, devoting most of its activities to the manufacture of lime for agricultural and chemical purposes. Maine's few feldspar quarries produce approximately twenty-five per cent of all the feldspar used in this country.

A highly important factor in the concentration and development of industries has been the exploitation of water-power on Maine rivers. From the earliest days, when streams and tidal rivers were used to run grist and corn mills, this natural resource has been increasingly put to use, until today Maine ranks seventh among the States in developed water-power. The developed and undeveloped energy is estimated at more than 1,200,000 horse-power. Maine is the only State whose laws prohibit the distribution of its power resources outside of its boundaries. There are now seventy-six public utility plants in the State, with seven companies controlling ninety-three per cent of the total generated power.

COMMERCE

Maine commerce has followed closely every turn in the course of the State's economic and industrial history ever since the 'Virginia' took a cargo of Maine furs and sassafras root to England in 1608. The purchase and barter of furs for export to Europe were mainly responsible for the penetration of the Maine wilderness and the establishment of forts and trading posts; the Massachusetts Bay Colony was keenly interested in the Maine fur trade and fisheries. Early commerce consisted chiefly in the export of such products as pipe staves (wood for the manufacture of oil and wine casks), clapboards, fish, fish oil, and salt fish — trade that soon gave way to the more important export of masts and timber. Another commercial item, of no great note but certainly unusual, consisted of scalps. During the period of the Indian wars, extending from the middle of the seventeenth to the mid-eighteenth century, French and Indian scalps frequently brought prices of from five to one hundred pounds.

There was, necessarily, a lull in commercial activity during the Revolution; but ninety-nine vessels cleared from Portland alone in the year 1787, all but ten of them bound for foreign ports. In the years between the end of the Revolution and the War of 1812, comfortable fortunes were amassed by local merchants; and this era of commercial prosperity is reflected in the number of impressive mansions built along the coast, especially during the first decade of the nineteenth century. Circumstances were ideal for the advancement of lucrative trade; there are few coastlines with more numerous land-locked harbors suitable for the fitting-out of vessels while safely protected from interference. It has been noted that only the Dalmatian coast of the Adriatic and the gulfs of the Grecian peninsula can compare with the Maine coast in this respect.

The embargo of 1807 and the War of 1812 brought commercial activity very nearly to a standstill all along the coast, although more than one Maine pocket was enriched by the proceeds from smuggling and privateering operations. As related to industry as a whole, it is noteworthy that the War of 1812 stimulated the growth of glass, woolen, metal, cotton, and other manufactories all over the State, as the citizens were deprived of their maritime livelihood. The State had been predominantly commercial up to this period, shipping on an average of 150,000 tons yearly, and had been created a separate district for the more satisfactory administration of maritime affairs more than thirty years previously. The influx of foreign goods after the War of 1812 had a disastrous effect on home industry, the demand for agricultural produce fell off, and Maine lost 15,000 inhabitants as its farmers rushed West during the 'Ohio Fever' of 1815-16.

By 1848, the number of vessels engaged in foreign commerce ran well into the hundreds. The West Indian trade, which had engaged the attention of Maine merchants for decades, was flourishing, sustained principally by the rapidly growing lumber industry. Cargoes of lumber were bringing profits of three hundred and four hundred per cent, and more than half the adult population of the coast towns was engaged in ocean navigation. Ships whose keels had been laid in Maine shipyards, from Kittery to Eastport, strained at their hawsers in ports all over the globe. Yankee shipmasters, whose hands were often as accustomed to turning the pages of a Bible as to wielding a belaying pin, brought back ships the holds of which were redolent with the odor of West Indian molasses, rum, spices, and China tea, or with the stench of a cargo of slaves. Among the principal foreign and coastwise imports at this time were molasses, sugar, salt, iron, flour, corn, and coal; while lumber, shooks, leather, agricultural produce, and ice were a few of the chief exports. The ice exporting industry, which occupied an important industrial position between 1840 and

1890, is now practically non-existent in Maine, due to the ice-harvesting of rivers elsewhere and to electrical refrigeration. Ice, shipped south as ballast at a negligible cost, once brought profitable returns; during the 1880's and 1890's, the excellent reputation of Kennebec River ice was so widespread that London ice companies spuriously flaunted the name 'Kennebec Ice' on their carts.

Checked temporarily by the effects of the panic of 1857 and the Civil War, Maine commerce appeared to increase steadily thereafter. In the year 1872, the total value of imports and exports at Portland was $45,000,000; while the same city's share of the 'in transit' and trans-shipment trade of the United States for February of that year was more than $5,000,000, or approximately five-sixths of the whole. In this same year, also, the Bangor lumber export trade reached its record value of shipments, nearly $4,000,000; while lime-producing Rockland was exporting more than 1,000,000 casks of lime annually. Yet, however imperceptibly at first, Maine shipping had begun to enter its decline. The causes were varied, some of comparatively recent development, yet all contributing to the falling away of Maine maritime commerce. A few of these factors have been the introduction of steam power in navigation, heavy tonnage and property taxes, pilotage fees, the use of steel, the competition of British tramp steamers, the lack of demand for fishing vessels, and the appearance of barges in coastwise trade. The industrial development of the State at large demanded increasing amounts of raw materials, yet maritime commerce reached its last high point during the World War. For the period of 1928-33, the average annual foreign imports and exports amounted to only 884,632 short tons, while domestic receipts and shipments were a little more than 3,500,000 short tons.

Maine commerce today is divided into the three classes of coastwise, intercoastal, and foreign traffic, the last-named being the one most seriously undermined by present conditions. Coastwise bulk traffic consists largely of coal, petroleum, pulpwood, sulphur, newsprint, and textile raw materials; lighter coastwise traffic has been to a large extent replaced by rail and highway transportation. A small amount of trade with the West Coast has developed within the last few decades. Maine's participation in foreign commerce is but a fraction of its former extent, particularly as regards export traffic. The State has little bulk cargo for the support of foreign shipping; and the important export of Canadian grain, which reached a maximum of 43,000,000 bushels shipped through Portland in 1915-16, has become a thing of the past due to the effects of Canadian, British, and American tariff policies in diverting the trade elsewhere.

Maine needs larger and more efficient distribution centers if it is to be assured of a revival of its foreign trade. The present lack is one of the reasons chiefly responsible for the fact that, in 1930, fifty-nine per cent of Maine's manufactured products flowed through the port of New York, nearly eleven per cent through Boston, and only thirty per cent through the State's own ports.

It is evident that full advantage is not being taken of the possibilities of Maine seaports for foreign trade. The State is further handicapped by not being near the primary markets, and it is possible that both railroad and highway freight systems could be better co-ordinated, especially in their relation to maritime commerce. Maine is today primarily an importing State. A revival of a profitable grain trade and coastwise shipping would be of the greatest benefit to both imports and exports, and would prepare the way for a restored commerce. Should the present commercial status be remedied, authorities would no longer be obliged to admit that a potential trade of $50,000,000 is being diverted from Portland, the State's largest seaport.

THE MAINE FARM

THE first settlers came to Maine's rocky shores, not to wrest a livelihood from the thin soil, but to exploit native resources of fish and lumber that seemed to them inexhaustible. They naturally built their towns along the coast and on the banks of navigable streams; but as the population increased and the forests were cut back from the water, the cleared land was taken up for farms. Constantly repulsed by Indians and ever at war with the elements, the Maine settlers were of necessity self-sufficing.

Their first crop of any importance was one that had been the staple of the aborigines — corn. It suited the requirements of the settlers; it could be stored through the winter and used as food for animals and humankind alike. On the farms of Captain John Mason along the Piscataqua and in Berwick, at the time of his death in 1635, there were several water-powered corn-grinding mills, the first of their kind in New England, and three hundred head of cattle. Since plenty of game was to be had from the near-by forests, cattle were kept only for fresh supplies of milk, butter, and cheese. Corn and cattle go together. Until the fertile bottom-lands of the Ohio and Mississippi valleys were opened and transportation facilities increased so that farmers in Maine were able to buy corn superior to their own at a price below their own production costs, corn remained the chief agricultural product of the State. When it ceased to be an important crop, the production of beef and pork fell off proportionately.

As Maine's settlement grew, lumbering and fishing flourished, but the home-making type of farm continued to spread through the territory. Not until after Maine became a State in 1820, however, were there agricultural exports of any importance. During the period of trade restrictions caused by the Jefferson Embargo and the following War of 1812, shipping and shipbuilding, until that time among the greatest of Maine's industries, met with an effective set-back, and men turned more and more to the handicrafts and to farming. The extensive use of horses in lumbering operations brought about a demand for hay, and this became an important cash crop. By 1900, lumbering operations had given way to pulp cutting, horses were replaced by machinery, and hay (though still an important crop in relation to dairying) had declined in value.

Sheep and cattle were driven overland to Massachusetts markets in the early days. In 1820 more than 4000 cattle and 3000 sheep were thus exported. In that year there were in the State more than 48,000 oxen, 17,800 horses, 95,000 cattle, and 66,500 swine. But even then, the number of horses was rapidly increasing because of the demand for them by lumber operators and the growing popularity of Maine-bred race-horses.

During the period of the trade barriers, the shortage of wool brought about what is now called the 'Merino fever.' As soon as the embargo was lifted, farmers returned to the Downs breeds they had formerly favored. The raising of mutton sheep and beef cattle increased until after 1870, when competition from western producers brought about a decisive change; between 1890 and 1900 the number of beef cattle in the State decreased one hundred thousand head. Market competition and the need for a crop giving higher cash returns shifted beef-raising to land of less value per acre. Industrial centers of Maine and Massachusetts offered ready markets for dairy products, and the change was made from beef to dairy cattle. Sixty cheese factories were built, and the production of farm butter increased; although the manufacture of these products never achieved great importance and has been declining since 1900, the number of dairy cattle has been constantly on the increase. Improved facilities for refrigeration and transportation have made it possible for Maine farmers to supply the larger cities of southern New England, as well as their own industrial centers, with fresh milk and cream, and to fill the increasing demands of summer residents within the State. Throughout all of southern Maine, dairying is now a major industry.

Since 1820 a wide diversity of products has been cultivated, with varying degrees of success. Early attempts were made to grow wheat, oats, barley, rye, apples, beans, peas, and other fruits and vegetables, even hops and silk from silkworms. With the development of the West, the raising of wheat ceased to be of importance in Maine, although it is still harvested in Aroostook and the inland counties, where modern machinery can be used. The growing of rye has practically ceased, but more than one hundred thousand bushels of barley are raised annually. Now that potatoes have become a very important crop, the production of oats has increased, because their cultivation fits into the rotation schedule in the potato areas; some four million bushels are produced annually. Buckwheat, also important in crop rotation, is grown to some extent.

After the opening of the West, Maine's agriculture underwent a period of rapid change. Between 1850 and 1870, State leaders, in order to promote farming, encouraged favorable legislation and the development of agricultural societies. Bounties were put upon the cultivation of certain products, such as wheat. An exemption of five hundred dollars in the valuation of farms was made against unpaid mortgages or incurred debts. New land was put on the market in two hundred-acre plots at fifty cents an acre, with the opportunity of working off the purchase price on town roads over a specified period of years. Fairs and exhibits helped to standardize varieties of products. Finally, with a change in farm enterprises and the new access to railroad transportation, agriculture became stabilized and increased in importance.

Aroostook County, settled by defenders in the Aroostook War, rapidly drew farmers from southern Maine. Because of the special fitness of soil and climate, potatoes early became a crop of great importance. Starch factories were built and formed the chief outlet for the crop; but not until the completion of the Aroostook railroad in 1894 did the county attain national importance for its potato production. Maine now raises nearly fifteen per cent of the United States potato crop, ranking first among the States in number of bushels produced and sixth in number of acres under cultivation. Storage opportunities, aided in part by the climate, make it economically advisable for southern States to depend upon Maine potatoes for seed stock. Government inspection, experimentation, and control of disease and insect pests have increased production and improved the quality of the crop. Maine potatoes today account for more than half the cash value of the State's total agricultural output, and some potatoes are raised in every county. The best producing area extends out of Aroostook County south and west into Penobscot and Somerset Counties. Here the land is especially adapted to potato-raising, facilities for transportation are available, and the crop is of high quality.

Apples are a staple crop in Maine. The small varied orchard of the past is rapidly disappearing as apple-raising becomes more specialized. The Baldwin, Ben Davis, and Greening varieties, once favored, have given way to the McIntosh, Delicious, and Northern Spy. Great quantities of these latter varieties are exported annually or made into cider. In 1933, the State's production of apples exceeded a million and a half bushels, but in the severe winter of 1933–34 many trees were killed and production dropped nearly a million bushels in a single year.

With the comparative increase in land values, creating a need for crops giving higher cash income per acre, cultivation of sweet corn, poultry-raising, and roadside and market gardening have assumed considerable importance. Sweet corn for canning or market is best grown in conjunction with dairying, because of the value of its stalks for ensilage and because it gives an outlet for barn manure. Farmers co-operate with canning factories toward producing a uniform and superior crop by using hybrid seed from a single source. The amount of Maine canned corn is increasing rapidly; in 1936, fifty thousand cases of twenty-four cans each were placed on the market. The area producing the most sweet corn extends from west to east through the south-central part of the State, including Oxford, Androscoggin, Kennebec, and Waldo Counties, and the southern parts of Franklin, Somerset, and Penobscot Counties. This is also the area from which comes the greater part of the milk exported to the Boston market.

Poultry has always been raised in Maine, but until recent years only in farm flocks of limited number and with egg production varying according to season. With the demand for uniform eggs of good quality and the development of rapid transportation, the raising of poultry has steadily increased. In 1936, the production of poultry in Maine rose to 1,713,000, and the egg production rose to more than 190 million.

Market or roadside gardening is a fairly recent development. As industrial towns grew, the demand for fresh vegetables increased, and nearby farmers began to cater to the ready market. Increasing numbers of summer residents also created a new and large demand for fresh farm and dairy products. Automobile transportation benefited the farmers relatively distant from cities, and roadside stands rapidly became profitable marketing centers for fresh farm goods. Market gardening is an important enterprise in the coastal belt, where rocky land and high property valuation prevent general large-scale farming.

With the growth of the canning industry, blueberries for canning and shipping have increased in economic value. About eighty-five per cent of the country's canned blueberries originate in Maine, and almost all of those come from the so-called 'blueberry barrens' of Washington County. The canning industry has also brought an increase in the cultivation of peas and beans.

The number of farms in Maine has been decreasing since 1880 — from 64,000 in that year to 39,000 in 1936. Although a considerable number of farms have increased in size, the total number of acres under cultivation has also decreased considerably. Tenant farming has never been popular in Maine; the majority of persons in the rural sections own their property outright, and take pride in handing it down intact from one generation to the next. Despite the general transition away from the self-sufficient farmer type, Maine continues to raise most of its own food supply. The culture of bees and the raising of small fruits on most farms throughout the State are among the survivals of a pioneer economy. The average Maine farm, with its well-kept fields, large barns, and trim white house surrounded by hardy orchard trees, attests to a hard-won and frugal security less common, perhaps, in other rural sections of New England.

FROM WATERWAYS TO AIRWAYS

TRANSPORTATION in Maine has always been conditioned by those geographic and climatic features which have had such a lasting effect on many varying phases of the State's life. Improvement in travel facilities has not reduced the distances from point to point within the State, has not altered the depth of snow or eliminated the effects of frost on the highways. From forest trail and canoe to the airplane, every link in the history of American transportation, with the exception of the stagecoach, is being used in Maine today. Large areas of the northern wilderness can be reached by no other means than those employed four centuries ago, walking and canoe, or by the latest development in transportation, the airplane. Luxurious trains speed through miles of forest which have not altered since the days when one was lucky to be able to drive from Kittery to Portland in a four-wheeled vehicle. Long the chief means of transportation for the settler, traveler, and merchant who gained access to the interior through the coastal towns or by way of the larger rivers, water-borne traffic now retains only a small fraction of its former importance.

The earliest recorded transportation system in Maine was that used by the Indians, an unusually comprehensive network of routes which required no cost or labor for maintenance — the waterways. By rivers and streams, alternating with 'carries' from lake to lake or to other rivers, the Maine tribes could thread their way over most of the State with a minimum of effort. The waterways were of particular importance during the autumn when inland tribes sought the more clement and favorable living conditions along the coast, as the primitive Red Paint People doubtless had done before them. Hunters and sportsmen today continue to use many of the old Indian highways.

One of the longest trails (meaning by 'trail' a combination of waterways and 'carries') was that between what is now Quebec and the mouth of the Kennebec River. The journey was made from Quebec, up the Chaudière to Lake Megantic, the Chain of Ponds, Dead River, to the Kennebec and down; this constitutes the Arnold Trail of today. Another trail followed the same route to the Forks of the Kennebec, then it turned eastward along the Kennebec by various ponds, Moosehead and Chesuncook Lakes, and so on down to the Penobscot and Penobscot Bay. Another series of waterways and 'carries' linked the Penobscot and Kennebec, starting from the Sebasticook River at Winslow. Three well-defined overland trails led from Rockland Harbor to Mill Stream, the Wesseweskeag, and St. George's River. Indians from the Penobscot also came down the St. George's to New Harbor, where they turned off over a 'carry' to the Sheepscot waters. A main trail went up the Sheepscot to Eastern River, the Kennebec and Androscoggin, and Merrymeeting Bay where, near Brunswick, a three-mile 'carry' gave access to Casco Bay. Again, a route lay between Gardiner and the Sandy River district by way of Cobbosseecontee Stream, Lake Maranacook, Greeley's Pond, Norcross Pond, etc., into the Little Norridgewock. Among other well-known Indian trails were the Abnaki, or Saco, from Saco to Fryeburg; the Pequawket, from Portland to Fryeburg; the Ossippi into the White Mountains; and the long Mohawk Trail, originating in Massachusetts, crossing the New Hampshire line into Maine, and passing through Naples, Farmington, Skowhegan, Bangor, and thence to Eastport and Calais. Parts of many of these early Indian routes are now automobile highways.

The early settlers, as well as those who came later, availed themselves of the same means of transportation used by the Indians. It goes without saying that Maine history, the State's social and economic growth, would have been something entirely different without its major waterways. There would have been no development of the industrially prominent river towns, and the lumber industry would have been negligible; the settling of the rich Aroostook region, for example, would certainly have been delayed had it not been for the St. John, Madawaska, and other rivers in the northeastern region. Land transportation in Colonial Maine was not a thing to be undertaken lightly. Indian trails and paths were gradually supplemented by woods roads and 'mast ways,' the latter so called because they were used for the transporting of wood — more specifically, timber to be converted into masts. One of these 'mast ways' ran between High Pine and Kittery, another between South Sanford and Berwick.

During the seventeenth and eighteenth centuries Maine towns were often rebuked and fined for their failure to maintain roads. In 1653, the Massachusetts commissioners could get no farther than Wells for want of roads; and they ordered the inhabitants of Wells, Saco, and Cape Porpoise to 'make sufficient roads within their towns from house to house, and clear and fit them for foot and cart travel, before the next county court under penalty of 10 pounds for every town's defect in this particular,' and to 'lay out a sufficient highway for horse and foot between towns within that time.'

Stagecoach lines of any extent did not come into existence until after the Revolution. The first stagecoach began operating in 1787 between Portland and Portsmouth, requiring three days for the journey. The advertisement stated that 'Those ladies and gentlemen who choose the expeditious, cheap and commodious way of stage traveling, will please to lodge their names with Mr. Motley. Price for one person, passage the whole way 20 shillings.' Five years later, an enterprising citizen made the first attempt to carry passengers between Portland and Hallowell by way of Wiscasset, making two trips weekly by sleigh in winter, and one trip a week by coach in summer. In eastern Maine, transportation was much slower in developing. For a long time there were no roads, and until 1800 no communication with interior towns was possible except by foot. As late as 1801 it was easy to get lost in going from Belfast to Bangor by land, and even in 1804 no one would attempt to bring a load of goods across country from Augusta.

One of the early transportation concerns of the Maine inhabitants was that of the postal service. Mail was entrusted to ships, or to men making the journeys through the woods by foot or horse. A post route between Portland and Boston was established in 1775, but the weekly service was very irregular. In 1790 there was only one post road in Maine; this ran along the coast southwest of Wiscasset and connected with the post road to Boston. For some years afterwards there was no post service east of Wiscasset. An arrangement had been made in 1788 whereby the mails came to Portland from Boston three times a week. The first express service between Portland and Boston was a tri-weekly schedule by water which was maintained in 1839.

As the population increased, land transportation began to expand. Stagecoaches between Boston and New York and Bangor operated in relays as early as 1816. At about this period, and a little later, more than fifteen stage lines were operating out of Hallowell alone. Lines increased along the coast and up the major river valleys, and travel conditions improved. By 1825, stages made the trip between Bangor and Portland in thirty-six hours, the fare being $7.50. Two years later, almost daily stagecoach service was possible between Portland and Dover, Portsmouth, Kennebunk, Hallowell, Augusta, Brunswick, Wiscasset, Waldoboro, Bath, Conway, Waterford, Paris, Alfred, Yarmouth, Gorham, and Saco.

It should be borne in mind that throughout the period of the stagecoach, and even after the coming of the railroads, the most important means of transportation for freight and passengers was by water.

Railroad transportation in Maine is distinguished in that one of the first railroads in New England began operating between Bangor and Old Town in 1836. Another early road, running from Whitneyville to Machiasport, was begun four years later; one of its primitive locomotives, 'The Lion,' is now in the Crosby Laboratory at the University of Maine. The Moosehead Lake Railway, a two-mile narrow-gauge road at Northeast Carry, remained the crudest in the State until it was destroyed by the fires of blueberry pickers in 1862. Locomotion was provided by draft animals, the tracks were originally fifty-and sixty-foot pine logs, and the first wheels were merely wooden disks of pine. A charter had been issued to the Portland, Saco and Portsmouth Railroad coincidentally with that of the Bangor–Old Town line, but the former did not begin operating until 1842.

Within the next half-century, there were thirty-one railroads, including branch lines, in the State. Of the roads operating at that time which are still in use, the Atlantic and St. Lawrence division of the Grand Trunk Railway between Portland and Montreal was opened to travel in 1853. The story of how Portland wrested from Boston the position as Atlantic terminus for this road is one of the most curious in Maine's railroad history. The Boston and Maine Railroad in Maine was completed in 1873, and the majority of the roads within the State began operating in the quarter-century between 1850 and 1875. The Consolidated Maine Central Railroad in 1881 comprised the Portland and Kennebec Railroad, between Portland and Brunswick, Augusta, and Bath; the Somerset and Kennebec Railroad, between Augusta and Skowhegan; the Androscoggin and Kennebec Railroad, between Danville and Waterville, and the extension between Danville and Cumberland; the Penobscot and Kennebec Railroad, between Waterville and Bangor; the Androscoggin Railroad, between Brunswick and Leeds Junction and Lewiston; and the Leeds and Farmington Railroad, between Leeds Junction and Farmington. Leased roads at the time were the Belfast and Moosehead Lake line between Belfast and Burnham, and the Dexter and Newport Railroad.

The Boston and Maine Railroad provides train and bus service between Boston and Portland, where connections are made with the Maine Central Railroad and busses to all points in Maine with the exception of Aroostook County, which is served by the trains and busses of the Bangor and Aroostook Railroad. Service between Maine and Canada is furnished by the Grand Trunk Railway, a part of the transcontinental Canadian National Railroads, and by the Canadian Pacific Railway.

Maine railroads now operate over more than two thousand miles of track. Accelerated schedules and an increasing number of modern air-conditioned coaches add to the convenience and comfort of the traveler. The railroads are of especial advantage here during the winter months, when highway travel is occasionally uncertain and hazardous. Special trains are at the disposal of visitors to Maine's summer camps and resorts, while 'snow trains' and other winter accommodations have been added to the system. Electric railways are on the decline, but nearly two hundred miles of this type of transportation are still in operation.

Steamboat transportation antedated the railroad by more than a decade, the steamboat 'Kennebec' making a trip between Portland and North Yarmouth in August, 1822. Two years later the 'Patent,' 'strong and commodious and elegantly fitted up for passengers,' began running between Portland and Boston. Steamboat lines gradually became more numerous, and before very long steamers were touching at nearly all the important coastal and river towns. Boats even steamed up the Kennebec as far as Waterville, and competition became so keen that at one time the fare between that city and Boston was only one dollar. One of the earliest iron steamships in America, the 'Bangor,' was built in 1845 to run between Bangor and Boston. Trans-Atlantic transportation by steam first affected Maine when boats began plying between Liverpool and Portland in 1853. Water transportation to the latter port reached its height in the fifties, with two hundred and forty-six sailing vessels and 12 steamships calling at Portland regularly. Among the larger steamship lines, the Portland Steam Packet Company, the Maine Steamship Company, the International Steamship Company, the Kennebec Steam Navigation Company, the Bath–Boothbay Steamship Company, and the Boston–Bangor Steamship Company eventually became associated as the Eastern Steamship Lines. Previous to the World War, the Allan, Leyland, and White Star trans-Atlantic steamship lines operated out of Portland, but this traffic has been discontinued.

The handicaps of climate and distance have been progressively overcome, and today Maine is well served by modern and efficient means of transportation. Much of the State which could not be reached by highway a quarter of a century ago is now accessible. Generally speaking, there is a concentration of roads in the southern half of the State, but more remote sections are rapidly being opened to automobile traffic. Although the majority of the roads are town-built or third class, the greater number of the many highways improved within the last two decades have been gravel-surfaced; and in addition, there are several hundred miles of concrete roadway. An extensive motor freight service is on the increase in Maine, and more than a score of intrastate and interstate bus lines provide highway transportation.

Water transportation to and from Maine has fallen off to an alarming extent from its former estate. Freight cargoes are today but a small fraction of those carried in the past, when imports and exports sometimes amounted to tens of millions of tons annually. With the exception of a few local steamship lines, passenger traffic by water completely died out when the Eastern Steamship Lines completed their summer service between New York and Bar Harbor for good in 1936. Efforts are being made to revive the decadent shipping industry, and to emphasize the State's advantages in harbors and navigable rivers as well as its relative proximity to European ports.

The most recent of all forms of transportation is represented in Maine by the Boston and Maine and Central Vermont Airways, which provides daily plane service to major points. There are eleven airports, three of which are lighted with directional radio range beams. Other airports and landing fields are being built. Five beacon towers on the Bangor–Boston route are in process of construction (1937). By January, 1937, the Works Progress Administration had supervised the painting of one hundred and eight town markers, airport symbols, and meridian markers throughout Maine. Maine's inland waterways — the same rivers, lakes, and ponds which once served the Indians — are of particular value to aviators and to those who wish to reach those sections of the State which are practically inaccessible by other means of transportation. Efforts are under way to make Portland the Atlantic terminus for a projected transoceanic air service.

From Indian trails to airways, transportation in Maine has developed along lines which parallel those of other States. The means used have been identical with those all over the nation; only in particular aspects as influenced by its natural setting and climate has Maine differed.

RACIAL ELEMENTS

AT THE beginning of the nineteenth century, Maine's population was representative of English, French, Scotch-Irish, Welsh, Irish, Dutch, German, and Acadian French stock. Men from western England began group settlement of the province as early as 1623 at Kittery, though there had been scattered settlers in the territory before that year. This stock combined with that of the Scotch-Irish, who followed soon after, to produce that shrewd, dry, somewhat dour type known as the Yankee — a name which later came to be applied to all New Englanders of this same general ancestry. These people weathered the protracted Indian wars, and their settlements grew slowly but steadily along the coast. By 1662 there had begun, as well, a gradual infiltration of Quaker settlers, whose frugal and peace-loving ways have helped to mold the Maine character.

In 1740, General Samuel Waldo imported forty families from Brunswick and Saxony to settle in Waldoboro, supplementing a Moravian colony established there a year earlier; and succeeding years brought more Germans to this section of Maine. Many of them, however, later emigrated elsewhere. Dresden was settled by German Lutherans, accompanied by French and Dutch immigrants of the same faith.

Irish settlers were especially plentiful in York, Lincoln, and Cumberland Counties; it was they who gave Limerick its name, after the city in the old country. In 1808, Irish Catholics were numerous enough in the vicinity of Damariscotta to build a place of worship, now the oldest Roman Catholic church building in New England.

The French, from their early but unsuccessful settlement of 1604, held control of the land east of the Penobscot River until 1759, when they relinquished all their claims in what is now Maine. At one time this territory had been controlled by the New Amsterdam Dutch, who were driven out only when the French returned in stronger force. Although the French were not active colonists, many of the Huguenot settlers early gained prominence in Maine. Today, especially in the coastal towns, there still live members of the old French Protestant families who strive proudly to keep their blood and their tongue as purely French as when their ancestors first came here. These people are not to be confused with the Canadian French, nor the latter with the Acadians who, refusing to swear allegiance to England or Canada, settled along the St. John River when they were exiled from their homes in Nova Scotia. Many of these people still preserve intact their language, religion, and customs.

In the middle decades of the nineteenth century, a flood of westward emigration from Maine aroused fears for the future and led to a venture in colonization. A group of Swedish settlers was imported in 1870, their colony being known as New Sweden. Their enthusiasm brought more settlers of the same nationality after them, and Stockholm shortly came into being.

As a result of the fact that Maine has no schools for industrial training, notwithstanding the National Government's offer to pay half the cost of trade schools, there has been since 1869 until recent years a continual importation of workmen from Scotland and England, and from the French-speaking sections of Canada, for specialized labor in the State's factories and mills.

Northern European peoples, particularly Finns, have joined the Canadian French in the lumbering industry; and Norwegians, Swedes, and Icelanders are engaged in the coastal regions in fishing, shipping, and quarrying. The many Russians, Lithuanians, and Poles who live in Maine have, like the Finns, settled most thickly in Knox County.

The growth of the cities has brought to the State a large number of Jews, Italians, Greeks, and Syrians, most of whom live in Waterville and Millinocket; and a scattering of other southern European nationalities, along with some Albanians, Turks, and Orientals.

Maine's small Negro population, numbering about one thousand, is chiefly resident in Bangor and Portland. Most of these Negroes are descendants of the servants of wealthy landowners and shipping families of post-Revolutionary days. They have, in some instances, intermarried with Indians, who today slightly outnumber them; and to some extent also with whites, particularly in certain more remote coastal sections.

The people of present-day Maine are predominantly of English-Scotch-Irish ancestry, with a generous proportion of French, and in lesser degree of German, blood. Most of the other nationalities represented are as yet more or less unassimilated. The Canadian French, who constitute about one-eighth of the State's total population, have lived in Maine since earliest times, yet they still keep their racial individuality, attending French churches and French schools. The census of 1930 gave the number of French-Canadians and Canadians living in Maine as more than 73,000.

FOLKLORE AND FOLKWAYS

BESIDES a considerable body of folklore peculiar to Maine, the State also possesses a larger body of racially inherited lore, particularly that of Great Britain and of France. The comparative isolation and independence of many a 'down-East' community have helped to preserve not only old customs, beliefs, and legends, but even characteristics of speech that hark back to Elizabethan or earlier days. The familiar use of the word 'butt'ry' for 'pantry,' and of the old Anglo-Saxon word 'gore' as a unit of land measurement, are obvious examples.

Maine is rich in an inherited knowledge of herbs and cure-alls, spells, weather signs, and omens which has gradually become characteristic of most rural sections through the country, and therefore does not require treatment as a cultural feature peculiar to Maine or even to New England. In sending forth pioneers to build up new territories to the west, Maine and its neighboring States contributed as well a great treasury of saws and sayings, songs and stories, which became a part of the common heritage in far distant regions, and are now only Maine's or New England's as the sociological or literary scholar may trace them back to their original source. Nevertheless, there is still a good deal of folklore, much of it as yet unrecorded, that is indigenous to the Pine Tree State.

There was a time in Maine when nearly everybody sang and composed his own songs. And he who was especially gifted as singer or story-teller was a person of consequence in his community, like the minstrel of an older day. It was as if the unlettered populace unconsciously sought and found in this way an esthetic relief from the harsh facts of their daily existence. As a result, there gradually came into being many stories and poems, some of them local and temporal, some universal and lasting. They were a sort of communal product, just as were the ancient English and Scottish ballads that are still recited or sung by many Maine folk; and they originated wherever men came together, in logging camps in the deep woods and in fo'c'sles on the sea. Verse or prose, they were passed on and further embellished by denizens of the village store or by idlers on the lee side of a wharf whittling shavings in the sun and passing plug or jug from mouth to mouth. This material is a heritage not widely known today, even in Maine itself.

Folklore and Folkways 77

Maine lore, particularly that of the lumberman, has been best recorded in the books of Mrs. Fannie Hardy Eckstorm. Her 'Minstrelsy of Maine,' a collection of folk-songs and ballads native to the State, preserves much of this rich inheritance. No anthology of American balladry or sea chanteys is without its share of Maine's songs and poems. Most of the ballads are the recordings of actual or reputed happenings. A hitherto unpublished example is 'The Mark Bachelder Tragedy,' which begins as follows:

> 'Twas on December twenty-fifth,
> A time not long ago;
> An awful tragedy was played
> In the town of Sebago.
>
> It was at Leslie Kenison's
> Upon a Christmas night;
> That then and there these persons met,
> To drink, and dance, and fight.
>
> And one Mark Bachelder was there,
> The bully of the town;
> And this man, Leslie Kenison,
> Was bound to knock him down.
>
> So Kenison did seize a stake,
> And struck him on the head;
> Inflicting wicked, cruel blows,
> Until they thought him dead.
>
> They dragged his lifeless form away,
> And quickly put him in his sleigh;
> Started his horse and sent him home,
> There to freeze and die alone.

Detectives investigate the crime; Bachelder is buried by a grieving family; and Kenison is sentenced to four years in prison. The convict's parting words are familiar ones:

> And now, young men and maidens all,
> Take warning thus by me;
> And e'er abide on virtue's side,
> And shun bad company.

Other ballads there are of greater poetic excellence, no doubt, though most of them have now been collected and published. All have a strong popular appeal. Many of the more exciting are concerned with local heroes, whose feats of strength or skill have become legendary — as, for example, John Ross, the big boss of the Penobscot drive. But more often the fabulous stories are told in prose form. And tall tales they are! There was the man who shot five bears with one bullet, the man who shot one bear for each day in the year, the man who invented the slow bullet, and the man who fashioned a curved rifle-barrel so efficient that when he shot from his door he had to pull in his head to escape the bullet coming around the house. These stories have survived to whet the imaginations of contemporary narrators, such as that member of the famous Coffin family who invented doughnuts that turned themselves over in the cooking fat and jumped out when they were done.

There is, however, a characteristic sort of Yankee humor which manifests itself more in understatement than in exaggeration. This humor plays a prominent part in everyday life. In Maine great expanses of water which elsewhere would be known as lakes are called ponds. A housewife says: 'Don't know what I've got; I'll just scratch around and see, but I'm afraid there's not a thing to eat in the house' — and then goes on to produce a meal of exceptional size and quality. Many of Maine's own writers have capitalized on this sober-sided Yankee wit, and none more successfully than he who was known as Artemus Ward.

What commonly passes for the Maine vernacular in print and on stage, screen, and radio is a libel on the 'down-Easter's' manner of speaking. In reality, there are as many Maine dialects as there are States in the Union. A skilled listener acquainted with Maine speech should be able to identify the community to which any Maine person speaking his home dialect belongs. Variations in the vernacular between one community or region and another do not lie in the use or misuse of words, but in changes of inflection and timbre. Thus it is next to impossible accurately to reproduce the Maine vernacular in printed words. The common speech of Maine people of English-Scottish-Irish stock is probably as nearly pure, in being free from corruptions and in retaining old forms intact, as any of this country, with the possible exception of that of the Carolina and Kentucky mountaineers. The peculiarities of Maine speech are its nasal qualities, slurred enunciation, and dropped syllables, with a hesitancy in delivery.

The Maine Yankee is not nearly so taciturn as a stranger might at first consider him, but it is a rule that words are not to be wasted. Get him talking, however, and he will tell you stories a-plenty. Less restricted to Maine than woods yarns and the ballad, but none the less typical, are tales of sea serpents, 'ha'nted' houses, ghosts, and witches. Every year serious church-going people attest to the truth of such mysteries and monsters, and an almost limitless volume of material could be gathered about them. Although there was a time when Maine witches were given their 'comeuppance,' therapeutic magic has been practiced throughout the State to this day. Indian legends and pirate stories abound. Corners, fields, and brooklets have their own peculiar names and histories. Here occurred an Indian massacre; there a witch was tried and hanged; at this crossroads a suicide is buried; no one lives in that house because footsteps are heard there in the night. The shore is pock-marked with holes dug by hunters of treasure, who usually toiled in vain; while those who chanced to find the wealth in blackened pot or ancient chest are said to have lost it again through the machinations of the Evil One, or to have come to some grim and sudden end.

People in Maine have their own ways of doing things. And if those ways are not always the most efficient, there is usually a reason for them. While the reason may in many cases seem to rest only upon superstition or even narrow-mindedness, it has generally a deeper and firmer foundation. Any bit of folk-wisdom — a cure, a weather or planting sign — does not spring into being spontaneously. It is knowledge gained from experience, tried and found true by generations; therefore it is to be trusted.

EDUCATION AND RELIGION

EDUCATION

SUPERFICIALLY at least, the early history of education in Maine is for the most part identical with that of education in Massachusetts. But the settlers of Massachusetts showed a veneration for learning, and rapidly developed an excellent school system; whereas the settlers of Maine, far more widely scattered, long harassed by the Indian wars, and of less wealth and more primitive interests, were largely indifferent to the value of education and the need for its development. When school taxes became a real burden to the communities, 'moving schools' were organized which traveled from town to town, spending only a few weeks in each place. The situation was greatly improved after 1789, when Massachusetts adopted a law requiring liberal instruction for all children and college or university education for schoolmasters. After achieving statehood in 1820, Maine modeled her own school laws upon those of Massachusetts.

The first real school in Maine was the mission established on the Kennebec in 1696 by Father Sebastian Rasle, whose valuable work among the Indians suffered greatly from, and was finally ended by, the depredations of the English colonists. Other early Jesuit teachers were Father Romagne at Passamaquoddy and Father Bapst at Indian Island.

In 1794, the Massachusetts General Court granted a charter to Bowdoin College at Brunswick. Academies were founded at Hallowell and Berwick in 1791, and by 1821 there were twenty-five academies in the State. From this beginning, higher education in Maine has progressed slowly but steadily. The free high school law of 1873 brought about the opening of some one hundred and fifty high schools in the State. In 1863, a bill was passed which established normal schools at Farmington and Castine; and the Madawaska Training School was established in 1878 at Fort Kent expressly for the preparation of teachers to instruct the French settlers, exiled Acadians from Nova Scotia, in the St. John Valley. Today there are six teachers' training schools in Maine, and more than sixty private schools and academies in good standing, including parochial, Jewish, and Quaker schools and two Catholic academies for girls. The Portland Hebrew School was founded in 1884. Oak Grove Seminary in Vassalboro, a Friends' school for girls founded in 1849, is now nationally famous.

The rural or district school, heralded in American song and story as the cradle of the nation's greatness, has always been a problem in Maine. Modern educators have exploded the myth of the little red schoolhouse; and intelligent people no longer expect one teacher, too often inadequately trained, to instruct from six to eight grades in all the required subjects with any degree of success. It is increasingly difficult to find good teachers willing to undertake such work, and the communities themselves are often unable to support their schools adequately. And yet all over the State today there are many such schools, little changed in the last fifty or seventy-five years. In 1937, President K. C. M. Sills of Bowdoin College charged that Maine's schools have been going steadily backward in the past ten years. He said that between two hundred and three hundred schools in the State operate on an annual budget of less than three hundred and sixty dollars, and that a smaller proportion of the State income is now spent on its schools than was spent one hundred years ago. There is certainly need for educational pioneering here today, particularly in the more thinly populated regions.

Maine has four old and important colleges. The University of Maine, at Orono, was founded as an agricultural school in 1865, became co-educational in 1872, and was named the University of Maine in 1897. It maintains a faculty extension service, operating largely in rural areas. Bowdoin College at Brunswick, incorporated in 1794, is one of the oldest and most prominent of the country's smaller liberal arts colleges. Colby College, at Waterville, was chartered in 1813 as the Maine Literary and Theological Institute. From 1831 to 1842, as Waterville College, it was one of the first institutions in the country to experiment with manual training; women were admitted as students in 1871; and it acquired its present name in 1899. Bates College, at Lewiston, now non-sectarian, is an outgrowth of the Maine State Seminary, founded in 1855 by Free Baptists. It became a co-educational college in 1864. Considerably more than half of its alumni have entered the teaching profession.

Among the State's miscellaneous educational institutions are the Bangor Theological Seminary, established in 1814; Nasson College, founded at Springvale in 1912 for the practical training of young women, the first chartered college for women in the State; Westbrook Junior

College for Women, in Portland, the only school of its kind in the State, founded as an academy in 1831 and attaining junior college status in 1925; and the Maine School for the Deaf, the School of Fine and Applied Art, and the Peabody Law School, all at Portland.

RELIGION

The first Christian missionary to Maine was the Jesuit priest, Nicholas Aubry or d'Aubri, who preached to the Indians at Dochet Island in 1604. The first Protestant clergyman was the Reverend Richard Seymour, minister at the unsuccessful Popham Colony of 1607. Early Jesuit churches and schools were built in the wilderness by Gabriel Druillettes (1646) and Father Rasle (1696), both unusual for their scholarship and progressive ideas. Most of the Abnaki tribe were converted to Christianity by these men, and Father Rasle wielded tremendous influence over the Indians. Partly from fear of his power and partly from bigotry, he was persecuted and eventually killed by the English. But between him and his Protestant contemporary, John Eliot, there developed a mutual tolerance and esteem. Eliot's Indian converts at that time were spread widely through southern Maine. Most of the present-day Indians, however, retain a heritage of Jesuit teaching and are staunch Catholics.

Today, although the Congregational, Baptist, Methodist, and (in some cities) Roman Catholic churches are strongest in Maine, nearly every denomination in the country is represented here. There are, besides those mentioned, Episcopalian, Free Baptist, Unitarian, Universalist, Advent Christian, Friends, Seventh Day Adventist, Christian, Latter Day Saints, Christian Science, Hebrew, Presbyterian, Greek Orthodox, Lutheran, Evangelical, and 'Church of God' churches in Maine. Many unusual sects, some of them peculiar to Maine alone, still flourish throughout the State, often in segregated colonies where they are free to worship according to their particular tenets, unmolested by curious and more conventional neighbors.

The Shakers, or members of the 'United Society of Believers in Christ's Second Appearing,' organized some of the first religious colonies in Maine. Their settlements at Alfred and New Gloucester, established in 1793, were active for many years. The Alfred village was abandoned in 1925, and is now owned and occupied by a Roman Catholic school for boys; but the New Gloucester settlement, though greatly diminished, still continues.

Shaker doctrines greatly resemble those of the Quakers, except that they hold to complete celibacy. They recruit new members by adopting orphans and making converts. They are famous for their piety and industry, and are always valuable citizens.

Less commonly known are various religious societies which have sprung up in Maine from time to time, sometimes gaining wide notice, but more often subsiding quietly with the death or dispersal of their founders. Maine life has a certain frontier quality favorable to revivalistic practices, and a Puritan temper in its people seems to produce zeal and fanaticism. Often a discontented or disqualified pastor of an organized church gathers together a small flock of followers, usually good but ignorant country folk eager for a faith they can comprehend and a leader they can see, and thus a sect is born. Many such have in time achieved considerable power and influence.

Among the oldest of the religious groups peculiar to Maine are the Bullockites, a society of primitive Baptists, who still worship, though infrequently, in their more than century-old meeting house at Porter in Oxford County. Less permanent were the Higginsites of Carmel. When it became known that their leader, the Reverend Mr. Higgins, was accustomed to drive the devil from children of the sect with whips, his fellow citizens decorated him with tar and feathers and escorted him from their town. Shortly thereafter the colony was discontinued. In Scarboro in the early 1800's there appeared a Scotch-Irish preacher named Cochran, remarkable for an irresistible personality and a singularly sweet voice. Under his leadership, Cochranism grew and flourished all through York County and spread into New Hampshire. His followers gathered each Sunday in the woods to join in simple rites of song and dance. This unusual method of worship in an age of bleak Puritanism achieved understandable popularity. York County churches were soon emptied, and their preachers exhorted vacant pews in vain. But with increasing strength, Cochranism more openly took on colors strangely resembling free love. This the righteous were not long in suppressing. Cochran took himself westward, but he was not easily forgotten.

Perhaps the most unusual organization of all, the Palestine Emigration Association, came into being in 1866. Under the leadership of a discredited Mormon minister named Adams, one hundred and fifty-six crusaders — men, women, and children — set out for the Holy Land, proposing 'to commence the great work of restoration foretold by the old prophets, patriarchs, and apostles as well as by our Lord himself.' The expedition sailed from Jonesport, and actually arrived and founded a colony in Palestine near Jaffa, where they were beset by every sort of hardship. The leader took to drink, and in little more than a year those of the band who had survived came straggling back to their homes.

But this was not the only crusade from Maine to the Holy Land. The Sandfordites, whose temple, Shiloh, in Durham, is now a famous landmark, once set out in three white ships to visit Jerusalem. They were forced to return in great distress, however, when the Lord failed to send them manna in lieu of the provisions they had not believed it necessary to provide. Of all Maine's religious cults, this is the most important, since it is of national scope. It flourished with most fervency at the turn of the last century, as the 'Church of the Holy Ghost and Us,' under the Reverend Mr. Sandford, an evangelist with convincing powers. He was later jailed and convicted for exploiting his flock, many members of which were found to be existing in extreme misery and want. Nevertheless, the church is today of considerable strength, despite its rigorous and primitive doctrines.

Other and less conspicuous manifestations are the Free Thinkers of Fort Fairfield; 'A Wayside People of the Triune God,' established at Litchfield in 1900; the Reverend F. W. O'Brien's 'Forward Movement' and People's Church, founded at Bath in 1898; and the more recent Holiness Church at Kingfield, formed by a group of literal believers organized to oppose the liberal trends of modern times.

Aside from religious groups interesting mainly because of their oddity, Maine can boast of several unusual and highly valuable organizations. The first 'radio parish' in the United States was formed at Portland in 1926, broadcasting over Station WCSH, with the Reverend H. O. Hough as pastor. The broadcasts are designed primarily for persons who have no opportunity to attend regular church services. They are now supported by nine denominations, and enjoy great popularity. The Young People's Society of Christian Endeavor was originated at Williston Church in Portland by the Reverend Francis E. Clark in 1881. The Society's membership now numbers several millions, and Williston Church is today a shrine for Christian Endeavorers from all parts of the world. A State Interdenominational Commission, organized in the middle of last century, came into prominence under President William DeWitt Hyde of Bowdoin College. It has been copied in seventeen other States.

The Bible Society of Maine was established at Portland in 1809. It distributes annually thousands of copies of the Bible, printed in the fifty different languages that are spoken in the State. Another important organization is the Female Samaritan Association of Portland, founded in

1828, and maintaining since an unbroken record of splendid philanthropic work throughout the State. A more modern type of social service is that provided by the International Institute of the Y.W.C.A. of Biddeford and Saco, in educating the foreign-born in domestic and practical arts.

The Seacoast Mission, an independent philanthropic enterprise supported by individual contributions, has its headquarters at Bar Harbor, and by means of its boat 'Sunbeam' it brings religious, educational, hospital, and recreational facilities to the inhabitants (particularly the children) of the islands and lonely outposts of the Maine coast. Its work at Christmas time is especially praiseworthy.

ARCHITECTURE

MAINE architecture has reflected the conservative, substantial, and practical characteristics of Maine people from the time the first roof was raised in the State to the present day. Climatic conditions and the abundance of superior-quality wood, sole basis of construction until about the nineteenth century, led to the evolution of architectural types in Maine common to the New England States as a whole. Maine architecture of the eighteenth and early nineteenth centuries (and, to a considerable degree, that of today, since many of the architectural traditions of those centuries have been upheld) was highly satisfactory from an esthetic as well as a practical point of view. Eminently suited to its time and its place, the State's architecture expressed a people and a way of living, it 'belonged' to its particular background and landscape. Even though their designs were derived elsewhere, were adaptations of existing forms, the better architectural examples were more than imitations; they had a definite indigenous quality peculiar to themselves. A sane and humanized relation to the environment characterized the development of Maine's architecture from period to period.

It is assumed that the earliest Maine dwellings were huts of branches, rushes, turf, and thatch, often built into a hillside, such as were found farther south in the early seventeenth century. Such dwellings were familiar to England in that period, due largely to the scarcity of wood for building purposes. Contrary to popular belief, the log house or cabin, which is still found here occasionally, was not native to Maine or New England. The type was unknown in England, and was presumably introduced to America towards the middle of the seventeenth century. English half-timbered methods of construction were employed in Maine, but proved unsatisfactory due to extremes in temperature and excessive snows and rains.

In respect to the two major standards of structural beauty and practicality, early Maine architecture admirably fulfilled both requirements. As elsewhere in New England, native architecture, particularly that between 1760 and 1820, influenced later architecture throughout the country, although it had little effect upon any other than domestic design. Architectural types prevailing in the State until well into the nineteenth century fall into several divisions: defensive garrisons, farm houses, manor houses, meeting-houses, public buildings, schools, and jails. Considering the long period of intermittent French and Indian warfare, extending from 1675 to 1763, it is remarkable that there are any existing buildings which were erected prior to 1765. The need for protection produced such defensive buildings as the McIntire Garrison House (1660–90) at York, the Fort Western blockhouses (1754; restored), and Fort Halifax (1754) at Winslow, in which simplicity, strength of design, and defensive requirements were stressed. The Maine garrison house or blockhouse was, in effect, an adaptation of English and medieval fortifications, as evidenced by such a feature as the overhang, which made it possible to protect the walls beneath by firing upon the enemy from the projection of the second story. Of all the architectural types in Maine, this was the slowest to change; little or no alteration in form occurred in defensive buildings between the McIntire Garrison House and Fort Edgecomb (1808).

Because of the rarity of existing buildings erected before 1730, it is difficult to trace the early architectural development in Maine, although it doubtless corresponded to that of Massachusetts and Connecticut. The ordinary farm house remained unchanged in design during the last three-quarters of the eighteenth century, whereas the meeting-house underwent clearly defined changes between 1760 and 1820. The plan of the typical Maine house was patterned after that farther south, the type which prevailed throughout the State during most of the eighteenth century having been evolved from an earlier design which consisted of one, two, or three rooms with a central chimney, and a half-story in the roof above. The characteristic eighteenth-century house was a rectangular structure, with a central entrance hall, a huge central chimney (usually seven or eight feet square) built behind the stairs, two spacious rooms on either side of the hall, a central kitchen at the rear of the chimney, and two small rooms filling out the rear corners of the rectangle. On the second floor there were usually two large rooms at the front of the house, called 'chambers,' and two small corner 'bedrooms' at the rear of the first floor. A rough 'lean-to' was often added afterward at the rear of the house. No exact architectural balance was sought, and it was customary for nearly all houses to be built with the front facing the southern, or warmer and more protected, side.

The framework of the early Maine house consisted of sills, plates, girts, and 'summers' or girders, and was constructed with the utmost care. Timbers were hewn, while all pieces of the framework were broad-axed or adzed until nearly as smooth as if they had been planed. Boards, studs, and light joints were sawed; joints between braces, girts, and posts were mortised and tenoned. Roofs were commonly gabled, with the ridge parallel to the road. Roof boarding covered the roof framework, and at an early date, before the use of shingles, roofs were occasionally thatched with river sedge. Ridgepoles were a later development, a ridge purlin, or horizontal member, being used on the early buildings to support the common rafters. With the exception of those on defensive buildings, there is no very early example in Maine of the overhang.

The exteriors of eighteenth-century houses were covered with clapboards, with or without sheathing. No outside cornices existed in the earlier architecture, although subsequently there were cornices of moderate projection with a bed mold. These gradually became elaborate, bed molds becoming profusely ornamented; and in the early nineteenth century, cornices were used across gabled ends, and the rake molds became as heavy as horizontal cornices. Early small and narrow casement windows were replaced by double-hung windows, three lights (panes) wide by five or six high, and later by still wider twelve-light windows. Much of the glass used was imported. Shutters were built either in one leaf, covering the entire window with a track on the window stool, or in two parts. Entrances were merely frontispieces, built without a projecting hood or canopy over the door, and were of three types: flat entablature (the horizontal member over the entrance), pediment and broken pediment (the triangular ornamental space over the doorway), and scrolled pediment. Sidelights are usually associated with nineteenth-century construction, while the use of the broken frieze (that section of the entablature lying between architrave and cornice) and of the architrave (the lowest division of an entablature) above fluted pilasters is an odd departure from classic precedent. Circular heads of doorways were common, while elliptical heads occurred after 1800. Front doors were broad and low, and simple molded entablatures with pilasters formed the usual design.

The interior woodwork of front rooms in the eighteenth- and early nineteenth-century houses centered about the fireplace, the fireplace wall usually being paneled. Two broad panels appeared over the fireplace itself, and an elaborate bolection molding surrounded the fireplace opening. In more formal houses, the moldings and horizontal panels were flanked by narrow fluted pilasters. The remaining parts of the fireplace wall were completed with vertical panels to the doorway, and a small horizontal panel above it. Wood cornices gave height and scale to the low-studded rooms, and nearly always there were dadoes the height of the window sills. Staircase newels were from two and a half to three inches square, and skirt moldings were cut to elaborate and interesting forms. Hand-rail moldings were often mitered to form the top of newels, and the handrails themselves were small and delicately wrought. The bead and bevel molding was the one most frequently used, serving as panel mold for interior doors, shutters, wainscot, dadoes, paneling, cupboards, and outside doors. A large cove, or concave, molding was characteristic of outside caps of windows; while some form of cyma recta, a molding of reverse curve at the top of the cornice, was commonly the dominant ceiling molding.

Cellars in early Maine buildings, if built at all, were usually under only part of the house, and they were used chiefly for the storage of food. Cellar walls were either finished with mortar of a poor quality or left unfinished. Chimneys were of under-burned brick laid in puddled clay, great care being taken in the construction of the brickwork. It is notable, however, that the woodwork of many old houses is in much better condition than the masonry, because of the inferior brick and mortar that had to be used. Fireplaces were large, their hearths finished with tiles seven or eight inches square. Bricks were not uniform in size and in all Colonial work were hand-made — as in the McLellan House (1770-74) at Gorham. Flemish bond was the common design for good brickwork, being used especially in the construction of important façades.

In the Colonial period, and later, iron was scarce in Maine and in great demand. Hardware was hand-wrought, and frequently showed much delicacy and refinement of design, as well as a fine sense of scale. Hand-wrought nails were of two types: a thin pointed nail for finishing work, and a larger and stronger nail for heavier construction. In sharp contrast to the many neatly painted white homes of today were the red-painted or unpainted houses of an earlier period. The paint first used on the exteriors was usually of a dark red color, called Indian red, in which red ocher was commonly mixed with fish oil. Although one or two rooms might be painted, only the well-to-do could afford this practice until well along in the eighteenth century. Records indicate the possible use of hangings or tapestries in the homes of the wealthy.

The characteristics of the typical Maine house before the period of the Greek Revival have been outlined. The more pretentious manor houses, of which the earliest recorded example in Maine is the William Pepperell House (1682) at Kittery Point, were somewhat similar in general architectural plan, but were larger and more elaborate. Other examples of this type are the Sarah Orne Jewett House (1774) at South Berwick, and the Lady Pepperell House (1760) and Cutts House (1783) at Kittery Point. Many of these manor houses represented precisely what the term implies: they were the 'big houses' in the English, almost feudal, sense of the word, the centers of prosperity and culture. Indeed, several of the pre-Revolutionary landowners, such as Dr. Sylvester Gardiner of Gardiner, were to all intents and purposes 'lords of the manor,' operating their estates under a feudal system of tenancy.

Even before the close of the eighteenth century, Maine had a considerable number of fine mansions, scattered all along the coast and on the major waterways; and after 1800, houses of great pretentiousness were not rare, as shipmasters and merchants became increasingly wealthy. Many Maine houses were built in the first decade of the nineteenth century, an important period in residential building in all eastern American cities. Houses at Wiscasset, which was then at the height of its prosperity, represented the 'apogee of the Georgian style as the culmination of colonial and early national architecture.' Visitors to Maine often express surprise at the many fine old houses which now stand in isolated sections of the coast. The explanation is that at the time of their erection Maine was still a predominantly maritime State — all wealth came from the sea. Hence, successful Maine men commonly built their beautiful homes with their doorstep on the shore and the sea for their front yard. When industrial interests turned inland and transportation developed along highways and railroads, many mansions became isolated because of their location on remote peninsulas all along the coast.

The mansions of the late eighteenth and early nineteenth centuries are characterized by larger scale, higher ceilings, and more elaborate detail. It is possible that much of the molding and other interior detail of modest houses was copied and simplified from the more pretentious buildings. Maine carpenters and carvers, deriving their designs for moldings, cornices, entablatures, portals, and façades from English patternbooks, nevertheless brought their own particular skill and originality to bear on their work. Adapting English Georgian architecture to their own ends, the architects used their materials intelligently, retaining a delicacy and refinement of treatment even after the style became ornate and heavy in England. Simplicity without crudeness was sought; and architectural charm was the result.

Cornices on the more elaborate early nineteenth-century houses show far more detail, windows are larger and have more complex moldings, and the entrance motives of the larger homes are outstanding features of the buildings. Although the work was usually executed by local artisans, the designs were far richer than those of the more modest buildings, and the influence of the Renaissance in England is obvious. Exceptionally fine interior work is found in the mansions built between 1790 and 1820. The elliptical arch for door heads and recesses was adopted, the Palladian window appeared, as did side lights in connection with entrance doorways, as well as porches and free columns. More generous lighting, space, and circulation were provided. Frequently, however, the demands of economy produced the architectural restraint which is a salient element of the best in Colonial-Georgian design, such as is found in the William Nickels House (1807-08) and the Abiel Wood House (begun 1812) at Wiscasset. It is regrettable that more houses representative of the period under consideration, as well as those of a few decades earlier, are not extant. Fire, such as that which destroyed so many mansions in Portland in 1775 and again in 1866, is responsible for this lack, while numbers of otherwise excellent examples have been marred by remodeling and alterations.

The Alna Meeting-House (1789) is probably the most satisfactory example of another architectural type found in Maine. Simply but sturdily constructed, with windows on all four sides, the building rests securely on a dry foundation of large squared slabs of granite over a rubble wall. As on most of the old meeting-houses, the outside finish is plain; cornices are unimportant, rake molds are flat, and windows are finished with simple architraves. Galleries run around three sides of the interior, which is dominated by a splendid two-story pulpit. Great skill of design and beauty of workmanship went into the old pulpits, which often resembled the Alna pulpit in height, and had a canopy and a high and elaborate enclosure for the preacher. The box pews in the Alna galleries are set at varying levels, several seats being hinged so that the worshipers might more comfortably stand to sing. Whether the pews are of box form or more nearly like the present-day arrangement, board dadoes about three and a half feet high are common features of the early meeting-houses.

Old stone buildings in Maine are rare. The Old York Gaol (1653) and the old Oxford County Jail at Paris Hill are interesting examples of this comparatively rare type of structure. Occasionally small stone buildings which were originally used for schools are found in remote districts, but they are not at all common. The Wiscasset Courthouse (1824) is a fine example of brick work. Its entrance, an elliptical niche with half-ellipsoidal dome, is unique as an exhibit of bricklaying.

It is unfortunate that the names of the architects responsible for the designing of seventeenth, eighteenth, and nineteenth century Maine houses, in particular the mansions and manor houses, were not preserved. Records too often report only that Captain this, Colonel that, or General someone else 'built his house' in such and such a year — as if the gentlemen referred to went to work themselves with axe, saw, and adze and created their homes. Mention has been made of the fact that domestic woodworkers took many of their designs from English sources. Similarly, the designs for general architectural plans as well as for details were borrowed from English books and from the work of English architects. The best carpenters of the Colonial period, and later, were carpenter-architects, cabinet-makers, and often skilled woodcarvers. It should be remembered that many Maine carpenters were also shipbuilders, ships' carpenters, and carvers of figureheads — men to whom a fine appreciation of line and form became almost instinctive. It has been pertinently stated that no better education relating to beauty of lines can be obtained than in the designing of ships.

Wealthy Maine landowners often had their homes designed by architects from Massachusetts and other States; and the work of such architects as S. P. Cockerell, Robert Mitchell, Thomas Major, James Hoban, and Stephen Hallett may well have affected the design of some Maine mansions constructed between the 1760's and 1830's. The influence of Charles Bulfinch, designer of the State Capitol at Augusta, and of Samuel McIntire, the Salem architect-carpenter, was doubtless felt in the State's architecture. Several Bangor houses have been accredited to Bulfinch, but the claim is no more authenticated than the assertion that Sir Christopher Wren designed a few Maine churches and mansions. A number of Portland homes, such as the Sweat, Shepley, and Churchill mansions, are attributed to the distinguished Boston architect, Alexander Parris. Aaron Sherman of Duxbury, Massachusetts, designed and built the Ruggles House (1819) at Columbia Falls, one of the State's more elaborate examples of the Colonial tradition as embodied in nineteenth-century architecture. Although only a carpenter by trade, Sherman designed several other noteworthy buildings in Columbia Falls and Machias.

Maine felt the influence of the beginnings of the Classic Revival in the mid-eighteenth century, and shared in the Greek Revival, extending roughly from 1820 to 1850. In this Hellenic movement, not only were features of Greek architecture adopted, but Maine towns were given Greek names such as Milo, Troy, and Athens. Variations on the Greek temple-home began to appear, although the Colonial traditions were carried through. Houses were built with end rather than side facing the street; Greek colonnades, columns, entablatures, bold and heavy moldings, and extensive variations on Doric, Ionic, and Corinthian designs were used. Somewhat later, a Gothic influence began to appear in the architecture of college buildings, churches, and public buildings. The Georgian and the Gothic were frequently combined, as in the beautiful First Congregational Church at Kennebunkport. Although Maine architecture variously adapted and interpreted the influences of the Neo-Classic, Gothic, and Romanesque revivals which swept the country, it assimilated nothing new from its immediate environment.

Following the decline of the Greek Revival, there is little to distinguish Maine architecture from that of the rest of the country. Examples of the later nineteenth-century architecture, when design ran wild and buildings abounded in profuse and meaningless detail, are to be found in the State's larger cities, particularly Portland. The Georgian and Greek Revival traditions were not altogether abandoned, however; no passing phase could alter the fundamental soundness and simplicity of these traditions.

Maine followed the general architectural trends of the twentieth century toward a readaptation of the classical forms and the increasing use of iron, steel, and stone in construction. Although a number of public and private buildings in Maine reflect the latest developments in modern architecture, there have been few experiments with ultra-modern design, and the majority of homes follow the usual traditions. A few radical departures in house-building have been carried out in some of the larger cities, such as Portland, and the Waldo Theater (1936) at Waldoboro is but one of several fine examples in the State of contemporary architecture applied to special fields. The architecture of the Maine farmhouse, with its usual series of sheds, workrooms, and storage-rooms joining barn and dwelling for purposes of warmth and convenience, remains basically unchanged. That Maine people on the whole are not unmindful of their architectural traditions is indicated by the care and appreciation bestowed upon their more select old houses, as in Wiscasset, Alfred, and Belfast, and by such valuable work as the reproduction of the beautiful mansion, 'Montpelier,' in Thomaston.

THE ARTS

THE New England tradition of active practice and patronage of the arts — something more than a general appreciation of esthetic values — is still alive in Maine. A relatively large number of writers and artists were born in the State or have done much of their work here, and each year many more are attracted to its green hills and bright harbors. Some come each summer to find rest, or to seek inspiration and material for their work; some make their permanent homes here, to enjoy peaceful activity among beautiful surroundings the year round.

Maine has lost some of her traditional vehicles of culture, while new developments and facilities have turned her people away from communal activity in the arts. But these losses are not without their compensations. New media, the radio and the cinema, offer larger opportunities for the enjoyment and appreciation of artistic expression. And even today the old-fashioned community 'sing' has not been displaced entirely. Fiddles still zip and whine in village ballrooms. Little groups in schools, granges, 4-H Clubs, and churches still gather in the evenings for orchestra practice or to rehearse 'the Play.' Each year new talent is revealed by the State-wide contest in high school dramatics that culminates at Bowdoin College in the spring. Occasionally the product of solitary, perhaps unencouraged, labor with chisel, brush, or pen is brought to light, and a new and original contribution to the art of Maine is recognized and acclaimed.

LITERATURE

Maine's literary heritage is an old and enduring one, rich in names the mention of which anywhere in this country evokes instant recognition. As early as 1800, books were being published in the Province by a 'lady novelist' who achieved national reputation under the pen names, 'A Lady of Maine' and 'A Lady of Massachusetts.' The work of Madam Wood (the name by which she later came to be known) was published in Baltimore and in Portsmouth, New Hampshire, as well as in Portland. She was one of America's first popular novelists. Born Sally Sayward

Barrel at York in 1759, she was in the course of her long life a resident of York, Wiscasset, and Portland, was twice married, and had three children, whom she helped to support by the proceeds of her writing. She died in 1854, when she was more than ninety-five years old. In most of her romances, the better known of which were 'Julia,' 'Amelia,' 'Dorval,' and 'Tales of the Night,' her aim was to develop an American style and to use American scenes and characters, an unusual literary ambition in a period when all genteel Americans aped in manner of life and thought the prevailing modes of England and the Continent. 'Why,' wrote Madam Wood, 'we should not aim at independence, with respect to our mental enjoyments, as well as for our more substantial gratifications, I know not. Why must the amusements of our leisure hours cross the Atlantic? and introduce foreign fashions and foreign manners, to a people, certainly capable of producing their own.' In an introduction to one of her novels she declared: 'The following pages are wholly American; the characters are those of our own country. The author has endeavored to catch the manners of her native land; and it is hoped no one will find, upon perusal, a lesson, or even a sentence, that authorize vice or sanction immorality.' It is said of Madam Wood that, after reading some of Scott's novels, she became so dissatisfied with her own work that she gathered as many of her books and manuscripts as she could and destroyed them.

Perhaps the earliest fiction to be written and published in Maine was an anonymous work, printed at Hallowell in 1797, called 'Female Friendship, or the Innocent Sufferer: a Moral Novel.' The earliest volume of Maine verse, 'The Amaranth,' by Eliza S. True, was advertised as 'Calculated to Amuse the Mind of Youth without Corrupting their Morals.' 'The Village,' a didactic and stilted poem obviously influenced by Pope and Goldsmith, appeared in 1816 from the pen of Enoch Lincoln. It reveals little of the ability that made its author, in 1827, the sixth governor of his State at the age of thirty-three, or of the qualities that gave him wide personal influence throughout his mature life.

Seba Smith (1792-1868), who founded Maine's first daily newspaper, *The Courier*, at Portland in 1829, early became known as a humorist and as a satirist of the down-East Yankee type later more shrewdly portrayed to a far wider audience by Charles Farrar Browne (1834-67). The latter, internationally known as 'Artemus Ward,' died in England before he had reached the full height of his literary power, and is buried at Waterford in Oxford County, where he was born.

Nathaniel Willis (1780-1870), first editor of Maine's earliest Democrat-Republican newspaper, *The Eastern Argus*, founded *The Youth's Com-

panion in 1827, a periodical characterized in its day as 'the most important single educational agency in America.' The *Companion*, though published in Boston for most of the hundred years of its existence, was always a vehicle for Maine writers; its most popular spinner of tales was the scientist C. A. Stephens (1844-1931) of Norway Lake, who estimated that he had written more than three thousand stories for the magazine; its first subscriber was a little girl in Maine; and the majority of its successive editors were men from Maine, among them Arthur G. Staples, a well-known journalist.

Two of Willis's children achieved prominence that overshadowed their father's. Nathaniel Parker Willis (1806-67) was a poet, journalist, and critic of great contemporary influence, though he is little read today. His sister, Sara Payson (Willis) Parton, better known as 'Fanny Fern' (1811-72), a popular novelist and essayist, is best described as a pleader of special causes, most frequently that of women's rights. The influence of her liberal mind, particularly on the everyday life of New York at that time, was of more lasting importance than any of her literary works.

Another Maine literary figure distinguished among his contemporaries was MacDonald Clarke, 'the mad poet,' born at Bath in 1798. He went to New York as a young man and joined the 'Bohemian' circle in which the younger Willis and his sister moved. His work, now almost wholly forgotten, enjoyed some esteem in its time. Brilliant and eccentric, he lived in continual poverty, befriended by the more successful of his fellows, notably Willis. He died in 1842 in the asylum on Blackwell's Island, drowned in his cell by the flow of water from an open faucet. Shortly before his death, it is recorded, he was heard to say: 'Four things I am sure there will be in Heaven — music, little children, flowers, and fresh air.'

There could be no greater contrast to Clarke's melancholy life than the happy and extraordinarily industrious career of Jacob Abbott (1803-79), perhaps the best known of his remarkable family and the author of some two hundred books for young people, the most popular of which were published as the 'Rollo Series.' His brother, John S. C. Abbott (1805-77), was famous as a teacher and historian. A small museum in the tower of Hubbard Hall, the library at Bowdoin College, houses a collection of material pertaining to the Abbott family, including manuscripts of some of the books of Jacob Abbott, doubtless Maine's most prolific writer.

Henry Wadsworth Longfellow was the first writer of outstanding distinction to be associated with Maine. Born at Portland in 1807, he was educated there and at Bowdoin College, where he subsequently taught

OF ARCHITECTURAL INTEREST

DOMESTIC architecture in Maine developed simply from the early Colonial structures of New England to evolve, in the late eighteenth century, into two general types. An example of the most prevalent of these is the story-and-a-half farm cottage pictured here; combining simplicity, economy, and sturdiness, it is a style well adapted to the Maine scene. On the other hand, the homes of the merchant and ship-owning class achieved varying degrees of refinement and architectural grace, culminating in such elegance as that of the Nickels-Sortwell House and occasionally in such frivolity as the decorations of the so-called 'Wedding Cake' House.

Architectural detail usually combined simplicity and strength, as in the hardware shown in the Old Jail at Paris Hill, but it could be very elaborate, as in the carved woodwork of the Means House. Native craftsmen of the State, their names now forgotten, often left enduring monuments to their skill and ingenuity, as the delicate work on the façade of the Ruggles House or the gracious sweeping stairway of the Black Mansion.

An example of twentieth-century building is St. John's Church in Brunswick, in which a modern interpretation of conventional ecclesiastical Gothic has been successfully worked out in native stone.

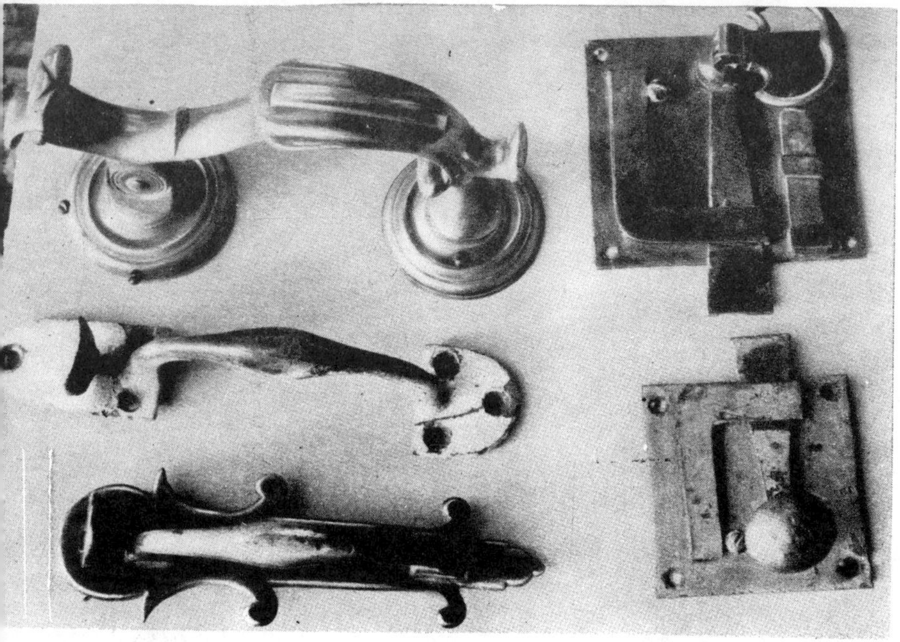

OM THE OLD STONE JAIL, PARIS HILL

THE HEARTH IN THE MEANS HOUSE, PORTLAND

DOORWAY, MAJOR REUBEN COLBURN HOUSE, PITTSTON

FARM COTTAGE NEAR BAR HARBOR

CARVED DOOR CASE, MEANS HOUSE, PORTLAND

ST. JOHN'S CHURCH, BRUNSWICK

NICKELS-SORTWELL HOUSE, WISCASSET

RUGGLES HOUSE, COLUMBIA FALLS

DOORWAY OF THE RUGGLES HOUSE

STAIRWAY OF THE BLACK MANSION, ELLSWORTH

'WEDDING CAKE' HOUSE, KENNEBUNK

and was librarian for six years (1829–35), before leaving to become professor of modern languages at Harvard (1836–54). Although the poetry that brought him highest acclaim was written after he left the State, Maine may call Longfellow her own. The life and scenery of this region doubtless would have been more strongly reflected in his work if literary convention had not led him constantly to classic mythology and to European models and themes. Nevertheless, in 'My Lost Youth' and other of his most popular poems, much of his early experience of the coast and country life in his native State is described feelingly. At Portland, his birthplace near the harbor and the Wadsworth-Longfellow House, with its lovely garden, are shrines visited by his admirers from all over the world. The Longfellow Room in the Bowdoin College Library contains a valuable collection of the poet's books and manuscripts.

Nathaniel Hawthorne, Longfellow's classmate and friend, at whose suggestion 'Evangeline' was written, is less specifically a Maine figure. Born in Salem, Massachusetts, Hawthorne spent most of his youth at Raymond on Sebago Lake, entering Bowdoin College in 1821. His first novel, 'Fanshawe,' anonymously issued from a Brunswick printing shop in 1828, is a romance of Bowdoin and Brunswick. Since Hawthorne himself subsequently withdrew this novel from the booksellers and had most of the copies destroyed, it is now a very rare and valuable collector's item.

Henry David Thoreau made several excursions into Maine, and some of his impressions are recorded in 'The Maine Woods,' posthumously published from his manuscript journals in 1864. Thoreau's treatment of nature, though often poetic in style, is marked by a scientific exactness quite opposed to the emotional and sentimental approach of many of his fellow naturalists. Joe Polis, an Old Town Indian guide, may have had some influence on Thoreau's philosophy. Doubtless reflecting his interest in the Maine wilderness were the last words which Thoreau uttered as he lay dying of consumption in 1862; they were 'moose' and 'Indian.'

John Greenleaf Whittier, though he never lived in Maine and visited the State only occasionally, used considerable Maine material in his poems. One of his most successful ballads, 'The Dead Ship of Harpswell,' embodies a famous legend of Casco Bay; and the heroine of the poem, 'Maud Muller,' was a young girl whom Whittier had met in York.

Harriet Beecher Stowe wrote 'Uncle Tom's Cabin' while living in Brunswick, and during the period of her Maine residence she also gathered material from the near-by salt-water country for her romance, 'The Pearl of Orr's Island.'

The novelist and editor, William Dean Howells, for many years one of

America's most prominent literary figures, owned summer homes at Kittery Point and York Harbor, and some of his novels show the influence of the Maine environment.

The first important book about Maine written by a native of the State was Sarah Orne Jewett's 'Country of the Pointed Firs,' a landmark in the so-called local-color movement in American literature. Miss Jewett (1849-1909) was born in South Berwick, the daughter of a country physician. Her delicate vignettes of rural New England life, beginning with 'Deephaven,' her first book, have come to be recognized as of lasting importance.

Kate Douglas Wiggin (1856-1923), author of 'Rebecca of Sunnybrook Farm,' 'The Birds' Christmas Carol,' and other stories that are likely to hold a permanent place in the affections of young readers, was also a Maine writer. Born in Philadelphia of Maine parents, she spent her childhood and most of her later summers in the State, finally making her permanent abode here (at 'Quillcote,' in Hollis). Mrs. Riggs' private library, which she bequeathed to Bowdoin, is housed as a unit in the College Library.

Today in Maine, Laura E. Richards (born 1850), particularly remembered for her 'Captain January,' continues in spite of advanced years to write fiction and poetry for children, much of it with a Maine background.

Among Maine writers of the nineteenth century who were of importance in their time is Elijah Kellogg (1813-1901), the gentle preacher of Harpswell and friend to boys. He was known particularly for his 'Elm Island Series,' concerned with heroes of the Maine coast and its islands, and the 'Whispering Pines Series,' stories of Bowdoin College. Elizabeth Akers Allen (1832-1911), wife of the sculptor Benjamin Paul Akers, a Portland newspaperwoman and verse writer, is remembered chiefly for her poem entitled 'Rock Me to Sleep.'

Under the pen-name of 'Sophie May,' Rebecca Sophia Clarke (1833-1906) attained wide popularity as the author of the 'Little Prudy' and 'Dotty Dimple' series, and other books for young readers. Arlo Bates (1850-1918), born in Maine and a graduate of Bowdoin College, gained distinction as a teacher and man of letters in Boston; Henry Johnson (1855-1918), Bowdoin professor and poet, translated Dante's *Divina Commedia* and *Vita Nuova*; Harriet Prescott Spofford (1835-1921), novelist and short-story writer, was a valued contributor to *The Atlantic Monthly*; Nathan Haskell Dole (1852-1935), poet and translator, described his native State in 'Maine of the Sea and Pines.' The famous humorist Edgar Wilson Nye (1850-96), known to readers and lecture audiences everywhere as 'Bill' Nye, was born at Shirley, in Piscataquis County, but left the State at the age of two when his parents moved to the Middle West. John Kendrick Bangs (1862-1922), although not a native of Maine, retired to Ogunquit from New York in middle life, his reputation as a humorous writer and lecturer already secure. Henry Milner Rideout (1877-1927), novelist and teacher, utilized the general background of his Maine boyhood and youth in at least two of his books — 'Beached Keels' and 'Admiral's Light.' The stories and verses of Holman F. Day (1865-1935) portray the Maine Yankee with keen insight and a rare sense of humor.

Edwin Arlington Robinson (1869-1935), recognized as one of America's foremost poets, was for many years Maine's outstanding writer. Born at Head Tide in Alna and brought up in Gardiner, he wrote his earlier poems in and of Maine. Gardiner is believed by some to be the 'Tilbury Town' of this poetry, in which he immortalized many persons he had known in his early youth. Robinson left Maine as a young man and returned only rarely. After his early characterizations in 'The Children of the Night' and 'Captain Craig,' the Maine element is not a major one in his poetry; but his style, with its subdued cadences and terse, often crabbed, turns of speech, was shaped to a great extent by the Yankee environment of his youth. In his way a profoundly 'literary' poet, Robinson yet had the strength that comes from a closeness to the land and an awareness of the simple people whose roots are in the soil and whose language and customs preserve the full flavor of the race. Though not always original in form or message, Robinson's poetry speaks in a special voice, and reveals a dry but vivid personality. It was the reserved, cynical, but intensely human Yankee in Robinson that gave life to his poetic creations.

Edna St. Vincent Millay, one of America's favorite modern poets, was born in Rockland and now spends part of each year on one of the most romantic spots of the Maine coast, Ragged Island in Casco Bay — the 'Elm Island' of Elijah Kellogg's stories. Her poetry, though seldom treating of Maine subject-matter in particular, is redolent of the sea and often descriptive of the rugged shore and hardy people who live along it. Chiefly influenced by the metaphysical and cavalier poets of England, Miss Millay has less of the New Englander's tense cadences of speech, wry humor, and salty expression.

Robert P. Tristram Coffin, on the other hand, is a Maine poet whose subject-matter is drawn almost entirely from his native State —

> This is my country, bitter as the sea,
> Pungent with the fir and bayberry.

A Brunswick man, teacher at Bowdoin, and 1936 Pulitzer Prize winner, Mr. Coffin hymns the virtues of the self-sufficient life of the Maine small farmer and fisherman. More successful in his verse, perhaps, than in his novels, he clings to the bedrock and gnarled beauty of his own small field. Like him, but in a less poetic and personal way, Mary Ellen Chase of Bluehill also writes of the former Maine coastal life in all its independent and picturesque aspects. Both of them are retrospective, dealing with a world that is past — Miss Chase with the shipbuilding and shipowning aristocracy, Mr. Coffin with the yeomanry of farm and fishing grounds.

Like them in depicting changing or past scenes are their fellow novelists, Gladys Hasty Carroll, author of 'As the Earth Turns,' Rachel Field, Elizabeth Hopestill Carter, and Gerald Brace. Miss Field, a Chicagoan converted to Maine, has also written a number of lyrics. Other contemporary Maine poets are Wilbert Snow of Spruce Head; Harold Vinal of Vinalhaven, editor of *Voices*, a prominent American poetry journal; and Harold Trowbridge Pulsifer of East Harpswell, former editor of *The Outlook* and citizen-by-adoption of Maine.

Other writers who must be mentioned are Ben Ames Williams, whose tales of the woods and inland country have won considerable popularity (his village of Fraternity, familiar to readers of his stories in the *Saturday Evening Post*, is in actuality the town of Searsmont, Maine); Kenneth Roberts, whose 'Arundel' and subsequent novels of the sea and the York County region, noted for their accuracy as to fact and locale, are in the best tradition of American historical romance; Margaret Deland and Booth Tarkington, both summer residents of long standing whose novels often reflect the Maine background; and Lincoln Colcord, who writes with knowledge and understanding about the sea.

No account of Maine's contribution to literature would be complete without some mention of Thomas Bird Mosher (1852–1923) of Portland, a man who devoted several decades of his life to the publication of *belles-lettres* in choice editions, gaining a unique position both for the remarkable taste which he evidenced in the selection of material and for the distinctively beautiful form which he gave to that material. Many of the prefaces in his book publications and in *The Bibelot*, which he issued as a monthly periodical for twenty years, were written by him and indicate literary ability of a rare sort.

ART

The art of Maine's early days found its expression in the crafts, most notably in woodcarving. Since shipbuilding was one of the State's first great industries, there was ample opportunity for the native artist to work on mastheads, bowsprits, figureheads, and the like. Some striking examples of such work have been preserved in museums in various parts of New England and in private collections in Maine. The largest of these latter is that of the Sewall family at Small Point, and another belongs to Booth Tarkington in Kennebunkport. Countless examples of beautiful woodwork exist today in Maine's old houses. It must be remembered, however, that much of this work was frankly derivative from earlier creative developments in southern New England. Until recent years, the work of Maine artisans in stone, glass, and metals has been at best rather primitive. There were only two recorded silver-working establishments in the State before 1830, and no glass works of any importance until after 1863, when the famous Portland glass began to be made. A collection of Portland glass is on exhibition at the Maine Historical Society in Portland.

Pioneer and Colonial life in Maine, rendered harsh by continual struggle with the elements and uncertain by constant Indian warfare, left little time for such esthetic development as Boston and Philadelphia early enjoyed. Most of Maine's great houses were not built until the nineteenth century; and their furnishings, though usually objects of taste and beauty, were commonly brought from other countries by seafaring members of the families. Tombstone designs and work in iron and other metals were dignified enough. So were the early paintings, often appealing because of their simplicity, but invariably crude; their value today is chiefly historical. Weaving and rug-making, quilting and embroidering, and other household arts, however, showed a high degree of skill in technique and design.

Any account of the painters and sculptors who have lived and worked in Maine must be limited to those who were closely associated with the State, whether or not they were native to it. Although there has never been a Maine school or movement in painting, the State, particularly its varied coast, has for years attracted a great number of summer artists. Certain noted artists, too, have been residents of the State the year round, spending part or all of their lives here.

In Colonial times, both Joseph Badger (1708-65) and Joseph Blackburn (*fl.* 1753-63), among the first painters of the New World, made many portraits of Maine persons. Badger was originally a coach and house painter who, although never attaining great eminence for his portraits, was for a time foremost in his profession in Boston. Copley is believed by some to have studied with him. Some of his portraits, distinguished by a certain charm in spite of their stilted mannerisms, still hang in the ancestral homes of Maine's old families. Little is known about the artist Blackburn except that he traveled extensively and lived at different times in Boston, Portsmouth, and possibly elsewhere in New England. It is conjectured that he was an Englishman working in this country under an assumed name. His painting, though not strikingly original, is superior to Badger's. It does not, however, equal the work of Robert Feke (about 1705-50), a native of Rhode Island, some of the very best examples of which are the Bowdoin portraits, probably executed in Boston and now in the possession of Bowdoin College. Feke was especially successful in reproducing the color and texture of fine fabrics.

For several years after the passing of the Boston group of Colonial artists that included Smibert, Copley, and Gilbert Stuart (who is known to have done some portraits in Maine), there seems to have been little painting of any distinction in the State. But later, Portland had an artist of her own in Charles O. Cole (1817-58), who achieved local fame with his portraits of prominent citizens. Today, examples of his work and of Badger's may be seen among the old portraits in the collection of the Maine Historical Society. The Walker Art Gallery at Bowdoin College has a remarkable collection of Badger, Blackburn, Feke, and Stuart portraits.

Winslow Homer, called 'the most powerful representative of open-air painting in America' and 'the most thoroughly American' of our painters, is unquestionably the foremost figure among Maine artists. Born in Boston in 1836 of Maine parents, Homer finally settled in this State in 1884, in the studio at Prout's Neck which he built himself. Here he lived until his death in 1910. During this period he became more and more absorbed in the battle of land and sea, in 'man's unbreakable courage against the overwhelming powers of nature.' Though a realist and always the illustrator, adept in catching the drama of his scene, Homer was primarily interested in color — whether the lush brilliance of Florida and the Bahamas, where he sometimes spent his winters, or the harsh brightness alternating with the cold grays of the Maine seacoast.

The nineteenth century witnessed the birth and early development in

Maine of several prominent American artists, most of whom eventually left the State to complete their training and their work. Some of these men were Eastman Johnson (1824-1906), portrait and *genre* painter; J. Foxcroft Cole (1837-92), landscape painter; Frederic Porter Vinton (1845-1911), portrait painter; Ben Foster (1852-1926), landscape painter and art critic; and Joseph Cummings Chase (born 1878), portrait painter.

Maine also produced in the nineteenth century two sculptors of note, Benjamin Paul Akers (1825-61) and Franklin Simmons (1839-1913). Akers was the son of a wood-turner of Saccarappa. A dreamy youth, known to his schoolmates as 'Saint Paul,' his aspirations were literary rather than artistic. Some of his early essays were published in *The Atlantic Monthly*. In 1849 he turned to sculpture as a profession and went to Boston to study. Some months later he opened a studio in Portland, where one of his commissions was for a portrait bust of Longfellow. Later he went to Rome, receiving in Europe the recognition of his talents to which he long aspired. His 'Dead Pearl-Diver,' produced in Rome and described in Hawthorne's 'The Marble Faun,' is probably his most famous piece of work. This idealized marble figure is today in Portland's Sweat Museum. Akers's meticulously finished work reflects the classicist taste of his period.

Franklin Simmons was in his youth an itinerant artist, wandering the Maine countryside. Later he made his way to Washington, and finally to Italy, where he lived until his death. He eventually attained considerable prominence, and in 1898 was knighted by the King of Italy. His seated portrait statue of Longfellow and his Civil War monument, 'The Republic,' have prominent places in Portland. His 'Penelope,' an idealized marble figure now in the Portland Museum as part of the Franklin Simmons Memorial Collection, is considered his best work. Simmons was possessed of tireless energy, and executed more than one hundred busts and monuments.

Since Winslow Homer, many leading American artists have spent their summers in Maine, but few have made the State their home and drawn as heavily upon its scenes for material as he did. At the present time the colorful artist, Waldo Peirce, resides at Bangor; and Stephen Etnier, of a younger generation, lives and works on his island near Popham. Robert Henri spent many summers in Maine, as did Emil Carlsen, whose marine paintings depict some of the variety of the Maine coast.

Two outstanding artists who have found inspiration in the Maine scene are Rockwell Kent and John Marin, each of whom uses a highly specialized medium of expression. Kent found the Maine coast, with its broad planes of sea and its background of jagged rock and pointed trees, an admirable setting for his idealized portraits, which seem to be made with the flat sweep of a chisel. The cold brightness and angular beauty of Maine seem to have affected him as they did Winslow Homer, but in Kent's work they are given more formalized expression.

Marin, a New York modern, has painted many aspects of the Maine coast. Since his work is marked by a suppression of detail and all unimportant passages, he has been able to find here scenery of the simplicity and strength which his method seems to demand. Although his work is sometimes baffling, it is probable that future critics may look to it for the sharp quality of the northern seascape and landscape which in this part of the country is peculiarly Maine's. Stephen Etnier seems to combine something of the spirit of both Kent and Marin, with a human quality added; in spite of his prevailing gray mood, he may finally succeed them as an interpreter of Maine and the sea.

Many other artists in Maine are doing interesting and valuable work, much of which may be seen at exhibitions held from time to time in the State by art societies and other groups. Summer studios of leading painters are scattered along the coast, each forming the nucleus for a colony of artists, pupils, and admiring followers. Among those who have such studios are John P. Benson and Russell Cheney, at Kittery; Charles H. Woodbury, at Ogunquit; Mildred Burrage, at Kennebunkport; Alexander Bower, on Cape Elizabeth; Edward W. Redfield, at Boothbay Harbor; Jay H. Connaway, at Monhegan; and Carol Tyson, on Mount Desert. Many of the colonies maintain summer art schools, such as that at Boothbay Harbor. Two of America's best known contemporary sculptors have studios in Maine — Robert Laurent at Ogunquit, and William Zorach at Georgetown, where the late Gaston Lachaise also worked in the summer.

There are two permanent museums of importance in Maine: the Walker Art Gallery at Bowdoin College and the L. D. M. Sweat Memorial in Portland, the latter a Georgian mansion of architectural and historical importance with an adjoining art gallery containing examples of the work of nineteenth-century painters and of many Maine artists. The Portland Society of Art, owner of the Sweat Museum, also conducts a School of Fine and Applied Art, the only school of its kind in the State. The Walker Gallery contains notable collections of American colonial portraits and of classical and modern art.

The most important private art collection in the State is that of Booth Tarkington at Kennebunkport, consisting principally of paintings by prominent English artists of the eighteenth century.

THE THEATER

Although the last stronghold of the 'legitimate' stage as a continuous cultural influence passed out of existence in Maine when the time-honored Jefferson Theater in Portland was demolished, the increasingly popular summer playhouses scattered through the State are more than making up for its loss, and the amateur work of high schools and other groups keeps the spirit alive in communities inaccessible to the presentations of professional players. Lakewood, near Skowhegan, established in 1901, was the pioneer among summer theater colonies. This and the Ogunquit Playhouse at Ogunquit bring each year to Maine talented actors, producers, designers, technicians, and playwrights, who participate in experimental dramatic productions that often later achieve Broadway success. The work of the summer theaters, always interesting, is nationally important, for they are becoming more and more the training schools for both stage and screen. Other dramatic groups are the Mount Desert Island Players, formerly the Surry Players; the Garrick Players at Kennebunkport, organized in 1933; and the Theater-in-the-Woods at Boothbay Harbor, opened in 1934. There are many lesser groups, not so professional as these, but no less eager and hard-working.

Two native daughters of Maine who have achieved prominence on the American and English stage are Maxine Elliott (Jessie Dermot) and her sister Gertrude, now Lady Forbes-Robertson. Both were born in Rockland.

MUSIC

From the day when the seaman's child had chanteys for lullabies and the woodsman's babe was sung to sleep with rollicking ballads, music has played an important part in the cultural life of Maine people. The State is rich in a heritage of balladry, folk-songs, and dance music equaled only by that of some of the southern States. Through several generations, songs of English, Scottish, and particularly Irish origin have been preserved — sometimes within a single family. Today scholars and musicians are finding in Maine an almost untapped source of old folk-music and poetry. For example, within only eleven days of actual field work in September, 1928, within a small area of eastern Maine, one collector took down 199 valuable old airs, most of which are reproduced in Barry, Eckstrom, and Smith's 'British Ballads from Maine' (New Haven, 1929).

Churches have always fostered and encouraged singing, and today the most active congregations are often the ones that lift up their voices with greatest fervor. Indeed, Maine's chief cultural activity lay for years in the field of music. One would expect this in a State which has produced such great musical artists as Emma Eames, Lillian Nordica, and Annie Louise Cary. John Knowles Paine, one of America's earliest composers, was a Maine man.

Today nearly every town and city has one or more musical clubs, among which Portland's Rossini Club is outstanding, comprising as it does many gifted and highly trained performers. Periodical concerts and annual festivals are held in most cities, with Bangor, assisted by the facilities of the near-by University of Maine at Orono, usually taking the lead. For nearly a third of a century, the Maine Music Festivals were the most important events on the calendar for every music lover in the State. The world's great artists were brought here, and Maine's own chorus of carefully chosen singers from all parts of the State was especially trained for the occasion. The concerts, beginning at Portland, were repeated in all the other large cities. But the death of William R. Chapman, the motivating spirit behind the festivals, marked their end within the last decade. Today it is encouraging that the possibility of their revival in the near future is under active discussion.

Musical activity has changed considerably in the past twenty years, and has come to take a subordinate place in the cultural life of the State. The Maine State Opera Company, organized in 1933, lasted but one season. Music in the colleges, though diligently cultivated, has not the popularity it once knew. The colleges, however, as well as outstanding civic groups, bring to the principal Maine cities each year musical artists of national or world prominence.

A significant cultural movement is under way in the recently developed summer music camps. In most summer camps, opportunities are provided for the study of music; but not until the Eastern Music Camp was opened in 1931, on Lake Messalonskee in Sidney, did Maine have a summer school devoted exclusively to music. This ambitious experiment, offering an eight-weeks program of musical education, has received deserved acclaim. Twice a week it presents excellent concerts, under such eminent guest conductors as Walter Damrosch and Howard Hanson. Music camps have also been established at Castine, Vinalhaven, and other places through the State.

There are several important summer colonies of musicians, for the most part along the coast and usually centering around some single prominent artist. At Kneisel Hall in Bluehill, weekly concerts of chamber music are the result of classes carried on by the children of the late Franz Kneisel. Camden has been called the summer harp center of America, and there is much musical activity at Bar Harbor during the season.

Interesting work is being done in the C.C.C. camps and in W.P.A. groups with band and orchestral music, providing through government agencies the facilities for musical training which many could not otherwise obtain. But perhaps the most favorable portent for music in Maine is the enthusiasm for playing and singing that is evident in the public schools. This is fostered by a high school band and orchestra contest staged throughout New England. The State's training schools are sending out to the public schools teachers who have been given a thorough groundwork of musical knowledge, which many of them supplement with a playing knowledge of several instruments.

HANDICRAFTS

CRAFTS in early Maine were very similar to those in Massachusetts. The things people made with their hands were necessities, but that they were necessities did not prevent them from being beautiful also; often, indeed, the discipline of necessity made for beauty. The objects produced have some of the chief characteristics of their creators — simplicity, sturdiness, practicability, spiced with unpredictable quirks of Yankee ingenuity. The outside influences upon Maine craftsmanship, though slight, included English, greatly simplified; French through Canada, in floral motifs for rugs and embroidery; and Oriental, from objects brought home by ships in the China trade. There are stenciled trays that bear two Oriental figures with parakeets on their hands, surrounded by familiar New England flower and leaf motifs. The articles women made for their homes with needle, loom, and hook are full of artistry, and represent a large proportion of the early craftwork of Maine.

The old New England art of making hooked rugs originated in Maine and Nova Scotia. The earliest and best rugs represent truly native craftsmanship, for the designs were original and the material was of wool from home-raised sheep, carded and spun at home, and dyed with home-made colors. Designs were inspired by familiar objects. The most beautiful were floral and wreath patterns, probably partly French in origin, free and intricate in design, with large cabbage roses, small harebells, daisies, goldenrod, and other native flowers surrounded and entwined by large scroll-like leaf motifs, on a white or nearly white ground. The finest of these reveal as much esthetic sense, beauty of design, and mastery of craft as a piece of glazed terra cotta or a stained-glass window. Pictorial rugs were common, though not so fine; a cat curled on a hearth, landscapes quite lacking in perspective, marine patterns with ships, compasses, shells, and anchors — these are a few of the subjects used. There were also many geometric patterns.

The very earliest rugs were made on hand-loomed linen, but this was soon superseded by burlap or sacking. The design was sketched on the background material in free-hand. When stamped patterns were put on the market in the nineteenth century, much of the beauty of design disappeared. Many early rugs were hooked, not only of wool yarns and woven materials, but contained also bits of calico and cotton. Characteristic of Maine and Nova Scotia was the practice of creating an effect of relief either by hooking parts of the design higher than the rest or by contrasting clipped and unclipped areas.

Colors for rugs, and for clothing and embroidery as well, were ingeniously concocted from a variety of materials. Extract could be purchased for black and indigo for blue; but browns and dull greens came from white maple, butternut, sumac, and hemlock bark, and from sweet fern; and yellow from onion peelings and urine. Until housewives could buy vermilion, reds were extremely difficult to create. Beet root made a rich magenta, but had no permanency, and the same was true of various berries. All colors were set with copperas and lye, the latter being obtained by pouring boiling water over wood ashes.

After the early nineteenth century, the art of making hooked rugs almost vanished. The few that were made were cheap in material, coarse in technique, and of stamped design. However, popular interest in antiques has brought about a revival of this old craft, and many women are again making rugs. They are not creating original designs, however, but are trying to copy the old. Few of these copies equal the beauty of the old patterns, and the sincerity of creative craftsmanship is missing.

Braided rugs are even earlier than hooked rugs in the country as a whole, but are not particularly native to Maine. They are now being made by hand extremely well at the Old Sparhawk Mills in South Portland, where local artisans design the rugs, dye the materials to match any given color scheme, and sew the rugs exactly as they were originally made. In the Williamsburg, Virginia, restoration these rugs were used throughout.

Weaving in the early days was a universal craft, scarcely less important than cooking. Cottons, linens, woolens, and other fabrics such as 'linsey-woolsey' or 'luster' (a glazed linen and wool material) were made by every housewife. There has been a recent revival of weaving at Limerick, Maine, where the women used yarn from the Limerick Yarn Mills for hand-loom weaving of excellent yard goods, scarves, curtains, etc., which they sold through a central shop. However, the closing of the mills in 1932, and their subsequent reopening under new management to make different types of yarn, brought this very worthy enterprise to an end; although some of the women continue to weave there.

Quilts were made in Maine, as in the rest of New England. Many of the best ones were not of patchwork, but derived their beauty from intricate quilting and lovely materials. One of the finest old quilts in

Maine, belonging to Mrs. Charles Crosby of Waterville, is made of indigo-blue linsey-woolsey backed with a light-weight yellow homespun blanket, and quilted in an extraordinarily fine and beautiful pattern of the familiar New England pineapple, feather, and shell motifs.

Crewel embroideries were also done in Maine in the seventeenth and eighteenth centuries. Yarns of home-produced wool, spun and dyed at home, were sewed into bold and decorative leaf and flower patterns on homespun cotton petticoats, bedspreads, and hangings. Colors were prepared as for hooked rugs, with often many gradations of one hue as the wool was removed from the dye pot a little at a time. The motifs of flowers arranged on long twisting stems were similar to those which appear on rugs and quilts. But the patterns often showed much originality and inventiveness in the use of bird, animal, monogram, basket, and ribbon motifs. The finest crewel embroideries in Maine are the bedspread and hangings made between 1745 and 1750 by Mrs. Mary Bulman of York and now in the 'Old Gaol Museum' at York. The Redington Museum at Waterville has a very fine spread of the same period.

Innumerable lesser related crafts practiced in early Maine included the making of dolls, embroidered pictures, plain samplers, mourning samplers in black and white, needlepoint work, etc.

Of the decorative crafts associated with the shipbuilding industry, the most interesting in the great middle nineteenth century period of sail was woodcarving. Although carving for the decoration of ships had been done in Europe for hundreds of years, the figureheads, trailboards, mast-sheaths, etc., carved in Maine, New Hampshire, and Massachusetts represent an artistic development as genuine, native, and inventive as any craft at any time. Colonel C. A. L. Sampson of Bath was probably the most famous of the Maine carvers, and his decorations for hundreds of ships built in that town went far around the world. At his death in 1881 his business was bought by William Southworth, who had conducted a carver's shop in Newcastle and had learned the trade from Edward S. Griffin of Portland. Other Maine carvers were Seavey of Bangor, Harvey Counce of Thomaston, and Woodbury Potter of Bath. Each of these men maintained a shop with apprentices, near the shipyards. Southworth carved more than five hundred figureheads, spending about eighteen days to a figure and receiving from two hundred and fifty to four hundred dollars for each. The material used was pumpkin pine, common on the Maine coast at that time; and the subjects were usually life-sized females, although Indians, military figures, and even birds and animals were fairly common. They were brightly painted. Sampson's famous 'Belle of Bath,' 'Belle of Oregon,' 'Western Belle,' and others were gleaming gold and white. Although many of the figures seem generous in proportion, they have extraordinary realism and grace. Sampson frequently portrayed his figures in stylish dress blown swirling backward in the wind, with head erect and one arm extended, creating on the whole an effect of life, strength, and beauty. Although the figureheads were the most spectacular, many smaller decorative pieces were carved to adorn the ships. Nearly always the stern bore a carving in relief partially or entirely surrounding the name of the vessel; these commonly depicted cornucopiae of fruit, eagles with spread wings, crossed flags, portrait heads, and even landscapes embellished with gold or white scroll-like leaf forms. Many a pilot house was topped with an eagle or a rooster. Billet-heads of curling acanthus leaves, lovely in design, were sometimes used instead of figureheads.

In all of these pieces the carving is bold and direct. The tools used were few and simple. One can accurately judge the size and curve of the chisels from the long, even grooves in leaves and drapery. The use of tools and material to best advantage, with no attempt to camouflage either, is evidence of the sincere craftsmanship that went into their making.

The use of carved decoration spread beyond the adornment of ships and crept into the homes and public buildings of coastal towns. Weathervanes, architectural details, insignia for public buildings, chests and other furniture, reveal the hand of the ship carver. Edbury Hatch of Newcastle, apprentice to Southworth, adorned his house with carved leaves, flowers, animals' heads, snakes, and the Maine seal; and for a Japanese print of a dog treeing a cat he carved a frame in which chubby New England cats and dogs in high relief chase one another.

There are very few skilled carvers in the State at the present time. Lloyd Thomas, a young resident of Camden, decorates chests with full-rigged ships and other nautical motifs much in the manner of the old-time carvers. Colby Williams of Wiscasset carves miniature oxen, drawing wagons and sledges, which are of fine craftsmanship. Karl Von Rydingsvard of Portland is a talented carver who not only works in the New England tradition but does chests and screens of Gothic or Elizabethan style.

The making of ship models became an important art in nineteenth-century Maine. So-called half models, beautifully finished and mounted on a flat background, were made for every new vessel, and are now frequently used for decorative purposes. Ship models, from one inch to four feet in length, fully rigged, have been made ever since ships were built, usually by the builders or sailors of the ships thus reproduced. They reveal much delicate and patient craftsmanship. Two of the men still making ship models are Frederic W. Snow of Kennebunkport and Mr. Candage of South Bluehill, the latter a former old sailor.

Early Maine cabinet work, while similar in general to that in the rest of New England, was cruder and more provincial. Much of the furniture was adorned with stenciled leaf, fruit, and flower motifs, and occasionally a landscape — often against a black background. Bronze powders of various shades were applied through the stencil, with little cloth bags or powder puffs, to tacky paint. Intricacy of cutting, delicacy of shading, and the gradual building up of a pattern from a number of stencils are characteristic of the best work. Trays and boxes were also stenciled in bronzes, and floors and walls were sometimes stenciled with colored paint.

Stevens Plains, now a part of Portland, was the center of activity for a number of metal workers in the late eighteenth and early nineteenth centuries. Zachariah Stevens, born in 1778, was the founder of a tin industry which in the early 1800's employed thirty or forty men in that locality. This early tinware consists of charming little chest-like boxes, trays of various shapes, tea caddies, etc. It is painted (most frequently in black though sometimes in yellow or white) and decorated in Japan colors with small leaves and bright red, green, and yellow flowers. Tinsmiths traveled through the countryside selling their wares, at the same time buying up at a low price much old pewter to melt for tin.

Pewterers were also working in this region at the same time. Allen and Freeman Porter established the trade; they were succeeded by Rufus Dunham, who worked in Stevens Plains until 1882 and maintained a shop employing from twenty-five to thirty artisans. The making of pewter as such came to an end very soon after 1845, when Britannia ware became popular. Much fine old pewter was undoubtedly melted to go into the new and inferior metal.

Metal craftsmanship in Maine at the present time is in general confined to the making of jewelry. This art is taught at the School of Fine Arts in Portland and at many of the summer camps, and is practiced with skill and artistry by a few persons — chiefly Miss Madeline Burrage of Kennebunkport and Mr. Ernest Gookin of Ogunquit.

Decorative hand-wrought iron is made by Ernest Wright of Camden, and by Charles Westcott, Jr., a blacksmith of Bluehill, who works from designs by Mrs. Lucie Barbour. Mr. Weston of Bremen carries on the traditions of his father and grandfather in the making of wrought iron;

he has many of his grandfather's designs for brackets, latches, chandeliers, etc.

Ceramics were of no importance in the history of the crafts in Maine until the twentieth century. Because of the exceptionally fine quality of the clay available there, the Bluehill region has become a center for this craft.

The only systematic effort now being made to foster handicrafts in Maine is by the Extension Service of the United States Department of Agriculture. There are many, however, who hope that the plan for a Maine Crafts Guild will eventually receive sufficient private and State support to make such an organization possible.

II. SEAPORTS AND RIVER TOWNS

AUGUSTA

City: Alt. 120, pop. 17,198, sett. 1629, incorp. town 1797, county seat 1799, city 1849, State Capital 1832.
Railroad Station: 348 Water St., for M.C. R.R.
Bus Stations: Hotel North, 264 Water St., for M.C. Transportation Co., Grey Lines, and Augusta–Belfast Stages.
Airport: Winthrop St., 0.5 *m.* west of business district, for B. & M. Airways.
Accommodations: Two hotels.
Swimming: Togus Pond, Threecornered Pond, Lake Cobbosseecontee.
Information Service: Augusta Chamber of Commerce, City Bldg., Cony St., E. end Kennebec Bridge; Maine Development Commission, State House, State St.
Annual Events: Maine National Guard Muster, 2 weeks, July; Annual Boy Scout Carnival, on or near Feb. 22.

AUGUSTA, State capital and Kennebec County seat, rises in a series of terraces and sharp inclines east and west of the bisecting Kennebec River. It is at the head of river navigation; although forty-five miles from open sea, there is an approximate tide range of four feet. The city differs from most Maine communities occupying both sides of a river in that it has not developed into two separate municipalities, or twin cities. The majority of its industrial and business establishments, as well as an extensive residential area, are on the west side of the river. Yet business, industries, and residences are so segregated that the casual visitor seldom realizes that the city is more than a pleasant residential community grouped about the center of the State's political activity.

The social groups common to an industrial city of the size and type of Augusta are augmented by a wide variety of county, State, and Federal employees. The predominating racial groups are of English and French-Canadian descent. The latter, making up approximately 15 per cent of the city's population, is largely concentrated in the northwestern section. More than half of the population own their own homes, and, although there are a few tenement areas, there are no slums or highly congested residential sections. On the other hand, like many Maine cities, Augusta suffers from lack of adequate modern apartment and lodging-house facilities.

The Augusta city government is of the mayor-council type (two-year term), but distinguished from the usual municipal administration in that the mayor directly controls all the fields of government. He appoints the heads of departments without confirmation by the city council and does not require the council's permission to remove the appointees from office.

The Kennebec has flowed through all Augusta's history and shaped the course of its development. To the Indian, the *Manitou Kennebec* ('river-god') was not only a highway and a source of food; at times it was an angry god that crushed canoes and swallowed its victims or swept away entire villages when in flood. To the early traders the river gave ingress to the treasures of the Kennebec Valley, furs and fish; later it carried wealth for the men of Augusta in the form of lumber, brought prosperity in trade through river traffic, turned the city's mills, and provided a lucrative harvest in ice from its frozen surface. Today, long after the Indians and traders, the ships and the ice harvest have departed, the river continues to supply the city with wealth in another form — water-power. And still, too, it strikes out at man's bridges, dams, and buildings when in flood.

The Indians called Augusta *Cushnoc* (also *Koussinock* and *Cusinock*). The name has been given several interpretations: one, that the site was so called because 'the tide runs no farther up the Kennebec'; another, that it meant 'the consecrated place,' since the Indians held annual meetings here and seemed to consider it in a sense hallowed.

Sacred or not, Cushnoc was of value to the Plymouth Colony of Massachusetts. Trade on the Kennebec was begun immediately after the grant of the Kennebec Patent in 1628-29. In 1628 the Plymouth men established a trading post on the approximate site of Fort Western, 'ye most convenient place for trade.' John Howland, the 'lustie yonge man' who was washed overboard during the 'Mayflower' crossing and nearly lost, was the first agent in command of the Cushnoc post. In 1634 he shared this office with John Alden, immortalized by Longfellow's 'The Courtship of Miles Standish.' Alden was falsely accused of murder because of two deaths in that year arising from a dispute with a rival company over the trading rights at Cushnoc. Miles Standish made frequent trips to the post, and Governor William Bradford is said to have visited it. Captain Thomas Willett, later Governor of New York, was a successor of Howland and Alden, and another notable commander of the post (1647-53) was John Winslow, brother of Governor Edward Winslow of Massachusetts. Winslow was an intimate friend of Father Gabriel Druillettes, the Jesuit missionary, making him welcome at the post on several occasions.

Fur trading was highly profitable to the Pilgrims, so much so that it is said that their debts to the Merchant Adventurers of London for the expenses of the 'Mayflower' expedition were paid with furs brought from the Kennebec. After more than thirty-two years of trading, amicable relations with the Indians were severed by the Indian wars, and English occupation at Cushnoc was abandoned for more than three-quarters of a century. However, industry and the white man's civilization had gained their first foothold in Cushnoc, and the Plymouth patent was the foundation of future land titles.

Augusta

During the middle of the eighteenth century the 'Proprietors of the Kennebec Purchase' sought to bring settlers into the region. In 1754, Fort Western was erected on the east bank of the river. Named for Thomas Western of Sussex, England, a friend of Governor William Shirley, the fort was one of three built on the Kennebec in 1754: Fort Halifax, the northernmost, about sixty-five miles from the mouth of the Kennebec, near the present town of Winslow; Fort Western, about forty-five miles from the river's mouth; and Fort Shirley, on the site of the present town of Dresden. Captain James Howard, the first and only commander of Fort Western, was Augusta's first permanent settler and a strong influence in the early development of the city.

The defeat of Montcalm at Quebec in 1759 made the Kennebec safe for pioneers, and the fort was dismantled (except the garrison building, the only one extant in Maine built prior to the Revolution) without ever having been attacked. The Benedict Arnold expedition gathered here for a week in September, 1775, before starting on the first leg of its Quebec journey.

A few miles south of the fort a settlement, called Hallowell, had been made in 1762. At the time of its incorporation into a town, in 1771, Fort Western was included. The two settlements became known as the Fort and the Hook, the latter name taken from Bombahook Stream at Hallowell. At this time the western side of the Fort settlement began to outstrip the eastern, aided by the industrial advantage of a sawmill at Bond Brook. Lumber was an important source of wealth, and in many instances pine boards took the place of currency. In 1780 the town voted to pay each of its Continental soldiers 2500 feet of pine boards plus the other bounty granted.

On the whole, however, the settlement at the Hook advanced more rapidly in wealth and population than the Fort, and rivalry gradually arose. In 1796, the Hook's leadership was threatened by Fort inhabitants who sought construction of a bridge to replace the ferry that ran from the foot of Winthrop St. to the Fort landing. To the chagrin of the Hook people, the first bridge over the Kennebec was completed at Augusta that same year. The resultant jealousy between the settlements necessitated a division. Hallowell retained its present name, and the Fort became Harrington, after Lord Harrington, when it was incorporated as a separate town, February 20, 1797. The name, however, was not agreeable, probably because the Hallowell wits corrupted it to 'Herringtown,' and on June 9 of the same year it was changed to Augusta. Accounts of the origin of the name differ, but one interpretation is that the town was called Augusta in honor of Pamela Augusta Dearborn, a daughter of General Henry Dearborn, the prominent Revolutionary soldier who was elected Representative to the Continental Congress from the Kennebec District in 1783. Two years after its incorporation Augusta became shire town of Kennebec County.

After the turn of the century, Augusta entered upon a new era of development, although Hallowell was the social and commercial metropolis of the region. The settlers' struggle for possession of the land against the claims of the proprietors came to a sharp focus in Augusta. In 1809, Paul Chadwick, one of a party of surveyors sent out to establish a land claim in Malta (Windsor), was murdered by squatters disguised, in Boston Tea-Party style, as Indians. Seven of the squatters were put in the Augusta jail. Shortly after, about seventy men descended upon the town in an attempt to release the Malta prisoners, and the community was thrown into a state of turmoil. Several companies of soldiers were called out from near-by towns to guard the courthouse, jail, and the homes of some of the land proprietors, and a cannon was placed on the west side in a position to sweep the bridge. There was continual rioting, and it was deemed necessary to keep the guard for six weeks, until after the prisoners' trial. Fortunately for the general peace, they were found not guilty. 'The Malta War,' as it was called, was one of the most serious disputes between settlers and landowners in Maine; it cost the Commonwealth of Massachusetts over $11,000 for supplies and military services rendered.

River traffic on the Kennebec had already entered upon an era that was to see a whole fleet of schooners plying weekly between Augusta and Boston by 1840. Freight from deep-water vessels was often transferred to long boats at Augusta and thence towed up-river through the rapids by oxen, which were driven through the shoals when there was not enough room to permit their passage along shore. Augusta had its share of the more than five hundred vessels built between Winslow and Gardiner, thousands of tons of shipping were owned in the city and neighboring communities, and it was not rare to see a score or so of vessels berthed at Augusta wharves. Although the arrival of the first train in Augusta in 1851, announced by 'wild screams such as locomotives are rarely permitted to utter,' predestined the decline of the river trade, schooners and tug-drawn barges conducted a profitable export business into the present century, exchanging cargoes of ice or lumber for produce and coal. Steamboat travel to Bath and Boston was inaugurated in 1826, and six years later a line ran up-river to Waterville.

The establishment of a United States Arsenal at Augusta in 1828 and the founding of the State Hospital eleven years later, two events contributing to the town's prestige, supplemented the even more important occasion of 1832, when Augusta became the State capital.

By 1849 the population of Augusta had increased (8225 in 1850) so that the town was authorized to adopt a city form of government. At no period had wealth been so great or indications of prosperity more marked. A cotton factory and sawmills at the dam, constructed in 1837, were in full operation, while the tonnage of ocean and river traffic was increasing. However, various checks, such as the gold rush of '49 and the Civil War, interfered with the city's development. Steamboat traffic, like that of the sailing vessels, fell off in time because of railroad competition and the lack of patronage. In 1865 a devastating fire razed nearly all of the business district.

Augusta

Various distinguished men visited the city during its mid-nineteenth century period of growth. General Winfield Scott made Augusta his headquarters for three weeks in 1839 while negotiating the settlement of the northeastern boundary dispute at the conclusion of 'the Aroostook War.' General U. S. Grant stopped in the city on several occasions, and in 1867, General Phil Sheridan visited Augusta as a guest of the State. A local account of the visit runs: 'General Phil Sheridan rides into Augusta. School children sing "Sheridan's Ride" from elevated steps.... Phil rides off in closed carriage after singing, and wasn't seen again.... Mothers checked up on their daughters to see if they had gone for a ride with Sheridan, but none were missing. This was known as Sheridan's Second Ride, but no poem was ever written about it that we know of today.'

Six Augusta citizens have become Governors of Maine. A native son, Melville W. Fuller (1833–1910), became Chief Justice of the U.S. Supreme Court (1888–1910), writing 829 decisions during his twenty-two years of office.

Lumber and the paper industry, textile mills, publishing houses, and the shoe industry figure largely in the history of Augusta's economic development. Forty-two industries employ nearly two thousand men and women, exclusive of hundreds of others in governmental and commercial employ. Augusta is the trading center for more than 75,000 city and suburban residents. The presence of the State and county departments has had much to do with Augusta's progress; were it not for these, it is questionable whether the city would be much more than a small industrial town. But as the capital of the State of Maine it has the characteristics of a secure, political-industrial metropolis.

TOUR 1 — 2.7 m.

E. from E. end of the Kennebec Bridge on Cony St.; R. on Bowman St.

1. *Fort Western (open daily in summer 9–5; adm. 10¢ and 25¢)*, Bowman St., and the land it occupies are probably as replete with historic associations as any place along the Kennebec River. On the site of the Plymouth trading post, established a few years after the landing of the Pilgrims in America, a fort was erected in 1754 as a protection against the Indians. The fort consisted of two blockhouses, a building for storerooms, barracks, officers' quarters, and parade grounds, the whole enclosed by a palisade. The original garrison house has been restored and furnished with Colonial antiques, and reproductions of the original blockhouses and palisades have been built by William Howard Gannett, a descendant of the fort's first commander. One room, chiefly devoted to collections from the Southwest, is dedicated to W. Herbert Dunton, native Augusta artist and illustrator.

2. A *Boulder and Tablet* south of Fort Western commemorate the passage of the Benedict Arnold expedition in September, 1775. The tablet was placed by the Second Company, Governor's Foot Guard, of New Haven, Connecticut, to record the services of its members participating in the Quebec campaign.

Retrace to Cony St.; R. on Cony St.; L. from Cony St. on Willow St.

3. The *Kennebec Journal Offices*, 20 Willow St. The *Journal*, Augusta's daily paper, is one of the few newspapers in the country with more than one hundred years of continuous publication to its credit. It has been claimed that the *Journal* was the first of the American press to advocate Abraham Lincoln for the Presidency. James G. Blaine, Maine's only Presidential candidate, was closely associated with the paper, having been its editor prior to his active participation in politics.

Retrace to Cony St.; L. on Cony St.; R. from Cony St. on Arsenal St.

4. *Augusta Lumber Company Mill* (*open*), 108 Arsenal St., is one of the remaining few of the 160 sawmills once situated on the Kennebec River. The mill, established in 1861, employs about 100 men in addition to 300 to 500 in the woods during the logging season.

5. The *State Hospital*, end of Arsenal St., established in 1896 as the Maine Insane Hospital, occupies the buildings of a former National Arsenal. In 1828, work was begun on the arsenal's main building 'for the safekeeping of arms and munitions of the United States for the northern and eastern frontier.' Later 15 buildings were erected, eight from blocks of undressed granite. The 40-acre lot was enclosed by an 8-foot fence set in a granite foundation, and a heavy granite wall and wharf were built on the river bank. The arsenal proper, a three-story building, 100 feet by 30 feet, had storage space for several thousand boxes of muskets and barrels of powder. Ammunition was prepared here during the Mexican War, and, during the Civil War, the arsenal buildings were closely guarded against burning by rebel agents. From the Civil War until the close of the century, when the supply of powder ran out and no further appropriations were made, sunrise and sunset salutes were fired from the arsenal. Among the commanders stationed here were General O. O. Howard and Lieutenant Anderson, hero of Fort Sumter. The State Hospital acquired the use of the buildings in 1897, and the Government later deeded the property to the State. Besides the hospital buildings, there is a 400-acre farm connected with the institution. Three hundred employees care for and supervise approximately 1500 patients.

Retrace to Cony St.; R. on Cony St.

6. The *Reuel Williams House* (*open by permission of owner*), SW. cor. Stone and Cony Sts., was erected during the first decade of the 19th century. It is a dignified building of the early Federal type, architecturally plain except for its fine doorways and Palladian windows. Noteworthy among the 13 large rooms is the Octagon Room, bearing its original wallpaper depicting scenes in the Hawaiian Islands, which was hand-painted in Paris in 1806. The Metropolitan Museum of Art in New York has

several panels of these scenes, as has a Philadelphia museum, but the Williams House contains the entire series in perfect condition. The paper, as well as a carpet that was hand-woven in Paris, was purchased in France by James Bowdoin, patron of Bowdoin College, and presented to Mr. Williams. The house contains many pieces of antique furniture, portraits, and a bust of Reuel Williams by Paul Akers. Williams (1783–1862) was one of Augusta's leading citizens and a prominent figure in State affairs. In 1847, President Polk and James Buchanan, then Secretary of State, were his guests while visiting Augusta.

7. *Cony High School*, SE. cor. Stone and Cony Sts., had its origin in the Cony Female Academy, founded in 1818 to provide 'instruction gratis to ... a number of orphans or other females under 16 years of age.' The present wedge-shaped high-school building was dedicated in 1930 and is thoroughly modern in equipment and curricula; about 850 students are enrolled.

Retrace Cony St. to Kennebec Bridge.

8. *Cushnoc*, a small island about a quarter of a mile north of the bridge, is visible only at low water. Navigation past Old Coon, as the early settlers called it, was difficult and dangerous, and many boats were sunk attempting the passage. About 1820 an effort was made to drag the island from its bed. One hundred yoke of oxen were procured, mill chains were fastened around the island and linked with the team, and the oxen headed upstream along the river bank. The first terrific pull succeeded only in throwing the hindmost yoke of oxen into the river. Subsequent attempts throughout the day effected no more than broken chains and crescendos of curses that rivaled the combined ox-power in volume. The island is still there.

9. *Kennebec Dam*, just north of the bridge, was first built in 1837. The structure, which was partially destroyed four times, was entirely rebuilt in 1870. The drainage waters from an area of more than 5000 square miles pour over the 22-foot face of the dam, supplying the city with 7150 horsepower.

AUGUSTA. POINTS OF INTEREST

1. Fort Western
2. Boulder and Tablet
3. Kennebec Journal
4. Augusta Lumber Company
5. State Hospital
6. Reuel Williams House
7. Cony High School
8. Cushnoc
9. Kennebec Dam
10. Edwards Manufacturing Company
11. Hazzard Shoe Company
12. Macomber Playground
13. Blaine House
14. State House
15. State Park
16. Jacataqua Oak
17. Kennebec County Jail
18. Lithgow Library
19. South Congregational Church
20. Camp Keyes
21. Ganeston Park

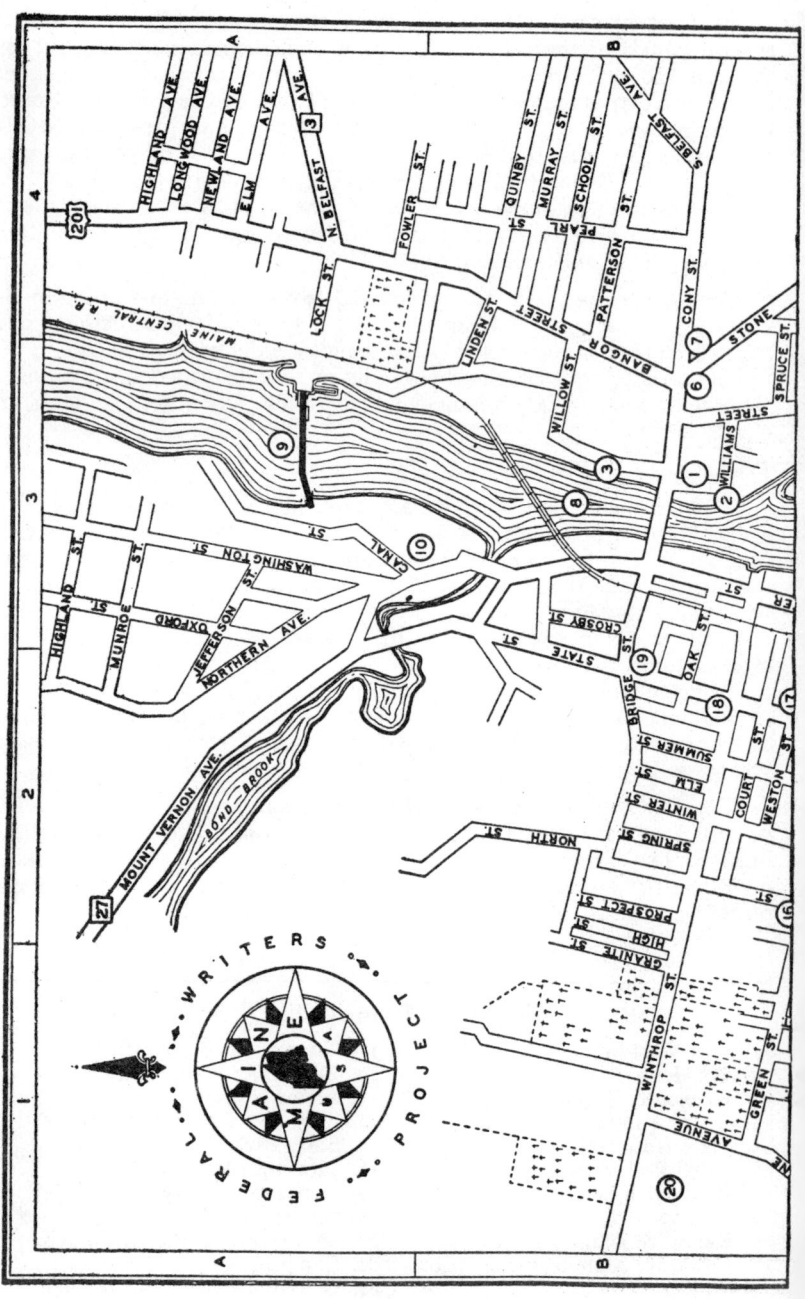

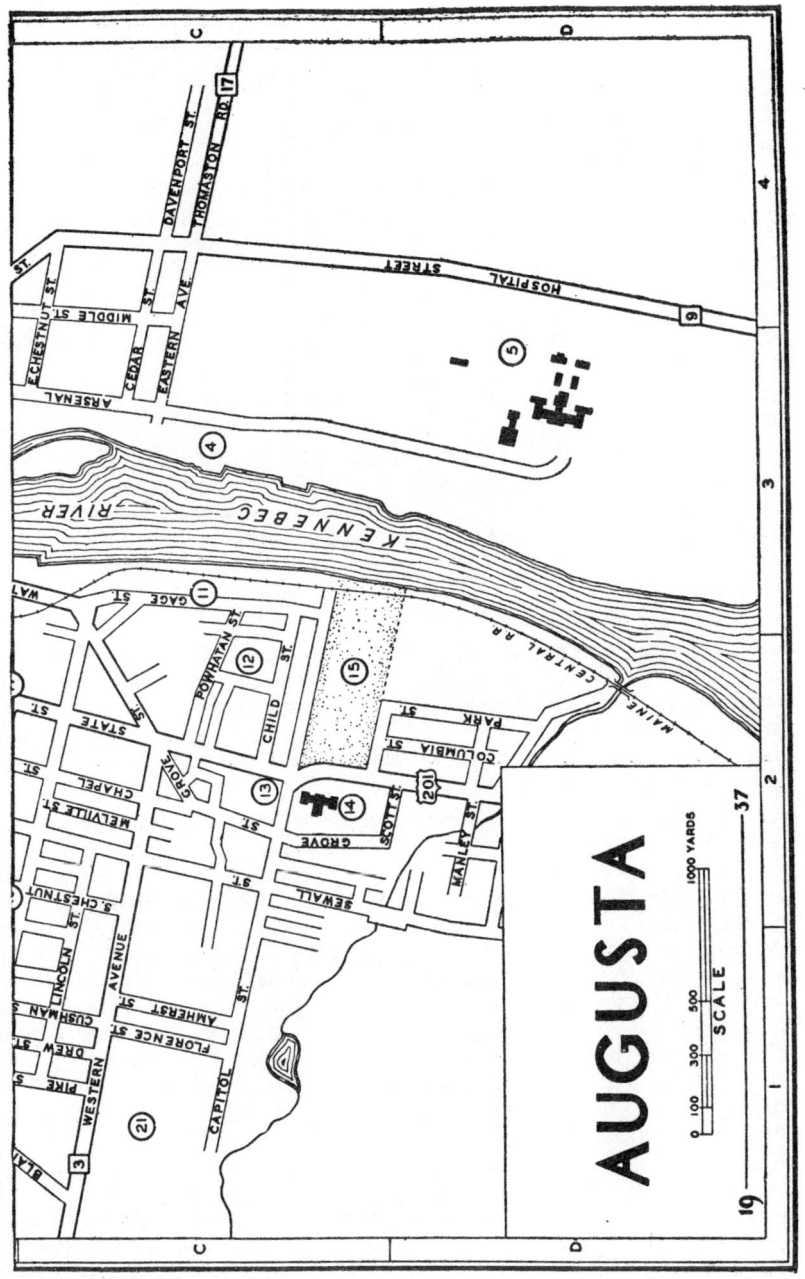

TOUR 2 — 5.5 m.

W. from Kennebec Bridge on Bridge St.; R. from Bridge St. on Water St.

10. *Edwards Manufacturing Company Mill* (*visitors' permits at office*), cor. Canal and Water Sts., is Augusta's largest industry. Established in 1845 by the Kennebec Lock and Canal Company, it was rated (1934) the sixth largest cotton mill in Maine. The company employs about 1200 workers and produces cotton cloth used chiefly in New England and the Midwest. The plant is modern and has attractive grounds kept in excellent condition. Exhibits from the mills are shown annually at the Eastern States' Exposition, Springfield, Massachusetts.

Retrace Water St. to junction of Water, Gage, Grove, and Green Streets; left on Gage St.

11. *R. P. Hazzard Shoe Company's Factory* (*open*), 61 Gage St., where approximately 575 skilled workers are employed in the manufacture of shoes, represents an industry which has attained a prominent industrial position in Augusta as well as in neighboring districts during the last few decades. Production at the Hazzard plant is about 4500 pairs of shoes daily.

R. from Gage St. on Child St.

12. *Macomber Playground* (R), Child St. between Valley and Center Sts., is a children's playground maintained by the city. The idea of a 'children's court,' wherein the children act as policemen, lawyers, and jury, was instituted here in 1930. The plan was at once successful, and it has been adopted by playgrounds throughout the country.

L. from Child St. on State St.

13. The *Blaine House,* or *Executive Mansion* (*open weekdays, except Sat.,* 2–4), NW. cor. Capitol and State Sts., is a spacious two-story residence of Classic Revival design, surrounded by landscaped grounds. Built shortly after 1830, the building was purchased by James G. Blaine, 'the plumed knight' of State and national politics, in 1862. This was the Augusta home of Blaine's family during his political career, and was the scene of numerous social and political gatherings. Here Blaine received news of his nomination for the Presidency, and of his 'rum, Romanism, and rebellion' defeat in 1876. Three of his children and three grandchildren were born here. In 1919, his daughter, Mrs. Harriet Blaine Beale, presented the house to the State as a memorial to her son, killed during the St. Mihiel drive in September, 1918; it was to be used as the official residence of the chief executive.

Remodeled under the direction of the architect, John Calvin Stevens, the old house retains its original design. The study is preserved as it was in Blaine's time. The silver service in the State dining-room was recovered from the cruiser 'Maine' ten years after its sinking in Havana Harbor.

14. The *State House* (*open daily* 8–5), SW. cor. State and Capitol Sts., provides offices for various State departments, the executive chambers, the House of Representatives and Senate chambers, the Maine State Library, and the State Museum. Built of Hallowell granite, the central section of the building embodies the strong architectural characteristics of its designer, Charles Bulfinch, and somewhat resembles another work of his, the Massachusetts State House. Rising upon a knoll above the surrounding city, the four-storied building has a 300-foot front with colonnaded portico in the center portion, and two 75-foot wings facing east. The cornerstone was laid in 1829, and the original structure completed three years later. In 1911, it was enlarged according to designs by G. Henri Desmond, necessitating the demolition of almost all the old building save the front and rear walls. At this time the grounds were graded, additions made to the wings, and a dome added, surmounted by a statue, representing Augusta, the city, designed by W. Clark Noble of Gardiner, and made of copper plated with gold.

A *Museum* on the first floor contains specimens of animals, birds, military relics, an aquarium, and scores of historic curios. The *Hall of Flags* on the second floor houses Maine's battle flags. The *Maine State Library* on the second floor has over 200,000 volumes of general reference, literature (but no contemporary fiction), legislative reference, genealogy, documents, a legal library of 60,000 books, and volumes about Maine and an ever-increasing collection of the works of Maine authors. Scattered about the building are many portraits of Maine governors and other eminent personages.

15. *State Park*, a 20-acre tract between Capitol and Union Sts., stretching from State St. before the capitol to the banks of the river, offers pleasant vistas and walks over more than a mile of paths. Thousands of trees and shrubs, rustic seats and benches, an artificial pond, and other landscaping effects make the park one of the most attractive spots in Augusta. There is also an arboretum, and the park presents one of the few places in the State where students in dendrology or horticulture can find a large variety of plants for study purposes. Landscape architects and the Forestry Department are using the park to determine what plants will thrive in this locality. Historically the park is of interest because of its Civil War associations. Maine regiments were encamped here during the war, and for at least two winters the soldiers weathered the rigors of the climate before setting out into the heat of southern campaigns, some even in Texas. At the end of a long lane of trees is a marble shaft marking the grave of Enoch Lincoln, Maine's sixth Governor. During his administration the capital was removed from Portland to Augusta and work begun on the new building. Lincoln's 2000-line poem, 'The Village,' having its setting in Fryeburg and written while he was a lawyer there, was the first book of poetry published in Maine.

Retrace State St. to Green St.; L. on Green St.

16. The *Jacataqua Oak*, an immense old tree standing at 81 Green St., is associated with one of the most romantic of the legends of the Kennebec.

Jacataqua, an Indian princess, who had been taken from her Abnaki tribal home on Swan Island, was being held at Fort Western when the Arnold expedition arrived there in 1775. Of mixed French and Indian blood, the girl had been educated at a convent in Quebec and was unusually intelligent and attractive. Aaron Burr, later Vice-President of the United States, but at that time only a youth of 19 accompanying the expedition, became enamored of Jacataqua, and the Jacataqua Oak is supposed to have been the scene of their love-making. Burr and the princess are accredited with having killed the bear which was the main course of the feast at the fort prior to the departure of the expedition. The story of Jacataqua is told by Kenneth Roberts in the historical novel, 'Arundel.'

Retrace Green St. to State St.; L. on State St.

17. *Kennebec County Jail*, SE. cor. State and Court Sts., was the scene of a lurid event in Augusta's history. Joseph Sager of Gardiner, accused and convicted of having poisoned his wife, was condemned to be hanged in January, 1835. A gallows was erected at the southwest corner of the jail, and Sager was brought to the scaffold still protesting his innocence, while the minister in attendance read a manuscript 'partly by narrative and partly by exhortation' that the murderer had prepared. Between 8000 and 12,000 persons attended the execution, there was much jeering and throwing of stones, and 'liquor flowed freely and was disposed of by the barrel.' The trap that was sprung under Sager and a whipping-post used in earlier days are in the basement of the courthouse near-by.

18. *Lithgow Library* and *Reading Room* (*open weekdays* 10-9), NW. cor. Winthrop and State Sts., is a solidly designed structure of Maine granite, architecturally of the Romanesque-Renaissance order, built in 1895 after designs by Joseph Neal and Alfred Hopkins. The library occupies the site of one of Augusta's early hotels, the Cushnoc House. In its book room six stained-glass transom windows, designed by Charles Willoughby of Augusta, later a curator at the Peabody Museum of Archeology and Ethnology, Cambridge, treat historic subjects important in the annals of the city. In addition to nearly 18,000 volumes, the library houses the collection of the Kennebec Natural History and Antiquarian Society, an organization now inactive. The collection, unclassified and uncatalogued, contains scores of items pertinent to Augusta and New England history.

19. *South Congregational Church*, 62 State St., is the oldest of Augusta's 11 churches, although the present structure, built of granite in Gothic design, was not erected until 1866. The parish dates to 1771, the first building being completed in Market Square 11 years later. In 1836 Roman Catholics established a church on the east side. Their present church, St. Mary's, on Western Avenue, was built in 1927; a stately granite structure of a modified Norman-Gothic design, it is considered the most beautiful of Augusta's churches. The growth of the French population, with increased lumbering and mill employment, assumed such proportions that a second Catholic church was necessary. St. Augustine's,

corner of Washington St. and Northern Ave., erected in 1915, is an impressive structure dominating the northern section of the city and plainly visible from the South Congregational Church.

Retrace State St. to Winthrop St.; R. on Winthrop St.

20. **Camp Keyes** is at the summit of Winthrop St., on a flat, almost treeless, plateau nearly a square mile in area. The 43d Division of the National Guard meets here every fifth year for its encampment and muster. Here are the local military headquarters and the training school for recruits to the Maine State police force. Up the eastern slope of the hill and extending onto the plateau are several of the city's cemeteries, while the four runways and the hangar of the Augusta airport are adjacent to the infantry barracks and other buildings. A revolving beacon sweeps the sky nightly. Some of the best views of the city and valley, as well as of the surrounding country, can be had from this hilltop.

S. through Camp Keyes Drive to Western Ave.; L. on Western Ave.

21. **Ganeston Park** *(open: no motoring)*, rear of the W. H. Gannett residence, 114 Western Ave., is the largest of Augusta's several parks. It was created several years ago when William Howard Gannett set aside 475 acres of wooded land for the use of the public. There are opportunities here for hiking, horseback riding, picnicking, and winter sports. Ganeston Park was made a State Game Preserve and Bird Sanctuary by the legislature in 1930.

Points of Interest in Environs:

> Veterans' Administration Facility, Togus, 4.6 *m.* (*see Tour* 17); Lake Cobbosseecontee, 6.8 *m.* (*see Tour* 13); Belgrade Lakes, 18.1 *m.* (*see Tour* 12).

BANGOR

City: Alt. 100, pop. 28,749, sett. 1769, incorp. town 1791, city 1834.

Railroad Station: Union Station, Exchange and Washington Sts., for M.C. and B. & A. R.R.s.

Bus Stations: Union Station, for M.C. Transportation Co., Bangor House, 174 Main St., for Grey Line and Quaker Stages.

Airport: Bangor Airport, 3 *m.* NW. on Cooper Rd., for B. & M. Airways.

Accommodations: Three hotels.

Fishing: Bangor Salmon Pool, May – June.

Swimming: Bull's Eye Pool, 1.5 *m.* north on Valley Ave., Pushaw Pond, 4 *m.* north on Essex St.

BANGOR, the third largest city in Maine and the county seat of Penobscot County, sprawls upon the hills along the west bank of the Penobscot River. Twenty-three miles from deep-sea anchorage and at the head of tidewater, the city faces in another direction the hundreds of miles of historic and playground areas that lie to the south along Penobscot Bay and eastward. Kenduskeag Stream enters the city from a northerly direction, running through the central and business districts from which other hills rise sharply to residential Bangor.

Were it not for its advantageous geographical position, Bangor might well be a city of ghosts: the ghosts of hordes of lusty caulk-booted river-drivers, of merchants, mariners, and mill hands of a dozen nationalities, who once swarmed about the present vital city. The lumber industry, largely responsible for Bangor's growth, is now restricted to pulp-wood operations at Brewer across the river, while the days when scores of vessels filled the Penobscot at Bangor are long departed. Today, the city is predominantly commercial. In addition, it is a focal point for thousands of tourists who pour through the city each year over highways which were once well-beaten Indian trails along the Penobscot.

The first authentic record of the site of present-day Bangor occurs in Samuel de Champlain's journals. Champlain, cruising out of St. Croix in September, 1604, piloted his sixteen-ton vessel up the Penobscot until, as he writes, 'we came to a little river [the Kenduskeag] in the vicinity of which we had to anchor. [We] could not have proceeded more than half a league on account of waterfall [Treats Falls] which descends a slope of some seven to eight feet.' The explorer landed 'to see the country,' went hunting, and found the locality 'most pleasant and agreeable.' He was much impressed by the oaks which originally covered the site of Bangor, and from which the present Oak and Grove Streets derive their names. The place was an important Indian rendezvous, and Champlain conferred here with the Etchimin Indian chief, Bessabez. Champlain's tactful and courteous conduct at this time was largely responsible for the amicable French-Indian relationships which lasted as long as the French had control of Acadia.

Bangor's early history, begun by the settlement of Jacob Buswell of Salisbury, Massachusetts, in 1769, was the usual one of a slowly growing pioneer community whose chief revenues were derived from the exportation of fish, furs, and lumber. The settlement was known as Kenduskeag Plantation until 1787, and as Sunbury from 1787 to 1791. In 1779, the Revolutionary expedition against Castine under the command of Commodore Richard Saltonstall and General Solomon Lovell was routed by a British fleet commanded by Sir George Collier. Retreating to Kenduskeag Plantation, the Americans destroyed their own fleet of nine ships and fled westward through the forest. With them went the settlers, except those who were unable to leave and who later were obliged to take an oath of allegiance to the British Crown. Twelve years later, the community had recovered sufficiently to petition for incorporation. The Reverend Seth Noble, Bangor's first installed pastor, was sent to Boston to obtain the incorporation from the General Court. It is said that, while the clergyman was attending to the town's registration, he was humming the old hymn tune known as 'Bangor.' When the clerk, filling out the necessary papers, asked Noble the name of the community, the pastor misunderstood the question and replied with the name of the hymn, and thus the latter name was written into the incorporation papers.

By the turn of the century, Bangor was beginning to enjoy a brisk export trade in lumber. But embargoes, and the War of 1812, with British ships lying off-shore and threatening the very life of the Penobscot Bay settlements, made financial gain possible only by privateering or the running of contraband. In September, 1814, a British fleet and army descended upon the defenseless town and forced its unconditional surrender. Considerable plundering and pillaging followed notwithstanding the town's petition that life and property be spared and the giving of a bond to assure the delivery of certain vessels, then under construction, to the British at Castine. Four years later, the most important news on the first day of the year was an announcement in *The Eastern Argus* that 'Mr. Holmes had a new suit of clothes before he went to Congress.'

Between 1830 and 1834, the early boom in lumber and allied industries resulted in an increase in Bangor's population from 2808 to 8000. The forests were cut back and away from the Penobscot, up the river to the East Branch and West Branch — that great woods country which produced men and legends as integrally a part of Maine as its pine trees. Bangor's rise to eminence coincided with the 'pine period' between 1820 and 1860, when real lumbermen rather scorned the lowly spruce. After the Civil War, as the supply of pine became depleted, spruce began to come into its own as a forest product, until today the cut of spruce considerably exceeds that of the other species. Millions of logs were tumbled down the Penobscot to be converted into lumber, clapboards, laths, shingles, and staves in the Bangor mills. In the 1850's, Bangor was probably the leading lumber port of the world, while in the sixties and seventies it was second only to Chicago in the extent of its lumber shipments. In the peak year of 1872, nearly 250,000,000 board feet, valued at $3,233,958.53, were handled here.

For approximately fifty years in the middle of the nineteenth century, a section of the city which compared with San Francisco's Barbary Coast in its palmy days flourished in the vicinity of Washington, Hancock, and Exchange Streets. This part of Bangor was known as the 'Devil's Half-Acre.' Here were the taverns and grogshops, the lodging-houses and brothels, which catered to the teeming life of the busy seaport. In the spring, when hundreds of lumbermen and rivermen thronged into Bangor fresh from the log-drives with a winter's wages and the accumulation of a winter's thirsts and hungers, the population of the Half-Acre swelled. After months of hard and dangerous labor, the men of the North Woods were ready for relaxation; and there was nothing half-hearted in the way they went about it. Today, there is no trace of this riotous quarter, where salt-water shellbacks and tall-timber men swapped tales, drinks, and blows.

The pulse of Bangor quickened during the exciting days of 1834–36 when land speculation was at its height in Maine. Land which sold for only a few cents an acre in the morning might command a price of as many dollars in the afternoon; townships and lots were sold over and over again 'sight unseen.' Brokers' offices were established in Bangor, a courier line was set up to Boston, and the city overflowed with speculators, gamblers, and the human flotsam and jetsam which is always attracted by the prospect of 'easy money.' One company, after advertising extensively in New England and New York papers, held a land auction at which 'champagne from the original bottles [was poured] into huge washtubs from which each man helped himself at his own sweet will.' The Baltimore *Niles' Register* of June, 1835, contained this item: 'It is rumored that one evening last week, two paupers escaped from the Bangor almshouse, and though they were caught early the next morning, yet in the meantime, before they were secured, they had made $1800 each by speculating in timber lands.' The bubble burst when people stopped long enough to look at the lands they had purchased; and the web of dishonest surveyors' reports, deception, and swindling fell to pieces.

Essential to the lumber industry were the ships, many of them Bangor-built and Bangor-owned, which sailed with pine boards and brought back molasses, sugar, and rum from the West Indies. From April until late November, the harbor was crowded with vessels of all rigs and sizes, ranging from bay coasters to full-rigged ships. Records show that as many as seven hundred vessels of from four hundred to four thousand tons have been anchored in the harbor at one time. A brisk trade was developed with the United Kingdom and the Continent, while many coasters carried cargoes to all ports along the western Atlantic seaboard. The harvesting and shipping of Penobscot River ice in the vicinity of Bangor flourished between 1840 and 1890.

Beginning with the construction of the 'Red Bridge' in 1791, scores of vessels were launched at Bangor, to carry that name all over the globe. The 'Thinks-I-to-Myself' was one of the Bangor vessels captured by the British during the War of 1812; it was later reported as a privateer under British colors. The 'Gold Hunter,' Bangor-built, was the first to carry a band of adventurers around the Horn to California in the gold rush of '49. The age of steam navigation was inaugurated at Bangor with the arrival of the steamboat 'Bangor' from Boston, in May, 1824. This wooden side-wheeler was later engaged in conveying pilgrims from Alexandria, Egypt, to Mecca — but not until its white coat had been painted black to satisfy the Mohammedans, who refused to embark on a vessel that flaunted their mourning color. Still later, the 'Bangor' was used as a royal yacht by the Sultan of Turkey. Another ship of the same name, one of the first American steamboats with an iron propeller, was built in 1845 to run between Bangor and Boston.

Many of Bangor's twenty-eight churches are architecturally important, and a survey made in 1935 revealed some eighty residences dating from more than a century ago. Charles Bulfinch, distinguished Boston architect who assisted in designing the National Capitol, surveyed a hundred-acre lot in Bangor about 1830 and laid out the streets lying south of State Street. Some of the older streets, particularly Broadway, Essex, Hammond, Ohio, and State, contain many fine old houses of Federal design. These were built mainly by the early gentry, prominent landowners and merchants. In addition, there are many later homes of varied design, stately structures built by 'lumber barons' of the city's boom days, from 1840 to 1880. Growth and civic improvement have gone on undeterred by several public disasters, such as the $3,000,000 fire which swept through the business district in 1911.

Henry D. Thoreau, describing Bangor as it was in 1846, wrote: 'There stands the city of Bangor, fifty miles up the Penobscot, at the head of navigation for vessels of the larger class, the principal lumber depot on this continent, with a population of twelve thousand, like a star on the edge of the night, still hewing at the forest of which it is built, already overflowing with the luxuries and refinements of Europe, and sending its vessels to Spain, to England, and to the West Indies for its groceries — and yet only a few axe-men have gone "up-river," into the howling wilderness which feeds it.'

From its nineteenth-century background of 'luxuries and refinements' in the heyday of Maine lumbering, Bangor, unlike many towns with a similar background, has forged ahead to become one of the State's most important cities.

TOUR — 1.8 m.

N. from Hammond St. on Central St.

Norumbega Parkway, crossing Kenduskeag Stream to Central St., is of historic interest because of the associations of its name with Bangor. 'Norumbega,' the old Spanish word meaning 'the country of the Norwegians, or Northmen' (also interpreted as Penobscot Indian, signifying 'still-water-between-falls'), was once applied to Penobscot Bay and vicinity. Norumbega Parkway, a garden spot in the midst of the city, was developed in 1933, financed by a bequest from Luther M. Peirce. The park's high, vine-covered walls overlook pleasant, landscaped walks.

BANGOR. POINTS OF INTEREST

1. Old City Hall
2. Joseph Garland House
3. Bangor Theological Seminary
4. Hannibal Hamlin House
5. Symphony House
6. Bangor House
7. Memorial and Davenport Park
8. Peirce Memorial
9. Bangor Historical Society and Public Library
10. Samuel Veazie House
11. Boutelle House
12. Grotto Cascade Park
13. Bangor Salmon Pool

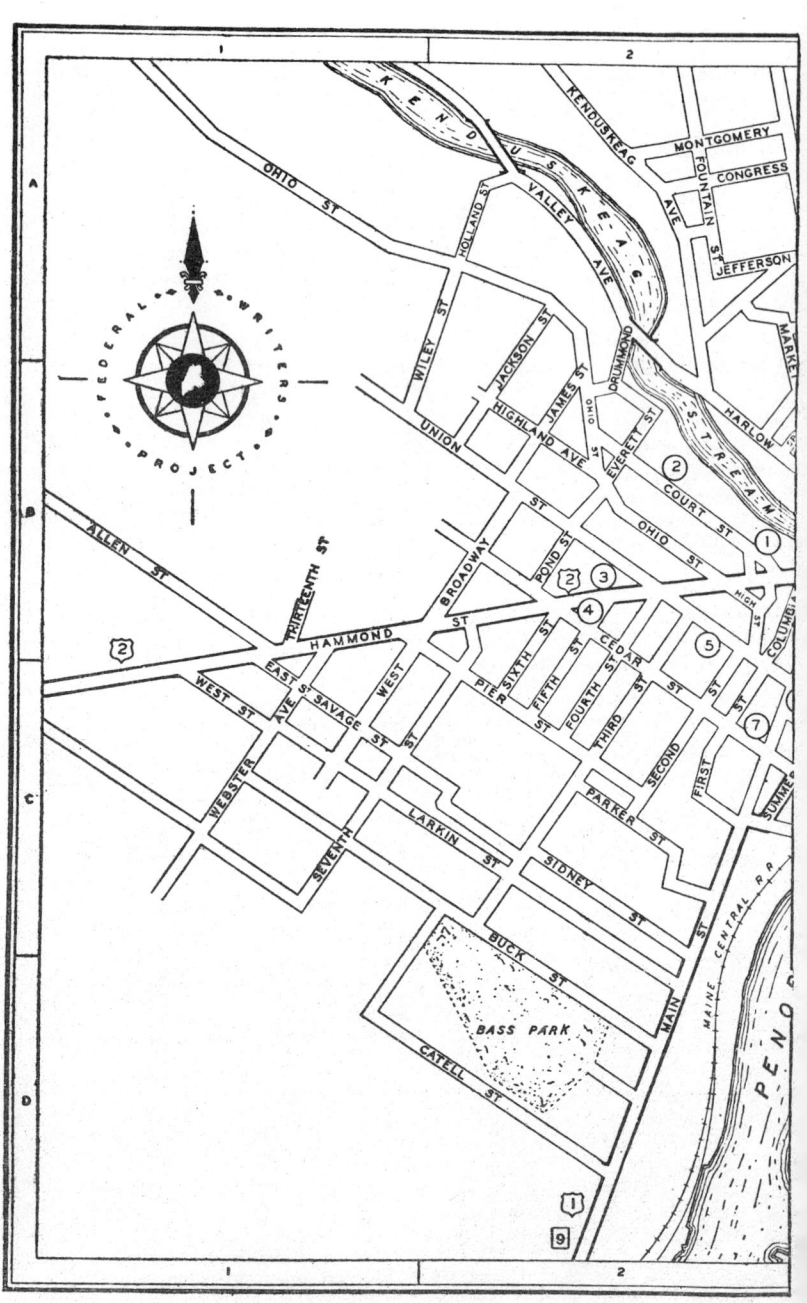

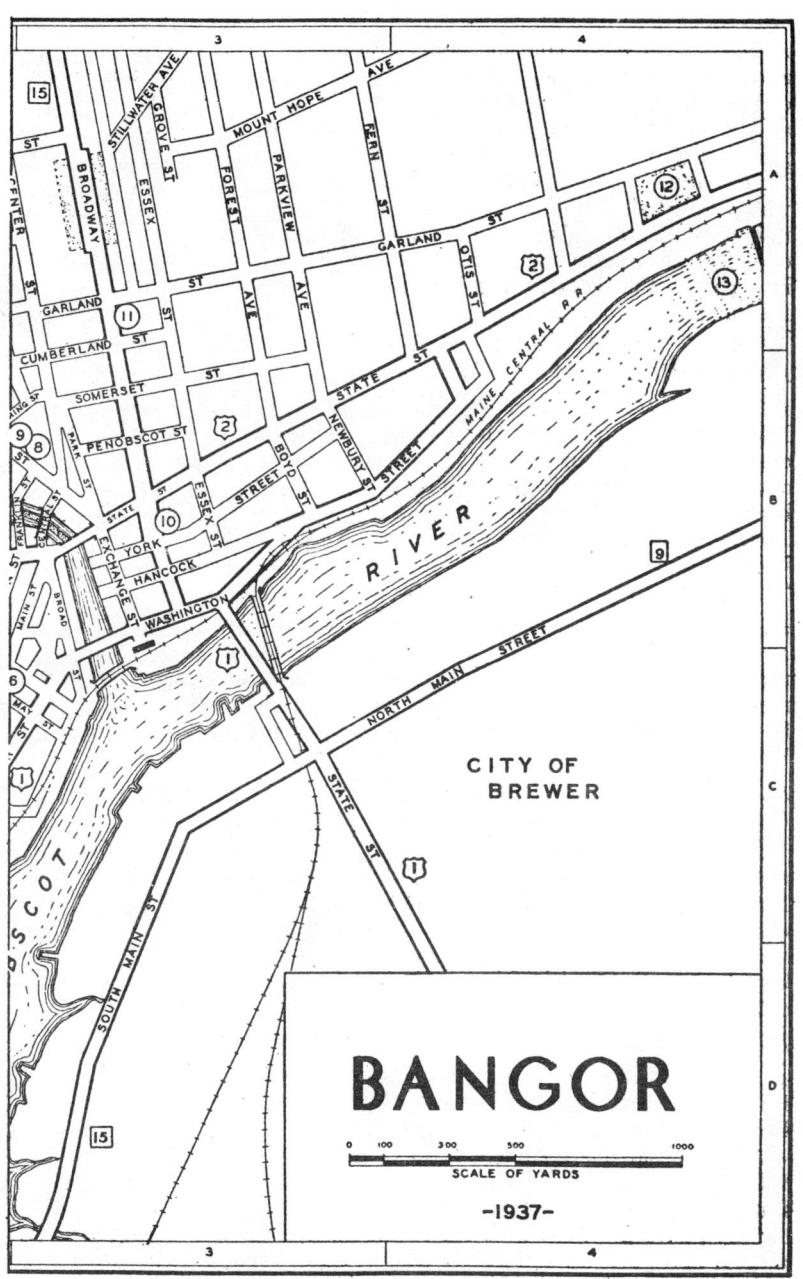

Kenduskeag Mall, a continuation of the parkway, lies between Central and State Sts. The name 'Kenduskeag' (also 'Condeskeag' and 'Kadesquit') signified 'eel-catching place,' from the Indian days when the stream abounded in that fish. The name was applied to Bangor until its incorporation in 1791. A bronze plaque and a boulder commemorate the landing of Samuel de Champlain, who is believed to have come ashore somewhere near this spot in 1604. Near the boulder are two cannon, one a relic of the Spanish-American War, and the other a piece recovered from one of the American ships sunk off Bangor during the Saltonstall retreat in 1779. In the center of the Mall rises a well-executed bronze statue of Hannibal Hamlin, Vice-President under Lincoln. The work of Charles E. Tefft, it was paid for by public contributions and unveiled in 1927.

Retrace to Hammond St.; R. from Hammond St. on Court St.

1. *Old City Hall*, Court St., was one of the buildings occupied by the British troops during their invasion in 1814. Built in 1812, the hall was designed for religious purposes as well as for the administration of town and county affairs. The town's early legal proceedings were carried on here. The old building, though, missed Bangor's first lawsuit when Jacob Buswell in 1790 brought suit against one David Wall, 'Yoeman,' for calling him 'an old damned, gray-headed bugar of Hell,' and for calling 'the Rev. Seth Noble a damned rascall.'

2. The *Joseph D. Garland House (private)*, 117 Court St., was built in 1830 after designs accredited to Richard Upjohn. The structure bears out the better features of the traditional Greek Revival architecture. Built of red brick, it stands on high ground amid giant elms, its pillared porticoes, front and rear, commanding prospects up and down the Kenduskeag Valley.

L. from Court St. on Boynton and Hudson Sts.; L. from Hudson St. on Union St.

3. The *Bangor Theological Seminary (open)*, NW. corner Union and Hammond Sts., the oldest institution in Bangor and the only one of its kind in Maine, New Hampshire, and Vermont, was incorporated as the 'Maine Charity School' in 1804. In the rigorous days of its past, when the students got their water from a well on the campus and used stoves and oil lamps, they could save ten cents a week on board by not drinking tea or coffee.

R. from Union St. on Hammond St.; L. from Hammond St. on Fifth St.

4. The *Hannibal Hamlin House (visitors by permission)*, NE. corner Fifth St., is associated with one of Maine's most distinguished citizens. Hannibal Hamlin moved from his native town of Paris Hill to Hampden where he resided for twenty years, building an extensive law practice. From 1862 to 1864, he was Vice-President of the United States under Lincoln, served as United States Senator from 1869 to 1881, and as Minister to Spain from 1881 to 1883. While Vice-President, Hamlin came to Bangor and purchased the Fifth Street house which was later left to the Theological Seminary by his son.

R. from Fifth St. on Hammond St.; R. on Union St.

5. *Symphony House* (*private*), 166 Union St., combines architectural and historic interest. Presumably designed by Richard Upjohn, it was built by one of Bangor's pioneer lumbermen, Isaac Farrar, in 1833–36. Constructed of red brick brought from England, it is architecturally of modified English Renaissance design. The slate for the roof was imported from Bangor, Wales, and a circular room is finished throughout with solid mahogany brought from San Domingo. The house was occupied at various times by Owen Davis, the playwright, and Gene Sawyer, author of the 'Nick Carter' series. It is now owned by the Bangor Symphony Orchestra.

6. *Bangor House*, SE. corner of Main and Union Sts., survives from stagecoach, schooner, and steamboat days. The original hotel, retained in the present building's annex, was built about a century ago. The old house had a huge kitchen fireplace where meats and fowl were spitted over the open blaze, and a large dance-hall built over the dining-room. Presidents Grant, Arthur, Harrison, and Theodore Roosevelt, as well as Stephen A. Douglas and Daniel Webster, were distinguished guests. In 1882, Oscar Wilde, on his American tour, made his only stop in Maine at the Bangor House, en route to New Brunswick. He spoke before an audience in a hall appropriately decorated with sunflowers, and was considerably booed and hissed by the vulgarly curious. It is recorded that no respectable young lady, no matter what her claims to being one of the intelligentsia, was permitted to attend the gathering.

R. from Union St. on Main St.

7. *'Remember the Maine!' Memorial* is in *Davenport Park*, NW. corner Main and Cedar Sts. A granite, wedge-shaped monument, surmounted by a bronze shaft bearing an American eagle, it was erected by the city in 1922. On the monument are the original shield and scroll recovered from the battleship 'Maine,' blown up in Havana Harbor in 1898.

OTHER POINTS OF INTEREST

8. *Peirce Memorial*, Harlow St. opposite Franklin St., is a bronze statue of three river-drivers, equipped with peavies and cant-hooks, breaking a log-jam. It commemorates Bangor's lumber industry. The memorial, the work of Charles E. Tefft of Brewer, was presented to Bangor by Luther M. Peirce.

9. *Bangor Historical Society*, 145 Harlow St., has its rooms in the *Bangor Public Library* (*open* 9–9, *weekdays*), one of the largest and best endowed of the State's libraries. The society's collection of historic objects includes relics of the Colonial and Revolutionary periods, the Civil War, Indians, the prehistoric Red Paint People. There are also collections of portraits, prints, and paintings, and antique furniture, and Chinese and East Indian art objects.

10. The *Samuel Veazie House*, NE. corner Broadway and York St. (*Jerrard Apartment House*), was built in the 1830's by one of Bangor's foremost citizens and lumber barons, General Samuel Veazie (1787–1869), who rose from the rank of ensign to general in the War of 1812. He moved to Bangor in 1832, and about 1850 purchased the Bangor, Old Town, and Milford Railroad (originally the Bangor and Piscataquis Canal and Railroad Company), one of the first railroads in New England. At the time of his death, Veazie owned all the fifty-two lumber mills between Bangor and Old Town.

11. The *Boutelle House* (*private*), 157 Broadway, was built in 1834 by the Smith Brothers, constructors of the Bangor, Old Town, and Milford Railroad. The design is attributed to Charles Bulfinch. The four Doric columns of the front support an entablature consisting of an ornamental architrave frieze, with carved wreaths and a cornice. An attractive balustrade surrounds the porch roof. Doric pilasters form the framework of the recessed doorway, as well as that of the leaded side-lights, and support a carved entablature in place of the conventional leaded-glass fan. During stirring political campaigns of the last century, distinguished speakers, such as James G. Blaine, William McKinley, Senators Eugene Hale, and William P. Frye, reviewed torchlight parades from the balcony.

12. *Grotto Cascade Park*, State St. at Summit Ave., is the newest of Bangor's city parks. An artificial 45-foot cascade terminates in an artificial pool and fountain, bordered by flowers and rocks. Colored lights, submerged in the fountain, combine with the electrically regulated spray to give the effects of sunset, moonlight, twilight, and other color illusions. The park's development was the first Government work relief project in the city.

13. *Bangor Salmon Pool*, right from State St. opposite the Bangor Waterworks, is known for its excellent fishing and for a custom, connected therewith, of presenting the season's first salmon to the President of the United States: the pool is the only one of its kind in the country within a city's limits. The days are over when shad, alewives, salmon, and sturgeon were, with furs, major stocks in trade for the early settlers, yet the gamey 10 to 30 pound Atlantic sea salmon still fight their way up over the falls each May and June to spawn.

Points of Interest in Environs:

University of Maine, Orono, 8 *m.* (*Tour* 4); Indian Reservation, Old Town, 13.2 *m.* (*Tour* 4); Dorothea Dix Memorial Park, Fort Knox, Black Mansion (*Tour* 1, *sec. c*); Acadia National Park, Cadillac Mountain, Mount Desert, Bar Harbor (*Tour* 2).

BRUNSWICK

Town: Alt. 65, pop. 7604, sett. 1628, incorp. town 1738.
Railroad Station: Maine St., for M.C. R.R.
Bus Stations: 150 Maine St., for M.C. Transportation Co.; 148 Maine St., for Grey Line and Quaker Stages.
Accommodations: Three hotels.
Swimming: Mere Point, Harpswell, Gurnet, Orr's Island, and Bailey Island.
Annual Events: Bowdoin College for intercollegiate sports; Maine Open Handicap Golf Tournament, April 19.

BRUNSWICK is a community where commerce, industry, and education flourish in well-balanced proportions. Famous as the seat of Bowdoin College, it is locally better known as the trading center for a large spread of coastal villages and summer resort regions to the east and south of the town. The township extends between the Androscoggin River and Merrymeeting Bay on the one hand and the northern reaches of Casco Bay on the other, the town proper growing out fanwise from the mill district at the falls of the Androscoggin where the population is heaviest. The terrain is a comparatively flat expanse on a broad, sandy coastal plain. Brunswick's growth has been according to plan; its streets are well laid out, most of them still unpaved, running at right angles to Maine, Bath, Harpswell, and Pleasant Streets. Maine Street, 198 feet wide, is second only to that street of Keene, New Hampshire, which is the widest main street in New England.

Early in its history the town was a lumbering center, leading the State in lumber export in 1820. The opening of a cotton mill in 1809, said to have been the first in the State, was the beginning of Brunswick's industrial development. When in 1843 Aaron Dennison began making paper boxes at the rear of his father's house at 8 Everett Street, he laid the foundation for the now internationally known Dennison Manufacturing Company, which in 1894 was removed to Roxbury, Massachusetts, and now has large factories in Framingham, Massachusetts, and elsewhere in this country. Incidentally Dennison, having perfected a method for making the works of watches by machinery, established the Boston Watch Company, now the Waltham Watch Company of Waltham, Massachusetts. The major industries in Brunswick today are a textile mill and paper and box manufactories.

With the growth of the pulp and textile mills in Brunswick the population has increased steadily since 1880. At present between 50 and 60 per cent of the people are of French-Canadian stock, chiefly of native parentage.

Brunswick was named in 1717 for the city and one-time duchy of

Brunswick, Germany, but, being a region long associated with Indian history, it was already replete with Indian names. At least three tribes, the Pejepscots, the Canibas, and the Anasagunticooks, had inhabited the territory. Tradition has it that the shores of Merrymeeting Bay, being accessible by water and rich in fish and game, were frequently used by Maine Indians as gathering-places for feasting and tribal ceremonies. The bay, a rendezvous for thousands of migrating ducks and Canada geese (see *The Nation's Northeast Corner*), was called *Quabacook* (Ind.: 'duck-water-place'), and is still one of the chief duck-hunting resorts on the Atlantic coast.

The Indians called the region, near the falls of the Androscoggin, *Ahmelahcogneturcook* ('place of much fish, fowl, and beasts'). And so it was to Thomas Purchase, the first known trader (about 1624-28) with the powerful Canibas and Anasagunticooks. He was so successful in curing and exporting salmon and sturgeon at the falls that an English company stationed an agent near this commercially strategic point. In 1688, a dozen years after the first settlement that had grown up around the post had been abandoned during the Indian wars, Governor Andros established Fort Andros at Pejepscot, as the place was then known. Two years later, both the fort and the new settlement were destroyed by Indians. In 1699, a treaty with the Indians was ratified, and after a group of eight men, known as the Pejepscot Proprietors, had purchased and plotted most of what is now Brunswick (1714-15), Fort George was erected near the site of Fort Andros in 1715. Yet seven years afterward, during Lovewell's War, the town was again destroyed by Indians. But in a few years the settlement had begun to develop uninterruptedly, and Fort George was dismantled in 1737.

Even before the Indian wars were over, Brunswick had begun to plan its municipal and economic development. In 1717, its citizens voted to construct a road twelve rods wide, extending from the south bastion of Fort George to the head of Maquoit Bay. Maine Street between Cabot Mills and the beginning of the Mall retains the original proportions. The first dam across the Androscoggin, highly important in Brunswick's industrial growth, was built in 1753, and has been many times replaced. A canal, which can still be seen, was built about 1797 from Merrymeeting Bay to the New Meadows River to facilitate lumber transportation. But since both ends of the canal were of the same level and there was no current, the logs refused to move in either direction and the lumbermen were forced to abandon the undertaking. Through the early part of the nineteenth century, ships were built in Brunswick, on the river and on Harpswell, Middle, and Maquoit Bays, but no trace remains of either the shipbuilding or lumbering industries today.

Brunswick has been the birthplace of many noted people, perhaps the best known of whom were John S. C. Abbott (1805-77), historian, and George Palmer Putnam (1814-72), founder of the publishing house of G. P. Putnam's Sons. A man who left his mark upon the local scene was Samuel Melcher, 3d (1775-1862), a son of one of the town's first families, who with no formal artistic training became a master builder and designed houses and churches of great beauty. Some of Maine's loveliest churches were done by Melcher, most outstanding being the old church in Wiscasset (*see Tour* 1, *sec. b*). Samuel Melcher, though a very old man at the time, supervised the delicate woodcarving in the Bowdoin College Chapel and, always willing to learn, even late in life he used to walk to Boston to observe the trends in architecture developing there and in towns along the way. In a small sphere he was a great artist.

Bowdoin College has, of course, greatly influenced Brunswick's position as a cultural center. The college was founded in 1794, but because of financial difficulties it was not actually in session until 1802. Seeking the patronage of a family both wealthy and sympathetic to education and the arts, the founders wisely hit upon the name of James Bowdoin, Governor of Massachusetts, for their new college. John Hancock, Governor after Bowdoin's death and his bitter personal and political enemy, so the story goes, delayed the starting of the college some two or three years by declining to sign a document to incorporate an institution with a name so odious to him and to his political adherents, and not until after his death in 1793 was the college granted official status. Governor Samuel Adams signed the bill on Midsummer's Day, 1794.

The Honorable James Bowdoin, the Governor's son, fulfilled the hopes of the founders by giving generously of land and money to the college, bequeathing it as well his collection of Dutch and Italian masters, many of them gathered while he was United States Minister to Spain and France. This, the first private collection of European art to be made by an American and brought to this country, is in the Walker Art Building. It reveals the excellent taste and discrimination of its owner, who was one of the first of a series of New England gentlemen of culture who combined the life of refinement with a commercial and political success. Governor Bowdoin, himself powerful, wealthy, and aristocratic, was the grandson of a penniless refugee from religious persecution, Pierre Baudouin, who landed at Casco in 1687. The Governor, who Anglicized the family name, was the first president of the American Academy of Arts and Sciences, a friend of Washington and Franklin, and a figure of political prominence during the Revolution.

Although Bowdoin College is not large, it has a history, interesting as it is varied, of nearly one hundred and fifty years, during which it has grown rich with tradition and has enjoyed high scholastic standards and attainments, many of its professors having achieved international reputation. In proportion to its size, the number of prominent statesmen, scholars, authors, scientists, financiers, and business men who have been graduated from Bowdoin is impressive. A few leaders most closely identified with the college are: Nathaniel Hawthorne and Henry Wadsworth Longfellow; Rear Admiral Robert E. Peary, discoverer of the North Pole, and Commander Donald B. MacMillan, Arctic explorer; Thomas B. Reed, Speaker of the House of Representatives, and Senator William P. Frye; William Pitt Fessenden, Secretary of the Treasury under Lincoln, Hannibal

Hamlin, fifteenth Vice-President, and Franklin Pierce, fourteenth President of the United States.

There has always been gathered about Bowdoin a circle of intellectual and literary people which, though small, has definitely made its influence felt all through Maine for a century and more. The college brings numerous lecturers, well-known speakers, and musical organizations to Brunswick each year. Series of public lectures on various subjects in special fields, given by ten or more authorities, are sponsored by the college every two years. These Institutes, as they are called, have included lecture series on modern history, modern literature, the fine arts, the social sciences, the natural sciences, politics and economics, and philosophy.

TOUR 1 — 3.5 m.

W. from Maine St. on Pleasant St.; R. from Pleasant St. on Union St.

1. The *Gilman Mansion* (1799) (*private, open by special permission: small fee*), cor. Union and Oak Sts., a 24-room white Colonial structure, rises imposingly among the fountain elms of its small park. Once the Great House of the town, with a long view down the river, its wide lawns sloping to Maine Street and along the Androscoggin, it is now hemmed in by the tenement homes of mill workers. Samuel Melcher 3d, native craftsman and master builder, began construction of the mansion in 1798 (at that time he was working also on Massachusetts Hall, Bowdoin's first building) for Captain John Dunlap, whose great-grandchildren live in it today. To be shown this house is to be led through the pages of a family history, for here are ancestral portraits — some by Badger (*see The Arts*); McKeen family relics — for the Gilmans are also directly descendent

---

BRUNSWICK. POINTS OF INTEREST

1. Gilman Mansion
2. Site of Fort Andros
3. Falls of the Androscoggin
4. Site of Fort George
5. Emmons House
6. Governor Dunlap House
7. Pejepscot Historical Museum
8. Harriet Beecher Stowe House
9. Chandler House
10. Hawthorne House
11. President's House
12. Bowdoin Pines
    Bowdoin College:
13. Seth Adams Hall
14. Memorial Hall
15. Massachusetts Hall
16. Winthrop Hall
17. Maine Hall
18. King Chapel
19. Appleton Hall
20. Hyde Hall
21. Hubbard Hall
22. Walker Art Gallery
23. Searles Science Building
24. Sargent Gymnasium
25. Dudley Coe Infirmary
26. Moulton Union
27. First Parish Church
28. Chamberlain House

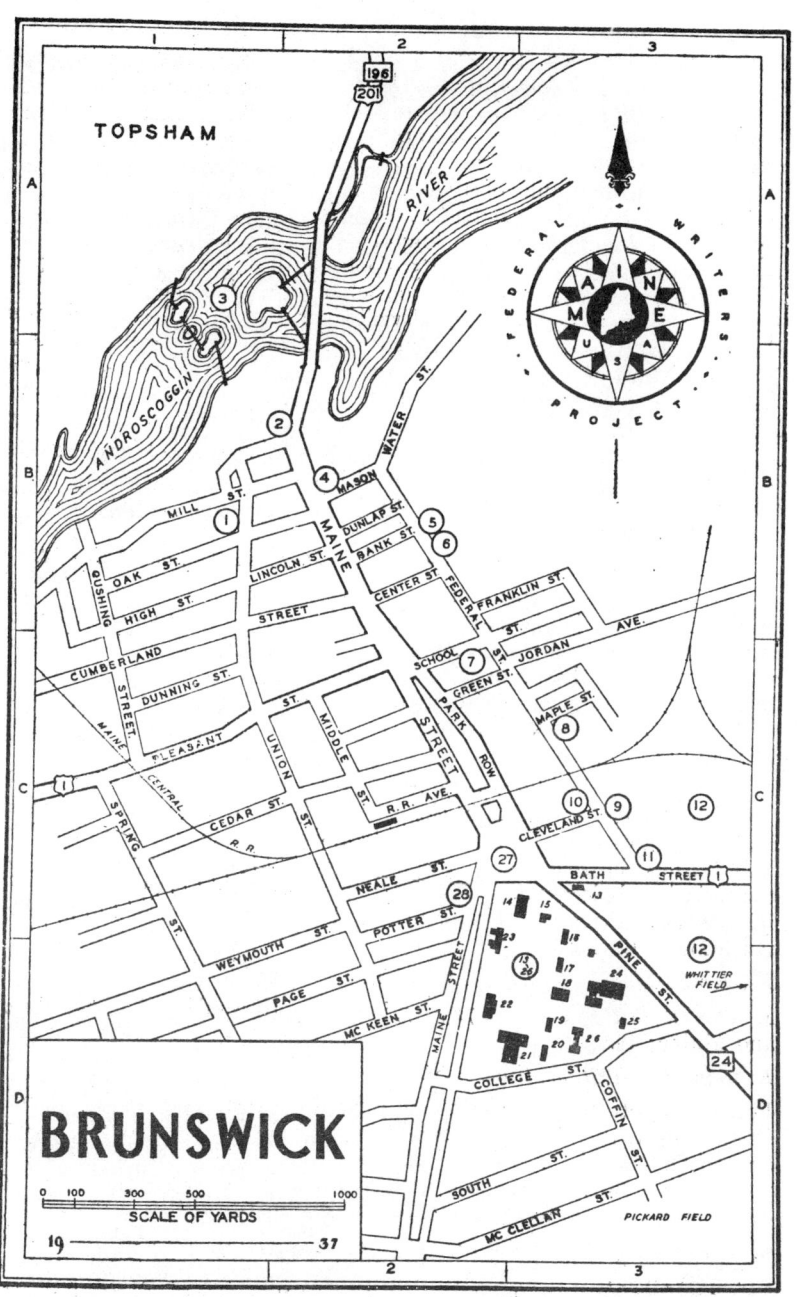

from Joseph McKeen, the first president of Bowdoin College; period costumes; antique dolls and toys; old books and documents; and valuable furniture. Its exterior, which had a balustraded roof and arched dormer windows, was doubtless more impressive before the mansion was remodeled by David Dunlap in 1841, but much of the original interior is retained, including nine of the old open fireplaces. A charming hall stairway with mahogany banisters ascends to the third floor in a sweeping curve. The fine white paneling of the principal rooms was cut from Brunswick pine boards. The full 50-foot length of the house is occupied by two identical rooms opening into each other so that they make a great formal drawing-room. The gilded wallpaper and crystal chandeliers in these 'parlors' were imported from France. Many people important in Maine's history have lived in this house or were entertained here: David Dunlap, who represented the District of Maine in the Massachusetts legislature from 1810 to 1817; Robert Dunlap, Governor of Maine, 1834–38, and member of Congress; and Congressman Charles J. Gilman, father of the present owners. At the S. side of the mansion, between its long ell and Oak Street, is the more than century-old garden, worth seeing at any time during the summer.

R. from Union St. on Gilman Ave.; L. from Gilman Ave. on Maine St.

2. A tablet in the corner of the *Cabot Manufacturing Company's Millyard*, by the river bank, marks the *Site of Fort Andros* (1688–90), Brunswick's first fort. The Cabot Company, largest of Brunswick's industries and a pioneer in the production of rayon goods, is the successor of the Brunswick Manufacturing Company, incorporated in 1809 and believed to have been the first to operate a cotton mill in Maine. It, too, occupied this site.

3. The *Falls of the Androscoggin* are best viewed from the Brunswick-Topsham bridge, named in honor of Frank J. Wood, whose efforts made its building possible. In spring when the river is in flood the spray of the falls washes the roadway of the bridge and their thunder reverberates through the whole river section of the town. Topsham, a quiet residential village directly across the river in Sagadahoc County, seems like a continuation of Brunswick.

Retrace on Maine St.; L. on Mason St.

4. The *Site of Fort George*, 1715–37, is marked by a tablet (L), cor. Mason and Maine Sts.

R. from Mason St. on Federal St.

Federal Street, lined with very old elms, is Brunswick's chief residential street. On it, the oldest and most beautiful houses of the town preserve an atmosphere of dignity and serenity. Even those which have been modernized, along with those neglected, retain beautiful doorways and other characteristic features of Colonial design.

5. The *Emmons House* (1814) (*private*), 25 Federal St., a white Colonial structure with, at one time, considerable charm, now greatly altered, was for many years the home of Henry Wadsworth Longfellow (*see*

PORTLAND) when he was Bowdoin's first professor of modern languages. Here he is said to have written his novel, 'Outre Mer.'

6. The *Governor Dunlap House* (*private*), 27 Federal St., formerly an elegant mansion, is now an apartment house. For many years the three-story wooden structure was the home of one of Brunswick's oldest and most outstanding families (*see above, Gilman House*), a recent descendant of which, Major-General Robert Dunlap of the U.S. Marine Corps, lost his life in 1931 at Tours, France, while attempting heroically to save a peasant woman from a landslide. A collection of the medals awarded to him may be seen at Hubbard Hall, Bowdoin College (*see below*).

R. from Federal St. on School St.

7. The *Pejepscot Historical Museum* (1825) (*open weekdays, July and August, 3–5*), 12 School St., formerly a church, was acquired by the Pejepscot Historical Society in 1891. The simple little weather-stained museum houses a fine collection of historical material; domestic, foreign, Indian, and military relics; currency exhibits; period costumes, trinkets, and portraits.

Retrace to Federal St.; R. on Federal St.

8. *Harriet Beecher Stowe House* (1806) (*open: gift shop in rear*), 63 Federal St., was the home of Mrs. Stowe while writing 'Uncle Tom's Cabin' and other works. While living under its high-pitched roof, she wrote to her husband: 'Our air-tight stoves warm all but the floor, heat your head and keep your feet freezing....'

9. The *Chandler House* (1806) (*private*), 75 Federal St., like the Gilman and Governor Dunlap Houses, was constructed by Samuel Melcher and has a history of elegance and fine living. Built for Parker Cleaveland (*see below*), it is architecturally the most distinguished of Brunswick's houses. Its sagging balustrades and weathered walls retain their original 18th-century delicacy in spite of the ravages of time and weather. The five tall chimneys leaning precariously over the ancient roof are mute evidence of the many fires which were once needed to heat the beautifully paneled rooms within. The small panes of the windows still occasionally reflect the glow from the open hearths, and the Colonial antiques cherished from generation to generation furnish, still intact, the gracious interior.

10. In the *House* (*private*) at 76 Federal St., Nathaniel Hawthorne had a room for part of his student days. Since it was almost directly across the street from the residence of Professor Cleaveland, young Nat could watch visitors come and go from the front door opposite his window, and, the story goes, it was also possible for him to see the Cleaveland's attractive servant girl who always answered the door. Hawthorne, a shy youth, never tried to know the girl, but would sit for hours at his window waiting for her to appear in the doorway across the street.

11. The *President's House* (*private*) 85 Federal St., home of Kenneth C. M. Sills, President of Bowdoin College, is an excellent example of a

modified Mediterranean type of architecture popular with retired sea captains of a century ago. These substantial houses peculiar to Maine's seacoast towns have an appearance of dignity, and often contain excellent examples of woodcarving or of fine glasswork, as that in the sidelights of the entrance door here. Square structures of board siding or of brick, characterized by solidity rather than grace, they are generally two-and-a-half or three-storied, the top floor windows, small and oblong, peeping out from under the heavy eaves of the hip roof which is invariably surmounted by an ornate cupola.

R. from Federal St. on Bath St.

12. The *Bowdoin Pines*, occupying a small area east of the college campus, overshadow Bath St. (L), the main highway. These trees, tall, erect, and carefully preserved, have grown up with the college and share in its history.

L. from Bath St. on Harpswell St.; enter Bowdoin Campus at Harpswell St.

Bowdoin College is most impressive when viewed from the inside of its compact quadrangular campus, which may be approached from any of several memorial gateways. (*Guides provided at college office, Massachusetts Hall; all buildings open at discretion of college authorities.*)

13. *Seth Adams Hall* (1860–61), across Harpswell St. from the campus on the triangular field known as 'the Delta,' is a classroom building which formerly housed the Maine School of Medicine (1821–1921), and its top floor is still occupied by a collection of medical exhibits.

14. *Memorial Hall* (1868) (*NW. end of campus, near Bath St.*), an architectural 'white elephant' built of local granite in the so-called 'General Grant Gothic' style, contains classrooms and an auditorium. Erected as a memorial to the Bowdoin men participating in the Civil War, it contains, among other important paintings, the best known portrait of Nathaniel Hawthorne.

15. *Massachusetts Hall* (1802) (*left from Memorial Hall*) houses the administrative offices of the college. In this square Colonial structure of painted red brick, the first building of the college to be constructed, lived President Joseph McKeen and his family, his faculty of two, and Bowdoin's first class of eight boys. Many years later it was rebuilt, the second and third stories forming a hall for faculty meetings and for the exhibition of the Cleaveland Cabinet, a valuable and extensive collection of geological specimens made by Professor Parker Cleaveland of Bowdoin, one of America's first geologists. In 1936 the interior of the building was restored more nearly to its original form, and the Cleaveland Cabinet was removed to the science building. Two interesting features of Massachusetts Hall are the graceful curved stairway opposite the front entrance, and in the office of the president, the open fireplace, complete with black caldrons and swinging cranes, which has been left as it was when the room was the college kitchen.

16 and 17. *Winthrop Hall* (1822) (R), named after Governor Winthrop of the Massachusetts Bay Colony, and *Maine Hall* (1808), where Haw-

thorne roomed, are dormitories. Longfellow's room, 27 North Winthrop, is marked with a marble tablet on the outside wall.

18. *King Chapel* (1845–55), a twin-spired structure of rough granite designed by Richard Upjohn, is considered a fine example of modified Romanesque style, unusual for the time when it was built. It represents a departure from New England's architectural conventions in that it is modeled on the plan of an English school chapel. It contains, besides the large organ presented by the late Cyrus H. K. Curtis, music rooms, and class and conference rooms.

19 and 20. *Appleton Hall* (1843), named for Bowdoin's second president, and *Hyde Hall* (1917), named for the seventh president, are also dormitories.

21. *Hubbard Hall* (1902–03) (R), the college library (*open daily* 8.30–10.30 *during college term; daily except Sundays,* 10–4, *during vacation; library privileges available to the public*) was designed by Henry Vaughan of Boston. It is constructed in the collegiate Gothic tradition of brick, granite, and limestone, with a high battlemented tower which dominates the south side of the campus. At both ends of the façade are projecting bays whose balustrades and gables relieve the long lines of the steeply pitched slate roof, while oriel windows give charm and light to the four large rooms in the wings. The college library includes the private library of the Hon. James Bowdoin, one of the largest and most complete Longfellow collections, the exhaustive Isaac W. Dyer collection of Carlyliana, the Guild German Dialect Collection, the Huguenot Collection of American-French writings, an extensive library of Mainiana, valuable sets of 19th-century periodicals, and an important Arctic exhibit. In the second floor hall are hung the portraits of Bowdoin's presidents. An art room contains a creditable collection of books and pictures for study of the fine arts.

22. The *Walker Art Gallery* (1894) (R) (*open daily* 10–12, 2–4; 2–4 *Sundays and holidays*) has been called one of the best small museums of the country. Designed by Charles F. McKim in a style derivative of the Romanesque and built of brick, limestone, and granite, the building was one of the first and most suitable of its kind, serving as a model for other museums. Niches containing busts of Greek characters adorn the façade. In the interior, four tympana under the arches of the central dome, each 26 feet wide, contain murals symbolizing the artistic achievements of Athens, Rome, Florence, and Venice, executed by John LaFarge, Elihu Vedder, Abbott Thayer, and Kenyon Cox respectively. The James Bowdoin collection of drawings and paintings contains rare sketches by artists as diverse as Rembrandt, Breughel, and Tintoretto, as well as many important American Colonial portraits by Badger, Feke, Gilbert Stuart, and Copley (*see Maine and the Arts*). Stuart is said to have journeyed to Maine four times to make copies of the famous original of his portrait of Thomas Jefferson. The Warren collection of Classical antiquities is particularly valuable, containing rare and even unique objects of special interest to archeologists. Also important are the carved As-

syrian tablets, the Coffin collection of etchings, and many noted paintings, including a well-known portrait of Longfellow, and several Winslow Homers. Exhibitions of the work of contemporary artists are held in the Museum from time to time.

23. The *Searles Science Building* (R) houses a small museum of botanical and zoological specimens.

Cross campus R. to driveway.

24. The *Sargent Gymnasium*, erected in honor of Dudley Allen Sargent, pioneer in physical training and the circus strong man who became Bowdoin's first athletic director, has been in recent years supplemented by a cage with an indoor track and a swimming pool, the latter given by Cyrus Curtis.

25 and 26. The *Dudley Coe Infirmary* (L) and the *Moulton Union*, containing cafeteria, lounge, recreation rooms, and offices, complete the campus buildings.

East of the campus behind Sargent Gymnasium and across Harpswell St. is *Whittier Field*, with its memorial grandstand, where the major athletic events of the college take place; and south on the campus driveway behind Moulton Union, down Coffin St. and beyond Longfellow Ave., is *Pickard Field*, where the practice grounds, tennis courts, and the newly constructed *Pickard Field House* (1937) are situated.

Return to Bath St.

27. The *First Parish Congregational Church*, across from Bowdoin College at the junction of Harpswell, Maine, and Bath Sts., is known as 'the College Church' and 'the Church on the Hill.' Designed by Richard Upjohn, architect for Trinity Church, New York City, and erected in 1846 on the site of a previous structure designed and built by Samuel Melcher, it is a good example of the Victorian Gothic. It is constructed entirely of wood. A tall spire which originally surmounted the steeple was several times struck by lightning and finally destroyed; it has never been replaced. Dr. Calvin E. Stowe, husband of Harriet Beecher Stowe, was professor of religion at the college and preached in the church. One Sunday while sitting in her pew, which is now marked by a commemorative *Plaque*, Mrs. Stowe had a vision of the death of Uncle Tom which inspired that scene in her book. From the pulpit of this church Longfellow delivered the poem, '*O Morituri, Te Salutamus,*' written for the 50th anniversary of the graduation of his class at Bowdoin (1825). Bowdoin's commencement exercises are always held here.

28. The *Chamberlain House (private)*, cor. Maine and Potter Sts., nearly opposite the First Parish Church, was built in 1808. When first made a teacher at Bowdoin, Longfellow set up housekeeping in this house, to which he brought his bride. At that time it was a cottage, consisting only of the present second and third stories. Later, when General Joshua Chamberlain (1828-1914) came to live there, these were brought forward and jacked up so that the floor below might be built under them. Thus the building was transformed from a poet's cottage in a field to a gen-

eral's mansion on a busy street. Chamberlain, a Bowdoin graduate, was a professor at the college when he obtained leave of absence to serve in the Civil War. He participated in 24 engagements and was wounded six times. He received the Congressional Medal of Honor for his defense of Little Round Top at Gettysburg, and left the service with the rank of Major-General of Volunteers. The General became President of Bowdoin, was elected Governor of Maine in 1866, and, as Major-General of the State Militia, kept peace during the riotous winter of 1878-79 when the Democrats and Greenbackers combined to gain control of the State Legislature (*see History*).

OTHER POINTS OF INTEREST

29. *Mere Point*, 7 *m.*, south on Maine St., is one of several coastal resorts near Brunswick. A *Memorial Boulder and Tablet*, 0.1 *m.* right from main road beyond entrance to Mere Point Colony, commemorates the round-the-world flight of U.S. Army pilots in 1924. The bronze tablet was erected in 1925 in a field near the point where the American aviators first landed in the United States. A record of the flight, which started in Seattle, Wash., but was never fully completed, is inscribed on the tablet, placed here under the auspices of Percival P. Baxter, at that time Governor of Maine.

At the tip of Mere Point the waters of Maquoit and Middle Bays merge into the wider reaches of Casco Bay with a breath-taking prospect of many wooded islands and distant hazy shores. Birch Island (*see Island Tours*) is at the left of Mere Point in Middle Bay.

30. The *Old Colonial Houses of Topsham*, 0.5 *m.* north along State 24 right from Maine Street across Frank J. Wood Bridge, combine beauty and utility in their architectural designs. Many of these houses, whose owners could look down on the river from their windows to see their ships anchored in the calm waters below The Falls, have been little changed since they were built during the prosperous shipping days in the early nineteenth century. Some of the loveliest of these dwellings were designed and built by Samuel Melcher, 3d.

31. *Merrymeeting Bay*, famous duck-hunting ground, 4 *m.* north on State 24 (*see Tour 10*) (*see Sports and Recreation*).

HOULTON

Town: Alt. 340; pop. 6865; sett. 1805, incorp. 1831.
Railroad Stations: W. end of Florence Ave. for B. & A. R.R.; NW. of Main and Military Sts. intersection for Canadian Pacific Ry.
Bus Stations: Feeley Drug Co., Market St., for Grey Lines.
Airport: 2 *m.* E. on US 2.

U.S. and Canadian Customs & Immigration Stations: 2.5 *m.* E. on US 2.
Accommodations: Three hotels.
Hunting and Fishing: Guides available.
Swimming: Nickerson Lake, 5 *m.* SW. on State 166; Carry Lake, 7 *m.* N. on US 1.
Annual Events: Houlton Fish and Game Club field day, September.

ATTRACTIVE and tree-shaded, Houlton combines the qualities of the old-fashioned country town with those of a modern city. The seat of Aroostook County, one of the richest potato-raising regions in the United States, and focal point of the northernmost part of Maine that is actively developing its assets as a recreation area, Houlton has become a large commercial center. Yet, in spite of the heavy traffic of motor trucks and automobiles over its smooth pavement, Market Square, the spacious heart of the town's business district, retains an atmosphere reminiscent of creaking wagon wheels and patient horses tethered to sidewalk hitching posts. And the residential sections, sweeping upward and away from the Meduxnekeag River through the center of the town, have a leisurely, almost rural air somehow paradoxical to their broad streets and well-kept appearance that would do credit to a modern suburb. It is doubtless the lack of crowding and the many fine old elms — as old, some of them, as Houlton itself — that preserve so well the dignified atmosphere of a New England town.

Houlton lies in a shallow natural bowl between wooded ridges. To the east the terrain rolls upward to the town line where, adjoining the highway, the frontier between the United States and Canada has the usual custom houses and markers, and is fortified only by a few bushes and a dilapidated fence. At the west end of the town the fertile land is traversed in a general north and south direction by a large esker or 'horse-back,' which is considered one of the world's outstanding examples of this type of glacial formation. An esker is a ridge of gravel created between the walls of a crack or groove in the glacier and left standing as the ice receded. Besides being a trading center for most of Aroostook, Houlton is the shipping point for potatoes produced in the surrounding farm regions. Although early in its history it was known as a lumbering town, most of the operations were actually carried on along the rivers to the north, especially on the Allagash, the Aroostook, the Meduxnekeag (Ind. 'where people go out'), and the St. John.

Lumbering operations near Houlton began in a small way. The first settlers made a business of turning out limited quantities of shingles and boards, which they rafted to Woodstock and Fredericton. A sawmill was erected in 1810 by Aaron Putnam, one of the fathers of the settlement, when Houlton's first dam was built across a small creek. Early lumber drives were worked under severe handicaps, the greatest of which was the necessity of trucking the rafts around Jackson Falls. Since potato farms quickly supplanted the wooded districts of Aroostook, the lumber industry, never as extensive as in Penobscot and Somerset Counties, soon ceased to be of primary importance.

When, in 1799, the citizens of New Salem, Massachusetts, petitioned the legislature of the Commonwealth for money with which to found an academy, they were granted, as was customary, a piece of land in the wilderness of Maine, to sell it if and as they could. This grant is now the south half of Houlton; the northern part is a section of the Williams College grant, presented at about the same time to the Williamstown, Massachusetts, institution. A group of New Salem men purchased the academy land. Of the original thirteen, however, only three — Joseph Houlton, from whom the town eventually took its name, and Aaron and Joseph Putnam — ever actually saw the land. These men established their settlement in 1805. They found that ingress to their new home was not only arduous but dangerous, for beyond Old Town the District of Maine was largely unexplored forest, dense, and trackless. The journey to the site of Houlton had to be accomplished by way of a complicated system of waterways and carries from the Penobscot, or up the St. John River to Woodstock and thence through the woods. Development of the land was slow. The newcomers had to struggle for their existence as if on a distant frontier, for supplies were brought in to them only after infinite labor, and the growing season was very short. A cow was a luxury, and every piece of mill machinery was worth its weight in gold.

In 1822, William H. Cary of New Salem came to Houlton, where he built the spacious house on the hill above the present Canadian Pacific Station. He, with his son, Shepard Cary, founded Cary's Mills, a combination of foundry, carding, and grist mills, thus establishing the town's first industry of importance. Members of this family contributed to the political, social, and economic development of their town and State.

A road built in 1827 connecting Houlton with Baskahegan greatly facilitated transportation, and Houlton finally ceased to feel itself set apart from the world when in 1828 it was the garrison for seven companies of United States Infantry. The National Government purchased twenty-five acres of land; the Hancock Barracks were constructed and a parade ground was laid out, and Houlton found itself the northeasternmost military station in the United States. A new era of prosperity began. The presence of the post stimulated local trade, gave the people a market for their produce and labor, and attracted more settlers to the town. Finally, in 1832, the construction of the military road (now Maine 166) between Houlton and Bangor was completed.

With the outbreak of the so-called Aroostook War (1839) that climaxed the old border controversy, Houlton jumped into national prominence. Twelve companies of Maine militia were sent in, and through the bitter cold of the long winter they subsisted on hardtack and salt pork and what little food the overburdened inhabitants could spare them. Major R. M. Kirby, in charge of the army post, refused to take any part in the 'war' for fear of placing the United States Government in a compromising position. The dispute was finally settled, and the national boundary established. Eight years later, the Government withdrew its troops and the post was abandoned.

Houlton thereupon entered upon an economic slump from which it began to recover in 1862 when the New Brunswick Railway (now the Canadian Pacific) was built from St. Andrews, New Brunswick, to a point on the Woodstock turnpike only five miles from town. By 1870 the branch had been extended into the town so that communication with the seaboard by way of New Brunswick was opened. The following year the European and North American Railway (now the Maine Central) was completed from Bangor to Vanceboro, thereby giving Houlton rail connections by a circuitous route with the cities to the south. Up to this time Houlton had to market its products in New Brunswick, and now not only the town itself but the whole of Aroostook County was able to capitalize on its agricultural resources. In 1894 the Bangor and Aroostook Railroad reached Houlton; within a few years it had extended its line through the northern territory as far as Fort Kent. By this linking of Houlton and the surrounding country with the great national markets, a new prosperity was brought to the people of Aroostook; they expanded their farming operations, the population began to increase rapidly, and Houlton was prominent in the development of the country.

The railroads remain of first importance to the continued economic success of this region, for the difficulties of highway transportation are considerable. In spite of the efficiency of modern snow-removal equipment and the improved conditions of the roadways, drifting snow often renders motor traffic completely helpless; heavy trucking over the unsurfaced roads of the country is possible only during a short period of the year. Houlton therefore remains chiefly important as a railroad shipping center.

TOUR 1 — 4.5 m.

N. from Market Sq. on North St. across Meduxnekeag River Bridge.

1. The *Black Hawk Tavern* (L), 22 North St., built in 1813 and now a tourist home, was erected by Samuel Wormwood for Aaron Putnam, one of the first settlers, and is the oldest house in Houlton. Constructed of wood cut and sawed on the site of the building, the house was walled up with brick on the outside in an attempt to make it bullet-proof. In the course of alterations the original roof was replaced by one of much steeper pitch and all but one of the stone fireplaces that were formerly used to heat each room are closed up. The first county court was held in the northeast room of the second floor; — the corner that was occupied by the judge's bench is still marked by a four-foot wainscoting. The first county jail was a dungeon in the basement of the building; there was no provision made for ventilation, and the rings in the wall to which prisoners were chained are still visible.

Retrace North St. to Market Sq. R. on Bangor St.; R. from Bangor St. on Florence St.

HOULTON. POINTS OF INTEREST

1. Black Hawk Tavern
2. Potato Warehouses
3. Houlton Grange
4. Peabody House
5. Ricker Classical Institute
6. Garrison Hill
7. Cary's Mills
8. Transatlantic Radiophone Station

2. *Potato Warehouses*, in the Bangor and Aroostook railroad yards, provide storage for thousands of barrels of potatoes. In these modern, well-equipped buildings potatoes are graded and sorted in preparation for shipping to all parts of the world. The annual shipment is nearly 2,000,000 bushels.

L. from Florence St. on Potato Row to Bangor St.; L. from Bangor St. to Grange St.

3. *Houlton Grange*, with a store at Green and Grange Sts., is second in size to Webster Grange, Rochester, New York, the largest in the world. The Houlton Grange originated a system of mutual fire insurance among its members, a practice widely adopted because of low rates and proved success. The extensive operations of the Houlton Grange also include a flour mill and warehouses.

L. from Grange St. on Green St.; R. from Green St. on Court St.

4. The *Peabody House (private)*, 98 Court St., built by Amos Pearce about 1826, is the oldest Houlton residence the original exterior of which remains unchanged. A feature that distinguishes it from its neighbors is the absence of eaves. In its front hall under the narrow, winding stair a smokehouse, complete with hooks, stepladder, and other meat-curing equipment, is intact. The town's original post office occupied the room to the right of the hall. Many of the original fireplaces are retained, and the rooms are furnished with antique furniture, old dishes, candlesticks, etc., belonging to the Peabody family, the present owners.

Retrace Court St. to Military St.; R. on Military St.

5. *Ricker Classical Institute* (1847) (*open during school year*), Military and High Sts., is the oldest secondary institution in Aroostook County. A privately endowed co-educational preparatory school and junior college, it is affiliated with Colby College and the Maine Baptist Convention.

OTHER POINTS OF INTEREST

6. *Garrison Hill*, a 583-foot elevation 1 mile east of the town on Military St., is the site of the Hancock Barracks (1828-47). Although all traces have disappeared of the military post's barracks and other buildings, the former parade grounds provide an excellent vantage point for a panoramic view of the town and surrounding country.

7. *Cary's Mills*, 2 miles west of Houlton on State 166 (Bangor St.), is a small settlement founded by Shepard Cary, the son of one of the early prominent citizens of the town. Cary was largely instrumental in opening much of the Aroostook timberland, since he actively engaged in developing large-scale operations on the Allagash and St. John Rivers. Besides conducting numerous local business enterprises, he was highly influential in county and State affairs, serving term after term in the Maine House and Senate, and as Congressman in 1844. The Houlton library is named in his honor.

8. The *Transatlantic Radiophone Receiving Station*, 3 m. (*see Tour* 4).

LEWISTON—AUBURN

Cities: Lewiston, alt. 196, pop. 34,948, sett. 1770, inc. city 1861; Auburn, alt. 210, pop. 18,571, sett. 1786, inc. shire town 1854, city 1869.
Railroad Stations: Bates St., Lewiston, and Main St., Auburn, for M.C. R.R.; Lincoln St., Lewiston, for Canadian National Rys.
Bus Stations: 204 Main St., Lewiston, and 240 Court St., Auburn, for M.C. Transportation Co., Blue Line, and Maine–New Hampshire Stages; 169 Main St., Lewiston, and Elm House, Auburn, for Affiliated Greyhound Lines.
Airport: 5 *m.* SW. on State 121 and Hotel Rd.
Accommodations: Eight hotels.
Swimming: Taylor Pond, Auburn; Sabattus Lake, Lewiston.
Annual Events: Maine State Fair, 1st week in Sept.; numerous winter sports events.

LEWISTON and AUBURN, known as the 'Twin Cities,' face each other across the Androscoggin River at Lewiston Falls. Divided by the river, each city is a distinct municipality, yet the two are closely interwoven socially and industrially. Both are justified in claiming to be the industrial heart of Maine. Lewiston, the second largest city in the State and primarily a textile city, is also the seat of Bates College, while Auburn, Maine's fourth largest city, is an important shoe manufacturing center and the Androscoggin County seat. Both cities were the objects of nation-wide attention during the shoe strike in the spring of 1937, involving, as it did, a test of the National Labor Relations Act.

The general traffic bridges and two railroad bridges join Lewiston, on the east bank, with Auburn on the west. Strong as the bridges have been in binding Lewiston and Auburn together, there have been occasions when they have, in a sense, separated rather than joined the two cities. Many residents of one city work in the other, and during the strike of 1937, the bridges became barriers guarded by militia and police who sought to prevent strikers of one city from entering the other. Again, the bridges have often been the scene of pitched battles, usually induced by high-school rivalry, between the youth of the two cities. Relationships between the two cities were severed during the flood of March, 1936, which ripped out South Bridge and made North Bridge impassable.

Auburn conveys the impression of being more of a residential city than Lewiston. Auburn residences seem more remote from the industrial areas. New Auburn, that section of the city lying south of the Little Androscoggin and largely inhabited by workers in the cities' mills, is a comparatively new development, almost a distinct village in itself. This section of the city lost 250 buildings through fire in 1933, and was entirely isolated for two and a half days during the floods in March, 1936. Tenement districts are concentrated near the great textile mills in Lewiston; one such district near the riverfront, is known as Little Canada because of its predominating French-Canadian population.

Lewiston may well be called a bi-lingual city, since practically every business finds it necessary to employ at least one French-speaking person. The present population of Lewiston is between 65 and 70 per cent French-American origin, while Auburn has only 25 per cent of this nationality, largely concentrated in New Auburn. This large French-speaking population supplies most of the workers for the textile mills and shoe factories. Lewiston has a charter form of government, with mayor and seven aldermen. In recent years these municipal officers have usually been of French-Canadian origin. The city's parochial school system is almost as extensive as the public school system.

Lewiston is a strongly Democratic city in a Republican State. In 1932, Louis Jefferson Brann, a resident of Lewiston, was elected Governor of Maine on the Democratic ticket. Auburn, on the other hand, is conservative Republican. In the 1936 presidential election, when Maine was one of the two States in the nation to vote Republican, an Auburn native, Wallace H. White, Republican, defeated Governor Brann for election to the U.S. Senate.

The two cities' combined industrial establishments number more than one hundred and employ in the neighborhood of 14,000 persons. Auburn, with nearly a score of shoe manufactories, leads in this industry that commands more manufacturing establishments than any other in Maine. Lewiston, a textile center manufacturing cotton, woolen and rayon goods, also has several shoe factories.

The Twin Cities, situated in a rich agricultural district, are the trading center for thousands of people, and are important distributing points for the State's industrial and commercial life, agriculture and dairy production.

The original patentees of the present site of Lewiston and Auburn received what became Bakerstown Township in New Hampshire in 1736, but not until 1768, owing to technical difficulties of location, were the agents of the proprietors granted the tract of land along the Androscoggin. Terms of the grant were that fifty families in as many houses should settle upon the claim before 1774, 'the houses to be 16' × 20' with a seven foot stud and the name of the town, Lewistown.' It is doubtful if the specifications were complied with, since the early growth of the two cities was unusually slow and the first Lewiston settler, Paul Hildreth of Dracut, Massachusetts, did not build his log cabin within the present city limits until 1770. The 'Plantation of Lewiston and Gore' ('gore,' a triangular piece of land left when surveyors' calculations do not result in an even division of land into townships) was incorporated in 1795. Auburn grew up even more slowly. The mid-nineteenth century was almost at hand before the town separated from Minot, 1842; its present land area of about sixty-five square miles was attained in 1867, when

Auburn, already shire town, annexed Danville. Auburn's name supposedly was taken from the Auburn of Oliver Goldsmith's poem 'The Deserted Village.'

The first woolen mill in Lewiston had begun operations in 1819, preceding the first cotton manufactory by twenty-five years. Exploitation of the water-power of the Androscoggin River began with the formation of the Androscoggin Falls, Dam Locks, and Canal Company in 1836. This enterprise was reorganized six years later as the Lewiston Water-Power Company — for the purpose of employing available water-power for textile manufacture. In the fifties the remarkable water-power advantages of this location attracted Boston business men engaged in similar industries. Other companies were established here within the succeeding thirty years. They purchased much land in this region, took over all the chartered rights and privileges of the existing power companies, constructed a system of canals for distribution of water-power, and in time built the several large textile mills that form the industrial background of Lewiston. These mills, granted unusually generous charter rights for the purchase of power, own almost exclusively the power rights on this section of the river through control of the Union Water-Power Company.

Auburn lays claim to being the home of the shoe industry in Maine because it was still a part of Minot when the Minot Shoe Company was incorporated in 1835, in what is now West Auburn. Shoe manufacturing in the present city limits was begun a year later by two brothers, Martin and Moses Crafts, and within a few years the city had definitely assumed its position as a leader in the industry. Early shoe manufacturing was crudely conducted and the products were coarse, heavy articles. Work was cut out in a small room or shop by the manufacturer himself, sometimes aided by a cutter or two, and then sent to dwellings in the community where the men and women finished the shoes. All work was done by hand until about 1850 when the first labor-saving machine was introduced. Fifteen years later, shoe manufacturing was a $1,000,000 industry, and the factory system was generally adopted by 1870 when the city's twenty-one factories produced more than 2,000,000 pairs of shoes annually. In 1917, one Auburn factory was making 75 per cent of the world's entire supply of white canvas shoes. Under normal conditions, the shoe factories now produce between 60,000 and 70,000 pairs of shoes and moccasins daily, and have a total weekly payroll of more than $100,000. Including the shoe factories, there are about fifty industrial plants in Auburn with an annual production value of more than $22,000,000.

Secluded from the city's busy industrial life, yet having its influences upon Lewiston's social and civic activities, Bates College was incorporated as the Maine State Seminary in 1856. Originally the Parsonfield Academy, Parsonfield, the college was founded by Free Baptists under a charter providing that it should be free from denominational control, yet that education and religion should be inseparably connected. The location of the college was disputed by other towns, but Lewiston's central location and subscriptions by local business men towards the building fund won the distinction. A college course was instituted in 1863 and the seminary's name was changed in honor of Benjamin E. Bates of Boston, who gave $200,000 to the college. Bates was one of the first New England colleges to become co-educational, and in 1907 it became one of the associated colleges in the Carnegie Foundation for the Advancement of Teaching. Bates initiated international debating and has won victories from some of the largest colleges in this country and abroad. Out of approximately 6000 alumni (1936), nearly half have entered the teaching profession; Bates is first among New England colleges in the number of its graduates who are principals of New England secondary schools.

POINTS OF INTEREST

LEWISTON
Tour 1 — 5.4 *m.*

Union Square, a broadening of the main thoroughfare from below the junction of Main and Sabattus Sts. to Lisbon St., is the commercial heart of Lewiston, and the natural distribution center for the bulk of highway transportation in and out of the Twin Cities. Streets radiating from the square lead to the business and industrial sections of the city. In the days of horse-drawn vehicles, Union Square was Haymarket Square, a busy mart for farmers with their hay, grain, and farm produce from outlying agricultural districts.

S. from Union Sq.; L. on Canal St.

1. The *Canal* (R), supplying several of the large mills with power, was begun in 1845 by the Lewiston Water-Power Company and completed in 1863–64. Running from the river above the dam the canal, 62 feet wide and less than a mile long, seems like a quiet stream flowing through the heart of the city.

2. The *Buildings of the Bates Manufacturing Company (permit at office)* (R), Canal St., largest local textile mill, are across the canal. The mill manufactures cotton and rayon goods exclusively. Since the recent introduction of machinery for the making of candlewick spreads the mill has specialized in their manufacture.

3. *Boarding Blocks (private)* (L), Canal St., opp. the Bates Mill, are reminders of an earlier industrial period. These three-story, brick structures were built by the company for its employees, following a practice common among industrial establishments in the last century. Country girls, eager to get work in the mills though it meant working long hours for small pay, came to the city and created a demand for suitable lodging facilities. Mill owners erected these 'boarding blocks,' dividing them into tenements for groups of 15 or 20 girls, and let them to 'boarding mistresses.' Girls paid $2 a week for board and room and, under the maternal eye of the

boarding mistresses, the blocks were conducted as strictly as a girls' school. The blocks, occupied by millworkers' families, are the property of the mill.

4. The *Androscoggin Mill* (*permit at office*), manufacturing cotton and rayon, is (R) at the junction of Lisbon and Canal Sts.

5. The *Lewiston Bleachery and Dye Works* (*permit at office*) (L), Canal and Lisbon Sts., carries on the bleaching and dyeing processes for the Pepperell and Lady Pepperell products (*see Tour 1, sec. a*).

L. from Canal St. on Lisbon St.; R. from Lisbon St. on Ash St.

6. *St. Pierre et St. Paul, Roman Catholic Church*, NW. cor. Ash and Bartlett Sts., is one of the most imposing buildings in the two cities. Designed by T. J. O'Connell, Boston, the church was erected over a period of years, 1906–36, to administer to the largest French parish in Lewiston, under the Society of Dominican Fathers. Of modified French Gothic design, the principal façade with its two pinnacled towers suggests the 13th-century ecclesiastical architecture of Provence. The mass of the building is constructed of Maine granite. The pews and interior woodwork are of oak. The floors are tiled and the walls of the sanctuary and rectory are adorned with traceried panels. There is a choir gallery and organ over the narthex. The church auditorium with the transept galleries seats 2100. The cost of the completed building was approximately $1,000,000.

L. from Ash St. on Bartlett St.; R. from Bartlett St. on College St.

7. *Bates College* (*open*), Campus Ave., College, and contiguous streets, housed in 26 buildings, spreads over 75 level acres away from the center of the city. The lawns, gardens, elms, and maples of the campus form an appropriate setting for the ivy-clad buildings.

A path from the corner of College St. and Campus Ave. leads to the attractive English Gothic *Chapel*, while other paths from the rear of Cheney House and Rand Hall, women's dormitories, across College St. lead to the summit of *Mt. David*, commanding panoramas of Bates, Lewiston-Auburn, and the White Mountains more than 50 miles to the west.

Hathorn Hall, College St. (R) is the oldest campus building. Erected in 1855, it contains the Bates Little Theater and several recitation rooms.

LEWISTON–AUBURN. POINTS OF INTEREST

1. The Canal
2. Bates Manufacturing Company
3. Boarding Blocks
4. Androscoggin Mill
5. Lewiston Bleachery and Dye Works
6. St. Pierre et St. Paul
7. Bates College
8. Lewiston Armory
9. Lewiston Falls and Dam
10. Laurel Hill
11. Androscoggin County Court House
12. Goff Hill

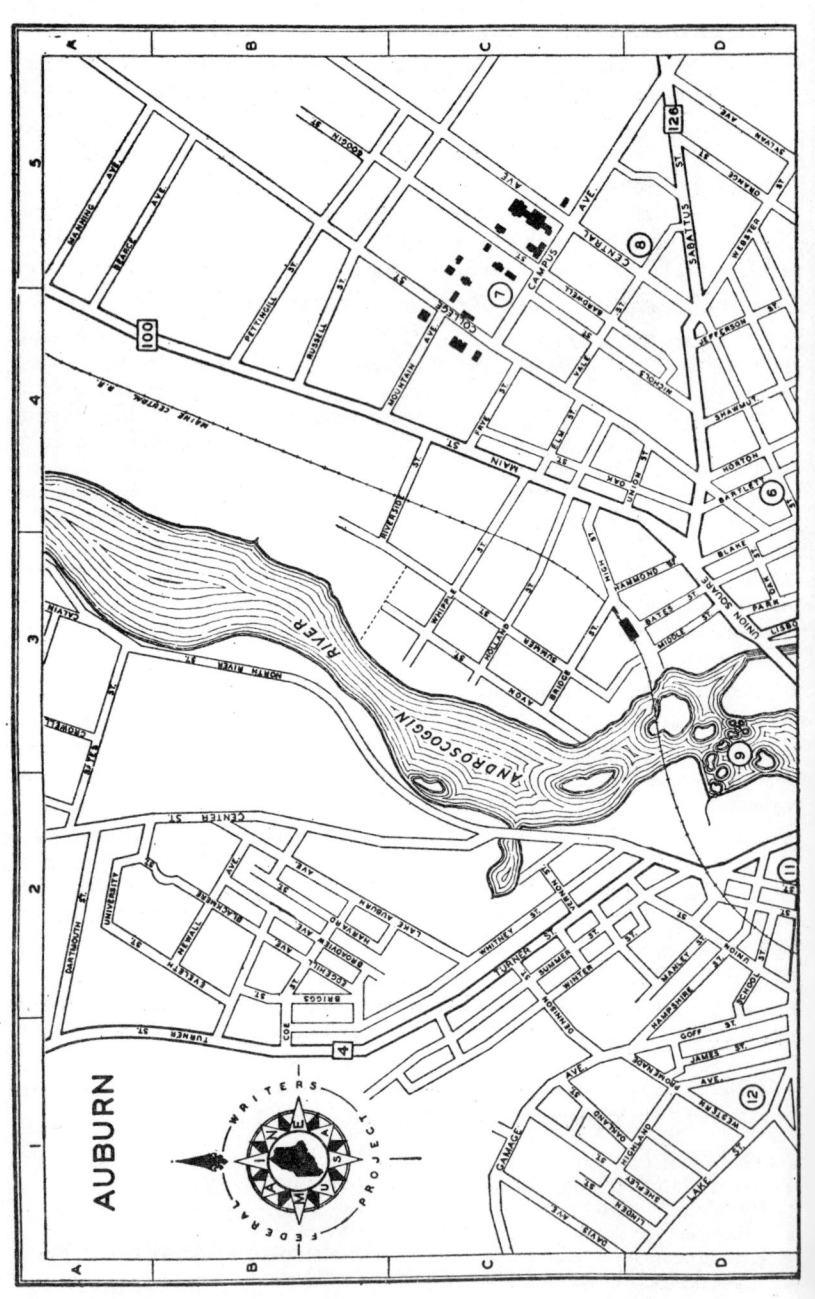

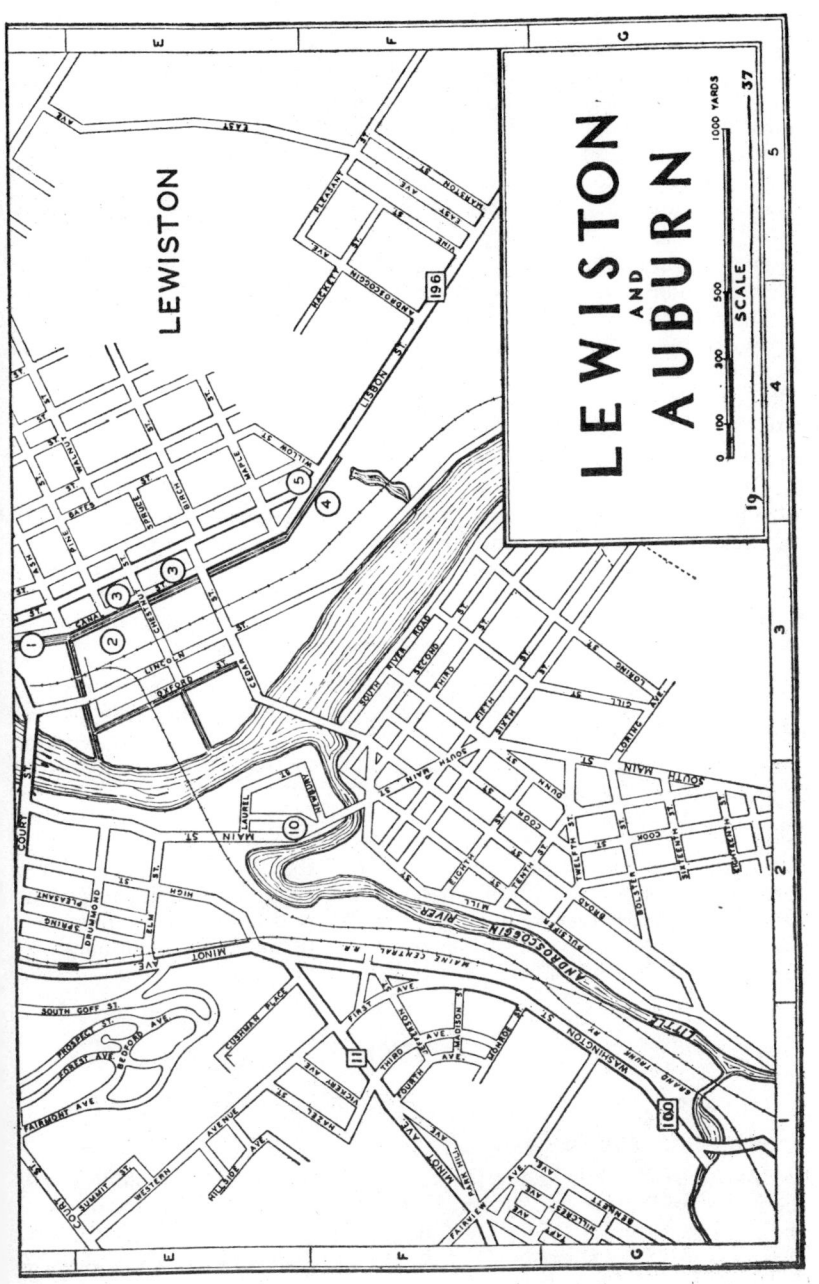

Carnegie Science Building, rear of Hathorn Hall, was made possible by a Carnegie endowment in 1908. Devoted to the departments of biology, physics, and geology, the building also houses the *Stanton Museum*, bequeathed to the college by Prof. Jonathan Young Stanton, one of the early instructors. The museum contains a valuable ornithological exhibit, including many rare and now extinct specimens collected in the United States and abroad. A collection of shells and an herbarium are also noteworthy.

Coram Library, Campus Ave. opp. Nichols St., contains more than 68,000 volumes, besides thousands of pamphlets, documents, and the 1800 volume Isaac L. Rice French Library. The classic columns of the library form an appropriate background for a Greek play presented each Commencement.

The athletic field was named for Alonzo Garcelon, prominent Lewiston citizen and Governor of Maine in 1879.

R. from Campus Ave. on Central Ave.

8. *Lewiston Armory*, Central Ave. and Vale St., constructed of light brick with limestone trim, somewhat resembles a fortress with its massive walls and corner turrets. The auditorium seating 6000 is one of the largest in the State. The building is used by the State for military drills, as well as for conventions and assemblies in the city. Troops were quartered in it for nearly a month in the spring of 1937, when 450 National Guardsmen were called out after street fighting during the shoe strike.

R. from Central Ave. on Sabattus St.; R. from Union Sq. on Main St.

9. *Lewiston Falls and Dam*, best viewed from North Bridge, are particularly spectacular during the spring freshets. Known at various times as Lewis Falls, Twenty-Mile Falls, and Harris Falls, an Indian legend is associated with the first naming. An Indian named Lewis, motivated by too much strong drink, embarked in his canoe above the falls. Losing control of himself, the canoe, and the situation, he stood in the boat as the water was about to engulf him and shouted that the falls should henceforth be known as Lewis Falls. The granite Dam, increasing the 40-foot natural fall of the river by more than 10 feet, was built in 1845, diverting the water into the canal which was begun in the same year. Another dam, a crude affair of timber, had been built in 1808.

AUBURN

Tour 2 — 2.2 m.

S. from Court St. on Main St.

10. *Laurel Hill*, Main, Laurel Sts., Laurel Ave., near the confluence of the Little Androscoggin and Androscoggin Rivers, was once the site of an Indian village and burial ground. It is claimed that the village on Laurel Hill was one of the strongholds of the Anasagunticooks, the Androscoggin Indian tribe, and that in 1690 the village and Indian fortifications were

attacked by a force of more than 60 English under the command of Maj. Benjamin Church.
Retrace to Court St.; L. on Court St.
11. *Androscoggin County Courthouse*, cor. Court and Turner Sts., was the center of legal controversies in March, April, May, and June, 1937, during the shoe strikes. Four of the 19 Lewiston-Auburn shoe manufacturers appeared at a hearing conducted by the National Labor Relations Board to answer complaints by the Committee for Industrial Organization, charging them with unfair labor practices under the Wagner Act. The rooms of the Androscoggin Historical Society (*apply Clerk of Courts, 2d floor*), in the courthouse, contain many items of interest, such as Indian implements and articles pertaining to local history. A *Mural*, 'Law, the Defender of Civilization,' by Harry Cochrane of Monmouth, is in the courtroom.
W. on Court St.
12. From *Goff Hill*, one of Auburn's fine residential sections, views of the two cities, the Lewiston Falls and the river, and the surrounding countryside can be obtained.
Points of Interest in Environs:
Deer Rips Dam, 3 *m.*; Gulf Island Dam, 4.4 *m.*; Mount Apatite, 3 *m.*; Lake Auburn, 4 *m.*; Auburn Fish Hatchery, 6 *m.* (*see Tour* 11)

PORTLAND

City: Alt. 50, pop. 70,810, sett. 1633, incorp. town 1786, State Capital 1820–31, city 1832.

Railroad Stations: Union Station, 222 St. John St., for B. & M. and M.C. R.R.s; Grand Trunk Station, cor. Fore and India Sts., for Canadian National Rys.

Bus Stations: 159 High St., for B. & M. and M. C. Transportation Co.s, Checker Cab (Manchester, N.H.), Maine–New Hampshire Stages, Vermont Transit Lines, Portland–Conway, N.H. Stages; 600 Congress St., for Affiliated Greyhound Lines; 593 Congress St., for Liberty Motor Tours.

Airports: Portland City Airport, Westbrook St., for B. & M. Airways, Inc.; 266 St. John St., for B. & M.–Central Vermont Airways.

Ferry Service: Casco Bay Lines, Custom House Wharf; Peaks Island Transportation Co., Portland Pier.

Accommodations: Sixteen hotels.

Information Service: Maine Publicity Bureau, cor. St. John and Danforth Sts.

Swimming: East End Bathing Beach, Eastern Promenade.

Fishing: Casco Bay, salt water.

Yachting: Portland Yacht Club, Merchant's Wharf.

PORTLAND, Maine's largest city and Cumberland County seat, holds the economic and commercial key to a vast territory extending north and east to the Canadian boundaries. At its feet lies Casco Bay with its '365 islands' — one for every day in the year — a miniature New England Aegean. Portland itself was once almost an island, and even now access to the city without passing over water is possible only from the northwest. The metropolitan area, clustered on an arm of land shaped like a saddle, is almost entirely surrounded by the waters of Casco Bay, Back Cove, and Fore River. Lying between the two elevations, crowned by the Eastern and Western Promenades at opposite ends of the city, the central section of the city extends along a sagging ridge in a general east-and-west direction. Tall elms and other trees line the streets and shade the city's twenty-six parks. Portland owes much of its attractiveness to these trees that in summer hide its architectural deficiencies and make up for some of the ill effects of overcrowding.

Because of its geographical position in the State, Portland is a shipping port and railroad terminus as well as the Gloucester of Maine. Large ships from European and South American countries and the Orient, and smaller coasting vessels, meet in its harbor. Three railroads enter the city. Maine's highway travel, almost without exception, touches Portland before spreading fanwise to other sections of the State. During the tourist season the city is the hub for a vast resort region, and by air and water, rail and highway, vacationists pour into the city, and then by a dozen divergent routes make their way to summer homes and playgrounds to the north and east. At the city's very back lies Maine's most highly concentrated summer resort country. And because Portland is the chief city of Cumberland County, one of the most densely populated sections of Maine, it is also of considerable political, as well as commercial, strength.

Its history has little to distinguish it from that of any average large American city except perhaps the unusual amount of travail and suffering that have gone to building it to a position of security. It has risen and fallen again, not once, but three times. The Indians devastated it; as a prelude to the Revolution the British burned it; and in 1866, the 'great fire' again left it a city of embers. Its first years were marked by the struggles over conflicting claims for the land on which it grew — between England and France, between squatters and landlords, between individual citizens and great corporations. Then, in the nineteenth century it achieved great importance and wealth. That, too, is all of the past. Portland today lives on in a kind of somnolence that belies its past greatness and its present real activity and vitality.

The first recorded settlement on the site of Portland was made by Christopher Levett, 'the King's Woodward of the County of Somersetshire in New England.' Levett built a stone house on Hog Island or House Island (historians have not agreed on the site) where he and his company spent the winter of 1623–24. In the spring he returned to England, apparently with the intention of arousing interest in forming the city of York at a place he called Quack, near Casco, presumably the place where Portland stands. He left his house garrisoned with ten men. There is no indication that he ever returned, and no one can say what happened to the company left occupying the stone house.

The next settler to occupy the site for any length of time was an unscrupulous trader named Walter Bagnall, called 'Great Walt' because of his size. As early as 1628 Bagnall was living on the Spurwink River, not far from Richmond's Island, in a hut with a solitary companion known only as John P. Walt exchanged firewater and worthless trinkets with the Indians for valuable furs, and is alleged to have netted a profit of more than £400 (a considerable sum at that time) in less than three years, before he was killed in 1631 by the Indian chief Squidraset and other dissatisfied customers who had already begun to chafe under the 'beneficent' practices of traders of his type.

About this time George Cleeve and his family established themselves on the land now occupied by the city proper, which was known successively thereafter as Machigonne, Indigreat, Elbow, the Neck, Casco, and Falmouth; the name Portland, of English origin, was first given to Portland Head on Cape Elizabeth and to the sound between the Head and Cushing's Island. In 1630 a body of religious fanatics called the Husbandmen was granted a patent of land at Sagadahoc, that came to be known as 'the patent of the Plough,' after their ship the 'Plough.' They arrived in 1631, but dissatisfied with the location given them, scattered to other Colonies. Cleeve, ambitious and unscrupulous, ingratiated himself with Sir Ferdinando Gorges, proprietor of Maine (then called New Somersetshire) from 1635, and was appointed Deputy Governor of the Province. He was ousted from that office when it was shown he had acquired it by making false accusations against Gorges's previous deputies. Still determined to control the region, Cleeve proceeded to England, where he found a patron in a Colonel Rigby, who purchased the patent of the Plough, named the estate the Province of Lygonia, and put Cleeve in charge as deputy president. Cleeve returned and summoned his first court in Casco, 1643–44, where he proclaimed his authority over the land 'from Sackadehock to Cape Porpus, being about thirteen leagues in 'length.'

There ensued a tedious quarrel between Gorges's agents and Cleeve over the proprietorship of the Colonies of the Casco Bay region; it was taken to courts first in Boston and then in England. Finally Rigby's claims were upheld, and for a while Cleeve enjoyed virtual dictatorship of the Province of Lygonia. Rigby died in 1650 and Massachusetts assumed control of the whole region in 1652. Cleeve kept up an empty show of authority until 1658, when all the inhabitants of the Maine Colonies submitted to the government of Massachusetts. Ruined by his protracted litigations, he died in poverty.

All through this period and for some time to come the Casco region continued as the center of unhappy warfare between 'selfish promotors and contentious claimants.' 'No one,' wrote an early historian, ' could be sure of reaping the rewards of his labors and industry.'

Nevertheless, by 1675, Falmouth (as it was then called) had attained a certain real prosperity. There was a meeting-house on The Neck and more than four hundred settled inhabitants were within a short radius. But in that year Indian wars broke out, and in 1676 several attacks were made on the town itself. In a final ruthless assault that summer the Indians advanced on The Neck, killing and burning as they came, as far as the easterly foot of High Street, where the colonists made their stand. Many of the inhabitants finally took to their boats, some of them escaping to Salem, Massachusetts, where they were admitted as citizens. Others retreated to Jewell Island, far out in the bay, and there threw up bulwarks against attack. An early historian wrote: 'The doom of Falmouth was pronounced at once... it was crushed by a single blow.'

No permanent settlement was effected after this until 1716, when Samuel Moody received permission from the Massachusetts Government to take up land at Falmouth. At his own expense he built a fort and persuaded others to join him there. Three garrisons were established in the township, but Falmouth was never again molested by the Indians or by the French. The town entered upon a harmonious development that continued unchecked for more than fifty years. It acquired outstanding commercial importance, exporting lumber, fish, and furs in exchange for sugar and molasses from English, French, and Spanish ports of the West Indies and the Caribbean. Shipbuilding grew apace with commerce, and the export of masts for the British navy and merchant marine was a lucrative business. It was reported in 1765 that 'the ships loading here are a wonderful benefit; they take off vast quantities of timber; masts, car-raters, boards, etc....' By 1770 Falmouth was as prosperous as any of the Colonial cities; her citizens were sturdy, independent, and comparatively well-to-do.

Forebodings of the impending war were felt as strongly here as anywhere: strong resentment of the Stamp Act was manifest; and when Boston was closed by the Port Bill, Falmouth sent liberal supplies to the Massachusetts city. In May, 1775, a Tory sea captain, attempting to outfit a vessel for shipping masts, was restrained by a local committee which asserted that masts for the British navy were in the nature of military supplies and therefore could not legally be exported. The captain appealed to Captain Henry Mowatt of the British sloop-of-war 'Canceau,' which shortly thereafter dropped anchor in Falmouth Harbor. Falmouth, strongly Whig, became the scene of anti-British demonstrations; revolutionary sentiments were expressed everywhere. Companies of Militiamen, responding to the call from the Continental Congress, were assembled about town. In the midst of the excitement, Captain Mowatt, who was strolling about Munjoy Hill with his surgeon, was seized by a company of Colonials who maintained that he was spying on their activities. The British officer was released on parole, after giving his word to return when requested.

He did return, though not upon request. October 16, 1775, four British naval vessels and a store ship hove to off Portland. Mowatt, in command of this small fleet, sent word to the people of Falmouth 'to remove all human specie from the town' within two hours. Frantic parleys and efforts to arrive at terms of surrender were of no avail. It must be said for Mowatt, however, that he would have spared the city had the inhabitants agreed to surrender all large and small arms in their possession. But this ignominy the people courageously spurned. Accordingly, at 9.30 on the morning of October 18, Mowatt's ships opened fire on Falmouth. Discharge after discharge of bombs, grapeshot, and cannon balls rained upon the defenseless town. Since most of the buildings were upon the level land between India and Center Streets, they were within easy range. The bombardment continued throughout the day, and at night parties were landed to apply torches to whatever structures had escaped the shots. Four hundred and fourteen buildings, including a new courthouse, the town house, and the customs house, with many barns and warehouses, went up in the general conflagration. Nearly two thousand persons were left homeless, although none were killed and only one was wounded. Some members of the British landing parties were believed to have been shot down by the citizenry.

One prominent building that escaped the flames was the Widow Grele's tavern, a story-and-a-half structure in the heart of the city. The doughty widow refused to leave her house; whenever flames burst forth around it, she rushed out and extinguished them with pails of water. Since most of the public buildings had been leveled to the ground, in the days that followed one of the rooms of the widow's tavern was used for court sessions. Here county court was held for the duration of the Revolutionary War, and until 1787, when a new courthouse was built. The Widow Grele's tavern was a Portland landmark even into the present century.

A month after the Mowatt bombardment a visitor reported 'no lodging, eating, or housekeeping in Falmouth.' The British came and went, but they found little about the ruined wharves and buildings to make occupation desirable. The town, though, was never abandoned because it was still a central point for the assembling of military recruits, and in 1777 there were upwards of seven hundred people living here under conditions of extreme hardship.

Cheerless predictions as to Falmouth's future after bombardment, the Revolution, and the period of post-war stagnation proved groundless. The town, which took the name of Portland on July 4, 1786, was once more the scene of great commercial activity. Business began to expand in volume and variety, forts were constructed, bridges were built connecting the city with the surrounding country, and Maine's first banking house, the Portland bank, was established with a capital of $100,000. The Falmouth *Gazette*, Maine's first newspaper, appeared in 1785. Commerce with England, even more profitable than before, was restored, and the French Revolution gave new impetus to American shipping. In 1800, Portland's population was 3704, an unusually large number when it is considered that 97 per cent of the Nation's total population at this time was rural. When, in 1803, Commodore Edward Preble subdued the Barbary Coast pirates, making shipping safe in the Mediterranean, Portland, the commodore's home, basked in the acclaim that the world accorded him. The rise of Napoleon in France and the subsequent European conflicts furnished valuable markets for Yankee enterprise, and Portland especially profited in the subsequent shipbuilding boom.

The newfound prosperity experienced sudden decline in 1807 with the two-year Jeffersonian Embargo. The Portland waterfront was deserted; ships literally rotted at their moorings; hundreds of citizens lined up each day in Market Square to be fed from public soup kettles. From 1807 to 1809, the city experienced a depression more profound than any during its subsequent history.

Recovery came suddenly. The War of 1812 provided new stimuli for commerce and industry, and shipyards again hummed with activity. Fortunes were made overnight in privateering. The whole town assumed a new aspect of liveliness and enterprise. The war had a further beneficial effect in substituting land trade where traffic by sea was sometimes hindered or halted altogether. As men turned from the sea, land was cleared farther and farther inland, and new industries came into being. Portland became the metropolis for the new State developing at its back. It was to be expected that the year after Federalist Massachusetts voted the separation of Democratic-Republican Maine, Portland would be selected as capital for the new State. It held this position until 1831.

The city's progress through the nineteenth century was rapid. Chartered as a city in 1832, it continued to expand as the development of steam-driven vessels and trains increased transportation facilities. The first steamboat to ply Casco waters was a ferry, the 'Kennebec,' nicknamed the 'Groundhog,' which made her maiden trip across the harbor in 1822. Since the craft lacked both sail and oars, the passengers sometimes had to turn the paddlewheel themselves by treading on its blades when the faulty engines balked against the tide. The first railroad line, from Portland to Portsmouth, was opened in 1842. Other railroad and steamboat lines were soon established, and in 1853 the 'Sarah Sands,' first trans-Atlantic steamer to dock at this port, made a safe crossing from Liverpool.

To the Civil War, Portland contributed one-fifth of its total population, at that time 25,000. Maine was strongly pro-abolition, and Portland was a center of considerable agitation. During the war a young Confederate naval officer conceived a plan for entering Portland Harbor; his goal was the destruction of two gunboats lying there and the capture of a steamer in which to continue his already extensive depredations on the sea. Disguising his men as fishermen, he had no trouble bringing his small vessel past the forts and anchoring it near the wharves. That night he boarded and took the revenue cutter 'Caleb Cushing' and sailed her out of the harbor. The following morning the collector of customs and the mayor with a crew of volunteers manned the Boston steamer 'Forest City,' another crew took the New York boat 'Chesapeake,' and set out in pursuit, eventually overtaking the 'Cushing.' The Southerners aboard her, failing to find any ammunition, set her afire and were taken as prisoners from the lifeboats.

The war over, Portland resumed its accustomed activity. Then, on the afternoon of July 4, 1866, there occurred what was probably the greatest of Portland's series of catastrophes. A great fire almost wiped out the city. Starting in a boatshop on Commercial Street near the foot of High Street, and fanned by a strong southerly wind, it swept diagonally across the Neck to Back Cove and up Munjoy Hill. Except for a line of buildings on Commercial Street and another on Oxford Street, the whole lower and most densely settled area of Portland was brought to the ground during the fifteen hours the fire raged. Only by blowing up buildings in the path of the flames, and by the most strenuous efforts on the part of fire fighters was the rest of the city saved. Longfellow, viewing the city some weeks after the conflagration, wrote to a friend: 'I have been in Portland since the fire. Desolation, desolation, desolation! It reminds me of Pompeii. . . .'

Most of the public buildings, all the banks, half the city's churches and manufacturing establishments, and hundreds of dwellings were razed by the flames. The financial loss amounted to millions. Yet, despite the extent of the disaster, not a life was lost. Colonies of tents sprang up to shelter the homeless, and contributions of money, provisions, clothing, and building materials poured in from all parts of the country. Thieving and extortion were more than balanced by countless deeds of heroism and acts of generosity.

Rebuilding commenced immediately, with many improvements. Narrow streets were widened and crooked ones straightened; much of the congestion caused by poor planning was changed. Once more Portland bound up its wounds and settled down to serious business, and shipping and industry were soon vying with each other in the renewed commercial expansion. Unlike that of some cities that have grown around one industrial enterprise, Portland's business complexion has changed with the times. It reflected the rise and fall of such major industries as lumbering and wooden shipbuilding; it was marked by the changes in the industrial life of the United States as a whole; and recently it has clearly indicated Maine's decline as an industrial State and its rise as a vacation and resort region.

During, and shortly after, the World War period, Portland experienced great prosperity. Nearly all the grain from Canada was exported through this port, and the city had facilities for handling large import and export cargoes which other cities in the State could not accommodate. In consequence, commerce was thriving, and there was no lack of employment along the water front. At the same time real estate was booming, and much of suburban Portland as it is today was built.

As Portland achieved a solid worldly footing, its citizens turned toward cultural and intellectual interests. At one time it enjoyed a reputation as a theatrical city, with thriving stock companies of its own. Dramatic performances had their beginning as early as 1794 with a performance of a comedy, 'The Lyar,' and a farce, the 'Modern Antiques, or the Merry Mourners,' while the 'Learned Pig' was sung between the pieces 'with much success.' In 1796, Portland theater-goers had the pleasure of hearing nine-year-old Elizabeth Arnold sing at an evening performance in which her mother played the lead; she it was who later bore the child named Edgar Allan Poe. Portland's theatrical days were in their greatest glory in the 1890's. At that time the famous Jefferson Theater was opened (September, 1897) with 'Half a King,' starring Francis Wilson; and Joseph Jefferson, for whom the playhouse was named, was guest of honor. In the course of its brilliant career, it is said, the boards of the Jefferson were trod by every American actor of note except David Warfield. Today the site of the theater is occupied by an automobile service station. All present-day Portland can boast theatrically is an active Little Theater movement.

Music, too, has felt the pressure of changing tastes. At one time the Maine Music Festivals were held here, gathering together choirs, choral societies, and bands from all over the State and bringing the world's greatest musicians and singers to Maine. For nearly forty years the festivals were the chief events of the Maine season. At the 1897 festival Madame Lillian Nordica (*see Tour* 11) scored distinct triumphs, and again in 1912, when she made her last appearance before a Maine audience responding to encore after encore with 'Home, Sweet Home.' Portland still has its musicians, as frequent concerts and recitals testify, and there are many organizations providing opportunities not only for those who play and sing, but also for those who like good music.

Present-day Portland socially is an average American city, its commercial and industrial aspects redeemed somewhat by its heritage of New England culture. Its population is predominantly of Anglo-Saxon stock, with small Americanized groups of Irish, Jewish, Italian, and Scandinavian people. There is no rigid segregation, and the only pronounced foreign quarter that may be called such is that of the Italians. Portland has more than sixty churches and religious meeting-places, accommodating a wide variety of denominations. A complete parochial school system, a convent, and one of the two monasteries in Maine are operated by the Roman Catholic Church. The first radio parish in America was established over Portland's broadcasting station. The city's public schools lead all others of the State, and private institutions include a Hebrew school, a junior college for women, a girls' preparatory school, a Roman Catholic academy for girls, several business colleges, and specialized schools for the study of law and other subjects. State schools for deaf-mutes and for the blind are maintained here.

Portland's shipping, always of first importance since Colonial times, declined abruptly following the World War, but tonnage figures show it to be on an upward trend. The chief products shipped into Portland by water are pulpwood, baled pulp, coal, petroleum products, small amounts of sulphur and China clay, and package freight. Outgoing cargoes consist mainly of Solka, a local wood-pulp product that is sent to Japan; fish, potatoes, finished paper, newsprint, and package freight. Portland, nearer the North Atlantic fishing grounds than either Boston or Gloucester, leads Maine in the fishing industry. Always a commercial rather than an industrial center, the city has attracted the branches of many national companies, is the distributing point for chain-store units throughout the State, and is the home of numerous large wholesale concerns. Its trading population almost equals that of its own citizens. Its position as a headquarters and point of departure for the tourist and sportsman frequently comes near trebling its population at the height of the summer season.

Portland is very much alive. Here one may feel the social, economic, and political pulse of the State of Maine. Here are modern businesses on up-to-date streets in close proximity to fascinating old shops and alleys with the dust of another century upon them. Today's business and yesterday's history, new enterprise and old romance, are combined in this city which Longfellow in his old age remembered wistfully as 'the beautiful town that is seated by the sea.'

TOUR 1 — 2.2 m.

NE. from Monument Sq. on Congress St.

Monument Square, the busy junction of Congress, Middle, Federal, Elm, Center, and Preble Sts., was for generations Portland's forum, the center of the city's commercial, social, and political activity. A blockhouse built at this point in 1746 for defense against the Indians, and garrisoned with provincial troops, was abandoned two years later and sold to the county. A few years later a jail and jail-keeper's house were built adjoining the blockhouse. Since the jailer received only £15 annually for his services, he kept a tavern, called the Freemason's Arms. A loyalist sea captain, captured in 1780 while recovering iron from the wreck of Saltonstall's fleet (*see BANGOR*) wrote of the Falmouth Jail that he 'had neither bed, blankets, or anything to lay on but the oak plank floor, with the heads of spikes an inch high and so thick together that I could not lay down clear of them.' Small wonder that he broke jail and escaped after his first few weeks of imprisonment. The blockhouse jail was removed in 1797.

Up to the 20th century, Market Square, as it was then called, was the scene of all popular gatherings in the city, surrounded as it was by stores, hotels, public halls, and places of amusement. The central building, Military Hall (1825–88), was both 'town house' and market place. Military companies had their armories in the building and town meetings were held there. More than one riot took place in the square before the hall — one of them in 1856 when, during the mayoralty of the prohibitionist Neal Dow, a man was shot during the attempt of an anti-liquor-law mob to seize the city-owned liquors stored in the building. On holidays the square was always the focus of the city's life, and in the evenings crowds gathered about the peddlers and showmen who displayed their wares by the light of flaming torches.

1. The lofty *Monument* by Franklin Simmons, in the center of the square, was completed and dedicated in 1891, a memorial to the Portland men who participated in the Civil War.

2. On Congress St. (R) is the *Building of the Edwards and Walker Hardware Company*, a typical Maine concern, which was started 61 years ago as a general trading center and is still (1937) under the management of its founder. Priding itself on its conservatism, it is the largest house of its kind in Maine if not in New England. The Edwards and Walker Building was in stagecoach days the United States Hotel, and until the Civil War was Portland's premier hostelry; its outward appearance has not greatly changed since its heyday.

L. from Congress St. on Elm St.

3. The *Portland Society of Natural History Museum (open weekdays, 2–4)*, 24 Elm St., maintains a library of 5000 volumes dealing with natural history, geographical surveys, scientific treatises, abstracts, bulletins, and magazines. Museum exhibits, marked for inspection, include Indian relics, mounted North American fauna, shells, minerals, wood samples, paper, plant life, clothing, and household instruments. There is a fairly exhaustive exhibit of Maine specimens.

Retrace to Congress St.; L. on Congress St.

4. The *First Parish (Unitarian) Church* (1825), 425 Congress St., is second successor to the original Falmouth meeting-house that stood at the corner of Middle and India Sts., and served the Community from 1718 to 1746 as a place of worship, and for a time as courthouse. Parson Smith, first regularly ordained minister in Maine east of Wells, recorded in 1747: 'I prayed with the Court in the afternoon. Justice came drunk.' Smith, succeeding a series of itinerant ministers of whom one was the Rev. George Burroughs, who preached here in the 1670's and was hanged for witchcraft in Salem in 1692, attended to the theological, and also the medical, needs of his parishioners for 70 years. The church became Unitarian in 1809 and attained its greatest prominence under the Rev. Ichabod Nichols, who was called to the parish at that time. 'Old Jerusalem,' the second structure, occupied the present site from 1746 to 1825, when it was replaced by the stone church as it now stands. The former church was for years a Portland landmark, and the young Longfellow wrote a poem protesting its destruction. 'Old Jerusalem' withstood the Mowatt bombardment, although a cannonball, now embedded in the ceiling of the present church, with a chandelier suspended from it, penetrated one of its sides.

5. The *Portland City Hall* and *Municipal Auditorium*, 380 Congress St., occupies a plot of ground associated with city, county, and State government for more than 150 years. The first structure on this site was a two-story frame courthouse (1782–1816) whose cupola was surmounted by the carved weathercock now adorning the First National Bank Building. Gallows, stocks, and pillory had a prominent place in the first floor hall of the courthouse, and the whipping post stood outside its door. The first

capital conviction in the United States Courts after the adoption of the Constitution (Article I, sec. 8: 'The congress shall have power ... to define and punish piracies and felonies committed on the high seas ...') occurred here in 1790, when one Thomas Bird was sentenced to be hanged for piracy and murder. Bird's petition for pardon was refused by President Washington, and he was promptly executed on Bramhall Hill. A jail (1797–1859) and a jail-keeper's house were built in the rear of the courthouse, the former having a dungeon with chains, shackles, and ringbolts. The debtor's rooms in the attic 'were not so repulsive, yet those who were then confined in them — did not appear as if they were happy.' A new brick courthouse was erected in 1818 and, four years later when Maine became a State, it was used by the legislature. Until 1822, spirituous liquors were sold on the premises, a practice which was discontinued in that year 'during the sitting of the Court of Legislature.' Another building adjoining the courthouse had been erected in 1820 to accommodate the Senate and State offices, and was in use until the State capitol was removed to Augusta in 1831. At the time of Lafayette's visit to Portland in June, 1825, an awning was spread from the front of the statehouse to the elm trees lining the street before it, and the General held his public reception on a platform built from the entrance.

Two other city and county buildings on the site of the old courthouse, jail, and statehouse were built and burned before the construction (1909–

PORTLAND. POINTS OF INTEREST

1. Monument Square
2. Edwards and Walker Company
3. Portland Society of Natural History
4. First Parish Church
5. Portland City Hall
6. Cumberland County Courthouse
7. Lincoln Park
8. Birthplace of Fanny Fern and N. P. Willis
9. Cathedral of the Immaculate Conception
10. Eastern Cemetery
11. Henry W. Longfellow Birthplace
12. Thomas B. Reed Birthplace
13. Grand Trunk Station
14. Water Front
15. Old Post Office Building
16. Wadsworth Longfellow House
17. Museum Maine Historical Society
18. Birthplace of Cyrus H. K. Curtis
19. Cumberland Club
20. L. D. M. Sweat Museum
21. Sweat Mansion
22. School Fine and Applied Art
23. Storer-Mussey House
24. Dole or Churchill House
25. State Street Hospital
26. Deane House
27. Saint Luke's Cathedral
28. Milliken House
29. Shepley House
30. Mellen-Fessenden House
31. John Neal Houses
32. Longfellow Statue
33. Neal Dow Homestead
34. Fort Allen Park
35. First Civic Monument
36. Fort Sumner Park
37. Portland Observatory
38. Deering Mansion
39. Deering's Oaks
40. Thomas B. Reed Statue
41. Williston Congregational Church
42. St. Joseph's Academy
43. Tate House
44. Means House

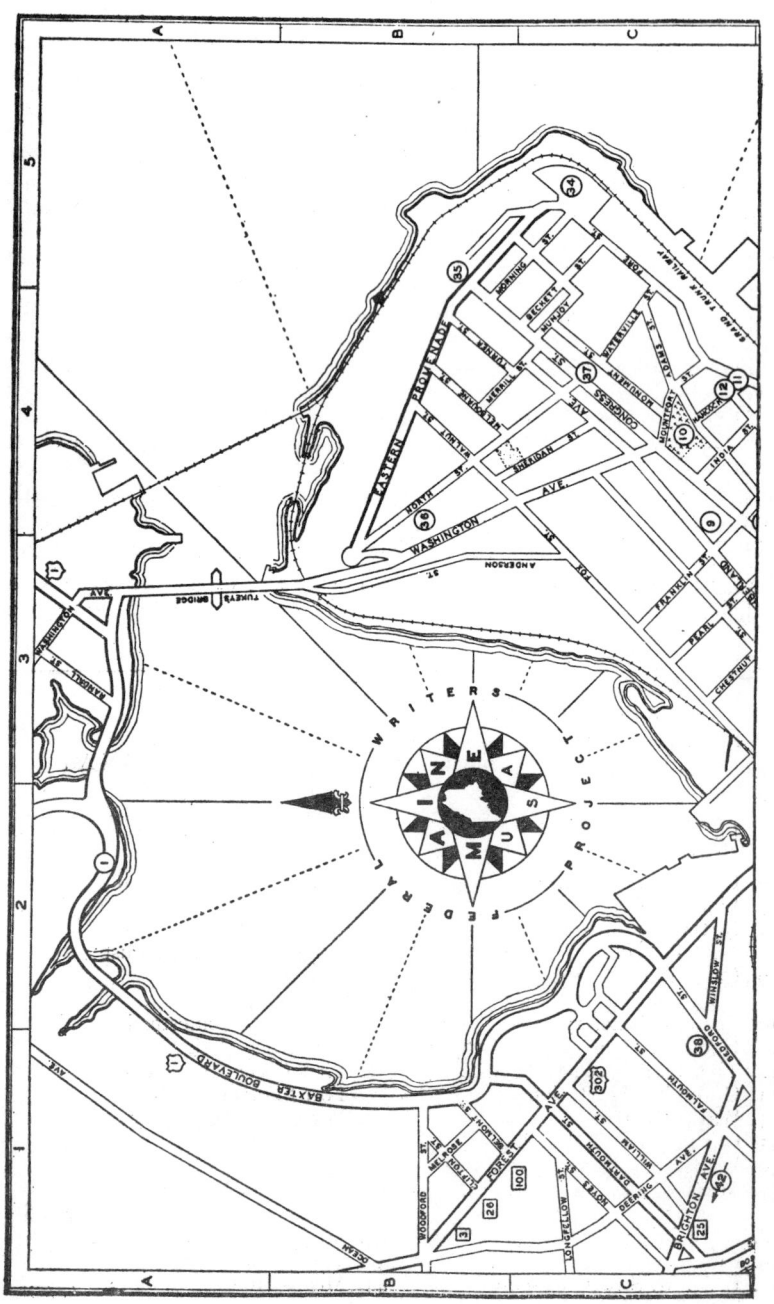

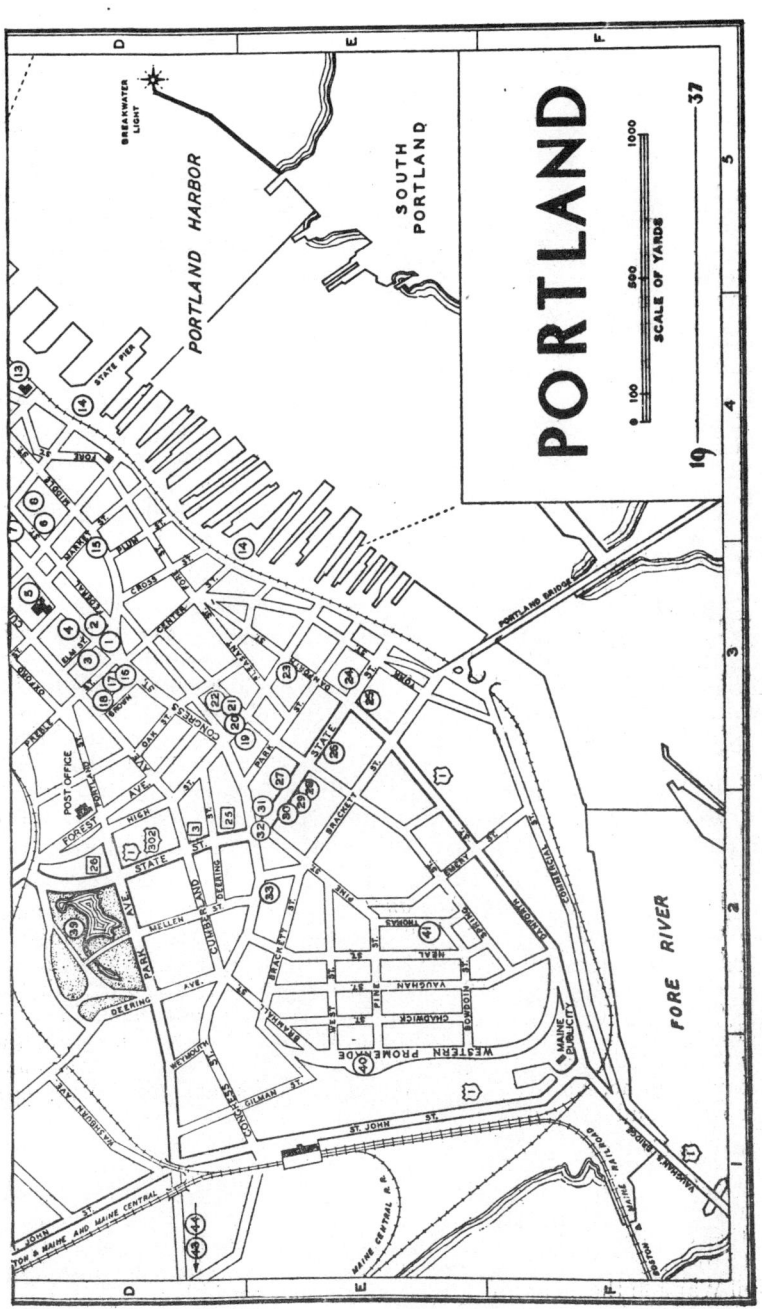

12) of the present city hall, designed by Carrere and Hastings of New York and Stevens and Stevens of Portland.

In the rear of the building a *Municipal Auditorium* with a seating capacity of over 3000, houses the *Kotzchmar Memorial Organ*, gift of the late Cyrus H. K. Curtis in memory of Herman Kotzchmar (1829-1908), composer, teacher, and for 47 years organist of the First Parish in Portland. The Kotzchmar organ, one of the largest in the world, is really eight instruments in one; it has 177 speaking stops and couplers, over 6500 pipes, and a carillon. Although there is at present no municipal organist, a series of summer concerts is sponsored by the American Guild of Organists, and each year many well-known musicians participate.

R. from Congress St. on Pearl St.

6. The *Cumberland County Courthouse* (1906-07) (*open weekdays*), NE. cor. Federal and Pearl Sts., an impressive neo-classic structure of Maine granite designed by George Burnham, houses the county governmental and judiciary offices and archives. Directly across, SE. cor. Pearl and Federal Sts., stands the *Federal Court Building*, a similarly impressive granite building, where the U.S. District Court holds its sessions.

Retrace to Congress St.; R. on Congress St.

7. *Lincoln Park*, bounded by Congress, Franklin, Federal, and Pearl Sts., occupies the heart of the city. Formerly a heavily congested residential area, it was set aside after the fire of 1866 by the city fathers as a 'protection against the spread of fire and to promote the public health.' The land was purchased for a public square and market place, designed accordingly in 1867, and named Phoenix Square. At the protest of the common council, the name was shortly changed to Lincoln Park. With the judicious planting of trees and the installation of a fountain in 1870 the spot soon became a welcome and restful breathing space in a section of the city which in the course of time has grown somewhat drab.

R. from Congress St. on Franklin St.

8. The *Birthplace of Fanny Fern and N. P. Willis* (*private*), 24 Franklin St., is an undistinguished gray house on a quiet street, with little about it to indicate that two famous children of a distinguished father were born and lived here more than a century ago. Here in 1807 was born Nathaniel Parker Willis and in 1811 his sister, Sara, known to thousands of readers as Fanny Fern. Their father, Nathaniel Willis, was the founder of the *Youth's Companion*; both children at an early age became even more famous than he, Nathaniel as an international journalist and poet, Sara as novelist and essayist (*see The Arts*).

Retrace to Congress St.; R. on Congress St.

9. The *Cathedral of the Immaculate Conception*, 307 Congress St., its main entrance facing Cumberland Ave., is the seat of the bishopric and the mother church for the entire Catholic diocese of Maine. Completed and dedicated in 1869 in spite of repeated setbacks in its building during the Civil War and the great fire of 1866, after which the bishop was obliged to

celebrate mass in the shed of the Grand Trunk Depot for want of a church, it has been remodeled once, in 1930. Apparently an agglomeration of several structures, the Cathedral is designed in a modified French Gothic style. The main building's lofty interior, resembling somewhat those of the cathedrals of Europe, is embellished with walls of Carrara, Brescia, Pavonazzo, Porta Santa, and Numidian red marble and adorned with delicately tinted ornament. The Stations of the Cross are executed in mosaic and the 18 stained-glass windows are of Munich glass.

10. The old *Eastern Cemetery*, extending below Mountfort St. from Congress to Federal Sts., has been in use for more than 250 years, and for more than two centuries of that period was the only graveyard within the city limits. The six acres of this crowded burial place, almost in the heart of the city, contain the graves of many of Portland's early and most prominent families. The oldest legible stone is dated 1717. Here, side by side, lie the bodies of the two gallant young commanders of one of the decisive naval battles of the War of 1812, Lieutenant William Burrows, commander of the victorious U.S. brig 'Enterprise,' and Captain Samuel Blyth, Commander of the British brig 'Boxer,' who were killed in action between Seguin and Monhegan September 5, 1813. Two days after the sea fight the 'Enterprise' arrived in Portland Harbor with the defeated British vessel. Then, to the accompaniment of booming guns and followed by nearly all the boats in the harbor, the officers' bodies were brought to shore in ten-oared barges rowed by ships' masters. Congress subsequently had a commemorative medal struck in honor of Lieutenant Burrows.

Near the graves of the commanders of the 'Enterprise' and the 'Boxer' is a memorial to Lieutenant Henry Wadsworth, the uncle for whom Henry Wadsworth Longfellow was named. In September, 1804, this 20-year-old officer was killed off Tripoli when the fireship 'Intrepid,' dispatched to destroy the Tripolitan navy, was blown up to save it from capture. A monument commemorating this event stands at the western front of the Capitol in Washington.

An impressive marble tomb marks the grave of one of Portland's famous citizens, Commodore Edward Preble (1761–1807). In 1803, President Jefferson chose Preble to command the forces sent to conquer the Barbary pirates. Sailing for Tripoli with the celebrated 'Constitution' for his flagship, Preble conducted so effective a campaign that the Barbary powers sued for peace at any terms. Pope Pius VII said of him that 'he had done more for Christianity in a short space of time than the most powerful nations have done in ages.'

R. from Congress St. on Mountfort St.; R. from Mountfort St. on Fore St.

Fore Street is as integrally a part of Portland as the far busier main thoroughfare, Congress St. Its crooked course, lined with rows of weathered, often ramshackle, brick and frame buildings, indicates the contours of the original Portland waterfront. Fore and contiguous streets — Love Lane, now Center St., Fish St., now Exchange, Lime St., now Market,

Fiddle Lane, now Franklin St., Turkey Lane, now Newbury St., Moose Alley, now Chatham St., Chub Lane, now Hampshire St., and King St., now India, the oldest street in Portland — were long the commercial and residential centers of the city, and comprise the district which suffered most from the fire of 1866. Longfellow recalled the Fore St. of his youth, with its 'black wharves and the slips... and the Spanish sailors with bearded lips,' when the fashionable residential section still lay east of Congress St. Here on Fore St. were the counting-houses, chandleries, slopshops, saloons, lodging-houses, and the warehouses crammed with West Indian goods. Wharves and piers were piled high with barrels of Jamaica rum, hogsheads of Porto Rico molasses, and the thousands of feet of lumber that were hauled in from the surrounding country by ox teams, a practice which occasioned a bit of popular verse, which with many variations, was repeated all over the globe:

> 'From Saccarap' to Portland Pier
> I've hauled boards for many a year;
> Since this hard work, with much abuse,
> I'm salted down for sailor's use.'

Later on in its history certain sections of Fore St. acquired an unsavory reputation. With the laying out of Commercial St. in the middle of the 19th century, Fore was relegated to a position of secondary importance, but suffered only slight diminution of activity. By the close of the Civil War, however, the center of the city's business had moved away, and while Fore St. today is by no means devoid of traffic, the turbulent bustle of its heyday is long past. Many of its buildings are the tombs of a former prosperity and, whereas midnight was once but another hour to the scores of brawling and carousing sailors who frequented the street, its silence is now broken only by an occasional, perhaps furtive, footfall or the caterwauling of the stray cats that live in the deserted lofts and cellars.

11. The *Henry Wadsworth Longfellow Birthplace* (1784) (*open: 1st July–Labor Day, 9–6; adm. 25¢, three for 50¢*), cor. Fore and Hancock Sts., is a plain three-story frame house that has long since given up any pretensions to elegance or beauty. At the time of the poet's birth, when his parents were visiting Stephen Longfellow's sister here, Casco Bay came nearly to the dooryard of the house. A white sand beach, a favorite location for administering the baptismal rites of certain fundamentalist denominations, stretched along the section now covered by railroad tracks. For a time the house was headquarters for the now disbanded International Longfellow Society. When the society attempted to restore the dwelling in 1914, it was found that the original doorway had been replaced by a cheap, glass-paneled door. A doorway more harmonious with the design of the house was found in another building, and a stately entrance with mullioned side-lights, arched transom, and molded architraves now ornaments the poet's birthplace. Not until 10 years or so ago was it discovered that the old house, from which the doorway had been removed, was also of considerable historic interest as the birthplace of John Knowles Paine (1839–1906), America's earliest noted composer.

Plain wooden plaques bearing the names and dates of Homer, Virgil, Dante, Shakespeare, and Milton are on the outside walls of the Longfellow House.

R. from Fore St. on Hancock St.

12. The *Thomas Brackett Reed Birthplace*, 15 Hancock St., now a storage warehouse, was the home of one of the leading political figures of Maine and the United States in the last quarter of the 19th century. Thomas B. Reed (1839–1902) grew up in this humble section of Portland where his friends were the 'Brackett Street boys' and the 'Center-Streeters' when 'beyond them in the unknown regions of Munjoy Hill, were savage and warlike tribes of whom we did not even know the names....' Graduated from Bowdoin in 1860, Reed later served Maine in its house and senate and as attorney general. In 1876 he was sent to Congress and was a member of that body for 22 years. Speaker of the House for three sessions, Reed won the sobriquet of 'Czar' Reed because of his autocratic rulings; he was responsible for much of the legislative procedure in use today. He was noted for his penetrating wit and humor as much as for his statesmanship. To one Representative's statement that he would 'rather be right than President,' Reed replied: 'The gentleman from Illinois will never be either.' Again, when informed that one member of the Senate was ill to the point of being out of his head, Reed remarked: 'He ought to come up to the House; they are all that way up there.' Although a great admirer of Theodore Roosevelt, he once said to the latter: 'What I especially admire about you, Theodore, is your enthusiasm at having discovered the Ten Commandments.' Possibly Reed's wit was keener and more malicious than he realized, and it may have had something to do with his small showing when running against McKinley for the Presidential nomination. He retired voluntarily from Congress in 1899 and made his home in Portland until his death.

Retrace to Fore St.

13. The *Grand Trunk Station* (1903), NE. cor. Fore and India Sts., occupies a site that has figured prominently in Portland's history from the days of Indian warfare to the era of modern transportation and commerce. Under the authorization of the Massachusetts Government, a stockade was built here in 1680. This stockade, on the site of Fort Loyal, stood on a bluff about 30 feet higher than the present level of the station. In the year of the fort's erection Thomas Danforth of Boston was appointed 'President of Maine,' and, invested with governmental authority, came to Falmouth Neck, where he held formal court within the fort's enclosure and established municipal government, the first ordered rule since Indians had destroyed the settlement in 1676. Grants of land were made, most of them in the India Street section, and a village was built along defensive lines. Ten years later the fort was enlarged into a strong fortification with four blockhouses and eight cannon. On May 17, 1690, nearly all the houses of the new community were destroyed by a force of 500 French and Indians, the inhabitants fleeing to the fort. After a three-day siege, during which the attackers had begun to undermine the defenses, the

fort surrendered. The French commanders assured the defenders quarter and liberty to march south, but as soon as the gates were opened, the English were abandoned to the Indians. The survivors, many of them women and children, were taken captive and forced to make the arduous 24-day journey northward to Quebec. Fort Loyal was fallen and deserted. Two years later a party under Sir William Phips (*see Tour 1, sec. b*) and Captain Church stopped to bury the bleaching bones of those who had perished within and around the fort.

Until the laying-out of Commercial St. and the filling-in of the land, the tidewaters of Clay Cove approached to within a short distance of the fort plot. In 1826 this location became the site of a marine railway, a horse-drawn cradle affair, which was the first approach to a modern drydock in this region. Much of the land now occupied by the station and railroad yards was for some time given over to the clean wood-and-tar atmosphere of a shipyard. Vessels of small tonnage for the West Indian trade were launched here, but not before the Cove had been filled with floating logs which, piling up before the sterns, lessened the momentum of the vessels so that they did not run aground on the flats.

In 1853 the old fort site assumed a new and international importance. In that year the Atlantic and St. Lawrence Ry., subsequently leased to the Grand Trunk Ry. Co. of Canada and now forming a part of the Canadian National Rys., was completed between the port of Portland and Montreal. Dispute between Boston and Portland as to which city should be the American terminus for the railroad was settled in unique fashion. A boat leaving Liverpool bore two special mail bags for Montreal, one to be left at Portland and one at Boston, the city from which the mail arrived first naturally becoming the choice for the terminus. A tug sent out from Portland intercepted the steamer, and in February, 1845, the Montreal-bound mail left Portland. Relays of horses, changed every seven miles, drew a sleigh northward through the snows of a severe New England winter. Three miles from Montreal a team of spirited horses and a stylish sleigh were given the driver, one Grosvenor Waterhouse. Bearing his immense figure erect, the American flag streaming out beside him from the whipsocket, Waterhouse urged his horses to a final tremendous burst of speed. The 255-mile drive was completed in the unparalleled time of 18 hours and 6 minutes, several hours ahead of the Boston mail. Thus Maine had demonstrated that Portland was the logical terminus for the projected railroad.

The present station is constructed of brick and rough granite, its façade surmounted by a square illuminated clock tower. East of the station the railway's two huge grain elevators raise their gaunt shapes above yards and wharves.

L. from Fore St. on India St.; R. from India St. on Commercial St.

Commercial Street, with the waterfront, is vitally important in the city's commercial life. In 1850 increased trade and the projected railway to Canada seemed to demand better and more ample transportation and terminal facilities than were possible on Fore St., which at that time bordered the water. Accordingly, in that year, Commercial St., 100 feet broad, more than a mile long, with a 26-foot space in its center reserved for the railroad, was laid out across tidewater, running over the heads of the wharves. The area between Commercial and Fore Sts. was later filled in; the drop between the levels of the two streets is noticeable today. Thus, leaving Fore St. stranded, Commercial St. has become the focus of maritime activity and trade. The days when the street was as crowded and busy as Congress Street of a Saturday noon today, and policemen patrolled the district in pairs, have gone within the past quarter of a century, but a semblance of the activity of a departed era is still found in the wholesale concerns and marine supply shops that border its length.

14. The Portland *Waterfront*, lying adjacent to Commercial St., has more than a score of wharves, chief of which is the $1,500,000 *Maine State Pier*. This pier, 1000 feet long, provides two ocean berths with a 35-foot depth at mean low tide on the east side and three berths with a lesser depth on the west side. Equipped with modern transit sheds and with ample equipment for the rapid handling of ships' cargoes, it has direct rail connections with tracks on Commercial St., and is the only public terminal served directly by all railroads entering the city. The boom days of 1812 when, according to Kenneth Roberts' novel, the 'Lively Lady,' 'there was free rum for the workers, and free food' on the waterfront, and those of the World War period, have declined, but fishing schooners and freighters from many countries can still be seen almost any day discharging or taking on cargo. At several wharves, gleaming cargoes of fish, one of which may be the spectator's lunch in some Portland restaurant, are taken out daily from the laden boats while flocks of gulls hover and flutter about waiting for scraps. Fussy little Casco Bay steamboats have replaced the packets and steamers of about a dozen companies that once plied between Portland and American and European ports. Naval vessels are occasionally berthed at a Portland pier. The ends of many of the wharves are more than a quarter of a mile away from the original shoreline, yet the essential flavor of old Portland, its history, and the dependence upon its position as a seaport, can best be sensed by visiting the waterfront.

At the wharf of the Casco Bay Lines are the little white steamers plying between Portland and island villages and summer resorts (*see Island Tours*).

R. from Commercial St. on Market St.; L. from Market St. on Middle St.

15. The *Old Post Office Building* (1871), cor. Middle and Exchange Sts., an elaborate marble structure with a Corinthian portico, was Portland's third post office on this site, the two preceding it having been destroyed by fire. In its day it was considered the finest of the city's buildings. Portland's (or Falmouth's) first post office was created in 1775 by Benjamin Franklin, Postmaster General of the United Colonies; Deacon Samuel Freeman, the postmaster, was not, apparently, overworked at his duties, for there was but one mail a week and only 84 letters were received during the first year. The document, signed by Franklin, which

created Freeman a 'deputy postmaster' can be seen in the rooms of the Maine Historical Society. Since January, 1934, when Portland's more capacious new post office was opened at 125 Forest Ave., this building has been occupied by the offices of various Federal bureaus.

Return W. to Monument Sq.

TOUR 2 — 1.7 m.

SW. from Monument Sq. on Congress St.

16. The *Wadsworth-Longfellow House* (1785–86) (*open weekdays 9.30–5; June 1–Sept. 15, adm. 25¢*), 487 Congress St., was the childhood home of the poet, Henry Wadsworth Longfellow. The dignified old house, built by Longfellow's grandfather, General Peleg Wadsworth (*see Tour* 15), was the first brick house in Portland. In 1815, after fire destroyed the gable roof of the original two-story structure, the present third story and hip roof were added. Set back from the street behind its high iron fence, rectangular, solid and simple, it is almost severe in its plainness, its only ornamentation being the Doric portico forming the front entrance. The 16 rooms open to the public are filled with documents, manuscripts, portraits, costumes, household utensils, and furnishings used by the Wadsworth and Longfellow families, items pertaining to early Portland history, and numerous personal belongings and souvenirs of the poet himself. A pleasant shaded garden with quiet walks lying behind the house has been restored and cared for by the Longfellow Garden Society. Although the view of Back Bay that added much to its charm in olden times is shut off by buildings, the garden today is much the same as it was when the poet walked there.

Henry Wadsworth Longfellow was born at the Fore St. home of his aunt February 27, 1807, and lived in the Congress St. house thereafter until he was 14. The poet's formal education began at the age of three, when, still in dresses and accompanied by a Negro servant, he went on horseback to a school on Spring St. Longfellow entered Bowdoin College in 1821, when he was only 14; and a few years after his graduation he became that college's first professor of modern languages. Later he was made a member of the faculty of Harvard University, and from that time his home was at Cambridge, Massachusetts, where he died March 24, 1882. After his death a memorial bust of the poet — the first American to be so honored — was placed in the poet's corner of Westminster Abbey. A replica of the bust is on exhibition at the Museum of the Maine Historical Society.

17. The *Museum of the Maine Historical Society* (*open weekdays 9.30–5; Sat. 9.30–12; adm. free*), at the rear of the Wadsworth-Longfellow House, contains a valuable historical and genealogical library for the use of the society members (*library privileges on request*). In addition to the library there are marked exhibits pertaining to Maine history, local history, and

archeology. The John W. Penny Collection of Indian relics and other articles (dating to the beginning of the 18th century) that belonged to Father Sebastian Rasle (*see Tour* 10) are especially interesting. There are displays of military equipment of the Revolutionary and Civil Wars, as well as documentary facsimiles, ship models, silverware and glassware, textiles, watches, clocks, and lamps and lanterns of other days.

R. from Congress St. on Brown St.

18. The *Birthplace of Cyrus H. K. Curtis* (1782) (*private*), 69 Brown St., a small two-and-a-half-story frame house, unpretentious and weatherbeaten, is identified by a bronze tablet on the door. Cyrus Herman Kotzchmar Curtis (1851–1934), editor, publisher of the *Saturday Evening Post* and other well-known periodicals, and long an active patron of education, music, and culture in the country at large, was for years one of Maine's outstanding philanthropists.

Retrace to Congress St.; L. from Congress on High St. at Congress Sq.

19. The *Cumberland Club House* (1800) (*private*), 116 High St., a Georgian structure in excellent preservation, has been at various times the home of some of Portland's leading families. It was designed from sketches by Alexander Parris, its lines similar to those of the Sweat Mansion (*see below*). Most of Portland's old homes are to be seen on High, Spring, Park, Danforth, and State Sts. within a small radius; they signify the worldly success and the dignified but cosmopolitan culture of the seafaring and trading class of Portland's youth.

20. The *L. D. M. Sweat Museum* (1908) (*open weekdays except Mon.* 10–4.30; *Sun.* 2–4.30), 103 High St., a gallery of ivy-covered yellow brick, was designed by John Calvin Stevens and attached to the rear of the Sweat Mansion (*see below*). It houses such famous works as Gilbert Stuart's portrait of General Wingate, Douglas Volk's portrait of Abraham Lincoln, and paintings by John Singer Sargent, Winslow Homer, and Chester Harding; a collection of paintings chiefly representative of 19th-century artists, outstanding among which are those of Maine's Harry W. Watrous; the Perry collection of 16-century Belgian tapestries; collection of Mexican and Indian potteries; all the work left by Franklin Simmons, famous Maine sculptor of the 19th century; and Paul Akers's marble figure, the 'Dead Pearl Diver,' known to readers of Hawthorne's 'The Marble Faun' (*see The Arts*). The museum holds monthly exhibitions of contemporary paintings, water colors, and prints, an annual photographic salon which is internationally known, and an annual exhibition of the work of local artists. The Portland Society of Art, owner of the museum, conducts in an adjacent building the Portland School of Fine and Applied Arts.

21. The *Sweat Mansion* (1800) (*adm. terms same as above*), cor. Spring and High Sts., is reached from the entrance hall of the Sweat Museum. It is a fine post-Colonial structure with a semicircular porch. It was erected by Hugh McLellan according to plans by Captain Alexander Parris, a distinguished Boston architect who designed several of Portland's

lovely houses of this period. At one time the home of General Joshua Wingate, whose wife was a daughter of General Henry Dearborn, Secretary of War in the Cabinet of Thomas Jefferson, it was known for years as the Wingate House. The mansion was left to the Portland Society of Art by the late Mrs. L. D. M. Sweat on condition that its furnishings, which are of the late Victorian period, be kept intact and unchanged.

L. from High St. on Spring St.

22. The Portland *School of Fine and Applied Art*, left from the Sweat Mansion on Spring St., only school of its kind in the State, holds daily and evening sessions through the academic year with an annual registration of about 65 students (*see Education*).

Retrace to High St.; R. from High St. on Danforth St.

23. The *Storer-Mussey House* (*open*), SW. cor. High and Danforth Sts., is now part of Portland's Children's Hospital, 68 High St., a charitable institution organized in 1908 and open to all children of the State of Maine. The old building of light-colored brick, now considerably enlarged, is a fine example of Federal architecture, presenting one of the best architectural studies of halls and stairways west of Wiscasset. The delicate details of the side-lights and the panels of the front entrance are exceptional, and the doors and fireplaces and the woodwork of the interior are in keeping with the appearance of the exterior. Set above a terraced lawn, it affords an excellent view of the harbor.

L. from Danforth St. on State St.

State Street is Portland's Beacon Street or Fifth Avenue. Here in the wave of prosperity occurring at the turn of the 18th century and the boom following the Embargo depression, the wealthy merchants and retired shipping men built their impressive mansions. In them were held the elaborate social functions of another day. Most of the old State Street houses retain their splendid and enduring charm, however dilapidated they may have become in the course of time, though some few have been unfortunately 'modernized.' Although to the casual visitor most of these historic doors are closed, and the stately interiors are not on exhibition, the graceful porticoes and fine architectural lines are evident. Many State Street homes today retain part of their original landscaped grounds and gardens. In this section are many of the city's finest churches.

24. The *Dole* or *Churchill House* (1801) (*private*), 51 State St., was designed by Alexander Parris for Joseph Ingraham, one of the town's wealthiest and most enterprising citizens. Although converted into a rooming and apartment house in recent years, its classic lines, with applied pilasters and ornamental cornice, are worthy of attention. In this mansion for many years lived one of Portland's famous citizens, William Pitt Preble (1783–1857), jurist, diplomat, and railway president. Under President Jackson he was U.S. Ambassador to the Netherlands; on his retirement from Government service in later life he became president of the new Atlantic & St. Lawrence Ry., and was largely instrumental in making Portland the terminus of the line.

Retrace on State St.

25. The *State Street Hospital* (1834), cor. Danforth and State Sts., formerly the Female Orphan Asylum, was originally the mansion of Captain John Dunlap of the famous Brunswick family, half-brother of Governor Robert Dunlap (*see BRUNSWICK*). Captain Dunlap's daughter Fanny, reared in this gracious home, became the wife of the poet, James Russell Lowell. Later the house belonged to Judge Joseph Howard, Chief Justice of Maine and U.S. District Attorney. Here in 1860, Judge Howard, then Mayor of Portland, entertained the Prince of Wales (King Edward VII).

26. The *Deane House* (1821) (*private*), 106 State St., was originally a joiner's shop with living quarters in the rear. About 1821 it was remodeled. A square hip-roofed frame structure with a long ell extending to the rear, its simple charm stands out in contrast to the more elaborate and ornate appeal of its neighbors. Here in 1825 was born Nathan Webb, a leading jurist of Maine and U.S. Circuit Judge.

27. *Saint Luke's Cathedral* (1855) (*open*), 137 State St., is architecturally one of Portland's finest churches, the work of Henry Vaughan, distinguished English architect who also drew the plans for Saint Stephen's Church in Longfellow Square. The cathedral, of early English Gothic design, is constructed of soft blue Cape Elizabeth ledge stone. Buttresses and copings, door and window sills, are of Nova Scotia freestone, alternating in red and gray. One of the outstanding features is the rose window in the Sanctuary. The reredos, an unusually beautiful native piece of wood-carving, was done by Kirschmeyer, considered the finest wood-carver in the world at the time (1925), under the direction of the noted church architect, Ralph Adams Cram. In the Codman Memorial Chapel (1899) is a 'Madonna and Child,' painted by John La Farge.

28. The *Milliken House* (1802) (*private*), 148 State St., much changed from its original appearance, was built by Neal Shaw, a rope-maker. Until rope-making machinery came into use the strands of hemp, in process of twisting, had to be pulled taut to their required length. The reaches of ground over which the rope was stretched were called ropewalks. Winter St., parallel with State, originated as a ropewalk.

29. The *Old Shepley House* (1805) (*public dining-room*), now the Portland Club, 162 State St., is the best preserved of the State Street houses. Designed from sketches by Alexander Parris for Richard Hunnewell, this three-story post-Colonial mansion was built of brick with frame walls in front and rear. The front doorway that replaced the original one is especially beautiful, with its leaded fan-light and side-lights. Over the door is an interesting Palladian window. The interior of the house has elaborate ceilings, fine paneling, and delicate mantelpieces. Many of the windows retain the original Belgian glass lights, marked with bubbles and other imperfections. On one window on the second floor someone has scratched with a diamond the names 'Lucy,' 'Annie,' 'Nellie,' and 'General George Shepley,' with the date July 19, 1816.

30. The *Mellen-Fessenden House* (1807), now the Monastery of the Precious Blood (*public chapel*), 166 State St., its former post-Colonial charm considerably altered, was built by Prentiss Mellen (1764-1840), statesman, U.S. Senator, and Chief Justice of Maine. In 1848, the house came into the possession of the Hon. William Pitt Fessenden (1806-69), lawyer, politician, and financier, godson of Daniel Webster and brother-in-law of Henry W. Longfellow. He served in the House of Representatives and Senate, and in 1864, was appointed Secretary of the Treasury by President Lincoln. Lincoln called him 'a radical without the petulant and vicious fretfulness of most radicals.' In 1934 the house was made the cloister of the Catholic Monastery of the Precious Blood, and seven Sister Adorers entered the building at the time, not to emerge until death. An eighth has since joined them.

31. The *John Neal Houses* (1836) (*private*), 173-175 State St., are impressively austere structures built of granite blocks. John Neal (1793-1876), prominent Portland lawyer, athlete, and poet, and a prolific writer, built these houses and settled here after an interestingly diversified career during which, at one time, he was self-appointed apostle of American letters in London, having gone there for the purpose of proving that there really existed an American culture. During his later life in Portland he greatly influenced many artistically gifted young people, such as Paul Akers. Number 173 was at one time the home of the Hon. L. D. M. Sweat.

32. The *Longfellow Statue* (1888), Longfellow Sq., occupies a central position at the junction of Congress, State, and Pine Sts. The seven-foot bronze statue, representing the poet seated in an armchair, one hand clasping a roll of manuscripts, is the work of Franklin Simmons (*see The Arts*) and cost $8500. The statue, a faithful portrait, is one of the city's prized possessions.

L. from State St. on Congress St.

33. The *Neal Dow Homestead* (1824) (*private*), 714 Congress St., is the home built by the ardent prohibitionist and author of the old Maine prohibition law, opposite his birthplace, 717 Congress St. The latter house was erected in 1800. Neal Dow (1804-97), through his ceaseless activity, aroused statesmen and citizens all over the world to the social ramifications of prohibition; he inaugurated legislation that in many sections is still the subject of political controversy. His home, a sedate, comfortable-looking brick house, painted gray, is still in the possession of members of the Dow family, and many of the rooms are kept much the same as when the great agitator lived there. On an escritoire still in the library, Dow drafted his famous Maine law, and the original manuscript lies there today. This house, so it is expected, will become a museum in the hands of the Women's Christian Temperance Union of Maine, to the members of which it is already a shrine.

TOUR 3 — 8.6 m.

E. from Monument Sq. on Middle St.; R. from Middle St. on India St.; L. from India St. on Fore St.

34. *Fort Allen Park*, junction Fore St. and Eastern Promenade, affords an exceptional and unobstructed view of Casco Bay and its islands. Fort Allen, named for Commander William Henry Allen of the sloop-of-war 'Argus,' who was killed in action in 1813, was hastily built on the site of previous fortifications in 1814 when it was rumored that a British fleet was approaching Portland. The fort mounted five guns and was manned by regular soldiers and volunteers. In September, 1815, between 5000 and 6000 of the Cumberland and Oxford County Militia were encamped in the vicinity of these fortifications on Munjoy Hill. It was doubtless to these that Longfellow referred in his poem, 'My Lost Youth':

> 'I remember the bulwarks by the shore,
>   And the fort upon the hill;
> The sunrise gun, with its hollow roar,
>   The drum-beat repeated o'er and o'er,
>   And the bugle wild and shrill.'

Fort Allen Park is landscaped with evergreens and other trees, shrubbery, and flower beds. Benches line the cement walks, and a large summerhouse where band concerts are often held during the summer fronts the harbor mouth. Two large Civil War cannon face seaward, and an eroded cannon recovered from the U.S. 'Maine' is mounted in cement on a rough ledge.

L. from Fore St. on Eastern Promenade.

Eastern Promenade, more than a mile long, begins at Fore St. and extends to Washington Ave., ranging in width from over 89 feet to nearly 150 feet. The parkway was laid out in 1836, when it was suggested that scenic drives be built along the heights at both ends of the city. Graceful trees arch above the promenade, and a circular drive has been added to allow the motorist a more leisurely enjoyment of the panoramic view of the outer harbor and Casco Bay.

35. The *First Civic Monument* of Portland, a graceful shaft of granite, rises opposite the eastern end of Congress St. on the promenade. This monument, dedicated in 1882, commemorates George Cleeve and Richard Tucker, the founders of Portland, and records four names the city has borne: Machigonne, Casco, Falmouth and Portland.

L. from Eastern Promenade on North St.

36. *Fort Sumner Park*, 60–80 North St., is the site of fortifications built in 1794 when Congress made an appropriation for coast defense. Named in honor of Governor Increase Sumner of Massachusetts, the fort had little to recommend its site except its elevation; during the War of 1812 it

was found necessary to erect new fortifications near the waterfront. In the spring of 1808 a company of 'sea fencibles' was organized here to 'do military duty at Fort Sumner': sentinels were stationed to watch for fires, and the firing of a cannon was to be the signal for the fire bells' ringing.

37. The *Portland Observatory (not open)*, opposite the junction of North and Congress Sts., rises 82 feet above Munjoy Hill. A heavy-timbered octagonal structure resembling a windmill, with 10-by-14 inch corner posts 63 feet long, it was erected in 1807 and for 116 years did active service in informing the townspeople of approaching ships and noting cases of distress on land and sea. The top of the tower is estimated to be 223 feet above sea level; the builders weighted the cribbing above the sill with 122 tons of stone to hold it secure against Atlantic gales. From the lantern deck of the tower there is an extensive view of the coast from Wood Island, off the mouth of the Saco River, to Seguin, off the mouth of the Kennebec, while inland the Presidential Range of the White Mountains and peaks farther south are visible. A lookout was once on duty from sunrise to sunset, and flags were flown from the observatory to announce homecoming vessels. President James Monroe inspected the tower during his two days' visit to Portland in 1817. The structure was pronounced unsafe in 1923 and since then has been closed to visitors, but observation rooms on the top of some of the high buildings in the downtown section adequately take its place.

R. from North St. on Congress St.; R. from Congress St. on Washington Ave.; L. from Washington Ave. on Baxter Boulevard.

Baxter Boulevard, an automobile route circuiting the Back Bay section of Portland, gives a fine skyline view of the city. The drive passes a sanctuary for migratory game birds, mostly black ducks, and the cove is dotted with flocks at all seasons of the year. City wardens usually have little difficulty protecting these birds, but boulevard residents once, upon investigating the strange actions of several ducks in the cove, discovered a most ingenious poacher. They noticed live birds apparently moored to one spot by a string attached to their mouths. It seemed someone with a fondness for duck and a genius for invention had contrived an elaborate snare; he laid out through the water a weighted string to which was attached a series of smaller strings on floats with baited fishhooks at their ends. The hapless ducks that swallowed the hook and line could only swim around in their usual way within a small radius. A casual observer watching them would suspect nothing amiss. At night the poacher arrived, pulled in his main line, and carried home a fine covey of birds.

At intersection W. end Baxter Boulevard and Forest Ave., straight to Bedford St.

38. The *Deering Mansion* (1804) *(private)*, 85 Bedford St., one of Portland's most beautiful and best-preserved old houses, is particularly interesting locally because it has been continuously the home of the Deering family, descendants of Nathaniel Deering, a shipbuilder, who came

here from Kittery in 1761. The house has become a veritable museum of Portland history. It is furnished much as it was and is kept in the same condition as when James Deering used to sail out to sea from his own wharf in the field below his house, when Back Cove waters extended over the land that is now Deering's Oaks.

L. from Bedford St. on Deering Ave.; L. into Deering's Oaks.

39. *Deering's Oaks*, lying between Deering and Forest Aves., is the largest public park area in Portland. Longfellow found that 'Deering's Woods are fresh and fair,' and so they have remained to this day. Less than a century ago much of the territory now occupied by the Oaks was still part of Back Cove, and a bridge along Forest Ave., built in 1806, spanned the waters directly northeast of the present park site. In 1689 the park was the scene of a long and bloody battle, when Major Benjamin Church and his men succeeded in defending the town and routing a large force of Indians. Deering's Oaks is popular at all seasons of the year. In summer there is swan boating on the pond, tennis and bowling on the green, while in winter the park is a rendezvous for skaters.

R. from Deering's Oaks on State St. to Longfellow Sq.; R. on Pine St.; R. from Pine St. on West St. to Western Promenade.

The Western Promenade, extending along a high ridge from Danforth St. to Arsenal St., is the counterpart of the Eastern Promenade at the opposite end of the city and was planned at the same time. Here is an excellent panoramic view of the Presidential Range and other peaks, South Portland, and Fore River. Directly below the Promenade on St. John St. are the Maine Central R.R. yards and Union Station. Along the parkway stand some of the finest homes of the city, overlooking a rich spread of sward traversed by walks and planted with flower beds, shade trees, and blossoming shrubs.

40. A *Statue of Thomas B. Reed*, executed in bronze by Burr C. Miller, stands midway of the Promenade. In a natural posture 'Czar' Reed dominates the scene here as he often did when ruling the U.S. House of Representatives.

L. from Western Promenade on Bowdoin St.; L. from Bowdoin St. on Clifford St.; L. from Clifford St. on Thomas St.

41. *Williston Congregational Church* (1876), 32–38 Thomas St., is the birthplace of the Society of Christian Endeavor. Here in 1881 the Rev. Francis E. Clark conceived the idea of organizing the young people of the world into one body for greater Christian growth. Twenty years later members of the society in America, Europe, Africa, and Australia joined in placing a bronze tablet over the main entrance of the church in commemoration of the founding of this movement.

OTHER POINTS OF INTEREST

42. *St. Joseph's Academy* (1881) *(open)*, 605 Stevens Ave. (3 *m. west of city*), is one of the State's most distinguished academies for girls. Conducted by the Roman Catholic Sisters of Mercy, its courses of study run

through the primary and high-school grades to special teachers' and business training classes. The enrollment is about 90, not limited denominationally. The extensive grounds of the convent, which includes the academy, formerly the gardens of a large private estate, are of great beauty. St. Joseph's Convent is the mother house of the Sisters of Mercy in Maine.

43. The *Tate House* (1755) (*open on application*), Westbrook St., Stroudwater (2.8 *m. west of city*), is of interest historically and architecturally. Restored by the Maine Society of Colonial Dames, the old house, much of its unusual wood paneling said to have been brought from England, was the home of George Tate, mast agent for the English Navy, who supervised the purchase and delivery of timber suitable for the construction of masts and spars, reserving with 'the King's Mark' trees of the right size and shape, regardless of the owners' wishes. Later he was employed in the same capacity by the Czar of Russia. A son, George Tate, Jr., left this home for the sea and subsequently joined the Russian Navy, spending 50 years of his life in its service and eventually becoming its First Admiral as well as a member of the Imperial Senate. The exterior of this house, said by some to be Portland's oldest dwelling, has never been painted. In the interior, the beautiful wainscoting retains the gloss of its original white paint, and there are fireplaces in nearly every room, one of which, in a tiny attic chamber, was used by slaves. The house overlooks the site of the old mastyard on Fore River.

44. The *Means House* (*private*), 2 Waldo St., Stroudwater, has an interior even more exquisitely paneled than the Tate house. This dwelling with its brick ends and hip roof was built by Major James Means after his return from the Revolutionary War, and it is said that he lavished money on its construction. His prodigality is manifest today in the delicate woodwork, deep windows, and stairways, which have been well preserved.

Points of Interest in Environs:

Casco Bay trips (*see Island Tours*); Cape Elizabeth (*see Tour 1, sec. a*).

WATERVILLE

City: Alt. 95, pop. 15,454, sett. about 1754, incorp. town 1802, city 1883, city charter 1888.
Railroad Station: 50 College Ave., for M.C. R.R.
Bus Stations: Elmwood Hotel, for M.C. Transportation Co. and Triangle Bus.
Airport: Municipal Airport, 3 *m.* from Post Office Sq. on State 11, for B. & M. Airways; reservations at M.C. R.R. Station.

IN TOWN AND CITY

THE peaceful Common before the old Wiscasset Courthouse contrasts sharply with the modern business areas of Maine's cities in this picture group. Yet many Maine towns have not grown so much as to have changed greatly in the past century; many, no doubt, resemble today the Machias here pictured as it looked to the local artist more than eighty years ago. As a matter of fact, the tranquillity of the old Village Green is found in the State's very heart — in the atmosphere of the Bulfinch-designed capitol set in its flowing lawns and beautifully kept shrubbery, in that of the Blaine House, as appropriate a symbol for Maine's tradition of gracious hospitality as the Jed Prouty Tavern and its counterparts have been for years symbols of Maine cheer. Even in the centers of the other large cities there can be found the quality of peace and serenity that is evident in the pictures of the swans at Deering's Oaks and of Lewiston's canal. And, finally, there is no greater feeling of peace to be found anywhere in New England than that which pervades its historic old graveyards, which, more often than not, are the centralizing feature of the small town.

WISCASSET COURTHOUSE

SWANS AT DEERING'S OAKS, PORTLAND

CANAL, ANDROSCOGGIN MILLS, LEWISTON

...D PROUTY TAVERN, BUCKSPORT

ANDROSCOGGIN RIVER AT RUMFORD

EAST MACHIAS, 1855

PHOTOGRAPH OF PAINTING

HEART OF BANGOR

PORTLAND BUSINESS ARE.

OLD CEMETERY AT WALDOBORO

BLAINE HOUSE (GOVERNOR'S MANSION), AUGUSTA

THE CAPITOL AT AUGUSTA

Accommodations: Four hotels.
Information Service: Waterville-Winslow Chamber of Commerce, 13 Appleton St.
Swimming: Municipal Pool, North St.
Annual Events: Winter Carnival, Feb.; Colby College, intercollegiate sports events.

WATERVILLE, lying on a broad terraced plain along the west bank of the Kennebec River at Ticonic Falls, is the seat of Colby College and an industrial center and railroad terminal. The stir of a manufacturing community is leavened by the quiet atmosphere of a college town and of the pleasant residential areas stretching westward to the near-by countryside. Factories lie close to the river, established on those Waterville shores which have witnessed so much in the past: the vivid life of a large Indian village across the river and the solemnities of Indian burial parties on the site of present day Waterville; the struggles of the discontented soldiery at Fort Halifax in the winter of 1755 who, 'being in a manner naked,' waited miserably for shoes, clothing, and supplies to be dragged up-river from Fort Western at Augusta; the shrill echoes from the snorting, puffing river steamers that churned their way to the city a century ago; and the thundering of logs, plunging over Ticonic Falls after their mad dash through the Five Mile Rips above the city, in the great days of the river-drivers.

While the falls of the Kennebec provide power for the operation of Waterville mills, the drainage basins in the vicinity (i.e., those of the Kennebec, Messalonskee Stream west of the city, and the Sebasticook River at Winslow) are equally important in the agricultural life of the region. There are numerous farms in the suburbs that supply dairy and farm produce for the larger city markets, as well as garden crops for local consumption. A worsted and a cotton mill, employing about 875 workers, are two of the city's chief industrial establishments. A shirt factory and an iron foundry, the oldest of Waterville's active industries, employ most of the remainder of the working population.

Ethnologically, Waterville presents an interesting racial grouping somewhat similar to that of other Maine manufacturing towns. Approximately 40 per cent of the population is of English ancestry while another 40 per cent is of French-Canadian, and 15 per cent is of Syrian, descent. The French-Canadians, or Franco-Americans, who have supplied the greatest growth in Waterville's population during the past century, began to arrive in 1827. Later, they came in increasing numbers as the cotton and woolen mills were established. The majority of these people have their own community in the district known as 'The Plains' south of the business district. Although they have retained their language and many of their customs, and have their own churches, parochial schools, and newspaper, the French elements have assimilated the English language and customs, and figure largely in the social, economic, and political life of the city. The Syrian population, concentrated along Front St.

and lower Union St., was first attracted to the city during the latter part of the nineteenth century by opportunities for work on the railroads and in the railroad repair shops.

Waterville's history was nearly identical with that of Winslow until 1802. The Canibas tribe of Indians, maintaining a large village along the banks of the Sebasticook and Kennebec Rivers opposite Waterville long before the coming of the English, held the central territory of the Abnakis and were surrounded by sub-tribes of allied blood. The Jesuits had already begun their successful missionary work among the Indians but a few miles farther north at Norridgewock, penetrating the State from Canada, when the first English trading post was established in 1653 at Teconnet, as the Indians called the Waterville-Winslow region. Successful trading relations were sustained until the outbreak of Indian wars in 1675, and for seventy-five years thereafter the Indians are reputed to have used the first trading post and two successive ones as forts.

The construction of Fort Halifax, forming the frontier and northernmost line of English defense on the river, was begun in 1754. With the fortifications as yet incomplete, Captain William Lithgow wrote Governor Shirley of Massachusetts concerning the state of affairs at Fort Halifax in January, 1755, and reported that 'the men in general seem very low in spirits, which I impute to their wading so much in ye water, in ye summer and fall, which I believe has very much hurt ye circulation of their blood and filled it full of gross humors....' Like the Indian village before it, the fort was strategically placed near the confluence of the Sebasticook and the Kennebec; thus, the Penobscot Indians were cut off from their travel route by way of the Sebasticook and connecting waterways to the Kennebec, and the war council meeting-grounds at Teconnet. The fort also commanded the vital Indian route northward to Quebec by way of the Kennebec and the Chaudiere River. However, despite the hardships and 'gross humors' of the Halifax garrison, the fort was never attacked by French or Indians; it was dismantled, with the exception of one blockhouse, in 1763. During the decade of military occupation, contact was maintained between Teconnet and the settlements to the south by a military (carriage width) road cut through the wilderness to Augusta, and by whale-boat express to Portland. The scattered settlements of the upper Kennebec were too young and unorganized to give much aid during the Revolution, yet the men of Teconnet did assist Benedict Arnold and his force in 1775 when they made their one-third mile portage around Teconnet Falls.

By 1800, it was becoming increasingly difficult to govern satisfactorily

---

WATERVILLE. POINTS OF INTEREST

1. Colby College Campus and Buildings
2. Coburn Classical Institute
3. Mayflower Hill
4. Redington Museum
5. Old Indian Burial Ground
6. Ticonic Falls

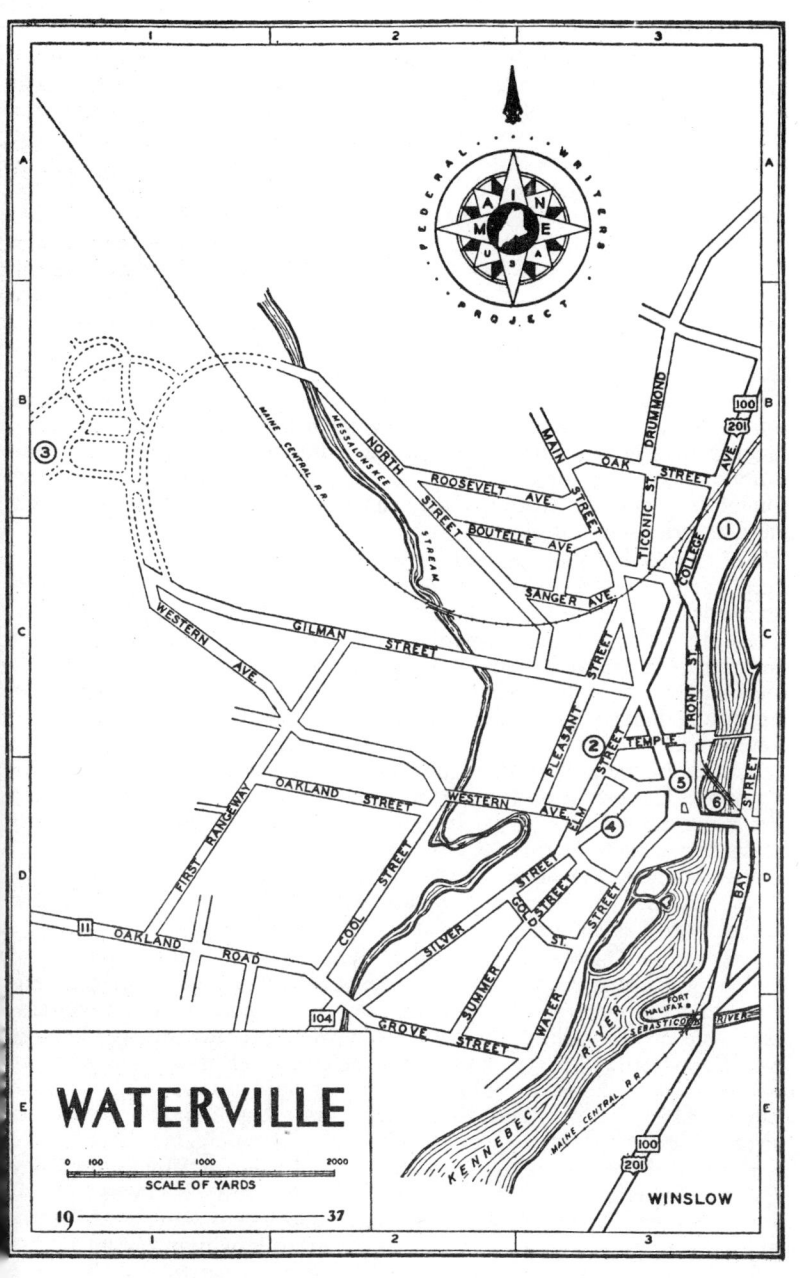

the settlements that had grown up on both sides of the Kennebec, Winslow and Waterville. Church services and town meetings were held alternately, and a double set of officials, including two tax collectors, caused dissension. A petition for separation was presented to the General Court of Massachusetts, and in 1802 Waterville, taking its name from the English 'water' and the French 'ville,' was incorporated as a town, with a population of 800. The new town grew rapidly, contributing towards the early nineteenth-century development of the Kennebec River valley. Passenger and freight service on the river was inaugurated in 1832 by the steamship 'Ticonic,' and competition in river traffic soon became so keen that the fare from Waterville to Boston was only one dollar. Despite the low steamship rate, the building of the Androscoggin & Kennebec Railroad in 1849 and the completion of the railroad to Portland and Bangor six years later precipitated the extinction of water-borne commerce up and down the Kennebec. The city's minor industries and small grist, corn, and lumber mills began to decline in importance after the Civil War. In 1873, five years after the construction of the dam at Ticonic Falls, the first of Waterville's large-scale manufactories was established.

One of the most important events in Waterville's history took place in 1813 when, upon the petitions of prominent Baptists in the State, a charter was granted to the Maine Literary and Theological Institution. Five years later, the 'Rev. Jeremiah Chaplin, with his family and seven students from Danvers, Mass.' ventured up the Kennebec, traveling by sloop to Augusta and thence by long-boats to Waterville, and began the theological department of the institution; and thus the nucleus of Colby College was formed. The power to bestow degrees was granted by the legislature in 1820, and the following year the name was changed to Waterville College. The theological department was short-lived, having been discontinued after 1825. In gratitude for a gift of $50,000 and other benefactions from Gardner Colby, a Boston merchant and prominent Baptist layman, the name of the college was changed to 'Colby University' in 1867. It became co-educational in 1871, and as such is now a small liberal arts college of about six hundred students.

The roster of Colby College graduates is distinguished for its list of seventy-one foreign missionaries in addition to thirty-nine college presidents, and numbers of ambassadors, generals, Senators, and Congressmen. One of the earliest of Colby's noteworthy graduates was George Dana Boardman (1801–31), a pioneer missionary to Burma and one of the two members of the college's first graduating class in 1822. Elijah Parish Lovejoy (1802–37), a graduate in 1825, was a prominent newspaper editor, strongly anti-slavery in his views and a courageous advocate of freedom of the press. First in Missouri and then in Illinois, Lovejoy expressed his convictions in the face of threats and mob violence. Shot by a mob of pro-slavery rioters in Alton, Illinois, twenty-four years before the outbreak of the Civil War, his death aroused widespread attention in the North and made Lovejoy one of the earliest martyrs in the cause of freedom for slaves. Benjamin Butler, Civil War general, Governor of

Massachusetts, and a figure in National politics, was graduated with the Colby Class of 1838.

The activities of several Waterville citizens have supplemented the cultural life of a college town. Robert B. Hall (1858–1907), a native of Bowdoinham and one of Maine's most prominent musicians, became a Waterville resident in 1890. Hall's compositions include about seventy-five band marches, many of which are played all over the country. Samuel Francis Smith (1808–95), at one time pastor of the First Baptist Church, Waterville, and professor of modern languages at Colby, wrote the verses of the anthem *America*, the tune of which he found while glancing through a book of German melodies; the melody itself is identical with that of the English 'God Save the King.' Professor Smith also composed 'The Morning Light Is Breaking.'

TOUR — 3.5 m.

N. from Post Office Sq. on College Ave.

1. *Colby College Campus and Buildings* (*information and directions at college library, first floor, Memorial Hall*) lie along the east side of College Ave., opposite and facing the M.C. R.R. Station.

At the southern end of the campus is *Memorial Hall*. Erected (1869) in honor of the Colby students killed in the Civil War, and allegedly one of the first Civil War memorial buildings in the North, the rubblestone and granite hall was designed by Alexander R. Estey of Boston. The style is modified Norman. On the second floor a reproduction of the 'Lion of Lucerne,' sculptured in marble by Millmore, surmounts a polished slab bearing the names of Colby's Civil War dead. The building contains many portraits, sculptures and objects of historic interest. Memorial Hall is now used as a library and chapel.

North of Memorial Hall lies *South College* (1821), the oldest campus building. A bell hanging in the hall was cast at the Paul Revere foundry in 1824. Among the several college legends associated with the bell is one concerning its travels. The bell was once removed by college students, shipped by freight collect to Harvard, and thence by the same means to the University of Virginia; the Virginia students in their turn dispatched it to Her Majesty, Queen Victoria, via New York, where it was finally traced by Colby authorities as it rested on a wharf preparatory to being loaded aboard a sailing packet.

Champlin Hall (1836), next north of South Hall, a square, plain red-brick structure typical of early nineteenth-century college buildings, was designed by Thomas U. Walter, architect for the Capitol extension, Washington.

North College (1822), north of South Hall, is a fraternity house. Like South College and Champlin Hall, North is a simply designed, two-story building of red brick, with stone and wood trim.

Northwest on the campus is *Coburn Hall* (1872), which houses a mounted collection of local birds, Maine minerals, and rocks. The two-story stone building is of modified Norman style and has a cupola.

Numerous residential halls, dormitories, and fraternity houses are in the vicinity of the campus, particularly along College Avenue.

Retrace to Post Office Sq.; R. on Elm St.

2. *Coburn Classical Institute*, Elm St., is a private college preparatory school founded in 1829 as Waterville Academy, and maintained under the auspices of Colby College until its incorporation under its own name in 1901. In 1883 Governor Abner Coburn of Skowhegan gave the present school building as a memorial to his brother and nephew. The red-brick building of indeterminate architectural design is surmounted with a tower. A circular dome was added in 1893 and equipped as an astronomical observatory.

Retrace to Post Office Sq.; L. on Gilman St.

3. *Mayflower Hill,* the site of the new Colby College Campus comprises 500 acres of land presented to the college by the citizens of Waterville at a cost of $100,000. The present campus, having become so restricted that expansion is impossible, is to be relocated on the northern and eastern slopes, which command views of the city, of Mt. Blue to the west and adjoining summits, and Messalonskee Stream to the southwest. Landscaping has begun with the assistance of the Works Progress Administration, although the construction of the new college buildings, at an estimated cost of $3,000,000, has not yet been started (1937). The new buildings, featured by a library with a 180-foot tower which is to be illuminated by flood lights, will be of modified Georgian Colonial design.

Retrace to Junction of Gilman St. and Western Ave.; R. on Silver St.

4. *Redington Museum (open weekdays except Mon.* 8–12, 2–4), 64 Silver St., presented to the Waterville Historical Society in 1927, was built in 1814 by William Redington, a Revolutionary soldier who underwent the hardships of the winter at Valley Forge. It is a white frame two-story Colonial building, with green shutters and granite foundation. On the front of the house, four Ionic columns support a portico with an ornamental balustrade. A few pieces of furniture that belonged to the grandfather of the builder have been retained. Museum pieces exhibited include Wedgwood ware, a watchman's rattle used in Boston when the Common was still a cow pasture, wood from the Connecticut Charter Oak, and a number of old maps and books.

R. from Silver St. on Main St.

5. An *Old Indian Burial Ground* once extended from what is now Temple Street to the site of the Lockwood Cotton mills. In 1905 six skeletons were unearthed at the junction of Main and Water Streets, while in the same year the remains of an Indian, buried in a sitting position, numerous implements and about two quarts of copper beads, were found when the foundations for the Crescent Hotel block were being prepared.

L. from Main St. to Ticonic Bridge.

6. *Ticonic Falls*, prominent in Waterville's history and industrial growth, are visible from Ticonic Bridge between Waterville and Winslow. Since the first bridge was thrown across the Kennebec at this point in 1824, the destructive force of flood waters has necessitated either total or partial reconstruction of the bridge on six occasions.

Points of Interest in Environs:

Fort Halifax, 1.1 *m.*, Winslow (*see Tour* 10); China Lake, 8 *m.*, China (*see Tour* 13).

III. HIGH ROADS AND LOW ROADS

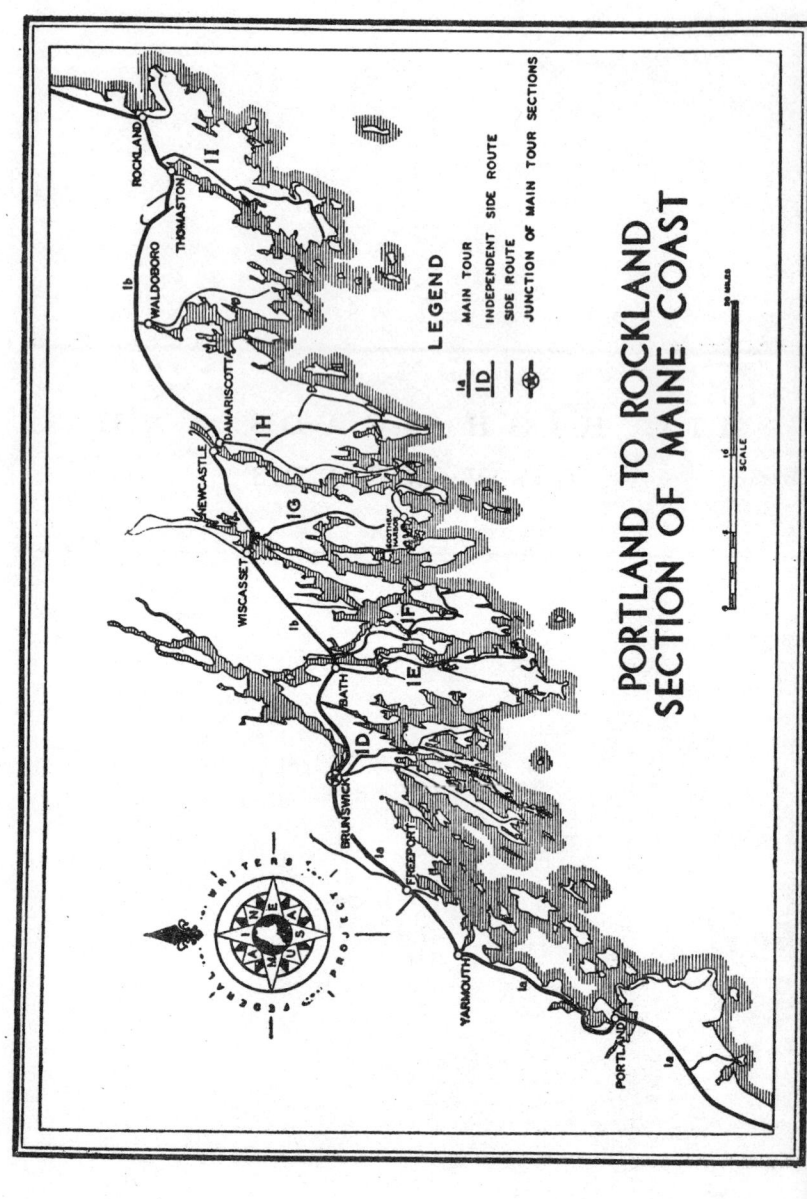

TOUR 1: *From* NEW HAMPSHIRE LINE (*Portsmouth*) *to* CANADIAN LINE (*Clair, N.B.*), 551.8 *m.*, US 1.

Via (*sec. a*) York Corner, Wells, Kennebunk, Biddeford, Saco, Portland, Falmouth Foreside, Yarmouth, Brunswick; (*sec. b*) Bath, Wiscasset, Thomaston, Rockland, Camden, Belfast; (*sec. c*) Searsport, Winterport, Hampden, Bangor, Brewer, Lucerne-in-Maine, Ellsworth; (*sec. d*) Cherryfield, Machias, Robbinston, Calais; (*sec. e*) Woodland, Danforth, Hodgdon, Houlton, Littleton, Bridgewater, Mars Hill, Presque Isle, Caribou, Van Buren, Fort Kent.

Hard-surfaced roadbed, three-lane at southern end. Northern sections sometimes impassable during winter storms.

US 1 in Maine runs close to the coast from one end of the State to the other, turns north along the Canadian boundary, and finally doubles back west along the St. John River. It runs through resort areas, rolling and rocky farm land, through primitive forests, and along the banks of broad rivers; it crosses high hills — locally called mountains — and blueberry plains. It connects the two ends of the 2500-mile coast line, which are but 225 miles apart by air line. It is this lower part of the route that is most frequented; the broken and jagged coast has a picturesque charm that has made it a favorite with summer travelers. South of Maine, land and sea have few rigid boundaries; the waves encroach and retreat, the land is washed away and built up. But on the Maine coast land and sea meet abruptly; that old devil sea at times comes dashing in as though it had been gathering force halfway around the earth to break the stubborn, granite headlands; it attacks with a roar, retreats, and returns to attack again.

There are two coasts of Maine. The coast known to most visitors has spruce-tipped hills and hard beaches dappled with the red, orange, green, blue, and white raiment of visitors, blue-green waters broken by tilting sails and the wakes of speeding motorboats, and a brilliant blue sky. The inhabitants of this land work night and day running hotels, boardinghouses, tourist camps, and lunch stands, piloting fishing and sightseeing boats, trying in a brief season to earn the wherewithal to keep their families during the rest of the year.

The second coast of Maine is for four or five months muffled in snow; travel is at times difficult and most hotels and many of the rooms in homes are closed. But this Maine has its own charm. The rural inhabitants, even though striving to add to their limited incomes, have time to relax and they accept the comparatively few visitors as members of their families, telling them long stories of grandfathers and uncles who never returned from the sea, of the great-aunt who heard voices, and other tales characteristic of a country that part of the year has almost pioneer isolation. There are other rewards for the visitor who comes to this coast out of season. The chowder and baked beans, made in family

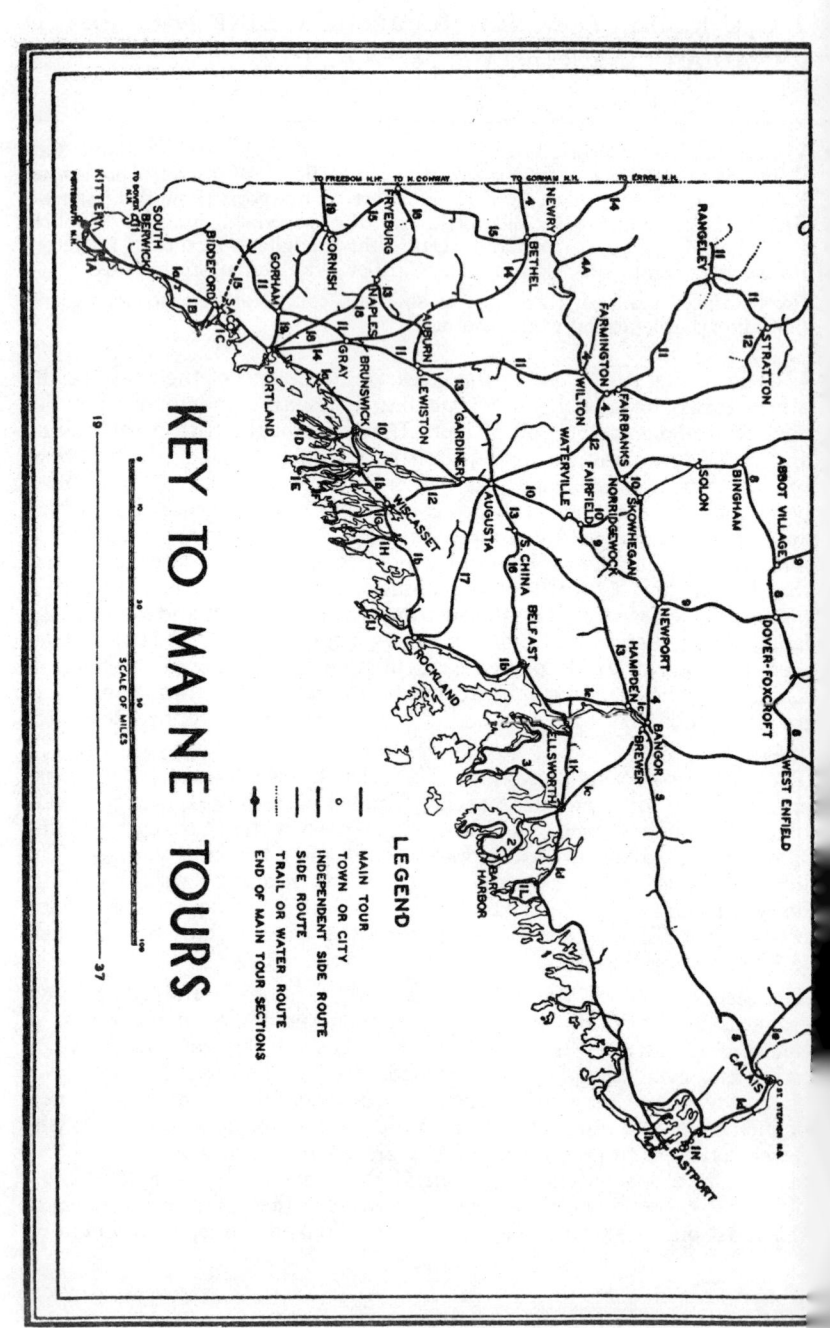

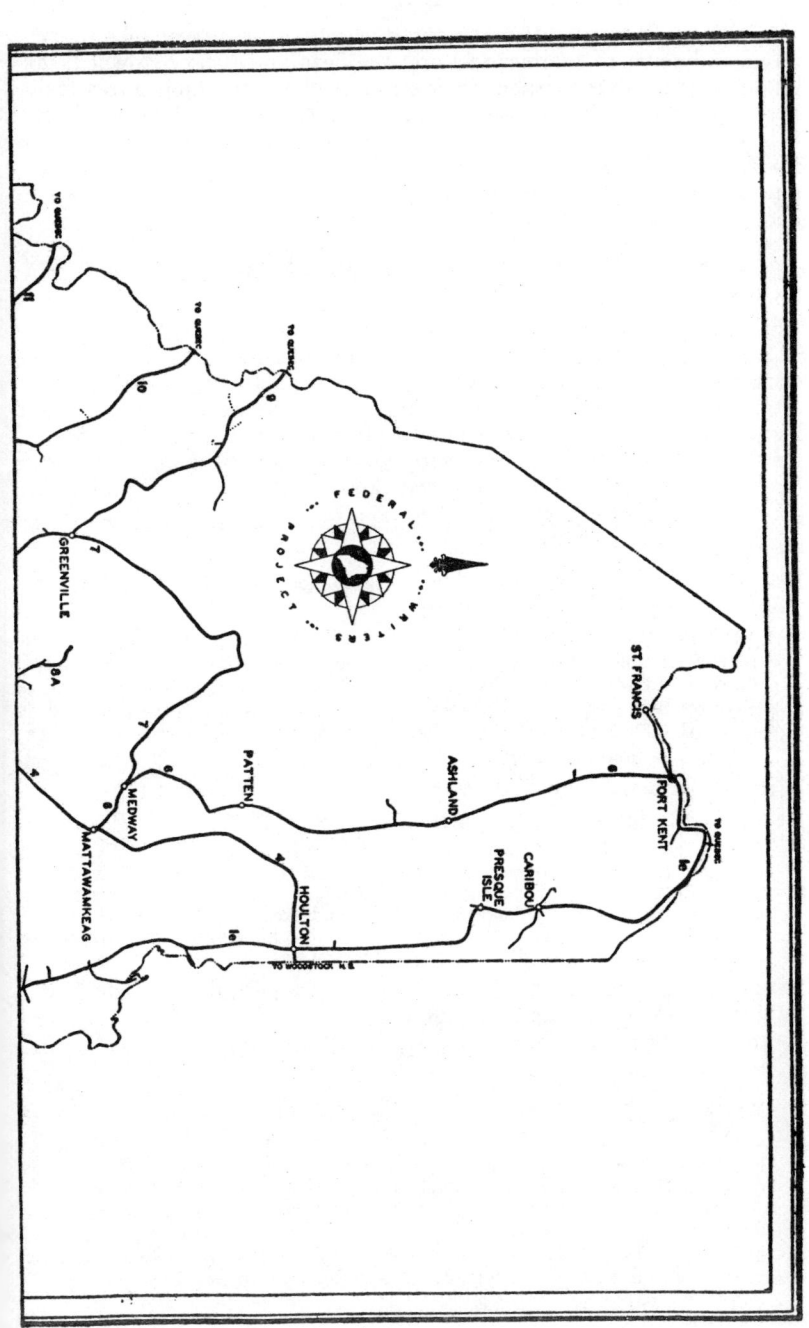

quantities and eaten after strenuous climbs over snowy hills, have a flavor unknown to summer visitors; the headlands, snow-crowned, take on an icy glaze that sharpens their strange silhouettes; and the sea makes acrobatic assaults that cause the very rocks to tremble. But the glory of this Maine is its sky, unreal saffron after the gray light that comes before the dawn, blue as Persian tiles for a brief time at midday, and an unearthly pale green streaked with rose in the late afternoon, turning the snow pale heliotrope with purple shadows.

Sec. a. NEW HAMPSHIRE LINE (Portsmouth) to BRUNSWICK, 76.9 m.

This section of US 1 is the main artery of entrance and exit from the State of Maine. The southern part runs through pleasant farm lands broken occasionally by pine groves, with open ocean (R) never far distant and often visible across wide stretches of marshland. Side routes branch (R) to historic and scenic spots on coastal peninsulas where the inhabitants are for the most part descendants of early fishermen and seamen, gaining their livelihoods from the summer colonists and tourists.

US 1 crosses the New Hampshire Line, 0 *m.*, in the center of the Portsmouth-Kittery Memorial Bridge.

Left at the east end of the bridge is a granite monument with a bronze plaque bearing the following inscription:

> THE PROVINCE OF MAINE. Originally extending from the Merrimac to the Kennebec Rivers, was granted Aug. 10th 1622 to Sir Ferdinando Gorges and John Mason, by The Council for New England, established at Plymouth in 1635 when Gorges received the Eastern portion extending from the Piscataqua to the Kennebec, which thereafter retained the original name of the Province of Maine.

Right at 0.5 *m.* is a junction with a tarred road (*see Tour 1A*).

At 6.7 *m.* is a junction with a tarred road.

> Left on this road is the *McIntire Garrison House* (*private*), 3.7 *m.* (L), built between 1640 and 1645 by Alexander Maxwell and restored in 1909 by John R. McIntire. As was customary in early garrisons, the second story overhangs the first so that beleaguered defenders could pour hot pitch and grease upon the enemy below. The building is constructed of heavy timbers interlocking at the corners and sheathed on the outside with weather-beaten shingles.

YORK CORNER (alt. 60, York Town, pop. 2538), 6.9 *m.* The Maine Publicity Bureau Information Building is R.

At 10.6 *m.* is a junction with State 1A (*see Tour 1A*).

CAPE NEDDICK (alt. 50, York Town), 10.8 *m.* Noticeable in this area are the well-built stone fences and rolling farm lands of southern Maine, with rock outcroppings typical of the New England glacial terrain.

> Right from Cape Neddick, on a winding gravel road; right at 0.5 *m.* and again right at 0.9 *m.*; the road passes through heavily forested country broken by summer estates and has splendid vistas of the ocean. The coast line becomes more rocky as the tip of the cape is reached.
>
> At 3.2 *m.* is the *Episcopal Memorial Stone Church* with bell in an arch of the roof over its entrance. The church stands on a cliff overlooking the sea.

Tour 1: From Portsmouth to Clair

At 3.3 *m.* is a trail to *Bald Head Cliffs*, against which the surf pounds continuously.

At 3.7 *m.* is the entrance to the *Ogunquit Cliff Country Club.*

At 5 *m.* is the junction with a road (R) leading 0.2 *m.* to *Perkins Cove* and its art colony. Grouped about the art school are small individualistically decorated cottages. The village abounds with art and antique shops and has several gaily decorated Chinese restaurants.

At 5.9 *m.* is the junction with US 1 in OGUNQUIT (*see below*).

At 12.8 *m.* (L) on a hill is a revolving *Airplane Beacon.*

At 14.1 *m.* (R) is the new *Ogunquit Playhouse* (*see below*).

At 14.5 *m.* is a junction with Agamenticus Road.

Left on this road is a *camp site,* 5.7 *m.*, at the foot of *Mount Agamenticus* (alt. 692), where the Indian 'Saint' Aspinquid was buried. This, the highest of the hills in this relatively low area, long used as a point of navigation in the days of square-riggers, is still so used by coastal vessels. A 15-minute climb from the camp site along a bridle trail leads to the *Fire Lookout Station,* from which is an extensive view of the sea in one direction with *Boon Island Light* in the distance.

According to tradition, in April, 1682, the 'Increase,' a trader between Plymouth and Pemaquid, was wrecked on an offshore island, its only survivors, three white men and one Indian, existing as best they could on the rocky shores. They were nearly ready to give up hope of rescue when one day in May they saw smoke rising from the summit of Agamenticus. This smoke was that of the burnt offerings of hundreds of Indians from all over Maine, converts of Aspinquid, who was a disciple of John Eliot; they had brought deer, moose, fish, and even rattlesnakes to sacrifice in the flames to the memory of their departed leader. Heartened by the smoke that indicated the presence of people on the mainland, the castaways gathered driftwood and themselves built a huge fire which attracted rescuers from the mainland. In gratitude for their salvation, it is said, the men named the island Boon. Boon Island Light was erected here in 1811.

OGUNQUIT (alt. 60, Wells Town), 14.9 *m.*, noted for many years only as a fishing village in a particularly beautiful situation, now has 16 hotels and is known for its colony of artists and actors.

The summer theater group, one of the largest in Maine, has been under the direction of Walter Hartwig for several years, and has nationally known stage and screen stars as guest artists. During the season a new play is presented each week. The Workshop, an interesting development that attracts students of the theater from all sections of the country, makes several presentations during the summer.

Among the many recreations here is fishing for tuna (*see Sports and Recreation: Salt Water Fishing*), which has become popular along the southern Maine coast in recent years.

At Ogunquit is the junction with a branch road to Cape Neddick (*see above*).

Between Ogunquit and Wells are (R) many glimpses of sand dunes, beaches, and the ocean. This section of US 1 is highly commercialized, appealing to tourist trade with road stands, restaurants, and cabins.

The *First Congregational Church,* 18.6 *m.* (L), stands on the site of the first church building in Wells, which was organized about 1643 by the Reverend John Wheelwright, who shared the beliefs of Anne Hutchinson, the English nonconformist. Wheelwright, who had been exiled from Massachusetts, settled at Exeter, but, when that was declared to be under the jurisdiction of Massachusetts, he migrated to this town with his family. About 1646 he made his peace with Massachusetts and returned to Boston. While a student at Oxford University he was apparently notable as an athlete, for Oliver Cromwell, his classmate there, said later in life that he had never felt as much fear before any army as before Wheelwright in competitive sports. The church he helped build at Wells was burned by the Indians in 1692.

At 18.8 m. is the junction with an improved road.

> Right on this road to WELLS BEACH (alt. 20, Wells Town), 1 m., a popular resort with a good bathing beach.

At 19 m. (R) is the *Joseph Storer Garrison House* (*private*), where 15 soldiers withstood a 2-day siege by 500 French and Indians in 1692. It is a weather-beaten, yellow, two-and-a-half story structure with a foundation of granite.

WELLS (alt. 50, Wells Town, pop. 2036), 20 m., is a small settlement in one of Maine's oldest townships. Covering a large area that originally included Kennebunk, the town was often the center of hostilities during the Indian wars which raged intermittently between 1650 and 1730. The names occurring most frequently in accounts of early Indian warfare are the names still most commonly heard in the town today. For most of its existence, farming has been the chief means of livelihood for the inhabitants. Increasing numbers of tourists and summer residents have afforded a large market for local garden produce.

The *Lindsey Tavern* (1799), 20.2 m. (R), now a tourist home, was a stagecoach stop on the old post road. Some of the original features of the interior, including stencilled wallpaper in the entrance hall, a Dutch oven in the dining-room, and hand-made door hinges, have been retained.

At 21.8 m. is the junction with State 9 (*see Tour 1B*).

KENNEBUNK (alt. 20, Kennebunk Town, pop. 3302), 25 m., is notable for its fine elms. The town, settled about 1650, was for nearly a century in almost constant dread of attack by Indians. By 1730, shipbuilding had begun along the Mousam River. This industry and an active trade with the West Indies made Kennebunk a town of importance until the beginning of the Revolutionary War. Soon after the Revolution, the Mousam River was again utilized in the development of industry. Small mills sprang up along its banks; shoes, twine, and lumber are still manufactured here. Kennebunk has one of the few municipally owned light and power plants in the State.

The *Storer House* (*private*), first house (R) on Storer St., was the home of General Joseph Storer, Revolutionary soldier and personal friend of Lafayette. This large, yet simple, structure is representative of the excellent taste in home building that characterized the post-Revolutionary period.

Kenneth Roberts, author of 'The Northwest Passage,' and other historical novels, was born in this house. Just beyond (R) is the spreading

Tour 1: From Portsmouth to Clair

Lafayette Elm, under which the French hero stood during the reception given in his honor in 1825 by the people of Kennebunk. The tree has grown so large that it has been necessary to prop up several of its massive limbs.

The *Bourne Mansion* (*private*) (1815), second house (L) on Bourne St., is a square three-story structure with four chimneys, two at each end of the building. The principal entrance, facing the garden, has a fan-light of thick leaded glass, a motif that is repeated above in the second-story window. Outstanding features of the interior are the curved staircase and the fine paneled fireplaces.

Five *Elms* (R), on Main St. near Fletcher St., are believed to have been set out on the day of the battle of Lexington. Directly back of the fourth elm is the *Nathaniel Frost House*, one of many fine homes built by prosperous merchants and shipowners in the town's period of greatest affluence.

The *First Parish Unitarian Church* (L), at the north entrance to Kennebunk village, was built in 1774 and remodeled in 1803. The fine steeple surmounts a three-story tower with front windows; over the open belfry is a four-faced clock which is beneath an octagonal lantern cupola with elliptical openings. In 1803 a bell cast in the Paul Revere foundry was placed in the steeple.

Right from Kennebunk on State 35 at 0.1 *m.* is the *Robert Lord House* (1800–03), similar in formality and dignity to the Sewall House, of the same period, in York. It is a massive, two-story, rectangular structure with a low hip roof and parapet rail. The symmetrical façade is finished with carefully matched siding simulating stone, and is broken by the lines of slender Doric pilasters, by a slightly projecting central pavilion with crowning gable pediment, and by a narrow belt course at the second-floor level. The elliptical fan-light of the entrance doorway and its dark louvred shutters are repeated in a large sentinel window in the pediment. In the second story is a triple rectangular window, its sections separated by slender paneled pilasters. The wall openings are framed with an unusually fine trim. The design of the parapet rail, although a trifle light in the absence of the usual corner posts, is notable for its delicately turned balusters. An older house (about 1767) forms a rear wing.

The *Taylor House* (1795–97), adjoining the Lord House, is notable for its three exterior entrances. Of similar proportions and detail, these doorways are designed with flanking pilasters, semicircular fan-lights, and crowning pediments. The interior is decorated with unusually fine putty-stucco ornament — a characteristic medium of the period used in simulating 'carved' ornament on flat surfaces.

At 0.6 *m.* is the junction with a tarred road.

Right here to a field road, 1 *m.*, leading R. to a granite monument marking the *Site of Larrabee Garrison House* (1720), overlooking Mousam River. A bronze bas-relief on the monument depicts the garrison within whose walls were five houses.

On State 35 at 1.2 *m.* is the yellow brick *Wedding Cake House* (*private*), one of the most extraordinary relics of the scroll-saw era extant. The house, apparently built some time before the decorations were added, is a square, two-story structure of good proportions with a central doorway and, above, a graceful Palladian window. At the corners have been added series of slim, elaborately ornamented wooden pinnacles that rise several feet above the low roof; these are duplicated on each side of the entrance and, in miniature, in front of a trellised canopy over the steps that lead to the doorway. In between these pinnacles at the tops of the first and second stories, has been suspended an elaborate tracery, raised to Gothic peaks over the entrance canopy and the Palladian window; the effect is that of the paper lace mat that is fastened above the old-fashioned valentines. A long barn, touching the rear of the house on the right, also has pinnacles and its small high windows are outlined by large wooden arches. A local legend — which, as S. Weir Mitchell said of the average family tree, is more genial than logical — is that the decorations were added by a sea captain whose bride had been deprived of her large wedding cake by his being ordered hastily to sea in an emergency.

Between Kennebunk and 30.6 *m.*, US 1 follows the post road established for early mail carriers.

BIDDEFORD (alt. 80, pop. 17,633), 33.6 *m.* The twin cities of Biddeford and Saco (*see below*), on opposite banks of the Saco River, are united historically, industrially, and socially. As a unit, they rank second in industrial importance in Maine; Biddeford is the industrial part of the union, Saco being predominantly residential. The population, strongly Franco-American, is employed in the three large textile and textile-machinery mills and the several smaller manufactories.

As far as is known Richard Vines was in charge of the first company of Englishmen to explore the site of Saco; he had been sent out from England in 1616 by Gorges, the most enthusiastic of the English promoters of settlement at the time, and others whom Gorges had interested in the enterprise (*see Tour 1B*). In 1629, Saco was granted to Thomas Lewis and Richard Bonython and a permanent settlement was made shortly thereafter.

It is said that about 1675 some drunken sailors, rowing in the river, saw an Indian woman and her infant in a canoe near-by, and determined to test a tale they had heard to the effect that Indian offspring swam from birth by instinct. They overturned the canoe; the woman reached the shore safely, but the child died a few days later as the result of the experience. Unfortunately for the settlers, the child was the son of Squando, an Indian leader, who executed terrible revenge on the whites.

The *Pepperell Manufacturing Company Plant* (*visited by permit*) (R) at 170 Main St., an industry established in 1845, occupies an area of 56 acres and manufactures nationally advertised cotton products.

The *Saco-Lowell Company Plant* (*visited by permit*), left of Main on Smith St., has built textile machinery for more than 100 years.

The *York Manufacturing Company Plant* (*visited by permit*), Main St. on Factory Island between Biddeford and Saco also manufactures textiles.

The *Lafayette House*, 20 Elm St., is a square, yellow, three-story house with a hip roof. It is on the property of the Diamond Match Company.

In Biddeford is a junction with State 9 (*see Tour 1B*).

SACO (pro. *Saw'kō*) (alt. 60, pop. 7233), 34.5 *m.*, is at a junction with State 5 (*see Tour 15*) and State 9 (*see Tour 1C*).

The *Cyrus King House*, 271 Main St. (R), now the rectory of Holy Trinity Roman Catholic Church, was built in 1807 by Cyrus King, member of the Scarboro family that produced the first Governor of Maine. A later occupant of the house was Horace Woodman, the inventor, who in 1854 devised the self-stripping cotton card and many other textile manufacturing appliances.

TOUR 1: From Portsmouth to Clair

Lyman Beecher Stowe, a grandson of Harriet Beecher Stowe, was born in Saco when his father was minister of the *First Congregational Church*, cor. Beach and Main Sts.

York Institute (*open weekdays* 1–4), 375 Main St., a small brick building erected in 1928, contains a collection of Colonial costumes and furniture, paintings, statuary, Maine minerals, Indian relics, and historical documents.

Thornton Academy, 438 Main St., a co-educational school of high standing in general preparatory courses, was founded in 1811 and now has 200 students.

North of Saco the wide highway passes through open hill country with many tourist camps, lunch stands, and filling stations along the way.

DUNSTAN (alt. 50, Scarboro Town), 40.2 *m.*, is at the junction with State 9 (*see Tour* 1C). Opposite the junction is (L) the *St. Louis School for Boys* conducted by the Sisters of Charity. Large residences in this vicinity have been converted into tourist homes and inns that advertise 'New England Shore Dinners' — steamed and fried clams, lobster stew, boiled and broiled lobster.

North of St. Louis School is (L) the *Scarboro Police Barracks*.

The highway crosses *Scarboro Marshes*, where underlying quicksands have caused great difficulties in road construction. Asphalt paving has been used, without cement surface, pending establishment of a solid base, for the surface invariably settles several inches within a few months after being repaired. In former days large crops of salt marsh hay were gathered on the hundreds of acres of marshland bordering the shore south of Portland. Seven-by-ten-inch oak slabs were fastened to the hoofs of the horses used in haying to keep them from sinking into the ground. Protected by game laws, plover, duck, and gulls feed uninterruptedly on the marshes where they formerly were hunted.

At 41.8 *m.* is the junction with a dirt road.

> Left on this road to *Scottow's Hill*. The first stagecoach road from Boston passed over this steep summit to avoid the marshes near the coast. At 0.6 *m.* (L) is the *King Homestead*, a two-story gable-end house with a long shed at one end.

At 41.9 *m.* (R) is the *Danish Village*, a tourist camp with cabins, patterned after the colorful little homes of a medieval Danish town, grouped about the Raadhus (town hall). Architectural details have been faithfully copied in the hall where meals are served, as well as in the individual cabins.

OAK HILL (alt. 100, Scarboro Town), 43.2 *m.*

> Right from Oak Hill on State 207 to (R) the *Hunnewell House* (*private*), 0.7 *m.*, built in 1684, known as the Old Red House. It stands in a 'heater piece,' a triangular plot of ground at a junction of roads so called in early days when snow-removal equipment, which contained a heater, was stored there. The timbers of this small one-and-a-half-story lean-to dwelling are hand-hewn and wooden-pegged. A trapdoor in the living-room floor leads to a shallow dugout used as a hiding-place during Indian raids.

SCARBORO (alt. 20, Scarboro Town, pop. 2445), 1.2 *m.* Most of the houses in this small village were built and inhabited by seafaring men. The *First Parish Congregational Church* (R), on the site of one built in 1728, is an attractive little white structure with a fan window in the front, and a belfry and spire.

The *Parson Lancaster House* (1766) (*private*), 1.5 *m.* on State 207, is a two-and-a-half-story unpainted dwelling with two huge elms in its front yard. Interesting architectural features include wide roof boards, single board wainscoting, white (pumpkin) pine paneling, HL hinges, hand-wrought latches, knobs, and locks, fireplaces with hand-carved woodwork, and a staircase with delicate balustrade. The floors, ceilings, and unpainted woodwork have the patina of age.

In the *Black Point Cemetery* 1.7 *m.* (L), the dark gray slate stones date back to 1739.

At 3 *m.* a road (L) leads to the popular bathing resort, *Higgins Beach.*

The private *Black Point Preserve and Game Farm*, 3.7 *m.* (R) on State 207, lies opposite the *Black Point Fruit Farm*, which has fine orchards. Small game, such as partridge, pheasant, and rabbit, roam unmolested in the small wooded preserve set aside by local residents.

Massacre Pond, visible (L) at 4.1 *m.*, was so named because in 1713 Richard Hunnewell and 19 companions were set upon near here and slain by a band of 200 Indians.

Opposite the pond is the fairway of the *Prout's Neck Country Club Golf Course* (*private*). At the seventh hole is a marker on the site of the first Anglican church in Maine, erected prior to 1658.

At *Garrison Cove*, 4.8 *m.*, the road emerges from the woods to a cliff from which is a splendid view of the bay with the white sands of Old Orchard Beach gleaming in the distance.

A *Marker* at 5.2 *m.* (R) indicates the spot where Chief Mogg Heigon, subject of Whittier's poem 'Mogg Megone,' was slain in 1677. This marker is at the east end of beautiful Garrison Cove on the site of Josselyn (or Scottow) Fort, headquarters for the defense in the first Indian war. Directly ahead is Black Point, its rugged shore line sweeping westward toward Old Orchard Beach (*see Tour 1C*).

The *Prout's Neck Yacht Clubhouse* (R), 5.1 *m.* on the ledges of the Point, commands a wide view of the Atlantic.

Left from the highway is a path leading to the *Prout's Neck Bird Sanctuary*, given to Scarboro by Charles Homer in memory of his brother, Winslow Homer, the artist.

PROUT'S NECK (alt. 40, Scarboro Town), 5.5 *m.*, is a pretentious summer settlement. Left is the site of the blockhouse where, in 1703, eight men under Captain John Larrabee for several days withstood a siege by 500 French and Indian marauders.

In 1633, Thomas Cammock and his wife Margaret moved from Richmond's Island to Prout's Neck, then called Black Point. Here they were joined by Henry Josselyn and for a short time, in 1638, by his brother John Josselyn. John's account of his visit, published as 'New England Rarities,' repeats stories of sea serpents, witches, revels, etc. Josselyn included a description of the native flora and of the Indians remarking, 'There are many stranger things in the world than are to be seen between London and Stanes.'

At 44.3 *m.* (R) is the old *Plummer House* (*private*), set well back from the street with its side turned to it. It is a one-and-a-half-story, gable-end house with central chimney.

The *Nonesuch River*, 44. 9 *m.*, so named for its remarkably crooked course to the sea, figured prominently in the affairs of Scarboro settlers and is mentioned in many early histories. Because it was impossible to bring

TOUR 1: From Portsmouth to Clair 211

boats of any size up this sharply winding tidal river, a canal was constructed, to follow the general course of the river. Instead of digging the entire canal by hand, the workers made a narrow ditch along the proposed course. The action of the tides carried away the loose soil, finally completing a project that would have required much back-breaking toil. Near the highway bridge, fishermen congregate in May for the annual run of alewives.

THORNTON HEIGHTS (alt. 80, South Portland), 46.1 *m.*, is a small residential community.

At 47.6 *m.* US 1 crosses Fore River, the southern boundary of Portland, on Vaughan's Bridge. Huge oil and gas tanks line the highway on both sides of the river, which separates Portland and South Portland.

At 48.7 *m.* is the junction with Brackett St., Portland.

> Right on Brackett St. crossing the *Million Dollar Bridge*, 0.2 *m.*, with Portland's waterfront (L). SOUTH PORTLAND (alt. 60, pop. 13,840), 0.9 *m.* at the mouth of Fore River, is a residential community, occupied chiefly by people working in Portland. It has several factories, however, among them being the Maine Steel, Inc. (L) on Second St., makers of snowplows and marine hardware.
> Left from Brackett St. on Cottage St. to Broadway, 1.2 *m.* Follow trolley line (L) to Shore Road. At 2.9 *m.* is the main gate (L) of *Fort Preble* (*open*), named for Commodore Edward Preble. It was built between 1808 and 1811 and enlarged during the Civil War. It commands a splendid view of Portland Harbor, the breakwater jutting far into the ocean, with Fort Gorges, an old unused stone fort near-by, and Peak's Island in the distance.
> Shore Road passes many beautiful estates.
> CAPE COTTAGE (alt. 30, South Portland), 4.7 *m.* Left is the northern entrance to *Fort Williams* (*open*), where the U.S. Fifth Infantry has been stationed since 1922. Organized July 24, 1808, the Fifth is one of the oldest Regular U.S. Army regiments. Its motto is 'I'll Try, Sir,' words spoken by Colonel James Miller in the battle of Lundy's Lane, July 25, 1814. During the Philippine insurrection it was stationed in the archipelago; in the World War it did guard duty in the Canal Zone and went to Germany with the army of occupation. Within the fortification near the shore is *Portland Head Light* (1791), the oldest lighthouse on the Maine coast. The white conical tower rises 101 feet above high water. From the hurricane deck of the tower, many of the 222 Casco Bay islands and the Cape Elizabeth shore can be seen. These islands are sometimes called the Calendar Isles because an official English report of 1700 said, 'Sd. Bay is covered from storms that come from the sea by a multitude of Islands, great and small, there being (if one may believe report) as many islands as there are Days in a yr.'
> At *Pond Cove* (L), 6 *m.*, the shore line cuts in nearly to the outer rocks, flinging spray across the highway in heavy weather.
> POND COVE VILLAGE (alt. 100, Cape Elizabeth Town, pop. 2376), 7.3 *m.*, is the center of a large town in which fertile soil is well adapted to the raising of garden truck.
> TWO LIGHTS, 11 *m.* (L), on the rocky point of Cape Elizabeth, is the neighborhood name for a group of cottages, two light towers and a Coast Guard station. There is a light only in the outer tower which is 120 feet high (*open*). The Coast Guard station, established in 1887, serves the coast from the Kennebec River to Biddeford Pool, with a personnel of only 14 men. A man is constantly on duty in the tower to receive distress signals by telephone, radio, or flares. The white Government buildings stand out sharply against the varied green of the shore foliage and of the ever-changing ocean. This exposed point, which bears the brunt of heavy seas after every storm, attracts scores of people who like to watch the magnificent display of surf as the huge waves batter themselves against the ledges.

PORTLAND (alt. 80, pop. 70,810) (*see PORTLAND*), 49.2 *m.* at Longfellow Square, is the point of departure for steamer trips to Casco Bay islands (*see Island Trips*).

Here are junctions with State 26 (*see Tour* 14), with US 302 (*see Tour* 18), and with State 25 (*see Tour* 19).

> Casco Bay (Ind.: *Aucocisco*, 'place of herons') was visited by most of the explorers who came along this coast shortly after 1600; all were attracted by it because of the safe anchorage offered by its deep waters and because the islands gave them places to land where they felt reasonably safe from the inhabitants of the country, on whom they looked with some fear. The islands are now much visited by summer visitors; some are fairly large, some mere dots on the water. On them hang countless legends of castaways, buried treasure, shipwrecks, and Indian gods. Many of the islands bear homely names given by the pioneers who displayed considerable imagination in finding resemblances to objects and animals in the rough profiles — Ram, Horse, Sow and Pigs, The Goslings, Turnip, and Whaleboat, are among them. Others have names derived from events that took place on them, or were given because of animals inhabiting them.
>
> The first settlement in the bay took place in 1623, when Captain Christopher Levett erected a stone house on one of the islands, probably YORK, or House, as it was formerly known.
>
> JEWELL ISLAND, one of the outermost, acquired by George Jewell in 1636, has the usual legend of vast treasure buried in it by Captain Kidd. Treasure-seekers, ignorant of the fact that Kidd never visited this part of the coast, tried every possible device to find the gold and jewels they believed to be there, sacrificing animals, using divining rods, and invoking the help of demented people believed to have second sight. Legends have grown up about the activities of the persistent diggers; one concerns a mysterious stranger who appeared, asking for the help of a skipper residing there. The visitor disappeared without anyone's having seen him leave the island and shortly afterward the captain showed evidence of great wealth; curious neighbors announced that they had seen the imprints of a large chest near a newly dug hole and a later treasure hunter reported the finding of a buried skeleton near-by.
>
> Large PEAK'S ISLAND, near Portland and a favorite resort of residents of that city, has various amusement devices; a number of Portland residents have year-round homes here.
>
> CLIFF ISLAND was the home of men who were accused of wrecking ships by decoying them to the rocks, in order to wreck them.
>
> EAGLE ISLAND, on the outer rim of the bay, was owned by Admiral Robert E. Peary, who made his home on its stony acres for many years.
>
> ORR'S ISLAND, accessible from State 123, south of Brunswick, was the scene of Harriet Beecher Stowe's story, 'The Pearl of Orr's Island.' Mrs. Stowe's former home stands on a hill near the ferry landing.
>
> BAILEY ISLAND, south of Orr's, was the summer home of Clara Louise Burnham of Chicago, who wrote a number of stories about the area.

At 54.8 *m.* is the entrance (R) to *Portland Country Club (open to public)*.

At 55.1 *m.* (L), is a marker indicating the near-by *Site of Fort New Casco*, which, erected in 1698, was also a trading post. The Indians of Maine had at first been very friendly with the English; it was only after they had been repeatedly betrayed, insulted, cheated, and assaulted that they became hostile and vengeful. The French, who have far less race prejudice than the English and therefore manage their relations with people of other races more amicably, soon won the friendship of the Indians and determined to use them in their efforts to drive the English from American

TOUR 1: From Portsmouth to Clair 213

shores. Maine, part of the territory that the French claimed longest, was particularly subject to attack. In 1703, a conference was held with the Indians at Fort New Casco and the settlers hoped for safer times; but within two months another attack came and the fort was the center of defense for the settlements of Casco Bay. The attack of a large force of Frenchmen and Indians was repulsed only by the arrival of an armed vessel. The fort was abandoned in 1716, when Massachusetts thought it was no longer necessary to maintain a garrison here.

The attractive castellated stone edifice (R) is the Episcopal *Church of St. Mary the Virgin*; directly opposite is *Falmouth Town Forest*, a well-kept grove of old pine trees.

FALMOUTH FORESIDE (alt. 100, Falmouth Town, pop. 2041), 57.1 *m.*, is a residential section of fine homes in an agricultural town on the shores of Casco Bay.

Underwood Spring (R), now exploited as a private commercial enterprise, is a natural curiosity, for though it has no perceptible source, it has a large flow of pure water unaffected by drought or freshet. The Abnaki Indians maintained a permanent settlement here, and Waymouth, the English explorer, wrote in his journal that the Indians allowed him to fill his casks at this spring.

Along the route here is an exceptional panoramic view (R) of Casco Bay and its islands.

At 61.4 *m.* (R), in the Westcustogo neighborhood (Ind.: 'clear tidal river'), is a *Burial Ground* dating back to 1732. Just beyond is a group of three large *Old Houses*. The most southerly of the houses is on the site of Royall Garrison House, part of the property purchased by William Royall in 1643. The house behind it stands on the site of the first church of Yarmouth built in 1729. The third house (1769) is on the site of the Loring Garrison of the 17th century.

At 62.3 *m.* is the junction with State 115.

> Left on State 115 is YARMOUTH (alt. 80, Yarmouth Town, pop. 2125), 0.4 *m.* This seaport town on Casco Bay was settled in 1658, laid waste by Indians in 1673, and resettled in 1713. Fishing and crab-meat packing are the major industries, which have supplanted the shipping and shipbuilding of the 19th century.
> *North Yarmouth Academy* (R), on Main St., was founded in 1810.

At 66.8 *m.* is the junction with a local road.

> Left on this road to the *Desert of Maine* (adm. 25¢), 2 *m.*, covering 300 acres and surrounded by forests and green farm lands. Such miniature Saharas are not unusual in coastal areas.
> The first patch of sand, noticed in the latter part of the 19th century, was about 30 feet square. The sand stratum is at present around the 300-acre (1937) area for a radius of 6 miles. In this circle a top layer of loam is either being covered or worn by frequent sandstorms. Some geologists believe the spot covers the bed of an ancient lake, perhaps formed by glacial deposits, for a glint of mica is apparent in the sand which is very fine in texture. Sandstorms constantly raise and lower the desert level as the erosion creeps outward, the sand covering everything in its path, creating 30-foot gullies and high dunes. The tops of trees once 70 feet high appear as bushes, and strangely enough are still alive. Among them is an apple tree which still blossoms and bears fruit.

FREEPORT (alt. 140, Freeport Town, pop. 2184), 68 *m.*, a pleasant, tree-shaded old village, is often referred to as the Birthplace of Maine, because the final papers for the separation of Maine from Massachusetts, which established it in 1820 as an independent State, are said to have been signed here by commissioners from Massachusetts and the Province of Maine, probably in *Jameson's Tavern* (1779), just north of the post office (L).

When Freeport was incorporated in 1789 it was named for Sir Andrew Freeport, the character in Addison's 'Spectator Papers' who represented the London merchant class. Whether the town namer admired Addison or, what is more probable, the prosperous conservative whom he presented, is unknown.

There was a time when Freeport had a prosperous shipbuilding business, but it is now engaged in shoemaking, crabbing, and crab-meat packing. The crab-meat is picked from the shells by groups of young women and shipped in iced cartons.

Freeport, like almost every other old town along this coast, has its story of an Indian attack. In 1756, Thomas Means, living near Flying Point, was surprised in his bed and scalped; his wife and infant son were killed by a single bullet; two other children crept into hiding and escaped. The Indians took Mrs. Means' sister Mary away with them to Canada, where she became a housemaid in the home of one of the French feudal lords. She was later rescued by William McLellan, whom she married.

> Right from Freeport on a dirt road to an old *Cemetery*, 0.6 *m.* (R), that is the burial place of many sea captains and seamen of the area.
>
> PORTER'S LANDING, 1.2 *m.*, the commercial center in Freeport's shipping days, is now a dignified residential section in which the old homes have been entirely modernized.
>
> At 2.7 *m.* is a four corners in SOUTH FREEPORT, the street (L) leading to the village center. South Freeport, at the mouth of Harraseeket River on Freeport Harbor, which is navigable throughout the year, has been a fishing center from its earliest days, assuming its greatest importance between 1825 and 1830 when as many as 12,000 barrels of mackerel were packed and shipped annually. Of late years it has specialized in crab-meat packing. In 1878 the 'John A. Briggs,' one of the largest wooden vessels built on the Maine coast up to that time, was launched here.
>
> Left, beyond the four corners, are the ruins of *Casco Castle*, once a picturesque summer hotel modeled after a medieval stronghold. The tower, all that remains of the hotel, which was burned in 1904, is a round solid structure of field-stone about 80 feet high with walls 3 feet thick. Standing on an eminence overlooking the bay, it has long been a landmark for fishermen.

At 68.9 *m.* is the junction with a dirt road.

> Left on this road is *Shiloh*, 10 *m.* (*services at noon Sun.*), which has received national attention from time to time as the home of the Holy Ghost and Us Society, a religious sect with Adventist beliefs, founded by the Reverend Frank W. Sandford, the 'Elijah' of the early 1900's.
>
> Sandford's cult brought converts from many parts of the world to pour their money into a common fund. Men and women sold their worldly possessions and turned the proceeds over to him. The colony flourished for a time, practicing various crafts. When the world did not end as he had predicted after ordering a

Tour 1: From Portsmouth to Clair 215

ceaseless night-and-day vigil of prayer in the high tower on the main building, Sandford announced that the Almighty had commissioned him to go forth and convert the heathen. When he prayed for means to accomplish this, a $10,000 check appeared. Forthwith, he purchased a 150-ton sailing vessel, the 'Coronet,' and set sail from Portland Harbor with a flowing beard, purple robe, sailor hat, and Bible underarm. Several voyages were made in various ships without noticeable results. During the last voyage, made in the 'Coronet' in 1912, after many hardships and privations, eight members of the party died of scurvy; when the ship returned to Portland Harbor, Sandford had trouble with the authorities. When he returned to Shiloh, two years later, he found his old power gone, his people scattered, and he subsequently dropped from sight. The buildings, on a high, windswept hill, are unusual. The square, hip-roofed, three-story main structure, on a high foundation, has a large five-story tower on its front, each story of the tower containing a large room and the top floor having protruding bay windows on each side; the tower is surmounted with a high-domed cupola supported by very slender columns. Between the main building and two-story, towered wings are three-story ornamental gateways with arched doors. Broad piazzas with balustrades on the roofs surround the three buildings.

In 1936, after many years of neglect, the place was repaired and the towers regilded. A small group of cultists lives here but does not welcome curious visitors. When rumors reached Portland of renewed activities under the leadership of Sandford's son and of the reconditioning of the 'Coronet,' reporters were sent to investigate; the residents refused to answer questions concerning the whereabouts of the elder Sandford.

Services are held in a well-carpeted room seating 200. During prayer all persons kneel with elbows on chairs, various members introducing the prayers as called upon by the speaker. While visitors are now invited to these services, none may inspect other buildings or the grounds at any time.

BRUNSWICK (alt. 30, Brunswick Town, pop. 7604) (see *BRUNSWICK*), 76.9 *m.*, is at the junction with US 201 (see *Tour* 10).

Sec. b. BRUNSWICK to BELFAST, 79.3 *m.*

East of Brunswick US 1 runs through the old shipbuilding city of Bath, crosses the Kennebec River, and gradually swings northeast to follow the western edge of Penobscot Bay. The countryside is fairly open with distant views of the ocean. Houses belong chiefly to the 19th century and there are few signs of recent prosperity. The area around Camden is particularly beautiful, the hills being covered with the evergreens that are increasingly present as the route moves northeast.

US 1 leaves BRUNSWICK (see *BRUNSWICK*) 0 *m.*

At 0.4 *m.* is the junction with State 24 (see *Tour 1D*).

BATH (alt. 50, pop. 9110), 9 *m.*, named for the ancient city of Bath, England, has a history of almost two centuries of shipbuilding, though its yards turn out comparatively few vessels today. Its heyday was in the wooden-ship era, though the first steel sailing vessel, a four-master, was built here. Naturally, many of its inhabitants have been shipmasters and shipowners, and the older homes are filled with souvenirs from far parts of the earth — printed India linens, teakwood chests, blue and white ginger jars from Canton, and strangely shaped sea shells. During the World War the local yards were active again, attracting several thousand workmen, but the revival was temporary. The chief event in local life still is, however, as it has long been, the launching of a new craft; and the townspeople follow the histories of Bath ships with pride.

Bath Iron Works (*visited by permit*), in the center of the city at Union and Water Sts. below the Carlton Bridge, was founded by General Thomas Hyde after his return from the Civil War. Some fairly large and many small Government vessels have been built here, including the battleship 'Georgia,' cruisers, and lighthouse tenders. Many fine yachts and sailboats have also come from this plant which built the 1937 America's Cup winner, the 'Ranger.'

Near-by are other shipbuilding works that can make any but the largest vessels.

The new *Davenport Memorial Building*, right on Front St., housing the Bath municipal offices, has in its tower a bell cast in 1805 at the Paul Revere foundry. The *Davenport Memorial Museum*, in the building, contains ship paintings and original half-models from which were built famous Kennebec merchantmen and vessels launched in other Maine ports, as well as many exhibits of importance in Maine marine history.

In the beautifully landscaped *City Park*, on Front St., is a cannon taken from the British man-of-war 'Somerset,' which was 'swinging wide at her moorings' in Boston Harbor when Paul Revere made his ride. The cannon was used for the firing of salutes at Bath until the latter part of the 19th century.

The *Apartment House*, 3 North St., corner of Front St., formerly a rather pretentious old home, was between 1915 and 1924 occupied by Madame Emma Eames (1867–   ), the operatic star, and her husband, Emilio De Gogorza, the baritone.

The home of Herbert L. Spinney (*open*), 75 Court St., houses a *Collection of Native Flora and Fauna*. Mr. Spinney was associated with the Smithsonian Institution for many years.

In Bath is the junction with State 209 (*see Tour 1E*).

> Left from Bath on Washington St., at 1.6 *m.* and opposite Harward St., is the *Old Peterson House*, on the river bank. The place is an architectural curiosity that was built (1770) by ship carpenters for the King's timber agent. The mass of the building is broad at the base and narrow at the top; the door jambs, windows, and window frames follow the lines of the house. The front lawn is the site of the dock at which were loaded the tree trunks that had been marked with a 'broad arrow,' indicating that they were sacred to the Royal Navy. These trees were intended for masts and were at least 24 inches in diameter. The resentment of the people of Maine against the commandeering of their best mast pines drove them into the revolt that became a revolution.
>
> Left from Washington St. on Harward St.; at 1.8 *m.* is the junction with High St.; left here to Whiskeag Rd.; right on the latter to (L) the *Stone House* (*private*), 2.1 *m.*, a structure with cathedral-like doors and windows that was erected in 1805 and became the home of Maine's first (1820) Governor, William King. It is said to have been built as a hunting lodge by Englishmen.

East of Bath US 1 crosses *Carlton Bridge* (50¢ *toll*) built in 1927, which spans the Kennebec River. It commands a sweeping view of the river, waterfront, and city.

TOUR 1: From Portsmouth to Clair

The Kennebec is one of the historic rivers of America. It was one of the earliest explored streams on the coast of North America; various adventurers had made fragmentary reports on it before 1600 and Champlain and Waymouth had explored it to some extent before 1606. It was named as one of the boundaries of various large land grants made during the race between the French and the British for control of the continent. In the middle of August, 1607, George Popham and Raleigh Gilbert, commanding the expedition promoted by Sir Ferdinando Gorges and Sir John Popham, sailed up the river, passing the place now spanned by the bridge in their search for a site for the colony (*see Tour 1E*) that was to send fur, sassafras, and other commodities back to England to make fortunes for the London investors. Two decades later it saw a steady stream of traffic to and from the trading settlement at the present Augusta made by the 'Undertakers' of Plymouth, and it was the rich cargoes that came down its waters that saved the Massachusetts settlement from extinction. Since that time the river has been the scene of continuous activity, of log-drives, ship launchings, commercial travel, power development, and, not least important, hunters' and fishermen's treks.

WOOLWICH (alt. 30, Woolwich Town, pop. 671), 10.2 *m.*, is on the east bank of the Kennebec River opposite the city of Bath. Shipbuilding and fishing for shad and sturgeon were the early industries, now replaced by farming, dairying, and orcharding. The canning of corn, peas, and beans is here rapidly increasing in volume.

In Woolwich is the junction with State 127 (*see Tour 1F*).

Left from Woolwich on State 127, to DAY'S FERRY (alt. 20, Woolwich Town), 3 *m.*, is the *Appleton Day House* (R), built in 1777 on the site of the Samuel Harnden blockhouse. It is a two-and-a-half-story frame house with a fireplace in each room. The chimneys and fireplaces are constructed of locally made bricks. There are three cellars under this house; legend has it that an underground passageway extending from the cellars to the river was built for use in times of Indian attack.

Nequasset Meeting-House, 11.6 *m.* (L), the oldest meeting-house east of the Kennebec River, was built in 1757. Here Josiah Winship, the first permanent pastor, was ordained in 1765, when there were but 20 families and only two frame houses in the settlement.

At 14.7 *m.*, is the junction with Montsweag Road, which is unmarked and in poor condition.

Right on this road, at 4.4 *m.*, is a view of *Hockomock Bay*, with its several islands.

At *Phipps Point*, 4.8 *m.* (R), in a private estate, is the site of Sir William Phips' home. Phips was born in Maine in 1651 of a poverty-stricken family and worked as a shepherd and ship carpenter until he was 25, when he went to sea; he learned to read and write in Boston and decided to make his fortune by treasure hunting, managing in 1683 to receive a commission from the English Crown for the recovery of treasure in a ship sunk off the Bahamas. He was successful in this enterprise, receiving £16,000 and a knighthood as his reward. He next commanded an expedition that captured Port Royal without difficulty but his second expedition to Canada failed. Through the wirepulling of Cotton Mather he was appointed Royal Governor of Massachusetts; he lacked the tact and education, however, to enable him to cope with the problems that confronted him and became involved in difficulties that resulted in his recall to England. He died there in 1695 during an investigation of the charges against him.

WISCASSET (Ind.: 'meeting of three tides' or 'rivers') (alt. 50, Wiscasset Town, pop. 1186), 19.3 *m.*, seat of Lincoln County, is a charming town with little more than half the population it had in 1850, when it was still a fairly important port on the west bank of the wide Sheepscot River. Its beautiful old homes, most of which were built by shipping merchants and sea captains, are now occupied in part by artists and writers who have been attracted by the distinctive charm of the place. The town, formerly much larger in area than it now is, was called Pownalborough in honor of Royal Governor Pownal until 1802. Settlement began here in the middle of the 17th century but the place was abandoned during King Philip's War and was not again occupied until 1730.

Open House Day is held annually in August (*adm.* $2), the funds going to the support of the town library. On this day the beautifully furnished old homes, some occupied by descendants of the original owners and others by summer residents, are opened to the public and collections of old and new craft work are displayed.

The *Nickels-Sortwell House* (1807-08), corner of Main and Fort Sts., one of the largest mansions of its period in Wiscasset, is a massive three-story structure with a one-story entrance portico, Corinthian pilasters, a long central Palladian window in the second story, and a large semi-circular window above it interpolated between the square windows on each side in the third story. This unfortunate arrangement of windows is a characteristic central motif of the façade in houses on the Maine coast. The inharmonious railing above the portico is a later addition (about 1890). An interesting variation in the detail of the main cornice is the omission of the modillions and the use of a double row of dentils in their place. The main portal with its elliptical fan-light and elaborately mullioned side-lights is particularly notable for slender pilasters and delicately carved transom rail and architrave. The face of the pilasters is carved in herring-bone pattern.

The *Abiel Wood House* (1812), cor. High and Lee Sts., though built a few years later than the Nickels House, is almost a duplicate of it. The Wood House, however, has greater distinction because of the more pleasing proportions of its Palladian window, and the lack of such superficial embellishments as the Corinthian pilasters. It was restored to its original lines in 1936.

The *Clapp House*, or Lilac Cottage, on US 1 opposite the Common, is an old story-and-a-half structure of unknown date, now painted white with green shutters. The front yard, which is fragrant with lilacs in the spring, is enclosed by a picket fence.

The *Lincoln County Courthouse* (1824), on the Common, contains a jail that was at one time a State prison. This building, the oldest in which court is still held in Maine, at one time resounded the rolling periods of Daniel Webster.

The *Lee-Payson-Smith House*, right on High St., opposite the library, is still owned by the descendants of Samuel E. Smith, who was Governor

TOUR 1: From Portsmouth to Clair

of Maine 1831-34. It was erected in the early 19th century and admirably illustrates the skill of the carpenter-architects of the day and their sensitive appreciation of classic detail executed in wood. The distinctive charm of this square, two-story frame house, with its clapboard front, brick ends, hip roof topped with a captain's walk, and low service wings, is found in its refinement of detail and subtle proportions, which attain an almost monumental quality. Perhaps the most notable feature of the exterior is the fine modillioned and dentiled cornices, both on the main section of the house and on the ells at the side; its thin acute-angle profile, combined with the low pitch of the roof, gives an effect of singular grace and delicacy. The Ionic pilasters, placed at some distance from the corners of the main façade, are carved in somewhat heavier detail. The open railing around the captain's walk, suggesting a Chippendale pattern, is very well proportioned to the mass of the house.

In the *Town Library*, High St. (*open weekdays* 2-5.30), is a very old piece of fire apparatus, a hand-drawn affair, equipped with two leather buckets, two cotton bags for use in carrying small articles from burning buildings, and a bed key for unfastening beds preparatory to their removal. The Wiscasset Fire Society, organized in 1801, though no longer active in a fire-fighting capacity, has maintained many of its old-time rules and regulations and members are still fined 10¢ if they are absent from meetings.

The *Tucker Mansion*, or Tucker Castle, east end of High St., was built in 1807, of curious architecture, and is said to be a copy of a castle in Dunbar, Scotland. The piazza was added in 1860. Inside, a slender spiral staircase with mahogany balustrades rises in the center of the hall. Patience Tucker Stapleton, daughter of a sea captain and author of 'Trailing Yew' and other stories, lived here in her youth.

At Wiscasset is a junction with State 27 (*see Tour* 12) and State 218.

> Left from Wiscasset on State 218 to (L) the old *Alna Meeting-House* (*apply at Walker House, next door, for admission*), 7.1 *m*. The original hand-hewn shingles are in place on two of the weather-beaten sides of this old structure, which was built in 1789, and on the north side are the original clapboards, shiplapped at the northeastern corner against the storms. Curiously designed hand-wrought foot scrapers grace the sides of the doorstep. The interior woodwork is very well preserved; the box pews, with carved spindles, seated nearly five hundred people. The raised hourglass pulpit, with a winding flight of steps and finely molded handrail, is paneled in contrasting dark and light wood; above the pulpit is an octagonal bell-shaped canopy and sounding board, and behind it is a long arched window flanked by fluted pilasters. The pulpit, with an arrangement for accommodating ministers of different heights, has been used by many men of varying oratorical talents since Parson Wood, the first minister, preached of fire and brimstone and fought in vain against the introduction of instrumental music.
>
> HEAD TIDE (alt. 40, Alna Town), 10 *m*. This tiny village, consisting of a few homes, one store, a church, and a sawmill, lies on both sides of the bridge that crosses the Sheepscot River. The second house (L) on the road beyond the store is the *Birthplace of Edwin Arlington Robinson* (*see Tour* 10).

Right at 20 *m*., at the east entrance of the long bridge over the Sheepscot River, is the junction with a tarred road (*see Tour* 1G).

NEWCASTLE (alt. 60, Newcastle Town, pop. 914), 26.7 *m*., is a pleasant little community with tree-shaded streets on the bank of the Damariscotta River, at a point where it widens considerably. Like many southern Maine towns, Newcastle was settled early in the 17th century, but the settlers, harassed by Indians, left their new homes repeatedly.

>Left from Newcastle on a local road is (R), atop a hill, the *Kavanaugh Mansion* (*private*), 2.6 *m.*, built in 1803 and once owned by Edward Kavanaugh, acting Governor of Maine in 1843. The two-story white building has an octagonal cupola, a balustraded roof, and a fine doorway with fan-light and side-lights under a semi-circular portico. Although slightly altered from its original form, it retains an old-fashioned charm.
>
>*St. Patrick's Roman Catholic Church* (*open*), 2.8 *m.* (R), built 1803–08, was dedicated by Father Jean de Cheverus (1768–1836), who became the first Roman Catholic bishop of New England in 1808. Bishop Cheverus came to America from France in 1796 and did some work among the Indians of the Maine coast. In the final year of his life, after his return to France, he was made a cardinal.
>
>This thick-walled old church has a 250-year-old altar-piece from France. Some of its paintings were taken from a Mexican convent during the Mexican War. The present altar is of the sarcophagus type, unusual in the United States; in the chancel is the original altar.

DAMARISCOTTA (alt. 30, Damariscotta Town, pop. 825), 26.9 *m.*, is a tiny village on low land in a bend of the Damariscotta River.

The digging of clams, which are served extensively in the many near-by summer hotels and eating places, and are shipped away in refrigerated cars, is an important local industry. The clammers, who live in shacks near the salt water during the summer, tap along the beaches at low tide, causing the clams, disturbed by the vibrations, to spout out tiny streams of water that betray their hiding places in the mud.

At Damariscotta is the junction with State 129 (*see Tour 1H*).

Between a white house and a barn at 28.4 *m.* is the junction with a dirt road.

>Left on this road, which runs through a pasture, to *Shell Heaps*, 0.5 *m.*, which have been explored, leaving the strata exposed. Between the bottom layer and the second, which is approximately 6 feet thick, is a layer of soil; in this second layer the shells are mixed with the bones of animals. The top layer, containing smaller shells, is covered with earth holding good-sized trees. The age of the heap is unknown but the bottom layer was undoubtedly deposited many centuries ago. The top deposit was made by the Abnaki Indians who came to this region in summer to catch fish and smoke them for winter use.

NOBLEBORO (alt. 170, Nobleboro Town, pop. 599), 31.3 *m.*, was part of the Pemaquid Patent and named, when incorporated in 1788, for Arthur Noble, one of the heirs of the proprietor.

At 37.8 *m.* is the junction with State 220.

>Right on State 220 to WALDOBORO (alt. 120, Waldoboro Town, pop. 2311), 0.7 *m.*, at the head of navigation on the Medomak River. It was named for General Samuel Waldo, proprietor of the Waldo Patent, which included this township and many hundred thousand other acres. The settlers, who arrived in 1748, were Germans who had received special encouragement from General Waldo. The town at one time had considerable prestige as a shipbuilding center, the first five-masted steamer, the 'Governor Ames,' having been built here.
>
>A seasonal local industry is the catching, packing, and shipping of alewives, commonly called herring. The village also has a pearl button factory and derives con-

TOUR 1: From Portsmouth to Clair

siderable income from the summer tourist trade. Many local boats are hired for deep-sea fishing, the catch including cod, cusk, hake, and halibut. Fly-fishing for mackerel and pollock is popular with visitors in this area. Occasionally gamey striped bass and very large tunas are secured in near-by waters.

The *German Meeting-House* (*open for services once a year*), on the west side of the river, was built between 1770 and 1773. The 36×45 foot building has a large entrance porch. Inside, a gallery overlooks a hand-made communion table and contribution boxes. The pews are unpainted. A cabinet contains a collection of old German books and mementos.

Near-by is the old *German Cemetery*, with many unusual and interesting inscriptions on grave markers. One bears the following:

'This town was settled in 1748 by Germans who immigrated to this place with the promise and expectation of finding a prosperous city, instead of which they found nothing but wilderness.'

On the eastern side of the river is the *Residence of John H. Lovell*, whose works on bees and pollination are accepted as authoritative by the U.S. Department of Agriculture.

FRIENDSHIP (alt. 90, Friendship Town, pop. 742), 10.1 *m.*, a fishing village of small neat homes, is at the end of a peninsula. Local travel here being generally by boat, small floats or wharves appear at the ends of the side streets, which slope sharply down to the shore. Pride in the building and care of small boats is traditional in Friendship, as is evidenced by the large number of well-painted craft in the bay.

In a small building on the grounds of Dr. William H. Hahn (L) is an extensive *Collection of Glassware* (*seen at convenience of owner*), consisting of about 1000 pieces, most of which are early American lamps. Dr. Hahn also has a collection of ruby glassware and some old Roman and Turkish metal lamps.

Salt-water fishing, from both sail and motor boats, is the chief pastime in the vicinity of Friendship, the coastal waters offering many kinds of fish. Casting for mackerel has become popular, but heavy catches are often made by trolling in the early morning and in the evening; these fish are as lively and agile as trout. Cunners, excellent pan fish 12 to 15 inches in length and up to 1½ pounds in weight, are usually caught on the incoming tides, with sharp hooks on straight poles baited with worms, clams, or periwinkles. Pollock, gamey as salmon, are caught with a fly rod by trolling bright flies in a swift current, or with herring attached to a colored spinner. The silver hake, which when fresh is one of the most satisfying foods for a hungry fisherman, can be caught from small boats near the shore.

As at other points on the Maine coast the skipper who takes parties out for deep-sea fishing is generally an entertaining fellow who knows the fish runs, as well as many fish stories; he furnishes tackle as well as good advice, and cooks a tasty chowder.

Clambakes, another popular diversion, can be arranged at reasonable rates, if assistance is wanted. A driftwood fire, built between granite boulders and reduced to embers, is used to steam lobsters, clams, and crabs in pails of seaweed; potatoes and corn, also cooked in seaweed, complete the menu.

Garrison Island (alt. 20, Friendship Town), off the extreme southern end of the peninsula but connected with the mainland at low tide, is the site of a fort built about 1755.

At 43.6 *m.* is a junction with State 137.

Left on State 137 is WARREN (alt. 70, Warren Town, pop. 1429), 1.3 *m.* In 1864, after the recovery of Mrs. Mary Baker Glover Eddy — then Mrs. Patterson — from a serious illness under the guidance of P. P. Quimby of Portland, Me., she came to this village with another Quimby pupil, who had become much attached to her. While here she gave a number of public lectures which she reported to the Portland healer in a series of charming letters. The title of one lecture she wrote was publicly advertised as 'P. P. Quimby's Spiritual Science Healing Disease — as opposed to

Deism or Rochester-Rapping-Spiritualism.' Her work here is considered by some as the beginning of her career as the founder of Christian Science.

At 47.7 m. is the junction with State 131.

> Left on State 131 is the entrance (L) to the *Knox State Arboretum* and the *Academy of Arts and Sciences*, 1.1 m. (*adm. free*). In the arboretum are specimen trees, shrubs, and wild flowers native to Maine. The museum, a two-story brick building, has a valuable collection of Maine minerals, Red Paint and Indian artifacts, two fine American bird collections, and a collection of sea shells and marine life indigenous to Maine.

Maine State Prison (*visiting hours Tues. and Fri.*, 2.30–4), 48.2 m., on Limestone Hill and surrounded by high gray walls of field stone, has accommodations for 300 prisoners. The first, and possibly the only, military execution in Maine took place on this site when Jeremiah Braun was hanged on the charge of having guided a British raiding party that in 1780 captured General Peleg Wadsworth, a grandfather of Henry Wadsworth Longfellow.

The prison site was sold to the State in 1824 by William King, Governor of Maine in 1820.

Capital punishment was abolished in Maine in 1876, re-established in 1883, and finally abolished in 1887 at the request of the Governor who said that it had not deterred crime.

THOMASTON (alt. 100, Thomaston Town, pop. 2214), 48.7 m.

> *Steamship service* to coastal points and Monhegan and other islands; schedules vary; inquire at wharves.

Thomaston, lying at the head of the long narrow inlet into which St. George River drains, is a favorite port of call of yachtsmen. Its main street has many attractive old homes with notable doorways. A trading post stood here in 1630 and occupation of the site was fairly continuous in spite of Indian attacks, though actual settlement did not begin until more than a hundred years later. Real development began after the Revolutionary War; Henry Knox, who had made a name for himself at the battle of Bunker Hill, who became a trusted adviser of Washington, and who was Secretary of War both under the Confederation and during Washington's first term as President, had married a granddaughter of Samuel Waldo, proprietor of the enormous Waldo Patent (*see above*). Through purchase and marriage he acquired a large part of the patent and, at the close of his Cabinet career, came to live in Thomaston, which had been incorporated in 1777. Knox made many plans for the development of his holdings, trying shipbuilding, brickmaking, lime burning, farming, lumbering, and many other industries, but, though an able military man, he was a poor businessman. His open-handed hospitality contributed to his failure to amass a fortune.

The community prospered, however, and was at one time active in shipbuilding, reaching its peak of prosperity and population about 1840, when its population was three times as large as it is today.

The plain frame *Cilley House* (*private*), 25 Main St., was the home of Jonathan Cilley, a Congressional Representative from Maine, when he

TOUR 1: From Portsmouth to Clair 223

was killed in a duel in February, 1838, on the old Bladensburg, Maryland, dueling ground, close to the District of Columbia Line. Cilley had risen in Congress to denounce an article that had appeared in an anonymous gossip column of a New York newspaper with a charge of immorality against another Congressman. He fastened the blame for the article on a Virginian, was challenged to a duel by William Graves, a Representative from Kentucky, and fell at the third shot.

On a hill (R) at 49.5 *m.* is *Montpelier (open daily* 10–6, *June* 1 *to Nov.* 1; *adm.* 50¢), a recent reproduction of the home built in 1793 by General Henry Knox *(see above)*. This large, imposing two-story and basement structure has a low roof surrounded by a balustrade and surmounted with a monitor that rises between the four inside chimneys. The central third of the façade is elliptical and ornamented by four engaged columns; the pedimented doorway is reached by a stairway leading to a wide roofless piazza. The 18 rooms of the house are furnished with old pieces, many of them from the original structure; they also contain many relics of the general and a portrait of him by Gilbert Stuart.

At 49.6 *m.* is (R) a junction with State 131 *(see Tour 1J).*

At 50.2 *m.* (R) is the *Lawrence Portland Cement Company Plant (not open to visitors),* one of the largest of its kind in New England. The quarry is between the highway and the plant.

ROCKLAND (alt. 40, pop. 9075), 53 *m.*, separated from Thomaston and incorporated in 1848 as East Thomaston, is a trading center and shire town for Knox County. The many summer residents and visitors have been a good source of trade. The city fronts on the fine harbor that the Indians called Catawamkeag *(great landing place).* Fishing, shipping, shipbuilding, and limestone quarrying have been the chief industries of the past.

The *Birthplace* (1892) *of Edna St. Vincent Millay,* the poet, is at 200 Broadway.

The *Community Yacht Club* and *Public Landing,* Main and Pleasant Sts., has floats, docks, and clubhouses for visitors.

At Rockland is a junction with State 17 *(see Tour 17).*

> Right from Rockland on Main St.; at 2 *m.* left on a tarred road; at 2.1 *m.* left to large triangular *Range Beacons*, 3.7 *m.* These open structures are used by vessels of the U.S. Navy in sighting their positions on the measured trial course off Rockland, which is marked by six buoys. New vessels and old ones that have been reconditioned are sent there for tests of speed and engine efficiency.
>
> OWL'S HEAD (alt. 40, Owl's Head Town, pop. 574), 4.6 *m.*, a summer resort, lies on the far end of a tree-sheltered cape. Visited by Champlain in 1605, it was then called Bedabedec Point (Ind.: 'cape of the waters'). The town was the scene of a bloody encounter in 1755 when Captain Cargyle, famous Indian fighter employing Indian tactics, killed and scalped nine braves, receiving a bounty of £200 each. During the Revolution and the War of 1812, British and American privateers were active in near-by waters.
>
> Left from Owl's Head to the heavily wooded *U.S. Lighthouse Reservation* at 5.3 *m.*

Owl's Head Light (open 9–11.30 *all year;* 1–5 *July–Aug.;* 1–3 *remainder of year),* was built in 1826, during the administration of President John Quincy Adams. The old white tower is only 26 feet high; but because of its situation, the light can be seen 16 miles at sea. In summer, yachts cruising in these waters are welcomed by three strokes of a bell. Snowshoeing parties from Rockland visit the snow-clad headland in winter.

At 5.7 *m.* the road ends. From this point it is but a short walk to the shore where the red and yellow quartz-streaked face of the headland, worn smooth by the pounding of the surf, rears itself nearly 100 feet above sea level. Tall spruce, their roots clinging tenaciously to the few inches of soil, crown the summit.

There is steamship service, also, from Rockland to the islands of Vinalhaven, North Haven, Deer Isle, Isle Au Haut, and Swan's Island which lie in broad Penobscot Bay and, to the east of it, in the Atlantic Ocean (*see Island Tours*).

NORTH HAVEN (pop. 476), about 12 miles from Rockland, at the mouth of Penobscot Bay, is a fashionable area with a number of summer estates. There is a flying field here.

VINALHAVEN (pop. 1843), is south of North Haven, with which it is connected by ferry. It also has many large summer homes. The town was settled in 1789 and when incorporated, 14 years later, was named for John Vinal of Boston. It has a larger permanent population than North Haven because of its active granite quarries, from which came the 51 to 55 foot monoliths of the Cathedral of St. John the Divine in New York City.

DEER ISLE (pop. 1226), on the eastern side of Penobscot Bay, is an hourglass-shaped area, about 12 miles in length. It has much charm but has received little development, which is a satisfaction to those who cherish its primitive character. Its permanent inhabitants are skilled boatmen, some of them having manned yachts in the international races.

ISLE AU HAUT (pop. 89), presenting a headland to the Atlantic some miles south of Deer Isle, is the administrative headquarters of Isle Au Haut Township, which contains about a dozen smaller islands. It is chiefly visited by the more hardy summer visitors. The near-by waters have been the scene of a number of wrecks.

At 54.3 *m.* is the junction with Waldo Ave.

Right on Waldo Ave. to the *Rockland Breakwater* which extends from Jameson Point nearly 1 mile across the harbor entrance and makes an excellent point from which to survey the city and environs. There is a *Lighthouse* at the end of the breakwater.

ROCKPORT (alt. 100, Rockport Town, pop. 1651), 59.4 *m.*, another town with a diminishing population, was set off from Camden in 1891. From the bridge at the southern end of the village is a remarkable view of the harbor and of the white lighthouse jutting out on the point. Goose River forms a V-shaped waterfront that has been landscaped by Mrs. Mary Louise Bok (*see below*). Unusually interesting are the *Old Lime Kilns* near-by.

Spite House (R), on Deadman's Point, was moved in 1925 over land and water from Phippsburg, 85 miles away, by Donald W. Dodge of Philadelphia. The story of this house is closely associated with the James McCobb House at Phippsburg Center (*see Tour 1E*). James McCobb, prominent Phippsburg citizen of his time, was three times married and built the so-called Minott House in Phippsburg for his second wife. Some time after his third marriage, the elder McCobb died while his son

Tour 1: From Portsmouth to Clair

Thomas was at sea. Mrs. McCobb, who had also been previously married, arranged a marriage between a son by her first husband and the sister of Thomas McCobb, thereby obtaining practical control of one of the largest estates in the section. When Thomas McCobb returned and learned of the marriage and its consequences, he became incensed and declared he would build himself a mansion large enough and sufficiently grand to overshadow the residence occupied by his stepmother. In 1806 he built this beautiful structure, which, from the day of its completion, has borne its present name.

CAMDEN (alt. 100, Camden Town, pop. 3606), 61 *m.*, one of Maine's loveliest towns, lies 'under the high mountains of the Penobscot, against whose feet the sea doth beat,' as Captain John Smith described the site. Champlain, who visited the Penobscot in 1605, named the Camden Hills the 'mountains of Bedabedec' on his map; so steeply do they rise from the blue waters of Penobscot Bay, that the magnificent yachts dropping anchor all summer long in the harbor seem from a distance to ride in the heart of the business district.

The town has developed rapidly as a small summer resort in recent years, the estate valuation now being more than half that of Bar Harbor. It has also become a winter sports center. The summer residents have taken particular interest in the landscaping of the town, a project that is stimulated by annual contests in which prizes are awarded.

Behind the *Camden Public Library*, Main St., is an *Amphitheater* with a seating capacity of 1500, landscaped with native trees, shrubs, and plants.

The old *Camden Opera House*, cor. Elm and Washington Sts., has been remodeled into a modern auditorium with elaborate interior decorations. Mrs. Mary Louise Bok, daughter of the late Cyrus H. K. Curtis, a summer resident for many years, has been a leader in carrying out many municipal improvements. A notable group of musicians, including Josef Hoffman, pianist, make their summer homes in Camden.

1. Left from Camden on Mechanic St., the southern section of State 137; straight ahead (R) from State 137 at 1 *m.*; left at 1.5 *m.*, passing a lake at 3.4 *m.*; left at 3.5 *m.* and again at 3.7 *m.* to the *Camden Bowl*, in which carnivals and competitive sports events are held in summer and winter.

2. Left from Camden on Mountain St., which enters the northern section of State 137, at 1 *m.*, is the junction with a trail leading to the summit of *Mount Battie* (alt. 800). From this height, occupied by cannon during the War of 1812, are beautiful views of Penobscot Bay and the surrounding hills. An area of approximately 6000 acres between Lake Megunticook and the seashore, including part of Mt. Megunticook, Mt. Battie, and Bald Mountain is being proposed for National park development.

At 71.7 *m.* is a junction with a gravel road.

Right on this road is NORTHPORT (alt. 140, Northport Town, pop. 413), 0.5 *m.*, near Saturday Cove, an arm of Penobscot Bay; many delightful woodland walks lead from the village to the shore.

At 78.3 *m.* is (R) the *Belfast City Park* with excellent camping and trailer facilities.

BELFAST (alt. 160, pop. 4993), 79.3 *m.*, a popular tourist center and seat of Waldo County, has parallel streets that follow a rolling terrain, which rises in a majestic sweep from the banks of the Passagassawakeag. Its highest points command a view over the island-sprinkled waters of Penobscot Bay.

The town was named for Belfast, Ireland, by a group of Scotch-Irish settlers who came to the place in 1770, after having tried settlement at Londonderry, N.H. Belfast was harassed by the British in 1779 and its settlers were driven away, but they successfully re-established themselves five years later. The city reached its peak of population in 1860 with 5520 inhabitants, but has since achieved prosperity by catering to the many summer residents and visitors.

Reminiscent of an earlier prosperity are the many fine old houses, whose chief interest lies in their variation on the standard 19th-century architecture.

The *James P. White House* (*private*), 30 Church St., is a simple white structure built in 1825. Fine old elms shade the broad lawn, which is surrounded by a picket fence.

The *Clay House* (*private*), 130 Main St., opposite Waldo Ave., was built in 1825. It is an attractive structure of the Greek Revival type with Doric columns.

The *Old Johnson House*, 100 High St., set in beautiful grounds, is a hip-roof structure with a lookout, built in 1812. The Corinthian columns on the front and sides may be later additions. Its shutters were the first used in Belfast.

The *Ben Field House* (*private*), 137 High St., is a large, square, hip-roof structure with a dentiled cornice, built in 1807.

The old *Blaisdell House* (*private*), 0.4 mile south of the center on High St., on spacious grounds, has a portico with four Ionic columns and an elaborately carved pediment.

At Belfast is a junction with State 3 (*see Tour* 16).

> 1. Left from the center on Main St., State 3; right at 0.2 *m.* on Waldo Ave. to the junction with Poor Mills Rd. at 1.4 *m.*; left here to the old *Joseph Miller Tavern*, 2.4 *m.* (R). It has the only salt-box roof left in Belfast, tiny panes in the windows, and no eaves, a characteristic of early building in the vicinity.
>
> 2. North from the center on High St. at 1.2 *m.* (R) is the *Otis House* (*private*), a one-and-a-half-story gable-end house on Nickerson Hill, overlooking the river; it was built in 1800.
>
> 3. Visible from Belfast's waterfront, and lying about 6 miles offshore in Penobscot Bay, is *Islesboro*, a long, low, tree-clad island reached from Belfast. (*See Island Tours*.)

Sec. c. BELFAST to ELLSWORTH, 61.3 *m.*

North of Belfast US 1 continues to follow the west bank of the Penobscot, running through scenic country to Bangor; at Bangor it cuts sharply SE. to reach the coast again, traversing placid farmlands that contrast with the wooded hills.

TOUR 1: From Portsmouth to Clair 227

US 1 leaves BELFAST (*see Tour 1, sec. b*), 0 *m*.

On the northern outskirts of the city, 0.5 *m*., the route crosses Passagassawakeag River on the *Belfast Memorial Bridge*, which is dedicated to Waldo County's enlisted men in the World War. From a hill beyond the bridge are seen, to the rear, the dark red warehouses of Belfast's waterfront. From US 1, between this point and Belfast, are a succession of views of the waters of Penobscot Bay and its islands.

At 1.9 *m*. is (L) *Stephenson Tavern* (*private*), a story-and-a-half house of simple lines, built in 1800; there is a well sweep in the front yard. The old pine sign, bearing a black horse and the name of Jerome Stephenson, is so weather-beaten that the painted horse and lettering stand out a quarter of an inch.

SEARSPORT (alt. 50, Searsport Town, pop. 1414), 5.9 *m*., has a small, compact business district on its main street (US 1). The rest of the village stretches along the highway, which affords many vistas of Penobscot Bay. In the heyday of New England shipping, Searsport was known as the home of expert seamen, and it has been the birthplace of many United States naval officers. As a terminus of the Bangor and Aroostook Railroad, it ships much of the annual potato crop of Aroostook County.

In an old brick house that was built in the village during the days of the town's prosperity, is housed the *Penobscot Marine Museum*, containing an unusually fine collection of relics and papers connected with the ships, shipowners, and captains of the days when the Penobscot was one of the most important shipbuilding centers of the Nation.

At 6.2 *m*. (R) stands the *Home of Lincoln Colcord*, a writer of sea stories and the son of a sea captain; he was born off Cape Horn. His home, for several generations the snug haven to which his adventurous forebears retired at the end of their voyages, is beautifully situated above the bay.

In this area US 1 passes many estates, also many farms that have achieved prosperity by catering to the needs of their summer neighbors.

STOCKTON SPRINGS (alt. 150, Stockton Springs Town, pop. 877), 10.1 *m*., has become relatively prosperous because of its fish canneries and fertilizer factories. In 1890 an attempt was made to exploit the spring for which the town was named but failed when it was found that sediment settled in the bottles when the water was ready to market.

Here is a junction with State 3 (*see Tour 1K*).

PROSPECT (alt. 90, Prospect Town, pop. 388), 14.6 *m*.

> Right from Prospect on State 174 is *Fort Knox*, 2.5 *m*., now a State reservation. The site for this fort was selected during the days of the heated boundary disputes with Great Britain, but work was not begun until 1846; the fort was never entirely completed, though troops were trained here during the Civil War. This massive structure was built of Mt. Waldo granite and commands one of the most beautiful views on the Penobscot River.
>
> A short distance beyond Fort Knox is the western approach to the *Waldo–Hancock Bridge* (*toll, 50¢*) on State 3 (*see Tour 1K*).

The granite ledges of *Mosquito Mountain*, 16.6 *m*., rise sharply (L).

At 17.4 *m.*, along both sides of the road, is the *Mt. Waldo Granite Corporation Plant* (*open to public*), with, near-by, the deep clefts from which countless tons of fine granite have been quarried.

Mount Waldo (alt. 1062), highest of several small peaks in this region, can be seen (L) at intervals. Mt. Waldo granite has been used in many public buildings.

The flat lands here bordering the river are one of the several points on the Maine coast where Captain Kidd is said to have buried a part of his treasure. A tinker who lived on the spot refused to allow searchers on the property; after his death a number of attempts were made to find the supposedly hidden jewels and gold. Legend has it that the hunters were frightened away by mysterious noises from the earth; no treasure has ever been found here.

FRANKFORT (alt. 180, Frankfort Town, pop. 468), 18.8 *m.*, a village shaded by huge century-old elms, belies its history of industrial prosperity. Log cabins first appeared here in 1756, and a permanent settlement was made in 1760. Shipbuilding began early and, by the time of the Revolution, Frankfort was important enough to draw the attention of the British Navy. Many of the 33 ships destroyed along the Penobscot in 1779 were tied up, or under construction, in this port. The English bombarded the settlement in 1814, subsequently occupying it.

In the vicinity of Frankfort, the road, which is very hilly and winding, affords many panoramas of the valley. Small farms cling to the hillsides.

At 20.9 *m.* (L) is the *Blaisdell House* (*closed*), built 1798, a two-and-a-half-story yellow structure with gable roof and two dormer windows.

WINTERPORT (alt. 80, Winterport Town, pop. 1437), 21.5 *m.*, whose name was derived from its position at the head of winter navigation on the Penobscot River, had at one time some importance as a shipbuilding community and a port. In the 1936 State election Winterport was the first and only town in Maine to use voting machines.

At 28 *m.* (R) is *Dorothea Lynde Dix Memorial Park* on the site of the Isaac Hopkins farm, on which in 1802 the prison and almshouse reformer, for whom the park is named, was born. When Miss Dix went to Boston as a young girl, she was so shocked by conditions in public institutions that she began a nation-wide campaign that resulted in marked reforms.

HAMPDEN HIGHLANDS (alt. 150, Hampden Town), 28.6 *m.*, has blue-green river vistas. In the latter part of May the numerous orchards in the township and in Orrington across the Penobscot blanket the countryside with translucent pink and white beauty and send forth a delicate scent that permeates the whole area.

HAMPDEN (alt. 80, Hampden Town, pop. 2417), 29.8 *m.*, on the banks of the Penobscot River, a suburban village flanked by farms, was settled in 1767, two years before Bangor, and for a long time rivaled that town in importance. During the War of 1812 the British drove the outnumbered militia from the settlement.

Tour 1: From Portsmouth to Clair

Here is a junction with State 9 (*see Tour* 13).

Huge piles of pulpwood are seen in the Penobscot (R) as the route passes through the outskirts of Bangor.

BANGOR (alt. 100, pop. 28,749) (*see BANGOR*), 34.8 *m.*, is at a junction with US 2 (*see Tour* 4).

BREWER (alt. 100, pop. 6329), 35.5 *m.*, is a city somewhat overshadowed by Bangor, across the Penobscot River. It was named for Colonel John Brewer who was one of the first settlers, as well as the first postmaster. Once famous for the wooden ships built in its yards, the city's present prosperity depends on the activity of pulp and paper mills.

Chillicote House, now an antique shop (L), at the corner of State and N. Main Sts., is a conspicuous landmark standing at the crest of a short hill that drops sharply to the east approach of the Bangor–Brewer bridge.

At 80 Chamberlain St. is the *Joshua Chamberlain House* (*private*). General Chamberlain, noted for his gallantry during the Civil War, received the Congressional Medal of Honor for his part in the defense of Little Round Top at Gettysburg; and as a further reward he was delegated to review and receive the arms and colors of the Confederate Army. In spite of repeated injuries received while in active service, he was able to serve his State as Governor (1867–71), and Bowdoin College as president (1871–83).

At Brewer is a junction with State 178 (*see Tour* 5).

At 38.1 *m.* is a sweeping view across valleys and mountains.

HOLDEN (alt. 190, Holden Town, pop. 543), 42.2 *m.* The Town Hall and Grange Hall (R) mark the corporate and social center of the township. The National Grange of the Patrons of Husbandry, of which the local lodges are members, was organized in 1867 by Oliver H. Kelley, an employee of the U.S. Department of Agriculture who felt the need of a fraternal organization to unite the farmers for social and educational purposes. The lodges became politically important, serving as local forums; they are particularly active in Maine. Grange suppers and meetings are open to the public and visitors who want to study the State are advised to attend the meetings, which are always advertised. The suppers are standardized — baked beans, ham, cold slaw, pie and cake.

EAST HOLDEN (alt. 100, Holden Town), 43.5 *m.*, is at a crossroads where overnight cabins outnumber the residences.

At 46.4 *m.* is a beautiful view of Lake Lucerne.

LUCERNE-IN-MAINE (alt. 440, Dedham Town, pop. 279), 46.6 *m.*, is a resort on the shores of Lake Lucerne, drawing winter sports enthusiasts as well as summer visitors. The *Clubhouse* (R), just off the highway, was the halfway house on the old Bangor–Ellsworth stagecoach route; it has been much remodeled. Thick woods nearly conceal (L) the huge log tourist lodge and tennis courts and (R) a golf course, bridle paths, hiking trails, and a bathing beach. This resort was carefully planned by the head of a lumbering firm who could not bear to see the natural beauty of the lake shore and hills spoiled.

ELLSWORTH (alt. 100, pop. 3557), 61.3 *m.*, the county seat and only city in Hancock County, was settled in 1763. The community has seen extensive lumbering operations, a period of shipbuilding, and an industrial era brought about by the development of its water power. A large part of the business district, and many of the old buildings, were destroyed by fire in 1933, but the center has been rebuilt. Today the town is a happy combination of gracious old homes and attractive modern business buildings. An example of this is the juxtaposition of the new *City Hall*, which shows a Scandinavian influence, and the old white *Congregational Church*, which dominate the business district from the east side of State Street Hill. The latter, built in 1812, has a portico with delicately fluted columns, and a slender spire.

The sparkling Union River flows through the center of the city, and from the bridge (R) a 60-foot falls is visible.

The *Black Mansion* (*open May* 30–*Nov.* 1; *adm.* 50¢), on W. Main St., built about 1802, was the home of Colonel John Black, land agent for William Bingham who owned large tracts of land east of the Penobscot River. Colonel Black's predecessor in the agency was his father-in-law, Colonel David Cobb, an aide-de-camp of General Washington. The two-story brick house, an elegant structure in the tiny frontier settlement, is of modified Georgian design, with one-story wings that may have been added after the main structure was built. An ornamental cornice and a balustrade surround the low roof. The main structure has no front entrance; four triple-hung, shuttered windows open out on a low porch with five Ionic columns, that runs the length of the main building and is surmounted with a balustrade. A notable feature of the interior is the gracefully curving staircase rising from the spacious hall that divides the house and parallels its front. Many of Colonel Black's possessions and those his wife inherited from her father are in the house; other articles have been added since the house became public property in 1928. Among the valued relics are a miniature of Washington by one of the Peales, a rare volume of the Colonial laws of Massachusetts, and a high-backed Dutch chair with a hinged seat that can be lengthened to form a couch or bed.

The *Public Library* (*open* 2 *to* 5), State St., once the Tisdale house, built before 1820, retains many of its architectural features, such as arched doorways and fireplaces.

At Ellsworth are junctions with State 3 (*see Tour* 1K *and Tour* 2) and with State 15 (*see Tour* 3).

Sec. d. ELLSWORTH *to* CALAIS, 123.9 *m.*

Following the coast for several miles, US 1 then passes through the hunting grounds of the Passamaquoddy Indians, which still provide good sport in season. Broad blueberry plains stretch out to the north, and numerous rivers and streams along the route provide excellent fishing.

Tour 1: From Portsmouth to Clair

US 1 leaves ELLSWORTH (*see Tour* 1, *sec. c*), 0 *m*.

At 1 *m*. is a junction with State 3 (*see Tour* 2).

At 3.6 *m*. is a magnificent view of the Schoodic Hills and Cadillac mountain, also various other hills rising from and around Frenchman's Bay.

The region through which US 1 passes here has small farms that look fairly prosperous, and much wooded land.

HANCOCK (alt. 40, Hancock Town, pop. 760), 9.1 *m*., was settled in 1764 and incorporated in 1828. In 1890 the township had a population of 1190; the decrease has been gradual.

At 11.8 *m*. is a striking view of Mt. Desert Island and its hills.

SULLIVAN (alt. 60, Sullivan Town, pop. 873), 12.3 *m*., a small hamlet, is the corporate center of a township whose many summer homes are spread out along US 1.

The *Stone Store* (*closed*), in the center of the village, is a two-story gabled building, constructed of heavy blocks of stone.

At 18.5 *m*. is the junction with State 186 (*see Tour* 1L), which rejoins US 1 at 21.6 *m*.

GOULDSBORO (alt. 80, Gouldsboro Town, pop. 1115), 22 *m*., is principally a summer resort and small trading center for the Grindstone Neck area. David Cobb made his home here from 1796 to 1808. During those years he was one of the most influential citizens of Maine. In 1795, he was appointed agent of the great Bingham estate (*see Tour* 1, *sec. c*), moving to Gouldsboro in 1796, and in 1802 was sent to the Massachusetts Legislature to represent eastern Maine.

STEUBEN (alt. 40, Steuben Town, pop. 684), 26.8 *m*., when incorporated in 1795, was named in honor of Baron von Steuben, inspector general of the Continental Army.

MILBRIDGE (alt. 20, Milbridge Town, pop. 1207), 32.3 *m*., lies at the mouth of the Narraguagus, its main street, which US 1 follows, paralleling the river. From the highway at the southern end of the village there is a fine view of the offshore islands (*boats and guides for deep-sea fishing*). Lumbering, lobster fishing, and farming are the main sources of livelihood. A knitting mill is also in operation.

A boat once frequently seen along the Maine coast and still occasionally found in some of the fishing villages of Nova Scotia is the pinky. ('Pinky' is provincial English for 'small.') These boats, pointed at both ends, have wide gunwales rising to meet in a stern overhang. In 1927, Howard L. Chapelle, naval architect and author of 'The History of American Sailing Ships,' revived the building of this type of craft in the Milbridge yard.

CHERRYFIELD (alt. 50, Cherryfield Town, pop. 1111), 37.8 *m*., lies on both sides of the Narraguagus River. The 'Belgrade,' a full-rigged bark that carried 56 local men around Cape Horn to California in the days of the gold rush, was built in this formerly active shipbuilding community. Today lumbering and blueberry packing are the chief industries of the town. The highway here turns north along the eastern bank of the river.

HARRINGTON (alt. 40, Harrington Town, pop. 862), 44.1 *m.*, was settled about 1765 and incorporated in 1797. Like many of the other villages between this point and Ellsworth, its air of comfort and prosperity depends largely on the money derived from the summer tourist trade. Pleasant Bay is a favorite spot for deep-sea fishing.

At 47.1 *m.* is the junction with a dirt road, known locally as the Jeff Davis Trail, which was cut in 1858 to enable members of the U.S. Coast Survey to transport supplies and heavy instruments to the top of Humpback, or Lead Mountain. Jefferson Davis, a close friend of Alexander Bache, superintendent of the Coast Survey, was a guest at the survey camp during the summer when the trail was cut.

>Left on this road is COLUMBIA (alt. 60, Columbia Town, pop. 409), 1.5 *m.*, settled soon after the Revolutionary War.

>The road continues in a northwesterly direction on a 200-square-mile plateau, where nearly 90 per cent of the country's blueberries are raised. Small brooks meander through acres of the low bushes, which in mid-June are covered with inverted bell blossoms. Blueberry packing begins in August and lasts through September. Men in large straw hats, women in sunbonnets, and barefoot children work from dawn to sundown raking, winnowing, and boxing the berries to be trucked to the canning factories.

>The blueberry industry has grown up in the wake of lumbering; the plants quickly cover the thin sandy soil after the trees are cut, and they need little cultivation. The land is burned over every third year to stimulate new growth. The spruce in this area was removed in the first quarter of the 19th century to provide masts and spars for ships built in the near-by yards. 'Blueberry plains' or 'barrens' as they are locally called, are privately owned and protected by the State. 'Bootleg berries' — those stolen by night pickers — are not so common as they once were.

COLUMBIA FALLS (alt. 60, Columbia Falls Town, pop. 583), 48.9 *m.*, was once a thriving lumber and shipbuilding center. Today the inhabitants depend on general farming and the blueberry industry for a livelihood. The prosperity that the town once knew is revealed by the many fine old homes in the vicinity.

The *Ruggles House* (*open*), constructed after a design by Aaron Sherman of Duxbury, Mass., who planned a number of homes in Washington County, was built about 1820 for Judge Thomas Ruggles, a wealthy lumber dealer. The house is notable for the delicate detail of its exterior trim. The interior woodwork, executed by an unknown English artisan, is unusually fine. In the drawing room are rope beadings on the cornices of the fireplace, done with great skill; exquisite carvings on the molding and delicate indentures on the chair rail of the wainscoting and on the frames and sills of the wide-shuttered windows. The house is in the process of restoration (1937), and workmen have uncovered rich mahogany-inlaid panels. Of particular interest is a swastika design which was carved with a common penknife below the mantel of the dining room. It is said that the villagers were so impressed by the delicacy of the work that they believed the carver's knife was guided by the hand of an angel.

Tour 1: From Portsmouth to Clair   233

Arthur Train used the Ruggles house as the setting for his short story, 'The House that Tutt Built.'

The *Maude Bucknam House*, opposite the post office, a yellow Cape Cod style dwelling with a wing, was built about 1820. It is notable for its woodwork.

The *Lippincott House*, opposite the Bucknam House, is a square, hip-roof house, with such interesting interior details as old-fashioned rope moldings and many fireplaces.

At 50.2 *m.* is a junction with State 187.

> Right on State 187, which cuts through the deep stillness of the woods and runs along the western shore of Englishman's Bay for several miles, presenting many attractive scenes, is JONESPORT (alt. 40, Jonesport Town, pop. 1634), 12.7 *m.* Although it derives considerable income from summer visitors, Jonesport's principal means of livelihood are fishing and sardine packing. Jonesport became famous as the background of a radio program, 'Sunday Night at Seth Parker's.' Island views, camp sites, fishing, and beaches are its resort attractions.
>
> In the harbor is *Beals Island*, reached from Jonesport by ferry. BEALS (alt. 40, Beals Town, pop. 524) is a fishing community on Beals Island, as well as a summer resort where the popular sport is deep-sea fishing.
>
> There is a faithful congregation of the Church of Jesus Christ of Latter-Day Saints at Beals. In 1865, G. J. Adams, a disgruntled Mormon elder from Philadelphia, succeeded in spite of local opposition in recruiting followers here. Prevailing upon many to sell their worldly goods, he organized the Palestine Emigration Association, issuing a religious publication, 'The Sword of Truth and the Harbinger of Peace.' After arrangements had been made with the Turkish Government, through the American consul, 175 members left on a 52-day voyage to Palestine in the barkentine, 'Nellie Chapin,' and settled near Jaffa. Beset by internal dissensions, misunderstandings with the natives, and disease caused by poor sanitary conditions, the colony was disbanded within a year and the survivors returned to the United States (*see Education and Religion*).
>
> *Barney's Point*, on the island, was named for Barney Beal, a son of Manwaring Beal, the first settler. The most colorful of the island legends are woven around the bold exploits and feats of strength of 'Tall Barney,' who always wore a butcher's coat and whose 6 feet 7 inches of brawn earned him fame as 'cock of the walk' from Quoddy Head to Cape Elizabeth; it was said that when he sat in a chair his hands touched the floor. Once, while he was fishing off Black's Island, armed sailors, objecting to his proximity to English territory, boarded his sloop, intent on capture at gun-point. Barney relieved the sailors of their guns, which he promptly broke over his knee and tossed back into the British boat. When the Canadian guards unwisely persisted in their intimidations, Barney twisted the arm of one until he broke the bone. In Rockland, Barney was said to have felled a horse with his fist, when a truckman drove too close to him. In a Portland saloon, without argument or assistance, he proved to 15 men the folly of deriding a 'down-easter.'
>
> *Perio's Point*, near the Freeman West Beal wharf, was named for Perio Checkers, an Indian, who is the only man known to have scaled the perpendicular side of the steep cliff at this point that still challenges climbers.
>
> In the past, shipwrecks in this vicinity were frequent. Companies were formed on the mainland to salvage boats and cargoes.
>
> The *Gravestone of Aunt Peggy Beal*, in the cemetery near the public square, reminds natives of how Aunt Peggy exorcised the powers of a witch, a Mrs. Thomas Hicks. Mrs. Hicks had the habit of borrowing from Aunt Peggy; if Aunt Peggy refused to lend what Mrs. Hicks wanted, it either died or disappeared. The last thing refused was a sheep, which died the following day. A Salem sailor, who claimed to know all about the handling of witches, told Aunt Peggy to build a hot fire and to

hold the sheep over it until it was scorched all over. This was done. 'Now,' he said, 'a boat will come over for something three times, and you must refuse each time, even though the witch tells you where the article is.' It all came about as the sailor predicted, so the story goes, and the day following the refusal of the third article, Mrs. Hicks was dead.

Separated from its larger but much less populous neighbor, Great Wass Island, by the *Flying Place*, a narrow strait, Beals Island affords views of surrounding islands and curious sea-wrought rock formations. Play of surf is most spectacular on stormy days in the Flying Place.

Great Wass Island Coast Guard Station is notable for its equipment and drills. The *Seacoast Mission Ship* regularly visits the island lighthouse.

In this area US 1 continues through blueberry plains; the homes show few evidences of prosperity, being weather-beaten and unpainted.

JONESBORO (alt. 60, Jonesboro Town, pop. 468), 57.6 *m*., a small farming community on the Chandler River, had a Revolutionary War heroine in the person of Hannah Weston, a descendant of Hannah Dustin, who became famous in the Indian massacre at Haverhill, Mass., in 1697. With a younger sister, Hannah Weston carried 50 pounds of lead and powder, collected from neighbors, through the woods from Jonesboro to Machias for use during the 'Margaretta' episode (*see below*) in June, 1775. The *Grave of Hannah Weston* is near the highway on the Charles Fish farm at the northern end of the village.

At 59.3 *m*. is the junction with State 1A.

Left on State 1A is WHITNEYVILLE (alt. 70, Whitneyville Town, pop. 229), 4 *m*., a small farming community on the western bank of the Machias River that is the terminus of an annual spring log drive. It is also a terminus of the Grand Lake–Machias Waters Canoe Trip (*see Sports and Recreation: Canoeing*). A marker near the river indicates the spot where the 'Margaretta' was beached, after being towed up the river following her capture, and concealed from the British by leafy boughs.

State 1A runs through wide blueberry plains and rejoins US 1 at Machias, 8.5 *m*.

MACHIAS (Ind.: 'bad little falls') (alt. 80, Machias Town, pop. 1853), 65.1 *m*., seat of Washington County, lies along the Machias River; the town formerly included what is now the town of Machiasport (*see below*). The gristmill in the center of the bridge across the river looks down on the narrow gorge through which the waters tumble and roar ceaselessly. From the bridge are seen the buildings of the *Washington State Normal School* on a high hill overlooking the town.

After the destruction of the Plymouth Colony trading post at Pentagoet by the French, the English in 1633 here established another post under command of Richard Vines, in a spot much closer to the French headquarters; La Tour, French Governor of Acadia, wiped it out almost at once. In 1675 Rhodes, the pirate, used the site as a base for repairs and supplies; a few decades later another pirate, Samuel Bellamy, came here for the same purpose, and, liking the place and deciding that it offered him security, determined to establish a permanent stronghold. Piracy was rampant along the Atlantic seaboard at this time, partly because of English and Spanish trade restrictions, designed to force colonists to buy from the mother country alone; this created a good market for stolen goods in the Colonies. Privateering provided good training for piracy, as Cotton Mather warned in 1704 in one of his 'hanging sermons,' and many men who started out to prey on shipping for their governments soon decided to keep the booty for themselves. Bellamy, from all reports, developed a Robin Hood philosophy on the matter; when he had captured a ship he would harangue its crew, invite them to join him, arguing that the men had as much right to rob as had the shipowners, who were merely powerful bandits who had had laws made to protect their operations.

When Bellamy determined to settle on the site of the present Machias, he erected breastworks and a crude fort before leaving for another expedition with three objectives — recruits, loot, and women. He had left the mouth of the river and was plundering along the Nova Scotian banks when, by mistake, he attacked a French naval vessel. His vessel, the 'Whidaw,' was almost captured before he managed to escape. Sailing south, he had further bad luck; he captured a New Bedford whaler, whose captain pretended to join him and agreed to act as a navigator through the dangerous reefs and shoals. The whaling captain did his part for a time and then deliberately ran his ship aground on a sand bar near Eastham, Mass. The pirate ship, following the lead of the whaler, went on the rocks, and Bellamy and most of his crew drowned.

In 1763 the first permanent English colony was established by settlers from Scarboro near Portland.

The Machias River has played an important part in the town's development as a commercial lumber and shipbuilding center. One of the few remaining 'long lumber' log drives in Maine takes place on the Machias River each spring. Logs are hauled over the snow to the landings, and when the ice goes out of the river they are shoved into the fast-moving water, which hurtles them downstream. When one of the numerous jams occurs, a daring river driver walks out on it to pry loose the key log; if this does not succeed the jam is blasted.

Burnham Tavern (open Sat. aft., June 1 to Oct. 1; small adm. fee), High and Free Sts., a plain two-story gambrel-roofed structure with the lower section of the roof broken back to a vertical wall with five windows, was built in 1770 by Joe Burnham. Beneath each of the four cornerstones of the building the owner placed a box containing a slip of paper inscribed with the words 'hospitality,' 'cheer,' 'hope,' and 'courage.' Over the door hangs the original sign, which reads: 'Drink for the thirsty, food for the hungry, lodging for the weary, and good keeping for horses.' Beneath the roof the townspeople gathered to plan their movements against the British and to discuss the exciting events of the day. Here Jeremiah O'Brien and his comrades planned the capture of the 'Margaretta' *(see below)*.

In the O'Brien Cemetery, about 0.3 *m.* from the center (R), is the *Grave of Captain O'Brien (see below)*. Just beyond the cemetery (L) is a marker indicating the site of his home.

Also on Elm St. about 0.5 *m.* from the center is a small stream called

Foster's Rubicon; the men of Machias met on its banks in June, 1775, to discuss the demands that they furnish lumber to be sent back to Boston for the building of barracks for the British troops. After a long debate in which part of the townsmen advocated compliance and part resistance, Benjamin Foster, a church leader as well as a rebel, sprang across the stream, inviting those who shared his views to follow him. The rebels went first, then those who had been wavering, and finally those who had advocated compliance; and the settlement as a whole was committed to the Revolution.

At 68 *m.* is the junction with a local road.

> Right on this road is MACHIASPORT (alt. 80, Machiasport Town, pop. 825), 4 *m.*, a typical Maine coast village where lumber shipping is now the chief activity.
>
> When news of the battle of Lexington reached this part of Maine in early May, 1775, Ichabod Jones, who had left Massachusetts because of the increasing disturbance to business caused in part by the Boston Port Bill, hastily left for Boston to secure his personal property. The Boston Port commander, however, refused to allow him to take his boat out of the harbor except to return to Maine for lumber to be used in building barracks for the increasing number of British soldiers. The armed schooner 'Margaretta' was sent along as a convoy to enforce the order. Meanwhile, public opinion in Machias had been inflamed and Captain Moore of the 'Margaretta' found a Liberty Pole in the little frontier coast town and citizens incensed at the idea of providing supplies for armies to be used against them. Led by Benjamin Foster and the fiery Irishman, Jeremiah O'Brien, the local citizens commandeered two boats, one of which, however, became stranded, and on June 12, 1775, closed in on the 'Margaretta'; in the fight that followed the British officer was mortally wounded and his boat captured. The following month the Machias men captured a British schooner from Nova Scotia. The British sent Sir George Collier with the 'Ranger' and three other boats to punish the rebels; Collier routed the local force from the breastworks they had hastily thrown up along the river and burned several buildings before his fleet moved on. The capture of the 'Margaretta' has been called the 'first naval battle of the Revolution'; the battle itself was not important, but it provided the Revolutionary leaders in Philadelphia with a talking point in urging the establishment of a navy.
>
> Machiasport was the terminus of the narrow-gauge Machias–Whitneyville R.R., built in 1841 to carry lumber from Whitneyville to Machiasport for shipping, and operated for 50 years by the Sullivan family of Whitneyville. One of the locomotives used on this railroad is now at the Crosby Laboratory, University of Maine, Orono.
>
> From *Wright's Lookout*, a bold rock at the top of Corn Hill, a few hundred yards back from the main street, is a splendid view of the Machias headlands and the western end of the Bay of Fundy.
>
> At the southern end of the village, on the western bank of the Machias River, is the State reservation holding the *Earthworks of Fort Machias*, or Fort O'Brien as it is locally called because it was erected in part through the activities of the O'Briens. After the Collier raid, Washington ordered a regiment of militia recruited and sent to protect the settlement. In 1781, Fort Machias was made part of the national defense. The British, however, did not return to the little town until 1814, when they took the fort and burned the barracks. The place was again fortified in 1863, during the Civil War, but was not attacked.
>
> At *Clark's Point*, 7 *m.* (L), are the so-called *Picture Rocks*. Figures somewhat resembling men, animals, and landscapes can be seen on a slanting ledge below the high-water mark. Some authorities who have examined the formations believe they are geologic, others that they are hieroglyphics.

EAST MACHIAS (alt. 60, East Machias Town, pop. 1253), 69.6 *m.*, is

Tour 1: From Portsmouth to Clair 237

divided by the East Machias River, the residential area and the business districts being on opposite sides of the stream.

On top of a hill across the river (R) is *Washington Academy*. A general interest in having a local school was shown as early as 1790–91, and a petition for help from the Government in the undertaking was transmitted to the General Court of Massachusetts in that year. The petition was granted, and Township 11, since known as Cutler, was given as an endowment for an academy, but it was not until September, 1823, that Washington Academy was opened.

In the *Library* (R), a brick building with two old millstones from an early gristmill set strikingly in the front wall, one on either side of the entrance, is a canvas showing a panorama of the community in the prosperous lumbering and shipbuilding days.

At 73 *m.* (L) is the graveled entrance to the *Summer Surveying School* of the Massachusetts Institute of Technology, on the shore of Gardner Lake; the neighborhood provides a variety of surveying problems.

Indian Lake (fishing and boating facilities), 76.6 *m.* (L), lies along the road, the blue of its waters enhanced by the dark green foliage of the dense forest surrounding it.

WHITING (alt. 60, Whiting Town, pop. 327), 82.2 *m.*, a village formerly called Orangetown, in an area where extensive lumbering operations are still carried on, is recognized by the large piles of lumber along the road near its center. The route passes a lumber mill on the Orange River, which has been dammed at this point to provide water-power.

In this area are long stretches of forests, broken occasionally by small scrubby farms. In spite of the extensive lumbering operations that have been carried on in what is now the State of Maine, the forests have not been seriously depleted. The country is full of game. Many rabbits are caught here and shipped to other parts of Maine, as well as to other States, for stocking game preserves.

At the rear of a small white church (L) is the *Grave of Colonel John Crane*, the first white settler. He was a member of the Boston Tea Party, and during the Revolution commanded one of the batteries whose fire diverted the attention of the British from the American forces in their capture of Dorchester Heights in March, 1776.

At Whiting is the junction with State 189 (*see Tour 1M*).

DENNYSVILLE (alt. 30, Dennysville Town, pop. 443), 91.5 *m.*, took its name from Dennys River which was named for an Indian chief whose hunting grounds were in this region. Swift Dennys River, where there is excellent fishing (*see Sports and Recreation: Fishing*), parallels the main street over which tall trees form an arch.

In 1786 the township land was granted to General Benjamin Lincoln of Hingham, Mass., who, at the surrender of Yorktown, was selected to conduct the British to the spot where their arms were deposited.

There is a fine *Salmon-fishing Pool* near the center of the village.

The *Lincoln Home* (*private*), 0.5 mile north of the center and facing the river, was erected in 1787 by artisans from Hingham, Mass., under the direction of General Lincoln's son, Theodore. It is a yellow, two-story structure. Theodore, who occupied the house, had large lumber interests and employed many Indians of the district. James Audubon, the artist and naturalist, was a friend of Theodore's son, Thomas, who assisted Audubon in making arrangements for an expedition to Labrador in 1833. Members of Lincoln's family still own and occupy the house, which contains many of the early furnishings, also old books and documents.

In the store of I. K. Kilby (R) in the village is a *Collection of Indian Relics* (*open*), found in the neighborhood.

WEST PEMBROKE (alt. 50, Pembroke Town), 96.7 *m.*, which seems part of Pembroke village, rather than a separate community, has a number of sturdy old homes. H. Styles Bridges, Governor of New Hampshire (1935–36) and U.S. Senator (1937–   ), was born here on September 9, 1896.

> Left from West Pembroke on State 214, an improved gravel road, is *Meddybemps Lake*, 10 *m.*, with excellent fishing (*boats and canoes for hire*) and a good bathing beach.
>
> This is one of the many hunting regions where the illegal practice of 'deer jacking,' less frequent today, was popular. The bright light of a hooded lantern or of a flashlight fascinates the fleet-footed animal, making him a target for the huntsman's bullet. When shot, the deer seldom drops immediately, but runs sometimes for hours, the hunter in hot pursuit. This phase, known as 'deer running,' develops fleet runners, particularly in deer-jacking expeditions when the law is pursuing the hunters as swiftly as the hunters are pursuing the deer.
>
> A story is told of a Washington County stripling who, left unwarned on sentry duty at Cedar Creek, Va., when a retreat was ordered, found himself alone facing the advancing enemy. He made his solitary retreat from Cedar Creek with the speed he had acquired in deer running in the Meddybemps region. He is said to have reported at Harpers Ferry, W. Va., 19 miles from his post, in advance of the dispatch bearer, who was on horseback.

PEMBROKE (alt. 80, Pembroke Town, pop. 965), 97.7 *m.*, is a village of pleasant homes along the bank of the Pennamaquan River. While the principal industries are now the packing of blueberries and sardines, the substantial, well-built houses recall the prosperity of the wooden-hull era, when extensive shipbuilding activities were carried on in the area.

The large, square, stone building of the *Old Iron Works* (R), resembles an old fort. The plant was established in 1828 with machinery brought from Wales. Much of the ore used came from bogs in the vicinity.

PERRY (alt. 40, Perry Town, pop. 992), 103.6 *m.*, lies on a double bend of US 1 where it crosses Boyden Stream. The houses are few and scattered.

At Perry is the junction with State 190 (*see Tour 1N*).

At 105.5 *m.* is a granite boulder (L) placed by the National Geographic Society to mark the *Forty-fifth Parallel of Latitude*, which is exactly midway between the Equator and the North Pole.

ROBBINSTON (alt. 60, Robbinston Town, pop. 582), 111.5 *m.*, is a village whose main street parallels the St. Croix River (*ferry service to St.*

TOUR 1: From Portsmouth to Clair   239

Andrews, N.B.). The smokestack of a sardine-canning factory that burned down sometime in the past is a landmark here. Fishing is the principal industry of the town, supplemented by sardine canning. In the spring when the herring are running, the fish weirs offshore can be seen from the road.

RED BEACH (alt. 90, Ward 9, City of Calais), 115 *m.*, takes its name from the color of the granite outcrop along the shore. The village lies along the main highway in a pleasant wooded area from which the wide island-dotted St. Croix is visible.

> Opposite Red Beach, in the St. Croix River, is *Dochet Island* (alt. 40), which is reached by rowboat.
>
> In 1603, Pierre du Guast, the Sieur de Monts, received the trading concession for Acadia, which, in the grand manner of the times, was defined as a territory extending from Cape Breton Island to a point well below the present New York City. In the following spring he set sail with his lieutenant, Samuel de Champlain, and fourscore colonists, including a Huguenot minister and a Catholic priest, landing on June 26, 1604, on this island, which he called St. Croix, where he expected to establish a trading post and settlement. So sketchy was knowledge of the New World at the time that the settlers brought with them part of the timber used in the erection of their buildings. Before winter arrived, the island held a storehouse, dining hall, kitchen, barracks, and a blacksmith shop, and carefully laid out gardens. An unusually severe winter and scurvy wrought such discouragement that in the spring of 1605 de Monts and Champlain sailed off south to find a more suitable place for the colony; in August, however, they decided to move it to the spot that is now Annapolis Royal, in Nova Scotia. Dochet Island was not entirely abandoned; for the French used it for a garrison at intervals for some years.
>
> This early settlement played an important part in the adjustment of the boundary question at the end of the Revolutionary War; both the United States and Great Britain acknowledged the River St. Croix as the point of departure in drawing the line, but Britain disputed the American claim on what river bore this name. Discovery of Champlain's map and the subsequent examination of the ruins of the early settlement decided the matter; had the British won their point, eastern Maine would probably now be Canadian territory.

At 122.2 *m.* is the *Saint Croix Golf Club (open to visitors)*, on the bank of the river.

CALAIS (*pron. Kal'is*) (alt. 82, pop. 5470), 123.9 *m.*, the 'international city' of Maine, is the only city in the State on the Canadian border. It is a port of entry and many of its citizens came from the Canadian Provinces. The city spreads out on a hilly terrain along the western bank of the St. Croix River, directly opposite St. Stephen, N.B. The mile-long main street, a wide thoroughfare lined with fine old elm trees, runs from the end of the International Bridge to the St. Croix Country Club at the southern end of the city. The business district is in the northern end of the city, close to the river; from the bridge are visible the docks that once played an important part in the city's industrial life. Encircling the business district are quiet streets with attractive houses surrounded by trees, broad lawns, and well-trimmed shrubbery. Handsome churches and modern schools add to the air of prosperity. The municipal affairs of Calais and St. Stephen are allied to the extent that the fire engines of the two communities clang back and forth across the International Bridge to answer alarms in what to each community is technically a foreign land. The

Calais water supply comes from St. Stephen, being piped across the river. United States and Canadian currencies are accepted in both cities.

The first settlers, who arrived in 1779, were attracted to Calais by the wealth of timber, the fertile soil, and the abundance of fish and game.

Calais early became an important lumbering center. The launching in 1801 of the 'Liberty,' the first vessel built in the community, marked the beginning of a profitable industry that lasted till the end of the 'era of tall ships.' In 1809, the Massachusetts Legislature named the settlement for the French port of Calais, as a compliment to France because of the aid rendered to the struggling Colonies during the Revolution. After 1820 the primitive backwoods settlement began to expand rapidly. Roads and bridges were built; churches and homes sprang up along the highways. In 1850, with a population of 4749, it was incorporated as a city.

In 1935, when the 'Normandie' made its maiden trip to America, the French city of Calais sent to the American Calais a hand-carved mahogany chest containing soil from its ancient cemeteries, four volumes of Calais history, and a dozen pieces of lace. In 1936 the American city shipped to France a tablet of red granite, taken from Dochet Island.

The *Mason House* (*private*), at the point (R) where Main St. turns toward the customhouse, was the home of Noah Smith, Jr. (1800–68). Smith, paternal grandfather of the writer, Kate Douglas Wiggin, is said to have been one of the last people who had official business with President Lincoln before his assassination; at that time he received the President's signature to a pardon granted to a young Calais soldier who had been convicted of treason.

Sec. e. CALAIS to FORT KENT, 210.4 *m.*

North of Calais, US 1 passes through a wooded area where the occasional villages have been chopped out of the wilderness; part of the country is so thinly populated that it belongs to the so-called wild lands, township-size units having no local government. Sportsmen and hunters who enter these areas should hire guides because only expert woodsmen can find their way about. The upper two-thirds of the route passes through the great potato-growing section of Aroostook County, where in summer the fields are undulating seas of green, broken in July by white and purple blossoms.

Aroostook County was involved in the long dispute between England and the United States over the boundary question, which was finally settled by the Webster-Ashburton Treaty of 1842. Before this time a series of border disputes and clashes had taken place, the best-known of which was the 'Aroostook War' of 1839–40, in which Maine men went north to expel Canadian lumbermen who, the 'Mainiacs' believed, were cutting lumber in United States territory. Many of the men who took part in this expedition went back to settle the border county; however, the development of the large area was very much hampered by lack of transportation facilities until the Bangor and Aroostook R.R. was completed; produce of

TOUR 1: From Portsmouth to Clair 241

the district had to be taken over to the St. John River in New Brunswick, or to a Canadian railroad, passing in a roundabout way through foreign territory before it reached the home markets. The line was extended to Fort Kent in 1902.

North of Van Buren, US 1 follows the northern boundary of Maine beside the St. John River from which wide undulating meadows spread to the edge of woodlands. In this area 90 per cent of the population is of French extraction, many of the people being descendants of the Acadians who were expelled from Canada during the French and Indian War, an event that was the basis of Longfellow's 'Evangeline.' These Roman Catholics still follow many of the customs brought by their ancestors from the coast of Brittany.

CALAIS, 0 *m.* (*see Tour 1, sec. d*).

MILLTOWN (alt. 85, Ward 1 of Calais), 1.5 *m.*, is, as its name suggests, a mill settlement on the banks of the St. Croix (R), many of the residents being employed in the cotton mills across the river. The monotony of the drab buildings here is relieved by the beauty of the swift St. Croix rapids. *Magurrewock Mountain* (L) rises precipitously almost from the edge of the road.

At 4.6 *m.* is the junction with a local road.

> Right on this road is BARING (alt. 100, Baring Town, pop. 204), 1 *m.*, an agricultural community named in honor of Alexander Baring, Lord Ashburton, England's representative in the Webster-Ashburton Treaty negotiations of 1842 (*see above*). Baring was the son-in-law of William Bingham (*see sec. c*).

At 6.9 *m.* (L) is a junction with State 9 (*see Tour 5*).

WOODLAND (alt. 130, Baileyville Town, pop. 2017), 10.1 *m.*, visible from US 1, is several hundred yards east of the highway on the banks of the St. Croix River. The community sprang into being in 1905 with the establishment of a paper mill whose huge stack and conveyor look down on a neat modern village. Large piles of pulpwood fill the river and line the shore near the railroad tracks.

Small quantities of gold have been found in *Wapsaconhagan Stream* at the south end of the village.

PRINCETON (alt. 210, Princeton Town, pop. 984), 19.6 *m.*, a small elm-shaded village (*guides and equipment for hunting and fishing*), lies at the southeast end of *Leweys Lake*, a headwater of the St. Croix River. The clear waters of the lake are excellent for both swimming and fishing and the near-by woods abound with game for the hunter. Princeton is the starting point of the Grand Lake–Machias Waters Canoe Trip (*see Sports and Recreation: Canoeing*).

> Left from Princeton on a dirt road to the *Adventist Camp Meeting Grounds* (*open*), 6 *m.*, on the shores of Big Lake (*bathing beach; cottages and camps for rent*).

US 1 now crosses a steel bridge to enter the *Unorganized Township of Indiantown*, a sparsely populated area, inhabited in part by the Passamaquoddy Indians. Granted to them by treaty in 1796, this section has always been their favorite hunting ground. Many fierce engagements between the Passamaquoddies and roving bands of Mohawks once took place here.

The road follows Big Lake shore about a mile.

At 21.9 m. is the junction with a dirt road.

> Left on this road 2 m., then sharp left on another dirt road, to an *Indian Reservation* (*open*), 4 m., at Peter Dana's Point on Big Lake. Many new houses have been built here for the Passamaquoddies, while near-by is a convent and chapel. These Indians hunt, fish, act as guides for the region, and make baskets for sale to visitors.
>
> Near the reservation is a *State Fish Hatchery* (*open*).

Just beyond (R) the junction are six *Log Cabins* used by the University of Maine Forestry Department as a field work base for forestry students.

WAITE (alt. 330, Waite Town, pop. 165), 28.9 m.

> Left from Waite on a local road is *West Musquash Lake*, 6 m., with sporting camps along its shores. The occasional splash of fish and the myriad symphonies of the deep woods break the stillness of this delightful spot.

At 29.6 m. is the junction with a narrow dirt road.

> Right on this road, which passes through thick woods, is *Tomah Stream*, 5 m., a ribbon of glistening waters flowing between deeply wooded banks, and named in honor of an Indian chief who aided the settlers of Machias during the Revolution.

TOPSFIELD (alt. 495, Topsfield Town, pop. 224), 35.1 m., an agricultural village, is in fine hunting country, and it is not unusual to see deer grazing in apple orchards not far from the road. The township is rich in cultivated fields, neat farms, and stretches of woodland dotted with lakes where hunting and fishing lure sportsmen from many distant points. The fire lookout on Musquash Mountain (L) is plainly visible.

> Left from Topsfield on State 16 to *Musquash Lake*, 4 m., a fine fishing ground.

BROOKTON (alt. 420, Brookton Town, pop. 240), 43.4 m., is a small village at a 'four corners.' The shores of *Jackson Brook Lake* (*cottages for hire*), where there is excellent fishing, are only a stone's throw right.

> 1. Right from Brookton on a local road to FOREST STATION (alt. 410, Unorganized Township of Forest City), 3 m., a stopping place on the Maine Central Railroad.
>
> FOREST CITY (alt. 444, Unorganized Township of Forest City, pop. 70), 12 m. Sporting camps have replaced extensive lumbering operations in this forest settlement on the shore of East Grand Lake.
>
> 2. Left from Brookton, on a dirt road, to *Baskahegan Lake*, 1.5 m., one of the largest bodies of water in this section. Surrounded by deep woods and canopied by the blue bowl of the sky, this wide sheet of water is ideal for the angler who wishes beautiful scenery combined with the prospect of a well-filled creel.

EATON (alt. 407, Danforth Town), 49.8 m., is a little woods hamlet that was once engaged in lumbering.

DANFORTH (alt. 387, Danforth Town, pop. 1462), 55.1 m., in the Baskahegan River valley, is the scene of much activity in spring and summer, when its two lumbering mills are in operation. Huge logs line the banks and float on the surface of the river. The sharp tang of fresh-cut wood fills the air as the saws buzz and whine and a great mound of yellow sawdust rises like a grotesque beehive on the river bank beside the spool mill.

TOUR 1: From Portsmouth to Clair

WESTON (alt. 720, Weston Town, pop. 323), 60 *m.*, lies in a setting of great natural beauty. From every point on the highway which runs along the side of a hill and then climbs abruptly to the summit, the view of East Grand Lake (R) is magnificent. Apple orchards, pasture land, wood lots, and hay fields slope from the homes that face the road, to the woods-fringed shores of the body of water. In the distance a chain of smaller lakes makes an intricate design in the dense forests that stretch to the green-clad Canadian hills.

ORIENT (alt. 460, Orient Town, pop. 161), 66.2 *m.*, a tiny community in the woods, owes its existence in great part to the fine hunting and fishing in the vicinity.

> Right from Orient on a local road to *Sunset Park*, 3 *m.*, on the north end of East Grand Lake (*boats for hire*), where there is a bathing beach.

NORTH AMITY (alt. 580, Amity Town, pop. 324), 74.2 *m.*, stretches out along the main highway on a high ridge of land, from the south end of which there is an excellent view of Mt. Katahdin.

CARY (alt. 435, Cary Plantation, pop. 241), 78 *m.*, is completely surrounded by dense woods.

HODGDON (alt. 470, Hodgdon Town, pop. 1054), 82.5 *m.*, is at the foot of *Westford Hill* (R), a tree-crowned elevation within easy walking distance of the main highway. Here the checkered pattern of Aroostook farmland meets the eye, the farmstead showing as on a picture map, with Mt. Katahdin's bold peak on the skyline (L).

HOULTON (alt. 340, Houlton Town, pop. 6865) (*see HOULTON*), 88.1 *m.*, is at a junction with US 2 (*see Tour 4*).

At 94.6 *m.* is a junction with Willey Road.

> Left on the Willey Road to two *Circular Depressions* (L), 1 *m.*, which are thought to be 'sink holes' or the beds of lakes that have long since dried up.
>
> At 2 *m.* there is fine fishing and swimming at *Carry Lake*, which is surrounded by a dense growth of pine and spruce that fills the air with a clean sharp scent.

LITTLETON (alt. 440, Littleton Town, pop. 1035), 95.5 *m.*, lies on a plain, its only distinctive feature being the long rows of potato sheds along the railroad tracks on the northern edge of the village.

In 1800, when the territory was still part of the State of Massachusetts, the southern half of this town, then unsettled, was granted to Williams College, and in 1801 the great forest-covered northern half was given to Framingham (Mass.) Academy. Settlements were founded here shortly after these dates, but the town was not incorporated until 1856.

During the latter part of the 19th century camp meetings, lasting several days, played an important part in the social life of such Aroostook communities as Littleton. They were held in pine groves or near lake shores, usually in August after the hay was in, people coming from long distances and bringing their own food and bedding. The living quarters were either rough bunkhouses or temporary shacks. Each camp ground had a tabernacle, often merely a long roof over ground covered with fresh sawdust; in front of the rows of pine benches was a platform holding the speaker's table or lectern, and the little organ with foot-operated bellows that supplied the music. During the meetings, held in the mornings, afternoons, and evenings, emotional fervor often reached a high pitch; but between times horse trading and the swapping of land, farm implements, patterns, and gossip, were carried on with zeal. Many Aroostook courtings began and were completed during these gatherings. Camp meetings are still held but the radio and automobiles have lessened the social need of them.

Visible from the highway (L) is a group of eskers, or 'horsebacks' as they are called locally, whose long ridges are remnants of the vast sheets of ice that covered this part of Maine during the glacial period.

MONTICELLO (alt. 415, Monticello Town, pop. 1467), 100.7 *m.*, settled in 1830, was incorporated in 1846. A small river divides the one-street village, which spreads over two hilltops.

Conroy and *Howard Lakes*, on the Wadleigh Road, are good fishing waters, and the surrounding woods afford excellent hunting.

BRIDGEWATER (alt. 415, Bridgewater Town, pop. 1235), 108.6 *m.*, with its neat, well-built homes along the main highway, is the principal settlement of this heavily wooded township. Near the village is *Portland Lake*, excellent for swimming and camping; *Whitney Brook* offers good trout fishing.

BLAINE (alt. 410, Blaine Town, pop. 1061), 114.3 *m.*, is a small farming village. Left is the old *Valley House (private)*, built in 1851 and known as a 'good bedded' hostelry in the days when a good bed was the most desired haven at the end of a day spent in a stagecoach bumping over the rough dirt road between Presque Isle and Houlton.

MARS HILL (alt. 710, Mars Hill Town, pop. 1837), 115 *m.*, takes its name from near-by *Mars Hill* (alt. 1660), a notable eminence in the low rolling country here. This hill entered into the hotly contested boundary dispute when Great Britain contended that this peak was 'the highlands which divide those rivers that empty themselves into the river St. Lawrence, from those that fall into the Atlantic Ocean,' named in Treaty of 1782; the United States maintained that the highlands were much farther north and nearer the St. Lawrence River.

> Right from the village on a short trail to the top of the mountain, from which there is an excellent view of the St. John Valley.

EASTON (alt. 580, Easton Town, pop. 1505), 126.2 *m.*, is a small village in a pleasant farm country.

PRESQUE ISLE (alt. 450, Presque Isle Town, pop. 6965), 133.2 *m.*, in the valley of the Aroostook River and surrounded by some of the most fertile land in Aroostook County, is a bustling center of trade with an up-to-date appearance.

The first explorers of this region came down the Arnold Trail from Canada to the Kennebec River, then overland; the first permanent settlers arrived at Presque Isle in 1820, but there were only 732 people in the township in 1860, the year after it was incorporated. Stories of pine trees so tall that 'the clouds were torn as they passed over them,' and of land rich in game, told by those returning from this northern area, in time tempted other adventurous souls to try their fortunes here.

Like the neighboring townships of Caribou, Fort Fairfield, and Mars Hill, Presque Isle plants more potatoes than any other crop. In addition, however, to the 10,000 acres of potatoes, the farmers of the town sow 4500 acres of oats and cut about 7000 tons of hay annually.

One of the principal industries of Presque Isle is the manufacture of potato starch. The improvement in the quality of the potatoes of the district has meant that fewer potatoes are used in the production of starch, but the mills still turn out thousands of pounds of this commodity each year.

The *Presque Isle Fairgrounds*, outer State St., are the scene of the annual Northern Maine Fair in September, providing a spirited carnival and holiday for people from all over 'the Aroostook.' The primary object of the fair is to promote agriculture in all its branches. There are also exhibits of handicrafts as well as the usual side shows, music, fireworks, and dancing. The major event, however, is horse racing. Enthusiasm and betting run high. Aroostook men are particularly interested in pacing and trotting; native-born sons are the drivers in many instances and their skill in the 'racing start,' a complicated and often long-drawn-out affair, evokes loud cheers or angry comment from the partisans in the grandstand. The light sulkies used in this type of racing occasionally lock wheels with resultant spills that add to the excitement.

Close to the hearts of the people of northern Aroostook is the name and memory of John R. Braden, one of the most famous pacers that ever appeared on Maine tracks. A *Granite Monument*, opposite the grandstand, tells the story of this great horse's record.

During the first week in March an annual Winter Carnival, sponsored by the Abnaki Club, is held with a lively program of sporting and social events.

> Left from Presque Isle on State 1A to *Aroostook Farm* (L) (*open*), 1 *m.*, a 275-acre experiment station. The United States Department of Agriculture, in co-operation with the University of Maine and the Aroostook County Farm Bureau, conducts farm research work here. Experiments in plant foods, soils, plant diseases, growing methods, and crop control are carried on, both in the field and in a modern, well-equipped laboratory.

CARIBOU (alt. 495, Caribou Town, pop. 7248), 145.5 *m.*, the potato-shipping center of northern Aroostook County, sends out thousands of carloads for seed and consumption.

Along the railroad tracks of this community on Caribou Stream are long potato warehouses with a capacity of 400,000 barrels. Offices of potato-protection societies, brokers, growers, and shippers occupy the buildings of the modern business district. During the growing and picking season the streets of the town teem with motor-trucks and the low-slung horse-drawn wagons used in transporting potato barrels. Conversation revolves around the possible price the crop will bring, and harvest time finds speculation rife on the trend of the potato market.

When the crops have ripened in the broad surrounding fields, an army of pickers arrives from all parts of the United States on their circuit of seasonal jobs. In the old days the farmers of Aroostook kept a 'shed room' for the farm hands. The pickers are still 'boarded' in the potato country where they are well fed and housed. Pickers are paid 10 cents a barrel and an unusually good worker can average 100 barrels a day during the harvest season. The farmers fare well in the good years and it is not unusual for the potato growers in the district to receive $5,000,000 for the year's crop.

In February the annual Aroostook Sportsmen's Show attracts large numbers of visitors; the climax of the event is the Bangor-Caribou Ski Marathon of about 170 miles.

The *Caribou Municipal Airport*, south of the village on US 1, the first municipal airport built in Maine, is the only port of entry (1937) for airplanes on the Maine-Canadian border. Its hangars accommodate 10 planes.

The *Aroostook* and *Little Madawaska Rivers* and *Caribou Stream*, flowing through the township, offer excellent trout and salmon fishing.

> 1. Right from Caribou on State 223 to a *State Fish Hatchery* (R) (*open*), 1 *m.*, which annually stocks the streams in this part of Aroostook with thousands of salmon and trout. Near the feeding ponds of the hatchery is a picnic grove.
>
> 2. Right from Caribou on State 161 is FORT FAIRFIELD (alt. 390, Fort Fairfield Town, pop. 5393), 13 *m.*, port of entry from Canada on the St. John River. It was named for a border fort which, in turn, was named in honor of Governor John Fairfield. The town was settled in 1816 by people from the Canadian Provinces, who played an important part in the Aroostook War (*see History*).
>
> The *Aroostook Country Club, Ltd.*, across the river and just over the Canadian border, was built during the prohibition era. It has a 9-hole golf course and a clubhouse used by citizens of both countries.
>
> 3. Left from Caribou on State 161 is NEW SWEDEN (alt. 865, New Sweden Town, pop. 898), 8.9 *m.*, a modern settlement that is the result of a successful immigration experiment of 1870. The legislature in that year appointed William Widgery Thomas, Jr., Commissioner of Immigration. Free farms had been offered by the State and Thomas, former consul at Gothenburg, Sweden, proceeded to that country in the spring, recruited a colony of 51 men, women, and children, and returned with them to this township in Aroostook, which had been set aside for their occupancy. Other people from Sweden followed and today's population consists of their descendants. Every 10 years festivities are held in commemoration of the founding of the community.

VAN BUREN (alt. 495, Van Buren Town, pop. 4721), 167 *m.*, named for President Martin Van Buren, is the largest of the northern boundary towns in population. The inhabitants are employed in lumber operations or in the potato fields. A bridge here spans the St. John River, which parallels the main street.

During the days when extensive lumbering operations were being carried on in the vast tracts of land at the head of the St. John River and its tributaries, the river was used to float the huge logs to sawmills and

TOUR 1: From Portsmouth to Clair   247

markets. At intervals booms, or floating chains of logs, were attached to piers and other structures on the banks to hold back the flow of logs. The five small islands in the river near Van Buren formed a barrier that could be utilized in forming one of these temporary dams and the place was the scene of great activity during the spring log drives. The air would be filled with the rumble of cracking ice, and the thunder and crash of the logs hurled against each other. Frequent jams occurred that had to be broken at considerable risk to the drivers who, here as elsewhere, were a wild, hard-drinking, dare-devil crew. Their feats, appetites, and vocabularies became matters of legend that filled every small boy in the community with envy. The spring drives continue but have lost some of their colorful character.

KEEGAN (alt. 450, Van Buren Town), 169.3 *m.*, is the site of the first French-Acadian settlement in the town. The lumber industry, the backbone of the community in the boom days, has dwindled to sporadic bursts of activity and lumber mills along the river are idle most of the year.

GRAND ISLE (alt. 510, Grand Isle Town, pop. 1408), 182 *m.*, is a village that, like other small ones in this area, is notable only for the ornateness of its church.

ST. DAVID (alt. 510, Madawaska Town), 187.8 *m.*, is the original place of settlement of the Acadian refugees who came to this region from Nova Scotia (*see above*). They had traveled along the St. John until they reached a village of the Malecite Indians, who permitted them to land on the forest-lined shores. Acres of meadowland and pasture were cleared, roads were built, and commodious farm buildings and smaller dwellings sprang up. Opposite, on the Canadian side of the river, is the Malecite Indian Reservation.

A large *White Cross*, at the rear of *St. David's Church* (R), 188.6 *m.*, marks the landing-place of the Acadians.

MADAWASKA (alt. 595, Madawaska Town, pop. 3533), 190.6 *m.*, a port of entry from Canada into the United States, has an atmosphere of industrial activity that differentiates it from other Aroostook communities on this route. At the northern edge of the village on Bridge St. are (R) the large *Fraser Paper Company, Ltd., Mills* (*visited by permit*). The establishment of these mills in 1926 brought skilled workmen and business to what had been a sleepy little river village. Large pipes that carry the paper pulp in liquid form span the St. John River and connect the mill here with the one at Edmundston, N.B.

FRENCHVILLE (alt. 501, Frenchville Town, pop. 1525), 197.9 *m.*, is strung out along a bend of the St. John River. As in near-by towns the inhabitants here are descendants of the French Acadians, and are dependent upon the potato crop for their livelihood. Scattered throughout the area are occasional sawmills, reminders of the once-active lumber industry.

Left from Frenchville on State 162 is ST. AGATHA (san tagat') (alt. 615, St. Agatha Town, pop. 1596), 4.5 *m.*, on the northwest shore of *Long Lake*, the starting-

point of the Fish River Chain of Lakes (*see Sports and Recreation*). There are
several sporting camps (*guides available*) along the shores of the lake which offers
excellent trout and salmon fishing.

At 200.1 *m.* are the imposing buildings of *St. Luke Church and St. Rosaire Convent.*

FORT KENT (alt. 530, Fort Kent Town, pop. 4726), 210.2 *m.*, is a port of entry from Canada. It was settled by French refugees from Acadia and, when incorporated in 1869, took the name of a fort that was erected here in 1839 (*see below*). Here, as in other villages along the river, the simple one- and two-story buildings are overtopped by the spire of the Roman Catholic church. Most of the population speaks a provincial French and, being strongly religious, observes the church feasts and fasts faithfully.

A Corpus Christi Procession, held on the Thursday following Trinity Sunday, which is the eighth Sunday after Easter, is the most impressive of these. This medieval splendor and pageantry is preserved in the colorful vestments of the priests and in the banners.

Fort Kent, on Main St. opposite Pleasant St., marked by a small heavily built *Blockhouse* (*open*), is a relic of the troubled days of the Aroostook War. Edward Kent was Governor of Maine in 1838 when plans were made for this fort to protect the lumber interests of the area, and it, as well as the township, was named for him. The blockhouse stands on a slight eminence and commands a view of the near-by St. John River. The sturdy timbers, the hand-wrought ironware of the doors and windows, and the weathered wood of the blockhouse show the painstaking workmanship of an early day.

A cannon that belonged to the fort is now on the greensward in front of the library in Fort Fairfield (*see above*), to the disgust of the citizens of Fort Kent. After Fort Fairfield had been torn down the citizens of that town came to regret that they had no souvenir of the Aroostook War. Someone there discovered that the custodian of the old Fort Kent cannon was very fond of strong spirits and arranged to have him liberally supplied with them while the cannon was moved away.

Fort Kent is at a junction with State 11 (*see Tour* 6). The village is the terminus of the Allagash River Canoe Trip (*see Sports and Recreation: Canoeing*).

> Left from Fort Kent, near the International Bridge, on a local road to ST. FRANCIS (alt. 597; St. Francis Plantation, pop. 1367), 16 *m.*, a small French settlement near the point where the St. Francis River flows into the St. John River. This woods-surrounded settlement is one of the northern termini on the Allagash River Canoe Trip.

At 210.4 *m.* (R) is the *International Bridge.* Clair, N.B., lies on the opposite side of the river.

TOUR 1 A : *From* JUNCTION WITH US 1 *to* CAPE NEDDICK, 15.4 *m.*, Unnumbered road and State 1A.

Via Kittery, Kittery Point, York, York Harbor, York Beach.
Two-lane tarred roadbed.

THIS route, an alternate to US 1 just north of the New Hampshire Line, follows the Piscataqua River near the sea.

An unnumbered road branches east from US 1 (*see Tour 1, sec. a*), 0 *m.*, at a point 0.5 *m.* north of the Portsmouth Bridge.

KITTERY (alt. 50, Kittery Town, pop. 4400), 0.3 *m.*, is the administrative center of a town, formerly much larger, that was incorporated October 20, 1647, as Piscataqua Plantation. The interests of the village center largely around the *Portsmouth Navy Yard* (*open to public*), the entrance to which is right. The yard, established in 1806, is spread over several islands in the Piscataqua River. Admiral Cervera and his staff, captured during the Spanish-American War, were technically held prisoners in the yard for a time. The so-called Portsmouth Conference, for the arrangement of the treaty of peace at the end of the Russo-Japanese War, was held here, the treaty being signed in the Supply Department Building.

Kittery has been interested in shipbuilding since its earliest days. The 'Ranger' was built in this yard in 1777 and the members of the crew were chiefly Kittery men. This was the ship, commanded by John Paul Jones and sent to France to carry word to the American commissioners that Burgoyne had surrendered, that received the first salute accorded a ship of the new Republic. Kittery yards also built the 'Kearsarge,' whose fight with the 'Alabama' was an important naval event during the Civil War.

At 0.5 *m.* (R) is a good view of the Navy Yard buildings. The highway proceeds between rows of beautiful, well-kept old homes.

The *Lady Pepperell House* (*private*), 2.1 *m.* (R), was built between 1760 and 1765 for the widow of Sir William Pepperell, soldier-merchant (*see below*). Lady Pepperell, born Marjory Bray, lived here till her death in 1789, always using her former title in spite of the Revolution that destroyed it, and demanding the deference to which she felt it entitled her. The house, an elaborate two-story structure of Georgian design with a hip roof and four large chimneys, is said to have been built by two skilled English carpenters. The ell in the rear is of later construction. The main façade is heavy and lacking in refinement, in spite of the corner quoins and the pedimented central pavilion, which is flanked by two pedestaled Ionic pilasters, whose richly carved caps carry a bellied fringe and cornice uniting them with the modillioned main cornice. The most interesting room in the house, said to be the work of Pelatiah Fernald, a local man, is the small one behind the parlor; it has a charming fireplace, paneled and finished flush with the closet on either side of it.

Opposite the house is the *First Congregational Church*, built in 1730 and remodeled and turned in 1874. The most interesting feature of the building is the pulpit; the steps on each side are of later date, but the central part, with delicate paneling and graceful lines, bears the date 1730. The church has a belfry and many-paned windows. In the cemetery near-by is the *Grave of Celia Thaxter*, the poet, who died in 1894.

Next to the church is the entrance to the long tree-bordered walk leading to the *Sparhawk House* (1742), classed among the really fine Georgian houses of America, and said to have been built by Sir William Pepperell for his son-in-law. Except for the addition of a rear ell and a cupola, the house has been little changed since it was built. The massive structure, now painted white, has a gambrel roof broken by end chimneys and, on the front, by five pedimented dormers. The many-paned windows of the first story on the front, and of both stories on the sides, have triple pediments. The entrance, with a 12-paneled door, richly carved pilasters, and graceful scrolled pediment, is the most interesting feature of the exterior. The house is of the central-hall type, with four rooms on each floor; the stairway, with a fluted newel topped with a pineapple motif, has richly carved and elaborately turned and twisted balusters. The parlor on the right, which is wainscoted and paneled, contains an octagonal chimney, the fireplace of which, with paneled overmantel, is flanked by delicately fluted pilasters. The reception room, also finished with fine raised paneling and having deeply recessed windows and window seats, is somewhat plainer in design.

At 2.4 *m*. (R) is the entrance to *Fort McClary* (*open*), which commands a view of the river.

The fort, now partly in ruins, was built in 1690 and called first Pepperell's Fort and later Fort William. The present name was given at the time of the Revolutionary War. The fort was garrisoned again during the Civil War, extensive repairs and additions being made. It is hexagonal in shape. The chief feature of interest now is the old blockhouse with overhang, which was built in 1812.

A winding road leads through a forested area to KITTERY POINT (alt. 40, Kittery Town), 2.8 *m*., one of the earliest settled sections of the town. It is now a fishing village and summer resort. The lighthouse on *Appledore Island* is visible from the point on a clear day.

In the center of the village is the *Pepperell House* (*private*), a weather-beaten two-and-a-half-story dwelling with gambrel roof. It was built in 1682 and was the home of the first William Pepperell, father of the baronet. The door and window casings still show the marks of hand cutting and the windows have the original lights, 12 in the upper sashes, 8 in the lower. Above the front door is a spread-eagle decoration of metal.

At a cement triangle, 3.2 *m*., bear right on Braveboat Harbor Road. At a fork, 6.3 *m*., continue left.

TOUR 1A: From Junction with US 1 to Cape Neddick   251

At 8 *m.* the road crosses *Sewall's Bridge* (1757); the original was one of the first pile bridges in America.

On the river bank (L) at the eastern end of the bridge is the large red, two-and-a-half-story *Sewall House* with a central chimney, shaded by fine old elms. This house was once owned by a member of the Sewall family, but there are no records showing that Samuel Sewall, the bridge builder, lived here. A cigar-store Indian on the river bank marks the supposed exit of a former secret passage built to enable those in the house to escape in case the place were attacked by Indians. This house, built in the early days of the 19th century, is designed with unusual dignity and restraint. The monumental façade, with its fine entrance portal, decorative Ionic pilasters, heavy dentiled cornice, and balustraded parapet, is finished with flush, matched siding in contrast with the clapboards at the sides. The lawn is enclosed by a delicate railed fence, notable for its urn-topped posts and square balusters; the latter are set diagonally to obtain the best play of light and shade.

The design of the main entrance is of exceptional charm and grace. Crowned by a fine dentiled cornice and elliptical fan-light, the eight-paneled door is flanked by finely modeled Ionic pilasters and engaged columns; their slender shafts having the classic refinement of entasis. The interior, with a delicately paneled stairhall and spacious salons is designed with a dignity in keeping with the exterior. The windows in the dining room on the left have sliding shutters. The parlor mantel is ornamented with a decorative frieze bearing the allegorical figures of Peace and Justice.

After passing (R) the *York Country Club (visitors admitted)*, and several attractive summer homes, the unmarked route at 9 *m.* becomes State 1A.

YORK (alt. 50, York Town, pop. 2532), 9.6 *m.*, one of the most attractive old coastal villages, is the commercial center of the near-by beach resorts. Generally known as Old York and now under the township form of government, York was settled as Agamenticus about 1624 by the Plymouth Company and was given a city charter and government under name of Gorgeana in 1641 by Sir Ferdinando Gorges. Thomas Gorges, a nephew of Sir Ferdinando, was the first mayor, and the little wilderness 'city' had a full set of officials, including aldermen and sergeants. In 1652, Gorgeana was reorganized as a town and called York after the English county of that name. In 1716 it was made the shire town of Yorkshire, now York County, by the legislature of Massachusetts.

After the battle of Dunbar, Scotland, in 1650, Oliver Cromwell found himself with many prisoners on his hands. More than 1000 of them were sent to the Colonies, 150 being apportioned to New England to be sold at £20 and £30 each for service to last six, seven, and eight years; the proceeds of the sale went to the captain of the ship. A year later, after the battle of Worcester, England, more bondmen were sent over, 275 of them to Boston on the ship 'John and Sarah.' Many were brought to Maine. The prisoners, after having completed their terms of servitude, were free to settle where they chose and twelve of them remained in York. The first Scot to settle in York (1657) was Alexander Maxwell who had been sold to George Leader of Berwick. After him came others from Dover and Exeter to form the section of the town known as Scotland.

As the friction between the Colonies and the mother country increased, the people of York took sides, most favoring the Colonial cause. They even had their own 'tea party,' when the sloop 'Cynthia,' with James Donnell as master, anchored at Keating's wharf with a cargo containing 150 pounds of tea for his uncle, Deacon Jonathan Sayward. The Sons of Liberty, much incensed, seized the tea and carried it to Captain Edward Grow's store for safekeeping. The next night a roving band of 'Pequawket Indians' entered the town, broke into the store, and carried the tea away.

This town, in which many important events in the State's early history occurred, saw the beginnings of industrial activity in Maine with the establishment of the first cotton mill. The York Cotton Factory Company was incorporated by the Massachusetts Legislature February 12, 1811.

York was once the home of Madam Wood, Maine's first novelist (*see The Arts*).

In the village is (L) a beautiful white *Church* (1747), its clock tower and spire surmounted by a weathervane and cock. The stained windows were added many years after its construction.

The lichen-covered slate headstones of the *Old York Cemetery* (R), dating back to the early part of the 18th century, bear many old-fashioned inscriptions beneath such somber and conventional designs as the weeping willow and the Grecian urn. Many of the headstones have crude death's heads with wings over the inscriptions with their old English spelling. One grave, completely covered by a large boulder placed between the headstone and footstone so the occupant could never escape, is called the *Witch's Grave*, said to be that of a woman executed for witchcraft and buried here in 1744.

Next (L) is the *Town Hall*, built in 1747 and rebuilt in 1882.

Farther along (R) is the *York Gaol (open in summer)*, now a museum. The large gambrel-roof building with frame ends is built around the stone jail, built in 1653; the walls of the old building form the sides of the later one. In the old part of the structure are dark cells. The place contains many old Colonial and Indian relics.

The *Wilcox House (private)*, opposite the jail, was originally a tavern. It stands on land leased for 900 years, 300 years of which have elapsed.

The fourth house (L) on Long Lands Road is *Coventry Hall (private)*, a large, handsome, two-story white house with ornamental balustrade around the edge of the flat roof. The entrance door has a fan-light and is framed by slender columns.

Opposite Coventry Hall is the *Woodbridge House (private)*, a two-and-a-half-story, hip-roof structure with dormers in front and an elaborate captain's walk on the roof.

At 10.2 *m.* is the junction with a tar-surfaced road.

CULTURAL LANDMARKS

THE pride of Maine, her distinguished sons and daughters, is accorded enough recognition within the State to refute satisfactorily the often-repeated saying about the prophet in his own land. Many communities throughout Maine boast a local museum dedicated to the memory of the celebrity who was born or who once lived there. The Longfellow houses are, of course, the most famous of these, and they reflect in their design the tradition of gracious living which the poet always represented. But the homes of Sarah Orne Jewett and Lillian Nordica are likewise shrines to many pilgrims, as are those houses made famous by transient human genius which are not open to the public, but which are constantly pointed to with pride by remembering neighbors. The L. D. M. Sweat Museum is at once a memorial to a prominent Portland family and a municipal art gallery.

Maine's educational institutions are here represented by four pictures. Fryeburg Academy is the old boarding-school where Daniel Webster started out in life at the age of twenty as a 'preceptor.' The view of the library at Bowdoin College, its central building, is an unusual one.

WADSWORTH-LONGFELLOW HOUSE, PORTLAND

LONGFELLOW'S BIRTHPLACE, PORTLAND

L. D. M. SWEAT MUSEUM, PORTLAND

FRYEBURG ACADEMY

ADMINISTRATION BUILDING. UNIVERSITY OF MAINE.

COBURN HALL, COLBY COLLEGE, WATERVILLE

WING OF BOWDOIN COLLEGE LIBRARY, BRUNSWICK

MADAME NORDICA'S HOMESTEAD, FARMINGTON

EMMA EAMES HOUSE, BA

QUILLCOTE, HOME OF KATE DOUGLAS WIGGIN, HOLLIS

REDINGTON MUSEUM, WATERVILLE

HOME OF JACOB ABBOTT, FARMINGTON

SARAH ORNE JEWETT MEMORIAL, BE...

Tour 1B: From Junction with US 1 to Biddeford 253

Right on this road and left at 0.1 *m.* to the *Sayward House* (*private*), 0.2 *m.*, a white two-story gable-end house with an ell that exactly copies the main structure.

YORK HARBOR (alt. 50, York Town), 10.3 *m.*, on a headland at the mouth of York River, has long been a fashionable resort. The shore estates and residences along the heavily shaded streets are dignified and impressive.

At 12.5 *m.* is the southern end of a 1.5-mile stretch of sand known locally as *Long Beach*, part of the York Beach resort area, with cottages (L) bordering the shore road. The wide beach, the delight of sea bathers and one of the most attractive in Maine, is unmarred by concessions. The Boon Island and Nubble lighthouses are visible from the beach.

At 13.2 *m.* is the junction with an improved road.

Right on this road to *Nubble Light*, 1 *m.*

YORK BEACH (alt. 20, York Town), 14 *m.*, is the busy center of the resort area. While having public amusement facilities, it is not garish.

At 15.4 *m.* State 1A joins US 1, near *Cape Neddick* (*see Tour 1, sec. a*).

TOUR 1B: *From* JUNCTION WITH US 1 *to* BIDDEFORD, 20.8 *m.*, State 9.

Via Kennebunkport, Cape Porpoise, and Fortune Rocks.
Two-lane tarred road.

STATE 9, winding through marshlands, from time to time reaches high ground with thick growths of pine and hemlock. It runs fairly close to the rocky shores and sandy beaches of a broad peninsula.

State 9 branches east from US 1 (*see Tour 1, sec. a*), 0 *m.*, at a point 1.8 *m.* north of Wells and runs through heavy forest growth broken at intervals by marshy inlets.

At 2.9 *m.* is the junction with a local road.

Right on this road to KENNEBUNK BEACH (alt. 15, Kennebunk Town), 0.9 *m.*, where great spurs of rock extend into the ocean, breaking a long stretch of white sand. Summer hotels and residences in attractive groves overlook the water.

KENNEBUNKPORT (alt. 20, Kennebunkport Town, pop. 1284), 4.4 *m.*, an elm-shaded resort village, was once the chief shipbuilding center of York County and a port of some importance. The old houses dating back to 1785, with their captain's walks, are reminiscent of the days when the occupants waited anxiously for the return on their investments by sea.

In the outskirts amid charming gardens are the summer homes of Booth Tarkington, Margaret Deland, Kenneth Roberts, and other writers and artists. Much of Tarkington's writing has been done aboard the 'Regina,' which is tied up near the River Club on Ocean Ave.

A gay event of the summer season here is the Water Carnival, held at night; the dark waters of the river then gleam with the reflections of hundreds of twinkling lights.

The *Garrick Playhouse* (L), on Temple St., is a summer theater in which plays are presented during the summer months as try-outs before the New York season.

A beautiful example of old New England church architecture is the *First Congregational Church* (1764), also on Temple St., with a stately columned portico and graceful spire.

The old *Perkins Mill* (L), on Mill Lane, a picturesque, weather-beaten structure perched on the edge of a stream, has been grinding grain since 1749, when there were but four houses in Kennebunkport.

The *Luques House* (*private*), corner Main and Union Sts., is a two-story gable-end house with a matching ell. It has a beautiful fan-light over the entrance door.

CAPE PORPOISE (alt. 20, Kennebunkport Town), 6.7 *m.*, is a year-around fishing village with summer residences along the shores; in summer the sheltered harbor is brightened by innumerable small boats. Inns here are famous for their sea-food dinners. Lobsters taken green from the cold sea waters are, within an hour, served piping hot in scarlet shells.

> Right from Cape Porpoise on a local road; from the summit of a small hill at 0.5 *m.* is a view of the colorful harbor where small, lightly wooded islands make irregular green patches on the blue surface. Here and there brown reefs shine with the spray of the surf. The white, cylindrical tower of *Goat Island Light* at the entrance to the outer harbor is visible from this point.

FORTUNE ROCKS (alt. 15, Biddeford), 13 *m.*, attracts many summer residents to its bold rocks and sandy beaches by the sea.

North of Fortune Rocks the highway passes *Three Fresh-Water Ponds* (L) not 50 feet from the salt spray of the surf.

At 14.1 *m.* is a junction with State 208.

> Right on State 208 to BIDDEFORD POOL (alt. 15, Biddeford), 1.2 *m*. The landscaped grounds of several large estates follow the curving shores of Fletcher's Neck, and cottages of every description cluster around the wharves on a deep narrow gut. Dories and lobster traps are scattered about the wharves, and all summer long stout fishing boats, light yachts, and cruisers lie at anchor in the saucer-shaped cove.
>
> At 2.2 *m.* (R), facing open ocean across the fissured rocks of the shore, is a *Coast Guard Station*.

A bronze marker (L), between two buildings, at 14.2 *m.*, marks the *Site of the Richard Vines House*, a thatch-roof log structure built in 1616, when Captain Vines and a crew of 16 men spent the winter here testing out the winter climate of Maine for Sir Ferdinando Gorges, who wanted to send out a group of colonists. Vines called the place Winter Harbor and he and his men were so comfortable that he reported enthusiastically that there had not been as much as a headache to plague them. During this winter he explored the Saco River and its banks.

The *Haley House* (*private*), 14.6 *m.* (R), is a salt-box house, built in 1730, that has had numerous additions. The weathered, clapboarded dwelling was built by Benjamin Haley, who did not agree with his neighbors on the character of the Indians and refused to take refuge with them in the Tarbox Garrison at night. One bitter evening he admitted two Indians who apparently judged him to be as hostile as others they had met and tried to snatch brands from the fire to burn the house. He succeeded in ejecting them and spent his nights in the garrison thereafter.

At 15.9 *m.* is a junction with a tarred road.

> Right on this road to HILLS BEACH (alt. 20, Biddeford), 1 *m.*, where small summer cottages and fishermen's homes straggle along the narrow spit stretching to Biddeford Pool. A landmark for seamen is a tall white *Monument* on Basket's Island (L).
>
> At the end of the point, 1.9 *m.*, a bronze tablet, facing the wharves of the pool across the gut, marks the *Site of Fort Hill*, built about 1688.
>
> The *Goldwaithe House* (1717), west of the fort site, was once known as the Jordan Garrison House. The high surrounding palisade of timber and stone with corner lookouts has disappeared, and the dilapidated two-story house bears no evidence of its former use.

At 16.1 *m.* (R) is the *Stella Maris Home*, a kindergarten boarding-school supervised by the Franciscan Brothers.

At 17 *m.* is the junction with Ferry Lane.

> Right down Ferry Lane to what is known as the Lower Ferry on the Saco River, where is the *Site of the First Hotel in Maine*, 0.4 *m*. The Saco court records for 1654 state that one Henry Waddock was granted the right 'to keep an ordinary to entertain strangers for their money.' Apparently the entertainment of guests caused some concern in the community, for the court made some very sharp rulings as to the conduct of drinkers. One of these regulations reads: 'Whoever is drunk pays 3s. 4d.; for drinking too much, 2s. 6d.; for sitting after nine at night, 5s., to be imprisoned until he pays, or sit in the stocks for 3 hours.'

At 20.4 *m.* is the junction with Alfred St.; right on Alfred St. then left on Main St. to US 1 at Biddeford (*see Tour* 1, *sec. a*).

TOUR 1C: *From* SACO *to* DUNSTAN, 9.6 *m.*, State 9.

Via Old Orchard Beach and Pine Point.
Two-lane cement and tar-surfaced road.

THIS loop route, an alternate to US 1 between Saco and Dunstan, skirts a 14-mile beach and then crosses marshland.

State 9 branches southeast from US 1 at Saco (*see Tour* 1, *sec. a*), 0 *m.*

At 0.9 *m.* is the junction with a local road.

> Right on this road to CAMP ELLIS (alt. 20, Saco), 4 *m.*, a beautiful spot on the northern bank of the Saco River at its mouth, with a rugged breakwater and a view of Biddeford Pool (R) and the Wood Island Light. Power boats with pilots can be hired here for a day's fishing on the 'grounds' (*see Sports and Recreation: Salt-Water Fishing*).
>
> A squatters' colony has grown to a sizable collection of cottages and shacks here on the spit, a piece of land made within the past 10 years by drifting sands that now cover part of the breakwater.

At 1.6 *m.* (R) is the stone clubhouse of the *Biddeford–Saco Country Club* (*open to visitors*).

At 2.2 *m.* is the junction with a local road.

> Right on this road to OCEAN PARK (alt. 15, Old Orchard Beach Town), 0.7 *m.*, a settlement of cottages where many religious organizations hold summer conferences. The *Baptist Camp Grounds* are left, 1.4 *m.* from the park.

At 3.2 *m.* is the junction with Union Ave.

> Right on this road to the *Methodist Camp Ground*, 0.2 *m.* (L), a natural amphitheater in a grove of old pines. Among the annual gatherings here each summer is that of the Salvation Army with its large Silver Band.

OLD ORCHARD BEACH (alt. 40, Old Orchard Beach Town, pop. 1620), 4 *m.*, with one of the longest beaches on the Atlantic coast, has been a popular resort for more than a century. Hotels and cottages crowd closely along the streets branching from the compactly built-up village. Roller coaster, fun houses, and scores of other concessions are centered here.

The *Pier*, over the beach, has a carnival promenade, its eastern side lined with confectioners' booths, games of chance, souvenir shops, and the like. The music of the merry-go-round at the entrance and the odor of popping corn and frying 'hot dogs' are among the attractions to many visitors. Well-known dance bands play during the summer months in the dance hall at the end of the pier. Because the Saco town line passes across the pier's end, its owners pay taxes in two towns.

Staples Inn, 1 Portland Ave., built in 1730, is still a lodging-house and, though remodeled, has the original panels and doors. The inn was built on land granted by the Council of Plymouth to Richard Bonython, one of the first settlers.

At 5.6 *m.* (R) is the *R. P. Hazzard Estate* (*private*), one of the show places on the ocean front in this section of the coast; it is recognizable by its stucco surrounding wall studded with mosaics. The small flat cement building (R), near the main house, is a guest house and an excellent example of modern architecture. All space has been utilized without sacrifice of line, and the interior seems spacious. It is beautifully furnished in a restrained modern style.

PINE POINT (alt. 15, Scarboro Town), 6.5 *m.*, is a residential settlement along the beach.

> Right from Pine Point a road follows the shore line, passing summer cottages and, farther along, the small homes of clam diggers who make their living from near-by clam flats; it then loops back to State 9, 1 *m.*

Tour 1D: From Brunswick to Bailey Island   257

The point of land (R) across from Pine Point is PROUT'S NECK (*see Tour 1, sec. a*).
At Pine Point the road swings left and soon crosses Scarboro Marshes.
At 9.2 *m.* (R) a marker indicates the *Site of the Birthplace of William King*, Maine's first governor (1820).
At 9.6 *m.* State 9 rejoins US 1 at DUNSTAN (*see Tour 1, sec. a*).

T O U R   1 D :   *From* BRUNSWICK *to* BAILEY ISLAND, 17 *m.*, State 24.

Via Great (Sebascodegan) and Orr's Islands.
Two-lane tar-surfaced and graveled roadbed.

THE transition from the mainland to the islands, lying in the northeastern part of Casco Bay, is hardly noticeable because of the narrowness of the channels; the road runs through a growth of pines that spread a carpet of tawny needles to the edge of the road. The rocky ridges along the highway terminate in ledges at the southern tip of Bailey Island.

State 24 branches south from US 1 (*see Tour 1, sec. b*), 0 *m.* at the eastern end of Brunswick.

At 0.5 *m.* is the junction with State 123.

> Right on State 123, which runs down an elongated peninsula, not more than 1.5 miles wide at any point, to NORTH HARPSWELL (alt. 60, Harpswell Town), 6.8 *m.*
> HARPSWELL CENTER (alt. 30, Harpswell Town, pop. 1364), 8.8 *m.* The *Congregational Church* (L) was built in 1843 for Elijah Kellogg (1813–1901), early pastor at Harpswell and author of several books for boys. While the structure is fundamentally of the usual New England type, the trim of the oversized steeple and the ogee arch of the entrance door are Gothic. A boulder on the lawn (R) marks the site of the first church, built in 1757. In the large old cemetery (R) are buried the Reverend Elisha Eaton (1702–64), first Harpswell pastor, and his successor, the Reverend Samuel Eaton, who died in 1822 at 86 years of age and in the 59th year of his ministry.
> WEST HARPSWELL (alt. 70, Harpswell Town), 12 *m.*, is a small village with excellent sea views.
> SOUTH HARPSWELL (alt. 30, Harpswell Town), 14.5 *m.*, offers deep-sea fishing facilities and boating. The peninsula here is very narrow, with summer homes grouped closely on barren rock. At the close of day the houses, silhouetted against a backdrop of sun-glinted sea, form a striking picture.

At 5.3 *m.* State 24 crosses a bridge over the gurnet, a narrow channel of rushing tides, to GREAT ISLAND, or Sebascodegan, locally known as East Harpswell, the 'Lost Paradise' of Robert P. Tristram Coffin, poet and novelist. A small summer colony at this point is called Gurnet.

At 6 *m.* is the junction with a dirt road.

> Left on this road to a briar-covered old *Cemetery*, 1.5 *m.* (L), one of many in this section of the State. The oldest gravestone, in an iron-fenced plot, bears the date September 24, 1774.
> CUNDY'S HARBOR (alt. 20, Harpswell Town), 5.2 *m.*, is a tiny fishing village catering to summer visitors who like deep-sea fishing.
> The road winds through pastures to *Cundy's Harbor Beach*, 6 *m.*, on a cove in East Casco Bay. On summer holidays and Sundays many inland families come here for boat trips, camping, clam-bakes, and swimming. The picnic ground is one of many recently developed at less widely known beach resorts on the Maine coast.

At 7 *m.* (L) is a small cove in which graceful seagulls feed; ahead is a fine seascape.

The *Gurnet*, 11.1 *m.*, a rugged inlet where incoming and outgoing tides rush furiously, has borne its name at least 200 years.

Here the highway cuts through a high cliff of gray stratified rock to reach a short bridge leading to ORR'S ISLAND. The highway, following the ridge of the island its entire length of 4.5 miles, commands a far-reaching view of East Casco Bay with its many craggy islands.

The *Orr Homestead* (*private*), 14 *m.* (R), a one-and-a-half-story yellow house near the cemetery, is occupied by descendants of the family for whom the island was named.

ORR'S ISLAND VILLAGE (alt. 40, Harpswell Town), 14.6 *m.*, a settlement of attractive summer homes, lies along a low ridge sloping to the shore. Deep-sea fishing is among the popular summer sports here.

At 15 *m.* (R) a footpath leads to a small white house near the shore known as the *Pearl of Orr's Island House* (*private*). This house is believed to have been the home of the heroine of Harriet Beecher Stowe's 'The Pearl of Orr's Island.'

South of the village the highway crosses Will Straits on *Bailey Island Bridge*, which spans the narrowest part of the channel, then curves to follow the line of a thin spit to solid ground. The bridge, considered to be one of great beauty, is built of uncemented granite blocks laid honeycomb fashion, similar to a breakwater; it thus holds more effectively against strong spring ice-jams than would a rigid structure, and is kept in position by its own weight. The tides flow freely through the large cells of 'the honeycomb.' It is said that the only other bridge of this type is in Scotland.

BAILEY ISLAND (alt. 30, Harpswell Town), 17 *m.*, is the southernmost summer settlement on this route. Steamers ply between Bailey and Portland, stopping at several other Casco Bay Islands. The *Wharf* (R) is the center of activities, boating and deep-sea fishing being the chief recreation of the summer residents.

A dirt road gradually rises for a mile to end on the ledges at the southern tip of the island, where is a magnificent view of the ocean. Mericoneag Sound and the numerous small islands of Casco Bay are seen (R), and 5 miles out is *Halfway Rock Light*, so called because it is midway between Portland Head and Seguin Lights. The 76-foot white granite tower, completed in 1871, appears to rise abruptly from the water, Halfway Rock itself barely showing above high tide.

TOUR 1 E : *From* BATH *to* FORT POPHAM, 17.5 *m.*, State 209.

Via Winnegance, Phippsburg, and Parker Head.
Two-lane tar-surfaced and dirt roads.

THE country gradually becomes more rugged as State 209 winds past fields and pastures, and past old farmhouses surrounded by snowball bushes and other informal shrubbery, to the mouth of the Kennebec River. The colors of the wild flowers here are made more vivid by the sea air.

State 209 branches south from US 1 at Bath (*see Tour 1, sec. b*), 0 *m.*
WINNEGANCE (alt. 20, City of Bath), 2.7 *m.*
At 3 *m.* is the junction with a dirt road.

> Left on this road to a *Tide Mill*, 0.4 *m.*, which until 1935 was used for cutting lumber. This old structure is a primitive forerunner of the mills and factories planned as part of the Passamaquoddy Power Project.

At 4.3 *m.* is the junction with a dirt road.

> Left on this road to a dwelling at 1.6 *m.*, to the rear of which is the *Site of Fort Noble*, a stronghold built in 1734. It faced down river to the wide waters at the southern end of Fiddlers Beach, forming an important defense of the Kennebec.

South of this point open fields and farmlands are less frequent, the road running through woods that thin at intervals, giving glimpses of the river.
At 5.9 *m.* is an exceptional view of the Kennebec (L); the white-spired Phippsburg church is visible, standing out against a green background.
PHIPPSBURG CENTER (alt. 20, Phippsburg Town, pop. 801), 7.1 *m.* On the left side of the village street is the *James McCobb House* (*private*), built in 1774, with a beautifully paneled interior. The hinges and bull's-eye glass of the entrance door are of interest to antiquarians. The town's first post office was established in the kitchen of this house, built by James McCobb, shipbuilder and trader. An old black walnut tree and three old lindens in the yard are noteworthy. Near-by is the site of Spite House, which was removed to Rockport (*see Tour 1, sec. b*).

> Right from Phippsburg Center on State 216; on the western shore of a small lake, 0.7 *m.*, (R) is a hillside, where in 1935 Indian skeletons were uncovered during road-building operations.

> Right from State 216 at 5.4 *m.* on a dirt road (sign, Aliquippa House) to the *Site of Ancient Augusta*, 6.3 *m.*, a fishing village established on Casco Bay in 1716. Hidden in juniper and bayberry growth on a knoll are the scattered bricks of a fort, built in 1716, by Dr. Oliver Noyes and his men as a protection against Indians. An enormous pit near-by may have been covered and used as a refuge or as a storehouse. The settlement remained until about 1821.

At 7.5 *m.* (L) stands an old brick store at the head of a former shipyard erected in 1806 by the McCobb family. The last square rigger built here slid down the ways in 1893. Formal launchings came into fashion on the peninsula in 1904, when engraved invitations were sent out for the debut of the five-master 'Marcus L. Urann.'

PARKER HEAD (alt. 30, Phippsburg Town), 11 *m.*, with small well-kept houses along its rough steep highway, was named for one of the pioneers who settled here about 1645. Clam flats along the shore provide the general means of livelihood.

At 12.8 *m.* is the junction with a dirt road.

> Left on this road to *Cox's Head*, jutting into the Kennebec, 0.9 *m.* (*private property*), a huge rock formation topped at the southern end by a ridge of earthworks built in 1812. Enthusiastic young recruits, who had expected to shoulder muskets on the battlefield, found themselves resentfully pushing wheelbarrows of earth up the steep incline to build the fortification.

Passing through a lovely stretch of woods, the road, bordered in summer by marsh grass and occasional clumps of purple iris or yellow lilies, soon reaches the sea.

At 15.9 *m.* (R), a few yards from the highway, ocean rollers break on a wide beach that still has few summer cottages and little resort development. Sea winds have carved the sands into high dunes, now overgrown with bayberry bushes.

At 16.5 *m.* (L) is the entrance to *Fort Baldwin* (*open*), a U.S. fortification whose armament was removed and whose 45-acre tract was purchased by the State in 1924. Its three batteries, built (1905-12) into the wooded side of Sabino Hill, are now cracked and broken. The batteries, named respectively for Patrick Cogan and John Hardman, officers in the Revolutionary Army, and Joseph Hawley, Brigadier General in the Civil War, were garrisoned during the World War.

The State reservation includes the *Site of the Popham Colony* (R), between the entrance gate and the shore. The information obtained by Sir John Popham, and particularly by Sir Ferdinando Gorges, from the Indians, who had been kidnaped and carried to England by Waymouth in 1605 (*see Tour* 1J), prompted them to finance a settlement on the shores of Maine. Acting under the Virginia Company Patent, Gorges sent out an expedition in 1606 under Captain Henry Challons; he disobeyed orders, however, sailing too far south, and was captured by the Spanish. This did not dampen the enthusiasm of Gorges; largely through his activities, a second set of colonists was sent out in the following year on the 'Gift of God,' commanded by George Popham, and on the 'Mary and John,' commanded by Raleigh Gilbert. The ships touched at Nova Scotia but sailed south to the country recommended by Waymouth and, on August 19, 1607 (O.S.), landed at this place. The group was hastily organized with Popham as president, the land laid out, and Fort St. George, a barracks, a chapel, storehouses, and houses were built. Immediately afterward the colonists built a boat of about 30 tons, described in the records as 'a pretty pynnace,' naming it the 'Virginia.' The careful manner in which Gorges selected the colonists, including among them capable craftsmen, should have made the settlement successful, but the winter was unusually severe and George Popham, an elderly man, and a number of the settlers died. In the following spring when one of the ships, which had gone to England for supplies, returned, it brought word that a financial backer of the expedition, Sir John Popham, had died; the next ship brought word that Raleigh Gilbert's brother had also died, an event forcing Raleigh Gilbert's return. Deprived of leadership and faced with the prospect of another hard winter, the settlers lost heart and sailed for England in September, 1608.

POPHAM BEACH (alt. 15, Phippsburg Town), 17.2 *m.*, is the center of a group of weather-beaten houses extending for half a mile across the point between the Kennebec River and the ocean. The settlement, facing two low barren islands known as the *Sugar Loaves*, with Seguin Light beyond them, has been an active summer colony since 1890.

Transportation can be arranged to *Seguin Island Light* (*open*), highest light above the sea on the Maine coast, which stands on an island off the mouth of the Kennebec. The original 38-foot tower was built in 1795 during President Washington's administration. The present tower (1857), 53 ft. high, stands 180 ft. above high tide.

Rough waters between Popham and Seguin keep the *Kennebec River Coast Guard Station* (R) busy during bad weather.

Fort Popham (*open until* 8 P.M.), 17.5 *m.*, an impressive granite and brick structure erected in 1861 but never completed, has been a State reservation since 1924. It was garrisoned in 1865–66, again in 1898, and men were stationed here during the World War. Built in the shape of a half-moon, the outer curve is a 30-foot wall of granite blocks pierced for musketry. Within the arc is a parade ground. A fine spiral staircase at each end of the fort leads to upper tiers. The top of the structure commands a sweeping view up the Kennebec in one direction and seaward in another.

Fort Popham Light is at the southern side of the fort. The white pyramidal bell tower, its top 27 feet above high water, is visible 7 miles at sea.

T O U R   1 F :   *From* WOOLWICH *to* FIVE ISLANDS, 15.3 *m.*, State 127.

Via Arrowsic and Georgetown.
Two-lane dirt road.

STATE 127 runs over a series of heavily wooded islands from whose hills are views of Sheepscot Bay and other islands, large and small. In the days when shipping was important on the Kennebec, many of the inhabitants of these islands sailed the seven seas; today agriculture, fishing, and clam digging combine to provide a livelihood for the people, who still live much as their fathers did, using kerosene lamps, hand pumps, and other out-moded appliances.

State 127 swings south from Woolwich (see *Tour* 1, *sec. b*), 0 *m.*

The *Drawbridge*, 0.6 *m.*, carrying the route across the Sasanoa River to Arrowsic Island, had until recently a toll gate.

The ebb tide of the Kennebec, which returns much more slowly than does the tide of the Sasanoa, meets the ebb tide of the Sasanoa at *Hell Gate*, 1.5 *m.* left of this bridge, in Sheepscot Bay. Great skill is needed to bring a boat up against this tide, reefs and shoals adding to the hazards.

At 2.2 *m.* the road bears L. through growths of spreading maples and silver birches.

The *Stinson Farm House* (*private*), 3.2 *m.*, built in 1751 by John Stinson, a magistrate of Yorkshire (now York County), stands back from the road (L) in a pine-fringed field. Only one room in the weather-beaten structure has the original hand-hewn paneling.

> Left from the Stinson House on a footpath to *Hockomock Point*, 0.2 *m.*, the site of the Clark and Lake settlement in 1650. Clark and Lake conducted a trading enterprise, placing groups of settlers in favorable situations to trade with the Indians. They bought Arrowsic Island in 1654, and during the following year built several dwellings, a warehouse, and a large barracks within a fortified enclosure. It was in their shipyard on this point that Sir William Phips (see *Tour* 1, *sec. b*) worked as an apprentice. There were 30 families here in 1670. Six years later the Indians burned all the settlements on the island. Cellar holes, overgrown by bushes, mark the places where the early houses stood.

ARROWSIC (alt. 25, Arrowsic Town, pop. 135), 6.3 *m.*, is marked by the *Town House* (R). Houses of the township are scattered, the oldest being on the shores of coves; others, plain little structures with their barns connected by sheds, are near the road.

At 7.5 *m.* is a junction with a dirt road.

> Right on this road to the old *Denny Cemetery*, 2.9 *m.* (R), nearly concealed by bushes, birches, and apple trees. Slate markers date back to 1729. Samuel Denny, an Englishman, built a blockhouse near this cemetery in 1728. An educated man, he acted as judge and bailiff, and the stocks in which he imprisoned offenders were still standing in 1800.
>
> Here, overlooking the Kennebec River, stood the old church mentioned in Arnold's report of his journey up the Kennebec to Quebec (see *Tour* 11). The river and Phippsburg Center are clearly visible from the open field where the church once stood.
>
> The *Watts' Garrison*, 3.1 *m.* (R), on Butler's Cove, was a brick structure surrounded by homes. The garrison was built by John Watts of Boston in 1714 and the town of Georgetown was incorporated in 1716 with this nucleus. All that remains of the settlement is a row of cellar holes with raspberry bushes growing up through a few decaying hand-hewn timbers containing hand-wrought nails.
>
> At the foot of the hill, 3.3 *m.*, near the river, are two old, rambling one-and-a-half-story buildings, crumbling and vacant, their doors swinging with the winds, reminders of the general desertion of these once busy lands.

Tour 1F: From Woolwich to Five Islands

Near-by (L), on what is now an island but which was once Squirrel Point, is a *Ruined House*, the only visible remains of the prosperous fishing settlement established by John Parker in 1629.

At 8 *m*, a steel bridge crosses Back River to the island of Georgetown, early known as Parker's Island.

GEORGETOWN VILLAGE (alt. 60, Georgetown Town, pop. 361), 11.9 *m*. Here are the general store, post office, town house, and near-by the two bridges that cross Robinhood Cove.

This township lies on hilly islands; the gradual settling of the continental terrain is very noticeable here. Stretches of marshland, formerly flooded only at high tide, are now waterways, navigable by small craft, even at low tide. Patches of land are at intervals cut off, more islands being created.

The shore line, where dulse, an edible seaweed, grows, is very rugged. Doubtless it was from such rocks as these that Moncacht-Apé, a Yazoo Indian, nearly three centuries ago gazed for the first time upon the great waters, fascinated and terrified by their expanse and their roaring as they lashed against the ledges only to fall back each time in huge billows of spent foam. An account written in French relates how this red man had traveled from the lower Mississippi Valley to the east coast seeking the place of origin of the North American Indians. The story is told of his first sight of 'the Big Water.'

> When I saw it I was so glad I could not speak. My eyes seemed too little to see it all. But the night came.... The water was close to us, but below. The wind was big and I think it made the Big Water angry. It made so much noise I could not sleep. I was afraid the blows made by the Big Water on our high place would break it, though it was made of rocks.... I was a long time without speaking to my friend. To see me always looking and never speaking he thought I had lost my mind. I could not understand where all this could come from. The wind went away before the sun came up and the Big Water was not as angry as it had been. I was surprised to see it coming back to us. That made me afraid. I got up and ran as fast as I could. My friend called to me that I had nothing to fear.... He said Red Men had seen the Big Water and that it was always traveling, sometimes going away, sometimes coming back. But he said it never came nearer the land at one time than another.... We went away so we could sleep far away from this noise which followed me everywhere. Until evening I did not speak of anything else to my friend.

FIVE ISLANDS (alt. 40, Georgetown Town), 15.3 *m*., has small boat connections with Bath. This popular residential village, with a good harbor, is at the mouth of the Sheepscot River; its unpretentious summer homes are built along the highway and rocky shore. A short beach (R) is a favorite spot for clambakes, and the little dance hall is a busy place when an occasional cruise of Boston yacht clubs brings a number of visitors to the harbor at 'Five' for a night. From the wharf, the center of village life, private speedboats ply back and forth between the sparsely settled and privately owned small islands near-by.

TOUR 1 G : *From* JUNCTION WITH US 1 *to* SOUTH-
PORT, 13.4 *m.*, Local road and State 27.

Via Edgecomb and Boothbay Harbor.
One year-round hotel at Boothbay Harbor.
Tarred and gravel roadbeds.

THIS route, skirting coves and inlets, runs down the peninsula, through fishing villages and the large resort area of Boothbay Harbor.

An improved, unnumbered road branches south from US 1 at the eastern end of Wiscasset bridge (*see Tour* 1, *sec. b*), 0 *m.*

At 0.3 *m.* is the junction with an obscure dirt road.

> Right on this dirt road to *Fort Edgecomb*, (*grounds open, though not the block-house*) 0.4 *m.* The grounds adjoining this octagonal wooden blockhouse command an exceptionally fine view of the Sheepscot River, with the long island of Westport in the foreground. Constructed in 1808–09 of heavy wooden-pegged square timbers of pine and ash from near-by forests, the building is well preserved. The first story, 27 feet wide and pierced for musketry, is overhung by a second story 30 feet wide with 12-foot posting, having square portholes and heavily shuttered windows. The narrow slits in the high tower were used by lookouts. The stockade and parade grounds have been obliterated, but the earthworks and the remains of the gun emplacements are still visible. The heavy armaments, consisting of four 18-pounder guns and one 50-pounder gun, were removed in 1816, never having been used in an engagement.

NORTH EDGECOMB (alt. 50, Edgecomb Town), 0.8 *m.*, is a small settlement of white houses, with lawns extending to the tree-shaded bank of the Sheepscot.

Left, opposite the post office, on the high riverbank is the *Marie Antoinette House* (*visited at convenience of owner*). This structure, built in 1774 by Captain Joseph Decker on Squam Island, from which it was much later brought to this spot, was inherited by Decker's daughter, the wife of Samuel Clough, captain of a merchantman that frequently visited France. In 1793 the captain became engaged in an enterprise, the details of which are somewhat obscure. According to romantics he was moved by the unfortunate situation of the imprisoned Queen of France to attempt her rescue with the aid of her friends; it seems clear, however, that he was merely hired by them to carry her to America on the 'Sally' when they had managed to effect her release. Some of her personal belongings and various articles that her friends thought might make her home in exile more comfortable and furnish it in a style befitting her rank were smuggled aboard the Yankee ship. The plan, however, like others with the same purpose, failed; the queen was beheaded and Captain Clough set sail hastily to escape possible punishment for his share in the enterprise. In the meantime the captain had written to his wife to give her warning of the guest she might expect to have for a time, carefully trying to reconcile

Tour 1G: From Junction with US 1 to Southport 265

her to the dismaying idea of sheltering royalty. He doubtless found his home polished and shining when he at last arrived — without the queen. The captain stored the queen's possessions in his home; some thought this was because of a personal devotion to her, but it seems more likely that his Yankee conscience made him uneasy about his right to dispose of the goods that had come into his possession in such an irregular manner. Gradually, as time passed and no one came to claim the cargo, the furnishings came into use in the large, plain, square house, now standing in North Edgecomb. Many stories are told of their later uses and wanderings. It is said that a satin robe, worn by the King of France on state occasions, was in time made into a dress by Mrs. Clough. A Wiscasset clockmaker discovered in the interior of an old clock a plate inscribed in French indicating that the timepiece had been presented by the maker to the Queen on the Dauphin's birthday. Other mementoes are at the Metropolitan Museum of Art in New York; a few articles still remain in the Clough House.

There is a legend that Talleyrand and Marie Antoinette's son, the Dauphin of France, were passengers on the return voyage of the 'Sally' and that both were guests at the Clough House for some time.

It is Captain Clough who is given credit for having introduced coon cats into Maine. He is said to have brought a cat home with him from some Chinese port, and that the present-day coon cats, seldom seen except on this coast, are descendants of this cat and one of the usual domestic breed. Local sages insist that the cat is a hybrid descendant of a house cat of China, Me., who mated with a wild raccoon, but the theory has no scientific backing. The coon cats, quite gentle and fragile, have long, frosty-gray hair; they are difficult to rear, being particularly susceptible to pneumonia, but some people have a profitable business raising them for sale.

At 1.5 *m.* is the junction with State 27; right on State 27.

EDGECOMB (alt. 50, Edgecomb Town, pop. 367), 3.4 *m.*, was formerly the home of the Wawenock Indians, who fished on the shores with bone-tipped spears and crude fishhooks of bone. The town was settled and incorporated in 1774. In 1850 it had a population of 1231, but the decrease since that time has been constant. There are few houses in the village, most of the inhabitants living on farms some distance apart.

The tradition that elderly Samuel Trask, one of the settlers of Edgecomb, was once a member of Captain Kidd's crew has furnished grounds for intermittent treasure hunting in this neighborhood. When Kidd was arrested and hanged, his estate was very small, giving rise to many stories of treasure buried by him, or by his crew for him. Edgecomb gossips said that Trask had been one of those delegated to hide part of the booty and that it had been buried near his clearing in Edgecomb. Since Kidd died in 1701 and Trask did not come to this neighborhood till 1774, such treasure, had it been trusted to a boy, would have had a long period of travel.

BOOTHBAY (alt. 80, Boothbay Town, pop. 1345), 9.6 *m.*, thought to have had a settlement in 1630, was first known as Newagen, and then as Townshend. It has an old *Meeting-House* (R) of early American design, with an old *Cemetery* in the rear. A new *Summer Theater* in Boothbay adds to its importance as a summer recreational center.

At 11 *m.* is the junction with a gravel road.

> Left on this road is EAST BOOTHBAY (alt. 30, Boothbay Town), 2.7 *m.*, a small fishing village and summer resort. A *Tide Mill* in the village is still used for cutting lumber after a century of service.
>
> OCEAN POINT (alt. 20, Boothbay Town), 6.4 *m.*, has steamer connections (*variable schedule, apply at wharf*) with Bath.
>
> The weather-beaten effect of the summer cottages on this exposed point of land is prized by the owners, who came here for the sea views and exhilarating air.

BOOTHBAY HARBOR (alt. 40, Boothbay Harbor Town, pop. 2076), 11.4 *m.*

> *Accommodations.* All types.
>
> *Steamers and Boats.* There is ferry service from Boothbay Harbor to Squirrel Island, and steamer service to Monhegan Island (*see Island Trips*). Sailboats and motorboats for fishing and other purposes for hire at wharves, with or without skipper.
>
> *Annual event.* Regatta third Fri. in Aug., sail and power boats, headquarters Boothbay Harbor Clubhouse.

This town is one of the most popular resorts on the coast; in addition to the summer residents and usual visitors, a number of artists and parents, whose children are in near-by camps, come here annually. Because of its summer importance the population of the town has gradually increased since it was separated from Boothbay and incorporated in 1889. The settlement, however, knew early days of prosperity, first as a trading center and later as a port and scene of shipbuilding. Well-kept homes line the few streets and the main street, sloping down to the wharves on the harbor, is lined with little shops that are busy all summer.

The harbor during the vacation season is a busy place, with small sailboats and outboard motorboats slipping about between the mahogany and grass-trimmed yachts. The down-east coasting schooner, mourned by lovers of the sea as gone forever has taken a new lease on life in the transportation of pulpwood to Maine paper mills. While this type of shipping is not as profitable as that of the small coasting vessel of the old days, it provides a living for the skipper and his small crew. These schooners, mostly two-masted, are beginning to be a common sight again in ports all along the Maine coast.

A favorite tale of the fishermen along the harbor here is of Luther Maddocks and his whale. In 1885 Maddocks decided that the exhibition of a whale at a Grand Army of the Republic reunion in Portland would be profitable. Capturing a 60-foot humpbacked whale, he towed it at high tide over a scow he had ingeniously weighted to a reef with rocks. When the tide receded, Maddocks removed the rocks, bailed out the water, and waited for another tide to lift his load. He towed his catch into Portland

Harbor, and, after a heated argument with the mayor, won the right to exhibit it, realizing $800 by the venture. He then sold the carcass for $150 to a company that wanted the hide and blubber. The company, having profited by the venture, sent the remains out to sea where it sank. Unfortunately, gas had begun to generate in it, and it soon floated inshore, to the annoyance of the inhabitants, who towed it out again. But the remains floated back in. The performance was repeated several times, though it was once lashed temporarily to a rocky islet. At length it came ashore at Old Orchard Beach, where another Yankee decided to profit by it; he exhibited the foul bulk as a 'sea-serpent' and special excursions were made from various points to view it. The directors of a Middle West museum that was building up a collection eventually heard about it and purchased the bones.

At 12.9 *m.* is the junction with a gravel road.

> Left on this road to a *U.S. Fish Hatchery and Aquarium* (*open* 8-6), 1.2 *m.*, at McKown's Point. It was established in 1903 for the conservation of marine life. The raising of flounders has supplanted the hatching of cod and lobsters. Eggs secured in the spring are placed in containers through which salt water, pumped by electricity and steam, runs continuously during the three weeks' hatching period. The aquarium has, among other exhibits, marine growths, crabs, giant lobsters, and rays. A large colony of seals is kept near the wharf.

SOUTHPORT (alt. 40, Southport Town, pop. 412), 13.4 *m.*, has steamer service to Boothbay Harbor and Bath. This widespread village catering to summer visitors is on a heavily wooded island separated from the mainland by a narrow channel.

TOUR 1 H : *From* DAMARISCOTTA *to* PEMAQUID POINT, 15.8 *m.*, State 129 and State 130.

Via Bristol, Pemaquid, and New Harbor.
Gravel road with short stretches of tarred surface.

SUPERB coastal scenery is offered by this route, which winds through small fishing hamlets, never far distant from the white surf. Here is seen the 'rock-bound coast of Maine' in all its beauty, with the waves flung high. In summer white sails always dot the stretches of open water.

State 129 branches south from Damariscotta (*see Tour 1, sec. b*), 0 *m.*

At 3 *m.* is the junction with State 130 which the main route follows.

> Right on State 129 is WALPOLE (alt. 40, South Bristol Town), 3 *m.*, a settlement of a half dozen houses on the east bank of the Damariscotta River. The *Old Presbyterian Church* (*services in July and Aug.*) was built in 1772 on the site of a church erected in 1766. Huge clumps of lilacs surround the white, green-shuttered

structure. The church resembles an ordinary two-and-a-half-story dwelling. Its ancient high-backed pews were accorded the dignity of paint for the first time in 1872, when repairs were made. The Bible lying on the heavy carved pulpit, surmounted by a sounding board, is dated 1793. A spacious gallery extends along three walls.

At 7 *m.* is the *Wawenock Golf Clubhouse* (*greens fee* $1.50; *meals served*).

SOUTH BRISTOL (alt. 80, S. Bristol Town, pop. 563), 13.5 *m.*, formerly shipping out fish in considerable quantities, is now largely dependent on summer visitors for a livelihood. The village, lying on an island — a fact difficult for those unfamiliar with the coast to realize, draws many people back year after year for the sake of the views of shining ocean and picturesque islands.

CHRISTMAS COVE (alt. 25, S. Bristol Town), 15.1 *m.*, is visited by coastal steamers (*variable service; apply at wharf*). This place was so named by Captain John Smith when he brought his ship to anchor here on Christmas Day, 1614. It is one of the '25 excellent good Harbors; In many whereof there is ancorage for 500 sayle of ships of any burthen: in some of them for 5000: And more than 200 Iles overgrowne with good timber, of divers sorts of wood, which do make so many harbors as requireth a longer time than I had, to be well discovered,' on which he reported after the voyage. It was Smith's report that helped to keep up the faith of Gorges in the possibilities of the land; Smith had announced that he would rather live in Maine than anywhere else, adding that if a colony there could not maintain itself, even if indifferently equipped, it ought to be allowed to starve.

The main route here follows State 130.

At 5 *m.* (L) is an attractive *Camp Site.*

BRISTOL (alt. 100, Bristol Town, pop. 1413), 5.9 *m.*, its homes built along the highway on a side hill, is known as The Mills. Midway, on the rising slope (R), a modern cemetery, with monuments of polished marble, looks down on an earlier burying ground and the ruins of an old sawmill (L) at the foot of the hill.

On the west side of Bristol St. has been placed a stone that helped form the walls of the little garrison in which the settlers of this region gathered to escape the Indians. Near this spot in the 1730's two young girls were shot down by Indians as they were going out to milk the cows.

PEMAQUID (alt. 60, Bristol Town), 10.5 *m.*

The *Harrington Burial Ground* (R) is the largest cemetery in this old section of Bristol. Many odd epitaphs are inscribed on the lichened gravestones, which reveal here and there the blurred names of early settlers, and dates as early as 1716.

At 12.5 *m.* is the junction with a dirt road.

Right on this road to PEMAQUID BEACH (alt. 20, Bristol Town), 1 *m.*, which has steamer connections (*variable schedules, apply at wharf*) with near-by shore villages. This is a fishing and resort village. The sandy beach, though short and narrow, is unusual on this long stretch of rocky coast.

The earliest history of Pemaquid is found in occasional references in the journals of early explorers. It was visited by David Ingram (*see below*) in 1569, by Captain Bartholomew Gosnold in 1602, by Raleigh Gilbert (*see Tour 1E*) in May, 1607, and by Captain Thomas Dermer in 1619.

Captain John Smith of Virginia, in describing his visit to Monhegan in 1614, said that opposite Monhegan 'in the Maine' in a port called Pemaquid, was a ship of Sir Francis Popham whose people had used the port for 'many years.' The Sieur de Monts, who, with Champlain, explored this coast in 1605, mentioned that

TOUR 1H: From Damariscotta to Pemaquid Point 269

settlements then existed in this vicinity. It seems probable that a group of Bristol (England) merchants maintained a fishing and trading center with a resident agent here as early as 1600 and more certainly in the following decade. The history of the 200 cellars (*see below*) and paved streets is not satisfactorily explained even by legend.

The first fort at Pemaquid, then called Jamestown, was a stockade named Shurt's Fort, built about 1630. The fort and settlement were destroyed by Indians or pirates in 1689. Fort Charles was built in 1677 by order of Governor Edmund Andros of New York; it was two stories high, with a stockade. The extensive, well-equipped Fort William Henry, built in 1692, was destroyed in 1696 by the French under Baron de Castin. Fort Frederick, named for the Prince of Wales, built in 1729 by Colonel David Dunbar under royal commission, was destroyed during the Revolution by local residents to prevent its occupation by the British. The little settlement suffered many depredations by the Indians in 1745-48 during the Fifth Indian War.

Next to Captain Kidd of another period, probably no pirate in Maine waters has been the subject of so many tales as Dixey Bull. In 1632 a band of French seized the Plymouth Company's trading post at Castine, and captured the sloop, goods, and provisions belonging to Bull, who happened to be there at the time as a trader. Fired by a desire for revenge, Bull assembled a crew of twenty-odd men to prey upon foreign, preferably French, shipping. His ventures meeting with little success, Bull attacked several small English vessels. When in 1632 Bull sailed into Pemaquid, sacked the trading post and near-by dwellings, he carried away booty amounting to $2500 in value. Bull's lieutenant was killed during the raid. The freebooter and his men continued raiding isolated colonies and attacking small vessels until, in November, the government at Boston dispatched a fleet of five sloops and pinnaces to capture him. Although the fleet cruised off the Maine coast for several weeks, it failed to find the pirate captain and eventually returned to Boston. There is no definite record of Bull's end, though one version has it that he was finally caught and executed at Tyburn, England.

A Reproduction of the Tower of Fort William Henry (*open* 2-6) faces the beach. Inside, the great rocky foundation of the old fort is seen, and showcases containing relics recovered from the site, copies of old Indian deeds, early military equipment, and many other articles. From the roof is an excellent view of the wooded bay shores.

A low stone wall encloses the old parade ground, with the fort in the left corner and the *Fort House* in the right. The house, built by Colonel David Dunbar in 1729, is a square two-story frame building with cupola, now a private residence. Bordering the stone wall are about 200 old cellars, some of them still open and others partly filled in; sunken paved streets, excavated some time ago, are now exposed in only one or two spots. A few yards from the rear of the fort enclosure, reached by a beaten path, is the old *Fort Cemetery*. Most of the stones are of slate imported from Wales and dated in the 18th century; the oldest legible inscription is that of Ann Rodgers, wife of Lieutenant Partrick Rodgers, who died July 1, 1758, in her 41st year.

NEW HARBOR (alt. 30, Bristol Town), 13.1 *m.*, is a compact fishing and resort settlement. The small boats riding in the harbor are particularly well built to withstand the buffeting of the rough waters outside. Along the wharves are scattered upturned dories, lobster pots with floats, drying nets, fish-drying stages, and all the appurtenances of fishing.

New Harbor was the home of Samoset, the Indian who, in March, 1621, startled the Pilgrims of Plymouth by appearing among them with the words, 'Much welcome, Englishmen.' He explained that he was a sachem and had learned the language from Englishmen engaged in fishing off Monhegan, and named many of the boat captains. He was apparently accustomed to English fare, eating without comment the food they offered him. On his next visit he brought with him Squando, who became a friend of the settlers. Chief Samoset was a magnificent figure, tall and straight, his body naked save for a loin cloth. The advice of these Indians enabled the Pilgrims to replenish their dwindling stores, a friendly act that was later repaid with treachery.

Samoset was entertained, with other Indian leaders, in 1624 in Portland Harbor by Captain Christopher Levett.

> Left from New Harbor on State 32 is ROUND POND (alt. 25, Bristol Town), 6.6 *m.*, a tiny village of well-kept homes and a post office, sloping down to a small cove on Muscongus Bay. Eighty years ago it was busy with shipbuilding, the making of sails and rigging, and as the home port of fishing fleets.
>
> *Loud's Island* (alt. 30, Bristol Town), lying 1.5 miles off Round Pond village (*rowboat ferry; irregular service*), is 4 miles long and 1.5 miles wide. It was formerly called Muscongus Island. By an oversight, the report of an early survey omitted mention of the island, though it was settled about 1745. The map of the coast did not show it, and it had the distinction of being subject to no government. A system of self-government, producing excellent results, was formed by the residents. The island is now included within the town of Bristol.
>
> Left from Round Pond village 2 *m.* on a dirt road; here stands the *Old Rock Schoolhouse*, built in 1836 of granite blocks nearly a foot thick, and chinked with plaster. In the small building eight rough benches, each accommodating three pupils, are formed by planks nailed at right angles to the walls. One of the oldest school buildings in Maine, it was abandoned years ago, but is kept in repair by a local organization.

PEMAQUID POINT (alt. 60, Bristol Town), 15.8 *m.*, the extreme tip of the peninsula, is marked by *Pemaquid Light* (*parking space* 15¢). The old light was established in the white pyramidal tower connected with the dwelling in 1827; the dwelling is no longer occupied. In 1934 an automatic illumination apparatus was installed in the old tower.

The point extends far out from the bordering land. A vast expanse of ocean sweeps before it and on its rocky shore a heavy surf pounds ceaselessly.

David Ingram with his companions, Richard Browne and Richard Twide, are thought to have visited the Bashaba Bessabez here in 1569 on their long walk from the Gulf of Mexico to Nova Scotia after they had been set ashore by Captain John Hawkins. Ingram's tales were so hazy on practical details and so embroidered by his imagination that it is impossible to identify anything he described with certainty.

TOUR 1 J : *From* JUNCTION WITH US 1 *to* PORT CLYDE, 14.5 *m.*, State 131.

Via St. George, Tenant's Harbor, and Martinsville.
Two-lane tar-surfaced route.

THE upper section of this delightful route follows the eastern bank of the broad St. George's River, then crosses the narrow peninsula to run along the inletted shore line, where it is swept by exhilarating breezes from the Atlantic Ocean.

State 131 branches south, from US 1 (*see Tour 1, sec. b*), 0 *m.*, on the eastern edge of Thomaston.

ST. GEORGE (alt. 90, St. George Town, pop. 2108), 5.2 *m.*, was named for the Georges Islands, a name given originally to Monhegan by George Waymouth in honor of England's patron saint and his own name saint. Waymouth visited the region in 1605, one year after the French had made a settlement on Dochet Island in the St. Croix River, claiming the whole northern part of the coast for France. Waymouth placed a cross on Allen Island, one of the present Georges Islands, to establish England's claim to sovereignty over the land. The village is near the site of a trading post established about 1630 by the English and maintained periodically until the Indian War in 1675.

The red granite *Memorial* on the village Green is to members of the Gilchrist family who served in the Revolutionary, Mexican, and Civil Wars.

Wilbert Snow, contemporary poet, was born on Whitehead Island in this town. His books of verse, 'Down East,' 'Inner Harbor,' and 'Maine Coast,' are vividly descriptive of the beauty of this area and narrate many of the old local legends.

Behind the white church (R), overlooking a cemetery on the bank of St. George's River, is the unmarked *Site of Fort St. George's*, built in 1809 and garrisoned during the War of 1812. Rugged earthworks 6 feet high and 50 feet long, overgrown by alders, are the only remains of the crescent-shaped rampart upon which 15-pounder guns were once mounted. The English ship 'Bulwark' captured the fort and spiked the guns in 1814.

TENANT'S HARBOR (alt. 30, St. George Town), 9.8 *m.*, is a village with stained and weather-beaten homes. The deep pits of granite quarries are visible from the highway, which provides a view out to the fir-topped islands.

At 11 *m.* is the junction with a dirt road.

Left on this road to the ELMORE NEIGHBORHOOD (alt. 25, St. George Town), 1.7 *m.*, on Hart's Neck. At the end of this road a footpath has been worn through the woods to the rough jagged shore where the intermittent boom and roar of

Spouting Horn, near-by, drowns out all other sounds. This waterspout is caused by the rush of the sea through a narrow passage under a ledge. On the incoming tide with a stiff east wind, the water is forced 40 feet into the air.

MARTINSVILLE (alt. 20, St. George Town), 12.1 *m.*, with its few houses by the roadside, is the village in which Sarah Orne Jewett (*see Tour* 11) once taught school. Her 'Country of the Pointed Firs,' written in the schoolhouse that stood on the site of the present school building (R), has this immediate area for its locale.

PORT CLYDE (alt. 30, St. George Town), 14.5 *m.*, has steamer connections (*variable schedules, apply at wharf*) with coastal villages and islands.

Life in this village on the tip of the peninsula revolves around the packing house and wharf where little fishing boats ride at their moorings.

The first hostile act of the English against the Indians is said to have been committed near here in 1605. Captain George Waymouth, in the 'Archangel,' visited here and found 'where fire had been made: and about the place were very great egge shelles bigger than goose egges, fish bones, and as we judged, the bones of some beast.' The party lingered on this pleasant spot, repairing their ship, catching lobsters and fish, and gathering the berries which grew in abundance. Establishing friendly relations with the Indians, the party traded knives and baubles for valuable furs and tobacco. Then, seizing five of the aborigines, they sailed away to display them in England. These Indians, Tahanedo, Amoret, Skicoworos, Maneddo, and Saffacomoit, attracted much attention in England. Three were held by Sir Ferdinando Gorges who presented two to Sir John Popham; these Englishmen were the chief backers of Waymouth's expedition. Sir John taught his Indians to speak English, in order to learn more about the country from which they came and to judge for himself the possible sources of wealth in it. Two of the Indians were sent back from England with expeditions sent out in 1606, for which they were to act as interpreters. The ship bearing the Indians was captured by the Spanish. Skicoworos, one of the remaining Indians, came back to Maine in 1607 on the 'Gift of God,' or on the 'Mary and John,' ships commanded by George Popham, brother of Sir John, and by Raleigh Gilbert, son of Sir Humphrey and nephew of Sir Walter Raleigh. This expedition first landed on Allen Island, which is between the end of St. George peninsula and Monhegan Island (*see Popham Beach, Tour* 1E).

TOUR 1 K : *From* STOCKTON SPRINGS *to* ELLSWORTH, 27.6 *m.*, State 3.

Via Sandy Point, Verona Island, Bucksport, Orland, and East Orland.
Two-lane tar-surfaced highway.

THIS route, through hilly farmlands offering views of the Penobscot River, is a short cut for the section of US 1 that loops north to Bangor. State 3 branches east from Stockton Springs (*see Tour* 1, *sec. c*), 0 *m.*

SANDY POINT (alt. 110, Stockton Springs Town), 3.2 *m.*, is an attractive settlement of green-shuttered, white frame houses retaining all the charm of old New England. The graceful façade of the white church in the center of the village looks toward Penobscot Bay, from which many men from this township departed for foreign ports. Immediately opposite the church is a small burial ground with many stones marked 'Lost' or 'Died at Sea.' The most pretentious monument is that in memory of Captain Albert Partridge; a globe of polished granite bears the names of the many distant ports he visited.

At 6.4 *m.* is the junction with a road leading (L) 0.3 *m.* into the Fort Knox reservation (*see Tour* 1, *sec. c*).

The *Waldo-Hancock Suspension Bridge* (*car and driver* 50¢), 6.7 *m.*, carries State 3 across the Penobscot River. The bridge, rising 137 feet above the river, was completed in the fall of 1931.

VERONA (alt. 80, Verona Town, pop. 228), 7.5 *m.*, is on an island in the Penobscot River. The last vessel built and launched in this former shipbuilding village was the 'Roosevelt,' which carried Commander Robert E. Peary on his final Arctic expedition, during which he is believed to have reached the North Pole.

State 3 crosses Verona bridge to enter Bucksport.

BUCKSPORT (alt. 80, Bucksport Town, pop. 2135), 8 *m.*, lies on the east bank of the Penobscot, the main street following the shore of the river. Directly opposite Bucksport are the gray ramparts of Fort Knox (*see Tour* 1, *sec. c*), which stands like a medieval castle at a high point of vantage on the river bank. The shopping and trading center of the village lies on the low ground near the river, and the residential area spreads on higher ground.

The *Maine Seaboard Paper Company Mill* (*visitors welcome*) was erected in 1930 in the northern part of the village. The mill can produce more than 1280 feet of 216-inch high-grade newsprint a minute. Although the mill was originally designed to produce 250 tons daily, an average daily production of 328 tons was reached in 1936. Paper makers from all parts of the world have made studies of the methods, high-speed machines, and other devices in use at this mill.

Opposite the mill is a group of Colonial-style company houses with landscaped grounds.

Franklin Street is lined with houses built for merchants and shipmasters of the early days of this town, which was settled in 1762 and incorporated in 1792. These old homes contain many souvenirs, pieces of bric-à-brac, and furnishings, gathered from all parts of the world.

North of Franklin Street, the buildings of the former Eastern Maine Conference Seminary crown a hilltop. Established in 1851 and discontinued in 1934 because of lack of funds, this former Methodist-Episcopal seminary was in 1936 reopened as Spofford Junior High School, a part of the public school system of the town. From the campus is visible the emerald beauty of Verona Island and the Waldo-Hancock Bridge, which looks like a shining ribbon of steel flung across the blue Penobscot.

On the south side of Franklin Street is the *Birthplace of William and Dustin Farnum*, stage and screen actors.

On the corner of Federal and Franklin Sts. is the *Doctor Moulton House*, an architecturally undistinguished structure, built in 1799 and occupied during the War of 1812 by the British, who came ashore and raided and burned property.

The *Jed Prouty Tavern* (1804), on the northeast corner of Main and Federal Sts., is known as the setting of the popular comedy, 'Old Jed Prouty.' This old white, three-story hostelry was a well-known stopping-place on the stage route between Bangor and Castine, the county seat. Here travelers sat beneath a great blackheart cherry tree growing among white rosebushes by the fence, and watched the busy river traffic while they waited for supper.

On the pages of the old register are 'Martin Van Buren, The White House,' written in bold letters; 'Gen'l Jackson — Hermitage'; the name of William Henry Harrison; and 'John Tyler, Washington.' After the last some person, apparently not an admirer, wrote, 'And the Old Nick is after him.'

In *Buck Cemetery*, near the entrance to Verona Bridge, a plain *Granite Obelisk*, visible from the highway, marks the resting place of Colonel Jonathan Buck, for whom Bucksport was named. Legend has it that, while living in Haverhill, Mass., prior to coming to Maine, Colonel Buck was called on, in an official capacity, to execute a woman condemned as a witch. It was said that the woman placed a curse on him; after his death the likeness of a leg and foot appeared on the side of his granite monument. The mark, undoubtedly a defect in the stone, reappears after every effort to efface it, and the townspeople call it the Witch's Curse.

ORLAND (alt. 180, Orland Town, pop. 891), 10.3 *m.*, with neat homes and churches, is an attractive village on the bank of the blue Narramissic River. Edwin Ginn, founder of the Boston publishing house that bears his name, was born here in 1838.

At Orland is a junction with State 175 (*see Tour 3*).

TOUR 1L: Gouldsboro–Winter Harbor Peninsula

EAST ORLAND (alt. 150, Orland Town), 14 *m.*, is a crossroads.

Left from East Orland on a gravel road to a *U. S. Fish Hatchery (open)*, 1.3 *m.*, established on the shore of Alamoosook Lake for the propagation of salmon and trout. The gravel road completely circles the wooded shores of the lake. Five Red Paint Indian cemeteries, together with Indian relics and workshops, have been unearthed during extensive archeological excavations carried on along the lake shore (*see Earliest Inhabitants*).

Right from the hatchery on a trail that extends about 2 *m.* along the course of Craig Brook to Craig Pond, then north to *Great Mountain* (alt. 1037), on whose slope is a deep *Cave* that burrows more than 60 feet into the center of the mountainside. The formation of walls and ceiling gives its several rooms a weird appearance.

At 27.6 *m.* State 3 rejoins US 1 in Ellsworth (*see Tour 1, sec. c*).

TOUR 1L: *From* JUNCTION WITH US 1 *to* JUNCTION WITH US 1, 16.6 *m.*, State 186.

Via Winter Harbor, Birch Harbor, and Prospect Harbor.
Two-lane tarred roadbed.

THIS route swings over a crooked and rolling road with many sharp curves and hills on the Gouldsboro–Winter Harbor peninsula, an exclusive summer resort area. Off the blunt southern end juts Grindstone Neck, from which are unsurpassed views over white-capped seas. Pointed firs crown wind-swept ledges along the jagged coast and from the western shores are superb views across blue Frenchman's Bay of Mount Desert Island with its forest-clad hills.

At 0 *m.* State 186 swings south from US 1 (*see Tour 1, sec. d*), on the western edge of West Gouldsboro.

The route follows the shore line of Frenchman's Bay for several miles.

SOUTH GOULDSBORO (Gouldsboro Town), 3 *m.*, is a small village on an inlet.

At 6.7 *m.* is the junction with a local road.

Right on this road is WINTER HARBOR (alt. 50, Winter Harbor Town, pop. 517), 0.3 *m.*, in an area identified principally with summer recreation and beautiful summer homes; its marine views, through the wide-mouthed harbor with its dozen islands, are famous. Although Frenchman's Bay, visible beyond Turtle Island, has been known to freeze, the sheltered harbor here with an average depth of seven fathoms, has never been frozen.

The road swings left at the end of the village and passes the *Grindstone Inn Golf Club (open June 15 to Sept. 15; 9-hole course)*, and *Swimming Pool*, and at 1.6 *m.* reaches GRINDSTONE NECK, a beautiful area with summer estates.

At 7.7 *m.* is the junction with an improved road.

Right on this road, at 3.8 *m.*, is an improved road (L) that winds its way 1 *m.* to the summit of *Schoodic Mountain*, locally called Schoodic Head (alt. 437). From this height the entrance to the Bay of Fundy can be seen northeast.

At 4.6 *m.* the main side road swings right and at 4.8 *m.* is the junction with a dirt road that leads 1.5 *m.* to the *U.S. Radio-Direction Finder Station* (*not open to public*).

At 5.2 *m.* is a parking site at the tip of the Schoodic Peninsula which is a part of Acadia National Park. There is a beautiful view of the ocean and Cadillac Mountain. The view at this point is particularly fine when the ground swells come rolling in against the rocks after a storm at sea. On the eastern side of Schoodic Peninsula is Wonsqueak Stream, locally called One Screech. It is said that an Indian became jealous of his squaw and, taking her out in his canoe, threw her overboard. Before the waters closed over her she gave one screech.

At 9.6 *m.* is BIRCH HARBOR (alt. 50, Gouldsboro Town). Tradition says that this beautiful harbor, which now has a summer colony, was so named for a thick birch grove along the shore. Today there are few birches, but the seascape is one of the finest along this section of the coast.

PROSPECT HARBOR (alt. 30, Gouldsboro Town), 11.6 *m.*, called Watering Cove in the early days of settlement, is a summer residential village.

Right from Prospect Harbor on a local road to COREA, 3 *m.* Here wind-swept dunes contrast with the otherwise rugged coastal scenery. A summer settlement tips the slender headland jutting out into the sea, while in a quiet cove are the cottages of fishermen, whose nets hang drying on rickety wharves.

Near-by is a lobster pound, a huge tank from which live lobsters may be selected before they are cooked in seaweed. Several Maine coast resorts have such pounds.

On the outskirts of GOULDSBORO, State 186 rejoins US 1 (*see Tour 1, sec. d*) at 16.6 *m.*

T O U R 1 M : *From* WHITING *to* LUBEC (*Treat's and Campobello Islands*), 11 *m.*, State 189.

Two-lane gravel road.

THE route runs through an area that makes clear why 'rock-bound' always precedes mention of the coast of Maine; on the mainland are high cliffs, the land rises abruptly from the rivers and bays, and the offshore islands are rugged. The area is particularly fascinating to inlanders, because both the villages and the people have distinctive characteristics, developed by long contact with the sea. The weathered wharves and canning factories are the centers of interest to visitors, as well as the centers of community life.

State 189 branches northeast from US 1 at Whiting (*see Tour 1, sec. d*), 0 *m.*, crossing Orange River.

Tour 1M: From Whiting to Lubec

At 1.6 *m.* (R) is a free camp site.

At 5.7 *m.* is the West Lubec Post Office.

   1. Left from West Lubec Post Office on a gravel road, along which are shafts of abandoned lead mines, is NORTH TRESCOTT (alt. 20, Trescott Town, pop. 365), 5.5 *m.*, on a point of land formed by the Cobscook River and an arm of Cobscook Bay.

   Cobscook Falls, visible at the road's end, are formed by high tides rushing with tremendous force through a narrow gut.

   2. Right from West Lubec Post Office, on State 191, is CUTLER (alt. 60, Cutler Town, pop. 492), 14.1 *m.*, a farming and fishing community on a horseshoe-shaped harbor. The town with its irregular coast line has numerous picnic grounds and camping spots.

At 9.8 *m.* is the junction with a local road.

   1. Left on this road, known as the North Lubec Road, which has many excellent views as it runs along a narrow neck of land that extends into Cobscook Bay. NORTH LUBEC (alt. 80, Lubec Town), 3 *m.*, gained notoriety from the Jernegan gold swindle (1896–98). Jernegan, pastor of a local church, claimed he had perfected a method of extracting gold from sea water by electrolysis. A stock company was formed and much stock sold throughout the country. A plant was erected on the shore; divers were sent to the bottom and came up bringing small quantities of gold. Large crews of workmen were imported and operations went on for a few months until Jernegan, having collected a considerable sum of money, disappeared.

   2. Right on the local gravel road is *West Quoddy Head* (alt. 40), 8 *m.*, the most easterly point of the United States, where a Coast Guard station and a lighthouse are maintained. From this point the high cliffs of Grand Manan Island are visible on a clear day.

LUBEC (alt. 80, Lubec Town, pop. 2983), 11 *m.*, has had greatly increased activity since the beginning of the Passamaquoddy Power Project (*see Tour 1N*). It is a picturesque seaside village with beautiful views of surrounding bays and coves.

Chaloner Tavern, Main and Cleaves Sts., formerly a stage-line terminus, has been used as a public house since 1804. Chaloner's, the Golden Ball, and Stearns' were the taverns in this harbor town in an earlier day when illicit border trade was profitable. Flour, bought in Canada for $4 a barrel, sold here for $8. Smuggling was rampant. Vessels hailing from Lubec or near-by towns took out papers for Spain or Portugal, sailed instead to some Canadian port where sugar, molasses, flour, and rum were loaded and returned with full cargoes. At any time of night innkeepers might be awakened by furtive knocks upon their doors.

The *Golden Ball*, now the Comstock House, is on Pleasant St. It is said the tavern keeper had a special room for deserting British sailors whom he recognized by their sea-soaked clothing, for they usually swam ashore. Generally they had money and he was glad to aid them in boarding a coaster at near-by ports. The story is told of an English officer who, looking for a hide-out, was tossed into the street when he displeased the innkeeper. The keeper's daughter went to the officer's assistance and later they were married.

Most of the old houses here face east, according to the former custom.

   On TREAT'S ISLAND (alt. 40, Lubec Town), in Cobscook Bay, reached from

Lubec by ferry, considerable construction in connection with the Passamaquoddy Tidal Project (*see Tour* 1*N*) has been in progress. The dam was to have run directly across the island.

A large granite *Shaft*, near the center of the island, is in memory of Colonel John Allen, Indian Superintendent for the Eastern District during the Revolution, who was chiefly responsible for keeping the Passamaquoddy Indians on the side of the colonists. Colonel Allen conducted a trading post on this island.

CAMPOBELLO ISLAND (Ital.: 'beautiful meadow'), though Canadian soil, is reached by a few minutes' ferry ride across Lubec Narrows. 1.5 *m*. from the ferry, the *Summer Home of President Franklin D. Roosevelt*, a large red house, is visible from the road. There is excellent fishing from the island, and the 30 miles of improved roads winding over it and passing many beautiful summer homes, provide magnificent panoramic views of the sea and the Maine coast.

TOUR 1 N : *From* PERRY *to* EASTPORT, 7.3 *m*., State 190.

Via Quoddy Village.
Two-lane tar-surfaced road.

THE route runs close to the shore of Passamaquoddy Bay, which, in sunlight, is intensely blue; beyond the islands dotting the water rise the hills of New Brunswick. This route is particularly delightful in the early morning, when the thumping of motor-boats and the tangy aroma of drying fish is a reminder of the area's fishing activities.

State 190 branches southeast from US 1 at Perry, 0 *m*. (*see Tour* 1, *sec. d*). At 0.7 *m*. is the junction with a gravel road.

Left on this road is *Pleasant Point*, 2 *m*., a 100-acre reservation established about 1822 and occupied by 300 Passamaquoddy Indians. The State appoints an agent to supervise the business affairs of the reservation but the Indians elect their own governor and may send a member of the tribe to represent them before the legislature. Houses on the reservation are of modern camp type and there is a fully equipped elementary school.

These Indians had accepted Roman Catholicism before there was extensive white settlement in the State and have remained devout communicants even though retaining some of their primitive ceremonies. After a conventional church wedding in the little brick church, for example, the dark-skinned, sleek-haired Passamaquoddies dance to the beating of drums and the chanting of old songs. Discarding ordinary dress, which differs little from that of the white people living around them, they don ancient costume and headdress, and paint their faces. They welcome visitors to these affairs and appreciate applause. While they do not make friends easily, once their initial shyness has worn off they belie their reputation for taciturnity and are excellent story-tellers.

The Passamaquoddies do some farming and occasionally work on the roads, but their livelihood is derived chiefly from fishing.

From the time of the Revolution, the men have been active in military service; many joined the northern troops in the Civil War. In the *Indian Cemetery* (R) at the top of the hill near the entrance to the reservation, is a monument to Moses

TOUR 1N: From Perry to Eastport

Neptune, killed at the Argonne in 1918, and another to the memory of Charles Nola, who was posthumously awarded the Croix de Guerre for remarkable courage and tenacity in defending an advance post until he was killed, in the World War. Most of the graves are marked by small wooden crosses with carved inscriptions. A *Dam*, a part of the Passamaquoddy Project, has been built between Pleasant Point and Carlow Island.

At 4.2 *m.* State 190 crosses a bridge to Moose Island. A short distance south of the bridge is *Quoddy Village*, in which 250 New England young men are learning (1937), in a National Youth Administration experiment, to choose careers compatible with their talents and abilities.

The boys occupy the 120 temporary cottages, nine permanent houses, the apartment buildings, the barracks and the mess halls formerly used by the laborers and engineers employed on the gigantic tidal project to harness the high tides of the Bay of Fundy. The youths have their own municipal government, run a newspaper, and do all the maintenance and service work.

In the exhibition building at Quoddy Village there is a working *Model of the Passamaquoddy Tidal Power Development Project* as originally planned, its purpose being the utilization of the high range of tides in the vicinity of Passamaquoddy Bay near Eastport.

This controversial project was undertaken by the United States Government in April, 1935, with Federal funds, work being placed under the supervision of army engineers. Actual construction was begun in February, 1936. Work was suspended in February, 1937, after the dams connecting Pleasant Point to Carlow Island and Carlow Island to Kendall Head (thus linking Eastport with the mainland) and a short dam between Treat and Dudley Islands had been completed. The estimated cost of the total finished project is between 37 and 38 million dollars.

> The idea of harnessing tidal power is not new; even in Colonial days there were small tidal mills along this coast and in other parts of the world, principally gristmills. But the Quoddy Project was the first large-scale attempt to manufacture power from the changes of the sea. At Passamaquoddy Bay is one of the few known possible sites in the world for such an undertaking; unusually high ocean tides (their average range from 13 to 23 feet) flow and ebb with great force through narrow channels connecting two large natural basins which are adjacent to each other and are almost entirely landlocked.
>
> The originally conceived International or 'Two-Pool' Plan of development embraced Cobscook Bay and all of Passamaquoddy Bay as well, the northern part of which is in Canada. In this plan, power would be generated continuously by controlling the flow of water into the two pools so as to keep them at variant levels, thus producing a powerful waterfall at a point between the basins known as 'the Carrying Place'; here the generating station would be installed. The Canadian Government's failure to co-operate in the international development limited the project to the single-pool plan. The planned operation of the latter is identical with that of the double pool, except that the lower basin would not be blocked off from the ocean and so would not remain constantly at low tide level, but would rise and fall with the ocean tide. Dams would run across the mouth of Cobscook Bay, the arm of Passamaquoddy from Estes Head on the southeastern shore of Eastport to Lubec Neck, crossing Treat and Dudley Islands, the top of the dam making a highway between Eastport and Lubec only two and a half miles long (at present it is 42 miles by road from Eastport to Lubec). That part of the dam already completed connecting Eastport with the mainland to the north replaces the old

wooden railroad trestle. The tide would flow in through filling gates between the islands and out through locks between Dudley Island and Lubec Neck and through a canal cut through 'the Carrying Place' between the northeast section of Cobscook Bay and the St. Croix River. The incoming and outgoing tides would here run large turbines to generate the power.

In this plan generation would continue seven hours out of the tide cycle of approximately twelve and a half hours. During the remaining time when Cobscook Bay was being refilled, the gap in power production would be taken care of by (1) a pumped storage plant, (2) tying in the project with existing power systems, (3) an auxiliary hydro-electric plant which could be constructed in the vicinity, or (4) a mechanical generating plant. The pumped storage reservoir, perhaps the most feasible of these devices, could be constructed in the vicinity of Haycock Harbor, over 100 feet above sea level; when the tidal power plant was not running, water would be released from the reservoir through an auxiliary set of turbines, thus furnishing continuous power. Pumps could operate as turbines during the flow of water back to the ocean, and likewise the motors driving the pumps could act as generators furnishing power.

The electricity generated at Quoddy would be greater than the combined capacity of all existing power stations in the State, and would supply cheap power to farms throughout Maine and to industries which might be encouraged to enter the region. It was hoped by advocates of the project that the newly created opportunities for manufacturing would bring about the development of the State's mineral deposits (*see Mineral Resources*).

EASTPORT (alt. 80, pop. 3466), 7.3 *m*., with its neighbor Lubec, has long been important in the fishing industry, though it is now less so than formerly. Fishing, like agriculture, has fallen on evil days. Centralized control of the marketing end of the business, the use of the high-powered beam trawlers that destroy millions of young fish, pollution of the streams in which the fish formerly spawned, and other factors have reduced many of the fishermen to abject poverty.

In this area the most valuable fish are cod, haddock, cusk, hake, pollock, halibut, and herring; the small herring are canned as sardines. Sardine canning began in Eastport about 1875 and since that time the women of the town, young and old, drop whatever they are doing, seize their aprons and knives, and rush to the factories when the siren gives warning of a new catch. The old folk speak of sardines as 'little fish biled in ile.'

The once worthless herring scales have become a valued by-product of the industry, now being carefully gathered for the making of an essence used to give iridescence to artificial pearls. Two plants here manufacture the product.

The town was settled in 1780, but European traders were here a hundred years earlier. The port had considerable prosperity after the passage of the Embargo Act of 1807, becoming the center of extensive two-way smuggling operations. The British ignored these activities until after 1812 when war was declared; in July, 1814, they captured the town, confiscating several vessels that were about to sail, loaded with contraband.

The *Site of Fort Sullivan*, erected in 1808 for the protection of the settlement, is on a high ledge behind the Shead Memorial High School; from the ledge is a magnificent view of the coast and islands.

The *George Pearse Ennis Art School* (*open*) is on High St. opposite

Boynton St. Many artists visit Eastport in numbers each summer because of the striking coast views and in spite of the fogs that are frequent in August.

Eastport Country Club Inn (open), on the outskirts of the city, maintains a 9-hole golf course.

Yachting and fishing are popular forms of recreation (*boats for hire*).

Campobello Island (see Tour 1M) is visible from the waterfront.

T O U R 2 : MOUNT DESERT ISLAND: *From* ELLSWORTH *to* TREMONT, 54.1 *m.*, State 3, State 198 and State 102.

Via Salisbury Cove, Hull's Cove, Bar Harbor, Seal Harbor, Northeast Harbor, Mount Desert, Southwest Harbor, Manset, and Ship Harbor.
Two-lane tarvia and cement roadbeds.

THIS route, one of the most scenic in Maine, winds through the fashionable summer resorts of Mount Desert Island and through Acadia National Park, dominated by Cadillac Mountain (alt. 1532). The island is one of the most dramatically beautiful spots in the world. Here eighteen hills — locally called mountains — and twenty-six lakes and ponds cover a rocky, wooded island that is cut nearly in half by a fiord. The circling highway presents ever-changing views of the island-dotted waters and the abrupt and broken coast of the mainland.

Mount Desert Island, as well as the rest of Maine and what is now the United States as far south as the Mason and Dixon Line, was included in the grant called Acadia that was made by Henry IV of France in 1603 to the Sieur de Monts. In 1604, Samuel de Champlain, making his second voyage to the New World, this time with de Monts as his patron, came down the coast after a colony had been established at the mouth of the St. Croix River, exploring the waters as far as Cape Cod. He is credited with the discovery of this island, which he named, possibly with a punning reference to the man who had sent him on the voyage, l'Isle des Monts déserts. A few years later a French missionary colony was established here, but this was speedily wiped out by the English, who had no intention of permitting France to establish a foothold in a country so rich in furs and forests. In 1688, Louis XIV granted the island as a feudal fief to the Sieur de la Mothe Cadillac — later founder of Detroit — who came to live on his domain. In 1713, Louis XIV was forced to cede the island, as part of a large slice of Maine, to the English. Massachusetts acquired control of it and granted the island to Sir Francis Bernard, its Royal Governor, for 'distinguished services.' Bernard visited the place in 1762 and was enchanted by its beauty. At the time of the Revolution Bernard's property in America was confiscated, but later his son succeeded in having half the island returned to the family; a granddaughter of Cadillac managed to gain control of the other half.

Several small settlements were made on the land at various times, but it was not until after the advent of the steamboat that the real development began. About the middle of the nineteenth century Mount Desert Island began to attract visitors and from then on its history has to some extent paralleled that of Newport as a fashionable summer resort.

In 1901 the State of Maine began a movement to preserve the beauty of the place by setting some of it aside as a public reservation. In 1916 control of the reserved area was transferred to the Federal Government; this control has been extended and the public lands are now called Acadia National Park.

ELLSWORTH (alt. 100, pop. 3557) (*see Tour* 1, *sec. c*), 0 *m*., is at a junction of US 1 (*see Tour* 1, *sec. c*) and State 15 (*see Tour* 3). State 3 branches south from US 1, 1.1 miles southeast of the center of Ellsworth.

At 7.1 *m*. (L) is the *Bar Harbor Airport* and modern flying field built under the supervision of the Public Works Administration.

At 8.8 *m*. is the drawbridge spanning Mount Desert Narrows, which separate the island from the mainland.

At SALISBURY COVE (alt. 20, Bar Harbor Town), 14.1 *m*., are (L) four buildings occupied by the *Mount Desert Island Biological Laboratory* (*open Wed. p.m.*), which provides research facilities and instruction.

At 16.4 *m*. (R) are trim pine and spruce groves; left is a view of Frenchman's Bay, which in summer is livened by dipping white sails and speeding motor-boats.

At HULL'S COVE (alt. 80, Bar Harbor Town), 16.8 *m*., a boulder in the village cemetery (R) marks the *Grave of Madame Marie Thérèse de Grégoire*, granddaughter of Cadillac, who once owned the island.

BAR HARBOR (alt. 70, Bar Harbor Town, pop. 4486), 19.9 *m*.

> *Accommodations.* Hotels, rooming houses, and restaurants, with wide price range.
>
> *Transportation.* Bus service in summer between Bar Harbor and B. & M. R.R. Station in Ellsworth. Regular and special boat trips to islands daily (*inquire on waterfront*). Power boats, sailboats and canoes for rent on waterfront. Daily sightseeing trips, 10.30, 2.30, and 4.30 on Frenchman's Bay, lasting 2 hrs.; $1 per person.
>
> *Information Services.* Headquarters Acadia National Park, Main St.; detailed maps for sale, free naturalist-guide service for park area. Bar Harbor Publicity Bureau, Main St., for information on hotels, boarding houses, sightseeing trips, etc.

Bar Harbor is the center of social and commercial life on the island. In summer the two business streets are lined with smart shops, branches of those on Fifth and Madison Avenues in New York City, and are filled with brightly dressed visitors and summer residents. There is a constant stream of arrivals and departures into Bar Harbor in connection with the gay house parties and entertainments given by the dowagers and debu-

TOUR 2: From Ellsworth to Tremont 283

tantes of the wealthy and nationally prominent families that own homes here. Yacht races, a marine tennis tournament, swimming, and numerous other competitive sports, as well as flower shows, garden parties, and the like, are prominent in the season's program.

Besides the visitors whose names are recorded weekly in the social columns of the metropolitan dailies there are those whose objective is the resort's beauty; they never tire of climbing the rocky slopes to find new vistas of the coast and sea.

The *Shore Club,* on the harbor, established by six of the leading hotels, is the social center for hotel guests, visiting yachtsmen, and summer residents.

The Mount Desert Players present Greek, Shakespearean, and modern drama in the *Casino,* on Cottage St.

Branching from the business streets are park-like sections containing churches, hotels, and residences.

> Right from Bar Harbor on Mt. Desert St. to Cadillac Mountain Drive. At 1.2 *m.* (L) is the *Kebo Valley Country Club* (*open July 4–Oct. 15, 18 holes*).
>
> The *Building of Arts,* 1.3 *m.* (L), with massive columns, and friezes of the Muses, has a terraced amphitheater at the rear where recitals are given during the summer season by well-known musicians.
>
> At 1.7 *m.* (L) is the entrance to *Acadia National Park,* which has 15,000 acres of mountain lakes. One section of the park is on the mainland, covering Schoodic Point, south of Winter Harbor (*see Tour* 1). The rocky summits, jutting cliffs, and forested slopes of the island rise so abruptly from the heavy waves of the open Atlantic that the roads and trails of the park provide an almost endless series of views that are breath-taking. The reservation is a wild-life sanctuary with a combination of woodland, lakes, highlands, and seashore that makes possible an amazing variety of vegetable and animal life; it is, moreover, in the band where the Northern and the Temperate Zone floras meet and overlap, and is directly on the coastal migration route of the birds. Vegetation grows here with exceptional vigor, and, among the many wild flowers in the forests and on the frost-split, lichen-clad rocks, are some of great rarity and others of exceptional beauty. In addition to the motor road, there are more than 200 miles of well-kept and plainly marked trails and bridle paths that thread their ways through the area to places where those who like solitude can find it without difficulty.
>
> At 2.6 *m.* the *Cadillac Mountain Summit Road,* a smooth, skillfully engineered ascent whose gradient never exceeds seven per cent, is entered. It winds up the mountain-side through heavy woods and past occasional open spots providing wide panoramas of exceptional grandeur and striking contrasts. Parking stations have been provided at intervals where the views are particularly beautiful. The sweep of sea, islands, coves, and inlets is increasingly wide as the road rises, and craft in the waters below become no more than toy boats.
>
> At 6.3 *m.* the road reaches the plateau that is the *Summit of Cadillac Mountain* (alt. 1532) and circles it. From the ample parking space here is a view of sea and land stretching far into the distance that is particularly impressive at sunrise or sunset. Many miles of the ragged, surf-silvered coastline are visible. To the south is the ocean, flecked here and there with boats; to the north is solitary Mount Katahdin, 110 miles away. Westward, the graceful outlines of the Camden Hills are visible.
>
> Easter sunrise services, largely attended, are held annually on the mountain-top.

South of Bar Harbor, at 21.3 *m.,* is a junction with Ocean Drive.

> Left on Ocean Drive; this 6-mile loop of highway follows the shore. Across

> Frenchman's Bay is a fine view of Schoodic Point, jutting far out to sea with the waves breaking grandly over it. After a storm at sea the ground swell that comes racing in against the headland makes a scene unsurpassed on the Atlantic coast.
>
> *Schooner Head*, 2.4 *m.* (L), a high, wave-washed cliff, named for its resemblance to a schooner, is said to have been cannonaded in 1814 by the British, who mistook its outline for that of a ship. In the cove on the south shore of Schooner Head is *Indian's Foot*, a marking in the rock resembling a footprint. The ledge at the southern end of the cove has been washed out by pounding waves and is known as *Anemone Cave*.
>
> *Great Head*, 3.4 *m.* (L), a high promontory reached by several paths, affords (L) a superb view of Frenchman's Bay with its many humped islands, and (R) the open ocean. In the cove formed by Great Head is a short sand beach.
>
> *Thunder Hole* is at 3.9 *m.* (L). As the waves dash against the rock the water rushes into a deep crevice with a terrific roar, rising to a height of 40 feet.
>
> From *Otter Cliff*, 4.4 *m.* (L), on a narrow point that descends steeply to the ocean on both sides, is an unmarred marine view.

At 21.7 *m.* (L) is the entrance to the *Roscoe B. Jackson Memorial Laboratory* (*open 3–5, weekdays except Sat.*), where biological research is carried on under the direction of Dr. Clarence C. Little, biologist, former president of the University of Maine and of the University of Michigan, and now managing director of the American Society for the Control of Cancer.

At 21.9 *m.* (L) Acadia National Park maintains a *Motor Camp* (*free*), equipped with electric lights, running water, laundry, barracks, and outdoor fireplaces.

At 22.3 *m.* is a junction with a tarred road.

> Right on this road is the *Sieur de Monts Springs and Park*, 0.3 *m.* In the *National Park Building* (information; maps), spring water can be sampled.
>
> Left here is the *Abbe Museum* (*open in summer; archaeologist in charge*), now part of the park property; it was erected and is maintained through the generosity of the late Dr. Robert Abbe, a New York surgeon, and his friends. It contains relics of the stone age of Indian culture.
>
> The spring (R), reached by a short path, is protected by glass and a canopy; named for the first proprietor of the area, the spring has a flow of 62 gallons a minute, the overflow being piped to supply a small trout pool.

At 23.9 *m.* (L) is the south entrance to Ocean Drive (*see above*).

At 26.8 *m.* is a junction with Cooksey Drive.

> Left on Cooksey Drive to the *Champlain Monument*, 0.4 *m.* (R), erected in commemoration of the explorer, Samuel de Champlain, who discovered the island in 1604.

At SEAL HARBOR (alt. 80, Mount Desert Town), 28.3 *m.*, are summer homes of John D. Rockefeller, Jr., and Edsel Ford.

In the settlement ASTICOU (alt. 80, Mount Desert Town), 29.5 *m.*, named for the Indian chief who lived in the area when the French settlement was made in 1613, is (R) *Thuya Lodge* (*open*), formerly the summer home of Joseph H. Curtis, the landscape architect. It has a small museum and a reading-room with many books of interest to the naturalist. The extensively landscaped grounds have a great variety of trees and shrubs. From the lodge is a broad view of the inlets of the shore and the Cranberry Isles.

Tour 2: From Ellsworth to Tremont

Left at 32.2 *m.* is NORTHEAST HARBOR (alt. 60, Mount Desert Town), whose summer residential section is entered over Peabody Drive; it has an 18-hole golf course. This village is a well-known yachting center and in August the Northeast Harbor fleet, made up of about 120 small craft, holds daily racing and cruising events and treasure hunts.

In the *Neighborhood House,* built with the aid of summer residents, and maintained through the proceeds of an annual vaudeville performance, dancing, theatricals, other amusements and social activities are held.

Visible from the waterfront are the three Cranberry Isles, their spruce-mantled cliffs rising two to four miles offshore. (*Reached by mail boats; variable schedules; inquire at wharf.*)

> Leaving the dock at Northeast Harbor, the small boat follows a southeasterly course for 4 miles between wooded islands to ISLESFORD (alt. 40, Cranberry Isles Town, pop. 349), on Little Cranberry Island. In this little village is *Sawtelle Museum (open in summer, free),* which contains Professor William Otis Sawtelle's collection of maps, documents, pictures, furniture, books, and memorabilia of all kinds illustrating every phase of the history of the Mount Desert Island area.
>
> Upon these islands, named for the vast cranberry marsh spreading over 200 acres on Great Cranberry, birds rare to this latitude come to nest. Leach's petrel, seldom seen except far out at sea, lays its eggs here. On the rocky cliffs and shores large colonies of herring gulls and the common tern have their breeding places.
>
> On near-by Sutton Island, the smallest of the Cranberry Islands and the one nearest Northeast Harbor, is the summer home of Rachel Field, the locale of whose 'Time Out of Mind' is this section.

North of Northeast Harbor, Sargeant Drive is followed along the clifftop beside *Somes Sound,* one of the few natural fiords on the Atlantic coast. The narrow inlet extends between 100- to 150-foot cliffs for 5 miles, cutting the island and its mountain range nearly in two.

At the head of the sound the route swings left into MOUNT DESERT (alt. 40, Mount Desert Town, pop. 2022), 39.7 *m.,* a small settlement generally known as Somesville. When Governor Bernard came to inspect the island in 1762, he found a man named Somes building a cabin here for himself.

At 41.5 *m.* (R) the road skirts *Echo Lake,* lying long and placid 90 feet above salt water. On the left looms *Acadia Mountain* (alt. 680).

At 43.6 *m.* (L) is *Saint Sauveur Mountain* (alt. 670), so named for the French settlement of 1613 on Fernald's Point (*see below*).

At 44.8 *m.* is a junction with a tarred road.

> Left on this road is *Fernald's Point,* 0.7 *m.* The hill at this point is the *Site of the Settlement of Saint Sauveur.*
>
> A party of French colonists, including Father Peter Biard and Father Ennemond Masse, had intended to establish a colony on the Penobscot River. Overtaken by a storm they landed in June, 1613, on the exposed southeast shore of Mount Desert Island, where, warned by friendly Indians that their position was too exposed, they came to Fernald's Point the same day. The party landed, planted a cross and celebrated Mass, calling the place Saint Sauveur or Holy Savior.

They then set about building homes and primitive fortifications on this beautiful hillside sloping to the sea.

In September, 1613, Captain Samuel Argall, acting under orders of the English in Virginia, destroyed the mission, set Father Masse and fourteen others adrift, and took Father Biard to Virginia; Father Masse and those with him finally reached Nova Scotia.

SOUTHWEST HARBOR (alt. 40, Southwest Harbor Town, pop. 888), 45.7 *m.*, is another resort village in a beautiful situation.

At 49.1 *m.* the neighborhood (L) bears the local name of SEAWALL, because the shore is a long natural wall of boulders that have been cast up by the sea.

Ship Harbor, 51.1 *m.* (L), is a tiny natural harbor extending to the edge of the road. In 1740, the ship 'Grand Design,' of 300 tons, loaded with passengers from the north of Ireland, struck on Long Ledge outside this harbor. Legend has it that after a night of terror they found that the ship had floated off the ledge and drifted through the narrow inlet into this refuge; this incident is said to be the source of the harbor's name.

TREMONT (alt. 40, town pop. 954), 54.1 *m.*, is in a town of the same name. This was originally a part of Manset; it was incorporated in 1848. The highway swings east, then north to Seal Cove, overlooking Bluehill Bay. A narrower road follows the western shore of the island, returning to the village of Mount Desert.

T O U R 3 : *From* ELLSWORTH *to* ORLAND, 62.6 *m.*, State 15 and State 175.

Via Bluehill, Sedgwick, Brooksville, Penobscot.
Two-lane tar and gravel roadbed.

THIS route, looping around the shores of one of the most beautiful and interesting of the many jagged peninsulas on the coast of Maine, follows the winding Union River south of Ellsworth, skirts lovely Bluehill Bay with many views of Mt. Desert Island to the east, meanders along Eggemoggin Reach with near-by Deer Island in view for several miles, and swings gradually north along Penobscot Bay. Many summer residents have built homes in this area. The now somnolent villages, which in the past seemed destined for an active commercial development, are in winter inhabited chiefly by fishermen and retired seamen.

Someone once wrote that the King's Council for New England had been guilty of 'confusing carelessness' in making land grants, but that censure is mild when applied to the French and English authorities in relation to

Tour 3: From Ellsworth to Orland

the grants covering this peninsula; probably no other area on the coast had quite as many bellicose and persistent claimants, in part, no doubt, because of its strategic position at the mouth of the Penobscot River, which provided entrance into the heart of the rich hinterland of Maine. Champlain inspected it on his trip south from the Colony at the mouth of the St. Croix when he was hunting a less rigorous home for de Monts settlers; Father Biard considered it in 1611 when exploring to find a site for the mission the Marquise de Guerchville proposed to establish; and it was one of the points selected by the Pilgrims as a valuable site for a trading post to obtain the furs that would make them rich. The French and English governments fought for its possession for nearly two hundred years.

State 15 branches south from US 1 at Ellsworth, 0 *m.* (see *Tour* 1, *sec. c*), which is also at a junction with State 3 (see *Tour* 1*K*).

At 5.6 *m.* (R) is the *Surry Theater*, one of Maine's several summer theaters, where noted players appear for a brief season.

SURRY (alt. 40, Surry Town, pop. 488), 6.5 *m.*, after its incorporation in 1785, became a busy fishing village. While the inhabitants still do some fishing to supplement their incomes, since the decline in prosperity of the individual fisherman, they have been largely dependent on catering to summer visitors for their livelihoods. Gaily painted summer cottages line the shores of Patten Bay. In winter this body of water, which freezes over, is covered with small tent-like houses, used by fishermen while catching smelts. In the spring the alewives rushing up Patten Stream to spawn are caught by the townspeople and smoked.

Between Surry and Bluehill, the route cuts across a subsidiary peninsula.

BLUE HILL VILLAGE (alt. 50, Bluehill Town, pop. 1439), 14 *m.*, is at the head of a pointed cove near *Blue Hill* (alt. 940), for which it was named. This hill provides a particularly impressive view of rugged Mt. Desert Island. Although the village is now chiefly known for its summer residential colony, it was a thriving seaport in the middle of the 19th century and before that had had industrial development. Within 40 years of its settlement in 1762, it had several small mills, including one that spun cotton yarn, and the lanes and harbor were echoing all day long with the steady pounding of hammers and sledges in the shipyards. Another source of early prosperity was the mining of minerals in Bluehill, chiefly copper, though occasional small deposits of gold were discovered and some chalk. The copper deposits, though not entirely exhausted, are no longer mined because of western competition.

One of the notable citizens of the town was Jonathan Fisher, to whom Mary Ellen Chase in 'A Goodly Heritage' devoted two chapters. In 1796, four years after his graduation from Harvard College, Fisher became the first pastor of the Congregational Church, which he served for 40 years. He was a man of broad interests and unusual energy. The *Jonathan Fisher House* (L), Main St., was designed and in part built by him; he made the paint for it from yellow ocher he discovered near-by, and constructed almost all the furnishings, including a clock that ran perfectly for 50 years. Not far from the house is his *Windmill*, which provided the power for machines that he devised for sawing wood, removing stones from the ground, and for splitting straws used in hatmaking.

In order that all parishioners might understand his weekly texts — and possibly for sheer joy in intellectual exercise — he read them in Hebrew, Latin, French, Greek, and Aramaic. When he died he left a volume of poetry for each of his children. The rugged hills of the peninsula were no impediment to the discharge of his clerical duties; it was not unusual for him to walk 35 miles to perform a baptism or to comfort a parishioner who was in distress.

It is not surprising that a town so long under the guidance of this intellectual man should in later years have been congenial to distinguished artists, authors, and musicians.

The musicians of the summer colony today hold weekly concerts in *Kneisel Hall*, on Pleasant St., formerly the studio of Dr. Franz Kneisel (1865–1926), the Roumanian violinist who was concert-master of the Boston Symphony Orchestra (1895–1903) and founder of the Kneisel Quartet, at one time the foremost chamber-music organization in the United States.

Mary Ellen Chase, born here in 1887, has preserved the memories of her childhood in this delightful old seaport in 'A Goodly Heritage'; the stories she heard in her youth were beyond doubt an inspiration for her novel 'Mary Peters,' a story of life and adventure on this coast.

State 175 is now followed south across another small inlet of Bluehill Bay.

BLUEHILL FALLS (alt. 25, Bluehill Town), 17.2 *m*. Here is the former *Summer Home of Ethelbert Nevin* (1862–1901), the composer, which is now (1937) occupied by his widow.

South of Bluehill Falls for about 8 miles the highway runs close to the western shore of beautiful Bluehill Bay.

At 17.9 *m*. (L), on the shore of the bay, are *Shell Heaps*, recently explored, that are relics of the days when the Indians came from inland to lay in a winter supply of fish.

SOUTH BLUEHILL (alt. 60, Bluehill Town), 18.2 *m*., is the home (1937) of Captain Otis M. Candage, who now has carved and built more than 100 miniature squareriggers and 200 miniature sloops and schooners since he gave up his boat 25 years ago.

State 175 swings across the head of the narrow peninsula to BROOKLIN (alt. 100, Brooklin Town, pop. 782), 26.3 *m*.

> Left from Brooklin on a narrow dirt road to *Naskeag Point*, 3 *m*., the far outer tip of the neck that is included in the township of Brooklin. In July, 1778, William Reed, working in a field near the shore here, saw the British sloop 'Gage' coming to anchor in a cove, preparing to land men. Hastily procuring his musket and sending

word to neighbors, he crept near the party of 60 men that was arriving in small boats and fired, killing two before they reached land. Fellow townsmen arrived, dragging an old swivel gun, which they filled with nails, filings, and pebbles, and fired. The landing force was at a disadvantage and returned to the sloop after two men had been captured and five badly wounded; before they left, however, they fired six houses and three barns, and seized some calves and hogs. Not being prepared to combat the inhabitants, whose irregular fighting methods had given the impression of more numbers and weapons than were actually there, the invaders came ashore the following day under a flag of truce and obtained the release of the captured men by returning the cattle.

Between Brooklin and Sargentville State 175, known as Eggemoggin Reach Drive, provides delightful views of the Reach and of Deer Island.

HAVEN (alt. 50, Brooklin Town), 27.2 *m.*, is part of the chain of resort villages along the Reach.

SEDGWICK (alt. 50, Sedgwick Town, pop. 699), 31.4 *m.*, is a village of neat white houses. The *Town Hall* (R), a handsome white structure on a hill overlooking the village, was built as a church in 1837, replacing the first church, built in 1794. Four columns ornament the front entrance and a weather-vane surmounts the attractive domed cupola. Daniel Merrill, first pastor of the early church, received an annual salary of £50. That the town was not particularly prosperous in the early days is shown by the official records which reveal that all unattached and unmarried females who could not find anyone to undertake their support were warned to leave town.

SARGENTVILLE (alt. 110, Sedgwick Town), 34.6 *m.*, has a ferry (*variable schedule; inquire at Guild's Wharf*) running to near-by Deer Island lying 1.7 miles off shore (*see Island Tours*). A new bridge (1938) will connect Sargentville and Deer Isle.

> DEER ISLAND is bisected by a motor road, State 172, that runs to DEER ISLE (alt. 30, Deer Isle Town, pop. 1266), 4.5 *m.*, on a wide cove of Penobscot Bay.
>
> At 10.1 *m.* is STONINGTON (alt. 50, Stonington Town, pop. 1418), a village in the center of the south shore of the island (*see Island Tours*).

At Sargentville State 175 turns due north across the head of the peninsula covered by Brooksville.

In a charming grove (R) at the crest of *Caterpillar Hill*, 36.7 *m.*, is a parking space and picnic ground from which is a broad and far-reaching view. Below the hill is Walker Pond and beyond it are the island-sprinkled waters of Penobscot Bay.

PENOBSCOT (alt. 25, Penobscot Town, pop. 708), 48.6 *m.*, is a shipshape village that opens the doors of its attractive little homes to summer visitors. This township is one of the few where stories of buried treasure have been justified. In 1840 a fortunate resident found about 2000 coins in a hillside near Bagaduce River; because most of the coins were French, though there were Spanish pieces of eight and 25 pinetree shillings and one sixpence, dated 1652, it was believed that the money might have been buried by the family of de Castin when they left for Canada in 1704; it is quite as possible, however, that this was pirate loot. The coins are now in the possession of the Maine Historical Society at Portland.

At 50.5 *m.* (L) the route follows the western shore of the small-mouthed triangular bay on which Penobscot lies.

At 53.9 *m.* is a junction with State 202.

Left on State 202 is CASTINE (alt. 80, Castine Town, pop. 726), 4.2 *m.*, which has boat connection with Belfast and Islesboro (*variable schedule; inquire at wharf*). As a popular resort this old village now has an 18-hole golf course. The more than 100 markers at various points indicate the pride that the residents take in their historic background.

Castine was for nearly two hundred years the center of a struggle by three nations for control of the peninsula. In 1629 the King's Council for New England granted permission to the Pilgrims to send Edward Ashley to establish a trading post at this point, then called Pentagoet. The post was, however, destroyed in 1631 by the same vigilant la Tour who wiped out the Vines-Allerton post at Machias. As Governor Bradford, first of the long line of Massachusetts men to succumb to the vice of history-writing, told the story: '... their house at Penobscot was robbed by the French, and all their goods of any worth were carried away.' The Englishman remained, however, and brought in new goods to be exchanged for furs. Meanwhile, Richelieu in France had sent out a new governor for Acadia with specific orders to keep the English out of the country east of Pemaquid and in 1635 Sieur d'Aulney de Charnisay, who had been given the task of carrying out this order, learned of the Pentagoet post from Indians and arrived to destroy it. The Frenchman, for some reason, resorted to the formality of forcing the agent to give him a bill of sale for the goods and left the members of the post with 'their shalop and some victualls to bring them home.' The Plymouth colonists were outraged by this and appealed to the Massachusetts Bay colonists for help; but the Bay leaders merely gave them their blessing and permitted them to hire a 300-ton ship and its crew. Miles Standish and 20 men accompanied the little ship in a bark, giving the captain advice on how he should proceed; but the captain, probably unwilling to risk damage to his boat, persisted in using up his ammunition by firing from a distance and after inflicting only a little damage the ship and bark left Pentagoet.

The Pilgrims again tried in vain to get assistance from the Bay Colony, warning the members of the menace of the encroachments of the French; the leaders in Boston not only declined to act but later on established friendly relations with the French on the coast. Bradford says that bay traders even furnished the French here with 'Poweder and shott' because it was to 'their profite.'

Meanwhile a Capuchin mission had been established here and when in 1646 the Jesuit Father Druillettes came down from Canada to establish a mission at Nanrantsouak (*see Tour* 10) he visited the fathers and received advice from them. In 1648 they built a Chapel of Our Lady of Hope on the site of the present village church of that name; in 1863 a copper sheet was found in the ground near the place with this inscription: '1648, 8 Junii, Frater Leo Parisiensis in Capuciorum Missione, posui hoc fundamentum in honorem nostrate Dominae Sanctae Spei.'

A few years later the English, under Cromwell's orders, took the place but they held it briefly, the French regaining possession in 1670. In 1673 Flemish pirates assailed the fort and kidnaped the governor.

Meanwhile there had appeared on the scene Jean-Vincent d'Abbadie, Baron de St. Castin (1652–1717). Castin, as he is usually called, had been in Quebec. Apparently neglected and deprived of the use of his wealth, the youngster at 15 started out in a canoe with three Abnaki Indians to inspect a royal grant that stood in his name at the mouth of the Penobscot. Pentagoet pleased him and he determined to stay there; when in 1673 the governor of the fort was carried away, Castin, then 21 years old, stepped into his place. The neglected lad, having lived with the Indians, had adopted many of their ways of life — even to the extent of marrying the daughter of a chief. By this time the French had begun to use the Indians to fight the English and they approved the establishment of friendly relations with the aborigines, but it is apparent from the rebukes Castin received that the government considered he was carrying the business rather far in this last respect.

Tour 3: From Ellsworth to Orland

Meantime he had in 1675 driven Dutch attackers away and in 1687, when the English in another attempt to take the place ordered him away, he had ignored the order. The following year Sir Edmund Andros came up to drive him away and, while Castin was off on a fishing trip, started pillaging. By 1693, when it seemed that the French were giving up their claim to this territory, Castin made some sort of arrangement with the English to accept the situation; but when Iberville three years later went down to attack Pemaquid, Castin led a band of Indians to attack from the rear. He was ordered back to France in 1701 and left expecting to return.

The little town had a period of peace until the Revolutionary War; in 1779, the British took it, remaining till 1783. The colonists made one attempt to take it back in an ill-starred expedition of 1779 that blighted Paul Revere's hopes of a military career and forced him to return to the unromantic job of casting cannon and the like for the army. There was a second British occupation, this time of eight months, during the War of 1812.

The *Bartlett House* (*open*), Perkins St. (1803), is a two-story yellow house once occupied by the British, and is distinguished by its large open fireplaces and attractive staircase.

The *Wheeler House* (1810) (*private*), opposite the Bartlett House, was occupied by the British paymaster in early days. Clapboards cover the bricks of this Colonial structure.

On Perkins St., near the shore, is the *Site of Fort Pentagoet*, erected by the French in 1635 and burned in 1722. It was originally a trading post built during the winter of 1613. It was later called the French Fort and was held by d'Aulney, de Castin, and others.

The *Wilson Museum* (1921) (*open 10–12 and 1–4 weekdays*), also on Perkins St., is a red-brick building containing anthropological and geological as well as Colonial and Revolutionary period collections. Dr. J. Howard Wilson, archeologist, who with his mother, the late Mrs. Cassine G. Wilson, gave the museum to Castine, is director and curator.

Fort Madison (*open*), on Perkins St., is yet another relic of the repeated military occupations of this delightful old town. This fort, occupied by the British during the War of 1812 but built by the Americans in 1811, has been variously called Fort Castin, Fort Porter, and United States Fort. It was rebuilt and occupied during the Civil War.

At various points in the village are vestiges of earthworks thrown up at one time or another during the nearly two hundred years in which four governments sought to hold the place.

Fort George (*open*), in Witherle Park, was erected by the British in 1779. Near-by are batteries built by the British in 1814–15, at the same time they built the canal that crosses the peninsula at its narrowest point.

The *Eastern State Normal School Buildings* are opposite the park.

The *Johnston House* (1805) (*open at discretion of owner*), Upper Main St., is one of the most attractive early houses in this historic community. It is notable for its fine self-supporting staircase. Of Federal design, the house has been restored recently. Its beautiful doorway under a Palladian window is somewhat marred by latticework.

The *Parson-Mason House* (1765) (*private*), Maine and Court Sts., a two-story yellow house, said to be the oldest in the town, has been considerably altered since it was built.

The *Old Meeting-House* (1790), on Court St., an attractive white structure with belfry and spire, is one of the oldest churches in Maine and is now owned by the Unitarian Society. It was remodeled in 1831.

The *Whiting House* (1812) (*private*), on Court St., is another Castine home that saw British occupancy. For many years a window pane in the house bore a crude drawing of the Stars and Stripes upside down with the inscription 'Yankee Doodle upside down,' scratched with the diamond of a British lieutenant.

The *Old Courthouse*, on Court St. opposite the Town Hall, is now the town library. The *Whitney House* (about 1800), near the Common, the *Dyer House* (about 1805), in Dyer Lane, and the *Abbott House* (about 1800), on Battle Ave., are among the many early Castine houses with the traditional central halls, wide staircases, and massive doors with leaded glass fan-lights and side-lights.

The route now follows the western shore of the narrow Castine Peninsula along Penobscot Bay.

NORTH CASTINE (alt. 110, Castine Town), 55.8 *m*. The *Old Devereaux House* (R), opposite a lobster pound, is a low-posted white house with central chimney, built in the 1780's. The dormers were a later addition. During the War of 1812, the Americans hid powder in a closet of the house. One day while Mrs. Devereaux was ironing, a party of British came to search the house. They failed to discover the powder for Mrs. Devereaux covered the closet with her freshly ironed clothes.

ORLAND (alt. 180, Orland Town, pop. 891), 62.6 *m*. (*see Tour* 1K).

TOUR 4: *From* HOULTON *to* NEW HAMPSHIRE LINE (*Shelburne*), 279.1 *m.*, US 2.

Via Houlton, Island Falls, Lincoln, West Enfield, Milford, Old Town, Orono, Bangor, Hermon, Newport, Skowhegan, Norridgewock, Farmington, Wilton, Dixfield, Mexico, Rumford, Bethel, and Gilead.

Mostly two-lane macadamized roadbed, open all year.

CROSSING Maine, between New Brunswick and New Hampshire, US 2 passes through five counties. The northern part of the route traverses the rolling potato fields of central Aroostook County, west of which rise great stands of birch, maple, and beech trees, full of wild game. A network of lakes, rivers, and streams teems with salmon, trout, bass, pickerel, and other game fish. Between Island Falls and Mattawamkeag lie 40 miles of desolate, wild country, from the wooded land of Silver Ridge Plantation to the wide stretches of the Mattawamkeag Swamp. South of Mattawamkeag the road parallels the Penobscot River, running through farming country and lumbering centers. Near Lincoln and in southern Aroostook County, the stark grandeur of Katahdin, Maine's highest peak, is visible.

Between Skowhegan and Rumford lies a region of lakes with the ancient forests coming down to their shores, and the mountains of the Rangeley group rising to the north. Between Rumford, thriving center of the pulpwood industry, and Gilead the road winds along the Androscoggin River, and past scenic hills and mountains to the New Hampshire Line.

HOULTON (alt. 340, Houlton Town, pop. 6865) (*see HOULTON*), 0 *m.*,

Tour 4: From Houlton to Shelburne   293

is at the junction with US 1 (*see Tour* 1, *sec. e*). East of Houlton, 2.5 *m.*, is the Canadian Boundary Line, 11.5 miles west of Woodstock, N.B.

At 3 *m.* is the *Trans-Atlantic Receiving Station* (L) (*open*) of the American Telephone and Telegraph Company, the first long wave receiving station of its kind. Oceanic service was begun January 7, 1927; at present, one-third of all traffic routed by way of England is handled here. This includes stations as far away as Australia. As part of the first international telephone circuit operated in connection with the telephone system of Great Britain, the station was established at Houlton because of its geographical position; that is, its comparative closeness to England, and its distance from the Equator, source of static disturbances; also it was the furthest point north in the United States reached by reliable telephone wire service. This station supplements the trans-wave radio telephone station of the Bell system in New Jersey. It receives the transmissions from the British long wave station at Rugby, England.

LUDLOW (alt. 510, Ludlow Town, pop. 361), 9.9 *m.*, single village of this farming township, consists of a cluster of dwellings along the highway on the northern shore of *Cochran Lake*, whose placid surface is broken by the swirl and splash of pickerel and salmon.

SMYRNA MILLS (alt. 579, Smyrna Town, pop. 442), 16.5 *m.*, a potato-raising center, lies deep in the valley on the banks of the east branch of the Mattawamkeag River.

DYER BROOK (alt. 620, Dyer Brook Town, pop. 262), 20.3 *m.* Several homes grouped around potato warehouses near the railroad station comprise this small village.

Many of the barns in this area were erected by barn raisings. Accumulating all materials, the proprietor would set a date, and farmers from the township and near-by territory would come and set to with a will, raising and boarding the frame work amidst much friendly laughter and shouting. At sundown the men and their families gathered near-by for a hearty meal laid on rough board tables beneath large shade trees; it was customary for the young folks to dance after supper in the new barn to the fiddling of square dances, jigs, and reels.

In the days when Dyer Brook was an active logging center, some of the villagers believed that if a man went seven nights at the same hour to the same place, the Devil would appear and talk with him on the seventh night. There is a tale to the effect that a log driver called Jack-the-Ripper carried out the conditions, and held converse with Satan who warned him to stay off the logs the following day to avoid an accident. Ignoring the warning, Jack jumped carelessly from log to log, working his way to the center of the drive. As he did so, a streak of red fire in the form of a pick-axe flamed up between the logs, a reminder of the warning. He went hastily ashore. From then on Jack was thought by his neighbors to be in league with the Devil. When his axe chopped, another was always heard in accompaniment. He was often heard conversing with a voice whose owner was invisible. Once he drove his axe into the hard trunk of a tree with such force the handle split. When he reached out to grasp the handle again, it became whole in his hands. Conclusive proof to residents of Dyer Brook that Jack-the-Ripper had acquired supernatural powers came when, after the combined efforts of several woodsmen had failed, Jack, single-handed, though unobserved, cleared a camp site of a huge tree that had blown across it during a storm.

ISLAND FALLS (alt. 450, Island Falls Town, pop. 1455), 27.5 *m.*, trading place for near-by farmers and center of a large area frequented by hunters and fishermen, has a lumber mill, a tannery, and a woodenware factory. The township contains much wooded wild land, two lakes, and numerous streams.

Northeast of Island Falls is *Pleasant Lake*, one of Theodore Roosevelt's favorite hunting and fishing spots. Several anecdotes are still told about him and his guide, Bill Sewall, a descendant of the first settler in the district. Driving up a rocky backwoods road one early spring, Roosevelt jokingly asked how one could tell the roads from rivers. 'No beaver dams in the roads,' was Sewall's reply.

South of Island Falls, US 2 passes through 20 miles of the Macwahoc woods to enter Township 1, Range 5. Through this township the route parallels Molunkus Stream.

MACWAHOC (Macwahoc Plantation, pop. 163), 56.5 *m.*, is a tiny settlement, the southernmost in Aroostook County on US 2.

At 63.8 *m.* the highway traverses a *Bridge* built on the unusual base of five bridges that have sunk successively in Mattawamkeag Swamp.

MATTAWAMKEAG (alt. 212, Mattawamkeag Town, pop. 461), 66.3 *m.*, with extensive train yards, is a junction for the Maine Central R.R. and Canadian Pacific R.R. at the point where the Mattawamkeag River flows into the Penobscot. Lumbering was once carried on extensively in this region.

In Mattawamkeag is a junction with State 11 (*see Tour* 6).

WINN (alt. 240, Winn Town, pop. 560), 68.8 *m.*, a little town clinging to the eastern bank of the swirling Penobscot River, was head of river navigation in the days when travel into this area was chiefly by boat.

LINCOLN (alt. 174, Lincoln Town, pop. 2970), 79.6 *m.*, named for Governor Enoch Lincoln, is a busy agricultural center in Penobscot County, and the only settlement of size between Houlton and Old Town.

Its most active industrial establishment is the *Lincolnsfield Woolen Mill* (*visitors by permit*), which manufactures woolen blankets, suitings, and the like.

Lincoln lies near *Mattanawcook Pond*, one of a chain of lakes and ponds running diagonally across the State. It is used for swimming and boating, and is a popular resort of local fishermen.

WEST ENFIELD (alt. 130, Enfield Town, pop. 1138), 91.6 *m.*, has the cutting of pulp wood as its chief industry.

Tour 4: From Houlton to Shelburne

Here is a junction with State 11 (*see Tour* 8).

PASSADUMKEAG (Ind.: 'quick water') (alt. 140, Passadumkeag Town, pop. 325), 96.6 *m.*, is on the northern bank of Passadumkeag Stream at its confluence with the Penobscot.

Specimens of Red Paint artifacts have been found near the settlement (*see Earliest Inhabitants*).

OLAMON (Ind.: 'red paint') (alt. 128, Greenbush Town, pop. 378), 101.1 *m.*, is at the mouth of the Olamon Stream as it joins the Penobscot River.

MILFORD (alt. 115, Milford Town, pop. 1203), 114.6 *m.*, is separated from Old Town by the Penobscot River and Old Town Falls. The river at this point was the scene of great activity in the heyday of lumbering. Huge sawmills in the two communities handled millions of logs from up river and each spring the West Branch drive was the center of interest. When the logs guided downstream by river drivers reached the booms, placed about two miles upstream, 200 or more men who had been waiting in 'driving boats' raced down the Penobscot to Milford or Old Town with the news. The approach of the winners was heralded by the firing of a cannon on Indian Island, and a general celebration followed.

The highway here swings right, crossing the Penobscot.

OLD TOWN (alt. 115, pop. 7266), 115.3 *m.*, was formerly a lumbering center (*see above*), and on the line of the State's first railroad, which was built in 1836 and extended between Bangor and the iron works on the Penobscot River.

Industrial activities today include the manufacture of woolens, wood products, paper, pulp, and toilet preparations. Better known, however, are the canoes manufactured here and sent to all parts of the world. At the *Old Town Canoe Company Factory (open to public)*, the entire process of modern canoe construction is demonstrated from the steaming and bending of the bows and ribs to the varnishing of the finished product. The presence of Indians working with modern equipment recalls the romance that hovered over the silvery birch craft so skillfully fashioned by their forefathers; they bring to mind the lines of Hiawatha in Longfellow's beautiful poem:

> 'I a light canoe will build me,
> That will float upon the water,
> Like a yellow leaf in Autumn,
> Like a yellow water lily.'

On INDIAN ISLAND (*reached by row-boat ferry: fare 5¢*) in the Penobscot River, off Old Town, is an *Indian Reservation (visitors welcome)*, the home of the remaining members of the Penobscot tribe, numbering about 400, a fragment of the once powerful Abnaki Nation. Although they neither vote nor pay taxes, the Penobscots own the island under State supervision and send a non-voting representative to the Maine Legislature.

The village, which centers around the main street extending back from the wharf, has a drab appearance, only the church, school, and parochial residence being painted. The Indians live in unplastered, weather-beaten structures, though the meagerly furnished rooms are scrupulously neat.

Although some of the Indians are employed at Old Town mills, they do not like to work in factories, and the men usually find employment in the woods, on the river, and as guides during the hunting and fishing seasons. Each spring a great many of the Penobscots leave the island for the seashore and mountain resorts, where they camp for the summer, selling baskets, handiwork, and curios to tourists. Both men and women are skilled in basket-weaving and the products of their handiwork are for sale in the shops on the island and near the ferry-landing in Old Town.

Many of the old customs are still retained. During the tribal celebrations (*visitors welcome*), held several times a year, centuries slip away and once again the island rings with the chanting of old songs, and flashes with the brilliance of the painted and ornamented men twisting and writhing in ancient ceremonial dances.

Wooden crosses mark most of the poorly kept graves in the *Two Cemeteries* on the island. The Catholic cemetery (1688) contains the remains of John Attean (1778–1858), governor of the tribe for over 40 years; John Neptune (1767–1865), lieutenant-governor for half a century; and other dignitaries of the tribe. Among those buried in the other cemetery are Andrew Sockalexis, runner and member of the American team in the Fifth Olympiad at Stockholm, Sweden, in 1912, and his brother Louis, Holy Cross graduate, and baseball player on the Cleveland American League Club.

In a small, tree-shaded grassy plot on the island stands a *Monument to the Penobscot Indians Killed in the Revolution*. A bronze tablet on the monument lists the names of the men who fought with the Continental forces.

A Catholic mission was established on the island in the 17th century and in the church here that romantic figure, the Baron Jean-Vincent de Castin (*see Tour* 3), took the daughter of Chief Madockawando for his bride, likely a diplomatic alliance. About 80 years ago the old church was replaced by the present frame building in which hangs a *Picture of the Crucifixion* painted many years ago by Paul Orson, an Indian artist who used the juice of berries for his colors and the tail of an animal for a brush.

Princess Watawasa, a singer and dancer, who assumed her title for stage purposes, is a native of the island. Another well-known Penobscot is Chief Needahbeh, known as Roland Nelson at the New York Sportsmen's Shows.

ORONO (alt. 80, Orono Town, pop. 3338), 120.6 *m.*, home of the State university, is an industrial as well as a college town. Canvas products, oars, paddles, paper, and pulp are manufactured in this former lumbering center.

The buildings and grounds of the *University of Maine* (L) (*open*) stretch for three-quarters of a mile along the northeastern outskirts of the village. The 500-acre campus, with its well-kept lawns and shade trees, overlooks the Stillwater River. So well hidden by trees are the modern brick and stone college buildings, some of which have Georgian and Gothic features, that no single one dominates the campus. Fraternity chapter houses of no architectural style line College Road from the campus south to the village center.

The University of Maine is a part of the State's educational system. Established originally as a State College of Agriculture and Mechanic Arts under the provision of the Morrill Act, approved by President Lincoln in 1862, the State of Maine accepted the conditions of the act the following year and in 1865 created a corporation to administer the affairs of the college. The institution opened September 21, 1868, with a class of 12 members and two teachers. Tuition was often paid in cordwood, or other local produce. By 1871, four curricula had been arranged —

Tour 4: From Houlton to Shelburne

agriculture, civil engineering, mechanical engineering, and elective — which gradually developed into the present college of agriculture, technology, and arts and sciences. The name, University of Maine, was assumed in 1899.

The College of Agriculture, the outstanding unit of the University, comprises the various departments of agriculture and husbandry as well as bacteriology, geological chemistry, forestry, home economics and horticulture. Although a four-year course is required for the degree of bachelor of science in agriculture, the college offers a two-year course and special short courses in these subjects which have become unusually popular. Its courses in forestry have been widely recognized. The University maintains a forestry camp in Indian Township near Princeton (*see Tour* 1, *sec.* e). Throughout the year extension lectures are given; and an extension service analyzes soils, studies animal and crop diseases, and distributes scientific and practical information to farmers.

The Maine Agricultural Experiment Station was established as a division of the University by an act of the legislature of 1887 as a result of the Hatch Act. Its offices and principal laboratories, besides the one at Orono, are at Highmoor Farm in Monmouth (*see Tour* 13), and Aroostook Farm at Presque Isle (*see Tour* 1, *sec. e*). The University also operates a marine biological station at East Lamoine on the shore of Frenchman's Bay.

The University buildings are best reached from the *Administration Building* (*campus guides and maps available*). Parking space is always available, and during the summer direction markers are posted along the drives.

The *Carnegie Library*, a two-story granite building with glass-enclosed central rotunda, houses the University library of 150,000 volumes and pamphlets, and also its art collection.

VEAZIE (alt. 70, Veazie Town, pop. 568), 124.2 *m.* General Samuel Veazie, a pioneer railroad operator, gave this community not only its name but also its claim to fame. In 1854 the General purchased the narrow gauge Bangor, Milford, and Old Town R.R., which ran through here, and it became known as the Veazie R.R. Completed in 1836 it was Maine's first railroad and one of the oldest in the country. The first rails were made of wood.

In 1834 the General had established the Veazie Bank. Just after the passage of the Federal Act (1866) taxing currency issued by State banks, officials of the Veazie banks refused to pay the tax. This led to the U.S. Supreme Court case, *Veazie Banks vs. Fenno*, in which the Supreme Court upheld the power of Congress to levy such tax. As a result the power to issue State currency was virtually taken from the States.

Veazie, originally called The Plains, was a part of Bangor until its incorporation in 1853.

BANGOR (alt. 100, pop. 28,749) (*see BANGOR*), 128.6 *m.*, is at a junction with US 1 (*see Tour* 1, *sec. c*).

HERMON (alt. 190, Hermon Town, pop. 1204), 136.9 *m.*, is near the railroad yards of Northern Maine Junction, a terminus of the Bangor and Aroostook R.R. at its junction with the Maine Central R.R.

The Millerites, disciples of William Miller who preached that the second coming of the Lord was imminent, won many followers here in the early 1800's. Contemporary newspaper accounts say his followers eventually numbered 50,000 souls, but this is doubtless exaggeration. A day in 1843 was set as the date of the coming, and the anointed were exhorted to prepare themselves. To be ready for heaven all the believers gave away everything they possessed and disposed of all their property. On the appointed day they donned ascension robes and climbed to hilltops so as to be as near heaven as possible. Some of them mounted the roofs of their houses. All day they stood looking into the sky. Nothing happened. After having been, so they thought, at heaven's very gate, they had to return to an earthly status made more difficult by the loss of their property. Miller attributed the dénouement to a miscalculation — whether on his part or the Lord's is not clear. Many of his followers, especially those in the town of Hermon, faithfully rallied around him once more, remaining loyal until his death in 1847. For many years small colonies of Millerites survived throughout the State.

CARMEL (alt. 170, Carmel Town, pop. 881), 144.3 *m.*, is in one of the oldest farming towns in Penobscot County. Bearing a name of Biblical derivation, Carmel, aptly enough, was the birthplace of a curious religious sect known as the Higginsites. The Reverend George Higgins, a local Methodist pastor in the early 19th century, started the sect; a village in the neighboring town of Levant is still called Higginsville. The Higginsites did not eat pork and believed in their ability to heal by faith. Tales of their religious activities were widely circulated and one, concerning the whipping of children in efforts to drive out the Devil, aroused the indignation of the townspeople, who determined to rid the town of Mr. Higgins. Calling him from his home late one night, a group tarred and feathered and drove him away.

ETNA (alt. 305, Etna Town, pop. 418), 147.9 *m.*

Camp Etna (R) is a campground on which spiritualists have held yearly meetings (*last week in Aug. and first week in Sept.*) since 1876, when Daniel Buswell, Jr., held the first meeting in a tent. Today there is a temple, built in 1880, seating 1100, a club house, and 78 cottages on the 80 acres of enclosed land. The *Grave of Mrs. Mary S. Vanderbilt,* a generous benefactor of the Campground Association, is marked by a conspicuous monument. In addition to the beautiful groves, the association owns the Camp Etna Hotel and Farm.

NEWPORT (alt. 205, Newport Town, pop. 1731), 156.8 *m.*, owes much of its beauty to *Sebasticook Lake,* sometimes known as Newport Pond, near the center of the town. The lake, 6 miles long, provides opportunities for bathing, boating, and fishing.

Here is a junction with State 7 (*see Tour* 9).

TOUR 4: From Houlton to Shelburne

PALMYRA (alt. 260, Palmyra Town, pop. 887), 161.1 *m.*, was in 1850 a prosperous lumbering town with a population of 1625. It is now the center of a small agricultural township.

CANAAN (alt. 230, Canaan Town, pop. 714), 172.7 *m.* Impressed by the fertility of the land, early settlers named their town for the land of milk and honey. It was part of the Plymouth Patent, but was not settled until 1770 when Joseph Weston of Lancaster and Peter Heywood of Concord, Mass., arrived.

SKOWHEGAN (alt. 190, Skowhegan Town, pop. 6431), 181.5 *m.* The original settlement of the town was made on the island of that name in the Kennebec River and even today, though the business and industrial area has spread to both banks, the island is to some extent the physical center. Long before the first white man came to the region in 1771, Indians knew the island, had explored the falls, had taken fighting salmon from the waters below it, and had named the place Skowhegan (*place to watch for fish*).

Among those who were born or have lived here are Abner Coburn (1803–85), one of Maine's Civil War governors who was prominent in the economic and cultural development of this section of the State; Daniel Dole (1808– ?), a missionary to the Hawaiian Islands who was instrumental in the establishment, and became president, of Oahu College, which prepares white students to enter universities; George Otis Smith (1871), a former director of the U.S. Geological Survey; Charles A. Coffin (1844–1926), first president of the General Electric Company; Artemus Ward (Charles Farrar Browne, 1834–67), American humorist, who was employed a few months in his boyhood in a Skowhegan printing office.

At the eastern end of Water St. is attractive *Coburn Park*, extending for nearly a quarter of a mile along the highway and named for Abner Coburn, who gave much of the land to the town.

A large granite boulder, on the *Site of Benedict Arnold's Camp* in the school grounds on the corner of Weston St., commemorates the passage of Benedict Arnold's army, September 29, 1775.

The *State Reformatory for Women*, housed in six modern buildings on Norridgewock Ave., was opened in 1916. Women delinquents over 16 years of age are confined in it.

The Skowhegan Fair Ground, Fairview Park, and an airplane landing field are 1 mile north of Water St., on Madison Ave. (State 147).

> Right from Skowhegan is State 147, an alternate and shorter route between Skowhegan and Solon (*see Tour* 10).
>
> At 5.1 *m.* on State 147 is LAKEWOOD, a resort on the shore of Lake Wesserunsett, with a hotel having a dining terrace overlooking the lake, and with a dance hall and other recreational facilities.
>
> Lakewood has had a summer theater since 1900, housed in the early days in an old amusement park. Admission at that time was five cents to those who arrived on the jiggling, bumpy trolley cars, ten cents to those who provided their own transportation, which was usually a buckboard drawn by plump horses. The plays, usually either Broadway successes presented by companies preparing to go on the

road with them or try-outs for New York presentation in the fall, are now performed in an attractive little structure of semi-Colonial design.

At 14.7 *m.* is the junction with US 201 (*see Tour* 10).

US 2 crosses the river, and on the southern edge of the city joins US 201 with which it is identical to Norridgewock.

NORRIDGEWOCK (alt. 180, Norridgewock Town, pop. 1478), 186.7 *m.*, derived its name from the Indian name for the place, Nanrantsouk ('smooth water between falls' or 'rapids'). Its early history is allied with that of the Indian village at Old Point (*see Tour* 10). When Somerset County, named for Somersetshire, England, was formed from the northern part of Kennebec County in 1809, Norridgewock became the shire town.

The *Norridgewock Bridge*, spanning the Kennebec, on US 201, is a four-span cement structure of the bowstring-arch type.

US 201, branching from US 2, turns right at the bridge (*see Tour* 10).

MERCER (alt. 280, Mercer Town, pop. 408), 194.4 *m.*, birthplace of Frank A. Munsey, the publisher, is a little settlement sheltered in a depression between two hills.

On the lawn of a small church (R) is a bronze tablet set in a large millstone commemorating what is believed to have been the *Largest Tree in New England*, an elm that was 32 feet in circumference.

At 198.6 *m.* is a junction with State 27 (*see Tour* 12).

NEW SHARON (alt. 340, New Sharon Town, pop. 750), 199.6 *m.* The homes of this settlement are built along the highway which slopes for a mile to the bridge over well-named Sandy River. Quantities of golden bantam corn for canning are raised in the broad rolling fields around this village.

FARMINGTON FALLS (alt. 335, Farmington Town), 204 *m.* When a party of six men led by Thomas Wilson, an early hunter, explored this country in 1776 with a view to settlement, they found the village of the Indian Pierpole and the remains of another Indian village and fort here at the falls. Pierpole became friendly with the white men and later aided them in establishing themselves — another example of Indian friendliness until the trust was betrayed.

At 208.3 *m.* (R) is *Stanwood Park* (*adm.* 10¢), a large zoo maintained by the owner as a hobby. The 500 clean, well-cared-for animals, in cages and fenced enclosures, include a collection representative of the State's wild life.

FARMINGTON (alt. 420, Farmington Town, pop. 3600), 210.1 *m.*, gateway to the Rangeley and Dead River regions, is the seat of Franklin County, and agricultural and trading center for this fertile valley along Sandy River. Fruitful apple orchards add to the incomes of many farmers here.

The first Farmington Falls settlers of the 1770's were joined by others who started clearings in various places along Sandy River; in 1782 eight families passed the winter in rough, snow-bound log cabins in the vicinity. The settlers were, for the most part, people of considerable culture and education. The first school of the settlement was opened in 1788 in the log-cabin home of Lemuel Perham, Jr. By 1790 there were 404 inhabitants, and in 1794 the town was incorporated.

Farmington State Normal School is on Academy St.

Here is a junction with State 4 (*see Tour* 11) and State 27 (*see Tour* 12).

WILTON (alt. 690, Wilton Town, pop. 3266), 218.7 *m.*, a busy industrial and farming settlement, stands at the point where Wilson Stream flows into Wilson Lake. The stream runs parallel with the main street of the village and a heavily wooded hill rises abruptly from the bank of the river.

Wilson Lake, along the highway just a few hundred yards west of the business district, has good recreational facilities and many summer camps on its shores.

The township was first called Harrytown for Harry, an Indian, who was the scourge of the whites in the area. In 1790, when Capt. William Tyng in an expedition against the Indians killed Harry, the township was renamed Tyngstown in honor of the captain. Abraham Butterfield, who later came from Wilton, N.H., paid the expenses of incorporation in 1803 for the privilege of renaming the place for his former home.

Here is a junction with State 4 (*see Tour* 11).

DIXFIELD (alt. 420, Dixfield Town, pop. 1518), 235.7 *m.*, in the shadow of the Sugar Loaves, twin hills, is at the confluence of the Androscoggin and Webb Rivers. The manufacture of paper boxes and wood-novelties is among the industries here.

MEXICO (alt. 460, Mexico Town, pop. 4761), 240.3 *m.*, is principally occupied by employees of the Rumford paper mills across the Androscoggin. Swift River, west of the village, passes through the township with a fall of 50 ft.

RUMFORD (alt. 610, Rumford Town, pop. 8726), 241.3 *m.*, high in the Oxford hills, where the Ellis, Swift, and Concord Rivers flow into the Androscoggin, is the home of New England's largest paper pulp mills. It is one of the most active towns socially in the State, and a popular winter sports center. Directly in sight of the business section, the magnificent *Falls* of the Androscoggin tumble down over a bed of solid granite, the water supplying power for the huge paper mills that employ most of the working inhabitants. The construction of a canal has placed the business section on an island, connected with the mainland by three bridges.

One thousand cords of pulpwood are used here daily (1936) and pulp piles rise high near the river.

The *Oxford Paper Company Mill* (*permit at office*), near Railroad Station, one of the largest book-paper mills in the United States, manufactures and prints book-cover labels, offsets, rotogravures, and lithographs.

Stephens High School, Congress St., offers the only course in New England for the study of the manufacture of pulp and paper.

The annual Winter Carnival, with competitive sports, is held in February under the auspices of the Chisholm Skiing and Outing Club.

> Left from Rumford on State 120 to the *Mt. Zircon Bottling Company Works*, 4.5 *m.* (L), which owns the *Moontide Spring*, the flow of which, the owners say, increases 20 gallons a minute during the time of the full moon. The spring bubbles high on a mountain reached by a 2-mile trail leading from the bottling works. This claim has never been scientifically investigated.

At 252.3 *m.* is a junction with State 5 (*see Tour* 4A).

NEWRY (alt. 630, Newry Town, pop. 188), 259.5 *m.*, is at a junction with State 26 (*see Tour* 14).

BETHEL (alt. 700, Bethel Town, pop. 2025), 266.5 *m.*, the center of a township in the delightful Oxford Hills, is built on both sides of the winding Androscoggin River, which, flowing gently here, soon drops away rapidly over numerous falls furnishing power for mills downstream. Behind the cluster of handsome residences with landscaped grounds on the slope of a low hill rise the rough foothills of the White Mountains. On August 22, 1781, it is said that a party of Indians attacked Bethel, carrying away a heavy plunder and three settlers. One of the captives escaped into the woods; the other two were held as prisoners in Canada until after the end of the Revolution.

On the brow of a hill is *Gould's Academy*, established 1836, one of the leading preparatory schools of Maine.

The *Chapman Home* (*private*), west side of Church St., was the former residence of the late Dr. William R. Chapman, organizer and conductor for 25 years of the former annual Maine Music Festivals (*see BANGOR; PORTLAND*), which were important musical events in the life of the State.

Directly opposite the Chapman Home is a quadrangular elm parkway. *Bethel Inn* (L), one of the best-known hostelries of Maine, was erected by Dr. John G. Gehring (1857-1932), whose home is beyond the inn at the far end of Church St. Dr. Gehring, a distinguished neurologist, late in life converted his residence into a sanatorium where he could give individual attention to patients suffering from nervous disorders. One of the wards of the New York Neurological Institute is named in his honor. In 1923 Dr. Gehring published a book, 'The Hope of the Variant.'

In Bethel are junctions with State 5 (*see Tour* 15) and with State 26 (*see Tour* 14).

GILEAD (alt. 710, Gilead Town, pop. 222), 276.6 *m.*, a tiny settlement near a railroad station, is on the northern line of the White Mountain National Forest. Behind it are tumbling mountain streams and below it the sweeping Androscoggin, cutting its way through forests of fragrant cedar and pine, the waters mirroring the beauty of the forest. Silvery birches spread a fragile web of loveliness over the highway.

> Left from Gilead on a good road, through White Mountain National Forest, to *Evans Notch*, 6 *m.* From the wooded area near the Notch are spectacular views of the Presidential Range of the White Mountains.

At 279.1 *m.* US 2 crosses the New Hampshire Line, 3.8 miles east of Shelburne, N.H.

TOUR 4 A : *From* JUNCTION WITH US 2 *to* SOUTH ARM, 25.6 *m.*, State 5.

Via Andover and The Notch.
Graveled roadbed.

THIS route, to the Rangeley Lake region, follows through the Ellis River Valley to the intervale of Andover where a long ridge of the Canadian border mountains far north can be seen. From a quagmire at the foot of Lower Richardson Lake, Black Brook seeps through dense vegetable matter, and flows beside the road in the heavily wooded area near South Arm.

At 0 *m.* State 5 branches northwest from US 2 (*see Tour* 4).

Visible from 1.4 *m.* (L), is a long, bare, high ledge on the side of Mount Dimmock.

At 3.6 *m.* (L) is the trail to *Newry Mine*, a 900-foot climb up Plumbago Mountain. The discovery of tourmalines here, in 1900, was followed by that of feldspar and pollucite. The mine is now inactive, its pollucite vein being considered exhausted. Pollucite, probably Maine's most valuable mineral — having had a maximum value of $20 per pound — is used in the manufacture of alternating current radio tubes.

At 10.7 *m.* (R) is *Andover Cemetery*, in the northern end of which is the *Grave of Molly Locket*, an Indian woman who was so constantly in demand by the settlers as a midwife that she neither had the time nor the need to establish a home of her own. Molly's second husband is said to have been Chief Sabattus, and although her gravemarker says she was the last of the Pequawkets, another tradition says two of her daughters were married to white settlers. The inscription reads:

> Mollocket baptized Mary Agatha,
> Catholic, died in the Christian Faith,
> August 2, A.D. 1816.
> The Last of the Pequakets.

ANDOVER (alt. 610, Andover Town, pop. 783), 11.7 *m.*, a small commercial settlement formerly important for its lumbering, now caters to summer campers. Throughout the entire township are visible the forest-cloaked Aziscoos Mountains which lie north of the Rangeley Lakes.

The Notch (Township C), 20.7 *m.*, formed by *Old Blue Mountain* (R) (alt. 3735) and *Parkhurst Mountain* (L) (alt. 2870), is barely wide enough for the road, which follows Black Brook. Old Blue towers sheerly above the road.

SOUTH ARM (alt. 1480, Township C, pop. 9), 25.6 *m.* Buried deep in the woods on the southern tip of Lower Richardson Lake, this little settlement with its half-dozen houses, wharf, and long rows of connected storage garages is the 'jumping-off place' for visitors on their way to hotels and camps scattered through the Rangeley Lake Region (*see Tour* 11*A*).

T O U R   5 : *From* BREWER *to* JUNCTION WITH US 1 (*Calais*), 87.5 *m.*, State 9, The Air Line.

Via Eddington, Amherst, Wesley, Crawford, and Alexander.

Two-lane, bituminous-topped, and graveled roadbed the greater part of the route; a few sections of narrow, unimproved dirt road; in winter it is not always passable.

Limited accommodations; gas stations long distances apart.

THIS inland route, most direct between Bangor and Calais, passes through a sparsely settled agricultural region, blueberry plains, and forests with winding trout streams; tote roads used by lumbermen lead into the woods at intervals. The more than 20-mile stretch between Beddington and Wesley is without habitation. Between Crawford and Alexander are lakes with sportsmen's camps.

This route, originally planned in 1838-39 as a military road during the Aroostook War (*see History*) to speed soldiers to the border through the wilderness, remained unfinished for more than 20 years after the boundary dispute was settled. Little more than a dirt lane, it was opened as a mail route in 1857 when Calais citizens became dissatisfied with mail service over the highway along the shore. When it was improved a few years later for the use of stages, travelers traversed it with uneasiness, fearing wolves in winter and bandits in summer.

BREWER (alt. 40, pop. 6329) (*see Tour* 1, *sec. c*), 0 *m.*, is at a junction with US 1 (*see Tour* 1, *sec. c*). State 9 branches northeast from US 1 here.

EDDINGTON (alt. 50, Eddington Town, pop. 487), 4.1 *m.*, with camps and tourists' homes, is a small farming community on the eastern bank of the Penobscot River.

The granite shaft, facing the river, is a *Memorial to Jonathan Eddy*, for whom the town was named. Eddy was a captain in the French and Indian wars, a colonel during the Revolutionary War, and the first magistrate appointed along the Penobscot River.

The banks of the river in this vicinity have yielded Red Paint deposits (*see Earliest Inhabitants*).

In Eddington, as in many inland villages before the days when sea food was brought to local stores, it was customary for the inhabitants to make annual trips to the coast to procure several barrels of sand and a quantity of clams. Each villager dug a hole in the earth of his cellar, filled it with the sand, and buried the clams in the sand, which was kept wet in order to keep the clams alive for use in the cold months. A story of clams thus preserved is told in connection with an old sea captain who had retired to this village. He had a clam-pit in his cellar, but he averred that instead of keeping his clams for food he used them as rat-catchers; he said he often went into the cellar and found a rat struggling against a clam that had closed its shell in a tenacious grip on the rat's tail.

> Right from Eddington village on a local road to a *Training Camp for Field Dogs* (*private*), 2 *m.*, on the eastern side of Eddington Pond. Here beautiful young bird-hunting dogs are trained until they can point out covies of birds, 'freeze' into a motionless stand, remain unflinching when a gun roars out at the rising birds, and then retrieve the kill for their master. The State and New England Field Trials for bird dogs were held here in 1935, and in May and September the Bangor Fish and Game Association holds annual bird-dog field trials at this camp.

State 9 swings right at Eddington.

CLIFTON (alt. 155, Clifton Town, pop. 156), 12.1 *m.*, is in a town where hills are composed of 'puddle rocks' or pudding stone, in which stones of many colors and shapes are held together by a conglomerate mass.

> Left from Clifton on a dirt road is *Chemo Lake* (*canoes for hire*), 0.7 *m.*, a wide sheet of water in summer reflecting forest-clad hills and blue skies. There is excellent trout fishing here.

AMHERST (alt. 30, Amherst Town, pop. 163), 24 *m.*, now a small farming community, was once supported by saw, grist, clapboard, and shingle mills, as well as a large tannery.

At 25.5 *m.* is a junction with State 179.

> Right on State 179 to a *Cannery* (*open*), 3 *m.*, in which great quantities of blueberries, hauled in from neighboring plains, are weighed, dumped in a long endless conveyor where they are carefully sorted, washed, packed in tins, and cooked under steam pressure, to be used eventually in pies and pan dowdies all over New England.

AURORA (alt. 315, Aurora Town, pop. 86), 26 *m.* Hunters and fishermen now use the *Village Inn*, formerly a stagecoach stop.

At 27 *m.* is the junction with a dirt road.

> Left on this road to *Great Pond*, 6 *m.*, where there is good trout fishing. This is a section with numerous hunting and sporting camps, for game is also plentiful.

Between 28.4 *m.* and 30.7 *m.* the road passes over the Whale Back, an alluvial ridge with an elevation of from 200 to 300 feet. Vast tracts of woodland stretch along either side, and in fine weather, Mt. Katahdin, 80 miles northwest, is visible. In this area the white flags of startled deer are often seen as they hurdle mossy logs to disappear into the dim forest. Occasionally, especially on crisp evenings, the long bellow of a bull moose echoes over the timberlands, and the staccato barking of the fox is heard in the stillness of the vast area.

At 40.8 *m.* is a junction with State 193.

> Right on State 193, 3 *m.*, to old *Beaver Colonies* and *Dams* on the west branch of

the Narraguagus. The broad-tailed, silky-furred workers are now rarely seen in this region, but the large dam and several sub-dams that they constructed still hold back the river waters over a considerable area, while cleverly built mounds appear like miniature brown igloos projecting from the water.

At 41.2 *m.* is a well-marked trail.
> Left on this trail leading about 1 *m.* to a fire lookout station on *Lead Mountain*. At the foot of the mountain is a Civilian Conservation Corps camp.
>
> For many years it was believed that veins of gold ran through Lead Mountain. Near-by settlements were often visited, so the story goes, by an Indian who offered small gold nuggets in exchange for a drink of rum. As he was usually intoxicated and apparently did no work to earn the gold, rumor spread that he knew of a lode on Lead Mountain. Finally a settler plied the Indian with enough rum to extract from him the story of a huge cave filled with nuggets, and the promise to lead him to the cave. It is said the two men left the settlement, but the white man never returned.

At 41.4 *m.* a bridge crosses the Narraguagus River, in which an annual log drive usually takes place about mid-April.

BEDDINGTON (alt. 530, Beddington Town, pop. 35), 41.8 *m.* The *Old Shoppe House,* now the post office, was for many years a stopping-place for stagecoaches. Jefferson Davis, later President of the Confederacy, is said to have resided in this old hostelry for several weeks during the summer of 1857 when he was visiting his friend, Alexander Bache, Superintendent of the Coast Survey, who was taking personal charge of work there and in the near-by Lead Mountain area. There is a local tradition that Davis, before leaving, placed a small chest in the innkeeper's charge, instructing the latter to turn it over to a person who would make a certain sign. The following autumn, on a windy night a stranger appeared on horseback, made the sign, and rode off with the chest. The villagers believed that the chest held documents that had some connection with the Rebellion.

At 49.8 *m.* is the entrance to a foot trail.
> Left on this trail, providing a stiff climb of about 1 *m.*, to the top of Peaked Mountain, where is a *Fire Lookout Station* from which is a view over vast blueberry plains, or barrens, as they are called.

At 54.3 *m.* is a wooden bridge crossing the Machias River, which was once famous for its log drives. Right is a *State Fish and Game Department Camp,* often used by wardens. Left is a free camp site.

WESLEY (Wesley Town, pop. 170), 65.1 *m.*, is on a high hill amid extensive blueberry barrens. From a *Fire Lookout Station (open),* virtually in the center of the village, is a panorama over great wooded areas, with Eastport, 32 miles away, visible on a clear day.

There is a story that during the Civil War three Federal recruiting officers were murdered here while trying to enforce draft requirements. During stagecoach days many robberies were committed at the foot of Wesley Hill, just beyond the village. This spot was still the scene of lawless activities during prohibition, when rum-runners in high-powered trucks brought contraband liquors from the Canadian Border; clashes with revenue officers were frequent.

Tour 5: From Brewer to Calais

At 69.1 *m.* (L) is a *Free Camp Site*.

At 72.4 *m.* is the junction with a local road.

> Right on this road to *Love Lake*, 0.7 *m.*, a small body of water surrounded by birch-clad hills. Water lilies grow in profusion here, many of the coves being likened to scenes portrayed by Monet. In the summer game is plentiful and quite tame near the lake; moose, knee deep in the water, munch lily shoots, and deer, silhouetted against a brilliant sunset, offer unusual opportunities to photographers. There are several small waterfalls in the streams that empty into Love Lake; *Seavey Brook*, toward the west, tumbles over a series of rocks, forming rapids.

CRAWFORD (Crawford Town, pop. 120), 76 *m.*, once the center of extensive lumbering operations, was the scene of many stagecoach robberies. Favorite yarns of early stagecoach travel tell of how, when deep snow impeded the progress of the coach, packs of wolves would follow the wheel tracks and were warded off only by the alertness of the drivers and the quick cocking and firing of hand-loaded and primed guns. Other exciting tales, many of them more frankly fiction but built around a fragment of truth, abound in this region. One concerns three brothers, living near Bangor, who became highwaymen and terrorized this district, stopping coaches several times a week and extracting all valuables from the passengers and their luggage. It is told that a passenger who had been robbed while traveling here, several months later in Boston recognized a man lounging in a tavern tap-room as one of the three bandits; accused, the man shouted his innocence, but a golden nugget, hanging from his watch chain, was found to bear the initials of the coach passenger.

Crawford Lake, in this town, has excellent bathing and fishing facilities. At *Cedar Cove*, on the eastern shore, perpendicular cliffs rising high above the sparkling waters are spoken of thus, by a local guide: 'The cliffs out there are a "high eyeful," and only the Devil knows how deep.'

At 81.2 *m.* is the junction with an oiled graveled road.

> Right on this road, ALEXANDER (alt. 420, Alexander Town, pop. 312), 0.4 *m.*, a small community on a high hill, carrying on some farming in a hunting region, overlooks *Meddybemps Lake* (R), which is 7 miles long, 3 miles wide, and has 52 islands dotting its placid surface. Many sporting camps are scattered along the shores of the lake which offers fine bass and perch fishing.
>
> In the *Corner Store*, near the village Center, hangs a large sign reading: 'After 40 years of credit business, we have closed our book of Sorrow.' This combination store, post office, information bureau, bank, and general gathering place is typical of the New England general store of the past. Here shelves of modern canned goods vie with bunches of fragrant pickling spices, dill-pickles in a barrel, beans in five- and ten-pound bags, penny candy, overalls, rubber boots, embroidery material and silks, and the heterogeneous mixture of merchandise required by village housewives and male 'bargainers.' In the evenings, the men gather around the potbellied stove set in its sawdust-filled square box — the latter for the convenience of tobacco 'chawers' — to settle problems ranging in importance from international affairs to fence disputes.

At 84.3 *m.* (L) is a *Free Camp Site*, maintained by the State Fish and Game Department.

At 87.5 *m.* State 9 joins US 1 (*see Tour 1, sec. e*), 6.9 miles southwest of Calais.

TOUR 6: *From* FORT KENT *to* MATTAWAMKEAG, 138 *m.*, State 11.

Via Wallagrass, Eagle Lake, Portage, Ashland, Patten, Sherman, and Medway.

Graveled or macadamized roadbed, narrow and rough in spots. Route not recommended except to reach sporting areas.

Accommodations infrequent except at sportsmen's camps.

THIS route, frequented chiefly by sportsmen, runs almost directly south. Small villages in this area are widely separated in the midst of forests, lakes, and mountains, with only occasional open farm land. Game abounds. Most of the people depend on guiding sportsmen, trapping, small-scale farming, and lumber operations for a livelihood. Between Fort Kent and Portage, the French Acadian villages are like those along the St. John River (*see Tour* 1, *sec. e*). Between Masardis and Sherman, the route crosses a fertile potato belt.

FORT KENT (alt. 530, Fort Kent Town, pop. 4726) (*see Tour* 1, *sec. e*), 0 *m.*, is at a junction with US 1 (*see Tour* 1, *sec. e*). The village is at the northern terminus of the Allagash River Canoe Trip (*see Sports and Recreation*).

FORT KENT MILLS (alt. 610, Fort Kent Town), 1.5 *m.*, was settled in the 1860's when the Bradbury Lumber Company began operations at this fine water-power site on Fish River. Extensive operations ceased about 1916.

At 7.3 *m.* is a junction with a dirt road.

> Left on this road is SOLDIER POND (alt. 590, Wallagrass Plantation), 1 *m.*, on the shore of a body of water named during the Aroostook Bloodless War (*see History*).

WALLAGRASS (alt. 820, Wallagrass Plantation, pop. 1145), 10 *m.*, is one of the series of French-Acadian settlements. In such villages as this the medallion of the Sacred Heart of Jesus is often seen on the doors of the homes, these people, like their ancestors, being devout Catholics.

EAGLE LAKE (alt. 602, Eagle Lake Town, pop. 1780) (*guides available*), 15.7 *m.*, is active during the hunting and fishing seasons. The town was settled about 1840 by French-Acadians and Irish emigrants.

Near the center of the village is the *Northern Maine General Hospital*, an important institution in this area where medical aid is hard to find.

The clear water of *Eagle Lake*, one of the deepest of the Fish River Chain, holds many landlocked salmon, and the streams flowing into the lake have abundant supplies of speckled trout. During the fall, hunting in the neighborhood is nearly always productive of the permitted quota of game.

Rufus McIntyre and Major Strickland, leading their 200 men north from Bangor at the time of the Aroostook War, were impressed by the large number of eagles hovering about, and gave the lake its name.

Tour 6: From Fort Kent to Mattawamkeag   309

In WINTERVILLE (alt. 1012, Winterville Plantation, pop. 408), 20.5 *m.*, guides are available.

> Right from Winterville on a gravel road to *Lake St. Froid*, 1 *m.*, another of the Fish River Chain, has an abundance of salmon, togue, and trout. Deer hunting in the vicinity is well rewarded. Along the headwaters of the near-by Red River are 17 ponds that, with 10 others along the headwaters of Nigger Brook, contain squaretail trout.

PORTAGE (alt. 641, Portage Lake Town, pop. 886), 36.6 *m.*, on *Portage Lake* is surrounded by dense forest growth. The lake is 60 miles from St. Agatha, a terminus of the Fish River Chain of Lakes Canoe Trip (*see Sports and Recreation: Canoeing*).

On fishing and hunting trips in this region guides frequently call attention to beaver dams and homes. Beaver, amphibious rodents common throughout Maine, are particularly numerous in the vicinity of Portage Lake. A full-grown beaver reaches a weight ranging from 25 to 40 pounds; its soft and velvety fur makes the pelt prized for luxurious garments. The beavers' activities, starting in the spring and continuing through the summer and fall, include the cutting of timber to build and repair their dams and houses, and the gathering of their winter food supply — the bark of poplar, white birch, and maple trees.

At the southern end of the lake is a large *Muskrat Settlement*. The houses, built of mud and grass and resembling small hay stacks about 3 feet in diameter and 2 feet high, are visible only when the level of the lake is low.

ASHLAND (alt. 75, Ashland Town, pop. 2198), 47.2 *m.*, commercial and industrial center of this area of Aroostook County, is an important shipping center for lumber and potatoes. The nine warehouses along the railroad tracks can hold 45,000 barrels of potatoes. There are several small sawmills in the vicinity, though this is not an active lumbering area at present; when the industry was at its peak, prior to 1916, daily shipments of 100 carloads were not unusual.

SQUA PAN (alt. 549, Masardis Town), 52.2 *m.*, a small settlement of woodsmen, is said to have been named for an Indian squaw who married a Frenchman named Pan.

At 52.7 *m.* (L) is a *Maine Forestry Service Station*.

MASARDIS (alt. 580, Masardis Town, pop. 584) (*bus service to Oxbow*), 56.4 *m*. During the Aroostook War in 1839, breastworks were built and artillery stationed here, at the confluence of the Aroostook River and St. Croix Stream.

Though lumbering operations are continued on a small scale, potato raising is the principal means of livelihood; the soil, chiefly 'caribou loam' — a local name for the exceedingly rich soil of the potato belt — is very fertile. There is excellent trout fishing in the streams about the town.

At 61 *m.* is the junction with a dirt road.

> Right on this road is OXBOW (alt. 620, Oxbow Plantation, pop. 176) (*guides available*), 5 *m.*, hunting and fishing center for sportsmen. Here, along the streams and lakes, are many privately owned hunting lodges as well as public camps.

Many large specimens of big game are taken from the forests. Small game such as partridge and woodcock is abundant, and togue, black bass, perch, and pickerel are plentiful. Jack Dempsey had his training quarters here before he fought Gene Tunney in 1926.

MORO (Moro Plantation, pop. 169) (*guides available*), 81.8 *m.*, is in a hunting and fishing area, with numerous public camps. Brook fishing for speckled trout is popular. There are beaver colonies here and there along the streams, and deer are often seen in the environs.

Moro guides are particularly skilled in making camp life comfortable and they are good cooks; in summer flapjacks and johnny-cake are served with fried trout. In the colder seasons game replaces the fish, and is served with bean-hole beans and salt pork. Codfish with salt pork scraps, and pancakes covered with black molasses make another memorable meal.

PATTEN (alt. 541, Patten Town, pop. 1278), 93.3 *m.*, is a busy lumbering and commercial community with a well-developed business section.

Several good woods trails leading from the village have been cleared recently. More than 20 ponds, in which salmon and trout fishing is carried on, are within a 30-mile area.

SHERMAN STATION (alt. 485, Sherman Town, pop. 1027), 100.2 *m.*, lies on the southern edge of the potato-raising country.

At 102 *m.* State 11 swings sharp right to climb a long, winding hill.

STACYVILLE (alt. 520, Stacyville Plantation, pop. 600) (*daily bus to Sherman Station*), 106.8 *m.*, is at the northern end of the long *Davidson Woods*; in the early days it was an important stage stop.

The Appalachian Mountain Club Trail to Mt. Katahdin (*see Tour* 7) starts here.

GRINDSTONE (alt. 322, Township No. 1, Range 7, pop. 34), 117.1 *m.*, is a tiny lumbering village in which woodsmen and their families live in frame buildings covered with tarred-paper. The East Branch of the Penobscot River at this point passes through a rocky gorge, causing many log jams during the drives. Before dynamite was used to loosen the jams, many river drivers lost their lives trying to dislodge key-logs. A story is told of how one pugnacious backwoods Frenchman, who was caught in a very perilous position on a jam, lifted his voice loud in prayer, promising that if he was saved he would never again fight man or beast. By luck he reached shore and found himself face to face with a huge bear. Remembering his vow, he hesitated; then, shouting a hasty plea to the Almighty for forgiveness, jumped on the beast with his knife.

For several years the Great Northern Paper Company took its pulpwood from the river here, hauling it overland by team to a plant at Millinocket. Grindstone is the terminus of the East Branch Canoe Trip (*see Sports and Recreation: Canoeing*).

MEDWAY (alt. 280, Medway Town, pop. 406) (*daily bus service to East Millinocket and tri-weekly service to Lincoln*), 126.8 *m.*, lies at the confluence of the Penobscot River and its East Branch which enters the main

Tour 7: From Medway to Greenville   311

stream through a rocky gorge. In early lumbering days the village was an important place; logs were sorted here and sent to Bangor in a segregated drive. The settlement is now small and scattered, the remaining inhabitants being employed at East Millinocket and Millinocket (*see Tour 7*).

Here is a junction with State 157 (*see Tour 7*).

At the northern end of MATTAWAMKEAG (alt. 212, Mattawamkeag Town, pop. 461) (*see Tour* 4), 138 *m.*, is a junction with US 2 (*see Tour* 4).

TOUR 7 :   *From* MEDWAY *to* GREENVILLE, 95 *m.*, State 157 and unnumbered road.

Via Millinocket, Katahdin State Game Preserve, Sourdnahunk Depot Camp, Ripogenus Dam, Kokadjo, and Lily Bay.

Road partly macadamized, partly graveled. Narrow woods road in middle section not recommended in wet weather. Private road with gates (*open* 6–6) between Sourdnahunk and Ripogenus Dam; permit from Great Northern Paper Company required at Bangor to cross dam.

Accommodations scarce; telephones for fire service only; 50 miles between gas pumps.

THIS route runs through several paper-making towns, and as a mere lane penetrates the heart of Maine's great North Woods, traversing 100 miles of unbroken forest with little sign of human habitation. It crosses the Katahdin State Game Preserve, above which looms Mount Katahdin, Maine's highest peak, crosses Ripogenus Dam, and skirts the southeastern shores of Moosehead Lake.

MEDWAY (alt. 280, Medway Town, pop. 406) (*see Tour* 6), 0 *m.*, is at a junction with State 11 (*see Tour* 6).

At EAST MILLINOCKET (alt. 340, East Millinocket Town, pop. 1593), 2.6 *m.*, the forest comes almost to the back doors of the small houses. The community grew up rapidly in 1907, when the dam and mill of the Great Northern Paper Company were completed. The economic existence of the population, about half of which is French-Canadian, depends upon the paper mill.

MILLINOCKET (alt. 359, Millinocket Town, pop. 5830), 12.3 *m.*, the easternmost settlement of importance on the route, became a boom town in 1899–1900 with the building of the *Great Northern Paper Company Newsprint Plant*, which has become one of the largest mills of its kind in the United States. It produces 620 tons of newsprint paper and 25 tons of wrapper paper in addition to 540 tons of ground wood and 200 tons of sulphurized pulp every 24 hours.

The town differs from many others in Maine in that it did not grow from a handful of early settlers, but sprang up overnight in answer to a labor need. Because of the advantages of manufacturing near the source of raw material, the Great Northern built its plant on the Penobscot River at a place where a 141-foot head of water-power furnishes abundant energy. The company established and operates a hotel, financed homes for the workers and their families, and constructed roads connecting Millinocket with the outside world; it likewise saw to it that stores were opened, schools built, and a government established. A year after the completion of the mill in 1900, the area was set off from Indian Township No. 3 and incorporated.

At 19.6 *m.* the route crosses the eastern boundary of Unorganized Township No. 1, Range 9; although without a name, this area is not without population during the summer months. Many residents of Millinocket have built summer homes on the shores of *Millinocket Lake* (R). *Black Cat Mountain* (L) is the most prominent feature of the landscape.

At 23.8 *m.* the route crosses the southern boundary of Unorganized Township No. 2, Range 9. Lakes in this area include *Pockwockamus Pond* at the western base of *Trout Mountain* (alt. 1440), and *Bottle Pond* to the south; *Rum, Tea, Mink,* and *Rat Ponds* drain through a boggy area into *Togue Pond.*

At 27.7 *m.* the route swings left.

At 30.2 *m.* the route swings right to a narrow, winding road to pass *Abol Pond* (R) at the foot of *Abol Mountain* (alt. 2306).

The southwestern boundary of the *Katahdin State Game Preserve* (*no hunting permitted*) is crossed at 32.8 *m.* This reservation covers Township 3, Ranges 9 and 10, and Township 4, Ranges 9 and 10, and includes *Baxter State Park,* in which is *Mt. Katahdin* (alt. 5267), the highest peak in Maine. In the game preserve are other peaks — *North Brother* (alt. 4143), *South Brother* (alt. 3951), *Owl* (alt. 3736), *Fort* (alt. 3861), and several lower ones. The 144 square miles of wilderness, containing heavy forests and numerous streams and ponds, is an ideal breeding ground for the moose, deer, bear, and smaller animals that make northern Maine one of the outstanding hunting grounds in the eastern part of the United States. Numerous trails and wood roads cross the area, but it is inadvisable for those unacquainted with the country to follow them without a guide.

Baxter State Park is reached by the Hunt and Abol Trails (*see below; also Sports and Recreation*), and by the Appalachian Mountain Club Trail from Stacyville (*see Tour* 6). The area, containing 9 square miles, was set aside for public use in 1931–33 by Percival P. Baxter, Governor of Maine, 1921–25, to be kept unspoiled and unexploited.

Mt. Katahdin (Ind.: 'highest land,' or 'high place') has had particular attraction for many people, in part because of its grandeur and in part because of its wilderness setting. Thoreau, who hated community life and the spoliation of natural charms, was one of the first to write at length about the mountain. He described it as 'a vast aggregation of loose rocks, as if at some time it had rained rocks, and they lay as they fell on the mountains, nowhere fairly at rest, but leaning on each other, all rocking-stones, with cavities between, but scarcely any soil or smoother shelf.' It is this formation that makes it one of the most difficult peaks to climb in the East. So far as is known, Charles Potter, a Boston surveyor, who managed to reach the top in 1804, was the first white man to stand on the summit. Forty-two years later, Thoreau wrote of the view from that point: 'The surrounding world looked as if a huge mirror had been shattered, and glittering bits thrown on the grass.'

The mountain always had a special fascination for the Indians, who wove many stories about it. According to one of them, the home of the Mountain King and his lovely but dangerous daughter Lightning was within it; they were served by the Thunders, fierce, giant warriors. Kinaldo, the hero, fell in love with the Mountain King's daughter, after having seen her beautiful face on the storm clouds, and left his tribe to seek her. At last he found her in the terrible depths, and she, returning his love, prevailed on her father to hold a great feast for him in his hall; during the feast she gave Kinaldo a potion that made him forget his former life. For a time they lived happily together, but one night he was wakened from his sleep by the tears of his favorite sister Winona, who had not ceased to pray for his return. Both the king and the mountain princess tried to prevent his leaving, but he persisted. At last the king gave him permission to go, but angrily warned him that those who had tasted the wine of Katahdin could no longer live long among men. Lightning bade her lover farewell, saying, 'Go, but tomorrow at sunset I come and thou wilt not forsake me.' Kinaldo made his way down over the rocks and at length reached his home village; he thought he had been away only a short time, but he found many changes had taken place and Winona was already a woman. In spite of his joy over seeing his friends and kinsfolk again, he was restless and uneasy. As evening came a storm began to gather over Katahdin and he heard the mutter of the Thunders, which did not add to his peace of mind. The Thunders came closer and a terror seized him; but suddenly he saw his loved one among the thunderheads. A blinding streak of lightning seemed to reach out and seize Kinaldo. When the storm cleared, Katahdin was bathed in glittering light and the dead warrior lay as asleep at the foot of the mountain.

Another story, a favorite of the Abnaki women, was of a girl who loved the mountain, imagining that it was a strong, handsome young man and praying that he would some day come to her. One day she went blueberry picking alone and failed to return; three years later she came into camp with a beautiful baby boy in her arms, who was marked by eyebrows of stone. Despite the gossip of the village, she gave no explanation of her absence and would not name the father of her child. The boy grew in beauty and stature and gradually the village people discovered that he had miraculous power; if he pointed his finger at bird, fish, or animal, it died,

He rarely exercised this power, however, until one terrible winter when there was little game and what there was was fleet and hard to kill. The miracles of hunting accomplished by the small boy set the tongues wagging afresh; night and day the women, old and young, teased the mother and such was their curiosity about the boy that they forgot how much they owed to his prowess and made insinuations about his paternity. Tired and angered by their cruelty and ingratitude, the mother at last burst forth: 'Fools, your folly kills you! You must have known from his eyebrows that this was Katahdin's son, sent to save you.' And she took her god-child and departed forever; from that time on the Abnakis were a doomed race, the white men stealing their hunting grounds and in time exterminating them.

At 33.6 *m.* (R) is the entrance to the Abol Trail (*see Sports and Recreation*).

At 37.4 *m.* (R) Hunt Trail (*see Sports and Recreation*) begins at *Camp Baxter* (*camp site*).

At 46.2 *m.* stands the *Sourdnahunk Depot Camp* of the Great Northern Paper Company. In summer the large number of horses pastured here, grazing and resting, are the only indication of the great lumbering activities of the region. The method of lumbering has been modernized, but tractors and other machinery have not entirely replaced horses.

At 58 *m.* the route crosses the eastern boundary of Unorganized Township No. 3, Range 12, and swings south.

At 59.3 *m.* is the *Ripogenus Dam*, 92 feet high, across the head of the deep Ripogenus Gorge. Although recent construction in various parts of the country has vastly exceeded this water storage in size, at the time it was built (1915–17) Ripogenus was hailed as a great engineering feat. It stores between 20 and 30 million cubic feet of water, which is released into the West Branch of the Penobscot River.

At 59.8 *m.* is the gate to the private road of the Great Northern Paper Company.

At 63.6 *m.* the route crosses the southeastern boundary of Unorganized Township No. 3, Range 12, near the deadwater of *Chesuncook Lake* (R); weathered driki, densely packed, rises in masses above its surface. There are fine views up the lake, which extends 18 miles to the north.

After a long stretch of woods the highway passes the southern end of *Ragged Lake*; due west is a splendid view of craggy *Spencer Mountain* (alt. 3035).

At 76.5 *m.* is the southern gate to the Great Northern's private road through the big woods.

KOKADJO (Ind.: 'Kettle Mountain') (Unorganized Township of Frenchtown, pop. 10), 81.3 *m.*, has a boarding-house and filling station. A large sign reads: 'This is God's country — Why set it on fire and make it look like hell?' In this township is *First Kokadjo Lake*, 6 miles long.

LILY BAY (alt. 1040; Unorganized Township of Lily Bay, pop. 5), 87.9 *m.*, has a lumberman's hotel, and a filling station.

South of Lily Bay the route borders the southeastern shore of *Moosehead Lake* (*see Tour* 9).

At 89.2 *m.* the route enters Gore A, No. 2. Forest-garbed *Baker Mountain* (alt. 3589) rises above the eastern part of the township and *Prong Pond* forms a blue patch on the southern boundary.

GREENVILLE (alt. 1040, Greenville Town, pop. 1614) (*see Tour* 9), 95 *m.*, is at the junction with State 15 (*see Tour* 9). The East Branch (Penobscot River) and Allagash River Canoe Trips (*see Sports and Recreation: Canoeing*) have their starting-point at Greenville.

T O U R 8 : *From* WEST ENFIELD *to* BINGHAM, 81.1 *m.*, State 11, State 155, and State 16.

Via Howland, Milo, Dover-Foxcroft, Guilford, and Kingsbury.
Good blacktop roadbed, with a short stretch of gravel through Kingsbury.

THIS route through woods and fields follows the winding course of the Piscataquis River, passing broad, tranquil ponds and large, prosperous farms extending to the outskirts of trim little towns.

The people of this section enjoy a comparatively steady, comfortable living, free from sudden booms and deep depression. Lumbering was begun here after the reckless boom period that left depleted forests and dead mill towns in its wake: production, now on a scientific basis, is kept at a constant level, thus providing regular employment.

WEST ENFIELD (alt. 140, Enfield Town, pop. 1138), 0 *m.* (*see Tour* 4), is at a junction with US 2 (*see Tour* 4).

HOWLAND (alt. 150, Howland Town, pop. 1605), 1.4 *m.*, entered from the east over a bridge spanning the Penobscot River, is an industrial and agricultural village at the confluence of the Penobscot and Piscataquis Rivers. Settled in 1818, it has grown up around large paper mills; corporation-owned houses are characteristic. In spring the rivers rise suddenly and the swirling waters toss logs and pulpwood high into the air. Many log jams result from this spectacular display.

LaGRANGE (alt. 310, LaGrange Town, pop. 468), 14.1 *m.*, lies in a fertile farming country, well adapted to cultivation. Since LaGrange was first settled, about 1823, the inhabitants have depended upon the soil for their livelihood, farm properties being handed down from one generation to another.

At LaGrange the route turns right on State 155.

BOYD LAKE (alt. 287, Orneville Town, pop. 284), 17.3 *m.* A few houses grouped on the highway at the point nearest the lake constitute this little settlement. This obscure town was once the home of the Maxim family, two sons of which played a not insignificant part in the destiny of mankind.

Hudson Maxim, brother of Sir Hiram Maxim, machine-gun inventor, was born here in 1853. He was an inventor in his own right. Smokeless cannon powder, a shock-proof high explosive for guns of large caliber, gun cartridges, and a new system for discharging high explosives from ordnance were among his contributions. He was paid $50,000 by the U.S. Government for his production of 'Maximite,' an explosive fifty per cent more powerful than dynamite, that could propel a projectile through heavy armor plate.

He was also deeply interested in the technique and scope of poetry. He published a weighty volume, 'The Science of Poetry and the Philosophy of Language.' Although, like his brother, he resided in England for many years, he was a frequent visitor to the United States. On one visit he was guest of honor of the Poetry Society of America; his remarks on that occasion are recalled for their scientific erudition.

For the first 18 years of his life he was known as Isaac, having been named for his father, who was also an inventor. Disliking the name, he had himself called Hudson.

MILO (alt. 295, Milo Town, pop. 2910), 25.3 *m.*, an industrial, commercial, and farming community, stands at a point where the Sebec River forms a junction with the Piscataquis, the combined waters furnishing power for several manufacturing concerns. With the establishment of a large spool mill in 1901, and the building of the Bangor and Aroostook Railroad car shops in 1905 at Derby (*see below*), the population of the town more than doubled between 1900 and 1910.

The *American Thread Company* (*permit at office*), employing nearly 400 people in full time, uses many cords of white birch in the manufacture of spools and box shooks. Other products manufactured in Milo are worsted yarn, and paper and excelsior made from the wood of poplar trees.

In towns like Milo, set in a heavily wooded area, the populace is in constant dread of that menace of the timberlands, the forest fire. Knowing that entire townships as well as thousands of acres of valuable timber may be laid waste, every able-bodied man, woman, and child springs into action when the first shrill scream of the fire siren pierces the hum of the mills. A moment's delay and the flames, leaping from undergrowth to treetops, may be caught by the wind and fanned quickly into a blistering, roaring inferno, hurtling through the resinous upper branches of the evergreens. Flames sometimes leap 30 feet into the black pall of smoke hanging above the crackling treetops.

As the trees crash to earth in a shower of flames and flying sparks, blazing embers are caught up on a current of acrid smoke and borne far in advance of the fire. Where each spark falls, a new blaze springs up, and in an incredibly short time the fire has reached conflagration proportions. Every means, from bucket brigades to backfiring, is employed to prevent such disasters.

Tour 8: From West Enfield to Bingham

Here is a junction with State 221 (*see Tour 8A*).

    1. Right from Milo on an improved road is *Schoodic Lake*, 8.3 *m.*, site of the former village of Lakeview where the American Thread Company once operated a spool mill. The view of the lake, noted for its trout fishing, is exceptional, with Mt. Katahdin looming darkly in the background.

    2. Left from Milo on a tarred road is DERBY (alt. 280, Milo Town), 1.6 *m.* The large *Car Shops* (*not open*) of the Bangor and Aroostook Railroad are the center of this community. The entire village is well landscaped with lawns and shrubbery around the plant, in front of residences and in the small parks receiving exacting care from company gardeners. The corporation houses are both comfortable and distinctive, and a playground with tennis courts and swimming pool has also been built by the railroad. This modern village, including marked and numbered parking spaces, is a surprising example of a planned municipality 'way up in Maine.'

SEBEC CORNER (alt. 440, Sebec Town, pop. 357), 31.7 *m.*

DOVER-FOXCROFT (alt. 330, Dover-Foxcroft Town, pop. 3742), 40 *m.* This enterprising mill town is made up of Foxcroft on the north side of the picturesque Piscataquis River and Dover on the south. The two communities, settled and developed separately, became one town in 1922. The water-power of the river is utilized in the manufacture of woolen goods in two mills owned and operated by the American Woolen Company which employs most of the population.

Dover-Foxcroft was the home of John Francis Sprague (1848-1926), prominent in historical research in Maine. Many Maine schools use his 'Journal of Maine History' as a standard authority. His writings appear among the collections of the Maine Historical Society (*see PORTLAND*), and among his published works are 'Sebastian Rasle,' 'Backwoods Sketches,' 'The Northeastern Boundary Controversy,' and 'The Aroostook War.'

Mrs. Lillian M. N. Stevens (1844-1914), president of the Women's Christian Temperance Union from 1898 until the time of her death, was born in Dover. She was instrumental in forming both the national and State organizations, and was likewise president of the latter from 1877 on.

John Colby Weston, first Maine man to enlist in the Civil War, was a native of Foxcroft.

Here is a junction with State 7 (*see Tour 9*).

At 40.6 *m.* is the junction with State 153.

    Right on State 153 to *Sebec Lake*, 4.5 *m.*, popular for salmon, lake trout, and bass fishing.

At 47.4 *m.* is the junction with State 24.

    Left on State 24 is SANGERVILLE (alt. 440, Sangerville Town, pop. 1225), 0.5 *m.*, a manufacturing and agricultural village, the birthplace of Hiram, later Sir Hiram, Maxim (1840-1916), the inventor of the machine gun which bears his name. At the age of 14 he started out to make his fortune, first by working in a carriage shop, then in the shop of a maker of 'philosophical instruments' in Boston, later in a shop in Montreal, Canada. He then turned his attention to applied science, and invented a smokeless powder, an automatic gas headlight for locomotives, a gas-generating apparatus, automatic steam pump, vacuum pumps, feed-valve heaters, engine governors, and many other devices.

In 1881 certain of his electric patents were put into 'interference' with Edison's, and in four trials, decisions were in Maxim's favor. The Maxim gun was completed only after he had acquired a fortune from other inventions following the establishment of his own factory in England. In the course of time the Prince of Wales (Edward VII) and other members of the nobility became convinced that the device was practicable. After a demonstration in Switzerland, the government of that country gave him an order, with Italy, Austria, and then England following suit. The gun with which he gave his demonstration in England is now in South Kensington Museum.

In the United States the gun was not accepted until the war with Spain (1898). It was used by many nations during the World War. Factories in Spain, Portugal, Sweden, England, and the United States were owned by Maxim for the manufacturing of a torpedo boat which he also designed. For his contributions to effective warfare, the inventor received honors and decorations from nearly every sovereign of Europe. He spent a great part of his life in England and was knighted by the British Government in 1901.

GUILFORD (alt. 430, Guilford Town, pop. 1735), 48.7 *m.*, spreading on both sides of the Piscataquis River, is an active industrial town chiefly engaged in the manufacture of woolens and wood products.

In 1803, a handful of men settled in what is now known as Guilford with 'a determination to admit on their part no person as a settler who was not industrious, orderly, moral, and well-disposed.' In 1806, the men residing in the township living so harmoniously together were called 'the seven wise men of Guilford.'

ABBOT (alt. 450, Abbot Town, pop. 524), 53.1 *m.*, is at junction with State 15 (*see Tour* 9).

KINGSBURY (alt. 520, Kingsbury Plantation, pop. 50), 66.3 *m.* This tiny village at the east end of Kingsbury Pond, guarded by an archway of tall pines, is engaged in lumbering operations in winter and is a small fishing resort in summer. For 50 years after Moosehead Lake became a sporting center in 1836, mail was brought south over Russell Mountain by pack-carrier to the Kingsbury Post Office.

At 78.4 *m.* the highway passes over a section of *Johnson Mountain* (alt. 1620), with a fine panoramic view of the Bigelow Range and the broad Kennebec River in the foreground.

BINGHAM (alt. 355, Bingham Town, pop. 1590) (*see Tour* 10), 81.1 *m.*, is at a junction with US 201 (*see Tour* 10).

TOUR 8 A: *From* MILO *to* KATAHDIN IRON WORKS, 20.5 *m.*, State 221 and unnumbered road.

Via Brownville.
Tarred roadbed to Brownville Junction; wide gravel to airport; then one-lane gravel road.
Accommodations include, besides a small hotel at Brownville Junction, sporting camps reached by buckboard or hiking from Katahdin Iron Works where reservations can be made and transportation arranged by telephone.

THIS route reaches a heretofore inaccessible hunting and fishing country.
At 0 *m.* State 221 branches north from Milo (*see Tour* 8).
BROWNVILLE (alt. 350, Brownville Town, pop. 1911), 5 *m.*, lies on both sides of Pleasant River near a dam.
On the far bank of the river north of the village, and visible from the highway, are long heaps of slate that show where quarrying was done until 20 years ago. Brownville slate won first prize at the 1876 Centennial Exposition in Philadelphia as the finest roofing slate in the country.
At 6.1 *m.* (L) is the *Maine Forest Station* of the Pleasant River District.
At 8.6 *m.* is the junction with a tarred road.

> Left here to BROWNVILLE JUNCTION (alt. 390, Brownville Town), 0.5 *m.*, which has a small hotel and the farthest north gas station on this road.

At 14.2 *m.* (R) is *Brownville Prairie Airport.*
At 14.7 *m.* the highway crosses a bridge of unusual construction. The floor consists of a long log on each side spanning the stream, with shorter logs fastened crosswise to them by rather loosely tied wire cable. Underneath is another cross-tied group of logs.
Towering pines of great beauty crowd close to the road north of the rolling log bridge; shorter hardwood and conifers, spruce predominating, mingle with the pines.
KATAHDIN IRON WORKS (alt. 580, Unorganized Township of Katahdin Iron Works, pop. 42), 20.5 *m.* A deposit of bog iron ore, a variety of hematite, was discovered about 1843 in the northern part of this town at the foot of Ore Mountain, and the development of the mine and the construction of the smelting mill were started. The property has changed hands several times. Because of lack of shipping facilities little work has been done in recent years.

Other valuable mineral deposits, including pigments and copper, can be mined but not profitably, because of the inaccessibility of the area. A large deposit of asbestos, said to be of excellent quality, has been surveyed but no attempt has been made to mine it.

Some of the old buildings of the Iron Works at the southern end of Silver Lake are now used as base headquarters in the lumbering operations of the Pleasant River Lumber Company.

The Gulf, also known as Little Jaws and the Grand Canyon of the East, on Pleasant River, is about 4 miles northwest; it cannot be visited except by trail. *Houston Pond* and *Indian Pond* are visited by canoes and trails. Little Wilson and Pleasant Rivers, noted for their beautiful waterfalls and cascades, canyons, deep gorges, and rugged profiles, are easily accessible by marked woodland trails. Trout fishing in the various waters is excellent.

T O U R   9 : *From* WATERVILLE *to* CANADIAN LINE (*St. Zacharie, P.Q.*), 168.9 *m.*, State 11, State 7, and State 15.

Via Benton, Pittsfield, Newport, Dover-Foxcroft, Greenville, Rockwood, and Pittston Farm.

Cement and tarred roadbed between Fairfield and Greenville; gravel and improved between Greenville and Rockwood; improved private road of Great Northern Paper Company between Rockwood and Canadian Line.

No filling stations and only fire-patrol telephones northwest of Rockwood; limited accommodations in same area.

THE southern section of this route runs through a country in which farming, quarrying, and some manufacturing are carried on. North of Greenville the route skirts the western side of Moosehead Lake, then runs through the broad forest lands owned by the Great Northern Paper Company, the scene of lumbering operations in winter.

WATERVILLE (alt. 95, pop. 15,454) (*see WATERVILLE*), 0 *m.*, a point touched on the Lower Kennebec Waters and Belgrade Lakes Canoe Trips (*see Sports and Recreation: Canoeing*), is at the junction of US 201 (*see Tour* 10). Between Waterville and Fairfield US 201 and State 11 are one route.

State 11 branches east from US 201 (*see Tour* 10) at FAIRFIELD, 2.9 *m.*

At BENTON (alt. 130, Benton Town, pop. 1156), 3.4 *m.*, the highway swings northeast.

At 5 *m.* is the junction with an improved road.

> Right on this road, which follows the eastern bank of the Sebasticook River, is BENTON FALLS (alt. 130, Benton Town), 1 *m.*, the oldest village in the area. The *David Reed House* (L), an inn of the post-road days, though vacant, is in a fair state of repair. The ell, which contains a kitchen with an old-fashioned brick oven, was built in 1813, a few years before the present two-storied main structure, which is square with a gabled roof. In the early days this place was a welcome sight to the

Tour 9: From Waterville to St. Zacharie 321

tired and thirsty travelers in the sparsely settled region. During the periods of militia training, the tavern was headquarters for the out-of-town men, who met at the bar to exchange gossip, elect officers, and conduct initiation ceremonies.

The *Asher Hinds House* (*private*), next to the Reed House, was built in 1830 by Hinds, a storekeeper who had been an early settler and was of some importance in local politics. The one-and-a-half-story house, an unusually attractive structure for the region and period in which it was built, has a recessed doorway.

The *Congregational Church*, built more than a century ago, contains a fine bell said to be the last sold from the Revere foundry in Massachusetts. This heavy bell, which had been brought by schooner from Boston without mishap, while being transferred to a scow for the last few miles of the journey, slipped off the planks into the river, where it lay for several days, to the distress of the settlers who had made considerable investment in this crowning glory for their church. The immersion did it no harm, however, and its tone is clear and mellow.

CLINTON (alt. 140, Clinton Town, pop. 1354), 9.2 *m.*, has a woolen mill and a refrigerator factory.

BURNHAM (alt. 155, Burnham Town, pop. 664), 14.6 *m.*, is on the Maine Central R.R. at the junction with the western terminus of the Belfast and Moosehead Lake R.R.

Right from Burnham on a good local road to WINNECOOK, 4 *m.*, small summer resort overlooking Unity Pond. The No. 1 fairway of the *Golf Course* (greens fee $1) parallels an Abnaki Indian migration trail; part of the hazard of No. 6 fairway is a large meteor.

PITTSFIELD (alt. 210, Pittsfield Town, pop. 3075), 21.7 *m.*, busy trading place for the surrounding agricultural section, includes among its local industries a small woolen mill, a shoddy mill, and a shoe factory.

Maine Central Institute (L), South Main St., was founded in 1869, and its first class had one member. It is a college preparatory institution.

Llewellyn Powers, Governor of Maine from 1897 to 1901, Carl E. Milliken, Governor from 1917 to 1921, and Hugh Pendexter (1875), poet and novelist, were born in this town.

NEWPORT (alt. 200, Newport Town, pop. 1731) (*see Tour* 4), 29.2 *m.*, is at a junction with US 2 (*see Tour* 4). State 11 north of this point is united with State 7.

Governor Lewis O. Barrows (1937–   ) is a native of Newport.

CORINNA (alt. 350, Corinna Town, pop. 1485), 35.6 *m.*, a compact settlement with two woolen mills, a small lumber mill, and a cannery, is the birthplace (1866) of Gilbert Patten, who, under the *nom de plume* Bert L. Standish, wrote the Frank Merriwell series of boys' books.

The route swings north on State 7 at Corinna.

DEXTER (alt. 480, Dexter Town, pop. 4063), 43.5 *m.*, an industrial community, lies on a hillside sloping down to the southern shore of Wassookeag Lake.

Dexter is the birthplace of Ralph O. Brewster, U. S. Representative (1935–   ) and Maine's 51st governor (1925–28).

Wassookeag School (R), on High St., a private college preparatory institution using modern teaching methods, has one teacher for every three pupils.

The *Amos Abbott Company Mill* (*open to public*), opened in 1820, has remained under the management of the same family for four generations. It was built in the wilderness when machinery and supplies were brought from Boston to Bangor in sailing vessels and then hauled by ox teams over rough logging roads to this place.

Between DOVER-FOXCROFT (alt. 330, Dover-Foxcroft Town, pop. 3742) (*see Tour* 8), 56.8 *m.*, and ABBOT (alt. 450, Abbot Town, pop. 524), 69.2 *m.*, State 15 and State 16 are one route (*see Tour* 8). The route swings left in Dover-Foxcroft and at Abbot State 15 turns right.

On State 15 is MONSON (Monson Town, pop. 1181), 76.6 *m*. Dense woods encircle this village perched high on a slate ridge, its hillsides cut by deep, slate-walled quarries, in which for 70 years the pit method of quarrying was carried on. The shaft method, operating with compressed air, has been used for the past five years. The ridge under the town, and for miles north, has a base of slate of the finest quality. Exhaustive experiments have demonstrated that the slate, because of its small mineral content, is better than any other for use in the manufacture of electrical goods.

Many brooks and streams near Monson afford excellent trout fishing.

At 83.1 *m.* is the junction with an improved road.

> Left on this road is SHIRLEY MILLS (alt. 1100, Shirley Town, pop. 197), 2 *m.*, the birthplace of Bill Nye, the humorist, who was born in 1850 and christened Edgar Wilson Nye. His family moved to Wisconsin three years later. From about 1878 until his death in 1896 his amusing letters and whimsical comments on the social and political life of the times gained him nation-wide fame. He traveled extensively through the United States, Canada, and Europe as a lecturer. The house in which he was born has burned; the site of the house is south of the post office.

GREENVILLE (alt. 1040, Greenville Town, pop. 1614), 90.5 *m.*, where guides are available, is the sporting center for the southern antler of the Moosehead region. Fishing, hunting, camping, canoeing, and mountain climbing (*see Sports and Recreation*) are the sports for which the settlement acts as a starting-point and supply base.

The village has hotels, sportsmen's camps, overnight cabins, and tenting space (*cap.* 2000, *reservations essential*), is on the Canadian Pacific and Bangor and Aroostook R.R.s, and has steamboat service (*variable schedule, apply at wharf*) to all points on Moosehead Lake.

Moosehead Lake (*see also Sports and Recreation*), greatest of all New England lakes, cuts through the almost trackless wilderness for a stretch of about 35 miles, hemmed by rugged mountains and flanked by the virgin forest. It is from 1 to nearly 20 miles in width, with a shore line of about 350 miles, and lies 1028 feet above the sea. The air is particularly invigorating. Since the first lake steamer was launched in 1836, it has been a famous recreational center. Many visitors have been enthusiastic about this primitive country; the poet, Whittier, wrote 'To a Pine Tree' after he had visited Moosehead and its forests.

In the center of the lake Mount Kineo (*see below*), an abrupt peak of

TOUR 9: From Waterville to St. Zacharie 323

flint, rises out of the deep waters. North of Kineo the lake is bordered by a plateau of densely covered wild land. Below Kineo the southern shore is dominated by Lily Bay, Baker, and Big and Little Squaw Mountains. Near the middle of the lower bay are the 2200 wooded acres of *Deer Island* and the sprawling expanse of *Sugar Island*.

Moosehead is a breeding ground of squaretailed trout, salmon, and togue; as the fishing season draws to its close, the bright scarlet of hunters' caps are but little brighter than the flaming autumn leaves dropping into the water along the shore, for Moosehead is as renowned for its plentiful game as for the excellence of its fishing.

GREENVILLE JUNCTION (Greenville Town), 92.3 *m.*, is the meeting point of the Canadian Pacific and Bangor and Aroostook R.R.s; it is on the southern shore of Moosehead Lake.

UNORGANIZED TOWNSHIP NO. 2, RANGE 6 (alt. 1600), 95.7 *m.*, with a hotel and camps (*guides available*), is commonly called Big Squaw Township and embraces an area of primitive beauty, in which some lumbering is carried on. The hotel and camps are headquarters for hunters and fishermen.

Big Squaw Mountain (alt. 3267), the chief landmark of the township, rises above the southern antler of Moosehead. There is an Indian legend that long ago Kineo, a great warrier of such bad disposition that he constantly quarreled with his fellow tribesmen and eventually left them to sulk, in time reached the mountain that now bears his name, rising between the two antlers of the lake. There he took up his abode, hunting each day in the neighboring forests, but always returning at night to his mountain. Resentment against the tribesmen who had scorned him increased as he grew more lonely. One evening as he sat looking down over the black waters of the lake he saw a bright blade of flame on what is now called Squaw Mountain; the next day he started south to investigate it secretly. Arriving at the summit at dusk, he found the embers of the fire and beside it his exhausted old mother, who had followed him to bring him back to his kinsmen; as she died she begged him to return. Kineo buried her by her fire and, grief stricken because he had been the cause of her death, obeyed her request. Since then, the Indians have called the mountain by the name it now bears officially.

At 98.7 *m.* (L) is a *State Fish Hatchery* (*open*), where, in more than 3 miles of runs and breeding pools, hundreds of thousands of landlocked salmon (*salmo Sebago*) are annually raised for distribution in various fishing waters.

UNORGANIZED TOWNSHIP NO. 1, RANGE 7 (alt. 1050, pop. 5), entered at 107.4 *m.*, is commonly called Sapling. Numerous small streams mirroring the delicate tracery of white and yellow birch, and affording excellent fishing, cut through this heavily wooded township on the western shore of Moosehead Lake and the banks of the Kennebec River.

MISERY GORE (alt. 1500), 110 *m.*, an unpopulated area 25 miles long and less than 0.5 mile wide at its widest point, is a sliver of land left by corrections of early surveys of township boundaries; it is not included in any township.

The southeastern boundary of UNORGANIZED TOWNSHIP OF ASKWITH (alt. 1400, pop. 56) is crossed at 110.6 *m.*; the area is popularly called West Outlet, but is also known as Taunton and Raynham. This township is renowned for its hunting and fishing, much game being found in the vast expanse of timber land, and the clear streams offering unusual opportunities for fishing. The west outlet of Moosehead Lake here forms the northern boundary of a *State Game Preserve* (*no hunting allowed*) which extends south through two townships to Squaw Brook.

ROCKWOOD (alt. 1050, Unorganized Township of Rockwood, pop. 315), 115.1 *m.*, sometimes known as Kineo Station, with hotels, camps, and cottages, has steamer service (*variable schedule, apply at wharf*) to points on Moosehead Lake (*see above*), on whose western shore the village lies. Just north of the settlement the road follows the shore of the lake, with excellent views to the north.

Across the lake which at this point is only about 1 mile wide, *Mount Kineo* (alt. 1806) thrusts itself above the waters and far-flung forests of the lake's eastern shores. This mountain, a round peninsula connected with the mainland by a narrow neck, is composed of flint. At the foot, broken and incomplete stone implements from early Indian workshops have been found. Many of the New England tribes came here for flint and it is believed that this mountain was also the source of the iron pyrites used by the Red Paint People (*see Earliest Inhabitants*) for fire stones.

At its southern base, on the lake shore, is the *Kineo House*, long a favorite with sportsmen and with lovers of primitive lake and mountain scenery.

The UNORGANIZED TOWNSHIP OF TOMHEGAN is entered at 118.2 *m.*; it lies between Moosehead and Brassua (bras'-a-wā) Lakes, in both of which are excellent fishing. Game abounds throughout the area, though hunters must not enter the State Game Preserve to the south.

At 138.6 *m.* is a junction with a gravel road.

> Right on this road, which follows the southern shore of *Seboomook Lake*, much of which is dead water, to SEBOOMOOK (Unorganized Township of Seboomook, pop. 24), 10 *m.*, a tiny, buried settlement of guides and woodsmen on the extreme northern shore of Moosehead Lake (*see above*).
>
> From Seboomook extends the 3-mile Northwest Carry to the Penobscot River (West Branch), a terminal of the Allagash River Canoe Trip (*see Sports and Recreation: Canoeing*).

Pittston Farm, 139.6 *m.*, surrounded by broad fertile fields, at a junction of the northern and southern branches of the Penobscot River, holds a collection of large, white buildings; it is one of the several isolated farms maintained by the Great Northern Paper Company for the care of horses in summer and the raising of produce to supply logging camps during winter lumbering activities.

At 140.2 *m.* is the junction with a local road.

> Left on this road to the deep-cut (40 feet) *Canada Falls*, 2 *m.*; about 1 mile north of the falls, along a trail, is *Grand Pitch*, another waterfall.

At 149.5 *m.* is the entrance to a trail.
> Right on this trail 6 *m.* to the *Green Mountain Fire Station* from which is a fine view over the great level plateau, a vast expanse of forest land and dead water.

At 152 *m.* is a *Log Storehouse* and *Stable* of the Great Northern Paper Company.

At 153.1 *m.* is the junction with a local road.
> Left on this road is *Penobscot Lake*, 5 *m.*, a forest-rimmed sheet of black water, across whose surface echo the calls of waterfowl and woods birds.

DOLE (Township 3, Range 5), 153.6 *m.*, with a residence and supply base of the Great Northern Paper Company, is almost buried in the dreary stretches of swamp land covering a considerable part of the township. Around Dole Pond, Long Pond, and Penobscot Lake, the forest struggles against the dead water overflow.

Boundary Cottage, 168.9 *m.* (R), 5 miles southeast of St. Zacharie, Que., is a customs office, near the entrance to a private road (*open* 7–8) of the Great Northern Paper Company, and is a headquarters for wood crews during the winter.

The mills and headquarters of the Great Northern Paper Company are at Millinocket and East Millinocket; the company conducts lumbering operations in all parts of the north country, and is particularly active in this section. When a cutting operation is started, tote roads are laid out through the forest for the transportation of the logs to the nearest point of shipment. These roads are simply slashes through the forest with the stumps often left in the ground. Snow covers the stumps and rough base in winter, packing down to a smooth sledding surface. Horses and oxen provided the early hauling power, but of late years tractors have been used in their stead.

TOUR 10: *From* BRUNSWICK *to* CANADIAN LINE (*Quebec, P.Q.*), 168.4 *m.*, US 201.

Via Topsham, Gardiner, Hallowell, Augusta, Vassalboro, Winslow, Waterville, Fairfield, Skowhegan, Norridgewock, Madison, Anson, Bingham, Jackman, and Moose River.

Two-lane, hard-surfaced road-bed; in winter often impassable north of Madison.

BEAUTIFUL river scenery characterizes the southern part of the route which follows the course of the Kennebec, past several power plants, then on through lumbering regions and fish and game country. Historic as well as scenic, the route also offers diversion at inland resorts.

BRUNSWICK (alt. 30, Brunswick Town, pop. 7604) (*see BRUNSWICK*), 0 *m.*, is at a junction with US 1 (*see Tour 1, sec. a*).

TOPSHAM (alt. 50, Topsham Town, pop. 2111), 1.1 *m.*, settled in 1730, rises above the Androscoggin River just before it empties into Merrymeeting Bay. Its history and industrial development is closely associated with that of Brunswick (*see BRUNSWICK*).

The *Aldrich House* (about 1800) (*private*), 26 Elm St., one of the masterpieces of the local builder, Samuel Melcher, has an unusually beautiful doorway.

> Right from Topsham on State 24, to a fork at 0.7 *m.*; right here to *Merrymeeting Bay*, 6 *m.*, a favorite resort of duck hunters. Great numbers of wild fowl stop here on their long migratory flights in the spring and fall (*see Sports and Recreation: Hunting*).

At 21.5 *m.* (R) is *Peacock Tavern*, a square frame two-story building, built about 1790 and still offering accommodations to travelers.

GARDINER (alt. 90, pop. 5609), 25.9 *m*. By a series of land grants under a system whereby the proprietor retained 500 out of every 900 acres of land, Dr. Sylvester Gardiner (1708–86), for whom the city is named, came into possession of 100,000 acres of land in the Kennebec country and applied himself with great zeal to its settlement and development as a feudal manor. He meant to give ownership of every foot of ground for miles around to his descendants, which would have made it possible for them to regulate the community as they chose; this dream was shattered by the Revolution.

Gardiner developed through the years, however, and by 1850 had become an industrial city. Shoe factories, paper mills, and woodworking establishments lie along Maine Ave. and Bridge and Water Sts., while the residential district covers the hills rising from the flat land along the Kennebec, and Cobbossee Stream. The area also developed culturally, contributing substantially to the world of letters (*see The Arts*). Shortly after his birth at Head Tide, Edwin Arlington Robinson (1869–1935) came with his family to Gardiner. A quiet boy, outstanding, it seemed, only for the brilliance of his great brown eyes, he lived and worked here, except for a short period given to study at Harvard, until his middle twenties, when he went to New York City. Robinson's 'Tilbury Town' is Gardiner and in his poems he has portrayed many of the village scenes and characters. In the fall of 1936 his admirers erected a simple *Granite Monument* on the corner of the Green to his memory.

Among other Gardiner authors is Mrs. Laura E. Richards, who at eighty-seven is still actively at work, her published works numbering more than seventy novels, biographies, and collections of poems and short stories. Several of her novels have Maine settings and characters; her 'Captain January' was made into a motion picture in 1936.

Kate Vannah (Letitia Katherine Vannah), prominent in literary and musical circles, is among the artists who have made their homes in Gardiner.

Oaklands (*private*), at the southern end of Dresden Ave., is the country home of former Governor William Tudor Gardiner, a direct descendant

TOUR 10: From Brunswick to Quebec

of Dr. Sylvester Gardiner. The somewhat grim, ivy-clad, 45-room granite structure is suggestive of an English manor of the Tudor period. The estate, one of the finest in Maine, extends along the Kennebec River.

In Gardiner is a junction with State 27 (*see Tour* 12).

FARMINGDALE (alt. 80, Farmingdale Town, pop. 1044), 26.9 *m.*

HALLOWELL (alt. 110, pop. 2675), 30.1 *m.*, legally a city in spite of its small population, is in a natural amphitheater formed by hills facing a bend in the Kennebec River. Its charm is not apparent from the highway.

Settled in 1754, it was named for Benjamin Hallowell, one of the proprietors of the Kennebec Purchase, who with Dr. Sylvester Gardiner (*see above*) owned the contiguous tracts of land now occupied by the cities of Gardiner and Hallowell. The city appears to have withdrawn from the waterfront at its feet where ships and wharves once clustered along the river, and streets were alive with traffic and commerce. Today industrial life is limited to the operation of two shoe factories and a few lesser establishments.

The *Vaughan Mansion* (*private*), at the southern end of Second St., a large, square two-story structure in spacious grounds, was the home of Dr. Benjamin Vaughan (1751–1836) who came to live here in 1797 and was influential in Hallowell's early commercial and cultural development.

The *Smoking Pine*, a huge tree on the southern bank of Vaughan's Stream, is said to give off a thin vapor under certain atmospheric conditions. It was Indian tradition that Assonimo's pipe of peace would continue to smoke so long as the Bombahook continued to flow into the Kennebec.

Old Hallowell Academy, Middle St., now a primary school, was the Academy at Hallowell Hook, the second institution of its kind to be established in the District of Maine (1791).

Worster House, a yellow-brick building on the corner of Second and Winthrop Sts., is a hostelry built in 1832. Its guests have included William Lloyd Garrison, President James Polk, Horace Greeley, Ralph Waldo Emerson, and Daniel Webster.

The *Hubbard House* (*private*), 52 Winthrop St., a neat one-and-a-half-story frame structure built in 1830, was the home of Dr. John Hubbard, Governor of Maine 1850–53. An attractive doorway with mullioned sidelights gives entrance to an interior preserved as it was in the doctor's day.

> Left from Hallowell on Winthrop St. to the *State School for Girls*, 0.7 *m.* (R). In 1871 nearly a thousand Portland women petitioned the legislature to make provision for the reform of young female delinquents; a private association was incorporated to administer the proposed institution for which, in 1872, Mrs. Mary H. Flagg offered $100,000 in money and Mrs. Almira C. Dummer contributed land. The first building was erected in 1875, and in 1899 the school was placed wholly under State control.
>
> *Hallowell Granite Quarries*, 2.5 *m.* (L), which now produce paving blocks, have produced granite of exceptional quality which has been used in many public build-

ings throughout the country. Hallowell granite is clear gray with a minimum of mica; it bears black tourmaline pinpoint markings.

AUGUSTA (alt. 120, pop. 17,198) (see *AUGUSTA*), 32.3 *m.*, is at the junction of State 27 (see *Tour* 12), State 9, and State 11 (see *Tour* 13), and State 17 (see *Tour* 17).

At 40.8 *m.* (R) is the *Birthplace of Holman F. Day* (1865-1935), poet and author. 'Up in Maine,' 'Pine Tree Ballads,' and 'King Spruce' are among his works.

VASSALBORO (alt. 120, Vassalborough Town, pop. 1815), 43.7 *m.*, settled about 1750 by immigrants from Cape Cod, was chiefly populated after 1780 by Quakers from New York.

Oak Grove Seminary (R), easily recognized by its castle-like main buildings, was established about 1844 by members of the Society of Friends and is still directed by Quakers. On the 330-acre campus, which overlooks Kennebec River from a hill, is the *Natanis Wild Life Sanctuary*, named for the Indian portrayed in Kenneth Roberts' novel 'Arundel.' In 1933, France awarded a medal to the school, now a college preparatory institution for girls, for the excellence of its French department.

WINSLOW (alt. 100, Winslow Town, pop. 3917), 50.1 *m.*, on the eastern bank of the Kennebec at its confluence with the Sebasticook River is closely connected industrially and historically with Waterville (see *WATERVILLE*) across the river.

The *Lithgow House*, north of the public library on Lithgow St., was built by Captain William Lithgow, first commandant of Fort Halifax (see *below*), and has been occupied constantly since 1754.

The *Blockhouse* (L), on the north bank of the Sebasticook River is all that remains of Fort Halifax, which was erected in 1754 by order of Governor Shirley of Massachusetts as the last in a series of defenses built along the Kennebec during the French and Indian Wars. No evidence has been found of its having been attacked by Indians, or the French. Two years before the close of the war, Captain William Lithgow (see *above*) was in command with a force of 130 men. Captain Ezekiel Pattee followed Lithgow as commander, and after the Peace of Paris in 1762, the fort was abandoned.

This structure, like others of its time, was designed in the manner of the old English forts. A stockade formed a square enclosure, in the southwestern and northeastern corners of which stood blockhouses; a row of barracks extended along the eastern side and there was a sentry box at the southeastern corner. The officers' quarters, a storehouse, and armory were housed in a two-story building with dormer windows, which extended east from the northeast corner. Two small blockhouses stood on the hill at the rear of the fort; both were enclosed by stockades, and one overlooked Ticonic Falls on the Kennebec.

The remaining weather-beaten blockhouse, built of hand-hewn timbers fastened together with wooden dowels, is typical of such structures used

TOUR 10: From Brunswick to Quebec

during the Indian wars. The upper story, with musket and lookout holes, overhangs the lower one, thus enabling the defenders to fire through the loopholes before the enemy could reach the door to force it in or get close enough to set the blockhouse on fire.

Winslow is within the boundaries of a former large village of the Ticonnets, and many Indian relics were unearthed on the western bank of the Sebasticook before the land was inundated in the building of Fort Halifax Dam.

In *Fort Hill Cemetery*, Halifax St., which dates from 1772, is the *Grave of Richard Thomas*, an early settler, who wrote the epitaph for his own gravestone:

> 'A Whig of seventy-six
> By occupation a cooper
> Now food for worms like
> An old rum puncheon
> Marked, numbered, and shooked
> He will be raised again
> And finished by his creator.'

Another epitaph in this plot reads:

> 'Here lies one Wood,
> Encased in wood.
> One Wood within another.
> The outer wood is very good,
> We cannot praise the other.'

From a *Red Paint Cemetery*, near the Fred A. Lancaster mill on Clinton Ave., have been taken ancient artifacts, including a number of finely finished hexagonal slate spearheads, a spearpoint of banded stone, and a large number of sheet-copper beads.

The large buildings (R), on the bank of the river are the *Hollingsworth Whitney Company Mills* (*permit at office*), manufacturing wood pulp and paper.

Ticonic Falls (R), which furnishes water-power for the mills, is visible from the bridge.

The highway here crosses to the western bank of the Kennebec.

WATERVILLE (alt. 95, pop. 15,454) (see *WATERVILLE*), 51.5 *m.*, is at a junction with State 11 (see *Tour* 9), which is united with US 201 between this point and Fairfield.

FAIRFIELD (alt. 115, Fairfield Town, pop. 5329), 54.3 *m.*, a manufacturing center of pulp, pulp-fiber products, and woolens, stretches along the west side of the Kennebec River. Here, in 1774, a few hardy pioneers settled in what was then a vast wilderness, paving the way for the busy industrial town of neat homes which long since have supplanted the first rude cabins.

One-half mile north of the business section, on the river bank, is a *Granite Seat* indicating the spot where Benedict Arnold and his men (see *Tour* 11) landed to repair their boats.

The *Keyes House* (*private*) (L), built in 1905, is probably the most fantastic architectural structure to be found along the route. Its turreted central section resembles the Castel Sant' Angelo at Rome, with turret and walls on either side crenelated in the manner of a medieval castle. It was formerly the home of Martin L. Keyes, founder of the Keyes Fibre Company.

State 11 branches right here (*see Tour* 9).

At 55.6 *m.* (L) is the entrance to the *Central Maine Sanatorium*, established in 1915 for the treatment of persons with advanced tubercular infections.

At 61.3 *m.* (L) is *Good Will Farm* (*open weekdays*), founded in 1889 by the Reverend George W. Hinckley. This institution has a three-quarter-million-dollar endowment, and receives no State aid. Its 40 buildings spread over 2600 acres, providing a home for deserving boys and girls from 9 to 20 years of age. In addition to receiving the usual secondary education, Good Will boys and girls help to operate the institution and are trained in various manual occupations.

Good Will Museum contains collections of minerals, flora and fauna, Indian relics and Red Paint artifacts, old and curious farm implements, and Colonial furniture.

At 69.1 *m.* is the junction with US 2, on the southern outskirts of Skowhegan (*see Tour* 4), and State 147 (*see Tour* 4), an alternate and shorter route between this point and Solon (*see below*). From this junction point US 2 and US 201, united, swing west, following the western bank of the Kennebec.

NORRIDGEWOCK (alt. 190, Norridgewock Town, pop. 1478) (*see Tour* 4), 74.4 *m.*, is at a junction with US 2 (*see Tour* 4), which here branches west.

At 75 *m.* is a junction with a dirt road.

> Right here to *Danforth Tavern* (*private*), 0.1 *m.* (L), a large frame structure painted yellow with green blinds. Built in 1807, it has undergone little alteration. Its hewn timbers are still held together with hand-wrought nails. There are more than 30 rooms and 12 fireplaces. A long central hall on the first floor has an arched ceiling.

Sophie May House, 75.1 *m.* (L), a red-brick structure with white columns, now a tourist home, was built in 1845 by Cullen Sawtelle (U.S. Representative 1845–47; 1849–51). It was the home of Rebecca Clarke (Sophie May) and Sarah Clarke (Penn Shirley), well-known 19th-century writers of juvenile stories. One of the most attractive homes in the vicinity, it has remained unaltered except for the redecoration of the walls and the remodeling of the kitchen. The hall has a graceful staircase with hand-carved ornamentation. The false floor in the attic, leaving a five-foot air space, is unusual in this State.

At 80.7 *m.* (L) about 100 yards from the road, is the *Father Rasle Memorial* (*see below*), an 18-foot granite obelisk, erected 1833.

At 81.1 *m.* is the entrance (L) to *Old Point*. Here, in a beautiful pine

OLD HOUSES AND OLD CHURCHES

EARLY Maine residents, when they could afford it, lavished their wealth freely on their buildings, but they were governed by an artistic restraint in so doing which was as much a part of their way of living as it was an esthetic ideal. The Lady Pepperell Mansion and 'Montpelier,' the reproduction of General Knox's Thomaston manor house, are examples of the very best in Colonial design. 'Montpelier,' inspired by Jefferson's 'Monticello,' is perhaps exceptional in its elegance, but both houses reflect a style and a society, that of the time immediately preceding the Revolutionary War, which is almost as significant as was *ante-bellum* feudal magnificence in the South. Churches, too, reflected the social ideal, and they stand today, more than do the great houses perhaps, as reminders of the period when even utilitarian structures were made to be lovely and when to create beauty was an enduring way of worship.

Good living and well-designed building were not limited to wealthy individuals and communities, however. Such hostelries as Burnham Tavern are today not at all uncommon in the State, and such fine simplicity as that of the Surry Church may be found in any little town in Maine.

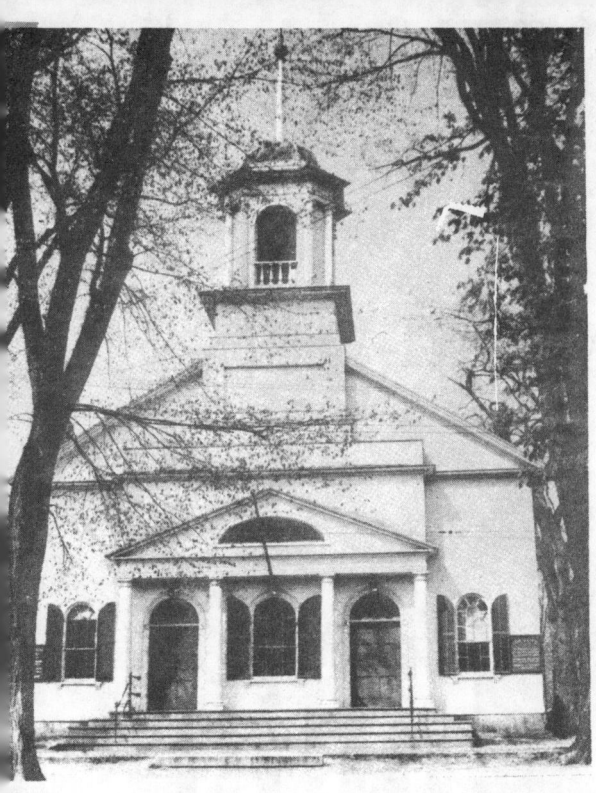

SECOND PARISH UNITARIAN CHURCH, SACO

CONGREGATIONAL CHURCH, KENNEBUNKPORT

LADY PEPPERELL MANSION AT KITTERY POINT

CHURCH AT PHIPPSBURG

McINTIRE GARRISON HOUSE, YORK

SWINGING SIGN OF BURNHAM TAVERN, MACHIAS

BURNHAM TAVERN, MACHIAS

ANDREW HOMESTEAD, SOUTH WINDHAM

FIRST PARISH UNITARIAN CHURCH, KENNEBUNK

WHITE CHURCH NEAR SURRY

MONTPELIER, THOMASTON

grove, is a public camping ground (*picnic tables, stone fireplace, spring water*).

This broad level stretch of land is the site of the Abnaki Indian village, Nanrantsouak, or Norridgewock. It lies on the Kennebec–Chaudière River route, long used by the Indians traveling between Maine and the Quebec region. As early as 1633, when the English were struggling to settle along the coast, Capuchin missionaries from Chaleur Bay were coming up the Kennebec River. After their visits to this section, the Norridgewock Indians asked the Jesuit mission in Canada for missionaries. By the middle of the 17th century the Jesuits had made numerous friends among their converts in the Quebec area, and the help they gave the Indians in various ways had gained them a wide reputation as desirable friends; as a result of reports of Abnakis who had come in contact with them at Quebec, they were invited to establish a mission at Nanrantsouak. Father Gabriel Druillettes undertook the task in 1646, leaving Quebec with some Abnakis, who led him up the Chaudière and down the Kennebec to the village, where he remained a few months and built a chapel. Later he went down the Kennebec to visit the Capuchin mission at Castine, stopping at the present Augusta, where he met John Winslow, the Pilgrim trader; Winslow, often alone with the Indians and in need of friendly relations with them, had gradually developed a friendly interest in them, and he and Father Druillettes had earnest discussions on the possibilities of converting them all to Christianity and civilization. The Jesuit returned to Canada in 1647.

At this time the leaders of the Massachusetts Bay Colony, determined to ignore the quarrels between Great Britain and France, which were harmful to business, were making overtures to the authorities at Quebec for a free-trade agreement. The French-Canadians, also bored by European quarrels, were prepared to make the agreement and hoped to form an alliance with the Massachusetts colonists against the militant Iroquois. Because the Abnakis surrounding the Pilgrim post on the Kennebec were the spiritual charges of Father Druillettes, he was selected to conduct the negotiations; he set out over his former route in September, 1650. After visiting Nanrantsouak he continued to Winslow's post, where he arranged to have Winslow accompany him to Plymouth and Boston. His negotiations there were not successful, in part, perhaps because the tightfisted colonists did not see any particular reason for spending hard-earned money to help protect the Canadians from a menace that did not at the time worry them. He returned to take up his work among the Abnakis with whom he lived until 1657.

Several well-known Jesuits were stationed here at one time or another, including Father Joseph Aubry and Father Sebastian Rasle; the latter was in charge from 1691 until 1724. Father Rasle brought ornaments and vessels from Quebec for the Indian chapel, made candles for it from bayberries, and trained a choir of 40 young Indians, whom he dressed in garments of the type used in French Catholic churches.

In 1701, the English authorities ordered the French missionaries to leave.

Colonel Winthrop Hilton's expedition went to Norridgewock in 1704-05, and burned all the church property. Father Rasle used a temporary bark chapel during the construction of a new church, which was not completed until 1718. During this period he broke both legs and was taken by canoe to Canada. On his return he learned a price had been set on his head. In 1722, Captain John Harmon and 200 men swooped down on the village while the warriors were hunting. The partly crippled priest and the old men of the camp hid while the party pillaged the church and the priest's dwelling, carrying off the dictionary of the Abnaki language on which Father Rasle had been working for years. Two years later Father Rasle met his death at the hands of a force under Captain Jeremiah Moulton who pillaged and burned the village. Finding themselves continually attacked, the Norridgewocks left, part of them going to Canada, many joining the Penobscots at Old Town.

Benedict Arnold on his Quebec expedition of 1775 (*see Tour* 11) followed in reverse the route down which came Father Druillettes in 1646. He and his men spent nearly a week at Old Point, preparing for the carry around Norridgewock Falls, about a mile north of Old Point. At the time of his visit all that remained of the settlement were ruins of an old Indian fort, a chapel, an old grave surmounted by a cross, and a covered passageway to the river.

According to a legend, Waban ('the morning'), son of a great chief and the first Norridgewock, was born at Old Point. Waban taught his people much, gave them food in abundance, cleared their streams and paths, and was kind to all creatures of the forest and stream. Although fierce and brave, he spared the birds, talked the language of all wild things of the woods, and became the greatest chieftain of them all. So great was his power that he did not die, but walked through the forest to the Great Spirit, and continued to clear the paths of his people for many generations.

MADISON (alt. 290, Madison Town, pop. 3956), 82.7 *m.*, named for President James Madison, is a manufacturing town, its chief products textiles and paper. The industrial development of the town did not begin until 1875, though Sylvanus Sawyer, first settler, cleared land near Old Point in 1773.

ANSON (alt. 290, Anson Town, pop. 2237), 83.1 *m.*, is a residential district for employees of the woolen and paper mills at Madison, directly across the Kennebec.

NORTH ANSON (alt. 295, Anson Town), 87.7 *m.* The route crosses the bridge over the *Carrabassett River* here, with views of the *Falls* (L) and the rocky river bed. The rocks, chiefly of slate schist, have been strangely carved by the water's action.

SOLON (alt. 395, Solon Town, pop. 852), 95.4 *m.*, is at the junction with State 147, a short-cut (*see above*) between this point and Skowhegan (*see Tour* 4).

Left from Solon on a gravel road to the railroad station, 0.4 *m.*, beyond which (200

TOUR 10: From Brunswick to Quebec 333

yards south) is *Caratunk Falls*, best viewed from the railroad bridge spanning the river. Extending V-shaped for 30 or 40 yards on either side of a point of land under the bridge, the falls drop 36 feet, sending up a cloud of spray and mist as the waters strike the jagged rocks below.

On the eastern bank of the river below the falls, an old road runs a few hundred yards to *Arnold's Landing*. Here in a quiet little cove, on a ledge near the water's edge, is an *Arnold Trail Marker*, surmounted by a flagstaff, with a tablet commemorating this as the spot where Benedict Arnold and his army landed October 7, 1775, remaining overnight prior to the carry around Caratunk Falls.

BINGHAM (alt. 355, Bingham Town, pop. 1590), 103.6 *m.*, is now generally identified with Wyman Dam (*see below*), which has caused a complete economic change in the town since its completion in 1931. Although the workmen that were here in the construction days have left, business activity is still on the upswing with the influx of tourists, who come each year to view the dam.

Bingham was first settled in 1785. The Bingham Purchase (*see Tour 1, sec. c*) was made up of two tracts of land, each of 1,000,000 acres, secured by William Bingham, a wealthy and influential Philadelphia banker in 1786, when the Commonwealth of Massachusetts, holding title to most of the unsettled land in Maine, undertook to dispose of a large area in the eastern part of the Province by lottery. Mr. Bingham drew several townships and bought others. General Henry Knox (*see Tour 1, sec. b*), already a large proprietor by reason of his acquisition of the remainder of the Waldo Patent, had secured a contract for a large piece of Maine's wild land, but his duties as Secretary of War under President Washington required his full attention, and he turned the contract over to Bingham, who had been active in financial matters during the Revolutionary War. This resulted in the purchase of the second Bingham tract.

At Bingham is a junction with State 16 (*see Tour 8*).

At 104.9 *m.* (L) is the combination earth-fill and concrete *Wyman Dam*, with a hydro-electric plant. The dam raises the level of the river 135 feet and has a total storage of eight billion cubic feet of water. The dam, 155 feet high and 2250 feet long, has created an artificial lake which provides water storage for the headwaters of the Kennebec, including Moosehead and Brassua Lakes, Indian Pond, and various other small bodies of water. The dam was completed after a two-year construction period by the Central Maine Power Company, and was named in honor of the company's president, Walter Scott Wyman.

At 113.7 *m.* a boulder with a tablet is the northernmost *Arnold Trail Marker* in the Kennebec section, and indicates the spot near which Benedict Arnold (*see Tour 11*) left the Kennebec River in October, 1775. The boulder, originally standing on the river bank, was moved to this point when the waters of artificial Wyman Lake flooded the lower slopes.

CARATUNK (Ind.: 'rough and broken') (alt. 560, Caratunk Plantation, pop. 169), 118.6 *m.*, lies near the Kennebec River not far from *Moxie Mountain* (alt. 2925). Near Caratunk the road runs close to the Kennebec River, with steep slopes covered with large boulders rising (R) above. (*Beware of falling rocks.*)

THE FORKS (alt. 576, The Forks Plantation, pop. 136), 126.3 *m.*, is at the confluence of the Dead and Kennebec Rivers. A quantity of red ocher (*see Earliest Inhabitants*) was found in this vicinity in 1935 when stone was blasted away for road construction. In the rocks were found two small openings leading into caves, which contained small quantities of the pigment; when the caves were further opened up, a pit holding great quantities of the material was found.

The Upper Kennebec Waters Canoe Trip (*see Sports and Recreation: Canoeing*) touches at The Forks.

> Right from The Forks on a dirt road to *Lake Moxie* and *Mosquito Mountain* (alt. 2230), 5 *m.*

At 129.1 *m.* (L) is an old tote (lumber) road, unfit for motor travel, leading to Spencer Stream, Spencer Lake, and the Dead River region, a popular hunting and fishing area 15 miles distant (*see Sports and Recreation*).

At 137.3 *m.* an entrance marker indicates a foot trail.

> Left on this trail to a fire warden's house, 2.5 *m.*, from which a steep trail leads to the *Fire Lookout Station* (*open*), on *Coburn Mountain* (alt. 3718). From the tower can be seen lakes and mountains to the north and west.

The *Parlin Pond Camps*, 141 *m.* (R), are the largest in this area on the main route where accommodations are widely scattered.

At 151.2 *m.* US 201 passes over *Owl's Head Mountain* (alt. 2380).

JACKMAN (alt. 1170, Jackman Plantation, pop. 1094), 152.3 *m.*, on the shore of Wood Pond, reaches its peak of activity as a resort center in the fall during the hunting season; in the winter it is a busy supply center for the lumber industry.

The *U.S. Immigration Station* (*must be visited by every person entering from Canada*), is just north of the tracks of the Canadian Pacific R.R.

Jackman is one of the terminals of the Attean Lake Canoe Trip (*see Sports and Recreation. Canoeing*):

MOOSE RIVER (alt. 1170, Moose River Plantation, pop. 277), 154.6 *m.* First settled in 1820 by Captain Samuel Holden, Moose River today has but one inn, *Holden House*, built in 1842 and now owned by one of the Captain's descendants. In the past many cattle were driven through here on their way from Boston to Quebec, and the drivers looked forward to a stop at this inn; it is now popular with lumberjacks.

At some distance from the highway, on either side, lumbering operations are in progress, though not as extensively as some years ago. Once operating in this region were the rugged, lusty lumberjacks who were supposed to 'sleep in trees and even eat hay if sprinkled with whiskey.' These were the woodsmen who never took off their red flannels from the time they hit camp in the fall until they came out in the spring; who never shaved; who chewed great hunks of tobacco, could spit 15 feet into a head wind and hit the mark, and roll off a lusty hair-raising stream of profanity.

Horse-play, stunts, story-telling, and singing of such chanteys as 'Little Brown Bull' constituted the social life of the old boys who sometimes

Tour 10: From Brunswick to Quebec

worked in the snow to their armpits, and who could stand upright on a rolling log in midstream as few can today.

Each spring the lumberjacks left camp and swaggered into the quiet villages to show the outside world what he-men were. They yelled for strong liquor and swore they'd leave no maid along the Kennebec. There were fights a-plenty, gory and bloody; when a man wore the imprints of a lumberjack's calked shoes, he was marked for life as a fighter.

Real 'bean-hole beans' were important in the 'feed' of lumber camps. Pots full of pork and beans were kept all night over rocks placed in the ground and brought to white heat. These were eaten with biscuits made by the camp cook or cookee who rose or fell on the quality of his output.

Lumbering today is no longer a pioneer adventure; it is an organized industry. Tractors, hauling logs over well-built roads, have replaced the oxen. Modern machinery has decreased employment. The keen spirit of competition has gone from the river drivers who once prided themselves on their strength, speed, and agility. Theirs was the job of following the drive of logs down the rivers to untangle the jams. Crawling across the logs in their calked boots until the key log was found and loosened, and then making their way back to shore as the logs started again, was no feat for the timid.

The lumberjack now lives more comfortably and the vigorous lumber-camp days are over. Even tobacco chewing is rare, for cigarettes, which formerly marked the user as worse than dandified, are preferred. White crockery, instead of tin plates and iron forks, is on the table, and the radio has replaced the fights and howling choruses that were the entertainment of the past. The camps, formerly as barren of femininity as a man-of-war, now furnish quite comfortable homes for women and children.

At 157.1 *m.* is a free camp site.

At 158.3 *m.* is the *U.S. Customs Office (all automobiles entering from Canada must stop for inspection).* From here is obtained the northernmost view of the chain of lakes that stretches through Jackman to Moosehead Lake.

At 168.4 *m.* US 201 crosses the International Boundary, 93 miles southeast of Quebec, Canada. The two *Line Houses*, serving food and liquid refreshments, were among the popular borderline resorts in motoring weather during Prohibition days, liquor being served in the Canadian half of the buildings.

TOUR 11: *From* NEW HAMPSHIRE LINE (*Dover*) *to* CANADIAN BOUNDARY (*Quebec*), 218 *m.*, State 4.

Via S. Berwick, N. Berwick, Sanford, Alfred, Gorham, S. Windham, Gray, Auburn, Turner, Farmington, Rangeley, Eustis, and Arnold Pond.

Two-lane macadamized road-bed between the New Hampshire Line and Rangeley; graveled and narrow dirt road-bed between Rangeley and the Canadian Boundary, not recommended in wet weather.

Accommodations scarce north of Rangeley.

STATE 4, roughly spanning the southwestern part of the State in a roundabout course, offers a wide range of scenery. The southern section traverses attractive villages having many old houses set on broad lawns; the northern section runs through the forested hills of the Rangeley Lake country, providing the chief highway approach to that popular hunting, fishing, and canoeing area. For a few miles the highway follows the route used by Benedict Arnold and his men on their unfortunate march to Quebec in 1775. North of Eustis the narrow road breaks through the wilderness relieved infrequently by camp sites.

State 4 crosses the New Hampshire Line, 0 *m.*, 3.7 miles east of Dover, N.H.

SOUTH BERWICK (alt. 110, South Berwick Town, pop. 2650), 0.6 *m.*, is an attractive old village near the home of Gladys Hasty Carroll, contemporary novelist, who uses New England as the locale of her stories. A dramatization of her novel, 'As the Earth Turns' (1933), is presented in summer by the townspeople.

The *Sarah Orne Jewett House* (*open in summer, adm.* 25¢), NE. cor. Main and Portland Sts., built about 1780 by John Haggins, is now owned by the Society for the Preservation of New England Antiquities, to whom it was bequeathed by Miss Jewett's nephew, Dr. Theodore Eastman. Several years after the house was erected, it was purchased by Captain Theodore Jewett, Miss Jewett's grandfather. This two-and-a-half-story clapboarded house with dormer windows is notable for its well-proportioned Doric portico and fine raised-panel door. The portico, with fluted columns that are reeded in the lower third and have simple stone block bases, is topped with a classic entablature and pediment. The door has dark louvered shutters and is framed with a delicately moulded and fluted architrave. It is probable that the portico was added in the early part of the 19th century.

From the center hall, considered one of the most beautiful in New England, rises a staircase of particularly fine design and detail; the raked dado on the stair wall is noteworthy. A large window of fine flowered glass illuminates the landing.

Tour 11: From Dover to Quebec

Books and folios fill the finely furnished library; old engravings, miniatures, carved ivory, and old silver ornament the parlor; old glass and rich dark mahogany fill the dining-room; and fine old willowware lines the cupboards of the kitchen, which has an open fireplace and rows of old kettles and pots. Four bedrooms, containing old mahogany four-posters with testers and valances, open off the upper hall. In the guest room, a narrow door opens into a hidden staircase that winds from cellar to attic. In Sarah Orne Jewett's room is the low desk on which a number of her books were written.

Sarah Orne Jewett was born in this house on September 3, 1849. Her greatest pleasure as a child came from accompanying her father, a country physician, on his rounds which took him into many remote farm homes. As the child sat in rural kitchens, while her father helped to bring babies into the world and tried to keep men, women, and children from leaving it, she saw much homely drama and tragedy, and heard many stories of the past; and as she and her father jogged along the back roads he talked with her constantly, telling her what he had learned in schools and elsewhere. Miss Jewett early began to write stories, her first being published in the *Atlantic Monthly* when she was only 20 years old. Eight years later, her first novel, 'Deephaven,' really a collection of episodes centering about one person, was published. 'A Country Doctor,' in which she portrayed her father's experiences, appeared in 1884, and her best-known volume, 'The Country of the Pointed Firs,' in 1896. In 1901, 'The Tory Lover,' a story of Berwick during the Revolution, brought her increased popularity and the degree of Doctor of Letters from Bowdoin College, her father's *alma mater*, the first honor conferred by that institution upon a woman. Miss Jewett's popularity was based on warmly sympathetic and often humorous portrayals of common people, which first appeared at a time when most writers of fiction were busy with scenes and people alien to the average citizen. Sarah Orne Jewett died at South Berwick, June 24, 1909.

On Portland St., just north of the Jewett House, is the *Eastman Community House (open)*, which at times was occupied by Miss Jewett; it also was bequeathed by her nephew to the Society for the Preservation of New England Antiquities.

> Right from South Berwick on Academy St. to *Berwick Academy*, 0.4 m. (L), one of the oldest preparatory schools in Maine. Its charter, granted by the General Court of Massachusetts, bears the signature, among others, of John Hancock. Samuel Moody, the first master of the academy, was paid an annual salary of £60, with the addition of sixpence a week for each pupil. The school, co-educational since 1828, now has about 150 pupils.
>
> At 2.1 m. (R) is the unoccupied *Simpson House*, a large, plain two-story structure, believed to be one of the oldest houses in Maine.
>
> On the opposite side of the road is the *Goodwin House (private)*, a large two-and-a-half-story structure that was the home of General Ichabod Goodwin, commander of the Berwick company during the Revolutionary War. At one time a band of thieves lived in the near-by Negutaquit Woods. A favorite local folktale tells how the General left for church one Sunday morning with an admonition to his small daughter, who was remaining at home with a servant, to be courteous to any guests

who might arrive during his absence. Shortly after his departure, the thieves approached, and the child, unaware of their identity and mindful of her father's orders, importantly assumed her rôle as hostess and asked the maid to prepare food for them. The visitors accepted the hospitality without comment, eating their fill; then they began to collect the family silver and other valuables, packing them in bundles. The child was puzzled and frightened, torn between a suspicion that something was wrong and a fear of violating the laws of hospitality; after she had seen one treasured object after another snatched up, she came forward timidly, offering her own silver cup as a substitute for her mother's possessions. The leader stared at her, abruptly told his men to leave the bundles, and led them away. The story is that sometime afterward, when the thieves had at last been jailed, the General, in talking with them, asked the leader why he had failed to take anything of value from the Goodwin home; the answer, according to the old wives, was that he could not do it after the little one had treated him 'for the first time in his life like a gentleman.'

The *Jonathan Hamilton House* (*private*), also on the left, and reached by a half-mile curving driveway, is a frame structure with hip roof, dormer windows, and four large chimneys. This house, in which Admiral John Paul Jones was a frequent guest, was built in 1788, by Colonel Jonathan Hamilton, and is mentioned in Sarah Orne Jewett's 'Tory Lover.'

At 2.3 *m*. (R), is an *Old Cemetery*, actually a group of family burial places where the oldest legible inscription is dated 1728.

NORTH BERWICK (alt. 230, North Berwick Town, pop. 1540), 7.3 *m*., is a village with tree-shaded streets and with landscaped lawns surrounding substantial old homes, some looking as they did when built and others remodeled. The town lands, settled shortly after 1630 as part of Kittery, and later included in the town of Berwick, were in 1831 set off as a separate unit and incorporated. Furs were dressed here in early days and the manufacture of plows was begun more than 100 years ago. Plows are still manufactured here, as are woolens, toboggans, and sleds.

Berwick sponge cake, familiar to many old-time travelers, originated here. When the railroad was built in 1842, William C. Briggs, a cripple, set up what he called a 'restorator,' a forerunner of today's station lunch counter. His wife, a cook of local fame, made a cake of such excellence that it became known over a wide area by the name of the town. All trains had a 10-minute stop at North Berwick and passengers would rush from the cars to the 'restorator' to buy large portions of the cake. Charles Dickens, the author, once stopped off to obtain some of the cake for a little friend accompanying him; she was Katie Smith, later Kate Douglas Wiggin.

At 12.1 *m*. (R) is *Bauneg Beg Country Club* (*open May–Nov.; greens fee $1.50, with member $1; Sat., Sun., holidays, $2*) with a 9-hole course. The course lies on the eastern side of Bauneg Beg Pond, a beautiful small body of water on the shores of which are stands of second-growth pine.

SANFORD (alt. 310, Sanford Town, pop. 13,392), 17.2 *m*., an industrial center, lies in the Mousam River Valley near the foothills of the White Mountains. The town, first known as Phillipstown in honor of Major William Phillips of Boston, original proprietor of land in this vicinity, was incorporated in 1768 and named for Major Phillips' stepson, Peleg Sanford, Governor of Rhode Island (1680–83).

Tour 11: From Dover to Quebec

Although the first mill was built in 1739, it was in 1867 that the town's real industrial development began with the establishment of a factory for the manufacture of carriage robes and kersey blankets.

The *Goodall Worsted Company Factory* (*open*), High St., manufactures Palm Beach cloth.

The *Sanford Mills* (*open*), High St., manufacturing mohair-plush fabrics, supply a large part of the automobile upholstery used in the United States.

Many of the residents of Sanford are descendants of early English immigrants, and some are French-Canadians who came in the last few decades to work in the mills and the two shoe factories.

> Left from Sanford on State 109 is SPRINGVALE (alt. 320, Sanford Town), 2 *m.*, a village occupied chiefly by people employed in the Sanford mills.
>
> *Nasson College for Women*, near the corner of Main and Oak Sts., was established as a vocational school for girls in 1912. It received its charter as a college in 1935, and confers the degree of Bachelor of Science in secretarial work and domestic science.
>
> Northwest of Springvale on the northern bank of Mousam River is *Indian's Last Leap*, two great boulders jutting out into the river from opposite banks. According to legend, an early settler, fleeing from a band of Indians led by Chief Nahanda, jumped from one boulder to the other — a distance of about 20 feet — clearing the stream in one leap. Chief Nahanda fell short in his leap, and, striking his head against the cliff, fell into the river and was drowned.

ALFRED (alt. 340, Alfred Town, pop. 883), 21.8 *m.*, is a typical New England village with quiet streets and dignified houses. The territory that includes Alfred was acquired in 1664 by Major William Phillips (*see above*), who bought a large tract of land from the Indian sagamore, Captain Sunday. This purchase was not recorded, but another deed signed in 1668 by Captain Sunday and preserved among the court records, conveyed 20 square miles of land, between Great and Little Ossipee and the Saco Rivers, to Francis Small of Kittery in exchange for two large blankets, two gallons of rum, two pounds of powder, four pounds of musket balls, 20 strings of beads, and several other articles. Captain Sunday's signature was the picture of a turtle. The first white settlement was made in 1764, nearly 100 years later. Alfred was the North Parish of Sanford until 1794, when it was incorporated, and its Indian name, Massabesic, changed to the one it now bears, given in honor of Alfred the Great. With the town of York, the original county seat, Alfred became a half-shire town in 1802. In 1832 records were removed from York and Alfred remained the shire town. It developed as a farming and lumbering community, and has changed little in the past half century.

The *Whipping Tree*, a large oak (R), on State 4 north of the junction with State 111, was used between 1800 and 1830 for the public flogging of certain types of offenders.

The *Courthouse* (R), cor. of Kennebunk and Main Sts., holds complete court records from 1636 to the present.

The *Holmes House* (*open*), opposite the village green (L), was built in 1802 for John Holmes, one of the first two United States Senators from Maine and chairman of the committee that drafted the State of Maine constitution. The most interesting feature of the exterior is an iron balustrade with a design of bows and arrows that rises from the eaves of the house. Among the traditions regarding this decoration is one that Senator Holmes had the pattern used to indicate his friendliness toward the Indians; another that it was his reply to those who believed he had Indian blood in his veins; and still another that it had romantic significance, the house having been built for Holmes and his bride.

At 23.5 *m.*, high on a hill overlooking Shaker Pond, formerly called Massabesic Lake, is the *Institute de Notre Dame*, a Catholic school for boys, housed in the buildings of a former Shaker settlement. For many years men of the former colony tilled the 1500-acre farm and cared for its herd of dairy cows, and the highly respected, primly bonneted ladies built up a profitable business selling baskets, knitted goods, and other wares. In 1931, the remaining members of the colony sold their holdings and joined the Shaker colony at New Gloucester (*see Tour* 14). The old buildings have been restored and new ones added since the estate came under the present ownership.

EAST WATERBORO (alt. 290, Waterboro Town, pop. 914), 29.7 *m.*, is at the junction with State 5 (*see Tour* 15).

HOLLIS CENTER (alt. 250, Hollis Town, pop. 1034), 34.7 *m.*, was the home of Freeman Hanson who invented the locomotive turntable, and Silas G. Smith who invented the locomotive snow plow.

BAR MILLS (alt. 150, Buxton Town, pop. 1574), 37.1 *m.*

> Right from Bar Mills on an unmarked road following the east bank of the Saco River across the Salmon Falls Bridge to SALMON FALLS (alt. 120), 1.3 *m.* The village lies on both sides of the river, about equally divided between the towns of Hollis and Buxton.
>
> Right from the bridge on the Hollis side is *Quillcote*, third house (L), for many years the summer home of Kate Douglas Wiggin (1859–1923), who wrote 'Rebecca of Sunnybrook Farm,' 'The Birds' Christmas Carol,' and other books popular among little girls at the beginning of the 20th century. The property was auctioned in 1937. Kate Smith, born in Philadelphia, was brought to Hollis as a child; later her family moved to California, where she became a pioneer in kindergarten work. In 1881 she married Samuel B. Wiggin and, after his death, George C. Riggs, but having acquired a literary reputation as Mrs. Wiggin she continued to use that name. The Quillcote house, a large two-and-a-half-story clapboarded structure built about 1805, stands well back on a lawn shaded by maples, elms, and apple trees, its gable end to the street. The wide pine boards were cut on the banks of the Saco. One of the five bedrooms was known as the 'painted room' because the walls were decorated by an itinerant young French artist who early in the 19th century did such work in a number of Salmon Falls homes. Two of the murals, depicting tropical scenes, were restored a few years ago. This room was occupied by Mrs. Wiggin's sister, Miss Nora Smith, until her death in 1934.
>
> The old Quillcote barn was transformed into an assembly hall, the interior decorated with autographed pictures of well-known writers and actors who were friends of Mrs. Wiggin and with drawings illustrating her books. The gilded weathervane represented a quill pen. The estate, owned by Mrs. Wiggin's niece, was maintained by the local Dorcas Society which she founded. Many well-known persons have lectured and presented entertainments in the hall for the benefit of local charities and other enterprises.

TOUR 11: From Dover to Quebec   341

South of the bridge is *Indian Cellar*, a large recess in the steep, rocky bank of the Saco, from which Indians are said to have attacked enemies passing along the river in canoes.

At 37.7 *m*. is the junction with State 112 at Emery Corner.

Right from Emery Corner on State 112 is *Tory Hill Meeting-House* (1822), 0.5 *m*. (R). This fine old white church of simple Georgian-Colonial architecture was erected on the site of the first frame church (1761). It has a rather high steeple and square belfry. Because the first pastor, the Reverend Paul Coffin, who came to Buxton early in the 18th century, was a Royalist as were many of his parishioners, the section became known as Tory Hill.

This church and the neighborhood provided the locale of Mrs. Wiggin's 'The Old Peabody Pew,' a dramatization of which is presented here annually in August. In the churchyard, with its far-reaching view of the Saco Valley and distant White Mountains, is an imposing *Celtic Cross* marking the lot in which were buried Mrs. Wiggin, her second husband, her sister, and her mother. The cross bears the words: 'The song is never ended.'

At 43.6 *m*. (L) is *Narragansett Park* where the Gorham Fair is held annually in August.

GORHAM (alt. 220, Gorham Town, pop. 3035), 44.6 *m*., first called Narragansett No. 7, was granted in 1728 to men, or heirs of men, who had borne arms in the Narragansett War in 1675. The first clearings were made here by Captain John Phinney, who, with his son, paddled up the Presumpscot River and settled on Fort Hill (*see below*).

The *Baxter Museum* (*open Wed., Sat. afternoons in summer; free*), on South St., contains relics of the Colonial, Revolutionary, Mexican, Civil, Spanish, and World Wars; it also has some Indian artifacts and a collection of rare coins. The museum, built in 1808, was the home of Percival P. Baxter, Governor of Maine 1921–24; it was presented to the town by his father, the Hon. James Phinney Baxter.

Western State Normal School (1805), in the square on a hillside (L), has a 12-acre campus shaded by many kinds of trees. William Corthell was principal of the school when it was known as Gorham Academy, and Kate Douglas Wiggin was at one time a student. *Russell Hall* (1934), a brick auditorium and gymnasium, designed in a modified Tudor style, resembles an old fortress.

The *Old Brick House* (*private*), 120 Fort Hill Rd., was built in 1773 by Hugh McLellan and his sons. The bricks were made near-by; the framework is held together with wooden pegs and hand-wrought nails. Many of the original furnishings have been retained and preserved, including some Hitchcock chairs. Elijah Kellogg mentioned this home in 'Good Old Times.'

On Fort Hill (L) is the *Site of Fort Gorhamtown*, erected in the first half of the 18th century as a defense against Indian attacks; the spot where the fort stood is marked by a large boulder. The hilltop provides a sweeping view of distant mountains.

The *Smith House* (R), on Main St., built in 1765, has been remodeled into a multiple dwelling. It still has the original raised-panel door and beautiful staircase; every room is paneled.

The *Crockett-Jewett-Broad House* (*private*), 129 Main St., built in 1765, is a well-preserved structure with large central chimney, roughly hewn, exposed corner-posts and wide granite entrance steps. The small-paned attic windows have the original glass and the cellar contains a large rain-water cistern.

In Gorham is the junction with State 25 (*see Tour* 19).

SOUTH WINDHAM (alt. 155), 49.1 *m.*, an industrial village, lies in two townships; the business section and most of the residences are in Gorham and the two major factories and the post office are in Windham.

On Depot St. is (R) the *Birthplace of John Albion Andrew* (*private*), Governor (1860–66) of Massachusetts; he was born in 1818.

At 49.7 *m.* is a junction with the River Road.

> 1. Right on this road to the two buildings (R) of the *State Reformatory for Men*, 1 *m.*, established in 1919.
>
> *Horsebeef* or *Mallison Falls*, on the Presumpscot River, in the rear of the reformatory, received the name from an incident that is said to have occurred while the mill and dam were under construction in 1740. Among the food supplied to the workers was a barrel of beef, which the men thought to be of a fine quality until the day the cook produced a pair of horse's hoofs from the bottom of the barrel. The remaining meat was dumped into the river.
>
> At 2.6 *m.* (L), is the *Parson Smith House* (*private*), a two-and-a-half-story structure built in 1764 by the Reverend Peter T. Smith, one of the early settlers. There are two large chimneys providing a fireplace in every room, the one in the kitchen being 10 feet wide.
>
> The Smith House is on the site of Old Province Fort, built so hastily that the first church was partly torn down to supply material for it; settlers lived within the stockade almost constantly between 1744 and 1751, a period in which Indian raids were frequent. After a few years of peace the raids began again; Ezra Brown, Ephraim Winship, four other men, and four boys went out to work in Brown's lot; Brown and Winship, who were at some distance from the others, were fired on and scalped by a band of 20 Indians led by Chief Poland. Four of the party hurried back to the settlement for help and in the fighting that followed Poland was killed.
>
> In *Smith Cemetery* (R) is the *John Anderson Tomb* (1807). Its door resembles that of a bank vault and is fastened by a lock, the combination of which is known by few, if any, now living.
>
> 2. Left on the River Road is NEWHALL (alt. 225, Windham Town), 0.5 *m.* In 1818, two Massachusetts men built a powder mill here by Gambo Falls; they later sold it to George G. Newhall for whom the settlement was named. The Russian government, while engaged in the Crimean War, placed huge orders with this mill.

At 52.3 *m.* (L) is the *Friends Meeting-House* (1849). Quakers began settling in this region in 1774.

WINDHAM CENTER (alt. 250, Windham Town, pop. 2076), 53.1 *m.*, is a small agricultural community.

FOSTER'S CORNER (alt. 210, Windham Town), 54.2 *m.*, is at a junction with US 302 (*see Tour* 18).

GRAY (alt. 310, Gray Town, pop. 1189), 61.5 *m.*, settled in 1762 as New Boston and incorporated in 1778, has a small, compact business and residential section, surrounded by well-kept and prosperous farms on elm-lined highways. Farming and canning have replaced manufacturing as the principal means of livelihood here. A woolen mill, one of the first in the United States, was erected in North Gray about 1770 by Samuel Mayhall.

Pennell Institute (R), on Main St., opened in 1879 and endowed by Henry Pennell, now serves the town as a high school.

In Gray is a junction with State 26 (*see Tour* 14).

At 65.6 *m.* is a junction with a dirt road.

> Right on this road to *Opportunity Farm* (*open to visitors*), 1 *m.*, with 260 acres of land, on a high hill overlooking most of Cumberland County. This home and school for boys between the ages of 8 and 15, was opened in 1912 and is supported by public subscription.

UPPER GLOUCESTER (alt. 340, New Gloucester Town, pop. 1866), 69.6 *m.*, is the center of a township granted to 60 inhabitants of Gloucester, Mass., in 1736. Eight years later Captain Isaac Eveleth came to advance the interests of the proprietors, who were offering £10 to one-year settlers, £20 to two-year settlers, and £30 to three-year settlers. A garrison erected on the high ground in 1753–54 was used by the settlers for the following six years.

AUBURN (alt. 210, pop. 18,571) (*see AUBURN–LEWISTON*), 78 *m.*, is at a junction with State 11 (*see Tour* 13).

At 81.1 *m.* (L) is *Lake Auburn* (*bathing prohibited; fishing and boating permitted*), a clear, sparkling lake fed by springs that is the water supply for the cities of Auburn and Lewiston. To guard this from pollution, the Auburn Water District is steadily taking over adjoining lands. Along the shores are beautiful birch and maple trees, and an occasional pine grove. Lake Grove, on the eastern shore, flourished as a resort in the early 1890's; families came here by horse-car from the near-by cities for Sunday picnics or to attend the open-air theater on week days. Many large fish have been taken from these waters, including landlocked salmon weighing up to 15 pounds. The 12-mile drive around the lake is picturesque and delightful.

TURNER (alt. 290, Turner Town, pop. 1362), 89.2 *m.*

> Right from Turner on a gravel road is TURNER CENTER (alt. 95, Turner Town), 2 *m.*, which was known for many years for its dairy products.
>
> *Leavitt Institute* (R) is a small preparatory school.

At 95.4 *m.* is a junction with State 219.

> 1. Right on State 219 is NORTH TURNER (alt. 280, Turner Town), 0.4 *m.*
>
> At HOWE'S CORNER (alt. 407, Turner Town), 3.6 *m.*, exact directions or a guide should be secured in the general store (R) for the hike to Devil's Den, 5.1 *m.* Dungarees and water-proofed shoes are essential in making this trip, as low, boggy land is crossed en route and the climb up the cave is rough.
>
> The *Devil's Den* is entered by a low aperture not easily discovered. The climber must 'inch' his way (R) and (L) over boulders to climb the cave whose four levels extend deep into a hill around a central passage extending upward 100 feet. When this place was first discovered some years after the town was settled, it was comparatively free of the soil that has since gradually obliterated the outlines of the different rooms. In the lower rooms there is some seepage that forms ice on the stone wall even in summer. The wall of the central staircase formed by great boul-

ders is always damp, while the accumulated soil in the rooms, with the exception of the lowest level, has a meal-like dryness. The central opening emerges onto the flat top of a great ledge from which the Androscoggin River, 2 miles east, is visible.

Legends of Indian occupation of these caves are surprisingly lacking, undoubtedly owing to the fact that the Indians retired from this area before the coming of the settlers.

2. Left on State 219 to *Bear Pond Park* (*open June 1 to Labor Day; boats for hire*) (R), 1.5 *m.*, an amusement resort in a long pine grove on the southern shore of Bear Pond. A casino (*roller skating*), hotel, cottages, and bath-houses are here.

LIVERMORE (alt. 504, Livermore Town, pop. 1113), 98.3 *m.*, is the corporate center of a farming town of several small villages in a fertile belt where orcharding and dairying are carried on.

At 99.3 *m.* is a junction with a wide gravel road.

Right on this road to the *Washburn Homestead* (*private*), 3 *m.*, a large two-and-a-half-story yellow house, built by Israel Washburn, father of seven sons — Israel, Representative from Maine (1851–61), Governor of Maine (1861–62); William D., manufacturer, railroad builder, Representative from Minnesota (1879–85), Senator from Minnesota (1889–95); Samuel, captain of a Union ship during the Civil War; Charles, U.S. Minister to Paraguay, and author of a history of that country; Cadwallader, banker, lumber and flour manufacturer, Representative from Wisconsin (1855–61; 1867–71), major general in the Union Army during the Civil War, Governor of Wisconsin (1872–74); Elihu, Representative from Illinois (1853–69), Secretary of State in Grant's Cabinet, U.S. Minister to France (1869–77); and Algernon, a merchant and banker of note.

LIVERMORE FALLS (alt. 390, Livermore Falls Town, pop. 3148), 106.1 *m.*, is a busy paper-mill settlement and shopping center for the farmers in the environs. A large part of the population is French-Canadian by birth or descent.

The *International Paper Company Plant* (*open to visitors*) produces 540 tons of ground wood every 24 hours.

CHISHOLM (alt. 380, Jay Town), 106.6 *m.*, is a densely populated industrial settlement, with large pulp and paper mills.

JAY (alt. 415, Jay Town, pop. 3106), 108.6 *m.* The business section lies (L) off State 4.

NORTH JAY (alt. 450, Jay Town), 111.8 *m.*, is famed for its white granite, the blocks for Grant's Tomb being among the many large pieces cut here. The *Stone Sheds* and *Quarries* are on the side hill (R).

WILTON (alt. 600, Wilton Town, pop. 3266), 114.6 *m.*, is at the junction with US 2 (*see Tour* 4).

FARMINGTON (alt. 420, Farmington Town, pop. 3600) (*see Tour* 4), 122.7 *m.*, is at the junctions with US 2 (*see Tour* 4) and State 27 (*see Tour* 12).

BACKUS CORNER (Farmington Town), 124.6 *m.*

Right from Backus Corner on a dirt road a short distance to (R) the *Birthplace of Lillian Nordica* (*adm.* 25¢), 0.7 *m.* The one-and-a-half-story cottage contains her collection of operatic scores and autographed pictures, and many personal effects.

Lillian Norton was born in 1859 of music-loving parents; when her musically promising sister, Wilhelmina, died suddenly, Lillian, then 15 years old, went secretly to have her voice tested, hoping to be able to achieve the success her ambi-

Tour 11: From Dover to Quebec

tious mother had anticipated for her older daughter. Though her high voice was light and unusually sweet, she was slow in reaching her goal, owing to both European and American prejudice against American-born musicians; she assumed the name of Giglia Nordica to disguise her nativity. Her early training was received in Boston; later, she studied under Sangiovanni, in Milan. She had a varied matrimonial career, the first marriage ending dramatically, after divorce papers had been filed, with the disappearance of her husband, an inventor, who had sailed off in a balloon. She died in Java in 1914 as the result of exposure suffered after a shipwreck off Thursday Island.

At 125.2 *m.* is a junction with State 27 (*see Tour* 12).

At 132.6 *m.* (R) is the *Birthplace of Elizabeth Akers Allen* (*private*), identifiable by a Victorian summer house. In this gazebo Mrs. Allen (1832–1911), newspaper woman and author, did much writing in her later years. She was thrice married, her second husband being Benjamin Paul Akers, a sculptor.

STRONG (alt. 505, Strong Town, pop. 877), 133.6 *m.*, the business center of this village lies (R) off State 4.

Maine's Republican party was founded in this town on Aug. 7, 1854, with temperance and opposition to slavery as the two specific planks in its platform.

At 138.5 *m.* (L) is *Mount Blue* (alt. 3187).

PHILLIPS (alt. 550, Phillips Town, pop. 1143), 140.8 *m.*, on picturesque Sandy River, is a large village surrounded by wooded hills. This area was virgin forest until lumber interests bought the timber. As the trees were cut and the lumbermen gradually moved northward leaving behind a stump-covered area, settlers came in who cleared the land and farmed it. The village, the cultural and commercial center of the sparsely settled country to the north, manufactures wood novelties. In the hills throughout the township are silica deposits.

MADRID (alt. 845, Madrid Town, pop. 207), 147.7 *m.*, is a small village on the fast-flowing western branch of Sandy River.

> Right from the village center in Chandler Mill stream is lovely *Small's Falls*, while a few hundred feet away in Sandy River, just before its junction with the Mill stream, is another series of cataracts.

At 153.5 *m.* is a junction with a local road.

> Right on this road, and then on a trail to *Saddleback Lookout Station*, 4 *m.* (*see Sports and Recreation: Hiking and Mountain Climbing*).

RANGELEY (alt. 1545, Rangeley Town, pop. 1472), 162.9 *m.*, is a trading center in the widely known Rangeley hunting and fishing area. It has seven hotels and numerous lodges and camps (*registered guides available for hunting and fishing*); steamboat service (*variable schedule, apply at wharf*) to points on Rangeley Lake (*seaplane base*). The three golf courses in the environs are 2000 feet above sea level.

Rangeley, within sight of beautiful Rangeley Lake, lies deep in the heart of a forest region that reaches across the Canadian border. Within a radius of 10 miles, 40 sparkling trout- and salmon-filled lakes and ponds lie between rugged evergreen-clad hills and mountains. This wilderness is the natural habitat of big game and many other kinds of wild life.

Rangeley Township, the village, the broad lake, and even the adjacent countryside, the Rangeley Region, received their name from Squire Rangeley, an Englishman from Yorkshire. Soon after his arrival here in 1825, he began the establishment of a great estate patterned after those of his homeland. He asked no price for his land, giving extensively of his acres to new settlers. He built a sawmill and a gristmill and constructed a ten-mile stretch of road through the wilderness to connect the settlement (and its great product, lumber) with the outside world. While developing his holdings, he made his home at Portland, where he had built a mansion on State Street, the city's 'Gold Coast' (*see PORTLAND*). For reasons now unknown, the Rangeley family did not remain in Maine, but took up residence in Virginia, where the Squire is said to have held vast acreage in what is now Henry County.

DALLAS (Dallas Plantation, pop. 211), 163.9 *m.* The highway is crossed by an old narrow-gauge railroad, no longer in use. Only a few years ago there was a network of these roads through the southern part of the State; trains hauled by miniature locomotives stopped at every cowpath. In this region in addition to the passenger service there was a heavy freight business, the small locomotive being able to pull 100 cars of lumber.

Green's Farm (Coplin Plantation) is right, 176.3 *m.*; on it is a massive two-story house with cupola, built about 1875. For a quarter of a century, Green's Farm and Maine hunting and fishing were synonymous to hundreds of out-of-State sportsmen, there being few lodges catering to this type of visitor.

At STRATTON (alt. 1170, Eustis Town), 181.5 *m.*, is a junction with State 27 (*see Tour* 12).

At 182.5 *m.* the road enters the southern end of the tract known as *Cathedral Pines*, a beautiful stand of tall Norway pines covering several square miles on both sides of the road. The northern end of the grove was the *Site of One of Benedict Arnold's Camps*, during his ill-fated expedition to Quebec in 1775.

The expedition led by Arnold was a quixotic project of the early days of the Revolutionary War. A few of the Colonial leaders believed that the French of Quebec, who had been under English rule since 1763, would be eager to join the revolt against the Crown; it was decided that Arnold should take 1100 men up through Maine and meet a force of equal size led by General Richard Montgomery, who would go north by way of Lake Champlain. Arnold and his men, who were poorly equipped and hastily assembled with little training, left Cambridge on September 13, 1775, and six days later had entered the Kennebec, Arnold planning to follow a route that had been explored and reported on by English officials. Progress up the river was slow, because of the time required to construct the boats necessary for the shallower waters, and the autumn rains had begun; many of the men became ill and had to be left behind. On October

TOUR 11: From Dover to Quebec   347

19, the diminishing band finally reached Eustis. From there they went up the northern branch of Dead River; on the 23d they lost several scowloads of provisions, which sank in the river. The weather increased in severity and many of the undisciplined Revolutionary heroes decided that they would go no farther. Arnold crossed the present international boundary line on October 25, and after the stragglers caught up with him, went down the Chaudière River. When Montgomery and Arnold met near Quebec, the former had 500 men left, the latter 510. The attack took place during a December snowstorm, and, though the troops entered the town, they were driven out with heavy losses; Montgomery was killed and Arnold was wounded.

At 184 *m.* is a junction with a dirt road.

> Left on this road to EUSTIS RIDGE (alt. 1460), 2 *m.*, from which there is a splendid view of the mountains, including Sugar Loaf (alt. 4237).

At 184.6 *m.* is a junction with State 149, a dirt road.

> Right on State 149 is FLAGSTAFF (alt. 1115, Flagstaff Plantation, pop. 179), 6 *m.* Lumbermen's homes occupy the cleared area of the high northern bank of Dead River. A tablet opposite the post office marks the *Site of one of Benedict Arnold's Camps* during his march through Maine. On arrival here, a party of men was sent to the summit of Mt. Bigelow to view the country beyond through which they were to pass. They erected a flag, and from this incident the town of Flagstaff received its name. Arnold found the cabin of Natanis, sometimes spelled Satanis, an Indian, on the site of the present village.
>
> DEAD RIVER (Dead River Plantation, pop. 82), 12.4 *m.* Near this point Arnold's expedition reached Dead River after making a portage from the Kennebec River.

EUSTIS (alt. 1185, Eustis Town, pop. 601), 186.3 *m.*, in a heavily wooded area, is a frontier village.

At 190.9 *m.* (R) is *Alder Stream Camp Site (public)*, near which, on Alder Stream, Arnold lost supplies (*see above*).

At 195.7 *m.* (R) is *Sarampas Falls Camp Site (public)*, the most northerly of a series of State Forestry camp sites in the area, which lies in a birch grove near a pebbly beach on Sarampas Stream; the camp is about 200 yards above the small falls mentioned by Arnold in his letters.

The route now crosses the southern boundary of CHAIN OF PONDS TOWNSHIP. Silvery birch and glossy green maple stand out among the dense evergreens here, and occasional ponds, traversed by Arnold, gleam through the silent darkly-green wilderness.

At 196.7 *m.* (L), on the side of Bag Pond Mountain, are what appear to be dumped carloads of bituminous coal, but are in reality deposits of broken slate.

At 197.2 *m.* is a watershed ridge (alt. 1360) where the road widens through a beautiful growth of white birch. The highway now cuts into the ledge (R) of *Mt. Pisgah* and *Mt. Sisk*, for about 5 miles, limiting the outlook to forest and rough ledge, with an occasional magnificent view (L) across deep gorges to the lovely *Chain of Lakes* shimmering against the wild rugged background of *Round, Snow, Indian Stream,* and *Bag Pond Mountains.*

At 206.5 *m.* is visible, to the rear and through the highway aisle, towering *Mt. Pisgah* (alt. 3325).

MOOSEHORN (alt. 1400, Unorganized Township of Coburn Gore, pop. 50), 217.9 *m.*, an apparent extension of Arnold Pond, is a new modern lumber-mill settlement replacing a settlement destroyed by fire in May, 1936. About 20 unpainted houses are grouped about the *Mill* (L), near the fragrant piles of freshly sawed lumber that lie drying in the sun.

At ARNOLD POND, 218 *m.*, State 4 crosses the Canadian Boundary, 137 miles south of Quebec. Arnold Pond, a sub-station of the Holeb-Jackman port of entry, is on the boundary, which follows the watershed of a low range of mountains whose green-mantled slopes stretch out for mile upon mile in either direction, the only visible gap being directly west. It was at Arnold Pond that Arnold's expedition is believed to have crossed the height of land. The *Customs and Immigration Station* (L) was erected in 1931.

TOUR 11A: *From* RANGELEY *to* HAINES LANDING, 9 *m.*, State 16.

Tar-surfaced roadbed, soft shoulders.

THIS route skirts four of the six Rangeley Lakes — 13-mile Mooselookmeguntic, 7-mile Rangeley (Oquossoc), Molechunkamunk, and Cupsuptic. The Rangeley region, with its beautiful lakes and streams full of trout and salmon, and its forested mountains and valleys rich in game, is a semi-wilderness of a kind very attractive to many sportsmen and difficult to match in the eastern part of the United States. Hunters and fishermen who come to this area need not live any more primitively than they care to, and can vary their days with golf, water sports, climbing, and other outdoor and indoor recreations.

Because the region is an important natural resource in a State deriving an increasing part of its income from visitors, the State is developing and protecting it. Fish hatcheries have been established at Oquossoc and other points for the breeding of salmon and trout, which are released annually to replenish the supply depleted by sportsmen. The Rangeley Game Preserve covers unorganized townships 5, Range 5, and 4, Range 6, and the southern half of 3, Range 5; to the northeast is the Bigelow Preserve.

At 0 *m.* State 16 branches west from State 4 at Rangeley (*see Tour* 11).
At 0.5 *m.* is the junction with an improved road.

> Right on this road, 4.5 *m.*, is a resort called LOG VILLAGE, established in 1889, the buildings of which are constructed of logs in a style suitable to the region.

Tour 12: From Wiscasset to Stratton

At 2.5 *m.* is a junction with a bituminous-topped road.

> Left on this road 0.7 *m.* to the *Rangeley Lakes Country Club* (*open to public*), with an 18-hole golf course, which has mountain and lake views in all sections; the lake breezes and the altitude (about 1600) make it a particularly popular course in summer.
>
> Near-by is a *Riding Academy* where mounts may be hired for following the many miles of lakeside and mountain trails that wind through groves of birch and pine.

At 7 *m.* is a junction with a dirt road.

> Right on this road, which soon becomes a tote road wandering along the northern shore of the Lakes and eventually enters New Hampshire. This road can be followed by car in mid-summer though the riding is rough; the opportunities for fishing compensate for this inconvenience.

OQUOSSOC (alt. 1510, Rangeley Town), 7.7 *m.*, is passed on the Rangeley Lakes Canoe Trip (*see Sports and Recreation*). This is the headquarters of the dog-sled postal service maintained in winter when many of the roads of the region are impassable for automobiles. Three times a week the team of Baffin Land huskies mushes through the woods carrying mail to Kennebago and Grant's. Although only 100 people are served, the average weight of the cargo is 400 to 500 pounds because of the merchandise sent in by parcel post.

HAINES LANDING (alt. 1490, Rangeley Town), 9 *m.*, has steamboat service (*inquire at wharf for schedule*) with other settlements on the lake. The village has a hotel that is surrounded by private camps and summer homes designed to fit the setting; it also has a general store and a store specializing in sport goods. The hotel and estate grounds have been landscaped with native shrubs and trees.

The paved motor road ends here, but rough roads and trails branch off along the heavily wooded shores of Lake Mooselookmeguntic.

TOUR 12: *From* WISCASSET *to* STRATTON, 117.8 *m.*, State 27.

Via Pittston, Randolph, Gardiner, Augusta, Belgrade, Kingfield, and Bigelow. Two-lane hard-surfaced roadbed.

BETWEEN Wiscasset and the Kennebec River, State 27 traverses a gradually rising terrain, then crosses the Kennebec and runs along the western bank; at Augusta it swings northwest past the Belgrade Lake chain, and runs through the valley of the Carrabassett River. There are many opportunities for canoeing, climbing, hunting, and fishing along this route.

WISCASSET (alt. 50, Wiscasset Town, pop. 1186) (*see Tour* 1, *sec. b*), 0 *m.*, is at the junction with US 1 (*see Tour* 1, *sec. b*).

DRESDEN MILLS (alt. 70, Dresden Town, pop. 629), 8.5 *m.*, is a small elm-shaded settlement on the southern bank of Eastern River.

At 10.6 *m.* is a junction with State 128.

> Left on this road to *Pownalborough Courthouse*, 2.8 *m.* (R), a large three-story white building built in 1761 as the seat of government for Lincoln County, which had been incorporated in the previous year. It stands within the limits of the former parade grounds of Fort Shirley, built in 1754 and first called Fort Frankfort. The court room is on the second floor; the lower floor has always been used as a dwelling. In Revolutionary days the records of the court were swollen by 'Tory trials' and proceedings involving the care and disposition of confiscated estates of absentee Loyalists.

At 16.2 *m.* is (L) the well-preserved *Major Reuben Colburn House*, built in 1765 by four Colburn brothers who came with their four sisters from Dunstable, Mass., in 1761. The plain structure, now painted white with green shutters, contains many of the original furnishings, including a brass-studded cradle, in which the children of the family were rocked.

Colonel Benedict Arnold (*see Tour* 11), and his officers were entertained by Major Colburn, September 21–23, 1775, in this home, while the soldiers built their own shelters on the grounds during the transfer of the army of 1100 men to 220 batteau built by Major Colburn for the expedition to Quebec.

The *Money Holes*, 16.6 *m.* (R), are the result of the usual legend of vast treasure buried by Captain Kidd. Thousands of tons of earth have been turned over, leaving several holes, one 80 feet deep, though not a single coin or jewel has ever been uncovered.

PITTSTON (alt. 55, Pittston Town, pop. 893), 17.1 *m.*, is a scattered group of houses on both sides of the road. In 1676 the first settler in the town, Alexander Brown, was killed by Indians. Dr. Sylvester Gardiner (*see Tour* 10), resident proprietor and manager of the Kennebec Purchase, lived here and was visited by Benedict Arnold.

From 1848 to 1900 enormous ice houses here were filled each winter and during the 'ice-boom' (1870–95) 15 to 20 vessels were often seen at one time loading ice for delivery to the cities farther south.

RANDOLPH (alt. 175, Randolph Town, pop. 1377), 19.1 *m.*, is a compact settlement on the eastern bank of the Kennebec. The town is a residential district for many persons employed in Gardiner's factories.

GARDINER (alt. 90, pop. 5609) (*see Tour* 10), 19.3 *m.*

Between Gardiner and Augusta State 27 and US 201 are one route (*see Tour* 10).

AUGUSTA (alt. 120, pop. 17,198) (*see AUGUSTA*), 25.7 *m.*, is at a junction of US 201 (*see Tour* 10), State 9 and State 11 (*see Tour* 13), and State 17 (*see Tour* 17).

At 31.1 *m.* (R) is a *Rifle Range,* used occasionally for target practice with light ordnance. Extending north for 3 miles is *Sidney Bog,* beyond which

Tour 12: From Wiscasset to Stratton 351

is a mile or two of wild land. Although the Bog has an abundant blueberry crop, it is left untouched because of the presence of 'duds' — unexploded shells from the rifle range — that lie hidden in the moss.

BELGRADE (alt. 255, Belgrade Town, pop. 978), 37.7 *m.*, is the small commercial center of a lake region. On the southwestern outskirts of the settlement is the *Minot House*, birthplace in 1872 of John Clair Minot, author and the literary editor of the Boston *Herald* since 1919.

BELGRADE LAKES (alt. 260, Belgrade Town), 44.8 *m.*, is a lake resort settlement on the eastern shore of *Long Pond*, a glistening sheet of water between beautifully wooded shores along which are scattered fine cottages and summer hotels.

The six large lakes of the Belgrade chain, connected by streams, provide opportunities for excellent fishing as well as for easy canoe trips suitable for the amateur canoeist and arduous journeys with 20-foot canoes for the paddle-hardened. In the waters of these lakes are landlocked salmon, lake trout, black bass, pickerel, and white perch, all gamey fish, valued by the visitors who throng this area during the fishing season.

ROME (alt. 530, Rome Town, pop. 398), 48.3 *m.*, a 'four corners,' is in the most rugged and least settled section of the Belgrade Lakes area, a heavily wooded and hilly country with several lakes. As the first green buds appear on damp brown branches in the spring, the woods here become alive with the songs of birds; scarlet-breasted robins and bluebirds usher in the spring days, and as the grasses grow higher, the humming of the locust and chirping of crickets blend with the soft calls of the Peabody bird, the meadow lark, and the chickadee. Later the raucous cries of blue jays and kingfishers echo over the surfaces of the lakes, whose tranquillity is occasionally broken by the splash of fish jumping for flies. As summer shadows lengthen and grow black near the marshlands, a chorus of frogs is heard, punctuated by the notes of whippoorwills and the laughs of loons.

Winter, in this region, has its own charms; the soft thud of snow falling from over-burdened pines, the deep, long-drawn-out boom made as the lakes finally freeze, and the faint vibration of 'northern lights' streaming to the zenith on clear cold nights, like a bright rainbow over a white world.

At 55.9 *m.* is a junction with US 2 (*see Tour* 4). Between this point and Farmington, State 27 and US 2 are one route (*see Tour* 4); also between Farmington and 70.1 *m.*, State 27 and State 4 are one route (*see Tour* 11).

NEW VINEYARD (alt. 610, New Vineyard Town, pop. 447), 78.9 *m.*, has an active sawmill and a woodworking mill.

In the northwestern section of this township are 4 ponds in lowlands surrounded by heavily wooded hills. Numerous small streams (*good fishing*) cut through the hillsides, and the few roads traversing the area are closely shut in by the luxuriant foliage of towering trees whose bases are buried deep in masses of tall, lacy ferns.

This is one of the Franklin County towns to which many of the early settlers came from the Kennebec River Valley. Going from the Massachusetts Bay Colony, or directly from England, to the Kennebec River Valley, their means were sufficient for proving their claims under the requirements of the Kennebec Purchase. After fulfilling the legal requirements there, they found themselves faced with a sizable levy, one of the impositions of lawless land agents; this they were unable to meet, and it forced them to push on to the Sandy River Valley.

NEW PORTLAND (alt. 507, New Portland Town, pop. 818), 85.5 *m.*, is the center of a township given to the people of Falmouth, now Portland (*see PORTLAND*), by the General Court of Massachusetts to indemnify them, in part, for their loss through the destruction of that town by the British fleet in 1775.

KINGFIELD (alt. 565, Kingfield Town, pop. 1024), 92 *m.*, with its cement bridges, wide streets, and modern stores and offices, a distinct surprise in this great woods area, is on a narrow intervale in the valley of the Carrabassett River. The Carrabassett, rapid at this point, created water-power for several mills when lumbering was an important industry here.

A heavily wooded grade rises sharply beside the river (R) north of Kingfield.

A boulder, opposite the Universalist Church, marks the *Site of the Residence of Governor William King*, who was the proprietor of this region, and Maine's first Governor.

Holiness Church, with headquarters in Kingfield, is a sect of militant conservatives, the older members of which belonged to various denominations and combined to preserve the old forms of worship. Their creed is evangelical and they interpret the Bible literally. The annual Holiness Camp Meeting is held in the neighboring town of Salem during the last week of August.

CARRABASSETT (alt. 842, Unorganized Township of Jerusalem, pop. 185), 102.3 *m.*, a small settlement on the edge of an unusually wide bottom-land by the Carrabassett River, is surrounded by deep forests. Several log houses have been built here because of the good protection they give against the severe cold that settles over the region in early fall.

At 109.2 *m.* is the entrance to a foot trail.

> Left on this trail, over rocky terrain in a forested country, to *Sugarloaf Mountain* (alt. 4237), about 4 *m.* and *Crocker Mountain* (alt. 4168), about 5 *m.* These two peaks are in the *Bigelow Game Preserve* (*no hunting allowed*), a vast wooded area taking in parts of Bigelow and Dead River Plantations, as well as parts of Township 4, Range 3, Crockertown, and Jerusalem. Here the big game, game birds, and smaller animals native to Maine roam unmolested by man.

BIGELOW (alt. 1305, Unorganized Township of Crockertown, pop. 10), 109.5 *m.*, formerly Bigelow Station, was a terminus of the Sandy River and Rangeley Lakes (narrow gauge) R.R. Except during midwinter lumbering operations, when the resounding chop of axes, the shouts of lumberjacks, and the aroma of bacon and beans fill the air, this settlement of a dozen log houses is a tiny ghost town.

At 116.7 *m.* is an entrance to a foot trail.

> Left on this trail, through hilly country, to *Hedgehog Hill* (alt. 2087), 1.7 *m.*, an irregular tree-clad eminence in a hunting region frequented by residents of central Maine.

STRATTON (alt. 1170, Eustis Town, pop. 601), 117.8 *m.* On the northwestern edge of the settlement is the junction with State 4 (*see Tour* 11).

T O U R   1 3 :   *From* HAMPDEN *to* NAPLES, 123 *m.*, US 202 (State 9, State 3) and State 11.

Via Augusta, Winthrop, Lewiston, Auburn and Mechanic Falls.

Two-lane macadamized and cement roadbed.

THIS inland route runs for the most part through thinly settled farmlands. In summer, cottage colonies are seen around the lakes passed at intervals.

HAMPDEN (alt. 80, Hampden Town, pop. 2417) (*see Tour* 1, *sec. c*), 0 *m.*, is at a junction with US 1 (*see Tour* 1, *sec. c*).

HAMPDEN CENTER (alt. 234, Hampden Town), 2.2 *m.*

WEST HAMPDEN (alt. 168, Hampden Town), 4.9 *m.*

NEWBURGH CENTER (alt. 256, Newburgh Town, pop. 551), 9 *m.*

At 13.2 *m.* the highway crosses a southern extension of *Pickard Mountain* (alt. 1221), locally known as Peaked Mountain because of its cone-like shape. The timber having been cut from its slopes, it is now a barren landmark visible over a wide area.

At 15.3 *m.* is a view (R) of a long range known as the *Dixmont Hills*. Near-by (L) is *Mount Harris* (alt. 1233), its timber-stripped slopes suitable only for the grazing of sheep.

DIXMONT (alt. 543, Dixmont Town, pop. 538), 16.3 *m.*, is at the junction with State 7.

> Left 2.7 *m.* on State 7 to the crest of *The Cliff* (alt. 980), on Mt. Harris. This precipice drops sheerly (R), and from a small parking space (L) is a view over an attractive valley below to the distant Camden Hills.
>
> At 6.7 *m.* the highway crosses *Great Farm Brook*, meandering across the Great Farm which lies on both sides of the road at this point.
>
> From *Thorndike Hill* (alt. 740), 7.9 *m.*, is a comprehensive *View of the Great Farm*, its original 1200 acres, now subdivided into 200-acre farms, extending across a narrow valley between the hills. Israel Thorndike (1755–1832), a wealthy Boston merchant, came into possession of the tract in 1806. He cleared the land, built a mansion of the Bulfinch type and created a beautiful country estate with

broad-lawns and large barns. He stocked the farm with imported Hereford cattle and merino sheep, and set out an orchard of 500 apple trees. Daniel Webster was one of the many distinguished guests who came from Boston by coach-and-four for the hunting and fishing at Mr. Thorndike's country place. One barn is all that remains of the original buildings, the others having been destroyed by fire.

TROY (alt. 474, Troy Town, pop. 651), 20.5 *m.*, is in a township purchased about 1800 by General Bridge of Chelmsford, Mass. for its timber. Pine was cut, sent down the Sebasticook and Kennebec Rivers and sold in Gardiner, at a time when 1000 feet of lumber could be sawed for one dollar. After the land was cleared, Indian corn, wheat, oats, and barley were raised on it, and several gristmills were operated on the ponds and streams.

UNITY (alt. 231, Unity Town, pop. 892), 27.1 *m.*, on the Belfast and Moosehead Lake R.R., is a small but active commercial center in this large, sparsely settled area. Before the establishment of trading centers such as this, the populace was dependent upon itinerant peddlers who during the last half of the 19th century walked about the country carrying packs of tinware, cotton goods, stationery, pictures, and dishes, as well as the latest news.

Frederic Hale Parkhurst (1864–1921), a native of Unity, arose from a sick bed for his inauguration as Governor of Maine and died 18 days later.

ALBION (alt. 305, Albion Town, pop. 923), 35.3 *m.*, is a settlement of well-built homes on a narrow fertile level plateau in a township notable for little hills and ravines of unusual shapes, believed to have been carved by receding glaciers.

East of Albion Corner, the old trees shading both sides of the road are known as the *Rum and Water Elms* because of an incident that occurred during the temperance agitation of 1845. Members of the village Washingtonian Society, a temperance group, and the anti-prohibitionists agreed to plant rows of elm trees on opposite sides of the road; the group whose elms made the finer showing was to be considered the one favored by Providence. The Washingtonians selected the south side of the street and the anti-prohibitionists planted along the north side. The 'rum elms' grew larger and today give broader shade than do the 'water elms.'

At 36.6 *m.* (R) is *Lovejoy Pond*, a small body of water with groves of silvery birch along its shores.

At 38.6 *m.* is the junction with a dirt road known as the Pond Road.

> Right on the Pond Road to the *Site of the Lovejoy Homestead*, 1.4 *m.* on the southern shore of Lovejoy Pond. Here was born Elijah Parish Lovejoy (1802–37), anti-slavery leader, and pioneer in defense of freedom of the press. Graduating with honors from Colby College (*see WATERVILLE*), he went to St. Louis, Mo., where he became interested in the ministry, and in freedom for the slaves. After attending Princeton Theological Seminary in New Jersey, he returned to St. Louis to preach and continue his fight against slavery. In 1833 he began to edit a religious paper called the *St. Louis Observer*, in which his anti-slavery views found expression. In Missouri, a slave State, his articles met with opposition, but this did not lessen his determination to gain freedom for the slaves. The opposition became so strong that he was forced to move across the river to Alton, Ill., to continue his work. Mobs attacked him and on several occasions his presses were destroyed, but he

Tour 13: From Hampden to Naples

procured new ones and demanded protection, as an American citizen, to carry on his work. While defending his press against a mob he was killed.

On a 93-foot granite shaft topped with a bronze statue of Victory, erected to his memory in Alton, Ill., are these words: 'As long as I am an American citizen, and as long as American blood runs in these veins, I shall hold myself at liberty to speak, to write, and to publish whatever I please on any subject, being amenable to the laws of my country for the same.'

CHINA (alt. 222, China Town, pop. 1164), 40.6 *m.*, is a well-shaded little village of old homes at the northern end of China Lake.

In 1818, when the town was incorporated and the name changed from Harlem to China — for a favorite old hymn — there was much controversy over boundaries. The postmaster, J. C. Washburn wrote: 'My house was in Winslow, my store across the road in Albion, and my potash works 40 rods S. were in Harlem.'

Between China and South China the road winds along the eastern shore of *China Lake*, 8 miles in length. The clear blue water of the lake, well below the level of the highway, lies in a long hollow between the hills. All along this attractive section of the route are farm houses and summer homes.

At 44.3 *m.* (L) is the old *Friends' Meeting-House*. Although the once active congregation is now widely scattered, Friends still gather together here at least once a year, the men on one side of the room and the women on the other, each person communing in silence with the Spirit and, if moved, rising to pray or address his brothers and sisters.

The *Summer Home of Rufus M. Jones*, 46.3 *m.* (R), Quaker minister and long a president of Haverford College, is on a hill sloping to the shore of China Lake, and commanding one of its finest views. The large pines that border the farm are 125 years old, and were planted by his ancestors. From the hill are seen Vassalboro and China Lakes with their small islands and to the west, the distant Kennebago Mountains. Rufus Jones, a descendant of Quaker missionaries, is the author of more than 40 books on ethics and on Quaker history.

SOUTH CHINA (alt. 209, China Town), 48.3 *m.*, is a small resort village at the southern end of China Lake. It has a public library that has been in existence 106 years.

At South China is a junction with State 3 (*see Tour* 16).

> Left from South China on State 32 to the *Site of the Birthplace of Leroy S. Starrett* (1836–1922), 1.3 *m.*, (L), inventor-manufacturer, who secured patents in 1865 for a meat chopper, a washing machine, and a butter worker. After three years of selling these, which were manufactured for him by the Athol Machine Co., he purchased controlling interest in the company and during the next 10 years as superintendent, invented a number of hand tools such as certain types of calipers, gauges, levels, and other precision instruments.

AUGUSTA (alt. 120, pop. 17,198) (*see AUGUSTA*), 59.8 *m.*, is at the junction of US 201 (*see Tour* 10), State 27 (*see Tour* 12), and State 17 (*see Tour* 17).

MANCHESTER (alt. 205, Manchester Town, pop. 492), 65 *m.* The two large old structures (R), somewhat remodeled, were inns from 1800 to

1850. Before the advent of the railroad, Hallowell, 4 miles east, was a busy river port and commercial center. The settlers of Winthrop, Readfield, and even those of Sandy River valley drove or rode horseback to Manchester, then known as The Forks, putting up in one of these inns at night. Early the next morning they would go on to Hallowell for trading, spending a large part of the day hauling their purchases up the two mile-long hills on their return journey. Stopping their second night at The Forks, they were ready for an early morning start over more level roads to their homes.

Right from Manchester on State 17 is *Monk's Hill Cemetery*, 2.6 *m.* (R), overlooking Lake Cobbosseecontee; here are buried the early Baptists of this section of the town of Readfield. In the cemetery is a monument to 'Elder Isaac Case, born in Rehoboth, Mass., Feb. 25, 1761, was ordained a Baptist preacher in 1783; came to Maine and gathered the first church in Thomaston, 1784, and was its pastor 8 years; came to Readfield 1792, gathered a church and officiated as its pastor till 1800. Died Nov. 3, 1852.'

Carlton Pond, 3.4 *m.* (L), less than 2 miles long and 0.5 mile wide, and almost hidden by hardwood and pine growth, is the source of water supply of the City of Augusta.

The *Methodist Meeting-House*, 4.3 *m.* (R), a plain white church with spire, overlooking Lake Maranacook, was the first Methodist meeting-house in Maine; it was dedicated in 1795 by the handsome and courtly Methodist clergyman, Jesse Lee (1758–1816), who traveled about on horseback. Lee, known as the 'apostle of Methodism' was born in Virginia, and from 1809–15 was Chaplain of Congress. The New England Conference of Methodists, with an attendance of 1500, was held in this sparsely settled community August 29, 1798.

Lake Maranacook, 7.7 *m.* (L), 7 miles long, with a heavily wooded shoreline, provides beautiful scenery as well as fishing and boating.

READFIELD (alt. 260, Readfield Town, pop. 881), 9.8 *m.*, a hill-top settlement, is the birthplace of two Maine governors, Jonathan G. Hunton (1781–1851) and Dr. John Hubbard (1794–1869). Governor Hubbard (*see Tour* 10) was known as the Father of Prohibition, having in 1851 signed Maine's first law prohibiting the sale and manufacture of intoxicating liquors in any part of the State.

The Kennebec Agricultural Society, formed here in 1787, was active for 30 years. In 1819 the society compiled statistics concerning the production of cider, the first recorded compilation of agricultural statistics in the State. Since 1856 its fair, known as Kennebec County Fair, has been held here annually.

KENT'S HILL (alt. 545, Readfield Town), 12.6 *m.*, overlooks Torsey Pond and the hills of Mount Vernon.

The *Maine Wesleyan Seminary* (L), commonly called Kent's Hill, overlooking a number of lakes in the surrounding valley is a co-educational preparatory school, founded in 1824 and fostered and largely supported by the Methodist Episcopal Church. As early as 1832 women were attending the seminary; in 1859 an act of Legislature authorized establishment of 'a female collegiate Institute.'

Right from Kent's Hill on State 134 is MOUNT VERNON (alt. 335, Mount Vernon Town, pop. 755), 20.1*m.*, a lovely spot lying among hills and near lakes. Near the village is the *Elizabeth Marbury House*, now a rest home for working women. Elizabeth Marbury (1856–1933), a play-broker, was long active in social, theatrical, and charitable affairs. After the World War she was decorated by the Belgian, French, and Italian Governments for her services during the conflict. In 1925 she bought the Higgins-Slocum farm of 68 acres and remodeled the house, furnishing it in old New England style. Her will dedicated the farm to its present use.

Not far from Marbury House is *Maine Chance (visited only by special permission)*, the property of Elizabeth Arden, the owner of beauty parlors and the manu-

TOUR 13: From Hampden to Naples 357

facturer of cosmetics. She has developed a resort open each summer to women who can afford to pay for an intensive course of physical training and treatment; the place is luxurious, with gay cabanas on the shore of a lake, with fencing and riding teachers, beautiful flower gardens, and various recreational facilities. Fresh vegetables are raised on the adjoining farm.

At 65.7 *m.* (L) are the grounds of the *Augusta Country Club*, with a clubhouse, tennis courts and an 18-hole golf course (*greens fee* $1, $1.50, $2); the latter lies on both sides of the road.

At 66.4 *m.* (L) is the entrance to *Island Park* on Cobbosseecontee Lake (*launch trips around the lake* 25¢: *swimming and boating facilities*). The park was developed 30 years ago as a trolley resort with hotel, outdoor theater, dance pavilion, and picnic grounds in a pine grove at the water's edge. Today there are many summer homes on the island.

Lake Cobbosseecontee (Ind.: 'place of abundant sturgeon'), is a popular summer and winter playground (*see Sports and Recreation*). The Winthrop Regatta is held here annually in August. Among other islands in the lake is *Lady's Delight*, about 1 mile from shore, where a small lighthouse (1908) is kept lighted in summer. The lake is a base for the State Forestry and privately owned seaplanes.

At 68.4 *m.* is a junction with an unmarked road.

> Left on this road is BAILEYVILLE (alt. 260, Winthrop Town), 1.2 *m.*, a settlement made by members of the Society of Friends in 1780.
>
> Ezekiel Bailey, a Quaker, began the manufacture of oilcloth by hand here about 1830. The business expanded into several factories and flourished until 1921 when the oil-soaked buildings burned.
>
> The Baileys were active members of the Society of Friends, contributing much to the Quaker churches and schools in the State, notably Oak Grove Seminary (*see Tour* 10). Regular services are still held in the *Meeting-House* (R).
>
> At 2 *m.* (L), in a pine grove on the hilly shore of Lake Cobbosseecontee, is a *Young Men's Christian Association Camp*. Six lodges are maintained under the auspices of the State organization for boys from 8 to 18 years of age. A leadership conference held here annually in the last week in June is an institution that originated in Maine and has been duplicated in other States.

WINTHROP (alt. 200, Winthrop Town, pop. 2234), 71 *m.*, is a compact, thriving settlement on low land between Lake Maranacook (N) and Lake Annabessacook (S). The town, first settled in 1765, was called Pondtown Plantation, probably because of the numerous bodies of water in the area; many lilies grow on the smaller lakes.

Shoes made by hand in Winthrop between 1800 and 1850 were sent as far south as New Orleans, and were also much in demand in 1849-50 among the men starting toward the California gold fields. Daniel Noyes Carr of Newburyport, Mass., came to Winthrop about 1809 and in 1820 opened one of the first temperance hotels in the State.

Oilcloth and woolen mills employ the year-round residents of this community, which is in summer a trading center for cottagers and campers living near the lakes.

At the *Bonafide Mills* (*permit at office*) (L), near the railroad tracks, more than 2 million square yards of felt-base oilcloth are made annually.

Right from Winthrop on State 133 at 6.5 *m.* in WAYNE (alt. 300, Wayne Town, pop. 464), is (L) the *Birthplace of Annie Louise Cary* (1842-1921), opera star, who lived here until her eighth year. Her voice developed a range running from low F to B above the staff and its purity was notable.

Left sharply at the Cary house on a dirt road to *Morrison Heights* (alt. 680), 8.3 *m.*, a picnic ground with a spectacular view over the surrounding countryside. An expanse of ledge on the hilltop furnishes numerous natural fire-places. Although the elevation of this conical hill is only about half that of several of the Kennebec County hills, the width of the surrounding valley makes possible a panorama. Androscoggin Lake stands out among the numerous bodies of water dotting the landscape. The trees in this area — birch, maple, sumac, and evergreen — are particularly beautiful in autumn.

At 77 *m.* is a junction with a tarred road.

Left on this road to *Monmouth Academy*, 0.1 *m.* (R), a large brick building housing a preparatory school founded in 1803.

MONMOUTH (alt. 285, Monmouth Town, pop. 1344), 1 *m.*, in the center of the Kennebec County apple belt, is a residential and commercial settlement on the eastern shore of Cochnewagan Pond.

The *Town Hall* (L), known as Cumston Hall, an ornate cream and white building with minarets and other Turkish architectural features, was designed by Harry Cochrane (1860–   ), a local muralist and writer. Mr. Cochrane has decorated many churches and public buildings throughout the State, and written 'The First Crusade,' a cantata, and 'History of Monmouth and Wales.'

Lorettus Sutton Metcalf (1837-1920), managing editor of the *North American Review* and founder and editor of *Forum*, and Benjamin Shaw, inventor of a machine for knitting hosiery, were natives of Monmouth.

Cochnewagan Pond (Ind.: 'the place of praying Indians,' or the 'place of battle') is said to have been the scene of a battle between the Mohawks of eastern New York and the Abnakis. The Mohawks made periodic journeys to Mt. Katahdin for flint, and in passing through the section that is now Monmouth, they killed much game that the Abnakis considered their property. Finally the Abnakis met the Mohawks in a sanguinary battle near Cochnewagan Pond. No one seems to know the date of the battle, but Indians, old when the first settlers came, were fond of telling of it.

Bears were troublesome to white settlers of the locality as late as 1810–15, but as most of the settlers were young, they not only survived these and other difficulties but managed to have good times as well. There are records of corn huskings with singing, dancing, and refreshments of brown bread, beans, and pumpkin pie.

At 79.3 *m.* (L), on a hill from which sunsets are particularly beautiful, is *Highmoor Farm (open)*, an Agricultural Experiment Station conducted by the University of Maine. The modern white farm buildings include a house and office for the manager, several barns, and a cold storage plant capable of holding 7500 boxes of apples. The 305-acre tract is principally given over to an orchard with about 2500 trees. Some fields are used for experiments with corn, potatoes, and other vegetables.

The first farm in the tract was purchased through an Act of Legislature in 1909 and according to law it should 'conduct investigations in orcharding, corn and other farm crops.' In 1925 an adjoining 30-acre tract was bought for a demonstration orchard.

A national egg-laying contest is conducted annually in the large, well-equipped *Poultry House* (R). The contest, open to poultry owners all over the country, was inaugurated in 1930 and competitors usually

Tour 13: From Hampden to Naples

number about 1000. In September, 1936, a Rhode Island Red, owned by Phillip Steele of Biddeford made the national record for consecutive egg-laying with 214 eggs in 214 days.

GREENE (alt. 295, Greene Town, pop. 784), 83.6 *m.*, was named for General Nathanael Greene.

At 89.2 *m.* is a junction with a tarred road.

> Right on this road, which follows the eastern bank of the Androscoggin River, to *Gulf Island Dam*, 2 *m.* (L). This dam, harnessing the Androscoggin River for hydro-electric generation and distribution, takes its name from an island that originally divided the Androscoggin at this point into two channels, but that now forms a part of the middle section of the dam. The valuable power project completed in 1927 was built by the Central Maine Power Company at a cost of about $5,000,000, and is operated by the Union Water Company at Lewiston.
>
> The plant has three turbines of 9000 horse-power, each under a head of 50 feet.

LEWISTON (alt. 196, pop. 34,939) (*see LEWISTON–AUBURN*), 91.7 *m.*

AUBURN (alt. 210, pop. 18,571) (*see LEWISTON–AUBURN*), 92.2 *m.*, is at a junction with State 4 (*see Tour* 11).

At Auburn State 11 swings west from US 202.

MECHANIC FALLS (alt. 280, Mechanic Falls Town, pop. 2033), 102.2 *m.*, is the center of a town with paper mills on the Little Androscoggin River. Paper-making was introduced here in 1850. Freeland O. Stanley, an inventor, was principal of the town's first high school, and early engines of the Stanley Steamer, one of the first automobiles, were built here.

Buffalo Bill, Kit Carson, Jr., and Texas Jack gave marksmanship exhibitions in the village, when it was the seat of the Evans Rifle Co.

An *Indian Totem*, unearthed on the river banks in this vicinity, is in the Poland Spring museum (*see Tour* 14).

Between 105.3 *m.* and 106.2 *m.* State 11 and State 26 are one route (*see Tour* 14).

TRIPP LAKE (alt. 320, Poland Town), 107.8 *m.*, is a popular summer resort in a long pine grove on the eastern shore of *Lake Tripp* (*bathing, boating, and picnicking*).

At 109.8 *m.* is a junction with a dirt road.

> Right on this road is WEST POLAND (alt. 359, Poland Town), 0.5 *m.*, on the southern shore of Lake Tripp. Stores here are patronized by several boys' and girls' camps near the lake.
>
> Left sharply from West Poland on a dirt road to *Agassiz Village* (*open*), 2.3 *m.*, on a wooded hillside at the southern end of Thompson Lake. This large camp for boys conducted on the village plan by the Burroughs Newsboys Foundation of Boston, Mass., is on property donated by Mr. and Mrs. Max Agassiz, in memory of Mr. Agassiz' grandfather, Dr. Louis Agassiz (1807–73), the scientist.

At 121.2 *m.* is a junction with US 302 (*see Tour* 18). Between this point and Naples, State 11 and US 302 are one route (*see Tour* 18).

NAPLES (alt. 280, Naples Town, pop. 641) (*see Tour* 18), 123 *m.*

T O U R   1 4 :   *From* PORTLAND *to* NEW HAMPSHIRE LINE (*Errol*), 100.3 *m.*, State 26.

Via Gray, Sabbathday Lake Village, Poland, South Paris, Bethel, and Upton.

Two-lane macadamized roadbed; in winter sometimes impassable between Bethel and Upton.

BETWEEN Portland and Norway, State 26 follows very closely the trail blazed by trappers and Indians between Canada and Portland; it extends through the beautiful mountain and lake counties of Androscoggin and Oxford, and affords interesting side trips to historic villages in Maine's 'back woods.'

PORTLAND (alt. 80, pop. 70,810) (*see PORTLAND*), 0 *m.*, is at the junction of US 1 (*see Tour* 1, *sec. a*), US 302 (*see Tour* 18), and State 25 (*see Tour* 19).

GRAY (alt. 310, Gray Town, pop. 1189) (*see Tour* 11), 17.4 *m.*, is at a junction with State 4 (*see Tour* 11).

State 26 swings left at Gray.

DRY MILLS (alt. 300, Gray Town), 20.5 *m.*

> Right from Dry Mills on a gravel road to the *Dry Mills Fish Hatchery* (*open*), 1 *m.*, a State-operated brook-trout hatching plant, the largest in Maine. Water supply and water temperatures are the most important factors in raising fish, and the supply at Dry Mills, said to be the finest for the purpose found in Maine, maintains a remarkably even temperature. Nearly all the brook trout used for restocking in the southern half of Maine, and breeders sent to other sections of the State and to other States, are produced at this hatchery. Fifteen million eggs, with less than eight per cent loss in hatched trout, were produced here in 1936.
>
> Adjoining the hatchery is the *State of Maine Game Farm* (*open*), the only farm of this type in the State, comprising 130 acres of land on a high hill; here ring-necked pheasants are bred for release throughout the State as game birds, open seasons on which are to be designated. More than 4000 birds are reared each year, and 10,000 eggs are annually distributed to persons interested in raising pheasants. Other types of pheasants less suited to the Maine climate are being bred experimentally; various types of native animals and birds are on exhibition.

SABBATHDAY LAKE VILLAGE (alt. 300, New Gloucester Town, pop. 1866), 25.3 *m.*, is one of the few remaining Shaker settlements in the country. The central brick building serves as dormitory, living quarters, and dining-hall, with a chapel in one wing. There are several large barns and a number of small workshops. The colony, established in 1793, declined in numbers during the last half of the 19th century; in 1931 the remaining members of the Shaker colony at Alfred (*see Tour* 11) joined the colony here. This small community adheres to the tenets of the faith and engages in farming and small industries such as woodworking, preserving, and needlecraft.

The Shakers, members of the United Society of Believers in Christ's

TOUR 14: From Portland to Errol

Second Appearing, originated in England around the middle of the 18th century when a group of spiritualists and Quakers formed a society called the New Lights. 'Mother' Ann Lee, a leader of the movement, came to America in 1774 after suffering much persecution in England. With a few believers, she established a colony near Albany, N.Y., and in 1793 colonies were organized in Maine at this place and at Alfred.

Originally called the Shaking Quakers because of their dancing movements during religious services, the Shakers have met little understanding. Their principles include the practices of religious and economic communism, purification of sin by confession, some practice of spiritualism, practice of complete celibacy, and the Quaker opposition to war and violence. The Shakers interpret the Divine Spirit as of dual nature, male and female. They believe that Christ represented the male principle, and that 'Mother' Lee, the female principle, manifested the second coming of Christ.

Men and women share equally in the work, offices, possessions, and religious practices of the colony. New members, now rare, turn over all they possess upon entering the society, and this, as well as all property descending by inheritance, belongs to the community as a whole. Married converts must separate themselves from their mates. In the past orphans were often adopted by the society and educated in its beliefs. The religious meetings are marked by singing and dancing, for which the Shakers find justification in the Scriptures. The dancing is not as frenzied as formerly, the 'shaking' being confined principally to marching with swaying bodies, and to a slight waving of hands. By means of the latter, the Shakers believe they shake out sin. Goodness is received from above on upturned palms.

The men wear long clerical coats and broad felt hats; the women, very full skirts and tight bodices of gray wool; sometimes the women also wear wide collars of the kind used in the 17th century.

Formerly a variety of woolen and wooden articles were manufactured and sold by the colonists, as well as fine basketry; most of the packing cases for Poland Spring water were made here. Today chocolate candy, preserves, jellies, and needlework are sold to visitors.

From the top of *Shaker Hill*, 26.7 *m.*, is a fine view of the surrounding country. The bleak four-story, square *Stone Building* (R) was once a Shaker community house. Near-by is (L) the old *Shaker Meeting-House*.

Poland Spring, 28.6 *m.*, is little but a cluster of hotels and the homes of those employed in them. In 1794, Jabez Ricker of Alfred secured land here from the Shakers of the Sabbathday Lake colony and established a home; two days after the Ricker family arrived, two travelers stopped at their door, asking for breakfast. This was the beginning of Jabez Ricker's career as an innkeeper. So many travelers continued to stop, asking for accommodations, that in 1796 Jabez and Wentworth Ricker opened the *Mansion House*. Near-by was a large spring of unusually fine water that had some local fame, but was not credited with unusual virtues until the summer of 1844, when Hiram, a grandson of

Jabez Ricker, drank copiously of the water while he was haying and insisted that it had cured him of a chronic dyspepsia. The guests of the hotel, which was by this time something of a summer resort, also sampled the waters and reported so enthusiastically on its effects that the hotel owners began to see the possibilities of commercial exploitation, this being the period in which the fashionable world of Europe and America was resorting to 'waters' for all ailments of the flesh. Poland Water is one of the few bottled waters that has continued to maintain a popularity.

The present *Mansion House* and the large *Poland Spring House* stand on the top of *Ricker Hill* (alt. 580), from which is a wide-spreading view of hills and lakes particularly beautiful at sunset. A part of the original Mansion House is incorporated in the present sprawling structure. Near the hotel is the *State of Maine Building*, erected in 1893 on the grounds of the Chicago World's Fair, and later brought here; in it are a library and, at intervals, exhibitions of paintings and other objects.

At 29.4 *m.* (L) is *Middle Range Pond,* the center of a group of five ponds, where is excellent fishing (*boating and bathing facilities on eastern shore*).

POLAND (alt. 310, Poland Town, pop. 1503), 31.2 *m.*, is in a town that is noted for its mineral springs; it spreads over seven prominent hills.

Between 32.2 *m.* and 33.1 *m.* State 26 is united with State 11 (*see Tour* 13).

At 38.8 *m.* (L) is the *Center Meeting-House,* a plain structure serving both as an interdenominational church and as a town hall.

Near the Meeting-House is a junction with State 121.

> Left on State 121, which crosses an old covered bridge over the Little Androscoggin River, to OXFORD VILLAGE (alt. 248, Oxford Town, pop. 1125), 1.5 *m.* The first settlement here on the northern shore of Thompson Lake was made in 1794. The *Woolen Mill* built in early days is still in operation. Near-by and directly opposite the post office is an old dwelling (R), long known as *Craigie's Tavern.* During stagecoach days, this was the village inn, famed as having the finest bar in a large area.

At 45 *m.* is the junction with State 117.

> Left on State 117 is NORWAY (alt. 387, Norway Town, pop. 3145), 0.5 *m.*, on the southern end of Lake Pennesseewassee, a manufacturing center for shoes, snowshoes, skis, sleds, moccasins, and totem poles. In summer the large colony on the southern shore of the lake is a place of much colorful social activity. The town has had a brilliant military history since the first regimental muster of Oxford County was held here; three Norway companies were sent to the War of 1812, one to the Aroostook War, eight to the Civil War, one to the Spanish-American and one to the World War. Major General George L. Beal and General Benjamin B. Murray of Norway served in the Civil War.

> In the center of the village is the *Weary Club* (R), founded by Fred W. Sanborn, editor and proprietor of the *Norway Advertiser-Democrat.* The club is designed to take the place of the now vanishing old-fashioned general store where village philosophers could gather by the cracker barrel, to practice their aim with 'tabaccy' juice and whittle the hours away. The Weary Club today is a glorification of the old country store, even to the pot-bellied stove and the cracker barrel. Members are supplied with pungent cedar sticks for whittling.

> Beyond the club is the *Norway Advertiser-Democrat Office* (L), where the humorist, Artemus Ward (*see below*), learned the printer's trade. Hannibal Hamlin (*see below*) was as a lad a chore-boy in the same office.

TOUR 14: From Portland to Errol   363

Directly opposite the *Advertiser* office is the former *Home of Sylvanus Cobb, Jr.*, author of 'The Gunmaker of Moscow' and many novelettes and short stories; it is now a filling station.

Among authors who live or have lived in Norway are Charles Asbury Stephens, writer of juvenile fiction; the later Don C. Seitz, former editor of the New York *World*; and Hugh Pendexter, author of many historical novels, who first came to Norway as a school teacher.

Mellie Dunham, who was selected by Henry Ford as the champion old-time fiddler, was a native of Norway; here he made the snowshoes used by Robert E. Peary on his trip to the North Pole.

> Left from the *Norway Advertiser* office, about 1 *m.* on a local road, to *Pike's Hill* (alt. 870), overlooking Lake Pennesseewassee (alt. 398). Outstanding among the 115 peaks in seven ranges visible by telescope from Pike's Hill are Old Spec, Mt. Washington, and Mt. Osceola.

At 2.6 *m.* on State 117 is a junction with State 118. Right here on State 118; at 7.7 *m.* the route swings left from State 118 to an unnumbered, improved road.

WATERFORD (alt. 400, Waterford Town, pop. 743), 11.3 *m.* The third house (L) beyond the post office is the *Former Home of Artemus Ward*. The earliest Yankee humorist in the State was Seba Smith, born in Buckfield; John Neal of Portland had some laughter in his soul; and 'Bill Nye' of Shirley was a later funmaker; but the one who earned the widest and most lasting fame was Charles F. Browne, best known as Artemus Ward (1834–67).

One of his letters tells this of himself: 'I was born in the State of Maine of parents. As an infant I abstracted a great deal of attention. The nabers would stand over my cradle for hours and say, "How bright that little face looks! How much it nose!"'

After his father's death, he learned the printer's trade, became a wandering printer and did some writing. Later he became known for his wit and humor in debating. He began writing as Artemus Ward in 1858. His letters attained immediate popularity and in 1860 he became editor of *Vanity Fair*. After its failure, he devoted the rest of his short life to lecturing. He died in Southhampton, England, of tuberculosis.

His first letter read thus:

The Plane Dealer

Pitsburg, Jan. 27, 1858

Sir:

i write to no how about the show bisnes in Cleveland i have a show consisting in part of a Calforny Bare two snakes tame foxies & also wax woks my wax works is hard to beat, all say they is life and natural curiosities among my wax works is our Saveyer Gen. Taylor and Dockter Webster in the ackt of killing Parkman. now Mr. Editor scratch off a few lines and tel me how is the show bisnes in your good city i shal have hanbils printed at your offis you scratch my back and i will scratch your back, also git up a grate blow in the paper about my show don't forgit the wax works.

Yours truly
ARTEMUS WARD
Pitsburg Penny.

ps pitsburg is a 1 horse town. A.W.

SOUTH PARIS (alt. 385, Paris Town), 46.6 *m.*, extends south from the business square on both sides of State 26. Here large-scale manufacturing of wood novelties is carried on; the *Mason Manufacturing Company*

Factory is one of the largest establishments in the world exclusively devoted to making children's toys.

At 48 *m.* is the junction with an improved road.

>Right on this road is PARIS HILL (alt. 803, Paris Town, pop. 3761), 1.5 *m.*, the earliest residential section of the township. Today it has a group of beautiful old homes.
>
>In Courthouse Square is (L) the *Old Stone Jail* (1828), a thick-walled stone building with monitor roof built as the Oxford County jail. Its use as a jail was discontinued in 1895 and it has since been converted into the Hamlin Memorial Library. With the exception of changes in the roof and the removal of cells from the interior, the building is in its original form. The heavy iron entrance door, grated windows, and small low door of the 'solitary' cell with its tremendous iron key, pique the imagination. There are many local tales of early imprisonment and romantic escape from this building whose grim walls are now softened by trailing ivy.
>
>Beyond the jail is the *Birthplace of Hannibal Hamlin* (1809–91), Maine's 23d governor, a U.S. Senator, and Vice-President of the United States under Abraham Lincoln. The house has been remodeled as a summer residence.
>
>*Lyonsden (private)*, Main St. at Tremont St. (L), built in 1808, was the home of the late Rear Admiral Henry W. Lyon, commander of the dispatch boat '*Dolphio*' in the Spanish-American conflict; it is now the home of his son, Captain Harry Lyon, the navigation officer in 1929 on the airplane 'Southern Cross' when it made the first trans-Pacific flight from California to Australia. The house takes its name in part from the lion's head decoration over the door, the figurehead of the 'Nipsic,' first vessel commanded by the Admiral.
>
>Directly across from Lyonsden is the *Baptist Church* (1803), a fine example of Greek Revival architecture. It has no spire and much of the interior has been altered.
>
>The *Carter House (private)*, Main St. (R), built in 1787 and the first frame house erected in Paris, is a one-and-a-half-story building considerably altered from its original form by the addition of dormer windows and a Greek Revival entrance.
>
>Just beyond the Carter House is *Old Brick (private)*, a flat-roofed, three-story brick building with a fan-lighted door, at one time occupied by General William Kimball, prominent in the Civil War, and later by his son, Rear Admiral William W. Kimball who took command of the first torpedo boat flotilla in the Spanish-American War. John P. Holland, inventor of the submarine, assured Kimball that the submarine was 'a subject that you must have credit for putting into practical shape and introducing.'
>
>The *Hubbard House* (L), a three-story structure, built in 1806, with flat roof and cupola, was formerly a private residence. It is now an inn.
>
>Right from Main St. about 3.5 *m.* on a dirt road to *Mount Mica* which has the most notable pegmatite exposures in the State. The mine has been the chief source of tourmalines (*see The Nation's Northeast Corner*).

Snow Falls, 52.8 *m.* (L), has a drop of 40 feet to the gorge of the Little Androscoggin River. The foundation of an old mill is visible on the opposite bank.

At 55 *m.* (R) is the *Maine Mineral Store*, a museum of Maine gems, particularly those of the immediate area, and a souvenir salesroom. On display are beryl and tourmaline crystals in their original state, and lepidolite, one of a species of mica that indicates likely areas for gem tourmalines.

Near the store is a junction with State 140.

>Left on State 140 is the village of WEST PARIS (alt. 486, Paris Town), 1 *m.*

Tour 14: From Portland to Errol

Feldspar, chiefly from the Bumpus Mine in Albany, is milled here before being shipped to potteries out of the State. There are also a spool mill, and manufactories of wood novelties, including snowshoes and a great variety of toys.

BRYANT POND (alt. 720, Woodstock Town, pop. 848), 62.5 *m*. Near the inn on the southern shore of the pond is a small *Mink Farm*.

At 65.8 *m*. is a junction with a gravel road.

> Left on this road, which follows the western shores of a series of lakes, to the *Greenwood Ice Caves*, 3 *m*. (L). Several hundred years ago landslides broke away huge boulders and piled them up in such a fashion as to form large caverns, one of which, called the Cathedral, is 30 feet in diameter and retains winter ice in its interior as late as July.

LOCKE'S MILLS (alt. 763, Greenwood Town, pop. 548), 66.3 *m*., is in a township that was the birthplace of Atherton Furlong, lyric tenor, author, and artist, some of whose pictures are in the Metropolitan Museum in New York City; he taught music to Annie Louise Cary (*see Tour* 13) and Lillian Nordica (*see Tour* 11).

BETHEL (alt. 700, Bethel Town, pop. 2025) (*see Tour* 4), 71.5 *m*., is at a junction with US 2 (*see Tour* 4) and State 5 (*see Tour* 15). Between this point and Newry, State 29 and US 2 are united.

NEWRY (alt. 530, Newry Town, pop. 188) (*see Tour* 4), 78 *m*., is at a junction with US 2 (*see Tour* 4).

NORTH NEWRY (alt. 675, Newry Town), 82.9 *m*., in an agricultural area in which feldspar is occasionally mined, is popular for its excellent fishing and hunting. *Poplar Tavern* (R), in operation for more than 100 years, was built in such manner that the rear abutted a ledge, affording rear ground-floor entrances to the second and third stories. The second-story porch affords a view of the dark bulk of Old Spec Mountain (L) and Puzzle Mountain (R).

In the woods near-by is *Diana Pool* (*bathing*). The old tavern was a popular vacation resort in the gay nineties.

At 87.4 *m*. (L) are *Screw Auger Falls*, where the swirling waters of Bear River have worn holes from 6 inches to 25 feet in depth in the solid rock of the river-bed; the holes look as though they had been made with an auger. The shallower holes in some instances have small waterfall showers of their own. The near-by ledges are attractive spots for picnics.

Farther along (R) is the *Old Jail*, a hole 75 feet deep and about 25 feet across, which affords fun and exercise for those who are ambitious enough to crawl down and climb up through to 'escape jail.'

At 89.6 *m*. is the junction with a path.

> Right on the path for a 5-minute walk into the woods to a deep gorge on Bear River; here is *Moose Cave*, where broken pieces of rock have fallen from the slope of Bald Mountain into the river and formed a cave, cold even in the hottest days. Upward from this point are cliffs cut bare by landslides.

Grafton Notch, 90.1 *m*., is formed by *Old Spec Mountain* (alt. 4150) and *Bald Mountain* (alt. 3996). On Old Spec is the highest lookout station in the State.

At 91.2 *m.* (L) is a junction with the *Mahoosuc Trail*, part of the Appalachian Club system of trails (*see Sports and Recreation: Hiking and Mountain Climbing*).

UPTON (alt. 1722, Upton Town, pop. 166), 99 *m.*, overlooks Umbagog Lake, the source of the Androscoggin River, which drains the Rangeley Lakes region. Camps for sportsmen provide facilities for boating, canoeing, riding, fishing, and hunting (*registered guides*).

At 100.3 *m.* State 26 crosses the New Hampshire Line, 8.7 miles southeast of Errol, N.H.

T O U R   1 5 :   *From* SACO *to* BETHEL, 102.9 *m.*,   State 5.

Via Waterboro Center, Limerick, Fryeburg and Lovell.
Two-lane bituminous roadbed; gravel roadbed north of Lynchville.

THIS route passes through a charming area of lakes banked by high hills. Between Fryeburg and Bethel the road skirts the eastern boundary of the White Mountain National Forest.

SACO (alt. 60, pop. 7244) (*see Tour* 1, *sec. a*), 0 *m.*, is at the junction of US 1 (*see Tour* 1, *sec. a*) and State 9 (*see Tour* 1C).

At 16.7 *m.* is a junction (R) with State 4 (*see Tour* 11) with which this route unites for about 1 mile.

WATERBORO CENTER (alt. 285, Waterboro Town, pop. 914), 20.7 *m.*, is a cross-roads with a scattering of stores and houses. Near-by *Little Ossipee Lake* (N) is a center of attraction for campers.

    1. Right from Waterboro Center on a gravel road to the lakeside *North Star Camp*, 2.5 *m.*, maintained by the Portland Young Men's Christian Association.

    2. Left from Waterboro Center on an improved road to a *Lookout Station* and *Camp Site*, 2 *m.*, on Ossipee Mountain (alt. 1050). A ski-trail built down the mountain-side by the Hockomock Ski Club was the scene of the Maine Interscholastic Ski Meet in 1935.

LIMERICK (alt. 535, Limerick Town, pop. 1199), 29.8 *m.*, settled in 1775, was on the old Pequawket Trail, used by the Sokoki Indians traveling from the Saco River to their principal village at Pequawket, now Fryeburg (*see below*).

The first town meeting was held in 1787 in *McDonald Inn* (L), a three-story structure still catering to travelers. Some of the rooms in the inn are wainscoted with knotless pine, while the walls of others are painted with land and seascapes created by some unknown artist long ago. The door and window trim is hand hewn.

TOUR 15: From Saco to Bethel   367

CORNISH (alt. 347, Cornish Town, pop. 753), 40.1 *m.* A deed at Kittery dated November 28, 1668, records the sale of territory including Cornish between the Great and Little Ossipee Rivers for such considerations as rum, blankets, and beads. The town — originally called Francisboro for the Indian trader, Francis Small of Kittery, who purchased the land from the Indian sagamore, Captain Sunday — is one of five townships included in the sale. After transfer of the property was confirmed by the General Court of Massachusetts, the first white settlement was made in 1776.

Here is a junction with State 25 (*see Tour* 19), following the old Pequawket Indian Trail. The bridge across the Saco River at this point makes a perfect half-circle and is banked to allow for the curve.

At 42.6 *m.* is a junction with State 113.

> Right on State 113 to the *Richard Fitch Tavern*, 1 *m.* (L), built about 1780 and now a private residence owned by descendants of Fitch. The tavern was the center of all local gatherings in the early days. The militia in every-day homespun and their officers in uniform assembled here under Captain Edward Small, to train and later to start their night's march to general muster at Raymond during the War of 1812.
>
> Just beyond is a dirt road (L) leading to the *Pierce Place*, a large, well-preserved square house with mansard roof built in 1787 by Josiah Pierce, an ancestor of the present owner. A fireplace is in each of the eight rooms which contain many old furnishings collected locally and abroad.
>
> At 3 *m.* (L), deep in a field on the Sanborn farm (*ask at farmhouse for explicit directions*) is a mammoth white *Pine Tree*. From its base, 10 feet in diameter, the dark ridged trunk tapers gradually, to a height of approximately 120 feet. Bluish-green branches thickly hung with clusters of long cylindrical cones form a broad irregular head on the lofty old tree.

In WEST BALDWIN (alt. 377, Baldwin Town, pop. 694), 43.6 *m.*, the largest settlement of the township, is the *Burnell House (private)*, near the center of the village, a large home erected in 1737. Typical of the period in which it was built are the windows with six lower and nine upper panes.

At 45.4 *m.* (L) a small picnic ground provides convenient parking space for viewing *Hiram Falls*, one of the attractions of this region. During the spring floods the falls are nearly obscured by a wall of foam.

HIRAM (alt. 382, Hiram Town, pop. 814), 47.9 *m.*, named for Hiram, King of Tyre, was settled in 1774 by Gen. Peleg Wadsworth, grandfather of the poet Longfellow (*see PORTLAND*).

At the outbreak of the Revolutionary War, several years after his graduation from Harvard, Peleg Wadsworth recruited a company at Kingston, Mass., and received a captain's commission, which was followed in 1778 by his appointment as Adjutant General of the Massachusetts militia. In the next two years he rose rapidly from being second in command in the attack on Castine to the post of commanding officer in the defense of the coast of Maine. While making his headquarters in Thomaston he was wounded by the British (*see Tour* 1, *sec. b*) and carried captive to Castine, whence he escaped. After the Revolution, General Wadsworth purchased 15,000 acres of forest land at 13¢ an acre in what was known as the Hiram or Wadsworth Grant.

> Left from Hiram on a dirt road to *Wadsworth Hall* (*open; adm.* 25¢), 1 *m.*, a large

two-and-a-half-story frame building with long ell, built in 1787 for the use of General Wadsworth's lumbermen. The General soon found it so much to his liking that he moved his family here. The house with its unusually high first story, was little changed by remodeling in 1875. The second floor rooms are paneled in white pine with bead and beveled joints and time has darkened the wood almost to the color of mahogany. One of the chambers has been preserved as it was when used by Longfellow. The hall in which the militia drilled during the War of 1812 was utilized as the first school and meeting-house in Hiram, and the first deed of the land, dated March 9, 1787, hangs here.

Among the other furnishings of the house are the general's desk, containing many of his semi-official documents, a braided rug made by his daughter, one of a pair of candlesticks given to General Wadsworth by General Lafayette, and an old fire set.

Spring's Tavern, 49.7 *m.* (L), an inn of Colonial days that is a tourist home, was built in 1796 by Captain Thomas H. Spring. Stagecoaches, traveling along the post road between Fryeburg and Portland, used to stop here for a change of horses while passengers and driver refreshed themselves in the tavern taproom.

EAST BROWNFIELD (alt. 399, Brownfield Town), 55.1 *m.*, is a small commercial center on the Mountain Division of the Maine Central R.R.

Left from East Brownfield, on State 160, which follows Shepards River, is the village of BROWNFIELD (alt. 426, Brownfield Town, pop. 688), 2 *m.*, an old-time community little touched by modern traffic and 20th-century progress. Tall, graceful elms shade lovely old houses.

At 57 *m.* is a fine view of Old Spec, Bear River Bald, Goose Eye, and North Peak Mountains.

FRYEBURG (alt. 429, Fryeburg Town, pop. 1582), 62.6 *m.*, a prosperous summer resort that is the oldest town in Oxford County, lies on a plain in the Saco River Valley. Wide, tree-arched streets and large well-kept residences characterize the village, once an Indian settlement known as Pequawket, said to have been visited by John Smith in 1614.

Pequawket was the home of Nescambiou, the only Indian knighted by the French. Nescambiou became identified with the French Colonial Army under General Iberville during the siege of Fort St. John in 1695. His leadership and fighting qualities and the desire of the French for an alliance with the Indians against the English, gained him an invitation to France in 1705, where King Louis XIV conferred a knighthood upon him. He returned to America a year later.

At the *Registry of Deeds*, in a small brick building (R), are copies of deeds in the handwriting of Daniel Webster, the orator and statesman, who was employed here in 1802 while he was preceptor of Fryeburg Academy. It has been said that at the time, Webster gave little promise of the remarkable career he was later to make for himself. He attended church with great regularity, was not averse to a draft of rum, and took evident pleasure in attending village dances, at which he earned a reputation for gallantry, rather than grace.

Several of his letters written from Fryeburg shed light on his life in this town. 'Nothing here is unpleasant,' he wrote in one, 'there is a pretty little society; people treat me with kindness and I have the fortune to find

TOUR 15: From Saco to Bethel

myself in a very good family. I see little female company, but that is an item with which I can conveniently enough dispense.'

Webster resumed the study of law after leaving Fryeburg Academy. His first case before a court was in defense of the Widow Amhead who had been sued by John Moss for $15, the price of a heifer she bought from him. Webster was obliged to plead the case before his own father, Judge Ebenezer Webster, and becoming completely confused, he closed his case by addressing the court:

'Your Honor, I never should have taken this case. Only a good lawyer could have won it. My client owes the $15, but I shall pay the $15 myself because I've failed the poor woman. The poor woman has toiled as no man in our hard working community has toiled. I'll pay it because it is unendurable that any woman should struggle as Mrs. Amhead has struggled and go down defeated by a mean man's cupidity.'

Moss shouted, 'Dang it! I don't want the money. All I want is an admission it was owed me. I'm satisfied, but you're the worst lawyer I ever heard, Dan Webster. All you have is a voice.'

A *Soldiers' Monument* (L), in Bradley Memorial Park, is on the first site of Fryeburg Academy. For a monthly salary of $20 Daniel Webster taught from January 1 to September 1, 1802, in the one building of the school, a log cabin that later burned.

Fryeburg Academy (R), founded in 1791, now has three modern buildings, and has been endowed by Cyrus H. K. Curtis (1850-1933), head of the Curtis Publishing Company, and by Colonel Harvey Dow Gibson, president of the Manufacturer's Trust Company of New York, who is an alumnus of the academy.

The *First Congregational Church* (R) on Main St., built in 1850, is an attractive structure with closed belfry, and an entrance portico with fluted columns.

Opposite the church is a boulder indicating the two *Meridian Stones* placed here in 1883 by Robert E. Peary, Arctic explorer, who was once a resident of Fryeburg. The stones indicate the true north, enabling surveyors to obtain the magnetic variation.

Fryeburg is at a junction (L) with US 302 (*see Tour* 18) which enters the village (R) at the northern end.

LOVELL VILLAGE (alt. 439, Lovell Town, pop. 645), 73.3 *m.*, is a commercial center on an intervale in an attractive resort area.

The township was settled in 1779 and named for Captain John Lovewell, leader of many expeditions against the Indians. Sabattus Mountain (alt. 1280) (*see below*) is the highest of the forest-covered hills near the village. Just northwest of Lovell Village and to the left of the highway lies the southern extreme of lovely *Kezar Lake*, whose pine-clad shores — which shelter many summer homes, among them a lodge owned by Rudy Vallee, radio and screen star — stretch between this point and North Lovell (*see below*), a distance of about 9 miles.

The 9-hole golf course of the *Lake Kezar Country Club* (*open to visitors, greens fee* $2) is near the southern end of the lake.

CENTER LOVELL (alt. 530, Lovell Town), 78.7 *m.*, consists of two stores, a gas station, and a half-dozen homes on a high terrace overlooking the lake. The tourist homes and camps here are screened from the highway by trees.

> Right from Center Lovell on a dirt road 3 *m.* to a trail up the eastern slope of *Sabattus Mountain*. The 1.5 *m.* trail is rough; a good part of it over a dried bed of a mountain brook. On the western side is a perpendicular cliff, which the more venturesome may scale by way of the *Devil's Staircase*, a peculiar formation of 250 natural rock steps embedded in the mountain side. The mountain appears to be one huge ledge of micaceous rock.

NORTH LOVELL (alt. 441, Lovell Town), 82.9 *m.*, a small neat village catering to summer people, has several delightful bridle trails winding through its environs.

EAST STONEHAM (alt. 629, Stoneham Town, pop. 164), 86.7 *m.*, is the only settlement in a hilly township, all but a very small section of which is included in the *White Mountain National Forest*. *Speckled Mountain* (alt. 2877), some miles west, is the highest in the town.

This section of the National Forest, with its superb scenery, is rough country, particularly attractive to the seasoned mountain climber (*see Sports and Recreation*).

Rattlesnake Mountain and *Square Dock Mountain* are seen (L).

At LYNCHVILLE (alt. 555, Albany Town), 92 *m.*, State 5 makes a sharp (L) turn to the north.

Bumpus Mine (*open to public*) (R), 94.2 *m.*, is one of the most productive feldspar mines in Maine; pink and green beryl is also mined here; the largest beryl crystal in the world was taken from this mine in 1930. The roughly circular pit with its sheer smooth walls of cream white feldspar has a ramp entrance on one side. When the more valuable clear pink or green crystals of beryl are found, they are usually removed at once.

From the beryl is extracted a silver-white metal, stronger and of lighter weight than aluminum; it is proposed to use beryllium as an alloy in the construction of airplane motors. Gem beryl is rarely found in this mine.

At 95.3 *m.* is the town house of ALBANY (alt. 647, Albany Town, pop. 309), the corporate center of a hilly, wooded township lying in the valley of Crooked River.

BETHEL (alt. 700, Bethel Town, pop. 2025) (*see Tour* 4), 102.9 *m.*, is at the junctions with US 2 (*see Tour* 4), and with State 26 (*see Tour* 14).

TOUR 16: *From* BELFAST *to* SOUTH CHINA, 32 *m.*, State 3.

Via Belmont, North Searsmont, Liberty, and Palermo.
Two-lane, hard-surfaced roadbed.

THE rolling farm lands and woods along this route are broken by still, deep lakes and small villages whose church towers stand out against the sky. The woodlands are a mixture of hardwood and pine with an occasional clump of fir or spruce.

BELFAST (alt. 160, pop. 4993) (*see Tour* 1, *sec. b*), 0 *m.*, is at a junction with US 1 (*see Tour* 1, *sec. b*).

BELMONT (alt. 398, Belmont Town, pop. 227), 6.6 *m.*, is a four-corners, formerly known as Green Plantation. The town was first settled by squatters who, having no legal right to the land, resorted to a ruse in thwarting attempts to eject them. When word of the impending arrival of unexpected visitors reached the settlement, the squatters would immediately don feathers, paint, and moccasins, and, when officers of the law arrived the little settlement would appear entirely deserted, except for a few loitering Indians who greeted the baffled visitors with stolid indifference. This subterfuge caused the squatters to be called the Green Indians.

NORTH SEARSMONT (alt. 235, Searsmont Town, pop. 613), 11 *m.*, is the center of a township in which is the summer home of the novelist, Ben Ames Williams, and the 'Fraternity' of his stories is recognizable as the northern and western half of the township.

LIBERTY (alt. 377, Liberty Town, pop. 516), 15.8 *m.*, on George's Stream and formerly the site of tanning mills and machine shops, now has no industries. The township was originally granted under the Waldo Patent, and early settlers, in order to maintain their rights to land titles, held a secret meeting and decided to take away the land agent's papers. Swearing themselves to secrecy, they seized the agent, took him to St. George Lake where they cut a hole in the ice, and threatened to drop him into the icy waters unless he gave up the papers. This he promised to do but later his kidnapers were arrested and tried in the old Wiscasset Courthouse.

Before a cemetery was laid out in Liberty nearly all the residents had private burying grounds in their back fields.

In early days when the nearest post office was in Wiscasset, the mails were very slow in winter, people in Liberty sometimes waiting weeks for replies to their letters. Even since the establishment of a rural delivery route 22 years ago, mail carriers have encountered difficulties in getting the mail through in winter, sometimes being obliged to leave their cars and proceed on snowshoes with such mail as they could carry.

Around 1843, a large group of Adventists, who were convinced the world was about to come to an end, gathered here. One ardent member turned loose his pigs and cattle and, with a few followers, went up to the top of near-by Haystack Mountain to await the cataclysm, only to return, disgruntled and sorely disappointed, to the task of collecting his scattered livestock.

More than a century ago Liberty was the home of Timothy Barrett, who, finding the village little to his liking, crossed to the opposite shore of George's Stream, where he laboriously dug a cave for his dwelling and built a floating garden of logs upon which he raised vegetables. He had few confidants, and his seemingly inexhaustible supply of money gave rise to rumors that Barrett was a former buccaneer, possibly a fugitive from Great Britain. After his death, kettles containing French coins were dug up near his home and the hollow rail of a near-by fence yielded $100 in gold coins.

Lovely *St. George Lake*, near-by, provides excellent fishing.

At 23.1 *m.* lies *Sheepscot Pond*.

When snow covers the green slopes, glistening against the background of pines, little red flags flutter on the icy surface of the pond heralding the arrival of the trap-fishing season. Spring traps, placed in holes cut through the ice, are attached to short wooden sticks with a tiny two-or-three-inch square bit of red cloth at the top. When the hungry fish rise to the bait, the spring snaps and the bright little flag bobs up to signal the bite. The fishermen are able to control several lines at one time. This manner of winter fishing is popular not only in this district but throughout the State.

PALERMO (alt. 345, Palermo Town, pop. 513), 26.9 *m.*, settled in 1778 by pioneers from New Hampshire, is principally an agricultural community.

SOUTH CHINA (alt. 209, China Town) (*see Tour* 13), 32 *m.*, is at the junction with State 9 (*see Tour* 13).

T O U R   1 7 :   *From* AUGUSTA *to* ROCKLAND, 45.7 *m.*, State 17.

Via South Windsor, Union, and West Rockport.
Two-lane tar-surfaced roads.

STATE 17 passes through peaceful agricultural country with gently rolling hills and skirts numerous small lakes and ponds.

AUGUSTA (alt. 120, pop. 17,198) (*see AUGUSTA*), 0 *m.*, is at the

Tour 17: From Augusta to Rockland 373

junctions of US 201 (*see Tour* 10), State 27 (*see Tour* 12), and State 9 and State 11 (*see Tour* 13).

At 4.6 *m.* (R) is the north gate of the *U.S. Veterans' Administration Facility*, a reservation containing 1752 acres that was the first institution established (1866) in the United States for disabled veterans. Though built as a home for Civil War Veterans, the place is now open to disabled men of all wars. It is a village in itself, with a number of barracks, a large modern hospital, an administration building, workshops, a chapel, a library, a theater, a clubhouse, a store, and officers' homes in landscaped grounds.

For many years the place was called the National Home for Disabled Volunteer Soldiers, though it was popularly known as Togus, a contraction of the Indian *Worromontogus*. By 1915, 50 years after the end of the Civil War, the number of members had been greatly reduced, several barracks were closed, and the canteen was discontinued. Today the home has over 700 inmates. The *National Cemetery* on the hill contains the bodies of many soldiers.

SOUTH WINDSOR (alt. 300, Windsor Town, pop. 565), 10.6 *m.*, is the center of a town first called Malta; it was the scene of land troubles between the proprietors of the Kennebec Purchase and the early settlers, who were without title. This eventually led to the so-called Malta War in which a surveyor, Paul Chadwick, was slain by a party of settlers disguised as Indians. Several members of the attacking party were jailed in Augusta, and troops were called in for six weeks to guard the jail, the courthouse, and the residences of the proprietors until after the Court trials.

Windsor shared with Vassalboro the honor of having furnished masts and spars for the frigate 'Constitution' which was built at Hartt's Navy Yard, Boston, and launched October 21, 1797.

Clara Barton (1821–1912), the nurse of Civil War days, who organized the American National Red Cross (first called the American National Association of the Red Cross), spent her summer vacations here as a child.

At 14.1 *m.* is a junction with State 218.

> Right on State 218 is NORTH WHITEFIELD (alt. 205, Whitefield Town, pop. 908), 3.1 *m.* An annual Game Supper is served by the Whitefield Fish and Game Club in the Grange Hall in mid-October. The supper of venison, rabbit pie, squirrel pie, partridge, and sometimes coon and bear, is followed by a dance.
>
> The town was settled about 1770, principally by Irish Catholics, who were attracted by the forests, and the streams convenient for floating logs to the sea. The early lumbering has been replaced by farming.
>
> Here is a junction with State 126.
>
>> 1. Right from North Whitefield on State 126 is *St. Denis Church*, 1.5 *m.* (L), a brick edifice with Gothic tower built in 1833 on the site of the first log church (1822). The bricks used in this building and in the abandoned Convent across the road were made by hand on the church grounds. The history of this church is closely linked with that of St. Patrick's in Damariscotta Mills (*see Tour* 1, *sec. b*). In 1818, the Reverend Denis Ryan, first Catholic priest ordained in New England, was named pastor of the parish.

Nearly opposite the church is *Whitefield Academy and Orphan Asylum* (R), a large ivy-covered brick structure built in 1871, and used until 1887, when the Sisters of Mercy and the orphans were removed to Portland.

2. Left from North Whitefield on State 126, which winds through an attractive wooded section to *Pleasant Pond*, 2.7 *m.* (L). Opposite the Pond is *Pleasant Pond Cemetery* (R), with vaults and granite boundary posts at the highway level. Laid out on 12 terraces, each about 4 feet above the one below it, on a steep side hill, with granite steps leading to the higher levels, this cemetery presents an unusual appearance. From the top of the hill is a broad view of Pleasant Pond and the surrounding farms.

The circular Jefferson *Cattle Pound*, 5.7 *m.* (R), is 30 feet in diameter with thick field-stone walls 8 feet high. The pound was built in 1829 by Silas Noyes at a cost of $28; it has been repaired recently. It was formerly used as a place to keep stray cattle until the owners came for them and paid for their keep.

From a slight elevation at 6 *m.* (R) the northern half of *Damariscotta Lake*, 8 miles long, is seen. This end of the lake is known as Great Bay. The placid body of water with its small wooded islands attracts many summer visitors.

The *First Baptist Church*, 7 *m.* (L), a white edifice with belfry, was built in 1808 and remodeled in 1891. On the lawn is a boulder with commemorative tablet to the first settlers of Jefferson.

At 7.3 *m.* (R) is *Baptismal Beach*, a stretch of shore on Damariscotta Lake, still used by the Baptists for baptism by immersion.

JEFFERSON (alt. 110, Jefferson Town, pop. 888), 8.5 *m.*, is composed of a group of neat white one-and-a-half-story houses, with comfortable rambling farmhouses on its outskirts. A number of oxen are used by the farmers in Jefferson. It is believed locally that the fields are unusually verdant in this region because the land is plowed deeply with the aid of these beasts.

Crescent Beach (*bathhouses, picnic grounds, and playground equipment*), 9.5 *m.*, at the northern end of Damariscotta Lake, has a gradual slope to deep water where a moored float, with diving board and tower, permits aquatic stunts. Damariscotta Lake is frequented by sail boat enthusiasts who cruise among the numerous islands and enjoy the view of Haskell's Mountain with its fire tower, and Bunker Hill with its shining white church and background of fir and spruce trees. The lake is a breeding ground for pickerel.

North Knox Fairground, 29.6 *m.* (R), is the scene of Union Fair during the last week of September.

UNION (alt. 105, Union Town, pop. 1060), 30.2 *m.*, its attractive business blocks facing three sides of the village green with its Civil War monument and band stand, is a thriving village far enough from large communities to be a commercial center in itself. Many of the substantial residences are on a steep side hill to the north and east. The small industries of the village include casket manufacturing, the seasonal canning of vegetables and the manufacture of wooden handles and boxes. A model milk plant has recently been built here for the use of the dairy farmers of the vicinity.

SOUTH HOPE (alt. 390, Hope Town, pop. 464), 35.6 *m.*, between Grassy and Fish Ponds, is the largest settlement in a hilly town that has a number of large lakes to the south. There are no special restrictions on fishing in these waters; ice fishing is permitted for all fish except bass.

At 38.4 *m.* (L) is *Mirror Lake*, a small pond at the foot of *Ragged Mountain* (alt. 1300), which shades it during the early part of the day. The rugged scenery and its reflections in the lake have been painted frequently by landscape artists.

WEST ROCKPORT (alt. 225, Rockport Town, pop. 1651), **39.9** *m.*
ROCKLAND (alt. 40, pop. 9075) (*see Tour* 1, *sec. b*), **45.7** *m.*, is at a junction with US 1 (*see Tour* 1, *sec. b*).

T O U R   1 8 :   *From* PORTLAND *to* NEW HAMPSHIRE LINE (*Center Conway*), 58.1 *m.*, US 302, The Roosevelt Trail.

Via Foster's Corner, Raymond, South Casco, Naples, Bridgton, and Fryeburg.
Two-lane cement or macadamized roadbed.

MILE after mile of delightful countryside is visible from this route as it twists along an almost unbroken chain of clear lakes, dips into broad valleys and winds through still, fragrant groves; at the western end sweeping suddenly over the crest of a hill it reveals the far-away peaks of the Presidential Range, which seem to vary in altitude with each atmospheric change. In summer the thick, dark forests form a somber border around the rich green of fertile farm lands, and when crisp fall nights bring the first touches of frost, woodlands flame into color, the scarlet and gold of their autumn foliage in vivid contrast to the brown fields.

The pretty little villages, grown gray in the shade of gnarled old trees, drowse peacefully. Every settlement along the way caters to summer visitors, the larger villages serving as trading centers for cottagers and campers.

Longfellow Square in PORTLAND (alt. 80, pop. 70,810) (*see PORTLAND*), 0 *m.*, is at the junction of US 1 (*see Tour* 1, *sec. a*), State 25 (*see Tour* 19), and State 26 (*see Tour* 14).

At 8.3 *m.* is a junction with a dirt road.

> Right on this road is HIGHLAND LAKE (Westbrook), **0.3** *m.*, a settlement near the south end of *Duck Pond*, a pretty little cottage-bordered body of water.

FOSTER'S CORNER (alt. 210, Windham Town), **13.3** *m.*, is at a junction with State 4 (*see Tour* 11).

NORTH WINDHAM (alt. 300, Windham Town), **16.1** *m.*

At 17.1 *m.* is a junction with a dirt road.

> Left on this road is *White's Bridge*, 1 *m.*, spanning the mouth of an inlet of Sebago Lake. At this point Chief Poland (Polin) of the Rockameecock Tribe assembled his warriors for an attack against the settlers who had gathered at Old Province Fort (*see Tour* 11). Below the bridge (L), at the mouth of the Presumpscot River and below the present dam, is an *Early Dam* built by the Indians.
>
> At the Harry Kennard home (R), is a *Collection* (*open to public*) of over 1000 Indian relics and Red Paint artifacts (*see Earliest Inhabitants*) including chisels, gouges, and pieces of pottery. Many of the artifacts are made of a stone entirely foreign to

this part of the State and some of them were discovered at an *Indian Burial Ground*, about 0.3 m. north on the shore of Sebago Lake, said to be one of the largest such burial grounds in the United States.

RAYMOND (alt. 295, Raymond Town, pop. 446), 21.8 *m.*, is on beautiful Jordan Bay of Sebago Lake with Panther Pond forming its northern border. Neat, well-kept residences line each side of the highway in the shadows of ancient elm trees.

Right of the highway is the *Morton Homestead (private)*, built in 1765; it has its original six-panel doors, pumpkin pine flooring and a wainscot made of a single board 27 in. wide and 13½ ft. long.

Also on the right is the *Hayden House (private)*, similar to the Morton Homestead in architectural style; it was built in 1786 and has its original hand-made clapboards.

The *Raymond Fish Hatchery*, on Panther Run connecting Panther Pond with Sebago Lake, has various buildings in which are rows of long tanks filled with water piped from the river. Salmon eggs are hatched in these vats, and the near-by pools harbor great numbers of fish. As many as 90,000 two-year-old landlocked salmon are released from the hatchery at one time.

Sebago Lake (Ind.: 'stretch of water' or 'place of river-lake'), with a length of 14 miles and a maximum width of 11 miles, in some places reaches a depth of 400 feet. Several small islands stud the broad sweep of water, and off the southeastern shore lies the green bulk of *Frye's Island*. The lake with its tributaries is the original home of the landlocked salmon (*salmo Sebago*), which propagate in great numbers and grow rapidly. These splendid fighters, often attaining a weight of eight pounds, rise best in the early months of the year, and in September. Hard hitters at fly or bait, landlocked salmon give a stiff fight until landed. Also in these waters are trout, togue, bass, white perch, smelts, pickerel, and an abundance of cusk that provides excellent catches during winter fishing through the ice. On the shores of Sebago Lake are many camps where hundreds of tanned youngsters spend the summer. The drinking water for Portland and its vicinity comes from this lake. During the summer a boat (*variable schedule, inquire at dock*) plies the waters of Sebago from the dock near the Sebago railroad station (*see Tour* 19).

At 23.7 *m.* (R), about 50 feet up from the highway, is *Pulpit Rock*, a smooth projection 5½ feet high and equally wide, on which, it is said, the Devil used to stand when preaching to the Indians. During one of his discourses, according to legend, a rash young chief had the temerity to laugh in the Devil's face, whereupon the Evil One rose in a passion and, stamping his foot, caused the ground in front of the pulpit to drop 50 feet. Nathaniel Hawthorne was very fond of this rock, where he spent many hours reading.

SOUTH CASCO (alt. 310, Casco Town, pop. 713), 24.7 *m.*, lies on a narrow strip of land between Thomas Pond (E) and Sebago Lake (W). Farmhouses comprise the residences of this small settlement, from which

TOUR 18: From Portland to Center Conway 377

well-cultivated lands extend into the hills overlooking Sebago Lake and the 14 Dingley Islands near the shore.

Left from South Casco on a local dirt road to a large wooden *Tower*, 0.3 *m.*, with a bell fire alarm. West of the tower, across the field, is a large *Rock and Shell Formation*, about 50 feet high overlooking a fine grove of pine on the shores of Dingley Bay on Sebago Lake. The variously shaped shelves of this formation terminate in a large, flat hood-like top shelf beneath which is a cave; in this, it is said, a 14-year-old girl was held prisoner by the Indians for three years. Her family, finally discovering her whereabouts, led an attack on the Indians and rescued her.

At 0.4 *m.* (R) is the *Manning House (private)*, built in 1810 by Richard Manning, an uncle of Nathaniel Hawthorne. A large square two-story structure with hip roof and massive chimneys, it has eight fireplaces with openings ranging from 45 to 56 inches in width. There is a Christian or 'witch' door with five panels, and the interior is decorated with wall paper 126 years old. All the window glass was imported from Belgium. In this house, Nathaniel Hawthorne visited for months at a time before the Hawthorne home (*see below*) was built. It was Uncle Richard who taught the budding literary genius the rudiments of mathematics, grammar and geography.

The frame *Murch House (private)*, on the left side of the road, was built in 1780 by Captain Joseph Dingley. It was originally a two-story house, but fire destroyed the upper part. The ground floor was preserved intact, and the house was later remodeled into the present story-and-a-half structure. At the rear of the Murch House stands an *Old Windmill*, its gaunt shape in drab contrast with the surrounding fields.

Just beyond this house the road crosses a bridge over *Dingley Brook*, which separates the townships of Casco and Raymond. The road continues out onto *Raymond Cape*, becoming a scenic shore route along a four-mile strip of wooded land projecting into Sebago Lake. On the tip of the cape, flint of the quality used by Indians in making their arrow and spear heads, skinning knives, and tomahawks, is frequently found.

Just after the road crosses the Dingley Brook bridge, at 0.5 *m.* (L), is the *Hawthorne House (open in summer)*, a remodeled two-and-a-half-story barnlike structure, now owned by the Town of Raymond and used for public meetings. This house was erected in 1812 by Richard Manning for his sister, Mrs. Hathorne, the mother of Nathaniel Hawthorne, who lived here in seclusion after the death of her husband. The boy, Nathaniel Hathorne, then about seven years of age, roamed the near-by hills, fished in local streams, and frequently sat on rocks in sunny spots, engaged in his favorite pastime of reading. One close companion of his boyhood days was William Symmes, a Negro boy of his own age. As there were few children in the community, he and Nathaniel would listen together to the tales of the men who congregated in Manning's store. Extracts from Nathaniel's diary show the deep interest he took in all he heard: 'Captain Britton from Otisfield was at Uncle Richard's today. Not long ago Uncle brought here from Salem a new kind of potatoes called Long Reds. Captain Britton had some for seed and uncle asked how he liked them. He answered, "They yield well, grow very long; one end is very poor and the other good for nothing." I laughed about it after he was gone, but Uncle looked sour, and said there was no wit in his answer and that the saying was stale. It was new to me and his way of saying it very funny. Perhaps Uncle did not like to hear his favorite potato spoken of in that way, and that if the captain had praised it he would have been called witty.'

Another entry reads: 'A peddler named Dominicus Jordan was today in Uncle Richard's store telling a ghost story. I listened intently but tried not to seem interested. The story was of a house, the owner of which was suddenly killed. Since his death the west garret window cannot be kept closed, though the shutters be hasped and nailed at night; they are invariably found open the next morning, and no one can tell when and how the nails were drawn.' (This Dominicus Jordan, under the name of Dominicus Pike, appears in Hawthorne's story, 'Mr. Higgenbotham's Catastrophe.')

Nathaniel Hathorne was graduated from Bowdoin College in 1825 and changed his surname to Hawthorne the same year. College vacations were spent at his Raymond home, and in later years, when a resident of Salem, Mass., he often spoke of his longing for this place. Another note from Hawthorne's diary of later years refers to Raymond: 'I have visited many places called beautiful in Europe and the United States but have never seen the place that enchanted me like the flat rock from which I used to fish.'

At 2.2 *m.* in a wooded section of the cape is a *Luther Gulick Girls' Camp* (Little Wohelo). The camp directly across the Lake (Wohelo) is the original Luther Gulick camp, said to be the first summer camp of its kind in the United States. Luther Gulick (1865-1918), pioneer in physical education, founded the child hygiene department of the Russell Sage Foundation, contributed a great deal to the advancement of the Young Men's Christian Association; with James Naismith, he devised the game of basketball, and with his wife founded the Campfire Girls organization. Although both Mr. and Mrs. Gulick are dead, the camps are maintained and directed by their son, Halsey.

At 4.6 *m.* is an open lot for parking. About 100 yards (R) near the shore of the lake is *Pulpit Rock*, pentagonal in shape and 7 feet high. Two natural steps lead up to its smooth top from which Chief Poland is believed to have addressed gatherings of his tribe, the Rockameecocks. Near Pulpit Rock is *Frye's Leap* (L), a cliff-top high above Sebago Lake, associated with an incident of pioneer days. After running several miles with a band of Indians in close pursuit, a Captain Frye came out upon the cliff. He escaped the Indians by diving into the waters far below, and swam into a cave formed by an overhanging ledge, in which he remained until nightfall, when he swam over to a large island, later named for him. In the same cave, the first chapters of 'The Scarlet Letter' were penned by Nathaniel Hawthorne. On the vertical faces of the cliff, which is formed of huge boulders 75 to 100 feet high, are paintings made with pigments in which the red men portrayed Indians, native animals, and hunting weapons. Once vividly colorful, these examples of Indian art have mellowed to soft hues, blending beautifully into the rock.

At 29.5 *m.* is a junction with State 11 (*see Tour* 13). Between this point and Naples, US 302 and State 11 are one route (*see Tour* 13).

NAPLES (alt. 280, Naples Town, pop. 641), 31.2 *m.*, with two golf courses (*open*), is a stopping point on the Songo River boat trip (*see Tour* 19).

Naples is entered from the east over an iron drawbridge, which spans a stream connecting *Long Lake* (R) and *Brandy Pond* (L); from the bridge is an exceptionally fine view of Mt. Washington and the surrounding hills, which seem to rise almost from the northern rim of Long Lake. On windwhipped Long Lake, seaplanes and sea-sleds, as well as fast cabin cruisers, find wharfing facilities.

The people of Naples take their politics so seriously that until a few years ago the town was openly divided, with two entrances to the public buildings, one for the Democrats and the other for the Republicans. In these buildings the seating plan was so arranged that each party had its own half of the room. This sharp party line was drawn even in the schoolroom, with the children of Republican parents seated on one side of the room and the children of Democratic parents on the other; the climax came when it became necessary to assign two teachers to each room to satisfy the rabid feelings of the parents. When a flagpole was erected on the village green by the Republicans, the Democrats, not to be outdone, had a flagpole erected on the same plot, with fitting ceremony. While such

Tour 18: From Portland to Center Conway

open expression of strong political feeling has disappeared to a certain extent, politics is still of paramount importance in Naples.

> Left from Naples on the Lake House Road, at the home of Harold Ridlon, 0.5 *m*. (L), is an interesting *Collection of Indian Relics* (*open*), consisting of arrowheads, stone skinning knives, and tomahawk heads, all well arranged and catalogued. These relics have been collected on the shores of Sebago Lake and are in an excellent state of preservation.

At 31.6 *m*. (R), in the rear of a cemetery on the shore of Long Lake, rests the partly exposed hulk of the freighter 'Columbia,' a 60-ton vessel, later christened 'The Ethel.' The 'Columbia' was the last of the fleet that carried lumber down Sebago Lake and along the canal to Stroudwater and the sea. First rigged as a schooner, she was later steam driven, and made her last trip in 1904. In the past, as now, the waters of Sebago and Long Lakes were subject to sudden and severe squalls, and the crews on these shallow freighters were hard put to keep them on an even keel.

At 32.7 *m*. (L) is *The Manor*, now an inn, but built as a home in 1799 by George Pierce, the first settler of Naples. The front and rear walls of the two-story, square structure are of wood, the side walls of brick. The house has four chimneys, a hip roof, and 24-light windows. The interior, with its original flooring, decorated cornices, wainscotting of single board width, six fireplaces, and a spacious hall with graceful balustraded stairway, retains much of its early appearance. From the Manor is a fine view of Long Lake and the White Mountains. The mineral spring on this property supplies excellent water; in 1935 when repairs were being made on the house, piping of hollow logs was found for conveying water from the spring to the house.

To the rear of the Manor is *Skid Hill* and a small group of pines known as the *Perley Pines*, some of them marked in pre-Revolutionary days with the 'broad arrow,' indicating that they were reserved for masts of the Royal Navy; the 'broad arrows' are still discernible. When Skid Hill was named, an unbroken forest of white pine stretched to Bridgton. Logs hauled to the hill were rolled down the hillside across the road and field to Mast Cove on the shores of Long Lake, there to be loaded on freighters and carried to the coast.

Seba Smith, one of the first prominent American humorists, recounted the exploits of a rough-and-ready crew that for many seasons made a festive occasion of cutting and loading the pine in this region. Smith was born in 1792 in a log cabin in Buckfield, of which his father had been one of the first settlers. After receiving some instruction at Bridgton Academy in Bridgton, where the family lived for a time, he obtained a loan for his education and entered Bowdoin College. An excellent student, he was of mild nature and inclined to oppose radical changes in the established order. After his graduation he became assistant editor of the Portland *Argus*, later purchasing a half interest. His 'Major Jack Downing Letters,' on contemporary political issues, first appeared in the Portland *Courier*.

At 33 *m*. (L) is the *Hayloft*, a house and remodeled barn on land that was a Revolutionary War bonus given to a Private Hill. To this veteran and his wife were born two sons, one of whom became Capt. Charles Hill, engaged in the clipper ship trade with the Orient. On one of his trips to China, Captain Hill and his crew are said to have removed several large idols from a Chinese temple and succeeded in bringing them back to the United States. Upon close examination, the exceedingly heavy idols were found to be filled with gold. The sum realized by Captain Hill, as his share, was around $300,000. With part of the money he added a fine two-and-a-half-story house to the old homestead, and used the old house as an ell. The spacious main house, which was built 80 years ago, overlooks Mast Cove. Chandeliers hanging from decorative ceiling rosettes brighten the large rooms and scatter shadows on the graceful balustrade and broad stairway in the wide hall, where for many years two of the huge idols reposed in odd contrast with the other furnishings.

After building the main house and losing most of the remainder of his stolen wealth, Captain Hill grew restless. With the hope of recouping his fortune, he once again set sail for the Far East; he was never seen again and it is possible that the priests, aware of his sacrilegious plundering, killed him when he returned to the temple.

BRIDGTON (alt. 360, Bridgton Town, pop. 2649), 40 m., is a trading center for the many summer and winter visitors of the environs, and has excellent recreational facilities.

Old elm trees grace the residential sections where well-kept old houses stand beside those of later architecture.

Bridgton is musically inclined, having a band, Fremstad Music Club, and church musical societies. Olivia Fremstad, the prima donna, was a summer resident of the town for several years, and many other musicians of note have become summer residents.

The *Pondicherry Mills* (*open to visitors*) (R) at Pondicherry Square were named for a French province in the eastern part of India. The mills have manufactured woolen goods and provided Bridgton with a means of livelihood for many years.

Highland Lake, the southern end of which is within the village limits, provides fine trout and bass fishing. At the village end of the lake is a *Rearing Pool* for trout.

Opposite the rearing pool is the *Walter Hawkins House* (*private*), a story-and-a-half structure built in 1770, but extensively rebuilt in recent years with the use of much of the old building material such as hand-hewn timbers and handmade nails. Among the furnishings are many old Bridgton pieces.

> Right from Bridgton on State 117 to *Bridgton Academy*, 3.6 m. (L), a co-educational preparatory school of high scholastic standing, first opened in 1808. The *Spratt-Meade Museum* (*open*) on the campus displays Indian artifacts, early American farm and home implements, butterfly, shell, and mineral collections, early books and manuscripts, and clothing of an early period.
>
> The village of NORTH BRIDGTON (alt. 370, Town of Bridgton), in which the academy stands, is a summer resort on the edge of Long Lake along the wooded shores of which are many estates.

In the Glines Neighborhood, 5.8 m. (Bridgton Town), in a neat little cemetery (R) beside the road, is the *Grave of Captain John Haywood*, hero of Bunker Hill. Private Haywood, in that battle, fought bravely and, when his captain fell mortally wounded, seized the sword from the captain's fingers, and springing upon the parapet, encouraged his men and directed their activities. Private Haywood became Captain Haywood in the course of time, survived the war, and returned to his old home at North Bridgton. On the slate stone at Captain Haywood's grave is an inscription that seems to have appealed to many people in the early days:

> 'Pause stranger, ere you pass by —
> As you are now, so once was I.
> As I am now, soon you'll be,
> Prepare for death, to follow me.'

At 43.7 m. *Pleasant Mountain* looms up ahead (left center).

At 45.7 m. a long bridge crosses narrow *Moose Pond* which extends on both sides of the bridge as far as the eye can see. This delightful spot where the green wooded slopes of Pleasant Mountain on the western bank are mirrored in the cold, sparkling waters has been little spoiled by the coming of civilization.

At 49.4 m. is a junction with a dirt road.

Left on this dirt road to a parking space at 1.5 m. where is the entrance to a well-defined trail leading to the summit of *Pleasant Mountain* (alt. 2007). This 2.5 m. trail, following an old coach road a considerable distance, has markers at frequent intervals and rustic benches at scenic points. Halfway up the trail (L) is a *Ranger's Cabin* built in a clearing. Near-by is a cold spring. Above this point the trail is more precipitous.

The *Fire Tower* (*open*), on the mountain summit is always manned by a fire warden. The glass-enclosed room, about 8 feet square, permits an unobstructed view for 30 miles with the naked eye, and 75 miles with glasses. It would be difficult to count the numerous mountain peaks, broken only by Lake Kezar to the north and six other lakes. To the southeast unwinds the broad silver ribbon of Casco Bay. Three other lookout towers, Kearsarge, Ossipee, and Blackstrap, are visible here. The wind sweeps across the summit of Pleasant Mountain with a velocity close to 50 miles an hour, and sings as it strikes the steel framework of the tower, which rises 50 feet into the air. The temperature at the top of the mountain is 20 degrees below that at the base.

At 54 m. is a junction with a dirt road.

Left on this road to a boulder, 0.3 m. (L), at the northern end of Lovewell Pond, marking the *Site of Lovewell's Fight*, May 8, 1725, when a company of 33 Massachusetts Rangers under Captain John Lovewell battled from dawn to dusk with 80 Pequawkets led by Paugus. During this battle, both the chief and Captain Lovewell were killed and afterward the Indians abandoned their seat at Pequawket and fled to Canada.

At 55.4 m. (R) is *Jockey Cap*, a gigantic 200-foot boulder near the roadside.

At 56.1 m. is a junction with State 5 (*see Tour 15*).

FRYEBURG (alt. 415, Fryeburg Town, pop. 1582) (*see Tour 15*), 56 m., is at a junction with State 5 (*see Tour 15*).

At 58.1 m. US 302 crosses the New Hampshire Line, 4 miles east of Center Conway, N.H.

TOUR 19: *From* PORTLAND *to* NEW HAMPSHIRE LINE (*Freedom*), 42.8 *m.*, State 25.

Via Westbrook, Gorham, Standish, Cornish, Kezar Falls, and Porter.
Two-lane hard-surfaced roadbed.

WEST of the industrial communities of Cumberland Mills and Westbrook, State 25 runs through a farming country with well-kept houses; crops in this vicinity are raised mainly for home use, with a small surplus for sale in local markets.

The countryside to the west is well wooded with pine, white birch, and some hemlock. In mid-April, hiding under dead leaves in the woods, are quantities of trailing arbutus; a few weeks later appear the pale-green stems and faint-yellow cup-like blossoms of wild oats, and as the season progresses, ladyslippers, and benjamins. In June great beds of lilies-of-the-valley are found near the edges of the woods. Hidden in the grass, yet spreading their perfume, sweet wild strawberries ripen as June draws to a close. The broad fields bloom in early spring, first with blue-white anemones, then with dandelions, buttercups, white daisies and black-eyed-susans, and in late summer with heavy growths of red clover and goldenrod.

PORTLAND (alt. 80, pop. 70,810) (*see PORTLAND*), at Longfellow Square, 0 *m.*, is at the junctions of US 1 (*see Tour 1, sec. a*), US 302 (*see Tour* 18), and State 26 (*see Tour* 14).

CUMBERLAND MILLS (alt. 70, Westbrook Town), 5.1 *m.* The fine brick buildings extending along the dam and both sides of the Presumpscot River are the *S. D. Warren Paper Company Mills* (*open to public*), Cumberland St. The plant, established in 1852, has grown from one little frame building that turned out less than five tons of the finished product daily, to the present great brick and concrete structure with nearly 60 acres of floor space, holding large, modern paper-making machines having a combined average daily production of 275 tons.

> Right on Cumberland St. to a dirt road; on this road is HALIDON, 2 *m.*, on the northern bank of the Presumpscot. It is one of several single-taxing communities founded by Fiske Warren, the paper manufacturer. Mr. Warren has the controlling interest of over 200 acres of the area; the tenants secure 99-year leases, pay the property tax of the City of Westbrook annually, and turn over the receipt to the trustees, as the only payment of land rental. Halidon has its own community meetings six times a year and elects officers; inhabitants of both sexes from the age of 15 may vote.

WESTBROOK (alt. 85, pop. 10,807), 6.1 *m.*, is an industrial city with a large French-Canadian population. In its early days the community was called Saccarappa. Westbrook and Deering were taken from the town of Falmouth in 1814 and incorporated in Westbrook Town.

Tour 19: From Portland to Freedom

The *Dana Warp Mills* (*open to public*), 347 Brown St., established in 1866, is one of the important cotton manufacturing plants of Maine.

The *Haskell Silk Mill* (*open to public*), 98 Bridge St., makes both rayon and high-quality silk goods.

The *Bean House* (R), on Bridge St. opposite the Dana Warp Mills, a three-story dwelling built in 1805 and divided into apartments, has a spiral staircase of great beauty, above which is a domed skylight.

Rudy Vallee, the orchestra leader, was brought to Westbrook when a young child and lived on Monroe Avenue. His father was the proprietor of a local drugstore for many years.

Benjamin Paul Akers (*see The Arts*), sculptor of the 'Dead Pearl-Diver' (*see PORTLAND*), was born here in 1825.

GORHAM (alt. 220, Gorham Town, pop. 3035) (*see Tour* 11), 10.5 *m.*, is at a junction with State 4 (*see Tour* 11).

WEST GORHAM (alt. 247, Gorham Town), 13.5 *m.*

The *Prentiss House* (*open*), in village Center (L), a two-and-a-half-story structure with hip roof, was the boyhood home of Seargent Smith Prentiss, who was born in Portland in 1808, and became a lawyer. He went to the South in 1832 and formed a partnership with John I. Guion; this firm attained a national reputation, in part because of Prentiss' oratorical ability.

On the edge of the village, left of the highway, is *Homeland Farms* (*open*), with a fine group of white painted buildings; cattle of this dairy farm were imported from the Isle of Jersey.

STANDISH (alt. 415, Standish Town, pop. 1317), 17.7 *m.*, a pretty village, settled in the late 1750's, was named in honor of Miles Standish. It lies in an area principally devoted to orcharding.

The *Marrett House* (*private*), next to the post office on the south side, a large two-and-a-half-story white house, built in 1789, became the home of the Reverend Daniel Marrett, on his appointment to the parish after ordination. During the War of 1812 when it was feared that Portland would be taken by the British, the coin from Portland banks was hauled by six oxen to Parson Marrett's house, where it was stored in a room the foundation of which had been strengthened for the purpose. The heavy locks, placed on the doors of the house at this time to protect the treasure, are still in place.

The frame *Unitarian Church* (R), built in 1806, is an example of the simplicity of early church architecture in Maine. It is now painted brick red, and has a square towered belfry and old-fashioned box pews.

> Right from Standish on a good dirt road to *Sebago R.R. Station*, 3 *m.*, the starting point for a delightful boat trip through Sebago Lake (Ind.: 'a stretch of water') and the Songo River into Long Lake.
>
> Leaving the dock near the Sebago R.R. Station, the small boat swings north toward the broader section of *Sebago Lake* (*see Tour* 18). On all sides tree-clad hills climb abruptly from rocky shores; *Rattlesnake Mountain'* gradually looms into

view (R). Toward the west the scenery becomes more rugged, with the *Saddleback Mountains* plainly visible. On a clear day, the sometimes snow-capped summits of the White Mountains are outlined in the distance.

After an hour's ride the boat swings into the waters of the *Songo* (Ind.: 'the outlet') *River*, rounding sharp bends, and pushing through reeds among which are often seen the sleek, brown bodies of muskrats, darting swiftly past the boat's prow. On either side, the river banks slope gently to the hills covered with pine and hemlock. The boat passes through several locks during the 1½-hour run. After a trip up this river, many years ago, Longfellow wrote his poem, 'Songo River':

> 'Nowhere such a devious stream,
> Save in fancy or in dream,
> Winding slow through bush and brake,
> Links together lake and lake.'

Entering *Long Lake*, a charming body of water with cottages, hotels, and summer camps scattered along its shores, the boat stops at NAPLES (*see below*).

A fork of roads at 19.7 *m.* is known as *Two Trails*. State 25, north of this point was the Ossipee Trail used by the Indians for travel between Maine and New Hampshire. The tribes of the two areas, bound by blood-ties, made frequent inter-tribal visits. The Pequawket Trail (R) was a short-cut from the lower Saco to the Indian village of Pequawket (*see Tour* 15).

At 23.2 *m.* a bridge spans the *Saco River*, here wide and turbulent in its broken rock bed, and a spot where the waters teem with logs during the spring drives. Only five million logs were driven down the Saco in 1935 as compared with the 60 million average of former years.

EAST LIMINGTON (alt. 240, Limington Town), 23.6 *m.*

Left from East Limington on a tarred road to the *Little Ossipee River*, 0.3 *m.*, on the northern bank of which is the *Site of an Indian Village*. Surrounded by woods, this permanent camp had a plentiful supply of fresh meat, which, with ground corn, formed the basic food stuff of the Indians. They stretched and tanned animal pelts for clothing, retaining the fur on their outer winter garments. The squaws set snares for smaller animals, and in spring collected maple sap in bark containers, boiling it down to sugar in much the same manner as is done today. After planting their corn the whole population went down the river to the sea, where the winter supply of fish was caught and smoked.

At 0.4 *m.* (L) is the *Chase Sawmill*, developed from the first small mill built by Deacon Amos Chase in 1773 on the same site.

At 0.5 *m.* (R) is the *Chase House* (*private*), deep set in a large lot and reached by a curving, maple-bordered driveway. The original plans for this large two-story octagon-shaped house surmounted by an octagonal cupola, which was built in 1810, were drawn by Mrs. Chase on an eight-sided collar box, which was the source of Captain Chase's inspiration for the house. The builder found it necessary to change the arrangement of rooms on Mrs. Chase's plans, as she had neglected to include a staircase in her design. On each of the eight façades of the house are twin windows in both stories. Captain Josiah Chase, father of the present owner, was a whaler out of New Bedford, Mass., and the house contains many mementos of his seafaring days. There are several whales' teeth carved and engraved and filled with colored inks; a small collection of shells; a reproduction of the Benjamin Russell drawing 'Sperm Whaling'; and photographs of the Maori Chief Tomati Waka, and of Thakomlan, King of the Fiji Islands.

NORTH LIMINGTON (alt. 310, Limington Town), 24.9 *m.*

Left from North Limington on State 11 is LIMINGTON VILLAGE (alt. 462,

TOUR 19: From Portland to Freedom

Town of Limington, pop. 747), 2.1 *m.*, on high land overlooking (W) a narrow valley and high wooded hills.

On the Main Street (R) is the *McArthur House* (*private*), a beautiful two-story weathered structure with gambrel roof and large central chimney, built in 1797. Across the front lawn run a row of large elms and a long line of spaced granite posts. To the rear is a large apple orchard.

The first floor of the interior is finished in black walnut. Among the old furnishings in the house are: four-poster beds, one of which is canopied with fine old lace; a small covered cradle that has been in the possession of the McArthur family for several generations; and a small piano. There is also a collection of rare editions of old books, some dating back to the 16th century.

Among treasured family possessions are a tomahawk given by Sitting Bull to Malcolm McArthur, graduate of West Point, 1865, and a letter from Malcolm to his mother in which he tells of going on expeditions under General Custer.

General William McArthur in 1861 organized the 8th Maine Regiment, 73 Limington men enlisting for service in the Civil War. After the war, he retired to his home to practice law and to cultivate an extensive apple orchard. He would walk through the fields with a cane and whenever the cane touched the ground, there he would plant a tree. When the trees were grown, every straight one, to the amazement of his neighbors, was cut down because, said the General, 'a straight tree is easier to bring up to bear good fruit than a crooked one.'

CORNISH (alt. 355, Cornish Town, pop. 763) (*see Tour* 15), 32.7 *m.*, is at a junction with State 5 (*see Tour* 15).

KEZAR FALLS (alt. 381, Parsonsfield Town, pop. 897, and Town of Porter), 36.5 *m.*, a good-sized settlement of neat small homes, is divided into two sections by Ossipee River. It has a village corporation, though the residents on opposite sides of the river are taxpayers and voters in separate towns.

The bustling village centers around the *Kezar Falls Woolen Company Mill* (*open by permit*) (R) along the river, which is wide at this point and held back by a long, curved *Dam* (L).

PORTER (alt. 407, Porter Town, pop. 883), 39 *m.*

Right from Porter on a dirt road to the *Bullockite Church* (*open last Sun. in May only*), 2 *m.* (L). In the early 1800's a religious battle raged in this locality, causing the Baptist denomination to be split. The dissenters, who were fundamentalists and led by Elder Jeremiah Bullock and Elder John Buzzell, emulated the example of the Disciples and for years the rite of washing one another's feet as a mark of humility was always a part of their services.

The severe simplicity of the large two-story building, which they erected in 1828, and the bleakness of its rough plastered walls and floor are relieved only by the beauty of the wainscoting of pumpkin pine, which has grown brown and satinlike with age. Square box pews, each with a small gate opening on the aisle, divide the floor of the church and face the high platform at one end. Here beneath the long fan-shaped window sat the elders, a delicate railing enclosing the benches reserved for them. When the church was built no provision was made for heat as it was the old-time belief that the love of God shown in the fervor of the congregation was sufficient to raise the temperature to a comfortable point. Later on the warmth of the meetings must have waned for a stove was set up downstairs and now many lengths of pipe twist along the ceiling under the gallery.

At 42.8 *m.* State 25 crosses the New Hampshire Line, 2.3 miles east of Freedom, N.H.

ISLAND TOURS

OF ALL Maine's physical attractions, perhaps her islands hold the greatest share of scenic riches. Thousands in number, they border her coast in a long fringe of interdependent but individual units, each with distinct features that make it stand out by itself. They have always been prosperous with the bounty of the sea, and many of them are still important fishing and lobstering centers. Others have achieved fame as shipping ports, or for some peculiar product of their own — as for example, the granite of the Penobscot Bay islands. Today they are principally summer resort centers, and from Casco Bay to Passamaquoddy Bay they are frequented by city folk who desire temporary retreat from the stress of modern living to the simplicity, privacy, and independence of insular life. More and more generally, artists and writers, yachting and fishing enthusiasts, sufferers from hay fever and other ailments, are acquiring summer homes on the coastal islands of Maine.

The tours described below may conveniently be taken from leading mainland points, and include some of the larger insular population centers, prominent summer resorts, and islands of special scenic, historical, or legendary interest. While numerous sunset or moonlight sails may be taken out of Portland and other ports, the following daylight cruises were selected as providing opportunity during the leisure of the voyage to enjoy some of the great body of descriptive material and native lore relating to almost every island. One should make inquiry at the various wharfs regarding steamboat schedules, as the service is variable.

TOUR 1: PORTLAND *to* THE ISLANDS OF CASCO BAY

A. To Orr's Island, via Peak's, Little and Great Diamond, Long, Little and Great Chebeague, and Cliff Islands, South Harpswell, and Bailey Island. Time: about 2½ hours.

B. To Gurnet, by same route as above to Bailey Island. Time: about 3 hours.

C. To Birch Island, via Cousin's and Bustin's Islands. Time: about 2 hours.

Casco Bay Lines. Custom House Wharf, Commercial St. (*see PORTLAND*).

The mainland shore of Casco Bay stretches from the end of Cape Elizabeth on the south to Bald Head at Cape Small on the north. These two points are more than twenty miles apart in a direct line; and between them, the lighthouse at Halfway Rock marks the center of the bay's outer border. The island-dotted waters of the bay cover an area of approximately 200 square miles. Geologists say that this was once the mouth of the Androscoggin River, and that the sandy inner islands were built up of sediment brought down by the stream and deposited upon jutting reefs. Finally blocking up its entire mouth in this fashion, the river eventually deviated to its present channel, joining with the Kennebec at Merrymeeting Bay. Steamers, ferries, small motor and sail craft ply the channels that weave among Casco's many islands, most of which are heavily wooded, with wild cliffs and crescents of smooth beach. Although any native of the bay region will say that the islands number 365, one for every day in the year, by official count there are actually but 222 'big enough for a man to get out and stand on'; and of these only 138 have sufficient acreage to be classed as good-sized islands. Besides those counted, there are, of course, innumerable rocks and ledges, shoals and 'knobs' — so many, in fact, that the eastern end of the bay is considered one of the most difficult sections of the entire coast to navigate. Single islands were generally named after early settlers, or they have retained their Indian designations. A few names, however, attest to the originality and imagination of the first inhabitants — as for example, Junk of Pork, Pound of Tea, Stepping Stones, Brown Cow, and Goosenest. Many of the names are used more than once: there are four Ram Islands, two Cushing Islands, two Crow Islands, and several Pumpkin Knobs.

These islands abound in pirate lore, Indian legends, and stories of the struggles between early colonists and the red man. The tales of Casco Bay have added their bright coloring to the tapestry of American literature. Whether the scene of a bloody battle or the former habitation of a famous chief, the site of an early settlement or a place of buried treasure, nearly every island can boast some exciting history of its own. And all possess in varying degree the rugged and sparkling beauty peculiar to the northern shores. Upon the larger islands there are summer colonies, summer hotels, and the villages of year-round inhabitants, most of them fishermen.

A. *Portland to Orr's Island*

This is a smooth-water trip of 44 miles, with stops at nine islands and opportunity to enjoy a memorable shore dinner at one of the hotels near the steamboat wharf.

From Custom House Wharf the steamer swings out into the water traffic of Portland Harbor, leaving behind it the activity of the water front — the busy docks, the noise of Commercial Street with its trucks and trains, and over all the shrill cries of the scavenging gulls. Soon the boat passes HOG ISLAND (L) with its formidable-looking *Fort Gorges*, in a commanding position on a reef, guarding the upper harbor entrances as well as the main ship channel. Completed about 1865, this bleak fortress has not been garrisoned for many years, for its short range guns made its period of usefulness a brief one.

Toward the right is HOUSE ISLAND, on which stands *Fort Scammell*, another old and abandoned harbor defense. As early as 1661, House Island was known by its present name, and an early blockhouse was erected here. During the rebuilding of the island fortification, early in the

Civil War, the original blockhouse, topped by a carved wooden eagle with extended wings, was replaced by the present fort — named for Colonel Alexander Scammell, a gallant soldier of the Revolution.

Rising in the background, beyond House Island, is the seamed granite shore of CUSHING ISLAND. Its history dates back to 1623, when Captain Christopher Levett took possession of its wild tree-covered area and built a strongly fortified house on its northern extremity. Cushing Island is now the year-round home of many Portland people, and has an active summer colony.

Several minutes out from Portland, the steamer docks at PEAK'S ISLAND (alt. 45, Insular Ward of Portland). With its summer hotels and cottage inns, churches, a hospital, and stores, this is more densely populated, both by permanent and by summer residents, than any other island in the Bay. In the early nineteenth century, Peak's was developed into one of the most popular recreational centers in the country, and many nationally known figures have summered here. Its woodland trails, well cultivated fields, and ledgy shores are colored with a history dating back to the early days of Falmouth, when the island was owned by Michael Mitton, son-in-law of Portland's first settler, George Cleeve (*see PORTLAND*). Mitton gained renown as a huntsman and fowler, and was much given to relating in detail the adventures that befell him. Perhaps the most amazing was his tale of the triton or merman who swam up and grasped the side of his boat, whereupon he seized a hatchet and with a single blow severed the hands of the son of Poseidon, who sank beneath the waves and was seen no more in the waters of Casco Bay. But the finny hands of the monster remained clinging to the side of the boat, and it was only with difficulty that Mitton pried them loose and flung them into the sea.

Longfellow's poem, 'The Wreck of the Hesperus,' is based upon one of the major tragedies in the annals of Peak's Island. The schooner 'Helen Eliza,' caught in the great gale of 1869, was driven ashore in the night and ground to pieces on the jutting rocks. Only one member of the crew of twelve was rescued — a lad who had previously been the sole survivor of a vessel which foundered in a hurricane off the West Indies. He decided to tempt fate no further, and retired from the sea to a farm in New Hampshire. There, ironically enough, he slipped off a log while crossing a small stream and was drowned.

Leaving Peak's Island, the steamer swings in a northerly direction, to dock at LITTLE DIAMOND ISLAND (alt. 27, Insular Ward of Portland), one of the prettiest islands in the Bay. It was formerly used as a part-time station for lighthouse service, and is connected with its larger sister island of Great Diamond by a narrow sand spit which is covered by water at high tide.

GREAT DIAMOND ISLAND (alt. 39, Insular Ward of Portland), formerly known as Hog Island, is the next stopping place. It has a select cottage colony, which maintains an excellent golf course. Great Diamond's precipitous sea walls fringed about with golden seaweed bound a greatly diversified surface — deep ravines, ragged elevations, and green slopes extending to the shore. On the east side, commanding Hussey's Sound, is *Fort McKinley* (*open*), a sub-post of Portland Harbor defenses, used as a summer training post by R.O.T.C., O.R.C., and C.M.T.C. units.

The steamer now enters *Hussey's Sound*, a water thoroughfare between the two Diamonds and Long Island. Straight ahead in the distance are Clapboard, Basket, and Sturdivant, three low-lying isles; while to the left, in the lee of Great Diamond, is Cow Island.

LONG ISLAND (alt. 40, Insular Ward of Portland), at which the steamer makes three stops, is one of the larger and most scenic in the island group. Excellent roads traverse its 1000 acres, which were well known to the Abnaki Indians long before white men came to the Casco Bay region. Stone implements, arrow heads of flint, and shell heaps found here bear testimony to the early red men's occupation. Ragged coast, sandy beaches, pine groves, and open fields, with shady paths and excellent roads, make walking a pleasure on Long Island. The hotels and inns here boast of the medicinal properties of the springs among the ledges.

Passing along the shoreline (R) of Long Island, the steamer enters the waters of *Chandler Cove* to dock at LITTLE CHEBEAGUE ISLAND (alt. 55, Cumberland Town), whose open fields run down to sandy beaches. It lies a short distance southwest from GREAT CHEBEAGUE ISLAND (alt. 70, Cumberland Town), where the steamer usually stops on its return trip. This, the second largest island in Casco Bay, has summer hotels, a nine-hole golf course, tennis courts, croquet grounds, and bathing and boating facilities. Numerous fine white-sand bathing beaches lie tucked in between its rocky cliffs, and many summer cottages are scattered over its 2000 acres. Twenty miles of gravel road, bright with clam shells, wind through fragrant pine and spruce groves, and through broad fields where many varieties of wild flowers, ferns, mosses, and berries grow in profusion. From its occasional eminences, the other islands of the Bay, with long reaches of water between them, may be seen stretching away as if in ordered arrangement; and from its western end at sunset, the reflected coloring in the water forms a striking foreground for Portland's Munjoy Hill, on the mainland.

Much excitement was once aroused here by the arrival of an old sailor who claimed to have been one of a pirate crew which many years before had landed at Chebeague and buried a great treasure. After prowling around for a time, the old fellow began digging in a secluded part of the island. Among those who offered to assist him in his excavations was a young man of the island. When his offer was curtly refused, the latter leaped over the rope with which the old man had enclosed the spot where he was digging; whereupon the treasure seeker, in a voice quaking with anger, cried: 'I call on God and you people to witness that within a year this young fool will be tied in knots even as I could tie this rope.' No one remembers now whether any treasure was found, but (as the story goes) in due time the young man received a severe drenching while out fishing, and was confined to his bed with an agonizing malady which drew up his arms and legs as if 'tied in knots'; and when he died, soon after, it was necessary to break the bones of his limbs in order to get his body into the casket.

Leaving Great Chebeague, the steamer rounds the tip of Long Island (R) to enter *Luckse Sound*, with the small HOPE ISLAND lying straight ahead. This latter was purchased in the early part of the present century by Senator George W. Elkins of Pennsylvania, who built a large mansion on it, 75 feet above the sea. At present Hope Island is the property of a private club; the clubhouse may be seen at the southern end of the island.

CLIFF ISLAND (alt. 38, Insular Ward of Portland), marked by sawtooth reefs, great coves, low sand bars, and beautiful pine groves, is an outlying island resort. Prominent among the legends kept alive here by year-round residents is the story of Captain Keiff, a notorious smuggler and pirate, who lived alone on the island in a log hut, and who on stormy nights would drive a horse with a lantern attached to its neck up and down the shore to decoy passing vessels into the narrow channel, where they would be wrecked on the treacherous reefs. From this practice he salvaged enough of the cargoes to net a considerable income. A grassy knoll rising above the island road where it turns into a deep ravine is still called *Keiff's Garden* — the reputed burying ground of the sailors whose bodies were washed ashore from the wrecks caused by Keiff's false signals. Close by is JEWELL ISLAND, for years a private estate.

Leaving Cliff Island, the steamer swings northeast. To the right lies EAGLE ISLAND, where lived the late Robert E. Peary. The Admiral's residence, a treasure-house of trophies from foreign lands, perches on a rocky promontory facing the mainland.

Ahead is the long slender bit of mainland known as *Harpswell Neck*, where the boat enters Potts Harbor to dock at SOUTH HARPSWELL (*see Tour* 1D).

From South Harpswell the steamer rounds Potts Point, the tip of Harpswell Neck, with HASKELL ISLAND lying to the right. A series of strange events took place on this fertile island about sixty years ago, when it became overrun by rats. An old lobsterman named Humphrey, who had built a shack on the shore, seemed to live amicably enough with the rats, even though they continually stole the fish from his bait barrel. But when winter came on, Humphrey's friends warned him of the danger of living alone with only rats for company. Nevertheless he persisted in staying. One day, Harpswell fishermen noticed that no smoke was rising from the chimney of the little shack and they could see no one stirring on the island, so they rowed out to investigate. When they opened Humphrey's door, they were met by a squealing swarm of rats. Driving them away, the men entered the cabin — to find that the old lobsterman had been eaten in his bunk. The horrified citizens of Harpswell and the neighboring islands armed themselves with sticks and clubs and converged upon Haskell Island. When they left they were satisfied that every rodent there had been exterminated. Yet next spring the rats were as numerous as ever.

But it was not long before Harpswell residents again saw smoke rising from the chimney of the hut where Humphrey had lived. Two young fishermen, Wallace and Bruce Mills from North Harpswell, had set up an establishment on Haskell, bringing with them for companionship and protection a dozen or more very husky cats. The war began. At first the cats had the worst of it, but they lived to emerge triumphant. They were almost as prolific as the rats; and, fed on fish and cared for by the Mills boys, they and their progeny grew to a size and strength unheard of among mainland cats. It was not long before the last rat met his fate. But not only the rats disappeared — Haskell, once a paradise of songbirds, became silent except for nightly yowls. The cats increased in number, and Wallace and Bruce were kept more than busy catching enough fish to feed them. With the young men they were docile enough, but any visitor who attempted to land on the island would be met by several hundred spitting and clawing furies.

One day a prospective purchaser from the city approached Haskell; here in this green and pleasant spot he saw an ideal place to build a summer home. But he did not land on the island; in fact, he left rather hurriedly. The owner of the island told Wallace and Bruce that something would have to be done. They were only squatters, and they and their cats had no legal right to usurp the island. But the boys would do nothing. Finally, however, they arose one morning to find an army of dead cats stretched before the shack. Someone had come in the night and poisoned them. The Mills boys were broken-hearted. They disappeared, and no one knew where they went. But never since has a cat been seen on Haskell Island — or a rat.

The steamer enters *Mericoneag Sound* to dock at BAILEY ISLAND (*see Tour 1D*). Of all the island treasure stories, perhaps the most satisfying is one told of a farmer-fisherman of Bailey Island, John Wilson by name. He was an impecunious and not overly ambitious soul, who one day surprised his neighbors mightily by sailing home from Boston in a handsome new sloop and buying the finest farm on Bailey. He set himself up in generous style, married, produced a fine family, and became a leader in his community. The reason for this sudden rise in life was finally revealed by Wilson after many years. He had been out duck-hunting, and a bird he had shot fell on a distant weed-covered ledge; as he went to retrieve it, his feet gave way beneath him, and he sank into a cavity between two rocks. Investigating this cavity, he found in it a heavy iron pot filled with pieces of Spanish gold. Wilson immediately took his find to Boston, and there exchanged it for $12,000 — in those days a large fortune.

The steamer leaves Bailey Island dock, to enter the waters of *Harpswell Sound*, an arm of Casco Bay partially enclosed by the shores of Harpswell Neck and Bailey and Orr's Islands. These waters are the locale of

Whittier's poem, 'The Dead Ship of Harpswell,' based on a legend current among Orr's Island folk.

On ORR'S ISLAND (*see Tour 1D*), which is connected by bridge with Bailey Island and with the mainland, is the *Pearl House*, home of the heroine of Harriet Beecher Stowe's novel 'The Pearl of Orr's Island.'

B. *To Gurnet*

This cruise follows much the same course as that taken on the trip just described, but from Bailey Island dock the steamer continues up Mericoneag Sound past Orr's Island. Visible between the latter and Bailey Island in the far distance is RAGGED ISLAND, the summer retreat of Edna St. Vincent Millay, Maine's famous poet, and locale of the Reverend Elijah Kellogg's widely read 'Elm Island Series' of books for boys. At one time, because of its isolated position, Ragged Island was a rendezvous for lawbreakers, in particular for a gang of counterfeiters who made their headquarters here for several years until finally routed by Federal agents.

The steamer follows the west shore of Orr's and Sebascodegan Islands for several miles, turning from Harpswell Sound into Harpswell Cove, then into Long Reach, and finally arriving at Doughty Cove, where it docks at GURNET (*see Tour 1D*), so-called from a narrow tide rip where the waters of the cove merge violently with those of the New Meadows River, a tidal river extending nearly twenty miles inland on the other side of Sebascodegan (or Great) Island. The stop-over at Gurnet provides opportunity for a shore dinner.

C. *To Birch Island*

A cruise through inner Casco Bay and its islands offers vistas of the mainland shores and glimpses of many of the islands touched on the Orr's Island trip. Leaving Portland, the steamer swings in a northeasterly course past Little and Great Diamond, with MACKWORTH ISLAND appearing at the left just off a promontory near the mouth of the Presumpscot River. In 1631, this bit of land was given to Arthur Mackworth by the powerful Sir Ferdinando Gorges, who was so favorably disposed toward Mackworth that he later made him deputy of the Bay. In 1808, James Rennie, a Scotsman, bought the island and promptly mortgaged it in order to build an elaborate mansion, where he and his charming wife entertained lavishly. Mackworth Island was occupied by a training camp during the Civil War; but since 1888 it has been owned by the Baxter family, whose members include the late James P. Baxter, at one time Mayor of Portland, and his son Percival P. Baxter, a former Governor of Maine. Opposite Mackworth, on the mainland at Martin Point, are the buildings of the U.S. Marine Hospital.

Continuing northeast, the steamer skirts the mainland shore, where many fine residences are visible from deck. About ten minutes out from Portland, the boat passes long and narrow CLAPBOARD ISLAND (L) which, twenty-nine years after all the area north and south of it had been

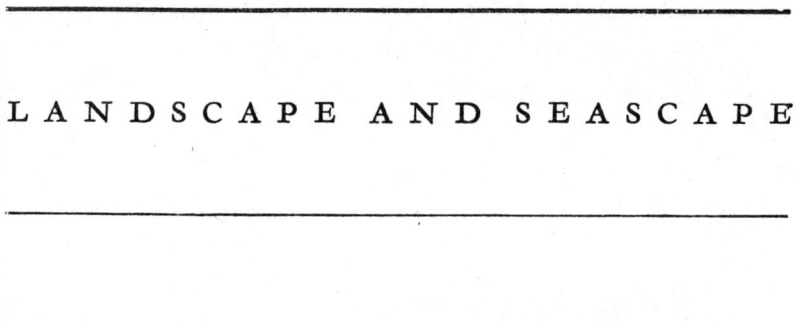

MAINE waters, whether stream, lake, or sea, and Maine's mountains and her valleys are known widely and speak for themselves with their own beauty. It is the natural loveliness of the State, in many places quite unspoiled, which is the chief cause of the conversion of many visitors to that mystic society of worshipers who will tell you that east of the Piscataqua even the very air is 'different.'

SCREW AUGER FALLS, GRAFTON

TRANQUILLITY

OFF FOR A CANOE TRIP, MEGUNTICOOK LAKE

AS SHADOWS DEEPEN

MOUNT DESERT ISLAND AS SEEN FROM SULLIVAN

PARLIN POND, SOMERSET COUNTY

WEST QUODDY HEADLIGHT AT SUNSET

THUNDER HOLE, MOUNT DESERT ISLAND

BAR HARBOR AND FRENCHMAN'S BAY, FROM CADILLAC MOUNTAIN

RIDING THE TIDE, BOOTHBAY HARBOR

PORTLAND HEADLIGHT

SNOW SCENE

forcibly annexed by the Massachusetts Bay Colony in 1651, was granted to Walter Gendall by the North Yarmouth Communities in recognition of his services at the time of the first settlement.

To the right lie LITTLE and GREAT DIAMOND ISLANDS, and not far beyond them is tiny BASKET ISLAND, with STURDIVANT ISLAND lying in the background a little offshore from Falmouth Foreside (*see Tour* 1, *sec. a*). The next stop is at COUSIN'S ISLAND (alt. 29, Yarmouth Town). This, like most of the more populous islands of Casco Bay, has its full measure of blood-stained history. To this wild spot, known to the Indians as Susquescon, John Cousins came and built his home in 1645. Other settlers followed, and at Cornfield Point, the north end of the island, land was cleared and the first crops sown. Game was plentiful here, especially in the spring, when it was customary for the colonists to join in an organized hunt of the wild animals which had crossed over the ice from the mainland, driving them across the island to Cornfield Point where, unable to escape, they were easily killed. During the Indian Wars, the few settlers who escaped the tomahawk fled to the mainland or to the refuge of island blockhouses. But the island was gradually resettled as soon as hostilities ceased, Rowland Hamilton, brother of Chebeague Island's first settler, being the first to return.

A cove adjacent to Cornfield Point has borne the name of *Dead Man's Cove* since the night, many years ago, when the sea cast ashore at this spot the mangled bodies of three sailors.

Not long ago, during the excavation of a cellar on the south end of the island, the skeleton of a man of extremely large stature, with an officer's sword lying across his breast, was uncovered. Both the skeleton and the sword, probably relics of a clash between French and English, were in a fairly good state of preservation, due to the dryness of the spot where they were found.

Cousin's is connected by a bridge with neighboring LITTLEJOHN ISLAND (alt. 30, Yarmouth Town), which is also a steamer stop. Littlejohn has been known by several different names, and has changed ownership many times. The east end of the island, with its numerous shell heaps, was long an Indian camping ground. Many fine Indian relics now in the possession of the Maine Historical Society were unearthed on Littlejohn.

To the north, after leaving the dock at Littlejohn, the mouth of the *Harraseeket River* is visible, with rocky *Wolf's Neck* extending out from its sparkling waters. To the southeast are the WHALEBOATS, two islands lying off the shore of *Harpswell Neck*, which rises in the background. Almost directly ahead is GREAT MOSHIER ISLAND, little changed since Hugh Moshier, a gallant adventurer, left the tarnished artificialities of London in the 1640's to settle here, where peace is broken only by the booming of white surf on rocky shores and the occasional cry of gulls. West of Great Moshier is LITTLE MOSHIER, a narrow isle which is the site of an early Indian burying ground. Northwest of Little Moshier is LANE'S ISLAND; here during the Indian Wars, when the hillsides echoed with blood-curdling yells of the painted red men, two white victims were horribly tortured to death.

BUSTIN'S ISLAND (alt. 28, Freeport Town), where the steamer next docks, is believed to have been the site of a mysterious lead mine where many years ago a person known as 'Swindler' Ransom procured a metal which he asserted could be transmuted into silver. Ransom appeared on the island out of nowhere, and succeeded in duping a respectable Portland silversmith and others into believing his claims. Finally one of the investors in his enterprise became suspicious and discovered that the black rod with which Ransom was accustomed to stir the ore while muttering strange incantations was really the source of the little ball of silver eventually produced. The finding of a thin rolled silver coin concealed in the hollow end of the black wand brought about Ransom's arrest, but his escape and disappearance were as sudden and mysterious as had been his appearance in this region.

An amusing tale is told on Bustin's Island of one Charles Guppy, an early resident, who conceived a novel plan to eliminate the labor of rowing to South Freeport for his weekly supplies. With the assistance of a neighbor, Guppy constructed a huge red kite which they tied by a heavy string to the bow of his dory, and set out from the mainland. Part way across to the island, a fierce gale of wind caught the kite and the dory's bow rose out of the water, while the panic-stricken inventors clung for dear life to keep from being tossed out of the craft. But they somehow managed to keep sailing in the direction of Bustin's; and before either had recovered sufficiently to reach the bow and cut away the kite, they went skimming up the beach, a full boatlength into the grass. Guppy and his friend thereupon decided that rowing had its advantages.

The steamer route passes (R) UPPER and LOWER GOOSE ISLANDS, lying end to end, and the GOSLINGS, tiny islets at the southern tip of Lower Goose. To the north are the waters of *Maquoit Bay* (pronounced *M'kwate*) with the shores of Freeport (*see Tour 1, sec. a*) rising in the background.

BIRCH ISLAND (alt. 41, Harpswell Town), the last boat stop, was so named because of its abundance of silver birch trees. Walter Merriman, ancestor of all of the Merriman name in Harpswell and its vicinity, emigrated from Ireland and became Birch Island's first settler. Several years after Merriman's arrival, a flourishing colony sprang up here, and the island wilderness soon became a little community of well-cultivated farms and comfortable homes, supporting a school with forty-eight pupils. In 1849, nearly fifty years after the inception of the settlement, most of the farmers abandoned their fields and orchards to join the great California gold rush. Today yawning cellar-holes and gnarled old apple trees scattered about the island are all that is left of the abandoned farms.

During the Indian wars, a sentinel was stationed on the steep hill on the west side of the island; and with the approach of the red men by water, a signal was given to the lookout at Harpswell, who spread an alarm which warned the settlers to take refuge in the blockhouse on near-by Shelter Island.

TOUR 2: BOOTHBAY HARBOR *to* SQUIRREL ISLAND

Ferry service. Virginia Landing, Townsend Ave. (*see Tour 1G*). Time: about 20 minutes.

Leaving the wharf, the boat emerges from among the small craft that crowd the waterfront of Boothbay Harbor, to speed through the open water of the outer harbor.

SQUIRREL ISLAND (alt. 40, Southport Town), connected by steamer with Boothbay Harbor and Bath, is the oldest summer settlement in the Boothbay region, and the scene of much social and recreational activity. The island is like a small city during the summer months; in the winter it is inhabited only by caretakers.

Squirrel was among the first points visited by early explorers along the Maine coast. Captain Waymouth stopped here in 1605, when he made his voyage to Maine, and undoubtedly Captain John Smith visited the island during his trip to Monhegan in 1614. Some of the early pirates who played havoc with shipping in Maine waters made use of Squirrel Island. On the east coast is *Kidd's Cave*, a curious tunnel-like cavern extending back into the solid rock 150 to 200 feet; it is so called because of a local belief that the privateer, Captain Kidd, used it as a hiding place for loot.

Before Squirrel became a summer resort it was owned by a local 'squire,' who sold it to a group of business men in Auburn and Lewiston. These men formed an association from which the present Squirrel Island Colony was developed. An interesting local story is connected with the death of Squire Greenleaf, the early owner, who moved to Boothbay Harbor after selling the island. He had always expressed a desire that when he died his body should be buried in sand from Davenport Cove, an inlet on the island's shore line. After his death a crew of men was sent over with a scow to Squirrel to get the sand for filling the Squire's grave. However, instead of going around the point and into the cove, the men decided that as long as the sand came from any part of Squirrel, it would meet the requirements; so they went ashore at a more convenient place, loaded the scow, and started back toward Boothbay Harbor. Almost immediately a storm came up, the harbor waters were churned into foamy waves, and several of the crew asserted that they saw a shadowy figure, vaguely resembling a wildly gesticulating Squire Greenleaf, walking on the water. Overcome by fear, the men shovelled every pound of sand overboard. Not until the scow was completely unloaded did the storm abate. They then went to Davenport Cove, reloaded their scow, and in perfect weather returned to Boothbay Harbor with the load of sand for the Squire's grave.

The founders of the summer colony realized that to secure desirable municipal improvements it would be necessary to form some sort of organization to collect taxes. Since no member of the colony, made up as

the latter was of temporary residents, had a vote in the town meetings of
Southport, it would not be easy to induce the town to appropriate money
for improvements on the island. A plan was evolved, therefore, from
which grew the Squirrel Island village corporation, the forerunner of all
village corporations within the towns of Maine. In this first corporation
the right to vote was restricted to property owners, whether men or
women. Thus, at Squirrel Island women's suffrage was given an early
trial.

One of the outstanding achievements of the village corporation is the
system of cement sidewalks threading the island, an improvement brought
about by women's votes and bearing directly on the economic development of the island. There are no delivery wagons or trucks on Squirrel,
and when housewives shop for supplies they trundle their purchases home
in wheeled carts, which when not in use may generally be seen standing
before the residences. Smooth walks nowadays make shopping easy on the
island. It is not unusual for the Boothbay steamer to have a long line of
carts aboard, when islanders sail for a day's shopping on the mainland.

TOUR 3: BOOTHBAY HARBOR *to* MONHEGAN ISLAND

Thomaston & Monhegan Steamboat Co. Eastern Steamship Co. Wharf,
Townsend Ave. (*see Tour 1G*). Time: about 2 hours.

From Boothbay Harbor a little steamboat runs outside into deep water,
bucking waves and swift currents on a 20-mile ocean voyage to the
natural harbor of Monhegan Island (*reached also from Thomaston and
Port Clyde*).

MONHEGAN ISLAND (alt. 40, Monhegan Plantation, pop. 109) has
three summer hotels. Monhegan, about 2½ miles long and 1 mile wide,
with a fishing village, and the adjacent islet of MANANA, both with
steep, ragged cliffs, attract many visitors.

Unusual marks on the ledges of Manana Island, scratches 4 feet long and
6 inches wide, have been used to support the beliefs of those who think
that Norsemen visited the island about A.D. 1000.

Fishing furnishes the livelihood of the residents of Monhegan, and fishing
brought the first visitors. It is thought that Basque, Portuguese, Spanish,
and Breton fishermen may have been taking rich cargoes of codfish from
these waters at the time Columbus discovered America. John and
Sebastian Cabot circled the island in 1498. David Ingram, who walked
from the Gulf of Mexico and through this region in 1569, gave the first
description of Monhegan, 'a great island that was backed like a whale.'
Captain George Waymouth visited the island in May, 1605, naming it St.
George's Island; and Champlain saw it later that summer. Captain John
Smith landed here in 1614.

A temporary settlement existed on the island in 1626. Another settlement was made in 1654, serving as a refuge for settlers from the mainland
until destroyed by the French, under Baron de Castin, in 1689. It was re-
occupied by fishermen about 1720. In 1717 the pirate Paulsgrave, some-

times known as Paul Williams, who was preying upon the shipping along the New England coast, sailed north to Monhegan, where he erected dwellings and a prison. Using the island as his base, he cruised the Maine waters for several weeks, capturing a number of vessels at sea and at Matinicus and Pemaquid. Although a man-of-war and an armed sloop were sent out from Boston to capture him, they were unsuccessful; he disappeared that year and was not heard of again. This pirate occupation has been the cause of much futile digging for treasure here.

During the Revolution and the War of 1812, privateering was carried on in neighboring waters. The battle in which the American privateer 'Enterprise' defeated the British brig 'Boxer,' September 5, 1813, occurred between Monhegan and Pemaquid Point.

All summer long, fishing smacks unload cargoes of green lobsters along the Monhegan waterfront. 'Cheap-livin' fish, lobsters are,' an old fisherman explained. 'Kin eat barnacles, seaweed, mud, anything. Even live in the well of a smack five or six months an' come out all right, 'less they chaw each other up, an' they're mostly doin' that. Don't seem to hurt much, though. I've found lots o' claws broke off in fights, an' they grow back just as good agin.'

Most of the lobsters caught average $10\frac{1}{2}$ inches in length, which is considered the standard market size; but occasional prodigies turn up to delight their captors. The largest lobster caught along the Maine coast, taken in Casco Bay about 50 years ago, weighed 36 pounds. Baby lobsters a few inches long are often seen scuttling for safety under their mothers' tails, and at times are found stranded in shells into which they have crawled near the shore. As they increase in size, their hard shells split up the back and are sloughed off, to be replaced by new ones. During the time of these periodical sheddings, the lobsters take refuge in crevices under stones or in the heavy eel grass. Though unwieldy in appearance and given little credit for velocity, the lobsters move rapidly, by preference backward. The large anterior claws, used to crack clams, are strong enough to take off a man's finger.

The island is covered by a network of trails. *Cathedral Woods* and *Burnt Head* are favorite spots with visitors. *Boar's Head*, one of the most unusual formations on the Maine coast, has the appearance of a fat neck and a triple chin beneath a snub nose.

Monhegan's art population is internationally known, Rockwell Kent being credited with having popularized the island as a resort for artists. He brought a group here, and started Monhegan's first art class on Horn Hill. Among the well-known artists who summer here are A. Bogdanove, Frances Cochrane, Alice Stoddard, Mr. and Mrs. Sears Gallagher, Mrs. William Clark Mason, and Frederick Dorr Steele.

The present *Monhegan Island Light*, near the center of the island built in 1850 of granite blocks, replaced a light erected in 1824. The top of the tower, which has a revolving light, is 178 feet above the water. On the western side of Manana Island is a trumpet fog signal that can be heard about 15 miles at sea.

TOUR 4: ROCKLAND to VINALHAVEN ISLAND

Vinalhaven & Rockland Steamboat Co. (Vinalhaven Line). Tillson Ave. Wharf (*see Tour* 1, *sec. b*). Time: about 1¼ hours.

The steamer swings out of Rockland Harbor past the Rockland breakwater (L), jutting far out from *Jameson Point* and tipped by a lonely lighthouse. To the right, a rocky and heavily wooded peninsula stretches out into the Atlantic, to terminate at *Owl's Head* with its slender white-towered *Lighthouse* (*see Tour* 1, *sec. b*). Taking a southeasterly course, the steamer enters an open section of Penobscot Bay. Ahead lie numerous small tree-covered islands. About half an hour out from Rockland, the boat passes HURRICANE ISLAND, green with scrub pine, the locale of Harold Vinal's poem 'Hurricane.' Swinging around the northern tip of this island, the steamer enters the waters of *Hurricane Sound*, formed by several small islands and the western shore of Vinalhaven Island. Ahead lies the bleak *Deadman Ledge*, while to the left is tiny POTATO ISLAND. Entering *Carver's Harbor* the steamer docks at Vinalhaven.

VINALHAVEN (alt. 40, Vinalhaven Town, pop. 1843) has a number of year-round and summer hotels and camps, with airplane as well as steamer service to the mainland. The long irregular eastern shore, endlessly pounded by ocean waves, is little populated, the island folk choosing to live in and near the village of Vinalhaven, on the hilly shores of Carver's Harbor. This village is at once a commercial, industrial, residential, and resort center. Fishing, largely monopolizing the waterfront, is the mainstay of existence. Sails are manufactured here; and because of its fine harbor in a long stretch of open sea, coastal vessels call here for supplies and equipment.

An irregular and much indented island, Vinalhaven has a maximum length of about eight miles. Except for the settlement at the southeastern end, it consists of wild rocky land, heavily wooded with scrub spruce and pine. It was named for its early colonizer, John Vinal, a Boston merchant. Near the center of the island is *Round Pond*, an attractive miniature lake, where lily pads float on the placid waters.

Natives look forward to another boom in Vinalhaven granite, which in the past has been quarried here in large quantities. The blue-gray granite of the deep *Quarry* on the northern edge of the village was at one time in great demand for public buildings; the 120-ton monoliths on three sides of the choir altar in the Cathedral of St. John the Divine, in New York City, were quarried here. At present no stone other than a small amount of paving material is cut on the island.

Harold Vinal, a descendant of John Vinal and a native of the island, has embodied much of the beauty of his island home in his poems and other writings.

TOUR 5: ROCKLAND *to* SWAN ISLAND

Via North Haven and Deer Isle.

Vinalhaven & Rockland Steamboat Co. (Swan Island Line), Tillson Ave. Wharf (*see Tour* 1, *sec. b*). Time: about 3½ hours.

Leaving Rockland Harbor, the steamer passes the breakwater and pursues a northeasterly course across blue Penobscot Bay. The SUGAR LOAVES (R), a series of brown moss-covered islets, mark the southern entrance to *Fox Island Thorofare*, a navigation route between the islands of Vinalhaven and North Haven — part of a group discovered in 1613 by Martin Pring. About midway in the 'Thorofare,' the steamer docks at the settlement of North Haven on North Haven Island.

NORTH HAVEN (alt. 50, North Haven Town, pop. 476) has airplane as well as steamer service to the mainland, and ferry service to Vinalhaven. Good roads connect the settlement with those at Bartlett and North Harbors.

The long irregularly shaped North Haven Island is well known as a summer resort. Its rugged shore line has many natural harbors, while little wooded headlands extend out into Penobscot Bay. Summer homes have been built on many of these headlands; and anchored offshore in summer, near almost all of the residences, comfortable cabin cruisers, or yachts are generally to be seen.

Anne Morrow Lindbergh has devoted a chapter of her book, 'North to the Orient,' to this town, which for several years was the summer home of her father, Dwight Morrow, former Ambassador to Mexico. Of her long flight across the top of the world, she wrote that its 'knotted end is held fast in North Haven.'

Leaving North Haven Island, the steamer continues east through the Fox Island Thorofare, past numerous small isles, and enters an open stretch of Penobscot Bay between the rugged *Calderwood Neck* (R), on Vinalhaven, and Deer Isle.

The next stop is at STONINGTON (alt. 50, Stonington Town, pop. 1418). This, the principal settlement on DEER ISLE, is a seaport with an unpretentious main thoroughfare from which extend short streets of homes of quarrymen, seamen, and fishermen. The skyline is broken by several tall derricks used in hoisting granite from the deep pits of near-by quarries. The entire island rests on a base of pink granite famous for its superior quality and unusual coloring. Many well-known buildings throughout the country are built of this granite; and the work of supplying the stone for New York's Triborough Bridge engaged 200 men for two years. A huge gang-saw, used here for cutting the granite into blocks, is said to be the largest in the world.

The fishing industry becomes of prime importance on Deer Isle in the periods when granite is not being quarried. Then wheeling white gulls appear out of nowhere to sail over the harbor, swooping down suddenly in flocks to snatch at fish as the fleets return home with their splashing cargoes. The *North Lubec Canning Company Plant* packs large quantities of sardines here. The fish are sorted for size, and after visceration they are dehydrated. Uniformed girls then cut them into the required length and pack them in tins, which are placed in machines to receive the proper quantity of either olive oil. or mustard, after which they are sealed and cooked. About 100 girls and 25 men are employed in this factory during the packing season, which extends from August to December.

The *Eastern Penobscot Archives Museum*, in the center of Stonington's business section, is a structure of long granite blocks, built against a high granite ledge. This museum was founded and is owned by Dr. B. Lake Noyes, who has spent thousands of dollars and devoted many years of research in making an extensive collection of geologic and historic relics, early documents, and antiques of the Penobscot Bay region.

Deer Isle, nine miles long and five miles wide, lying in Stonington and Deer Isle township, is very jagged in outline and nearly divided in two by deep inlets of Penobscot Bay. A narrow neck known as the *Haulover* connects the northern and southern sections. About 100 miles of hard-surfaced roads wind through the island's woods and fields, joining a number of little hamlets and twisting along the shore. Across stretches of sand or shingle beach, long reaches of ocean sweep towards distant Bluehill (*see Tour* 3) and the undulating hills of Camden (*see Tour* 1, *sec. b*).

The island is rich in legends of sea captains who made fortunes in slave-running and smuggling, and of the lawless adventures of roustabouts and human derelicts. In the old cemeteries are tombstones in memory of sea-faring men who died on the coast of Africa or lost their lives at sea in the China and East India trading days. In recent years many of the palatial yachts of millionaires have been manned from cabin boy to captain by Deer Isle sailors.

From Stonington, a mail boat may be taken to Isle au Haut.

>Leaving Stonington, this boat winds among the islands to the south, entering Isle au Haut Township as it approaches the waters of Merchant Island. As the boat nears the island, a peculiar haze will be observed hovering over the heights that rise above the sea.
>
>ISLE AU HAUT (alt. 35, Isle au Haut Town, pop. 89) has two small hotels and other accommodations. Champlain, upon sighting the island in 1604, named it, obviously enough, Isle au Haut. Three large and a number of small islands comprise the present township. Bold towering cliffs at the northern end of the island rise to a sheer height of 556 feet above sea level, offering from their summits an inspiring view of other islands and the peaked hills of the mainland, with Cadillac Mountain in the far distance.
>
>Near the eastern shore, scarcely 100 yards from the sea, is *Turner Lake*, with silver birches, cedars, and green maples fringing its steep banks. This mile-long lake, the peculiar amber-hued waters of which are fed by subterranean springs, has long been of interest to geologists.
>
>At *Money Cove* it is believed that Captain Kidd buried a part of his fabulous pirate treasure. Many legends have sprung up around this belief, but there has been no discovery to substantiate them.

Leaving Stonington on the main route, the steamer passes the southern shores of Deer Isle (L), with many small islands on the right. After crossing *Jericho Bay*, with *Naskeag Peninsula* (N) in the distance, and passing be-

tween MARSHALL ISLAND (R) and tiny HAT ISLAND (L), the boat swings north to enter *Burntcoat Harbor* and dock at Swan Island settlement.
SWAN ISLAND (alt. 50, Swan Island Town, pop. 576), with small hotels and other accommodations, comprises 5875 acres. It is one of the Burntcoat group of islands, whose fine harbors and good anchorage make them a haven for fishing craft.

Champlain visited these islands more than a century and a half before their purchase by Colonel James Swan. The latter, born in Fifeshire, Scotland, came to America in 1765, and despite hardships and privation succeeded in colonizing the Burntcoat group of islands. In 1808, he was arrested by the French government and confined in the St. Pelagie debtor's prison. Since he was not responsible for the debt for which he had been imprisoned, he remained in prison for 22 years rather than secure his liberty by accepting the charge and paying the debt. Lafayette, his close friend, tried to persuade him to the latter course; but it was not until Louis Philippe ascended the throne of France that Swan, with other imprisoned debtors, was released. An old and broken man, he died three days later.

The early colonists engaged in frequent bloody contests with the Indians. The final gesture of the aborigines against white possession of their ancient home came in the famous raid of 1750, when they descended on the island to perpetrate a cruel massacre. At this time Captain James Whidden, who won his commission under Sir William Pepperell, was living on the easterly end of the island with his wife and two sons. A daughter, Agibail Noble, with her husband and seven children, was visiting them. Early in the morning of September 8, a party of Indians slipped through the unlocked palisade gate and entered the house. Whidden and his wife escaped by taking refuge in the cellar, but the rest of the family and two servants were taken captive, carried up the Kennebec to Canada, and sold into slavery to the French at prices varying from $29 each for the adults to almost nothing for the thirteen months old Frances Noble. The forlorn condition of the baby appealed to a young French couple, who bought the child for a trifle and adopted her as their own. Baptized Eleanor in the Catholic Church, the little girl was carefully educated in a Canadian convent, and when finally taken away by agents from Massachusetts she left her foster parents with tears and protestations. Brought to new scenes and a new language on the Kennebec, she found that her mother was dead and her father reduced to poverty. It is known that she became a teacher and that she was twice married — first to Jonathan Tilton of New Market, later to John Shute. Her story is related in Drake's 'Tragedies of the Wilderness.'

TOUR 6: BELFAST *to* ISLESBORO ISLAND

Belfast to Castine Service. Eastern Steamship Wharf, Front St. (*see Tour 1, sec. b*). Time: about 20 minutes.

Leaving Belfast, the steamer takes a leisurely course to the southeast, with (R) the heavily wooded and rocky shore line of the mainland forming a striking setting for several small summer resorts. Rounding *Turtle's Head*, a headland marking the north end of Islesboro Island, the steamer passes by North Islesboro and the narrow neck of land that separates it from South Islesboro, to dock at Islesboro on Hewes Point.

ISLESBORO (alt. 40, Islesboro Town, pop. 697), with summer hotels and an island bus service, is the center of an exclusive resort region that includes several smaller islands. A nine-hole golf course, tennis courts, and excellent facilities for sailing, swimming, and fishing make the region a popular one with sports enthusiasts. There is steamer service to Prospect, Belfast, Camden, and Lincolnville.

Islesboro Township consists of North and South Islesboro (connected by a narrow neck of land to form Islesboro Island), Seven Hundred Acre Island, Job Island, and several small near-by isles. It was originally a part of the Waldo Patent, and was visited by the Church Expedition of 1692 in a campaign directed against the Indians. Islesboro Island, however, was not settled until 1769. During the War of 1812, when the British occupied near-by Castine (*see Tour* 3), the inhabitants of Islesboro found neutrality forced upon them. Winter in those early times was of such severity that the waters of Penobscot Bay froze as far out as Isle au Haut, and it was not uncommon for sleighs drawn by oxen to cross to the mainland.

Some farming and fishing is done on the island, but the chief means of livelihood comes from the many summer estates here. Among the well-known persons who regularly visit Islesboro are Lady Astor; Ruth Draper, the monologist; Richard Whitney, president of the New York Stock Exchange; and Charles Dana Gibson, the illustrator.

IV. SPORTS AND RECREATION

SPORTS AND RECREATION

MAINE'S scenic variety and beauty, and its exceptional facilities for recreation and sport, have been extolled by several generations of writers. The long line of coast indented by deep bays and flanked by romantic islands, the vast primeval forests, the innumerable lakes and waterways, the rich resources of game and fish — all these contribute to attract an ever-increasing host of those who seek pleasure, adventure, and health.

Hunting in the fall, sports on snow and ice in the winter, inland and deep-water fishing virtually throughout the year, and summer recreational activities of every kind — boating, swimming, mountain climbing, hiking, horseback riding, etc. — can be enjoyed in fullest measure here. Numerous boys' and girls' camps train youngsters in the appreciation and enjoyment of outdoor life; while State-wide tournaments enhance the competitive interest of such sports as tennis, golf, and archery, skeet and trap-shooting, 'coon' and bird trials.

But along with its many advantages for active sports and recreational exercise in the open, Maine has its own peculiar charm and stimulus for the seeker of restorative solitude and for the creative artist in whatever field, as well as for the nature student and the camera enthusiast. A list of the artists, writers, musicians, and others, living and dead, who have habitually spent their summers on the Maine coast would include many of the most prominent names in American cultural annals.

Although it might be termed the youngest of Maine's industries, the tourist and recreational traffic has developed with such mushroom-like rapidity that it now leads all others in the amount of revenue accruing to the State and its people. It is difficult to say precisely when this became established as a definite economic factor in Maine. As early as 1654, the Court at Saco granted one Henry Waddock the right 'to keep an ordinary to entertain strangers for their money.' Hunters, fishermen, and nature-lovers have been coming to Maine since Colonial times. Their numbers grew tremendously during the first half of the nineteenth century, and by 1850-60 many boarding-houses and hotels were devoted exclusively to entertaining them. Old Orchard, with its four-mile beach skirting the Atlantic, was officially dedicated to the resort business in 1840. Other sections of the Maine coast became popular as resorts well before the end of the century. Bar Harbor, for example, acquired its fame and a reputation for exclusiveness during the early 1890's. In 1920, it was estimated that the annual income from tourists and summer visitors was in the neighborhood of $30,000,000.

Today, the income from Maine's recreational and tourist traffic pours into many hands, from the roadside purveyor of fish stews and chowders to the collector of taxes on huge summer estates. According to the Maine Development Commission, a State promotional organization, the 1936 recreation trade amounted to $160,000,000, from approximately 1,000,000 visitors.

Because of their importance to the visiting vacationist and in the present-day economy of the State, a separate section of this Guide is devoted to detailed information concerning the principal sports and recreations that Maine affords, and the regions or routes where they may best be enjoyed.

FISHING IN INLAND WATERS

IT IS literally true that there is good fishing in almost any of Maine's more than 2200 lakes and ponds and 5000 rivers and streams. Each year thousands of fishermen take from the fresh waters of the State millions of fish of a wide variety, chief of which are the Atlantic, chinook, and landlocked salmon (*Salmo sebago* and *ouananiche*); brook trout (redspots or squaretails); brown, rainbow, and lake trout (togue); small-mouth black bass; white and yellow perch; pickerel; cusk; and smelts. Others not generally classed as game fish but good for eating are whitefish, hornpout (bullheads), eels, barvel (suckers), and shiners. Fly-fishing is increasing in popularity, especially in the quicker water of the thoroughfares and during the earlier season; deep-water trolling yields better results in the warmer summer months.

Shad and sturgeon, both formerly fish of value in Maine, are still occasionally taken in Maine waters. Shad is caught with hand nets in streams near the coast in early spring. Sturgeon, for the past fifty years a distinct rarity, has begun to be found again in Maine rivers, sometimes running to as much as 300 pounds in weight. The fisherman is lucky who brings home a good-sized sturgeon, for its roe, from which caviar is prepared, usually commands a high price in the markets.

Fishing through the ice is popular in all parts of Maine during the winter, both on inland and coastal waters. Salmon, trout, pickerel, smelts, and cusk are chief among the varieties caught. Smelt fishing through the ice of tidal streams with nets and flares at night is known as frost-fishing. Equipment and fishhouses can be rented from winter sporting camps or from guides.

The Maine Department of Inland Fisheries and Game annually liberates an average of 6,000,000 landlocked salmon and trout from the State's thirty-five hatcheries and rearing pools. Other hatcheries are being built, so that there will be a constant increase in the number of fish planted each year. Most of the stocked fish are of legal catching length when liberated.

The State can be roughly divided for the angler's convenience into eight regions, in each of which the fishing is diversified and good.

Sebago Lake — Long Lake — Oxford County Region: Sebago, Bunganut, Crystal, Kennebunk, Mousam, Highland, Thompson, Pennesseewassee, Long, and Kezar Lakes; Peabody, Hancock, Moose, Brandy, Woods, and Thomas Ponds; and a network of streams and rivers, including the Songo River.

Catch: salmon (*Salmo sebago*), cusk, black bass, perch, pickerel, and trout.

This southern region is noted chiefly for landlocked salmon and black bass, although it includes many good trout streams. Sebago Lake, one of the four lakes that were the original home of the landlocked salmon, is the first in the State to open in the spring. Cusk, usually considered a salt-water fish, is caught in only a few of the Maine lakes, and in those but rarely.

Rangeley Lakes Region: Rangeley, Mooselookmeguntic, Richardson, Umbagog, Loon, Parmachenee, Sawyer, and Kennebago Lakes; Quimby, Tim, Jim, Carry, Rowe Ponds, and Chain of Ponds; and a network of streams and rivers, including the Dead River and its tributaries.

Catch: trout, landlocked salmon (introduced), black bass, togue, and pickerel.

The Rangeleys are the natural home of the fighting trout, and it is only in recent years that these lakes have become famous for salmon fishing. The Dead River region is known for its cold waters, fed by mountain springs; some of the lakes in this section have an altitude of well over 1500 feet. There is good fishing here in the summer months, when the trout in warmer waters have become sluggish and no longer fight.

Belgrade Lakes Region: China, Messalonskee, Cobbosseecontee, Maranacook, Annabessacook, Androscoggin, Damariscotta, and Meguinticook Lakes; North, East, Great, Long, Webber, Three Mile, Branch, Biscay, St. George, and Pemaquid Ponds; and many small streams and rivers.

Catch: black bass, trout, salmon, pickerel, hornpout, smelts, yellow and white perch.

The Belgrade Lakes have been for many years the headquarters for bass fishing. Only recently has generous stocking made them excellent grounds for trout and salmon. There is good sport here from the time the ice goes out in the spring until well into the summer.

Moosehead Lake Region: Moosehead (*see below*), Brassua, Parlin, Lobster, Ragged, Kokadjo, Onawa, Sebec, Jo Mary, Seboeis, and Sebasticook Lakes; Long, Wood, Attean, Holeb, Misery, Pierce, Indian, Moxie, and Pleasant Ponds; the Kennebec and Moose Rivers and many streams.

Catch: salmon, togue, squaretailed trout, and other game fish.

Moosehead Lake, itself the center of Maine's chief sporting region, is the gateway to a vast region of almost unbroken wildland stretching to the Canadian border, where there are many waters which have not yet been explored by fishermen.

Allagash Region: Chesuncook, Allagash, Eagle, Chamberlain, Churchill, Umsaskis, Chemquasabamticook, Long, Musquacook, Munsungan, and Caucomgomoc Lakes; Long and other ponds; and Pine Stream and the Allagash, the St. John, and the West Branch of the Penobscot River.

Catch: squaretailed trout, togue, and salmon.

Ten ponds on the headwaters of Nigger Brook, which flows into the Allagash, provide the best location for squaretails in Maine, with the possible exception of the ponds at the headwaters of the Red River. The togue are still biting well in August in Munsungan Lake, and trout fishing is good throughout most of the season on the smaller tributaries of the Allagash, some of them still untried by fishermen.

Katahdin Region: Katahdin, Sourdnahunk, Millinocket, and Ripogenus Lakes; Kidney, Daicy, Shin, Chimney, and Togue Ponds; and mountain streams.

Catch: squaretailed trout, togue, and salmon.

This country is as rich in trout as it is in glorious scenery. Baxter State Park, which includes Mount Katahdin, is one of the finest natural fish and game preserves in existence.

Fish River Region: Long, Mud, Square, Eagle, St. Froid, Big Fish, Frost, Munsungan, and Portage Lakes; ponds along the waters of the Red River and Nigger Brook; and the Fish, Aroostook, Red, and Machias Rivers.

Fishing in Inland Waters 409

Catch: salmon and squaretailed trout.

From the foot of Long Lake to Big Fish Lake (Township 13 and 14, Range 8), a distance of nearly 100 miles, perhaps the best salmon fishing offered in the State may be had from the time the ice goes out to June 15, and again in the fall from September 1 to 30; salmon weighing 18 pounds were taken out of these waters in the fall of 1936. Seventeen small ponds on the headwaters of the Red River, with those on Nigger Brook, provide unsurpassed squaretail fishing. In August there is good stream fishing on the Fish, Aroostook, and Machias Rivers.

Grand Lakes and Schoodic Region: Grand, Big, Junior, Sysladobsis, Little Musquash, Meddybemps (*see below*), Spednic, Mud, East Grand, the Machias Lakes, and the Schoodic Chain; many small ponds; and Clifford, Amazon, and Grand Lake Streams, and the South Branch of the Little, the East Branch of the St. Croix, and the Dennys Rivers.

Catch: salmon, pickerel, trout, togue, black bass, and white perch.

The best bass fishing in Maine is found along the East Branch of the St. Croix River and on Spednic Lake of the Schoodic Chain. These lakes of eastern Maine lay claim to being the fisherman's paradise, for they provide not only salmon fishing (ouananiche, the Washington County salmon), but an abundance of all other kinds. At Grand Lake, from the time the ice goes out to July 1 and from September 1 to 30, there is excellent salmon, trout, and togue fishing; and in Big Lake, three miles away, there is fishing for salmon, black bass, and pickerel. The streams in this region offer excellent fly fishing, and many of the lakes give opportunity of fishing the same waters for trout, togue, bass, salmon, perch, and pickerel.

General open seasons and creel limits are as follows:

Open Season

Lakes and Ponds:
    Salmon, trout, togue; from time ice is out to September 30.
    Black bass (fly fishing only, limit 3 fish); June 1 to June 20.
    Black bass (bait, plugs, etc.); June 21 to September 30.
    White perch; June 21 to September 29.

Rivers above Tide Waters:
    Salmon, trout, togue; from time ice is out to September 14.
    Black bass (fly fishing, limit 3 fish); June 1 to June 20.
    Black bass (bait, plugs, etc.); June 21 to September 30.
    White perch; June 21 to September 14.

Brooks and Streams above Tide Waters:
    Salmon and trout; from time ice is out to August 15.
    Togue; from time ice is out to September 30.
    Black bass (fly fishing only, limit 3 fish); June 1 to June 20.
    Black bass (bait, plugs, etc.); June 21 to September 30.
    White perch; June 21 to August 15.

Creel Limits

Salmon, trout, togue, black bass, and white perch from streams and brooks:
    25 fish or $7\frac{1}{2}$ pounds, unless individual fish weighs over $7\frac{1}{2}$ pounds or last fish caught increases the combined weight to more than $7\frac{1}{2}$ pounds.
    Twenty-five fish, combined weight 10 pounds, from lakes, ponds, and rivers.
    Salmon and togue must be 14 inches or over in length.
    Trout   must be 6 inches or over in length.
    Black bass   must be 10 inches or over in length.
    White perch must be 6 inches or over in length.

As fishing varies in different localities, so does the equipment required. It is always advisable to consult a registered guide of the region where the fishing trip is to be taken about all accessories required and about accommodations. Guides are not required in every region, but for sportsmen unfamiliar with the country they are a practical necessity.

As a variation to the usual breakfast of pan-fried trout or other game fish with which guides cater to appetites of Gargantuan proportions, a meal of woods-style planked trout gives a treat only to be realized in the woods. The bark is cut from a live hardwood tree for about 18 inches above the ground, and the exposed wood of the tree chipped to make a flat surface. After cleaning a good-sized trout, it is pegged skin side in on the flattened surface, and a few strips of salt pork pegged just above it. A fire is built about two feet from the tree, the heat quickly searing the fish while the pork serves as basting. Another woods-style method of cooking trout is to cover the cleaned fish with an inch or two of wet clay and bury it in the hot ashes of the campfire for an all-night bake. In the morning, when the clay is broken open, the steaming aroma and the flakiness of the trout meat provide a treat for which Paul Bunyan would willingly have traded his celebrated ox.

The following are two of the more popular among the almost countless fishing trips that it is possible to make in the State of Maine.

DENNYS RIVER FISHING TRIP

From MEDDYBEMPS *to* DENNYSVILLE, 25 *m.*, 1–2 days.

Over Dennys River.

Accommodations at Meddybemps and Dennysville; camping sites along the river.

MEDDYBEMPS VILLAGE (*see Tour* 1, *sec. d*), a tiny settlement on the southern shore of Meddybemps Lake, is the starting-point for a canoe-fishing trip over the winding Dennys River, which varies in width from 75 feet to 200 yards between heavily wooded shores.

The canoe is put in at the source of the river on Meddybemps Lake; the first 10 miles of paddling are through deadwater, calm and peaceful as the surrounding dense woods and spreading meadows. Although lily pads on this stretch offer tackle hazards, the pickerel fishing is good, as it is along the whole length of the river. The pickerel, little brother of the pike, has a voracious nature and hits hard at moving bait. Striking with a savage rush, it will take flies, feathered lures, perch belly, or pork rind, offering good sport at seasons when other fish are sluggish. Pickerel run up to 6 pounds in weight.

At 6 *m.* down-river from Meddybemps, the deep-pooled Dead Stream empties into the river; this is good trout ground. Trout flies and trout streamer flies are good magnets for the redspots. Other tributaries flow into the Dennys for the next few miles of wooded country, where deer and small game are occasionally seen along the banks. This region is a favorite nesting place for ducks; they are heard constantly honking among the reeds and lily pads.

About 10 *m.* down the river, the slow Dennys suddenly breaks into swift

Fishing in Inland Waters 411

water for a 500-yard rip. This thrilling but navigable bit of fast water is the site of the old Gilman Dam. Deadwater, a splendid place for a fight with a tough squaretail, lies at the site of the old dam pool. The banks of the Dennys from this point are higher, ledgy in many places and verging into sand banks at others. The deadwater stretch continues for more than 1 mile, along an extremely winding course, before surging into the Bright Island Rips, a stretch of white water nearly one-fourth mile long.

Alternating stretches of deadwater and sudden rips, following the winding contortions of the river, bring the canoe into Dennysville.

DENNYSVILLE (*see Tour 1, sec. d*), 25 *m*., with its famous salmon pool, is one of the two places which offer sea salmon fishing in Maine, the only State where salmon may be taken with flies, fly spoons, and trolling lures. The pool here, like the one at Bangor (*see BANGOR*), swarms with hard-fighting Atlantic salmon, which may be taken after April 1. A battle with one of them is a memorable experience.

MOOSEHEAD LAKE FISHING TRIP

From GREENVILLE *to* MOOSEHEAD LAKE REGION.

Accommodations, guides, boats, and live bait available at Greenville and sporting camps on the lake shores.

GREENVILLE (*see Tour* 9), lying on Moosehead Lake's southern antler, is the gateway to a sprawling wilderness of thousands of miles of woods, lakes, and streams. Within this vast wildland area of Piscataquis and Somerset Counties lie more than thirty of the finest fishing grounds in the State, within a 50-mile radius of Greenville; while more than 100 ponds, streams, and rivers form a web of waterways filled with gamey fish.

Moosehead Lake, 1000 feet above the sea, stretches for 40 miles north of Greenville, With its 300 miles of wooded shores, and its deeply sheltered bays, it is 'tops' with anglers desirous of deep pools and fine trolling grounds. The fishing swings in with the passing of the ice — usually around the first of May — for a round of bait fishing and trolling lasting until the end of the month, when the water temperature rises. Fly fishing is supreme until the middle of July, and again in September. Moosehead salmon run from 3 to 10 pounds; togue (lake trout) from 5 to 20 pounds; and trout from 2 to 7 pounds.

The thoroughfare between Sugar Island and the eastern shore of the lake is good trolling ground for 'lakers' (togue). In early spring they will often take a streamer fly, although best results come from trolling; later on in the season, 'lakers' are taken by deep trolling. They like live or preserved smelts on a single hook, preceded by spoons.

Fly fishing in the pool below the dam across the source of the Kennebec River, about a third of the way up on the lake's western shore, offers plenty of thrills in taking out husky trout and salmon. Regular flies are best for salmon, but this pool is a good place to try out some streamer flies such as black ghost, plumed knight, or welsh rabbit. Trout here have a special liking for smaller-sized flies.

Many good trout, salmon, and 'lakers' are taken from the pools just off the mouth of the Kennebec by flies, and in deep trolling from a boat.

Reached from Greenville, either by steamer, canoe, motor, or hiking, are such good trout grounds as Attean, Parlin, Rainbow, and Onawa Lakes. The streams in the vicinity are well stocked with trout (redspots or squaretail), which range from the six-incher up to four pounds. They bite worms readily, take trolling baits like the salmon, and rise readily to the fly. When hooked, they do not leap from the water as frequently as salmon.

SALT-WATER FISHING

IN THE salt water off the Maine coast, rock cod, cunners, and summer flounders or plaice are caught from the rocks along the shore; while in deeper waters are found bluefish, Atlantic salmon, mackerel, cod, cusk, herring, flounders, haddock, silver hake, chicken halibut, perch, pollock, sea bass, tuna, bluefins (small tuna), swordfish, porpoise, mackerel sharks, shad, alewives, and smelts. Of non-edible fish, sculpins and skates are all too frequently found on the fisherman's hook.

From Kittery to Belfast, offshore salt-water trolling with heavy rods and reels for the giant tuna or 'horse mackerel,' weighing up to 1000 pounds, is becoming a popular sport. They are terrific fighters, equal to those found off Block Island or in California waters. Tuna fishing is a rather expensive sport, requiring specially constructed rods and reels and boats equipped with special rigging.

Deep-sea fishing is an old and popular pastime on the Maine coast. Nearly every fishing village has its skipper who specializes in taking parties out to good fishing grounds, furnishing lines, hooks, and bait, and providing a real down-East meal of fish chowder at noon. The catch on these trips usually includes haddock, cod, cusk, hake, halibut, and perhaps swordfish in season.

A new sport, not usually known elsewhere on the Atlantic coast, is fly fishing for mackerel. The striped sea bass, a game fish weighing up to 20 pounds or more, is taken close to shore with surf-fishing tackle and in rivers that empty into the ocean.

Information about tuna and other deep-sea fishing may be obtained from the yacht clubs in the various coastal towns. The average charge per party for a day's tuna fishing is $25; for deep-sea fishing, $15. No license is required for salt-water fishing. Boats equipped for tuna fishing are available at Ogunquit, York Harbor, Biddeford Pool, South Portland, and Portland. Necessary equipment, which may be rented by arrangement with the boatman, consists of large reel (either 9/0, 10/0, or 12/0), hickory or split bamboo rod with tip of at least 16-ounce weight, 36-thread line, 12-foot leader (of .035 inch piano wire), hooks (Pflueger-Sobey 11/0 or 12/0 are good), belt butt-rest, and shoulder harness.

TUNA FISHING OFF OGUNQUIT

For boats and equipment, inquire at Maine Information Bureau, Ogunquit, for Maine Tuna Club.

OGUNQUIT (*see Tour* 1, *sec. a*) is headquarters of the Maine Tuna Club, membership in which is open to all rod and reel sportsmen.

The specially rigged tuna boat cruises to an area about a mile offshore, where the 'horse mackerel' schools begin. Blind trolling brings only disappointment and strikeless hours, but if a school is located the sportsman is assured of a battle royal. The lure, a one-fourth to one-half pound mackerel, a squid, or a feathered plug, is skittered along about 30 to 40 feet behind the boat, which moves ahead between 4 and 6 miles an hour. Some sportsmen prefer a slower troll. Strong muscles, steady nerves, and quick movements are of paramount importance in tuna fishing. The fish, one of the fastest and strongest of salt-water game fish, is moving at express train speed when he strikes, and his terrific lunge carries him partly or completely out of the water. It is in the split second when he appears above the water that the fisherman must snap back his rod and set the hook firmly. The setting of the hook accelerates the amazing struggle of the tuna, whose fight has been likened to the battle of the Florida kingfish on a heroic scale. Between the short dashes of the fish the angler must recover his line; and much depends on the man at the wheel of the boat, who must swing the craft with the circling fish to keep lines from fouling.

A tuna battle may last from ten minutes to several hours, depending on the skill of the angler and the size and strength of the individual fish. Two sportsmen in a launch off Ogunquit one season hooked a tuna estimated to weigh about 1000 pounds, and the ensuing struggle lasted throughout many hours of a day and night, the fish towing the launch about 50 miles out to sea and back. Almost on the spot where he had taken the hook, the tuna swished his saw-like tail and cut the line for freedom.

When the fish has been tired, and gradually swung alongside the boat, he is caught and held on a gaff, a short pole with a large hook at its end, and then roped by the tail. Skillful gaffing and roping are necessary, otherwise a big fellow may be lost at the moment of apparent victory.

Commercial tuna fishing, as it is practiced by the fishermen and lobstermen off the coast, is perhaps not so thrilling a sport as that of the rod and reel, but it requires as great a degree of skill. The fishermen cruise offshore looking for the tuna, with one man or even two standing on the tiny platform built out from the bow of the launch keeping constant watch for the great fish. As soon as the prey is sighted, the fishermen overtake it and harpoon it with a specially constructed spear to which is attached a stout line with a float (usually a small cask) at its end. The tuna usually darts out to sea, dragging the float, which prevents the fish from going deeply below the surface and impedes its progress. The fishermen follow the float wherever it goes, sometimes heading straight to open sea for hours at a stretch. Eventually the tuna becomes exhausted by its long struggle and succumbs, or the fishermen overtake and kill it. This form of tuna fishing is easier and more certain than the rod and reel method, and the natives using it are far more likely to bring to land fine specimens of the 'horse mackerel,' which they sell at a good profit, than is a conducted party of even the most expert sportsmen.

HUNTING

WITH more than 75 per cent of its total area consisting of forestland and water, Maine offers excellent 'wild land' hunting. The vast acreage of the State provides a maximum of sport with a minimum of danger. The hunter is protected by a law passed in 1933 by the State legislature which stipulates that a hunter who accidentally shoots any person within the State shall be prohibited from ever hunting in Maine again.

ANIMALS

Moose are plentiful in Aroostook, Kennebec, Penobscot, Piscataquis, and Somerset Counties, and are to be found in increasing numbers along the coastal areas of Knox, Lincoln, and Waldo Counties, where they have become so numerous that an open season of a few days is occasionally declared on them.

From wardens' reports it was estimated that in October, 1935, there were from 100,000 to 125,000 deer in the woods of the six northern counties alone. The registered deer kill for the State in 1935 was 19,726. Deer are commonly found near cleared land, tote roads, and abandoned lumber camps. Early in the season they frequent old cuttings where there are plenty of raspberry bushes. Later, after the frosts, they take to the beech ridges early in the day, making for the swamps and thickets around noontime. Hunting is best after a light fall of snow. In dry weather, when the silence of the woods magnifies every sound the hunter makes, it is advisable to find a comfortable seat on a sunny ridge and sit perfectly still, waiting for the deer to make their appearance. The veteran hunter scorns 'bushwhacking' (leaving tote roads and woods trails to plow through the forest). When a deer is sighted and the hunter fires, there is a sudden crash as the startled animal attempts to flee, and the white flag of its tail shows over the 'blow-downs.' If the flag drops, it means a hit. When hunting is poor, it is best to head for almost inaccessible high land, for the big bucks travel from one ridge to another, resting spasmodically, and make for vantage points where they can command views of the surrounding country. One of these beautiful bucks with many-pointed antlers is well worth the difficult climb.

Black bear are numerous in Aroostook, Oxford, Piscataquis, Somerset, and Washington. Many sportsmen prefer shooting bear to deer, for it takes a skilled hunter to stalk and bring down one of these crafty beasts. Slow-moving by nature except when startled, and painfully near-sighted, it is astonishing how well they are able to take care of themselves. A running bear can sprint for more than 100 yards, especially on an upgrade where his powerful hind legs propel him over the ground at top speed. Accused of being sheep-killers, there was a bounty on them for years, and it is only recently that they have been classed as a game-animal, with a closed season. Bear meat, when properly prepared, is excellent eating, with a flavor much like that of pork. Bear liver is a real delicacy.

Bobcats are common. As they are a natural menace to deer, a considerable bounty has been placed on them ($15 in 1935).

Fox-hunting is popular in Maine, the cunning animal being found in abundance in every part of the State except Knox County. Foxes have fixed habits, and the best way to make sure of one is to learn his runways and then wait until he comes along. They are as destructive as they are elusive, destroying partridge eggs and chicks, and playing havoc with rabbit colonies. The number of foxes in this State is increasing steadily.

Raccoons are also increasing in number, and are plentiful in every county except Aroostook, Franklin, Knox, Penobscot, Piscataquis, Sagadahoc, and Washington Counties. They are usually hunted at night with dogs. Nearly all of the hounds used for this sport are imported from the South, a good coon dog costing $100 or more. But native dogs can be developed into good coon hunters; one Belfast dog has 500 raccoons to his credit in 13 years of active field work. In contrast to the southern raccoons, which are considered of good size if they weigh 20 pounds, Maine raccoons of 30 pounds are not at all uncommon — one caught at Sebago Lake weighed 35 pounds and measured 51 inches in length.

Many persons consider rabbit hunting a fine sport, and most persons agree that rabbits make very good eating. Maine rabbits keep to the surface of the ground, and do not 'hole in' like the smaller species found in most other States. They usually live in the low evergreen growths, but cold weather or lack of food in the heavily wooded areas often forces them to the swamplands, where they take to brush piles in old cuttings. It is said that there are more rabbit hounds in the Kennebec valley than in any other section of New England. These dogs, baying in sorrowful tones, find the rabbit and chase it in circles back to its starting place. The hunter needs only to stay where he first started the rabbit, and wait for it to arrive.

At one period, Maine white hares suffered from tularemia; but in 1935 they were once more admitted into Massachusetts for restocking purposes, the disease apparently having run its course.

Gray squirrels are now protected by law, but there is an open season on them each year.

BIRDS

Duck shooting is a very popular sport in Maine, and the shooting at Merrymeeting Bay is conceded to be the best anywhere on the Atlantic coast. The number of wild ducks in Aroostook County, and in the Machias region, has increased greatly. The common mallard and black duck are the most popular game birds of Maine, particularly the black duck, which is found in abundance, generally weighing about three pounds. A dozen or more varieties breed on the cool waters of the northern part of the State, and the hunter can be sure of finding sheldrakes, teal, pintails, and bluebills. There is no open season, however, on buffleheads, ruddies, wood ducks, snow geese, or Canada geese. The open season on ducks and geese is controlled entirely by the Federal Government; in addition to the Maine hunting license, it is necessary to have a Federal duck stamp.

Excellent hunting for woodcock is found anywhere along the coast, for the birds in flight stop to rest at every natural feeding place. Native woodcock are found inland, especially in central and western Maine. They are a shy bird and a real test for any bird dog. A dog is necessary for woodcock hunting, as the birds lie so close in the thickets that they are rarely flushed unless nearly stepped upon. For the best shooting conditions several heavy frosts must have been felt, since woodcock do not have to resort to eating worms in marshy runs while the foliage is heavy and food plentiful. When forced out of the thick woods, they are generally found in alder and birch runs with blackberry tangle beneath, or on sunny ridges with a brook below.

Hunting

The partridge (ruffed grouse), so-called king of all North American game birds, is native to Maine and protected by law. In 1935, there were grouse covers near every Maine city, although the shooting becomes progressively better toward the north. They are common in old apple orchards, blackberry bushes, and in open birch and alder growth.

The pheasants liberated in Maine every year are well able to withstand the winter cold, and many of them are found nesting in a wild state. Since many pheasants have appeared in Piscataquis County, where none have been liberated in recent years, it is clear that they are coming in from territory to the south and spreading throughout the State. Both black and ring-necked pheasants are found in Maine.

GAME AREAS

In order to list Maine's game resources, the State can be roughly divided for convenience into four sections, as follows:

SW. Section: York, Cumberland, Androscoggin, Sagadahoc, Oxford, Lincoln, Franklin, and Kennebec Counties, as well as portions of Waldo, Knox, Piscataquis, and Somerset Counties.

Game: moose, deer, bear, raccoon, fox, rabbit, woodcock, partridge, duck, and pheasant.

Moose are, as a general rule, continually protected by law, although in 1935 an open season of three days (November 28, 29, 30) was declared on bull moose in Knox, Lincoln, and Waldo Counties.

Bears are found in the northern portions of Franklin, Oxford, and Somerset Counties of this section.

Rabbits are hunted as a popular sport in all townships of Kennebec County. They are found in every part of the State.

Good woodcock hunting is common near Damariscotta.

A very famous duck-shooting ground is Merrymeeting Bay in Sagadahoc County, where the wild rice planted by Capt. Sam Nickerson has been attracting great hordes of the waterfowl since 1890. Planting the rice is now supervised by the State's Inland Fish and Game Commission. Lakeshore duck-hunting is excellent in the Belgrade Lakes region.

Flocks of pheasants abound in the vicinity of Damariscotta. The State Game Farm at Gray raises ring-necked pheasants, about 3000 of which are annually distributed throughout the State by the Inland Fish and Game Commission.

NW. Section: Somerset, Piscataquis, and Aroostook Counties.

Game: deer, bear, bobcat, lynx, fox, mink, otter, fisher, partridge, woodcock, snipe, duck (black duck, mallards, sheldrakes), and geese.

Moosehead Lake is not only the gateway to the big-game country but is a center for game-bird hunting. The woodcock found here are reported as being much larger and better than those found along the coast.

Partridge are shot here with rifles rather than shotguns.

NE. Section: northern Penobscot, eastern Piscataquis, northern Washington, and parts of Aroostook Counties.

Game: deer, bear, fox, rabbit, bobcat, lynx, otter, fisher, mink, woodcock, partridge, duck, and geese.

There is excellent woodcock hunting in alder swamps near Machias.

Popular duck-hunting grounds are found in the Grand Lake region and along Grand Lake Stream.

SE. Section: Hancock, parts of Waldo and Knox, most of Washington, and southern Penobscot Counties.

Game: moose, deer, bear, fox, raccoon, rabbit, woodcock, partridge, and duck.

Raccoon is particularly plentiful in Hancock County.

Woodcock flock near Ellsworth along the coast, and partridge and pheasants abound in the warmer regions near the coast.

A good duck-hunting ground is Pocamoonshine Lake in Princeton, Washington County.

At one time there was only one Fish and Game Association in Maine, and this was State-wide in scope. In recent years, many county and city organizations have been formed, all of them with large enrollments. Their purpose is not to encourage fishing and hunting, but to co-operate in the conservation of fish and game. This is accomplished by seeing to it that protective laws are passed, and then aiding in their enforcement.

Open seasons on game vary in different sections of the State and the game laws are frequently changed, so that it is always advisable to have a copy of the Maine Hunting Laws. This may be obtained from the Maine Publicity Bureau in Portland, together with a complete list of hunting camps, hotels, and farm inns. With judicious planning, the hunting season may be prolonged by moving from one part of the State to another; for example, with the varying seasons on deer in different sections, it is possible for a hunter to change his location so that he may hunt continually from October 16 to December 15.

CANOEING

FOR the experienced canoeist, there is no better way of becoming acquainted with the heart of Maine than by following any one of the courses that have been laid through the great maze of inland waterways penetrating the forests of the State. Hunting, fishing, hiking, and mountain climbing, all important features of Maine's outdoor life, can easily be made side issues to a leisurely but exciting journey by canoe over some one chain of Maine's lakes and streams. The hardships of the trip — aching muscles at the day's end, wet weather, insects — are far outweighed by the thrill of shooting rapids, the pride felt by the successful fisherman or hunter, the wholesome knowledge gained from association with the men of the woods, and the simple joys of life in the wilds.

Four of the most popular of Maine's long canoe trips, with approximate mileages, are given here in tour form. These trips require guides ($6–$8 *per day*), who will provide canoes and arrange for supplies.

ALLAGASH RIVER CANOE TRIP

From EAST SEBOOMOOK *to* FORT KENT, 156.5 *m.*, 8 days to 4 weeks.
Via Allagash and St. Francis, over the waters of the West Branch of the Penobscot River, several lakes, the Allagash and the St. John Rivers. 6 carries.
Guides and equipment obtainable at Greenville. Sporting camps and camp sites at intervals. Supply stores at settlements.

There are miles of quick water to challenge the sportsman's skill with the shod pole on this trip over forest waterways threading unbroken stretches of natural scenery still unspoiled. There are almost limitless opportunities for hunting and fishing; stirring rapids and lovely waterfalls tumbling into deep pools where great cream-bellied trout strike savagely at the fly; shallow side streams arched overhead with thick black spruce and pungent fir leading to still caverns and tiny lakes where wild game gather to feed and drink, and to sunlit glades in which deer are caught browsing.

The starting-point at East Seboomook (*see Tour* 9) is usually reached from GREENVILLE (*see Tour* 9) by steamer, a 40-mile trip up Moosehead Lake.

EAST SEBOOMOOK, at the end of one of Moosehead's arms, is a small lakeside settlement with a general store and several sporting camps. From here, dunnage and canoe are toted overland via Northwest Carry to the deadwater below Seboomook Dam. At 3 *m.* the canoe is put in on the *West Branch* of the Penobscot River, and the trip is actually begun.

Lobster Stream, 7 *m.* (R), affords a pleasant side trip for hunting and fishing through a heavily wooded waterway, where ducks, partridges, bear, and deer are frequently seen.

> *Lobster Lake,* 4 *m.*, at the end of Lobster Stream, is a secluded basin well known for its trout and salmon fishing. Wild game along its shores offer good opportunities for the huntsman and the camera enthusiast.

The canoe must now be snubbed down with the pole through several short rapids. The guide stands in the stern of the canoe, and, with quick deft movements of his pole (never a paddle), keeps the slender craft off the rocks. In the smooth water below the rapids, trout rise eagerly to the fly, and trolling brings gratifying results.

Half Way House, 13 *m.* (R), is an excellent camping site. Here the guide sets to, and in a short time the piny air is filled with the tang of campfire smoke and the aroma of broiling trout, fresh from the stream. After a rare meal and an hour by the flickering fire, sleeping bags and blankets are very welcome. The peaceful quiet of the great woods prevails until the guide's call, 'Come and get it,' awakens the canoeist to the good morning smells of fresh-made coffee and sizzling bacon.

The second half of the course on the West Branch passes Moosehead, Ragmuff, and Pine Streams, all good fishing waters. The West Branch flows into Chesuncook Lake near its northwest end, about 1 mile below the junction of Caucomgomoc Stream with the lake waters.

Chesuncook Lake, 23 *m.*, about 20 miles long, is surrounded by wilderness and hemmed in by the Katahdin and Sourdnahunk Mountain ranges. The fishing is good in the streams flowing into the lake, with an abundance of trout, salmon, togue, and whitefish — the latter, a particularly sweet-fleshed fish, running usually about a pound in weight. Flood waters on the lake, however, caused by the Ripogenus Dam, have diminished its attractions for sportsmen. The shores, lined with dead timber and sand banks, provide no suitable camp sites, and it is a dangerous place in which to be overtaken by dusk.

Caucomgomoc Stream, 24 *m.*, follows a northwesterly course to the lake of the same name. It is marked by quick water and running rapids, and gives a strenuous workout to the most hardened paddle-swinger.

Caucomgomoc Lake (Ind.: 'Gull Lake'), 35 *m.*, is a long body of water between high wooded ridges. Salmon is plentiful here. Just north of Caucomgomoc Stream is a fine camp site near the entrance to Ciss Stream, narrow, and winding, which leads 2.5 miles to Round Pond.

At *Round Pond Carry*, 43 *m.*, on the opposite shore, an old-time 'jumper sled' is provided for hauling the canoe to Allagash Lake. This is a log sled having a high crosspiece on which one end of the canoe is supported while it is being dragged over the tote road through the woods. There is an excellent camp site at the Allagash end of the Carry.

Allagash Lake, 46.5 *m.*, offers fine fishing and hunting in the shadow of Allagash Mountain. Deer are plentiful; and if he is fortunate, the traveler may catch a glimpse of a moose in the low marshy ground at the lake's edge.

Allagash Stream, 49.5 *m.*, is entered from the northeast end of the lake.

Allagash Falls, 53.5 *m.*, requires another carry. The shores of the pool below the lovely little falls provide a pleasant site for noon camp, where bird songs are accompanied by the music of falling waters. Berries are abundant in season near this spot, and a hatful of raspberries, quickly gathered, tops off the meal as no prepared dessert could.

Chamberlain Lake, 56.5 *m.*, is one of the most attractive bodies of water on the trip, with fine views of distant blue mountains in all directions and plenty of fat trout waiting to be caught. Here the State has developed pleasant camp sites, and provided conveniences for the camper.

Chamberlain Lake Dam, 62.5 *m.*, is directly across the lake. There is a 10-rod carry to the southwest shore of Eagle Lake, rich in trout, salmon, togue, and whitefish, and on its banks berries in abundance are found in season. The northern end of the lake narrows to a thoroughfare leading to Churchill Lake.

Main Water Thoroughfare, 72.5 *m.*, is entered from the southwest.

Churchill Lake, 74.5 *m.*, offers a wide blue vista, with water-lilies floating placidly in the foreground.

Chase Carry, 79.5 *m.*, lies at the north end of Churchill Lake. There is a tote here of approximately 1 mile to the Allagash River.

The *Allagash River*, 80.5 *m.*, is swift and full of rapids. The trip here becomes strenuous and exciting, as the canoe is poled through roaring swash past banks dark with evergreen. In a tight bad place in short rapids the canoes are sometimes 'roped down,' but the guide more often resorts to the pole and the art of 'snubbing her down.' Old-timers say that skill at snubbing down is fast vanishing from the Maine woods, and guides now prefer the less dangerous tenderfoot practice of roping the canoes down through the steeper pitches of water.

Umsaskis Lake, 81.5 *m.*, is entered from the southeast. There is a 5-mile paddle up-lake and through a narrow thoroughfare to Long Lake. Umsaskis provides excellent camp sites, and the fishing is good. When the canoeist takes more than he can eat at a single meal, he can keep his catch overnight by cleaning the fish, wrapping them in paper or leaves, and burying them in the ground.

Long Lake, 86.5 *m.*, is dammed at its lower end. Here is a 10-yard carry, after which the canoe is again put into the Allagash.

The *Allagash River*, 91.5 *m.*, is again quick with rapids and made dangerous by small falls for a distance of about 10 miles. It is not unusual to startle deer or bear drinking at the edge of the stream.

At 101.5 *m.* the Allagash broadens into *Round Pond*, the second body of water of that name on this trip. There is excellent fishing here, and good camp sites, one of which is provided and cared for by the State. The Allagash River is re-entered from the north end of Round Pond. The tempestuous waters soon become placid, and water-lilies on all sides float on the deadwater. Several streams, especially Musquacook, draining into the deadwater, offer good fishing; many of them, wandering through miles of unbroken forests, have never been tried by fishermen.

The *Allagash Falls*, 118.5 *m.*, shaded by some of the largest cedars in the country, are famous for their beauty. Their drop is more than 30 feet. There is a short carry around the Falls. The rapids below the Falls, a particularly turbulent pitch, is called the Horse Race. Again expert handling of the canoe is called into play.

ALLAGASH (Allagash Plantation, pop. 438), 130.5 *m.*, a frontier village settled by the English, but now largely inhabited by French-speaking people of Acadian descent, has grown up near the confluence of the St. John and Allagash Rivers. There is a small hotel here, and bus service to St. Francis. Canoeists often make this the terminus of the trip, but the latter may be continued to St. Francis by way of the St. John River.

At ST. FRANCIS, 142.5 *m.* (*see Tour* 1, *sec. e*), a Bangor and Aroostook train can be taken to Fort Kent.

FORT KENT, 156.5 *m.* (*see Tour* 1, *sec. e*), is the terminus of the present trip. However, if desired, the canoeist may continue to Van Buren (*see Tour* 1, *sec. e*), nearly 50 miles down the St. John.

EAST BRANCH CANOE TRIP

From GREENVILLE *to* GRINDSTONE, 141 *m.*, 2–3 weeks.

Via Kokadjo, Ripogenus Dam, Chesuncook Dam, Whetstone, Burntland, and Grindstone Falls, over several lakes, Umbazooksus Stream, and the East Branch of the Penobscot River. 12 carries.

Guides, equipment, and supplies available at Greenville. Trucking charges from Greenville to Ripogenus Dam, about $10 per canoe; Chesuncook Lake motorboat transfer, $6–$8; Mud Pond Carry charge, $5–$7 per canoe.

For those who want an exciting voyage through the wilderness, the East Branch canoe trip is suggested. The journey is so difficult, with its carries and rapids, that few guides care to make it; some persons consider it the wildest canoe trip in the Maine woods. The start is usually made at Greenville, although the canoe is not put into the water until Umbazooksus Stream is reached.

GREENVILLE (*see Tour* 9). Here canoes and dunnage are loaded on a truck for the 40-mile drive over a good gravel road to Ripogenus Dam on the SE. shore of Chesuncook Lake.

KOKADJO (Ind.: 'rippling waters'), 20 *m.* (*see Tour* 7) is a village on the shore of *Kokadjo Lake,* where there is good fishing.

Grant Farm, 32 *m.* Near here is Ragged Stream.

> Ragged Stream, winding through virgin timber, leads to *Ragged Lake,* 3 *m.*, which offers excellent fishing and hunting in season.

Ripogenus Dam, 40 *m.* (*see Tour* 7), across Ripogenus Gorge, is at the southeast shore of Chesuncook Lake. Here supplies and canoe are transferred to motorboat for the trip up the lake. It is not advisable to attempt to paddle Chesuncook Lake because of choppy waters and headwinds.

Chesuncook Dam, 58 *m.*, necessitates a short carry. Canoes are put in on Umbazooksus Stream for the mile run into Umbazooksus Lake, which is used principally as a thoroughfare.

Mud Pond Carry, 60 *m.*, is equipped with wagon and horses to haul canoes and dunnage to Mud Pond. The latter is a difficult thoroughfare to paddle because of its shallowness, and much dragging of canoes and wading are necessary to reach the small outlet leading into Chamberlain Lake. With the exception of this stretch, the going is all easy paddling over quiet water, with good camp sites always at hand and a variety of splendid scenery.

VACATIONLAND

THESE, too, are speaking pictures. They show some of Maine's advantages in the long-enjoyed but only recently discovered recreational resources of which resident and visitor alike are taking greater advantage every year. There is no season of the year in Maine which does not offer some exciting and vigorous sport; there is no time when the Maine landscape does not present some new and striking scene.

DREAMING OF A DUCK HUNT

ON THE BANK OF SOURDNAHUNK

TROTTING RACE ON THE ICE AT CAMDEN

WINTER SCENE, NEAR FRYEBURG

MORNING PADDLE ON MOOSEHEAD, MOUNT KINEO IN THE BACKGROUND

SAILS IN THE SUN

ALMOST IN THE NET, PLEASANT RIVER, GRAY

ICE FISHING, SEBAGO LAKE

AUTUMN TRAIL

HUNTING PARTY AT CAMP, KOKADJO

CAMP SITE NEAR MOUNT KATAHDIN

POPHAM BEACH

At *Chamberlain Lake*, 63 *m.*, the canoe is headed southeast to reach Three Mile Thoroughfare, an easily managed passage to Telosmis Lake, with splendid views of the Sourdnahunk, Katahdin, and Wassataquoik mountain ranges. Telosmis is best covered in a leisurely fashion, for it offers excellent fishing and some of its tributaries are fine trout streams with deep pools and small ponds caused by beaver dams.

At 73 *m.* the canoe enters the north end of *Telos Lake*. There is an old camping ground in a sheltering grove about halfway down the lake on the southeast shore. To the northeast, the general direction of the course, are *Telos Lake Dam* and *Canal*. The canal was built more than 100 years ago to prevent logs from going out of Maine by the Allagash and St. John Rivers into Canada. The short carry around the dam brings the canoe to the canal. This latter presents a thrilling shoot over white water that spills and wrecks craft not guided by skilled hands. Owing to the difference in the levels of Telos and Webster Lakes, whose waters it connects, the canal has become a roaring swash, capable of shooting a canoe the distance of three-fourths mile in less than two minutes. In such difficult waters some prefer to rope down their canoe, but most guides use the shod pole and snub the canoe down with sureness and great dexterity. From this point all the way down the East Branch, there is abundant opportunity for watching the guide work the fast-moving canoe among rocks and rapids, with never a mis-stroke or a smash — which would end the voyage then and there. The relief from poling to paddling comes in passing through the quiet and beautiful waters of the lakes. And from the passage in fast water, the contrast is sharp with the slowness of the carries, which must be made with leg and back power.

The Telos Canal drops the canoe into *Webster Lake*, 76 *m.* Tote roads leading to abandoned lumber camps, now almost buried in the thick underbrush of the forest, start from the shores of this lake, once an active waterway in lumbering days.

Webster Lake Dam, 79 *m.*, necessitates a short carry to Webster Stream.

> Left from Webster Lake Dam on a rough road is *Coffalos Pond*, 2 *m.*; here one can stand in the fields which border the pond and snap a fly into quiet pools where lurk fine trout waiting to break the surface the moment the lure lands on the water.

Webster Stream is followed for nearly 10 miles to Indian Carry, an overland trip that is most difficult even under favorable circumstances. With canoe carriage lacking, this shift of more than 3 miles must be made by man power, and has been known to take a full day with all hands hauling. The canoe is put in at Second (or Matangamonsis) Lake, where there is always good fishing and a fine choice of pleasant camp sites along the shore.

Three Mile Thoroughfare, 93 *m.*, winds to Grand (or Matagamon) Lake, which affords many fine views of Mount Matagamon and the Traveler Mountain Range. This is the last lake passed on the present trip. There are excellent camp sites along the shores, and the fishing is good.

At 100 *m.* the canoe enters the *East Branch* of the Penobscot River, and the traveling becomes even more interesting and varied than before.

Stair Falls, 106 *m.*, a beautiful cataract, makes a short carry necessary. From here through the four pitches of Pond, Grand, Hulling Machine, and Bowling Falls, and along the 15-mile run to the mouth of Wassataquoik Stream, the waterway runs through good deer and bear country. The traveling is continuously exciting, and the scenery is lovely beyond description. Camp sites are available in places of breath-taking beauty, the finest of all being in a pine grove on the bluff above Hulling Machine Falls. In this land of early frosts, the late August and September voyager enjoys a pageant of color in the variegated foliage.

Haskell's Rock Pitch, 108 *m.*, requires an arduous carry.

Bowling Falls, 112 *m.*, can be run at times, although it is safer to make a carry.

The mouth of the *Wassataquoik Stream*, 127 *m.*, marks the beginning of a stretch of white water, variously named Whetstone Falls, Burnt Falls, and Grindstone Falls. This stretch can be run, but in rush water it is best to make a long carry.

GRINDSTONE, 141 *m.* (*see Tour* 6), is the terminus of the trip.

DEAD RIVER AND MOOSEHEAD WATERS CANOE TRIP

From STRATTON *to* ROCKWOOD, 87 *m.*, 8-14 days.

Via Flagstaff, Dead River and Jackman, over Dead River, Spencer Lake, Fish Pond, Attean Lake, Wood Pond, Moose River, Brassua and Moosehead Lakes. 8 carries.

Guides and equipment obtainable at Stratton; sporting camps and sites at intervals; supply stores at settlements.

This is an easier trip, through somewhat safer waters, than those with courses laid to the northeast. Part of this trip covers streams followed by Arnold's men (*see Tour* 11) on the ill-fated expedition to Quebec. The region throughout is famous as a sportsman's country, and some of the biggest and most impressive of Maine's mountains can be seen to advantage from this course.

STRATTON (*see Tour* 11). The canoe is put in on Dead River, north of the village, near the forks of Stratton Brook and the South Branch of the Dead River. Pickerel fishing is good here, but bigger and more exciting quarry await the fisherman farther on.

FLAGSTAFF, 4 *m.* (L) (*see Tour* 11), is passed.

At 8 *m.* (R) is DEAD RIVER POST OFFICE (*see Tour* 11). The waters are quiet here and the paddling easy. From this point there is a trail (R) to Mt. Bigelow Fire Tower.

Bog Brook, 9 *m.*, where the Arnold expedition made its passage between West Carry Pond and Dead River, is at the right.

Long Falls, 12.5 *m.*, a series of cataracts extending about 1.5 miles, requires a long carry. Below the falls, the journey continues along a twisting course through low bog land and swamps to Grand Falls.

Grand Falls (also known as *Great Falls*), 17.5 *m.*, leaps from a broad ledge to plunge into a boiling misty cauldron below. A carry, made on the west bank of the river, is necessary at this point. A half-mile farther on, at the mouth of Spencer Stream, the Dead River bears east on its way to join the Kennebec at The Forks. At the junction of the Dead River and Spencer Streams are *The Norways,* an exceptionally fine stand of pine.

Little Spencer Stream, 19.5 *m.*, is entered; but because it is shallow and very rocky, many canoeists prefer to carry around it to Spencer Lake, or from Big Spencer Stream.

Spencer Lake, 23.5 *m.*, is surrounded by a heavy growth of towering pine and hemlock. Above the forest tower Tumbledown, Spencer, Hedgehog, Hardscrabble, and Hardwood Mountains. The lake is teeming with fish, and the surrounding country is full of game. A paddle of 7 miles to the north end of the lake brings the canoeist to Bratten's Camps, where horses may be hired to haul the canoe and dunnage across a carry of 6.5 miles, through a dense growth of cedar and fir to Moose River.

At *Moose River,* 37 *m.*, the canoe is put in the water to follow a course north through Fish, Chub, and Whipple Ponds, and Beaver, Horse, and Moose Brooks, to Attean Falls, where a short carry brings the traveler into Attean Lake.

Attean Lake, 48 *m.*, provides good fishing for the canoeist, who follows its east shore past three small wooded islands and the Attean Lake Camps and under the Canadian Pacific Railroad bridge to Wood Pond. After a paddle of 3.5 miles to the north end of Wood Pond, the canoe is headed into the Moose River to follow a 3-mile course beneath the Jackman Bridge and through the center of Jackman Village (*see Tour* 10) to Long Pond.

Long Pond, 62.5 *m.*, has many wooded bays and coves, along the shores of which game of all sorts is plentiful. Trout and salmon fishing is good here.

Long Pond Dam, 72.5 *m.*, requires another short carry. The canoe is again put in on Moose River waters, where it enters a fast run, Long Pond Rips, the most exciting section of the entire trip.

The 3-mile length of *Little Brassua Lake,* 76.5 *m.*, is crossed directly to Brassua Lake, which is entered on its west side. The course turns right here, and follows the southeast shore to Brassua Lake Dam, where a short carry must be made. The canoe is again put in on Moose River, which from here continues in a comparatively straight and unbroken course to Moosehead Lake.

Moosehead Lake, 85.5 *m.* (*see Tour* 9), is entered from the west. The canoeist follows the west shore south past Mount Kineo (L) to Rockwood.

ROCKWOOD (Kineo Station), 87 *m.* (*see Tour* 9), is the terminus.

RANGELEY LAKES CANOE TRIP

From RANGELEY VILLAGE *to* UPTON, 49.5 *m.*, 1 week.
Via Oquossoc and Haines Landing, over Rangeley, Mooselookmeguntic, Upper Richardson, and Umbagog Lakes.
Guides necessary; camping equipment recommended, although good accommodations are available along the route.

Traversing waterways in the scenic Rangeley region, this trip passes through several of the larger lakes of the Rangeley group.

At RANGELEY VILLAGE (*see Tour* 11), the canoe is put in on the east shore of Rangeley Lake, to follow westward along the north shore.

At OQUOSSOC, 8 *m.* (*see Tour* 11*A*), at the west end of Rangeley Lake, the canoe comes out for a carry to Haines Landing.

HAINES LANDING (*see Tour* 11*A*), 9.5 *m.*, is at the north end of Mooselookmeguntic Lake. Here the canoe is put in, and the journey continued along the west shore to Upper Dam, where there is a short carry to Richardson Lake. In front of the dam is the well-known Upper Dam trout and salmon pool. About one-fourth mile out from the dam in the lake is Dollar Island, on which is a camp site. Metalic Island, about 4 miles from the dam, offers a fine camp site for a few days' fishing stop.

At *Middle Dam*, 33.5 *m.*, another carry must be made before continuing to Sunday Cove over Rapid River. Unless the pitch of water is right, numerous carries are necessary over this river.

Sunday Cove, 41.5 *m.*, is on the northeast shore of Umbagog Lake. The course follows south from here.

UPTON, 49.5 *m.* (*see Tour* 14), is the terminus of the trip.

OTHER SELECTED CANOE TRIPS

WEST BRANCH TRIP. *From* RIPOGENUS DAM *to* NORCROSS, 36 *m.*, 4–10 days. Over the swift water of Upper Umbajackamegus, through Sourdnahunk Deadwater, West Branch of the Penobscot River, Ambajejus and Pemadumcook, and North Twin Lakes. Guides necessary.

ST. CROIX RIVER TRIP. *From* DANFORTH *to* CALAIS, 108 *m.*, 10 days–3 weeks. Over Spednic Lake and St. Croix River. Guides necessary.

FISH RIVER CHAIN OF LAKES TRIP. *From* ST. AGATHA *to* FORT KENT, 65 *m.*, 1–3 weeks. Over waters of Cross, Square, and Eagle Lakes, and Fish River. Guides necessary.

UPPER KENNEBEC WATERS TRIP. *From* THE FORKS *to* BATH, 120 *m.*, 1–2 weeks. Over waters of Dead River, Wyman Lake, and Kennebec River. Guides not necessary.

LOWER KENNEBEC WATERS TRIP. *From* GARDINER *to* GARDINER (loop trip), 100 *m.*, 8 days–3 weeks. Over Cobbossee Stream, Pleasant and Horseshoe Ponds, Cobbosseecontee, Annabessacook, Maranacook, and Messalonskee Lakes, and Kennebec River. Guides not necessary.

BELGRADE LAKES TRIP. *From* WATERVILLE *to* OAKLAND, 40–100 *m.*, 4 days–2 weeks. Over waters of East, North, Great, Ellis, McGrath, and Long Ponds, Belgrade Lakes, Belgrade Stream, and Snow Pond. Guides not necessary.

SACO RIVER TRIP. *From* FRYEBURG VILLAGE *to* LOVEWELL'S POND, 17 *m.*, 1–3 days. Over Saco River. Guides not necessary.

GRAND LAKE–MACHIAS WATERS TRIP. *From* PRINCETON *to* WHITNEYVILLE, 75 *m.*, 2–4 weeks. Over Big, Grand, and Dobose Lakes, and Machias River. Guides necessary.

SEBAGO LAKE TRIP. *From* PORTLAND (Riverton) *to* HARRISON, 60 *m.*, 4–10 days. Over Presumpscot River, Sebago Lake, Songo River, Brandy and Long Ponds, and Highland Lake. Guides not necessary.

PEMAQUID TRIP (fresh and salt waters). *From* DAMARISCOTTA *to* DAMARISCOTTA (loop trip), 70 *m.*, 3–7 days. Over Damariscotta River, Damariscotta Lake, Muscongus Bay, Pemaquid River, Boyd Pond, John's Bay, and Christmas Cove. Guides not necessary.

HIKING AND MOUNTAIN CLIMBING

THERE are more than 100 mountains 3000 feet or higher in the State of Maine. Few natives and fewer visitors realize that these mountains exist, and that they have so important a place in the list of the State's natural resources. With the wild forest land in which they are set, they form a vast and natural State park, where the nature-lover, the hiker, and the mountain climber may find nearly every type of trail, the challenge of rugged mountain peaks, meandering paths along forest-bordered streams, and panoramic views of mountains, lakes, and timber lands.

The Maine State Forestry Commission has built and marked trails from the principal State highways to lookout towers on mountain peaks and high hills. It has also constructed camp sites in those areas where private accommodations are lacking. These camp sites are situated near pure drinking water, and contain stone fireplaces, shelters with tables, and other conveniences. The Maine State Highway Commission map shows the location of these camp sites throughout the State.

Many of the shorter trails in Maine, especially those in the south where there is a more even distribution of population and an occasional village, follow dirt roads and abandoned county highways. Other trails start from small villages or from the main highways.

The longest and best known trail in the State is the *Appalachian*, comprising the first 265 miles of the 2054 mile continuous hiking trail from Mount Katahdin in Maine to Mount Oglethorpe in Georgia. The Appalachian Trail in Maine was the last part of the total route to be undertaken and was not completed until 1935, when the work of building it was finally adopted as a Civilian Conservation Corps project. The Maine section was the most difficult to build because its way lay through utter wilderness, far removed from centers of population, and there were no outing or mountaineering clubs in the State to aid in its construction. Nevertheless, the trail is today an easy, well-marked route. Throughout its distance the way is conspicuously marked by an unbroken line of white paint blazes facing the direction of travel. As the insignia of the route, this marking is further supplemented by metal markers which bear the A monogram and the legend 'Appalachian Trail — Maine to Georgia.' The paint used in the marking has a luminous quality which helps travel in the evening hours. A further helpful device is that known as the 'double blaze,' one blaze placed above another, which calls attention to a turn. This is the only blaze symbol adopted for uniform use on the entire Trail. Cairns — piles of stones built so as to appear obviously artificial — and paint on rocks also indicate the route where other marking is impossible. All side trails are marked by blue-paint blazes, and large wooden signs indicate the route and distances at important intersections. The Trail traverses a series of mountain peaks in a general southwest-northeast direction, and it has been so located that comfortable accommodations can be found at the interval of a moderate day's journey. Two of the trails treated in this section are part of the Appalachian system. (For full information, see 'Guide to the Appalachian Trail in Maine,' The Appalachian Trail Conference, 901 Union Trust Building, Washington, D.C.)

The following trips, selected for their scenic beauty, range from difficult climbs for the experienced to easy hikes for the novice. It should be understood that the mileages given are only approximate, as floods and frost may change the trails from season to season.

Sporting camps are fairly frequent in lake areas and small villages, and game and fire wardens will supply specific information on accommodations, communication facilities, and trail changes. There are telephones at all fire lookouts.

HUNT TRAIL

From BAXTER CAMP *to* BAXTER PEAK (alt. 5267), 5.2 *m.*, 1 day, blazed trail (part of Appalachian system). Via the Gateway and Thoreau Spring.

Caution advised, but no guide necessary. Trail markers are of three types: Appalachian 🅰 white paint blazes on rocks and trees, and cairns (small piles of stones). Area is State Game Preserve; no hunting.

Wending into the vast game area of Katahdin State Game Preserve and Baxter State Park, to reach Mount Katahdin, which Thoreau described as 'a vast aggregation of loose rocks,' the Hunt Trail leads into a district filled with the lore of woods and mountains and colored with legends of the Indians, to whom Katahdin was the home of the Mountain King, his sons the Thunders, and his beautiful swift daughter Lightning. Climbing the west side of the mountain, the trail affords spectacular views over the forest-rimmed bowl of the game preserve.

Baxter Camp (*see Tour* 7), a State camp, with custodian on the grounds all year, is the starting point of the trail, which leads through a growth of spruce, pine, and hardwood, with Katahdin Stream (R) visible at intervals. The trail crosses a rustic bridge at 1 *m.*, and bears left to follow the stream for some distance, before ascending to an altitude of about 1800 feet.

Seven Pennies Shelter, 2 *m.*, is a camper's lean-to just beyond which there are several steep bits of ground known as The Pitches; these are very slippery in wet weather.

The Cave, 2.6 *m.*, a huge slab of rock projecting from the mountain-side, offers shelter for a party of not more than six, and is a good stopping place for luncheon. From this point the trail becomes rocky, even the stunted growth of timber finally vanishing, and edges its way through the Boulders, a desolate stretch of huge granite rocks marked only by white paint blazes.

The Gateway, 3.6 *m.*, is the entrance to the plateau or tableland of Katahdin, a generally level stretch carpeted with several inches of moss.

Thoreau Spring, 4.2 *m.*, in a setting of tall grass and moss, lies at the end of the plateau. A bronze marker at the spring records the naming of the water supply in 1932. From here to the summit is a gradual climb of 300 yards.

At *Baxter Peak*, 5.2 *m.*, the end of the trail, a sign bears the legend: 'Terminus of the Appalachian Trail, A Mountain Footpath 2054 Miles Long to Mount Oglethorpe, Georgia.' The mile-high point of vantage affords an unexcelled panorama of Maine's lakes, streams, forests, and mountains.

SADDLEBACK MOUNTAIN TRAIL

From SADDLEBACK POND *to* SUMMIT OF SADDLEBACK MOUNTAIN (alt. 4116), 3.5 *m.*, 1 day. Marked trail; no guide necessary. Inquire at Rangeley (*see Tour* 11) for local road to the Saddleback Camps on the west side of the pond, where boats may be hired for the trip across the pond; or the old logging road that runs from the camps may be used to reach the trail entrance. Trail marked by horsehoe sign.

This short climb, along a rocky path bordered by pine and spruce, makes a gradual ascent to Saddleback summit, from which the view is especially attractive.

The *Ranger's Cabin*, 3 *m.*, a log building with porch, marks the first open ground on the trail. Near-by is a spring, and campers may use the open fireplace for cooking.

From this point the trail becomes steep and rocky, following an old stream bed that is slippery when wet. With the higher altitude, the trees beside the trail grow smaller and more wind-twisted, finally disappearing altogether about 200 yards from the summit.

The Summit, 3.5 *m.*, is barren rock relieved only by a few blackberry bushes and moss. Crowning the summit is a 75-foot *Observation Tower*, affording a fine view of the Rangeley Lakes and distant mountains.

SQUAW MOUNTAIN TRAIL

From SQUAW MOUNTAIN INN *to* SUMMIT OF SQUAW MOUNTAIN (alt. 3262), 3 *m.*, 1 day. Marked trail; no guide necessary.

Traversing an area rich in scenic beauty, this trail climbs to the summit of the peak which according to legend was named Squaw Mountain by Kineo, a mighty Indian warrior, because his mother died here (*see Tour* 9). Starting from *Squaw Mountain Inn*, 2 *m.* north of Greenville Junction (*see Tour* 9), the trail skirts the east base of Squaw Mountain for 1 mile, then gradually ascends.

The best spot for rest and luncheon is near the top of the mountain, where there are a fire warden's cabin and a spring. The *Fire Lookout Tower*, a short distance above the warden's cabin, affords a view of Moosehead Lake, numerous smaller lakes and streams, and Mount Kineo and Spencer Mountain.

MOUNT BLUE TRAIL

From WELD VILLAGE *to* SUMMIT OF MOUNT BLUE (alt. 3187), 1.8 *m.*, 1½ hrs. Marked trail; no guide necessary.

Trail entrance may be reached by motor by turning right at four corners in Weld Village (*see Tour* 4) and continuing 2 miles to the base of the mountain. The first stage of the trail is a moderate climb of a half mile to a fire warden's cabin, near which a spring of cold clear water bubbles from the rocks. The remainder of the trail is steep. The summit, a flattened crest with outcropping ledges covered with scattered evergreen growth, is crowned with a *Fire Lookout Tower*.

OTHER SELECTED MOUNTAIN TRAILS

MOUNT ZIRCON (alt. 2240) from Rumford. 0.7 *m.*, 45 min. Marked. No guide necessary; water at foot of trail.

RUMFORD WHITECAP MOUNTAIN (alt. 2197) from Rumford. 2 *m.*, 1½ hrs. Unmarked. No guide necessary; no water.

OLD SPEC MOUNTAIN (alt. 4150) from Grafton Notch (*see Tour* 14). 1.5 *m.*, 2½ hrs. Marked (over section of Mahoosuc Trail of the Appalachian System). No guide necessary; water at warden's camp.

OSSIPEE MOUNTAIN (alt. 1050) from E. Waterboro (*see Tour* 11). 0.3 *m.*, 20 min. Marked. No guide necessary; no water; fire lookout tower.

BALD MOUNTAIN (alt. 2572) from Carthage. 3.5 *m.*, 3½ hrs. Marked by cairns on ledges. Start at Hill's Pond; no guide necessary; no water.

PLEASANT MOUNTAIN (alt. 2007) from Denmark. 1.8 *m.*, 1½ hrs. Marked. No guide necessary; brook near trail.

SABATTUS MOUNTAIN (alt. 1280) from Lovell (*see Tour* 15). 1.5 *m.*, 1 hr. Unmarked. Guide advised; no water.

TUMBLEDOWN DICK MOUNTAIN (alt. 1740) from Gilead (*see Tour* 14). 1 *m.*, 1 hr. Unmarked. No guide necessary; no water. Ascent must be made without trail, over steep ledges.

STONE MOUNTAIN (alt. 1580) from Brownfield (*see Tour* 15). 1.5 *m.*, 1 hr. Unmarked. No guide necessary; no water.

CARIBOU MOUNTAIN (alt. 2828) from Mason. 3.5 *m.*, 2¼ hrs. Unmarked. Guide unnecessary; water near-by; shelter near summit.

STREAKED MOUNTAIN (alt. 1770) from Buckfield. 1 *m.*, 45 min. Unmarked, but well defined. Guide unnecessary; no water.

BEAR MOUNTAIN (alt. 1207) from North Turner (*see Tour* 11). 1 *m.*, 1 hr. Marked. Guide unnecessary; no water.

AGAMENTICUS (alt. 692) from Wells (*see Tour* 1, *sec. a*). 0.5 *m.*, 20 min. Marked. Guide unnecessary; picnic facilities at mountain base.

MOUNT KINEO (alt. 1806) from Rockwood (*see Tour* 9). 0.3 *m.*, 45 min. Marked. Guide unnecessary, but dangerous climbing (no guard rails); no water.

DOUBLETOP MOUNTAIN (alt. 3520) from Bradeen's Camps at Kidney Pond. 4.5 *m.*, 4 hrs. Marked. Guide necessary; no water.

TUMBLEDOWN (alt. 3600) from Weld (*see Tour* 4). 3 *m.*, 1 day. Unmarked. Guide unnecessary; water.

MOUNT BATTIE (alt. 800) from Camden (*see Tour* 1, *sec. b*). 1 *m.*, 1 hr. Marked. Guide unnecessary; water; stone observation tower.

CHAMPLAIN MOUNTAIN (alt. 1060) from Bar Harbor (*see Tour* 2). 1 *m.*, 1 hr. Marked. Guide unnecessary; water; National Park Service (Acadia National Park).

BIGELOW MOUNTAIN (alt. 4150) from Dead River (*see Tour* 11). 4.5 *m.*, 3 hrs. Marked (via section Appalachian System).

COBURN MOUNTAIN (alt.3718) from Township 3, Range 6 (*Upper Enchanted*). 4 *m.*, 3 hrs. Marked. Guide necessary; water at warden's cabin en route.

RIDING

HORSEBACK riding has come into its own in Maine within the past few years. The Maine Development Commission and the Maine Horse Association are completing a system of saddle trails which thus far covers more than half the State. The trails, marked by orange boards bearing a black horseshoe encircling the trail number, have been planned to utilize abandoned roads, old trolley-line beds, tote and dirt roads, avoiding as far as possible hard-surfaced highways and heavy traffic.

Experienced riders as well as beginners will find many interesting trips in Maine. The trails wind past mountains and lakes, traverse meadows and woods, follow rivers and streams, and pass through pastoral villages. Whether he is on the road one day or a week, the horseman will find adequate accommodations along the way. Visiting riders are offered the courtesies of numerous riding clubs throughout the State.

The two bridle path trips outlined here are representative of opposite types of terrain and scenery encountered by the horseman in Maine. The first, leaving a thriving city behind, strikes into the wilderness, and is never far from the lakes, mountains, and forests of northern Maine. The second passes through regions which are definitely rural, mountains and forests forming only distant impressive backgrounds to the quiet countryside.

SADDLE TRIP OUT OF BANGOR

From BANGOR *to* CHESUNCOOK VILLAGE, 136 *m.*, 8–10 days. State Trail No. 1.
Via Bradford Center, Lakeview, Brownville, Katahdin Iron Works, and Kokadjo.
Well marked and clearly defined trail after leaving Bangor city limits.

Eleven lunch and night stops (advance reservations should be made for accommodations for rider, and hay, grain, and tieup for horse); ample tieups at night stops; mounted guide service between Grant's Farm and Chesuncook Village obtainable at Grant's Farm.

Leaving Bangor, the trail wanders through a rural area gradually reverting to thick woods from the once fertile agricultural land of northwestern Penobscot County. The central section of the trail touches small villages which once bustled with activity as the trading centers of a prosperous farming area, but which now quietly drowse except during the hunting seasons, when red-capped gunners fill all available accommodations. The northern section, after leaving Katahdin Iron Works, follows tote and corduroy roads through the timber area north of Brownville Junction, where splendid lakes, well stocked with fish, lie gem-like in the vast dimness of great pine and spruce forests.

At 0 *m.* the trail starts from the *Bangor Fair Grounds* (*see BANGOR*) to follow Fair Grounds fence for 300 yards, then left on dirt road one-fourth mile to fork; left at fork on dirt road for one-fourth mile to junction with side road, then bear right and continue three-fourths mile to turn right on Webster Ave. Left from Webster Ave. to Silver Rd.; continue on Silver Rd. to Hammond St., then left across fields to dirt road paralleling car tracks for 1.5 miles. Bear left across field to large green barn and cross Union St. to follow stone wall one-fourth mile. Bear sharp right on Ohio St. and continue to red barn, then left for one-half mile to turn right on Finson Rd. Continue on Finson Rd. for 3.3 miles to join Broadway; right on Broadway for 200 yards, then left on Milo Rd. to cross railroad tracks (*watch for trail markers*).

DAVIS FARM (red barn), 19 *m.*
Lunch accommodations for any number. Stable for 15 horses.

Continue on Milo Rd. to U.S. Bench Mark 172 1/BM, and straight ahead through woods to BRADFORD CENTER, a small village that is principally a trading center for the surrounding farming area. There is fine fishing in Mohawk Stream (L) near State 221, along which the trail follows on leaving the village.

DOW FARM, 28 *m.*
Ten bedrooms. Stable for 10 horses. Telephone.
For the next 10 miles, the trail passes through a former agricultural area.

Many of the homesteads are decaying and uncared for, while the once rich farmland is gradually growing up to second-growth hardwood. Occasional small garden plots contrast with the neglected area surrounding them.

DEAN CAMPS, 40 m.

Four bedrooms (2 beds each), one cottage (3 beds), 2 stalls, tieup for 6 horses, hay and grain. Telephone. Lunch accommodations for 20 riders.

From Dean Camps, the trail swings through the outskirts of MILO (see *Tour* 8), an industrial, commercial, and farming community in a heavily wooded area near the junction of the Sebec River with the Piscataquis River. The trail follows Highland Ave. to cross a bridge, then first street right, and first road left.

The next few miles are through a heavily wooded section, where the menace of forest fire constantly lurks. Thousands of acres of valuable timber have been laid waste in areas such as this. Care should be exercised, for a lighted match or live cigarette carelessly dropped into the underbrush may be fanned by a slight breeze and cause a blazing inferno.

LAKEVIEW, 52 m.

Lakeview House: 20 bedrooms, 10 double stalls, 20 straight stalls, hay and grain. Telephone.

Once the site of a large mill of the American Thread Company, Lakeview is now almost a deserted village. Sprawling along the west shore of the long Schoodic Lake (noted for its excellent trout fishing), with the dark peak of Mount Katahdin looming in the background, are the dismantled mill property and the empty dwellings of its one-time employees.

Leaving Lakeview by returning over the Milo Road for 2 miles to take the second road right, the trail leads into BROWNVILLE (see *Tour* 8A), a small village lying on both sides of Pleasant River. The trail follows State 221 from Brownville.

ARBO HOME, 66 m.

Four stalls, 4 tieups, hay and grain. Telephone.

From Arbo's the trail runs straight through deep woods for 6 miles. Deer and other wild animals are occasionally seen along this road.

KATAHDIN IRON WORKS, 72 m.

Mrs. A. L. Green: 3 bedrooms main house, 1 cottage (5 beds), 16 stalls, hay and grain. Telephone.

Once the site of a bog iron mining venture, this small settlement is now used as base headquarters in the lumbering operations of the Pleasant River Lumber Co. Four miles northwest of here, and reached only by hiking, is *The Gulf*, a spectacular rocky canyon through which rushes Pleasant River. Near-by are several waterfalls and lakes (see *Tour* 8A).

Leaving Katahdin Iron Works over the Pleasant River bridge, the trail leads through splendid forest growth to the *Hermitage*, a private camp in a grove of towering pines. About 1 mile from the Hermitage, over a foot trail, are the *Screw Auger Falls* on Gulf Hagas Brook, a series of cascades with a zigzag descent of 125 feet.

MACLEOD CALL CAMP, 84 *m*.

Six cabins (2–5 bunks in each), stabling for 20 horses, hay and grain. No telephone.

There are no lunch stops or stables for 18 miles beyond this camp, and arrangements should be made here for a buckboard to carry luncheon and hay and grain along for the noon rest-stop.

KOKADJO, 102 *m*. (*see Tour* 7).

Inn: Accommodations for 20 persons, stable for 20 horses, hay and grain. Telephone.

Take first left road after leaving Kokadjo, then straight ahead for 12 miles.

GRANT'S FARM, 114 *m*.

Accommodations for 25 persons, stable for any number of horses, hay and grain. Telephone. Mounted guide service.

From Grant's to Chesuncook Village, the trail traverses an area densely covered with big timber. Winding through narrow aisles beneath fragrant balsam and along crystal-clear brooks which suddenly hurtle over rocky beds in a mass of foam and spray, with here and there beautiful vistas across wide lakes, the trail affords opportunity for seeing a part of Maine little known to the average rider.

CHESUNCOOK VILLAGE, 136 *m*.

Inn: Accommodations for 25 persons; stable for 25 horses in village.

This isolated settlement deep in the woods nestles on the shore of Chesuncook Lake, a popular fishing area and the starting place of many canoe trips. Sporting camps scattered along its pine-fringed shores are served by steamer.

SADDLE TRIP OUT OF AUGUSTA

From AUGUSTA *to* JEFFERSON, 24 *m*. State Trail No. 13.
Via North Whitefield.

Well-marked trail. Reservations for overnight accommodations for riders and stabling for horses at Del Andrews Camps in Jefferson should be made before leaving Augusta.

Following along a back road, with little motor traffic, this route winds through an area of diversified farming, where pastoral vistas over broad fields and rolling hills vie with views of blue lakes and wooded hillsides.

At AUGUSTA, the starting point, the trail follows US 201 from Water St. across the Kennebec River bridge. To the left is the dam at the head of navigation on this river, while (R) stands *Fort Western*, with its stockade and blockhouse of hand-hewn logs, built in 1754. The route continues straight ahead up Cony St., turning at the top of the grade to Stone St. (State 17).

At about 1 m., the trail leaves Stone St. to follow Hospital St. At the right is the *Augusta State Hospital*, with the granite buildings of the former United States Arsenal, on a side hill of the grounds. Farther along is a splendid view (R) of Augusta's west side, with the State House in the foreground, backed by the wooded expanse of Ganeston Park. Hallowell (*see Tour* 10) lies to the southwest.

At about 2 m., the trail joins State 226, and a left turn is made on a gravel road leading to the United States Veterans Administration Facility at Togus (*see Tour* 17).

Leaving Togus by the North Gate, the trail swings right on State 17, a hard-surfaced road which is followed 2.5 m. to the junction with a gravel road (R), on which it continues up Nolan Hill to join State 126 on Jay Ridge. The next few miles are through an area of wooded and farming country.

At about 13.5 m. (R) stands *St. Denis Catholic Church* (*see Tour* 17), erected in 1833 on the site of an earlier log church.

NORTH WHITEFIELD is reached at 15 m. (*see Tour* 17). In mid-October the Whitefield Fish and Game Club serves an annual game supper here, consisting of venison, rabbit pie, partridge, and sometimes raccoon and bear.

Leaving North Whitefield, the junction of State 126, State 218, a local road is reached. Following the local road southeast over Jones' Hill for 4 miles to the junction with a dirt road, the trail turns left on this latter and follows along the west shore of Dyer Long Pond for 2 miles, to rejoin State 126. It then bears right on State 126 for a 2-mile stretch through woods, to the junction of State 126 and State 213.

Swinging right on State 213, the trail follows along a ridge overlooking Damariscotta Lake, to reach its destination at Del Andrews Camps in the town of Jefferson, 24 m.

OTHER SELECTED SADDLE TRAILS

From NORTH POWNAL *to* WATERVILLE, 71.5 m., 3–4 days, Trail No. 3. Via Wales, Winthrop, and Augusta. Seven lunch and night stops.

From BRUNSWICK *to* AUGUSTA, 36 m., 1–2 days, Trail No. 4. Via Gardiner and Hallowell. Two lunch and night stops.

From INTERSECTION OF TRAIL NO. 3 *to* WATERVILLE, 34.5 m., 2–3 days, Trail No. 5. Via Readfield Depot, Rome, and South Smithfield. Three lunch and two night stops.

From BRUNSWICK *to* WEST AUBURN, 54 *m.*, 2-3 days, Trail No. 9. Via Lisbon Falls, Webster, and Lewiston. Three lunch and night stops.

From EAST RAYMOND *to* HACKETT'S MILLS, 18 *m.*, 1-2 days, Trail No. 14. Via Poland Spring. Three lunch and night stops.

From NORTH RAYMOND *to* RANGE HILL, 20 *m.*, 1-2 days, Trail 14-A. Via Webb's Mills. Two lunch and night stops.

YACHTING

MAINE'S many islands, providing almost continuous shelter for small sailing vessels, together with a variety of scenic beauty and an abundance of good harbors, have made the Maine coast a mecca for the yachtsman. Most of those who live on these shores during the summer months spend many of their waking hours in boats; and yacht racing — whether of small 12-footers in the juvenile class or of sea-going vessels handled by salty professionals — has become one of the important sports of the State.

Formal races are staged at the York County resorts several times during the season, especially at Kennebunkport, York Harbor, and Biddeford Pool; and there are, in addition, many impromptu events. Interest in small-boat racing at Portland is not so great as in former years; but several of the minor resort regions, such as the New Meadows River Basin, have formed their own regattas and hold regularly scheduled races. Boothbay Harbor has an annual program of weekly yachting events, which includes at least one ocean race during the summer.

At Camden there is a large class of so-called HAJ boats, identical in form and rig, all 30-footers, built in Finland several years ago and exported to this country. Semi-weekly races of these boats are held by the younger group of yachtsmen. Two series of races are arranged here each summer, and special events in connection with the Rockport Carnival and Regatta include a captains' race, a Labor Day race, and an overnight cruise. Competition in these races is keen; and the course, laid outside Camden Harbor, is a difficult test of the sailing ability of the young skippers, many of whom are girls.

At Dark Harbor on Islesboro Island there is equally enthusiastic racing activity. Several classes of one-design boats, principally 12-footers and 17-footers, participate in an annual series of summer races. A similar fleet at North Haven, farther out in Penobscot Bay, confines its activities chiefly to the sheltered reaches between North Haven and Vinalhaven.

The resorts farther east also have their fleets of one-design boats. At Bar Harbor and Northeast Harbor, the yachts are fewer in number but larger in size than in the Penobscot region and on the lower coast. Boats of the 'Bull's Eye' class are especially prominent in the Bar Harbor region.

The principal yachting event of the year in Maine is the annual Monhegan Island race, staged by the Portland Yacht Club. This attracts entries from as far south as Marblehead, Mass., and from all sections of the Maine coast. The boats race over a 100-mile course from Portland Head to Cape Porpoise, thence to Monhegan Island and back to Portland, usually finishing within 30 hours under favorable weather conditions.

Small regattas and regularly scheduled races are held on some of the larger lakes, particularly at Sebago and Moosehead, although in general motor boating is a more popular sport on fresh water.

WINTER SPORTS

FOR nearly a century ice skating, tobogganing, fishing through the ice, and harness racing on ice have been the chief winter sports in Maine. More recently, ice hockey has been developed from the original game played by the American Indians on dry land, and many teams representing Maine's schools, colleges, and private athletic organizations compete with each other and with groups from other States and from Canada in this brilliant, fast-moving sport. Yet not until the past few years has Maine become aware of the unusual facilities for winter sports available in various parts of the State. The leading colleges and schools, of course, have for many years presented programs of winter sports, but these activities are limited locally and only few persons are able to compete in them. But now most of the leading cities and towns — Lewiston, Bath, Augusta, Waterville, Bangor, Rumford, Camden, Fryeburg, North Berwick, Bar Harbor, Houlton, and Presque Isle — have their ski trails and jumps, toboggan runs, snowshoe trails, and skating rinks; and a winter carnival, with an ice palace and a carnival queen, is held in each of these communities. The more ambitious of the carnivals have horse and iceboat racing, even dog-sled competitions. There are always breathtaking exhibitions of skill on skates or skis, but there is a generally prevailing spirit of good-natured competition rather than the more bitter partisanship of strenuous athletic contests.

Maine's topography — rolling mountain slopes and high hills — the consistency of its snows, warm sunshine, good transportation, and the availability of accommodations are its chief attractions as a winter sports country. Civic developments of natural facilities are adding greatly to this list. Railroads operate 'snow trains' from Portland to Fryeburg, Rumford, Greenville, and other sports centers, and each winter finds Maine's highways in better condition.

Fishing through the ice is possible on many of the countless Maine lakes and ponds, or on the rivers (*see Hunting and Fishing*). Frost-fishing (smelting) is a remunerative sport enjoyed at night on tidal streams near the coast.

Harness racing on ice, an early sport in the State, is being revived at some of the winter carnivals. The straight course, laid on lake or river, has an advantage over the oval dirt tracks of the summer fairgrounds in that it gives opportunity for achieving greater bursts of speed and affords more favorable views of the race to the spectators. Horses are equipped with caulked shoes, and drivers are heavily dressed. Otherwise, the races, thrilling and fast as they are, are no different from those of the various county fairs held throughout the country through the summer and fall months. The same horses are run, and the regulation sulkies are used. Betting is unofficial and illegal.

Iceboats, run by sail or by propeller, are raced on many of the larger lakes and rivers. At Island Park on Lake Cobbosseecontee (*see Tour 13*), an iceboat regatta has been held for many years, the local residents competing in the fast and exciting races with vessels of individual design and manufacture. This regatta has become semi-official although there is at present no organized iceboat racing in Maine. Lake Cobbosseecontee continues as a center for the sport, certain of the iceboats raced there having been in use each season over a period of twenty-five years. Moosehead Lake is also becoming well known for its ice-sailing. There are several reasons why iceboating should grow in popularity in Maine. It is fairly inexpensive; the boats themselves are simple enough to build from easily obtainable materials. The only parts that cannot be produced by home manufacture are the steel runners (skates or 'shoes'). Even with the most modest craft it is possible to attain a high rate of speed — sixty miles an hour is not unusual. And in the open cockpit of the boat, with ice shavings flying from the runners and gleaming islands or wooded shore streaming by, the wind whipping the faces of the passengers, the sensation is one of really great speed, much greater of course than that which the boat actually attains. Even with the possibility of great speed, the sport cannot be considered a dangerous one. Being thrown from a fast-moving iceboat seldom brings more than a few bruises.

Dog-sled racing is another sport that is rapidly attaining prominence in the State. The races at Poland Spring have formerly drawn contestants from as far away as Alaska, and the events were given much publicity. Although some of the winter carnivals, notably Rumford, have featured dog-racing, Poland Spring has been most outstanding for the sport in Maine. Local racers, however, travel with their dogs into New Hampshire, New York, and Canada each winter to compete with enthusiasts from all sections of the northern part of the continent. Many Maine residents are breeding and training racing dogs; some of the animals come from Husky strains, some are Norwegian or Siberian dogs, some are of well-known hunting breeds, such as setters, and others are just mongrels. Often the fastest dogs have wolf blood in them. Chief among Maine's breeders and racers has been Mrs. E. P. Ricker of Poland Spring, the only woman champion dog-sled racer of the State.

The following is a selected list of a few of the winter sports offered in some of Maine's communities.

ANDOVER (see Tour 4).
Available facilities: Ski jumps.

BANGOR (see BANGOR).
Available facilities: Skating. Ski trails — Bald Mountain No. 1, 0.5 m. long, 20-25 ft. wide, 720 ft. vertical descent, 25° maximum grade, class in upper part is expert, class in lower part is intermediate; — Bald Mountain No. 2, 0.25 m. long, 20-40 ft. wide, 480 ft. vertical descent, 28° maximum grade, class is intermediate; — Ryder's Bluff, 0.5 m. long, 300 ft. wide, 20° maximum grade, class is intermediate and novice; — Graystone Farm Slope, 0.25 m. long, 150 ft. wide, 18° maximum grade, class is intermediate and novice; — Paradise Park, 0.37 m. long, 450 ft. wide, 28° maximum grade, floodlighted, class is intermediate and novice.

BAR HARBOR and ACADIA NATIONAL PARK (see Tour 2).
Available facilities: 50 miles of rolling carriage roads for cross-country skiing on island. Ski trails — South Face Trail on Western Mountain, 0.75 m. long, 15-45 ft. wide, 750 ft. vertical descent, 20° maximum grade, S. exposure, 6-12 in. snow, class is intermediate, lean-to shelter and parking space; — West Side McFarland's Hill, 0.37 m. long, 15-35 ft. wide, 350 ft. vertical descent, 28° maximum grade, SW. exposure, 8 in. snow, class is novice to intermediate; — Stemwinder on McFarland's Hill, 0.25 m. long, 10-60 ft. wide, 350 ft. vertical descent, 18° maximum grade. E. exposure, 8 in. snow, class is novice to intermediate; — The Loop on McFarland's Hill, 0.5 m. long, 10-60 ft. wide, 350 ft. vertical descent, 18° maximum grade, S. exposure, 8 in. snow, class is novice; — Open Slope on McFarland's Hill (20 acres), 75-600 ft. wide, 200 ft. vertical descent, 15° maximum grade. Ski tows — on McFarland's practice slope, 800 ft. long, 200 ft. vertical descent, 15° maximum grade.

BRIDGTON (see Tour 18).
Available facilities: Ski trails — several, information available locally.

CAMDEN (see Tour 1, sec. b): Camden Winter Carnival, dates tentative annually.
Available facilities: Ice boating, skating, hockey, harness racing on ice, Lodge House, and Hosmer Pond Snow Bowl (said to be the only permanent winter sports area of its kind in New England) for athletics. Ski trails — Spring Brook, 4 m. long, 8-12 ft. wide, 600 ft. vertical descent from apex 2 m. on either side, 15° maximum grade, N. by NE. exposure; — Cameron Mountain (from W. side Bald Rock Mountain on Spring Brook Trail to Zeke's Lookout), 1.75 m. long, 8-10 ft. wide, 500 ft. vertical descent, 23° maximum grade, NW. by W. exposure; — Zeke's Lookout (Spring Brook Valley up Mt. Megunticook, northwest along ridge to Zeke's Lookout, northeast to midpoint on Spring Brook Trail), 2.25 m. long, 8-12 ft. wide, 500 ft. vertical descent in 0.5 m., 22° maximum grade, NE. by E. exposure, class is intermediate and expert; — Mt. Megunticook Slope, 2 m. long, 8-10 ft. wide, 400 ft. vertical descent in 0.5 m., 20° maximum grade, NE. exposure, class is novice to intermediate; Cross Country Trail, 4 m. long, 7-12 ft. wide, 15° maximum grade. Ski jumps — practice. Ski tow — 1 electric, 900 ft. long, 186 ft. vertical ascent, slope flood-lighted for night use. Toboggan chute.

CARIBOU (*see Tour 1, sec. e*): Caribou Winter Carnival, dates tentative annually.
Available facilities: Skating on Aroostook River, dog-sled and horse racing, shooting, and other sports. Ski trails — 3; open slopes — 3; ski jumps — 1; ski marathon from Bangor to Caribou (longest ski race in the United States).

FORT FAIRFIELD (*see Tour 1, sec. e*): Fort Fairfield Winter Carnival, dates tentative annually.
Available facilities: Skating, horse racing on Aroostook River, dog-sled racing, skijoring, and sleighing. Ski trails — 1 cross country (30 miles long); open slopes — 2; ski jumps — 1. Snowshoe trails — 1.

FRYEBURG (*see Tour 15*): Winter Sports Carnival, dates tentative annually.
Available facilities: Ski trains — Stark's Hill No. 1, 0.75 *m.* long, 15–60 ft. wide, 26° maximum grade, class at top is expert, class at bottom is intermediate; — Stark's Hill No. 2, 0.75 *m.* long, 18–62 ft. wide, 30° maximum grade, class at top is expert, class at bottom is intermediate; — North Chatham Trail, now under construction (1937), will be for experts and intermediate, class at bottom is novice. Ski tow at Jockey Cap, 500 ft. long, 100 ft. vertical ascent. Snowshoe trail. Toboggan chute.

GREENVILLE (*see Tour 9*).
Available facilities: Toboggan chutes. Skating.

LEWISTON (*see LEWISTON — AUBURN*).
Available facilities: Skating rink. Ski trails — Sabattus Mountain, 0.25 *m.* long, 10–30 ft. wide, 1200 ft. vertical descent, 34° maximum grade, class at top is expert, class at bottom is novice; open slopes — large number undeveloped. Ski jump.

NORTH BERWICK (*see Tour 11*).
Available facilities: Ski trails, open slopes, and a ski tow under construction (1937).

PRESQUE ISLE (*see Tour 1, sec. e*): Winter Sports Carnival, dates tentative annually.
Available facilities: Ski jumps, skating rinks, toboggan runs, and snowshoe trails.

RUMFORD (*see Tour 4*): Rumford Winter Carnival, dates tentative annually.
Available facilities: Skating rink. Ski trails — Chisholm Trail, 1.5 *m.* long, 15–50 ft. wide, 1100 ft. vertical descent, 35° maximum grade, class at top is expert, class at bottom is novice; — Town Trail, 0.5 *m.* long, 10–20 ft. wide, 900 ft. vertical descent, 24° maximum grade, class is intermediate and novice; — Paxton Trail, 0.5 *m.* long, 12–18 ft. wide, 1500 ft. vertical descent, 24° maximum grade, class is intermediate and novice; — Woodrow Trail, 0.75 *m.* long, 15–40 ft. wide, 22° maximum grade, class at top is intermediate, class at bottom is novice; open slopes — 4; crosscountry ski trail (12 miles long). Ski jump (1935 eastern Championship 60-meter jump). Snowshoe trails — 15.

WATERVILLE (*see WATERVILLE*): Winter Sports Competitive, dates tentative annually.

CHRONOLOGY

1000–10 (*ca.*) The Norsemen, first Europeans known to have visited North America, probably explore coast of Maine.

1492 Era of active exploration in western hemisphere begins with Columbus' voyage.

1497–99 Explorations of John and Sebastian Cabot along entire coast of New England, forming basis for all future English claims to this region.

1524 Giovanni da Verrazzano, in service of France, explores to 35° N. Lat. First to give Aranbega (Norumbega) as a definite locality.

1525 Estevan Gomez, a Portuguese exploring for Spain, names the Penobscot *Rio de los Gamos* or 'river of stags,' because of many deer there.

1569 David Ingram and two other English sailors, marooned by Sir John Hawkins, make overland journey from Gulf of Mexico to Nova Scotia. Ingram later wrote account of their adventures, telling of splendors of mythical city of Norumbega on Penobscot River.

1580 John Walker, sailing for Sir Humphrey Gilbert, leads expedition into Penobscot River region.

1602 Bartholomew Gosnold, in bark 'Concord' out of Falmouth, England, takes back furs, sassafras, and cedar from Maine coast, his voyage causing renewed interest in New World.

1603 Martin Pring, sent by merchants of Bristol to trade with Indians, makes careful survey of Maine coast from the Piscataqua to the Penobscot, naming islands in Penobscot Bay 'Fox Islands.'

Henry IV of France appoints Sieur de Monts Lieutenant-General of La Cadie, giving him seignorial rights to territory between 40° and 56° N. Lat.

1604–05 Sieur de Monts with company of gentlemen-adventurers establishes colony on St. Croix Island (near present-day Calais); Samuel de Champlain makes extensive explorations and detailed maps of islands and coastline of Maine; colony disbands after hard winter and removes to Nova Scotia.

1605 Captain George Waymouth, in the 'Archangel,' lands at Monhegan Island; he trades with Indians, finally kidnaping five of them, whom he takes back to England.

1606 James I of England grants two charters 'to colonize Virginia'; one company, known as the London Company, being granted right to colonize 'Southern Virginia' (34° to 38° N.); the other, known as West of England Company (or Plymouth Company), given right to colonize 'Northern Virginia' (41° to 45° N.); the intermediate territory being open to either colony after having settled its original area.

1607 Sunday, August 9, at Allen's Island, colonists from the 'Gift of God' and the 'Mary and John' listen to sermon of Thanksgiving, first English service on New England soil.

	Popham Colony, called St. George, planted on Hunniwell's Point at the end of Sagadahoc Peninsula, by the mouth of Kennebec.
1608	A ship of 30 tons, 'Virginia of Sagadahoc,' first vessel constructed by English hands in New World, launched into the Kennebec at Popham Colony.
	Popham colonists give up their settlement and return to England.
1609	Henry Hudson, in the 'Half Moon,' during his search for a Northwest Passage, puts into Casco Bay to repair his storm-battered vessel after a tempestuous voyage.
	Father Pierre Biard, Jesuit priest, accompanies French traders into Maine and establishes first Indian mission at Indian Island on the Penobscot, beginning spread of Christianity among Maine Indians and friendly relations between them and the French.
1613	St. Sauveur, a mission and settlement, established by French Jesuits at entrance to Somes Sound on Mt. Desert Island; its colonists are shortly expelled as trespassers on English soil by Captain Samuel Argall of Virginia, who sets them adrift in open boats.
1614	Captain John Smith visits Monhegan Island and deserted Sagadahoc colony, sounds 'about 25 excellent harbors' on Maine coast, and makes map of region from Cape Cod to Nova Scotia, which he calls New England.
1616–17	Captain Richard Vines and crew of 16 men spend winter at mouth of Saco River to prove Maine climate not too severe for Europeans; names site Winter Harbor.
1620	Pilgrims land at Plymouth from the 'Mayflower.' Great Patent of New England, covering territory from Philadelphia to Gulf of St. Lawrence, issued by King James. Territory placed under a council at Plymouth, England.
	Permanent settlement established on Monhegan Island.
1622	Land between Merrimac and Sagadahoc (Kennebec) Rivers granted to Sir Ferdinando Gorges and Captain John Mason by Great Council of New England.
1623	First successful settlement on the mainland in Maine begun at Saco by Richard Vines and others; marks beginning of active settlement along coast west of Penobscot Bay.
	First sawmill in America in operation on the Piscataqua.
	Gorges attempts to establish general government for New England, sending Robert Gorges to Maine for this purpose, but is unsuccessful.
	Christopher Levett builds home on what is believed to be House Island in Portland Harbor; here he plans to erect city with funds from collection in churches throughout England on proclamation issued by the King. Although Levett fails, proclamation calls wide attention to possibilities for colonization in Maine.
1626–28	Trading post established at Pentagoet (later Castine) on the Penobscot by Pilgrims.
	Contention begins between British and French over Acadia-in-Maine, region between Penobscot and St. Croix Rivers.
1629	Plymouth Colony of Massachusetts granted territorial and trading rights to 'all that tracte of lande ... adionethe to the River of Kenebeke ... the space of 15 English miles on each side of the river.'

	Trading post established at Machias by Pilgrims; soon captured by the French.
	Pilgrims are able to pay most of debts incurred by 'Mayflower' expedition with furs from Kennebec region.
	Mason and Gorges divide their province: Mason takes land west of the Piscataqua and names it New Hampshire; Gorges takes land east of the Piscataqua and names it New Somersetshire.
1630–31	Plymouth Council (England), perceiving that its own authority may soon pass, grants eight patents to New England lands, including Kennebec, Lygonia, Waldo (or Muscongus), and Pemaquid grants.
1632	French raid English trading house at Pentagoet. Fort at Pemaquid attacked and demolished by notorious English pirate, Dixey Bull.
	English cede Acadia to France by Treaty of St. Germaine-en-Laye.
1635	Pilgrims remaining at trading post at Pentagoet driven out by French under De Charnisay.
	French claim as far west as Pemaquid and occupy to Penobscot River.
	Council of New England surrenders its charter to the King, who has become suspicious of liberties allowed colonists.
	Sir Ferdinando Gorges made Governor-General of all New England; sends his nephew, William Gorges, to colonies as deputy-governor.
1639	William Gorges organizes government of New Somersetshire, with first legally organized court in Maine held at Saco under his jurisdiction; returns home in same year.
	Gorges obtains charter from Charles I for region incorporated as 'The Province and County of Maine.'
	Thomas Purchase, first settler of Pejepscot on the Androscoggin (now Brunswick), assigns to Governor Winthrop of Massachusetts 'all the tract at Pejepscot.'
1640	Thomas Gorges appointed Deputy-Governor of Province of Maine.
	'First general court' (legislative assembly) under Maine charter established at Saco.
1641	Gorgeana (York) chartered as first English city in America under feudal tenure of Gorges.
1646	Father Gabriel Druillettes establishes Indian mission in the Norridgewock territory.
	Court of law upholds grant of Province of Lygonia as separate from Province of Maine.
1647	Sir Ferdinando Gorges dies. Parliament declares his grant invalid. Thomas Gorges nevertheless appoints Edward Godfrey deputy-governor.
	Piscataqua Plantation formed, including present towns of Kittery, North and South Berwick, and Eliot.
	Kittery, settled 1623, incorporated as town.
1650 (ca.)	Maine in great confusion as result of contradictory grants, Indian raids, pirates on coast, and lack of organized government.
1651	Massachusetts claims all Maine land south of lat. 43° 43' 12" with eastern point on Upper Clapboard Island in Casco Bay.
	Sir William Phips born at Woolwich.

1652 Province of Maine comes under jurisdiction of Massachusetts Bay Colony in spite of inhabitants' protest; Massachusetts General Court appoints commissioners to settle northern boundary of colony.
York (formerly Gorgeana) incorporated as town.
1653 John Wincoln of Kittery and Edward Rishworth of York, representatives from Maine, seated in Massachusetts General Court.
Wells, Saco, and Cape Porpoise (Kennebunkport) made towns.
1654 French lose control of all territory in Maine.
1655 Acadian Province confirmed to English, who hold it 13 years.
1658 Scarborough (settled 1630) and Casco (settled 1632) incorporated as towns.
Isles of Shoals and all territory north of the Piscataqua to the Penobscot (belonging to Massachusetts) made County of Yorkshire.
1660 Re-establishment of monarchy in England under Charles II results in tightening of Colonial government.
1662 First Quaker meeting in Maine held at Newichawannock.
1663 Strong feeling manifested between people of Maine and those of Massachusetts; Robert Ford of York County is fined by Massachusetts General Court for saying, 'John Cotton [of Boston] is a liar and has gone to hell.'
1664 Ferdinando Gorges, grandson of original proprietor, obtains royal order restoring his Province of Maine; Massachusetts judges expelled from province.
Charles II, planning an American empire, grants royal province to his brother, Duke of York, including region between the St. Croix and Pemaquid, to be called County of Cornwall.
Royal commissioners set up independent government in Maine.
1667–70 Treaty of Breda and supplementary articles give France disputed area east of the Penobscot, with Nova Scotia.
Baron de St. Castin, French fur trader, comes to New England.
1668 Four commissioners from Massachusetts convene at York, commanding people of Province of Maine to yield obedience to Massachusetts Colony. Royal agents forcibly ejected from Maine.
1672 Massachusetts formally extends its jurisdiction to Penobscot Bay.
1673 Dutch seize French fortifications at Pentagoet.
1674 Region between Kennebec and Penobscot Rivers organized as County of Devonshire.
New royal patent issued to Duke of York; Sir Edmund Andros becomes Governor of New York and Sagadahoc (County of Cornwall).
1675 King Philip's War begins in Maine; emboldened by conflict in Massachusetts, Maine Indians attack English settlements; Scarborough and Casco completely destroyed.
1676 Charles II decrees that Massachusetts does not have 'right of soil' in Maine and New Hampshire.
Dutch again capture fort at Pentagoet, but English drive them out.
Indian warfare continues; many settlements attacked and burned.
1677 Province of Maine purchased from Gorges' heirs by Massachusetts for £1250 sterling (about $6000).

	Indian hostilities continue. Governor Andros, fearing French aggression in Duke of York's Sagadahoc Province, dispatches a force from New York to Pemaquid.

1678 Commissioners from Massachusetts negotiate peace with Indians at Casco.

1680 Provincial government established by Massachusetts; Thomas Danforth appointed 'President of Maine.'

1685 James II replaces Charles II on English throne; Massachusetts Charter annulled.

1686 Sir Edmund Andros appointed Royal Governor of New England Colonies, and immediately starts aggression on Maine frontier.

1688 Baron de Castin, enraged by English attacks, organizes Maine Indians; many settlements along the coast destroyed. James II dethroned and replaced by William of Orange.

Andros attacks Penobscot and sacks stronghold of Baron de Castin, thus precipitating King William's War.

1689 People of Massachusetts imprison Governor Andros, and Danforth is restored as provincial president of Maine.

1690 French and Indians from Canada sweep Maine until only four settlements remain inhabited.

Sir William Phips takes Port Royal in Nova Scotia.

French capture Fort William Henry at Pemaquid, vantage point of eastern coast.

1691 Massachusetts obtains its second charter; Province of Maine now becomes District of Maine, including Colony of Sagadahoc between the Kennebec and the St. Croix.

Sir William Phips appointed Royal Governor of Massachusetts Bay Colony, helped by Cotton Mather and his faction.

1697 Treaty of Ryswick establishes peace between France and England; Acadian boundary remains undetermined, France claiming all land to the Penobscot.

1699 Mere Point (Brunswick) Treaty with Indians marks end of King William's War.

1703-13 Queen Anne's War (third Indian war). Only remaining settlements in Maine are Kittery, Wells, and York.

1722 Lovewell's War (fourth Indian war) begins with sudden raids on towns of southwestern Maine.

1724 English sack Norridgewock Indian village at Old Point, killing Father Sebastian Rasle, missionary-teacher.

1725 Colonial soldiers from Massachusetts defeat Pequawket Indians at battle of Lovewell's Pond, Fryeburg.

1726 Dummer's Treaty at Falmouth with 40 Maine chiefs brings better feeling and establishment of government truck houses for Indian trading.

1732-33 Massachusetts offers Maine land to settlers free to increase immigration into Maine. Resettlement definitely under way.

1739 Boundary with New Hampshire fixed by King George II and Council.

1743 Population about 12,000.

1744-48 King George's War (fifth Indian war) begins, causing temporary exodus of many settlers to other Colonies.

    1745 Louisburg captured by English soldiers and Colonial forces commanded by William Pepperrell of Kittery.

    1754 Sixth Indian war; Indians of Maine now struggling against complete extermination.

    1755 Acadians dispersed throughout American Colonies; many later settle along St. John River in Maine.

    1759 Quebec falls to the English. Massachusetts takes complete possession of Penobscot region.

    1760 Peace made with remnants of Maine Indians at Fort Pownal.

Cumberland and Lincoln Counties established.

Definite efforts made by land proprietors to attract settlers from other Colonies, British Isles, and Germany.

    1763 Peace of Paris; New France ceded to Great Britain.

    1764 Census is taken; population about 24,000.

    1774 Show of resistance to Parliamentary taxation in Maine towns, notably Saco, Falmouth, and Machias.

    1775 Benedict Arnold leads expedition from Augusta to Quebec by bateau and on foot.

Falmouth burned by British under Captain Henry Mowatt.

British vessel 'Margaretta' captured by Colonials at Machias — first naval engagement of Revolution.

Maine's first post office established at Falmouth.

    1776 Declaration of Independence; General William Whipple of Kittery a signer for New Hampshire.

    1777 Ship 'Ranger' launched at Kittery under command of John Paul Jones.

    1778 John Paul Jones sets sail for England in 'Ranger,' beginning his great naval career.

Continental Congress divides Massachusetts into three electoral districts, of which northernmost, including York, Cumberland, and Lincoln Counties, is called District of Maine.

    1779 British take Castine and build Fort George there; revolutionists fail to take fort. Other coast towns of eastern Maine occupied or cannonaded by British forces.

    1780 Constitution of Massachusetts adopted, giving Maine eight senatorial representatives.

    1781 Cornwallis surrenders at Yorktown; end of hostilities.

    1783 Treaty of Versailles; England recognizes independence of United States. St. Croix River set as eastern boundary of country.

    1784 Canadian Province of New Brunswick established, and long boundary dispute in the Aroostook begun.

    1785 Question of separation from Massachusetts arises, causing establishment of Falmouth *Gazette*, first newspaper in Maine, as organ to aid in agitation for separation.

    1786 Portland (formerly Falmouth, once Casco) incorporated as town.

1787 On adoption of United States Constitution, Maine is made a representative district, having 93 towns and plantations.
1788 Slavery abolished in Maine and Massachusetts.
1789 Hancock and Washington Counties established.
1790 Population 96,540.
1791 Portland Head Light, today the oldest lighthouse on Atlantic coast, established at Cape Elizabeth; Joseph Greenleaf, first keeper, appointed by George Washington.
1793 French Revolution; much political partisanship in America. The Clough House at Edgecomb (near Wiscasset) prepared as a refuge for Marie Antoinette.
Federalist and Democrat-Republican Parties formed in United States.
1794 Bowdoin College receives its charter from Massachusetts General Court; officially opens in 1802.
1795 General Henry Knox takes up residence at 'Montpelier,' his mansion in Thomaston.
1799 Kennebec County established.
The Portland Bank, first bank in Maine, opened.
1800 Population 151,719.
1801 Maine's first free public library founded at Castine.
1805 Oxford County established.
1806 Portsmouth Navy Yard built at Kittery.
1807 Embargo Act on foreign commerce passed by National Government; causes severe economic depression in New England. Much smuggling in Maine, centering around Eastport.
Henry Wadsworth Longfellow born at Portland, February 27.
District votes 9404 to 3370 against separation from Massachusetts.
Farmington Academy, later first State Normal School, incorporated.
1809 Embargo Act repealed.
Somerset County established.
Hannibal Hamlin, Vice-President of U.S. 1861-65, born at Paris (Maine), August 27.
First cotton mill in Maine established in Brunswick at falls of the Androscoggin.
1810 Population 228,705.
Great internal development in Maine resulting from Embargo Act.
England increases impressment of American sailors.
1812 War between United States and Great Britain seriously affects shipping on Maine coast. Smuggling between Canada and Maine practiced on large scale.
1813 American brig 'Enterprise' captures British brig 'Boxer' off Pemaquid Point.
Maine Literary and Theological Institute, now Colby College, established.
Corporal punishment totally abolished in Massachusetts and Maine.
1814 British seize and occupy Maine coast from the St. Croix to the Penobscot; Eastport on Moose Island declared to be part of New Brunswick.

Treaty of Ghent brings peace between United States and Great Britain.
1815 Foreign occupation of Maine soil ended.
Beginning of western migration, known as 'Ohio Fever,' which continued until about 1870, causing alarming decrease in Maine's population.
1816 Penobscot County established.
Year of the great cold, known as 'eighteen-hundred-and froze-to-death.'
1818 Waterville (Colby) College opened; obtained charter in 1820.
1819 Convention for framing State constitution meets at Portland, October 11.
1820 Maine admitted as a State to the Union; capital at Portland; William King elected first governor.
Population 298,335.
1825 Lafayette given enthusiastic reception on visit to Maine.
1827 Augusta chosen as site for State capital.
Waldo County established.
1830 Population 399,455.
Cumberland and Oxford Canal opened.
James G. Blaine, famous Maine statesman, born in Pennsylvania, January 31.
1831 Maine refuses compromise boundary solution offered by King of Netherlands.
1832 State capital removed from Portland to Augusta.
1834 Charles Farrar Browne ('Artemus Ward'), noted humorist, born at Waterford, April 26.
State Anti-Slavery Society formed.
State Prohibition Convention held at Portland.
1836 Bangor, Old Town, and Milford Railroad completed, first in State and one of earliest in country.
1838 Franklin and Piscataquis Counties established.
Earthquake felt throughout New England, vibrations lasting for 20 days after; chimneys and lighthouses thrown down.
'Aroostock War' begins. Serious hostilities between Maine and New Brunswick citizens avoided by mediation of General Winfield Scott.
1839 'Aroostock War' ends, and Aroostock County established.
Thomas Brackett Reed, noted statesman, born in Portland, October 18.
1840 Population 501,793.
Hiram Maxim, inventor of modern machine gun, born at Sangerville, February 5.
1842 Webster-Ashburton Treaty fixes northeastern boundary at last.
1846 Four-mile ice jam on the Penobscot floods Bangor and terrifies its inhabitants.
Sale of spirits forbidden in Maine except for medical or mechanical purposes.

Chronology 451

1847 Maine's first child labor law enacted.
1849 Bangor afflicted by cholera, causing 151 deaths; Mayor William Abbott dies in office.
   Sarah Orne Jewett, author of 'The Country of the Pointed Firs,' born at South Berwick, September 3.
   Maine adventurers sail in Maine ships around the Horn to California gold fields.
1850 Population 583,169.
   Edgar Wilson (Bill) Nye, humorist, born at Shirley, August 25.
1851 Prohibition enactment, known as 'the Maine law,' framed by Neal Dow, prohibits manufacture and sale of intoxicating liquors in any part of State.
1854 Androscoggin and Sagadahoc Counties established.
   Anti-slavery Whigs and Free-Soilers unite throughout country to form the Republican Party, which at once becomes very strong in Maine.
1856 Maine State Seminary, now Bates College, incorporated.
1857 Lillian Norton (Madame Giglia Nordica), noted prima donna, born at Farmington, December 12.
1860 Population 628,279.
   Knox County established.
1861–65 Civil War, to which Maine contributed 72,945 men and $18,000,000.
1862 Maine State College of Agriculture and Industrial Arts (now University of Maine) established.
1863 Confederates seize the 'Caleb Cushing' from Portland Harbor and put to sea, pursued by other Portland vessels; having no ammunition, they burn the boat and are taken prisoners.
1864 Bates College receives charter.
1865 Civil War ends.
1866 Great Portland fire of July 4 and 5 destroys 1800 buildings, with loss of over $6,000,000; aid rushed from all parts of country.
1869 Edwin Arlington Robinson, poet, born at Head Tide in Alna, December 22.
1870 Population 626,915.
   State colonization venture brings about establishment of New Sweden, with importation of Swedish colonists.
   Maine's popularity as summer resort region begins to be felt
   Railroad transportation by this time well established.
1873 State legislature passes law providing State aid for free high schools.
1875 Compulsory education bill passed by legislature.
1876 Death penalty abolished in Maine.
1879 Freak snowstorm in Portland, July 4.
1880 Population 648,936.
   Economic decline in rural areas begins to be marked.
1890 Population 661,086.
1892 New constitutional amendment requires education qualifications for voting.

1893 Severe economic depression, continuing to 1895, widely felt in Maine.
1898 Battleship 'Maine' blown up in Havana harbor; followed by Spanish-American War, to which Maine furnishes one volunteer regiment of 1717 men.
1900 Population 694,466.
1907 Widespread economic depression.
Largest dam of its time in New England built at Ellsworth.
1910 Population 742,371.
Resettlement of northeastern boundary controversy with Great Britain.
Democratic State victory for first time in 32 years; Frederick W. Plaisted of Augusta, elected Governor.
1911 Bangor fire causes more than $3,000,000 damage.
Direct primary adopted; initiative and referendum law passed.
1914 Outbreak of World War. 'Kronprinzessin Cecilie,' North German Lloyd liner with cargo of gold, interned at Bar Harbor.
Maine Public Utilities Commission created.
1915 Workmen's compensation law adopted.
1917 United States enters World War; Maine legislature passes emergency act providing for $1,000,000 in State bonds for war purposes.
Ripogenus Dam completed, great engineering feat in wilderness.
1918 End of World War, to which Maine contributed more than 35,000 men and more than $116,000,000.
1919 Lafayette National Park (renamed Acadia National Park in 1928) created by act of Congress.
1920 Centennial year. Maine receives new impetus toward forest conservation, permanent roads, and publicity for its vocational facilities. Celebration in Portland.
Population 768,014.
1921 Consolidation of leading Maine newspapers.
1923 City Manager-Council form of government established in Portland, resulting in adoption of plan by many other towns and cities of State.
1924 Winter port of English steamers changed from Portland to Halifax, N.S., because of tax on imported goods.
1929 Stock market collapse marks beginning of depression years; effects not felt immediately in Maine.
Popular vote on power question prohibits exportation of hydroelectric power from State.
1930 Population 797,423.
Wyman Dam at Bingham completed.
1931 State Administrative Code consolidates departments and agencies of Maine's government under five commissions.
Mt. Katahdin State Park given to State by ex-Governor Percival P. Baxter of Portland.
1932 Waldo-Hancock toll bridge dedicated.
Portland and Boston steamer service discontinued.
Pari-mutuel betting on horse racing legalized.

1933 Nation-wide bank failures cause general suffering in Maine's rural areas. Ninety-eight of Maine's 109 banks eventually reopen after moratorium.

Ellsworth fire causes $1,250,000 damage.

Maine ratifies repeal of 18th amendment.

1934 State prohibition amendment repealed.

1935 Construction begun on Passamaquoddy Tidal Power Project.

Eastern Steamship Lines, Inc., discontinue service between Boston and Bangor and Penobscot River ports.

1936 Maine suffers most disastrous floods in its history; $25,000,000 loss.

Eastern Steamship Lines, Inc., discontinue service between Portland and Bar Harbor and New York.

Construction on Passamaquoddy Tidal Power Project abandoned.

SELECTED READING LIST

THE following titles are chiefly those of relatively recent publications intended in most cases for the general reader rather than the specialist. For further references, the latter should consult Joseph Williamson's *Bibliography of the State of Maine, from the Earliest Period to* 1891 (2 volumes, Portland, 1896), together with the briefer and in many cases more up-to-date bibliographies contained in various specialized publications about the State of Maine.

GENERAL DESCRIPTION

Coe, Harrie B., editor. *Maine: Resources, Attractions, and Its People.* In 5 volumes, illustrated. New York, 1928-31.
Coffin, Robert P. Tristram. *Kennebec: Cradle of Americans.* Illustrated. New York, 1937. (In 'The Rivers of America' series.)
Dole, Nathan Haskell, and Gordon, Irwin L. *Maine of the Sea and Pines.* Illustrated. Boston, 1928.
Drake, Samuel Adams. *The Pine-Tree Coast.* Illustrated. Boston, 1891.
Dunnack, Henry E. *The Maine Book.* Illustrated. Augusta, 1920.
Hueston, Ethel. *Coasting down East.* Illustrated. New York, 1924. (Describes a motor trip through Maine.)
Nutting, Wallace. *Maine Beautiful.* Illustrated. Framingham, Mass., 1924.
Stanton, Gerrit S. *Where the Sportsman Loves to Linger.* Illustrated. New York, 1905. (A narrative of the most popular canoe trips in Maine.)
Thoreau, Henry D. *The Maine Woods.* Boston, 1864, and many later editions.
Thoreau, Henry D. *Canoeing in the Wilderness.* Edited and illustrated from photographs by Clifton Johnson. Boston, 1916. (The latter half of Thoreau's classic account of 'The Maine Woods.')
Verrill, A. Hyatt. *Romantic and Historic Maine.* Illustrated. New York, 1933.

HISTORY

Burrage, Henry S. *Beginnings of Colonial Maine.* Illustrated. Portland, 1914.
Burrage, Henry S. *Gorges and the Grant of the Province of Maine,* 1622. Illustrated. Augusta, 1923.
Burrage, Henry S. *Maine at Louisburg in* 1745. Illustrated. Augusta, 1910.
Burrage, Henry S. *Maine in the Northeastern Boundary Controversy.* Illustrated. Portland, 1919.
Dunnack, Henry E. *Maine Forts.* Illustrated. Augusta, 1924.
Elkins, L. Whitney. *The Story of Maine: Coastal Maine.* Illustrated. Bangor, 1924.
Hale, Robert. *Early Days of Church and State in Maine.* Brunswick, 1910.
Hatch, Louis Clinton, editor. *Maine: A History.* Centennial edition. In 5 volumes, illustrated. New York, 1919.
Holmes, Herbert E. *The Makers of Maine: Essays and Tales of Early Maine History.* Illustrated. Lewiston, 1912.
Maine Federation of Women's Clubs. *Maine in History and Romance.* By members of the Federation. Illustrated. Lewiston, 1915.
Maine Historical Society. *Documentary History of the State of Maine.* In 24 volumes, illustrated. Portland, 1869-1916.

Spencer, Wilbur D. *Pioneers on Maine Rivers.* Illustrated. Portland, 1930.
Sprague, John F. *Sebastian Raslê: A Maine Tragedy of the Eighteenth Century.* Illustrated. Boston, 1906.
Starkey, Glenn W. *Maine: Its History, Resources, and Government.* Revised edition. Illustrated. Boston, 1930.
Sylvester, Herbert M. *Maine Coast Romance.* In 5 volumes. Illustrated. Boston, 1904-09. (Deals with Maine pioneer settlements, 1605-90.)
(*See also* Proceedings and Collections of the Maine Historical Society, Portland.)

BIOGRAPHY

Gay, Maude Clark. *Five Women: Little Romances of Early Maine.* Illustrated. Wiscasset, 1930.
Little, George T., compiler. *Genealogical and Family History of the State of Maine.* Illustrated. New York, 1909.
Moulton, Augustus F., compiler. *Memorials of Maine: A Life Record of Men and Women of the Past.* Illustrated. New York, 1916.
Scales, John, editor. *Piscataqua Pioneers, 1623-1775.* Dover, N.H., 1919.
Spencer, Wilbur D. *Maine Immortals.* Augusta, 1932.

GOVERNMENT AND LEGISLATION

Dunnack, Henry E. *Manual of Maine Government.* Illustrated. Augusta, 1921.
Gordon, Ernest. *The Maine* [Liquor] *Law.* New York, 1919.
Hormell, Orren C. *Maine Towns.* Illustrated. Brunswick, 1932.
Hormell, Orren C. *Sources of Municipal Revenue in Maine.* Illustrated. Brunswick, 1918.
MacDonald, William. *The Government of Maine: Its History and Administration.* New York, 1902.
Maine Register, State Year-Book, and Legislative Manual. (Published annually since 1870.) Portland, 1937.
Whitin, Ernest S. *Factory Legislation in Maine.* New York, 1908.

ARCHAEOLOGY AND THE INDIANS

Eckstorm, Fannie Hardy. *Handicrafts of the Modern Indians of Maine.* Illustrated. Bar Harbor, 1932.
Moorehead, Warren K. *A Report on the Archaeology of Maine.* Illustrated. Andover, Mass., 1922.
Moorehead, Warren K. *Ten Years of Archaeological Research in the State of Maine.* Andover, Mass.
Smith, W. B. *Indian Remains of the Penobscot Valley and their Significance.* Orono, 1926.
Smith, W. B. *The Lost Red Paint People of Maine.* Bangor, 1930.
Starbird, Charles M. *The Indians of the Androscoggin Valley.* Lewiston, 1928.
Willoughby, Charles C. *Prehistoric Burial Places in Maine.* Illustrated. Cambridge, Mass., 1898.

GEOLOGY

Bastin, Edson S. *Geology of the Pegmatites and Associated Rocks of Maine.* Illustrated. Washington, 1911.
Bastin, Edson S., and Davis, Charles A. *Peat Deposits of Maine.* Illustrated. Washington, 1909.
Dale, Thomas N. *The Granites of Maine.* Illustrated. Washington, 1907.

Tebbetts, Leon H. *The Amazing Story of Maine.* Illustrated. Portland, 1935. (Relates to the State's geological history.)
Toppan, Frederick W. *Geology of Maine.* With map. Schenectady, N.Y., 1932.
Williams, Henry S., and Breger, Carpel L. *The Fauna of the Chapman Sandstone of Maine.* Illustrated. Washington, 1916.

FLORA AND FAUNA

Fernald, Charles H. *The Grasses of Maine.* Illustrated. Augusta, 1885.
Fernald, Merritt L. *The Portland Catalogue of Maine Plants.* Second edition. Portland, 1892.
Knight, Ora W. *The Birds of Maine.* Illustrated. Bangor, 1908.
Miller, Olive Thorne. *With the Birds in Maine.* Boston, 1904.
Rand, Edward L., and Redfield, John H. *Flora of Mount Desert Island, Maine.* Cambridge, Mass., 1894.
Ricker, Percy LeRoy. *A Preliminary List of Maine Fungi.* Orono, 1902.
Scribner, F. Lamson. *The Ornamental and Useful Plants of Maine.* Illustrated. Augusta, 1875.
Tower, Gordon E. *Forest Trees of Maine and How to Know Them.* Illustrated. Augusta, 1908.
Wilkins, Austin H. *Forests of Maine.* Illustrated. Augusta, 1932.
(*See also* Proceedings of the Portland Society of Natural History.)

COMMERCE AND INDUSTRY

Chadbourne, Walter W. *A History of Banking in Maine, 1799-1930.* Orono, 1936.
Chase, Edward E. *Maine Railroads: A History of the Development of the Railroad System.* Illustrated. Portland, 1926.
Wood, Richard G. *History of Lumbering in Maine, 1820-1861.* Illustrated. Orono, 1935.
(*See also* annual reports and miscellaneous publications of the State Department of Agriculture, Department of Labor and Industry, and Department of Sea and Shore Fisheries.)

WATER POWER AND RESOURCES

Barrows, Harold K. *Water Resources of the Kennebec River Basin, Maine.* Illustrated. Washington, 1907.
Barrows, Harold K., and Babb, Cyrus C. *Water Resources of the Penobscot River Basin, Maine.* Illustrated. Washington, 1912.
Clapp, Frederick G. *Underground Waters of Southern Maine.* Illustrated. Washington, 1909.
Pressey, Henry A. *Water Powers of the State of Maine.* Illustrated. Washington, 1902.

SHIPS AND THE SEA

Lubbock, Alfred Basil. *The Down Easters: American Deep-Water Sailing Ships, 1869-1929.* Illustrated. Boston, 1929.
Rowe, William H. *Shipbuilding Days in Casco Bay, 1727-1890.* Illustrated. Yarmouth, 1929.
Sterling, Robert T. *Lighthouses of the Maine Coast, and the Men Who Keep Them.* Illustrated. Brattleboro, Vt., 1935.
Wasson, George S. *Sailing Days on the Penobscot: The River and Bay as They Were in the Old Days.* With a record of vessels built there, compiled by Lincoln Colcord. Illustrated. Salem, Mass., 1932.

RACIAL GROUPS

Collins, Charles W. *The Acadians of Madawaska, Maine.* Boston, 1902. (Publications of the New England Catholic Historical Society.)
Lawton, R. J., compiler. *Franco-Americans of the State of Maine.* Illustrated. Lewiston, 1915.
New Sweden, Maine. *The Story of New Sweden.* Illustrated. Portland, 1896.

BALLADS AND FOLK-SONGS

Barry, Phillips; Eckstorm, Fannie Hardy; and Smyth, Mary W., editors. *British Ballads from Maine.* Frontispiece. New Haven, Conn., 1929.
Day, Holman F. *Pine Tree Ballads: Rhymed Stories of Unplaned Human Natur' up in Maine.* Illustrated. Boston, 1902.
Eckstorm, Fannie Hardy, editor. *Minstrelsy of Maine: Folk-Songs and Ballads of the Woods and the Coast.* Boston, 1927.
Gray, Roland P., editor. *Songs and Ballads of the Maine Lumberjacks, with Other Songs from Maine.* Map. Cambridge, Mass., 1924.

EDUCATION

Chadbourne, Ava H. *Beginnings of Education in Maine.* New York, 1928.
Chadbourne, Ava H., compiler. *Readings in the History of Education in Maine.* Bangor, 1932.
Hall, Edward W. *History of Higher Education in Maine.* Illustrated. Washington, 1903.
Stetson, William W. *Study of the History of Education in Maine and the Evolution of Our Present School System.* Augusta, 1901.
Survey of Higher Education in Maine. By the University of Maine, in co-operation with Bates, Bowdoin, and Colby Colleges. Maps. Orono, 1931.
(*See also* annual reports and miscellaneous publications of the State Department of Education.)

RELIGION

Allen, Stephen, and Pilsbury, William H. *History of Methodism in Maine, 1793-1886.* Illustrated. Augusta, 1887.
Clark, Calvin M. *History of the Congregational Churches in Maine.* In 2 volumes. Portland, 1926.
Dow, Edward F. *A Portrait of the Millennial Church of Shakers.* Orono, 1931.
Randall, Daniel B. *A Statistical History of the Maine Conference of the M.E. Church, from 1793 to 1893.* Illustrated. Portland, 1893.

ARCHITECTURE

Loomis, Charles D. *Port Towns of Penobscot Bay.* Illustrated. St. Paul, 1922. (In the 'White Pine Series of Architectural Monographs.')
Nason, Emma Huntington. *Old Colonial Houses in Maine.* Illustrated. Augusta, 1908.
Walker, C. Howard. *Some Old Houses on the Southern Coast of Maine.* Illustrated. St. Paul, 1918. (In the 'White Pine Series of Architectural Monographs.')

MUSIC

Edwards, George T. *Music and Musicians of Maine.* Illustrated. Portland, 1928.

The Press

Fassett, Fredrick G., Jr. *A History of Newspapers in the District of Maine, 1785–1820.* Orono, 1932.
Griffin, Joseph. *History of the Press of Maine.* Illustrated. Brunswick, 1872.

Guides and Recreational Handbooks

Appalachian Mountain Club. *The A.M.C. Guide to Paths on Katahdin and in the Adjacent Region.* Folding map. Boston, 1933.
Bangor and Aroostook Railway. *Atop Katahdin.* Illustrated. Bangor, 1922.
Bangor and Aroostook Railway. *In the Maine Woods: The Vacationist's Guidebook.* Illustrated. Bangor, 1937.
Clifford, Fred H. *Haunts of the Hunted: The Vacationer's Guide to Maine's Great North Country.* Illustrated. Bangor, 1903.
Clifford, Fred H. *In Pine-Tree Jungles: A Handbook for Sportsmen and Campers in the Great Maine Woods.* Illustrated. Bangor, 1902.
Emerson, Walter C. *When North Winds Blow.* Illustrated. Lewiston, 1922. (Descriptive of the Maine Lake country.)
Emerson, Walter C. *The Latchstring to Maine Woods and Waters.* Illustrated. Boston, 1916.
Maine Appalachian Trail Club. *Guide to the Appalachian Trail in Maine.* Folding maps. Augusta, 1936.
Maine Automobile Association. *Maine Automobile Road Book and Pine Tree Tour of Maine and the White Mountains.* Illustrated. Portland.
Maine Development Commission. *Maine, the Land of Remembered Vacations.* Illustrated. Augusta, 1936.

Miscellaneous

Barry, William E. *A Stroll Thro' the Past.* Illustrated. Portland, 1933. (Embodies much early Maine history and lore, especially of Kennebunk Village and adjacent region.)
Boardman, Samuel L., compiler. *Agricultural Bibliography of Maine, 1850–1892.* Illustrated. Augusta, 1893.
Brooks, Annie Peabody. *Ropes' Ends: Traditions, Legends, and Sketches of Old Kennebunkport and Vicinity.* Illustrated. Kennebunkport, 1901.
Coffin, Robert P. Tristram. *Lost Paradise: A Boyhood on a Maine Coast Farm.* Illustrated. New York, 1934.
Day, Clarence P., and Meyer, William E. *The Port of Portland and its Hinterland.* Illustrated. Portland, 1923.
Hasse, Adelaide R., compiler. *Index to Economic Material in Documents of Maine, 1820–1904.* Washington, 1907.
Maine State Planning Board. *Report* of 1934–35. Augusta, 1936.
McCorrison, A. L. *Letters from Fraternity.* With Introduction by Ben Ames Williams. New York, 1931. (Descriptive of life on a Maine farm.)
Varney, George J. *Gazetteer of Maine.* Illustrated. Boston, 1881.

(Of those novelists and poets who have written about the Maine scene and character, the more prominent are mentioned in the Literature section of the article on 'The Arts,' printed elsewhere in this volume.)

INDEX

Italic figures indicate the main references of the items concerned

Abbot, 318, 322
Abbott Company Mill (Dexter,) 322
Abbott, Jacob, 96
Abbott, John S. C., 96, 140
Abnaki Indians, *24–27*, 213, 220, 331, 358; crafts, 26; dress of, 25; economic status of, 25; elections of, 26; miscellaneous references, 213, 331, 358; nomadic life of, 27
Abolitionists, 43, 168
Academy of Arts and Sciences (Thomaston), 222
Acadia, 130, 234, 239, 248, 281, 290
Acadia National Park, *281–83*, 284, 440
Acadians, 37, 74–75, 241, 247
Accommodations, xxii
Adams, G. J., Rev., 83, 233
Adams Hall (Brunswick), 146
Adventist Camp Meeting Grounds (Princeton), 241
Adventists, 372
Agamenticus (*see* York)
Agassiz Village, 359
Agriculture (*see* Farming)
Agriculture, U.S. Department of, 113, 245
Air Lines, xxi
Airports: Augusta, 129; Bar Harbor, 282; Brownville, 319; Caribou Municipal, 246
Akers, Benjamin Paul, *103*, 183, 383
Akers, Elizabeth (*see* Allen, Elizabeth Akers)
Albany, 370
Albion, 354–55
Alden, John, 118
Alder Stream Camp Site (Eustis), 347
Aldrich House (Topsham), 326
Alexander, 307
Alfred, 82, 339–40
Alfred Courthouse (Alfred), 339
Allagash, 421
Allagash Falls, 420, 421
Allagash Region, 408
Allagash River Canoe Trip, *419–22*
Allefonsce, Jean, 29
Allen, Elizabeth Akers, 98; birthplace of (Farmington), 345
Allen, John, 278
Allen, William Henry, 187
Alna, 219
American Thread Co. (Milo), 316
American Woolen Co. (Dover-Foxcroft), 317
Amherst, 305
Anderson, Lieutenant, 122
Andover, 303, 440
Andrew, John Albion, birthplace of (South Windham), 342
Andros, Edmund, Sir, 33, 34, 291
Androscoggin County Courthouse (Auburn), 163
Androscoggin Falls (Brunswick), 144; (Rumford), 301

Androscoggin Mill (Lewiston), 159
Anemone Cave (Bar Harbor), 284
Anson, 332
Anti-liquor law riot, 171
Anti-masonry, 43
'Antiquities of the New England Indians' (book), 22
Apartment House (Bath), 216
Appalachian Trail System, 310, 312, 366, *428–29*
Appleton Hall (Brunswick), 147
Arbo Home, 434
Archeological Remains, 20
Architecture: architects, 92; character of, 86; Classic Revival, 92–93; early structures, 86–87; French and Indian Wars, effect of, 87; manor houses and mansions, 89–91; modern period, 93; public buildings, 91; stone buildings, 91; typical 18th-century house, 87–89
Argall, Samuel, Capt., 286
Arnold, Benedict, 329, *246–47*, 350; camp sites: *Eustis*, 346; *Flagstaff*, 347; *Skowhegan*, 299; expedition, 119, 348, 424; Trail Markers, 333
Arnold Pond, 348
Arnold's Landing (Solon), 333
Aroostook County, 65
Aroostook Country Club, Ltd., 246
Aroostook Farm (Presque Isle), 245
'Aroostook War,' *42*, 121, 151, 240
Arrowsic, 262–63
Arrowsic Town House (Arrowsic), 262
Art: collections, 104, 183; Colonial, 102; early, characteristics of, 101; modern, 103–04; 19th century, 102–103; woodcarving, 101
Arts (*see* Literature, Art, Theater, Music)
'Arundel' (book), 128
Ashland, 309
Askwith, Unorganized Township of, 324
Aspinquid, 26
Asticou, 284
Atlantic and St. Lawrence Railway, 180
Aubry, Nicolas, 82
Augusta, 117–29; development, 119–20; early settlement, 118–19; fur trading, 118; government of, 117–18, 120; population, 117, 120; racial groups, 117; social groups, 117
Augusta Country Club (Manchester), 357
Augusta Lumber Co. (Augusta), 122
Augusta State Hospital (Augusta), 436
Aurora, 305

Backus Corner, 344–45
Bacon, Daniel, Rev., 44
Badger, Joseph, 102
Bagnall, Walter, 165
Bailey, Ezekiel, 357
Bailey Island, 212, *258*, 391

Index

Bailey Island Bridge, 258
Baileyville (Town), 241
Baileyville (Winthrop), 357
Bald Head Cliffs (York), 205
Baldwin, 367
Bangor, 129–38, 440; architecture, 132–33; early history, 130–31; industry, 131–32; land speculation, 132; shipping, 132; War of 1812, 131
'Bangor' (ship), 72, 132
Bangor House (Bangor), 137
Bangor Salmon Pool (Bangor), 138
Bangor Theological Seminary (Bangor), 81, 136
Bangs, John Kendrick, 99
Bapst, John, Rev., 44
Baptists, 42
Bar Harbor, 282–84, 440
Bar Mills, 340–41
Baring, 241
Barn Raising, 293
Barney's Point (Jonesport), 233
Barrel, Sally Sayward, 94–95
Barrett, Timothy, 372
Barrow, Lewis C., Gov., 321
Bartlett House (Castine), 291
Barton, Clara, 373
Baskahegan Lake, 242
Bates, Arlo, 98
Bates College (Lewiston), history, 81, 157–58; buildings, 159–62
Bates Manufacturing Company Buildings (Lewiston), 158
Bath, 215–16
Bath Iron Works (Bath), 216
Bauneg Beg Country Club (North Berwick), 338
Baxter Boulevard (Portland), 188
Beaches: *Bristol*, Pemaquid, 268; *Harpswell*, Cundy's Harbor, 258; *Jefferson*, Baptismal, 374, Crescent, 374; *Kennebunk*, Kennebunk, 253; *Old Orchard*, Old Orchard, 256; *Wells*, Wells, 206; *York*, Long, 253
Beal, Barney, 233
Beal, Harriet Blaine, 126
Beal, Manwaring, 233
Beal, Peggy, gravestone of (Jonesport), 233–34
Beals Island, 233
Bean House (Westbrook), 383
Bear Clan, 26
Bear hunting, 415, 417
Beauchamp, John, 31
Beaver colonies and dams, 305–06, 309
Beddington, 306
Belfast, 225–26
Belfast Memorial Bridge (Belfast), 227
Belgrade, 351
'Belgrade' (ship), 231
Belgrade Lakes, 351
Belgrade Lakes Region, 408
Bellamy, Samuel, 234–35
Belmont, 371
Benfield House (Belfast), 226
Benton, 320
Benton Falls, 320
Bernard, Francis, Sir, 281–82
Berwick Academy (South Berwick), 337
Berwick Sponge Cake, 338
Beryl mining, 370
Bethel, 302

Bethel Inn (Bethel), 302
Betterment Act, 41
Biard, Pierre, Father, 30, 285–86, 287
Bible Society of Maine, 84
Biddeford, 208, 254–55
Biddeford Pool (Biddeford), 254
Biddeford Saco Country Club (Biddeford), 256
Big Squaw Township (*see* Unorganized Township No. 2, Range 6)
Bigelow, 352
Bigelow Game Preserve, 352
Bingham, 333
Bingham, William, 333
Birch Harbor, 276
Birch Island, 394–95
Bird, Thomas, 173
Black Hawk Tavern (Houlton), 152
Black, John, Col., 230
Black Mansion (Ellsworth), 230
Black Point Fruit Farm (Scarboro), 210
Black Point Preserve and Game Farm (Scarboro), 210
Blackburn, Joseph, 102
Blaine, 244
Blaine House (Augusta), 126
Blaine, James G., 122, 126
Blaisdell House (Belfast), 226
Blaisdell House (Frankfort), 228
Blockhouse (Winslow), 328
Blue Hill, 287
Bluehill, 287–88
Bluehill Falls, 288
Boarding Blocks (Lewiston), 158–59
Boar's Head (Monhegan Island), 397
Bog Brook, 424
Bok, Mary Louise, 225
Bonafide Mills (Winthrop), 357
Boothbay, 266
Boothbay Harbor, 266
Boston and Maine Railroad, 71–72
Boston Watch Company (Brunswick), 139
Boulder and Tablet (Augusta), 122
Boundary Cottage, 325
Boundary line, Maine and New Hampshire (1739), 36
Bourne Mansion (Kennebunk), 207
Bowdoin Art Collection (Brunswick), 141
Bowdoin College (Brunswick), history of, 141–42; buildings, 145–48; charter of, 80
Bowdoin College Library (*see* Hubbard Hall)
Bowdoin, James, 141
Bowdoin, James, Gov., 141
Bowdoin Pines (Brunswick), 146
Boyd Lake, 315–16
Braden Monument (Presque Isle), 245
Bradford, William, Gov., 118
Bradstreet, Simon, 35
Bray, Marjory (Lady Pepperell), 249
Brewer, 229, 304
Brewer, John, Col., 229
Brewster, Ralph O., Gov., 321
Bridgewater, 244
Bridgton, 380–81, 440
Bridgton Academy (Bridgton), 380
Bridle trips: Augusta, 435–36; Bangor, 433–35; miscellaneous, 436–37
Briggs, William C., 338
Bristol, 268–70
Brooklin, 288–89

Index

Brookton, 242
Browne, Charles Farrar (see Ward, Artemus)
Browne, Richard, 270
Brownfield, 368
Brownville, 319
Brownville Junction, 319
Brunswick, 139–49; Bowdoin College, 141–42, 145–48 (see also individual entry); economic development, 140; Indians and, 140; industries, 139, 140; noted citizens, 140–41
Bryant Pond, 365
Bucknam House, Maude (Columbia Falls), 233
Bucksport, 273–74
Building of Arts (Bar Harbor), 283
Bulfinch, Charles, 132–33, 138
Bull, Dixey, 269
Bullockites, 83
Bumpus Mine (Albany), 370
Burial grounds — *Indian:* Orland, 275; Perry, 278–79; Waterville, 196; Windham, 376; Winslow, 329. *White:* Andover, 303; Augusta, 373; Bristol, 268, 269; Bucksport, 274; Falmouth, 213; Freeport, 214; Georgetown, 262; Indian Island, 296; Machias, 235; Manchester, 356; Portland, 177; Scarboro, 210; South Berwick, 338; Whitefield, 374; Waldoboro, 221; Windham, 342; Winslow, 329; York, 252
Burnell House (West Baldwin), 367
Burnham, 321
Burnham Tavern (Machias), 235
Burnt Head (Monhegan Island), 397
Burr, Aaron, 128
Burroughs, George, Rev., 172
Bus Lines, xxi
Bustin's Island, 394
Buswell, Jacob, 130
Buxton, 340–41

Cabot, John, 28
Cabot Manufacturing Company's Millyard (Brunswick), 144
Cabot, Sebastian, 28
Cadillac, de la Mothe, Sieur, 281
Cadillac Mountain Summit Road (Bar Harbor), 283
Calais, 239–41
Calendar Isles, 211
Camden, 225, 440
Camden Bowl (Camden), 225
Camden Opera House (Camden), 225
Camp Ellis, 256
Camp Etna (Etna), 298
Camp Keyes (Augusta), 129
Camp site (Ogunquit), 205
Campobello Island, 278
Canaan, 299
Candage, Otis M., 288
Canibas Indians, 192
Canoe trips: Allagash River, 419–22; East Branch, 422–24; Dead River and Moosehead Waters, 424–25; miscellaneous, 426–27; Rangeley Lakes, 426. (See also Sports, Recreation)
Cape Cottage (South Portland), 211
Cape Elizabeth, 211
Cape Neddick, 204
Cape Porpoise, 254
Capital punishment, 222

Caratunk, 333
Caratunk Falls (Solon), 333
Caribou, 245–46, 441
Caribou Stream, 246
Carlton Bridge (Bath), 216
Carmel, 298
Carnegie Science Building (see Bates College)
Carrabassett, 352
Carroll, Gladys Hasty, 100, 336
Carter House (Paris), 364
Cary, 243
Cary, Annie Louise, birthplace of (Wayne), 358
Cary, Shepard, 154
Cary, William H., 151
Cary's Mills, 154
Casco, 376–78
Casco Bay, 164, 212, 213, 386
Casco Bay Islands, 211, 386–95 (see also individual entries)
Casco Castle (South Freeport), 214
Case, Isaac, 356
Castine, 290–92; Indians in, 290; Pilgrims and, 290; Revolutionary War, 291; War of 1812, 291
Castine Expedition, 130
Caterpillar Hill (Sedgwick), 289
Cathedral of the Immaculate Conception (Portland), 176–77
Cathedral Pines (Eustis), 346
Cathedral Woods, 397
Cattle Pound (Jefferson), 374
Cave, The, 429
Center Lovell, 370
Central Maine Power Co. (Bingham), 333
Central Maine Sanatorium (Fairfield), 330
Chain of Ponds, 347–48
Chaloner Tavern (Lubec), 277
Chamberlain House (Brunswick), 148–49
Chamberlain, Joshua, Gen., 45, 148–49; house of (Brewer), 229
Chamberlain Lake Dam, 420–21
Chandler House (Brunswick), 145
Chapelle, Howard L., 231
Chaplin, Jeremiah, Rev., 194
Chapman Home (Bethel), 302
Charter of 1639, 31
Chase House (Limington), 384
Chase, Mary Ellen, 100, 287–88
Chase Sawmill (Limington), 384
Chebeague Legend, 389–90
Cherryfield, 231–32
Chesuncook Dam, 422
Chesuncook Village, 435
Chillicote House (Brewer), 229
China, 355
Chisholm, 344
Christmas Cove, 268
Church of England, 41
Church of Jesus Christ of Latter-Day Saints, 233
'Church of the Holy Ghost and Us,' 84
Churches: *Baptist:* Paris, 364; Porter, 385; Whitefield, 374. *Congregational:* Augusta, 128; Benton, 321; Brunswick, 148; Ellsworth, 230; Fryeburg, 369; Kennebunkport, 254; Kittery, 250; Portland, 189; Saco, 209; Scarboro, 210; Wells, 205. *Episcopal:* Falmouth, 231; Portland, 185; York, 204. *Presbyterian:* Walpole, 267. *Roman Catholic:*

Augusta, 128-29; Lewiston, 159; Newcastle, 220; Portland, 176-77; Whitefield, 373.
Unitarian: Kennebunk, 207; Portland, 172; Standish, 383
Churchill House (Portland) (*see* Dale House)
Cilley House (Thomaston), 222-23
Cilley, Jonathan, 222-23
Circular Depressions (Houlton), 243
Civil War, 44-45
Civil War Monument (Portland), 172
Clapboard Island, 392-93
Clapp House (Wiscasset), 218
Clark and Lake Settlement, 262
Clarke, MacDonald, 96
Clarke, Rebecca Sophia, 98
Clark's Point (Machiasport), 236
Clay Cove (Portland), 180
Clay House (Belfast), 226
Cleaveland Cabinet, The (*see* Massachusetts Hall, Brunswick)
Cleaveland, Parker, 146
Cleeve, George, 165
Cliff Island, 212, 390
Clifton, 305
Climate, xxii, 5-6
Clinton, 321
Clough, Samuel, Capt., 264-65
Clubhouse (Lucerne-in-Maine), 229
Coast Guard Stations: Biddeford, 254; Jonesport, 234; Lubec, 277; Phippsburg, 261; South Portland, 211
Coastline, 201-04
Cobb, Sylvanus, Jr., home of (Norway), 363
Cobscook Falls (North Trescott), 277
Coburn, Abner, 299
Coburn Classical Institute (Waterville), 196
Coburn Gore, Unorganized Township of, 348
Cochrane, Harry, 358
Cochranism, 83
Coe Infirmary (Brunswick), 148
Coffin, Robert P. Tristram, 99-100
Colburn House (Dresden), 350
Colburn, Reuben, Maj., 350
Colby College (Waterville): As Waterville College, 42, 81; campus and buildings, 195-96; history, 194-95; Maine Literary and Theological Institute, 81
Colcord, Lincoln, 100; home of (Searsport), 227
Cole, Charles O., 102
College of Agriculture (Orono), 297
Columbia, 232
'Columbia' (ship), 379
Columbia Falls, 232
Commerce: Colonial, 59-60; exports, 50, 56, 58; from Revolution to Civil War, 60-61; imports, 56; later, 61-62; shipping, 63, 132; types of, 61-62
Commercial Street (Portland), 180-81
Community Yacht Club (Rockland), 223
Comstock House (*see* Golden Ball)
Congregationalism, 41
Consolidated Maine Central Railroad, 71
Cony High School (Augusta), 123
Corea, 276
Corinna, 321
Cornish, 367
'Coronet' (ship), 215
Council for New England, 31 (*see also* Council for Plymouth)

Council for Plymouth, 30-31
'Country of the Pointed Firs' (book), 272
Courtship of Miles Standish, The (poem), 118
Cousin's Island, 393
Cox's Head, 260
Craigie's Tavern (Oxford), 362
Cranberry Isles, 285
Crane, John, Col., grave of (Whiting), 237
Crawford, 307
Crockertown, Unorganized Township of, 352
Crocket-Jewett-Broad House (Gorham), 342
Cromwell, Oliver, 206
Cumberland Club House (Portland), 183
Cumberland Country Courthouse (Portland), 176
Cumberland Mills, 382
Cundy's Harbor, 258
Curtis, Cyrus H. K., 176, 183; birthplace of (Portland), 183
Cushing Island, 388
Cushnoc, 123
Cusinock (*see* Cushnoc)
Cutler, 277
'Cynthia' (ship), 252

d'Abbade, Jean-Vincent (*see* de St. Castin, Baron)
d'Aubri, Nicolas (*see* Aubry, Nicolas)
da Verrazzano, Giovanni, 29
Dallas, 346
Damariscotta, 220
Dana Warp Mills (Westbrook), 383
Danforth, 242
Danforth Tavern (Norridgwock), 330
Danforth, Thomas, *34*, 35, 179
Danish Village (Scarboro), 209
Davenport Memorial Building (Bath), 216
Davis Farm, 433
Davis, Jefferson, 306
Day, Holman F., birthplace of (Augusta), 328
Day House (Woolwich), 217
Day's Ferry (Woolwich), 217
de Castin, Jean-Vincent, 25-26, 33, *290-91*, 296
de Champlain, Samuel, *29*, 136, 225, 287, 281; Journals of, 130; Monument (Mount Desert), 284
de Cheverus, Jean, Father, 220
de Grégoire Marie Thérèsa, grave of (Bar Harbor), 282
de Monts, Sieur, 29
de Poutrincourt, Baron, 29
de St. Castin, Baron, 290
Dead Man's Cove (Cousin's Island), 393
'Dead Pearl-Diver' (statue) (Portland), *103*, 183, 383
Dead River and Moosehead Waters Canoe Trip, 424-25
Dead River Region, 408
Dead Ship of Harpswell, The (poem), 97, 392
Deadman Ledge, 398
Dean Camps, 434
Deane House (Portland), 185
Dearborn, Henry, Gen., 119
Dearborn, Pamela Augusta, 119
Dedham, 229-30
Deer hunting, *415*, 417, 418
Deer Island, 289
Deer Isle, 224, 289, *399*

Index 463

Deering Mansion (Portland), 188-89
Deland, Margaret, 100
Dennison, Aaron, 139
Denny, Samuel, 262
Dennys River Fishing Trip, 410-11
Dennysville, 237-38, 411
Derby, 317
Desert of Maine, 213
Devil's Den (Turner), 343-44
Devil's Half-Acre (Bangor), 131
Devil's Staircase (Lovell), 370
Dexter, 321
Direct Primary Law, 46
District of Maine, 38, 39
District Schools (see Rural Schools)
Dixey Bull, 269
Dixfield, 301
Dixmont, 353-54
Dochet Island, 239
Dole, 325
Dole House (Portland), 184
Dole, Nathan Haskell, 98
Dorcas Society, 340
Dover-Foxcroft, 317
Dow Farm, 433
Dow Homestead (Portland), 186
Dow, Neal, 186
Dresden, 350
Dresden Mills, 350
Druillettes, Gabriel, 32, 82, 118, *331*
Dry Mills, 360
du Guast, Pierre, 29
Duck-hunting, 140, *416*, 417
Dunbar, David, 36
Dunham, Mellie, 363
Dunlap, David, 144
Dunlap, Fanny, 185
Dunlap House (Brunswick), 145
Dunlap, Robert, Gov., 144
Dunlap, Robert, Maj.-Gen., 145
Dunstan, 209
Dunton, W. Herbert, 121
Dustin, Hannah, 234
Dutch attempt at colonization, 33
Dutch explorers, 30
Dutch West Indies Company, 33
Dyer Brook, 293
Dyer House (Castine), 292

Eagle Island, 212, 390
Eagle Lake, 308
Earliest recorded Transportation, 68
Earthworks of Fort Machias (Machiasport), 236
East Boothbay, 266
East Branch Canoe Trip, 422-24
East Brownfield, 368
East Holden, 229
East Limington, 384
East Machias, 236-37
East Millinocket, 311
East Orland, 275
East Seboomook, 419
East Stoneham, 370
Easter sunrise services (Bar Harbor), 283
Eastern Maine Conference Seminary (Bucksport), 274
Eastern Music Camp (Sidney), 106
Eastern Promenade (Portland), 187

Eastman Community House (South Berwick), 337
Easton, 244
Eastport, 280
Eastport Country Club Inn (Eastport), 281
Eckstorm, Fannie Hardy, 77
Eddington, 304
Eddy, Jonathan, memorial to (Eddington), 304
Eddy, Mary Baker Glover, 221-22
Edgecomb, 264-65
Education, 42, 80-82; first real school, 80; free high school law, 80; 'moving schools,' 80; normal schools, 80; rural schools, 81; colleges, 81-82
Edwards and Walker Hardware Company Building (Portland), 172
Edwards Manufacturing Company Mill (Augusta), 126
Eliot, John, 82
Ellsworth, 230
Ellsworth City Hall (Ellsworth), 230
Elmore Neighborhood, 271
Embargo Law of 1807, 39
Emmons House (Brunswick), 144-45
'Enterprise' (ship), 177
Eric the Red, 28
Etchimins, 24, 26, 130
Etna, 298
Etnier, Stephen, 103, 104
Eustis, 346-47
Eustis Ridge, 347
Evans Notch, 302
Executive Mansion (see Blaine House)

Fairfield, 329
Falls of the Androscoggin (Brunswick), 144; (Rumford), 301
Falmouth (see Portland)
Falmouth Foreside, 213
'Falmouth Gazette' (publication), 40, 167
Falmouth Town (see Falmouth Foreside)
'Fanshawe' (novel), 97
Farming, 63-67; blueberries, 66; dairy products, 64; decrease in, 66; earliest, 63; grain production, 64; home-making type, 63; market, 66; orchard, 65; potatoes, 65, 150, 240, 245-46, 309; poultry, 66; roadside market, 65; sheep and cattle, 64; sweet corn, 65-66
Farmingdale, 327
Farmington, 300-01, 344-45
Farmington Falls, 300
Farnum, William and Dustin, birthplace of (Bucksport), 274
Farrar, Isaac, 137
Fauna, 15-19
Federal Court Building (Portland), 176
Federal Street (Brunswick), 144
Federalists, 38-39
Feke, Robert, 102
'Female Friendship' (book), 95
Female Samaritan Association of Portland, 84-85
Fern, Fanny, 96, 176; birthplace of (Portland), 176
Fernald's Point, 285
Fessenden, William Pitt, Hon., 186
Field House, Ben (Belfast), 226

464   Index

Field, Rachel, 100, 285; summer home of (Cranberry Isles), 285
Financial panic of 1835, 55
Fire of 1866, 178
Fire Law, xxii
Fire Tower (Bridgton), 381
First Civic Monument (Portland), 187
First Hotel in Maine, site of (Biddeford), 255
First naval engagement of Revolution, 38
First Parish Church (Portland), 172
First Permanent English Colony (Machias), 235
First 'radio parish,' 84
First real school, 80
First representative body in permanent settlement, 31
First Train in Augusta, 120
Fish River Region, 408-09
Fisher House (Bluehill), 287-88
Fisher, Jonathan, 287
Fishing industry: decline of, 51; early, 50; later development, 50-51; principal varieties, 50-51; (see also Industry, Commerce, Sports)
Fitch Tavern (Cornish), 367
Five Islands (Georgetown), 263
Flagstaff, 347
Flora, 12-15
Flying Place, 234
Folklore: folk dialects, 78; folk wisdom, 79; folksongs, 76-78; folktales, 78-79; folkways, 76-82; speech peculiarities, 78
Folkways (see Folklore)
Fore Street (Portland), 177-78
Forest City, Unorganized Township of, 242
Forest Station, 242
Forests: Cathedral Pines, 346; Cathedral Woods, 397; White Mountains National, 370
Forks, The, 334
Fort Fairfield, 246
Fort Gorhamtown, site of (Gorham), 341
Fort Hill, site of (Biddeford), 255
Fort House (Bristol), 269
Fort Kent, 248, 308
Fort Kent Mills, 308
Fort New Casco, site of (Portland), 212-13
Fort Noble, site of (Bath), 259
Fort Pentagoet, site of (Castine), 291
Fort Settlement (Augusta), 119
Fort St. George's, site of (St. George), 271
Fort Sullivan, site of (Eastport), 280
Fort William Henry, reproduction of Tower (Bristol), 269
Forts: *Augusta:* Western, 119, 121; *Bristol:* Charles, 269, Frederick, 269, Shurt's, 269, William Henry, 35, 269; *Brunswick:* Andros, 140, site of, 144; George, 140, site of, 144; *Castine:* George, 291, Madison, 291; *Edgecomb:* Edgecomb, 264; *Fort Kent:* Kent, 248; *Great Diamond Island:* McKinley, 389; *House Island:* Scammell, 387-88; *Kittery:* McClary, 250; *Machiasport:* Machias (O'Brien), 236; *Phippsburg:* Baldwin, 260, Popham, 261, St. George, 260; *Portland:* Loyal, 35, 179-80; *Prospect:* Knox, 227; *Scarboro:* Josselyn, 210; *South Portland:* Gorges, 211, Preble, 211, Williams, 211; *Winslow:* Halifax, 119, 192, 328-29
Fortune Rocks (Biddeford), 254
Forty-fifth Parallel of Latitude, 238

Foster's Corner, 342
Foster's Rubicon, 236
Fox-hunting, 415
Fox Island Thorofare, 399
Frankfort, 228
Franklin, Benjamin, 181-82
Fraser Paper Company, Ltd. Mills (Madawaska), 247
Free Camp Site (Alexander), 307
Free high school law, 80
Free-Soil Party, 43
Freemason's Arms (Portland), 171
Freeport, 214
French and Indian War, 1744, 36-37 (*see also* History)
French influence, 33
French Revolution, 38
Frenchville, 247-48
Friendship, 221
Frost House, Nathaniel (Kennebunk), 207
Fryeburg, 368-69, 441
Fryeburg Academy (Fryeburg), 369
Frye's Leap (Casco), 378
Fuller, Melville W., 121
Furlong, Atherton, 365

Gannett, William Howard, 121, 129
Gardiner, 326
Gardiner, Sylvester, 326, 350
Garland House (Bangor), 136
Garrick Playhouse (Kennebunkport), 254
Garrison Cove (Scarboro), 210
Garrison Hill, 154
Garrison Island, 221
Gehring, John G., 302
Gendall, Walter, 393
Geography and Topography, 3-5
Geology, 6-8; Cambrian fossils, 7; Cenozoic era, 7; Devonian period, 7; ice age, 7-8; Mesozoic era, 7; Ordovician beds, 7; Paleozoic rocks, 6-7; Pre-Cambrian rocks, 6
Georgetown, 263
German immigrants, 31
Gilead, 302
Gilman Mansion (Brunswick), 142-43
Ginn, Edwin, 274
Glassware, collection of (Friendship), 221
Glines Neighborhood, 381
Goff Hill (Auburn), 163
Gold, 11
'Gold Hunter' (ship), 132
Golden Ball (*see* Comstock House), 277
Goldwaithe House (Biddeford), 255
Good Will Farm (Fairfield), 330
Goodall Worsted Company Factory (Sanford), 339
'Goodly Heritage' (book), 287-88
Goodwin House (South Berwick), 337-38
Goodwin Ichabod, Gen., 337-38
Gorgeans (*see* York)
Gorges, Ferdinando, Sir, 31, 32, 165, 251, 260, 272, 392
Gorges, Thomas, 31, 251
Gorges, William, 31
Gorham, 341-42, 383
Gosnold, Bartholomew, 29
Gould's Academy (Bethel), 302
Gouldsboro, 231, 275-76
'Governor Ames,' (ship), 220

Index 465

Government, 48–49 (*see also* History)
Grafton Notch (Newry), 365
'Grand Design' (ship), 286
Grand Falls, 425
Grand Isle, 247
Grand Lakes and Schoodic Region, 409
Grand Trunk Railway, 71
Grand Trunk Station (Portland), 179–80
Granite Quarrying, 398
Grant, Ulysses S., 121
Gray, 342–43, 360
Great Chebeague Island, 389
Great Diamond Island, 388–89
Great Farm (Dixmont), 353–54
Great Head, 284
Great Island, 257
Great Moshier Island, 393
Great Mountain Cave (Orland), 275
Great Northern Paper Company (Pittston Farm), 324, 325
Great Northern Paper Company (Sourdnahunk Depot Camp), 314
Great Northern Paper Company Newsprint Plant (Millinocket), 311–12
'Great Patent,' 30
Green Indians, 371
Greenback Party, 45–46
Greene, 359
Green's Farm (Coplin), 346
Greenville, 322, 441
Greenville Junction, 323
Greenwood, 365
Greenwood Ice Caves (Woodstock), 365
Grindstone, 310
Grindstone Inn Golf Club (Winter Harbor), 275
Grindstone Neck, 275
Guide Service, 308, 309, 310, 322, 323
Guilford, 318
Gulf Island Dam, 359
Gulf, The, 320, 434
Gulick, Luther, 378
Guppy, Charles, 394
'Gurnet,' 258, 392

Hahn, William H., 221
Haines Landing, 349
HAJ boats, 437
Haley House (Biddeford), 255
Half Way House, 419–20
Halidon, 382
Hall, Robert B., 195
Hallowell, 52, 58, 70, 119, 327–28
Hallowell, Benjamin, 327
Hallowell Granite Quarries (Hallowell), 327–28
Hamilton House (South Berwick), 338
Hamlin, Augustus C., 21
Hamlin, Hannibal, 43, 136; birthplace of (Paris), 364; house of (Bangor), 136; Statue of (Bangor), 136
Hamlin Peak, 4
Hampden, 228, 353
Hampden Center, 353
Hampden Highlands, 228
Hancock, 231
Handicrafts: cabinet work, 112; embroideries, 110; house and furniture carving, 111; in shipping industry, 110–11; influences on, 108; metal work, 112–13; quilts, 109–110; rugs, 108–09; ship models, 111–12; weaving, 109
Hanson, Freeman, 340
Harpswell, 257–58, 394
Harpswell Neck, 390
Harpswell Sound, 391–92
Harrington, 232
Haskell Island, 390
Haskell Silk Mill (Westbrook), 383
Hathorn Hall (*see* Bates College)
Haven, 289
Hawkins House (Bridgton), 380
Hawkins, John, Sir, 29
Hawthorne House (Brunswick), 145
Hawthorne House (Casco), 377
Hawthorne, Nathaniel, 97, 103, 145, 377–78
Hayden House (Raymond), 376
Hayloft, The (Naples), 379–80
Haywood, John, Capt., grave of (Bridgton), 381
Hazzard Estate (Old Orchard Beach), 256
Hazzard Shoe Company Factory (Augusta), 126
Head Tide, 219
'Helen Eliza' (ship), 388
Hell Gate (Woolwich), 262
Hermitage, The, 434
Hermon, 298
'Herringtown,' 119
Higgins, George, 83, 298
Higginsites, 83, 298
Higginsville, 298
Highmoor Farm (Monmouth), 358–59
Highways, xxi
Hiking, 427–32; Hunt Trail, 429; miscellaneous, 431–32; Mount Blue Trail, 430–31; Saddleback Mountain Trail, 430; Squaw Mountain Trail, 430 (*see also* Recreation)
Hill, Charles, Capt., 380
Hills Beach, 255
Hilton, Winthrop, 332
Hinds House, Asher (Benton), 321
Hiram, 367–68
Hiram Falls (Baldwin), 367
History: Abolition movement, 43; as part of Massachusetts, 32, 34, 35–36, 39, 40; Canadian boundary dispute, 42; character of inhabitants, 41–42, 47; Civil War, 44–45; commerce, 40–41; early explorations, 28–30: early missions, 30, 32, 33; early territorial changes, 32–33, 34, 38; education, 42 (*see also* Education); French and Indian Wars, 34–35, 36–37; French influences, 33; Industry, 40–41; King Philip's War, 34; political parties, 36, 38–39, 42, 43, 44, 45–46; Prohibition Movement, 43–44, 45, 47; religion, 41–42, 44 (*see also* Religion); Revolution, 37–38; settlement, 31–32; War of 1812, 39–40; water power legislation, 47; World War, 46–47
Hockomock Point, 262
Hodgdon, 243
Hog Island, 387
Holden, 229
Holden House (Moose River), 334
Holiness Church, 352
Holland, John P., 364
Hollingsworth Whitney Company Mills (Winslow), 329

Hollis, 340
Hollis Center, 340
Holmes House (Alfred), 339-40
Holmes, John, 339-40
Homeland Farms (Gorham), 383
Homer, Winslow, 102
Hook Settlement, 119
Hope, 374
Hope Island, 390
Hormell, Orren C., 49
Houlton, 149-54, 243, 293; as a military post, 151; communications, 152; early grants, 151; geologic formations, 150; in the Aroostook War, 151; industries, 150
Houlton Grange (Houlton), 154
House Island, 387-88
Howard, James, Capt., 119
Howard, O. O., Gen., 45, 122
Howe's Corner, 343
Howells, William Dean, 97-98
Howland, 315
Howland, John, 118
Hubbard Hall (Brunswick), 147
Hubbard House (Hallowell), 327
Hubbard House (Paris), 364
Hubbard, John, Gov., 356
Hudson, Henry, 30
Hull's Cove, 282
Hunnewell House (Scarboro), 209
Hunt Trail, 429
Hunting (see Sports)
Hurricane Island, 398
Hurricane Sound, 398
Husbandmen, 165
Hussey's Sound, 389
Hutchinson, Anne, 205
Hyde Hall (Brunswick), 147

'Increase' (ship), 205
Indian Cellar (Buxton), 341
Indian Island, 295
Indian Lake, 237
Indian Relics, collections of: Dennysville, 238; Naples, 379; Windham, 375
Indians: as state wards, 38; Canibas tribe, 192; French relations with, 33, 130; miscellaneous references, 140, 162-63, 213; Penobscots, 192; reservations: *Indian Island*, 295; *Princeton*, 242; Revolution and, 38; settlers' attitude toward, 36; villages, 25, 384 (*see also* Abnakis, Red Paint People)
Indian's Foot (Bar Harbor), 284
Indian's Last Leap (Sanford), 339
Indiantown, Unorganized Township of, 241
Industries: Beryl mining, 370; fishing, 50-51, 280, 397, 399-400; lumbering, 54-57, 119, 121, 131, 132, 139, 293, 295, 309, 335; miscellaneous, 57-59; quarrying, 58-59, 322, 398; shipbuilding, 51-54, 63; shoe, 57, 157, 357; textile, 57-58, 121, 139, 208
Information Bureaus, xxiii
Ingram, David, 29, 270, 396
Institute de Notre Dame (Alfred), 340
International Bridge, 248
International Institute of Y.W.C.A. (Biddeford), 85
International Longfellow Society, 178
International Paper Company Plant (Livermore Falls), 344

International Plan, 279-80
Island Falls, 294
Isle Au Haut, 224, 400
Islesboro, 226
Islesford, 285

Jacataqua Oak (Augusta), 127-28
Jack-the-Ripper, 293-94
Jackman, 334
Jackson Brook Lake, 242
Jackson Memorial Laboratory (Bar Harbor), 284
James I, 30
Jameson's Tavern (Freeport), 214
Jay, 344
Jefferson, 374
Jefferson Embargo, 63
Jernegan Gold Swindle, 277
Jerusalem, Unorganized Township of, 352
Jewell Island, 212, 390
Jewett, Sarah Orne, 98, *336-37*, 338; house of (South Berwick), 336-37
'John A. Briggs' (ship), 214
Johnson, Henry, 98
Johnston House (Castine), 291
Jones, Rufus M., 355; summer home of (China), 355
Jonesboro, 234
Jonesport, 233
Jordan, Dominicus, 377
'Journal of Maine History' (book), 317
Judiciary system, 48-49

Katahdin Iron Works, 11, 319-20, 434
Katahdin Region, 408
Katahdin State Game Preserve, 312
Kavanaugh Mansion (Newcastle), 220
'Kearsarge' (ship), 249
Kebo Valley Country Club (Bar Harbor), 283
Keegan, 247
Keiff's Garden (Cliff Island), 390
Kellogg, Elijah, 98
Kenduskeag Mall (Bangor), 136
Kenduskeag Plantation, 130
Kennard Home (Windham), 375
'Kennebec' (ship), 72, 168
Kennebec Agricultural Society, 356
Kennebec County, *39*, 57, 117, 119, 300
Kennebec County Jail (Augusta), 128
Kennebec Dam (Augusta), 123
Kennebec Journal (newspaper), 122
Kennebec Journal Offices (Augusta), 122
Kennebec Patent, 118
Kennebec Purchase, 352; Proprietors, 119, 327, *373*
Kennebunk, 206-08, 253
Kennebunk Beach, 253
Kennebunkport, 253-54
Kent, Rockwell, 103-04, 397
Kent's Hill, 356
Keyes House (Fairfield), 330
Kezar Falls, 385
Kezar Falls Woolen Company Mill (Parsonsfield), 385
Kidd, William, Capt., 212, 228, *265*, 350, 395
Kidd's Cave (Squirrel Island), 395
Kimball, William, Gen., 364
Kimball, William W., Rear Admiral, 364
Kinaldo, **313**

Index 467

Kineo House (Rockwood), 324
Kineo Legend, 323
King Chapel (Brunswick), 147
King Homestead (Scarboro), 209
King House, Cyrus (Saco), 208
King House, William, site of (Kingfield), 352
King Phillip's War, 34
King, William, 42; birthplace, site of (Scarboro), 257
King William's War, 34-35
Kingfield, 352
Kingsbury Plantation, 318
Kirby, R. M., Maj., 151
Kittery, 32, 249-51
Kittery Point, 250
Kneisel, Franz, 288
Kneisel Hall (Bluehill), 288
Kneisel Quartet, 288
Know-Nothing Party, 44
Knox County Historical Society (Thomaston), 23
Knox, Henry, Gen., 222, 333
Kokadjo, 314
Koussinock (see Cushnoc)

La Farge, John, 147
La Grange, 315
Lafayette Elm (Kennebunk), 207
Lafayette House (Biddeford), 208
Lake Kezar Country Club (Lovell), 370
Lakes: Allagash, 420; Attean, 425; Auburn, 343; Carry, 243; Caucomgomoc, 420; Chamberlain 420, 423; Chesuncook, 314, 420; China, 355; Cobbosseecontee, 357; Cochran, 293; Conroy, 244; Damariscotta, 374; Eagle, 308; Echo, 285; Grand, 423; Highland, 380; Howard, 244; Kezar, 369; Leweys, 241; Lobster, 419; Long (St. Agatha), 247-48, (Naples), 378, (Standish), 384; Lower Richardson, 303-04; Maranacook, 356; Meddybemps, 238; Millinocket, 312; Mirror, 374; Moosehead, 5, 322, 411-12; Moxie, 334; Musquash, 242; Portage, 309; Portland, 244; Ragged, 422; Sebago, 376, 408; Sebasticook, 298; Spencer, 425; St. Froid, 309; Tripp, 359; Turner, 400; Umsaskis, 421; Wesserunsett, 299; West Musquash, 242; Wilson, 301
Lakeview, 434
Lakewood, 299-300
'Lamson' (ship), 53
Land policy of Massachusetts, 39
Landlocked salmon, 376
Lane's Island, 393-94
Larrabee Garrison House (Kennebunk), 207
Latter-Day Saints, Church of (Jonesport), 233
Laurel Hill (Auburn), 162-63
Lawrence Portland Cement Company Plant (Thomaston), 223
Lee, Ann, 361
Lee, Jesse, 356
Lee-Payson-Smith House (Wiscasset), 218-19
Leif the Lucky, 28
Leverett, Thomas, 31
Levett, Christopher, 164-65
Lewiston-Auburn, 155-163, 441; history, 156-57; industries, 156-57; politics, 156
Lewiston Armory (Lewiston), 162

Lewiston Bleachery and Dye Works (Lewiston), 159
Lewiston Canal (Lewiston), 158
Lewiston Falls and Dam (Lewiston), 162
Lewiston Falls Legend, 162
Liberty, 371-72
'Liberty' (ship), 240
Libraries: *Augusta:* Lithgow, 128, Maine State, 127; *Bangor:* Bangor Public, 137; *Brunswick:* Bowdoin College (Hubbard Hall), 147; *Camden:* Camden Public, 225; *East Machias:* East Machias, 237; *Ellsworth:* Public, 230; *Lewiston:* Coram (see Bates College); *Orono:* Carnegie, 297; *Paris:* Hamlin Memorial, 364; *Wiscasset:* Town, 219
Lighthouses: *Bristol:* Pemaquid, 270; *Harpswell:* Halfway Rock, 258; *Kennebunkport:* Goat Island, 254; *Lubec:* West Quoddy, 277; *Monhegan Island:* Monhegan Island, 397; *Ogunquit:* Boon Island, 205; *Owl's Head:* Owl's Head, 224; *Phippsburg:* Fort Popham, 261, Sequin Island, 261; *Rockland:* Range Beacons, 223; *South Portland:* Portland Head, 211, Two Lights, 211; *York:* Nubble, 253
Lilac Cottage (see Clapp House)
Lily Bay, 314-15
Limerick, 366
Limington, 384-85
Lincoln, 294
Lincoln County Courthouse (Wiscasset), 218
Lincoln, Enoch, 95, 127
Lincoln Home (Dennysville), 238
Lindbergh, Anne Morrow, 399
Lindsey Tavern (Wells), 206
Line Houses (Moose River), 335
'Lion, The' (locomotive), 71
Lippincott House (Columbia Falls), 233
Literature, 94-100
Lithgow House (Winslow), 328
Little Canada (Lewiston), 155-56
Little Chebeague Island, 389
Little, Clarence C., 284
Little Diamond Island, 388
Little Moshier Island, 393
Little Spencer Stream, 425
Little Wohelo (see Luther Gulick Girls' Camp)
Littlejohn Island, 393
Littleton, 234-44
Livermore, 344
Livermore Falls, 344
Lobster fishing, 397
Lobster Stream, 419
Locke's Mills, 365
Locket, Molly, grave of (Andover), 303
Log cabins (Princeton), 242
Log Village (Rangeley), 348
Long Falls, 424-25
Long Island, 389
Long Pond Dam, 425
Long Reds, 377
Longfellow Garden Society, 182
Longfellow, Henry Wadsworth, 96-97, 144-45, 148, 178, 182; birthplace of (Portland), 178-79; statue (Portland), 186
Longfellow Square (Portland), 212
Lord House (Kennebunk), 207
'Lost Paradise' (book), 257
Loud's Island, 270

Louisburg, capture of, 37
Lovejoy, Elijah Parish, 354-55; homestead (Albion), 354
Lovell, 369-70
Lovell, John H., residence of (Waldoboro), 221
Lovewell's Fight, site of (Bridgton), 381
Lovewell's War, 140
Loyalists, 36
Lubec, 277
Lucerne-in-Maine, 229-30
Ludlow, 293
Lumbering and allied industries: condition influences, 54-55; development, 55, 56; phases of economic development, 54; pulp industry, 56-57 (*see also* Industry, Commerce)
Lumberjacks, 334
Luques House (Kennebunkport), 254
Luther Gulick Girls' Camp (Casco), 378
Lynchville, 370
Lyon, Harry, Capt., 364
Lyonsden (Paris), 364

Machias, 30, 32, 38, 92, 234-36, 290
Machias River, 235
Machias Seal Island, 18
Machiasport, 71, 236
Mackworth, Arthur, 392
Mackworth Island, 392
Macleod Call Camp, 435
Macomber Playground (Augusta), 126
Macwahoc, 294
Madawaska, 247
Madawaska Training School (Fort Kent), 80
Maddocks, Luther, 266
Madison, 332
Madockowando, 25-26
Madrid, 345
'Maine' (ship), 126
Maine Administration Code of 1931, 48
Maine Agricultural Experiment Station, 297
Maine and Central Vermont Airways, 73
Maine and New Hampshire Boundary (1739), 36
Maine Central Institute (Pittsfield), 321
Maine Chance (Mount Vernon), 356-57
Maine Department of Inland Fisheries and Game, 407
Maine Forestry District, 49
Maine Garrison Houses, 87
Maine Hall (Brunswick), 146-47
Maine Historical Society (Portland), 23
Maine Hunting Laws, 418
Maine Literary and Theological Institution (Waterville) (*see* Colby College)
Maine Mineral Store (Paris), 364
Maine Music Festivals, 106, 170 (*see also* Music)
Maine Seaboard Paper Company Mill (Bucksport), 273
Maine Society of Colonial Dames, 190
Maine State Pier (Portland), 181
Maine State Planning Board, 4
Maine State Prison (Thomaston), 222
Maine State Seminary, 81
Maine Steel, Inc. (South Portland), 211
Maine Wesleyan Seminary (Readfield), 356
'Major Jack Downing Letters' (Articles), 379
Mallison Falls (South Windham), 342

'Malta War,' 120, 373
Manana Island, 396
Manchester, 355-57
Manning House (Casco), 377
Manitou Kennebec, 118
Manning, Richard, 377
Manor, The (Naples), 379
Mansion House (Poland Spring), 361-62
'Marble Faun, The' (novel), 103, 183
Marbury, Elizabeth, 356
Marbury House (Mount Vernon), 356
'Margaretta' (ship), 38, 236
Marie Antoinette House (Edgecomb), 264-65
Marie, Henrietta, 3
Marin, John, 103-04
'Mark Bachelder Tragedy' (folk song), 77
Market Square (Portland) (*see* Monument Square)
Marrett House (Standish), 383
Mars Hill, 244
Martinsville, 272
Masardis, 309
Mason House (Calais), 240
Mason, John, Capt., 31
Mason Manufacturing Company Factory (South Paris), 363-64
Masonry, 43
Massabesic (*see* Alfred)
Massachusetts, union with, 32
Massachusetts Charter of 1691, 35
Massachusetts Hall (Brunswick), 146
Masse, Ennemond, Father, 285-86
Mattawamkeag, 294
Maxim gun, 318
Maxim, Hiram, Sir, 316, 317-18
Maxim, Hudson, 316
Maxim, Isaac (*see* Maxim, Hudson)
'Maximite,' 316
Maxwell, Alexander, 252
May House (Norridgewock), 330
Mayflower Hill (Waterville), 196
McArthur House (Limington), 385
McArthur, William, Gen., 385
McCobb, James, 224-25; house of (Phippsburg), 259
McDonald Inn (Limerick), 366
McIntire Garrison House (York), 204
McKeen, Joseph, 146
Means House (Portland), 190
Mechanic Falls, 359
Meddybemps Village, 410
Medway, 310-11
Meeting-houses: *Buxton:* Tory Hill, 341; *Castine:* Old, 291; *China:* Friends, 355; *Manchester:* Methodist, 356; *New Gloucester:* Shaker, 361; *Poland:* Center, 362; *Waldoboro:* German, 221; *Winthrop:* Quaker, 357; *Wiscasset:* Alna, 91, 219; *Woolwich:* Nequasset, 217
Melcher, Samuel, 142, 145, 148
Melcher, Samuel, 3d, 140-41
Mellen-Fessenden House (Portland), 186
Memorial Hall (Brunswick), 146
Mercer, 300
Mere Point, 149
Meridian Stones (Fryeburg), 369
'Merino fever,' 64
Merrymeeting Bay, 149

Index 469

Methodist Camp Ground (Old Orchard Beach), 256
Methodists, 42
Mexico, 301
Milbridge, 231
Milford, 295
Millay, Edna St. Vincent, 99, 392; birthplace of (Rockland), 223
Miller Tavern, Joseph (Belfast), 226
Miller, William, 298
Millerites, 298
Milliken House (Portland), 185
Millinocket, 311-12
Mills, Bruce, 391
Mills, Wallace, 391
Milltown, 241
Milo, 316-17
Mineral Resources, 10-11
Minot House (Belgrade), 351
Minot, John Clair, 351
'Minstrelsy of Maine' (book), 77
Misery Gore, 323-24
Missionaries (see Religion)
Mitton, Michael, 388
Mogg Heigon Marker (Scarboro), 210
Monastery of the Precious Blood (Portland), 186
Moncacht-Apé, 263
Money Cove (Isle au Haut), 400
Money Holes (Pittston), 350
Monhegan Island, 396-97
Monhegan Island Race, 438
Monmouth, 358
Monmouth Academy (Monmouth), 358
Monmouth Town Hall (Monmouth), 358
Monson, 322
Monticello, 244
Montpelier (Thomaston), 223
Monument Square (Portland), 171-72
Moody, Samuel, 166
Moose Cave (Newry), 36
Moose hunting, 417
Moose River, 334-35
Moosehead Lake Fishing Trip, 411-12
Moosehead Lake Region, 408
Moosehorn, 348
Moro Plantation, 310
Morrill Act, 296
Morrison Heights, 358
Morton Homestead (Raymond), 376
Mosher, Thomas Bird, 100
Moulton House (Bucksport), 274
Moulton Union (Brunswick), 148
Mount Blue Trail, 430-31
Mount Desert, 284-86
Mount Desert Island, 14, 29, 30, 281-86
Mount Desert Island Biological Laboratory (Bar Harbor), 282
Mount Desert Players, 283
Mount Vernon, 356-57
Mountain climbing (see Recreation)
Mountains: Acadia, 285; Agamenticus, 205; Bag Pond, 347; Battie, 225; Baxter Peak, 429; Blue, 430; Cadillac, 4, 276, 281, 283; Coburn, 334; Great, 275; Katahdin, 4, 312-14, 429; Kineo, 4, 322-24; Lead, 306; Magurrewock, 241; Mica, 364; Mosquito, 227, 334; Old Blue, 303; Old Spec, 365; Ossipee, 366; Owl's Head, 334; Pickard, 353; Pleasant, 381; Plumbago, 303; Ragged, 374; Sabattus, 369; Saddleback, 4, 345, 384, 430; Schoodic, 276; Squaw, 430; Sugarloaf, 4; Waldo, 228
Mowatt, Henry, Capt., 166-67
Mt. Katahdin, 312-14
Mt. Katahdin Legends, 313-14
Mt. Waldo Granite Corporation Plant (Prospect), 228
Mt. Zircon Bottling Company Works (Rumford), 302
Mud Pond Carry, 422
Municipal Auditorium (Portland) (see Portland City Hall)
Murch House (Casco), 377
Muscongus Grant of 1630, 31, 41
Muscongus Patent (see Muscongus Grant)
Museums, art: *Portland:* Sweat, 104, 183
Museums, historic: *Augusta:* Fort Western, 121, State, 23, 127; *Bangor:* Bangor Historical Society, 137; *Bar Harbor:* Abbe, 23, 284; *Bath:* Davenport Memorial, 216; *Brunswick:* Pejepscot Historical, 145; *Castine:* Howard Wilson's, 23, 291; *Gorham:* Baxter, 341; *Islesford:* Sawtelle, 285; *Portland:* Maine Historical Society, 182-83; *Saco:* York Institute, 209; *Stonington:* Eastern Penobscot Archives, 400; *Waterville:* Redington, 196; *Windham:* Kennard Indian Collection, 375
Museum, industrial, *Bridgton:* Spratt-Meade, 380
Museum, marine, *Searsport:* Penobscot, 227
Museums, natural history: *Brunswick:* Searles Science Building, 148; *Fairfield:* Good Will, 330; *Lewiston:* Stanton (see Bates College); *Portland:* Natural History, 21, 172
Music: Folk music, 105-06; organizations, 106; summer camps and colonies, 107
Muskrat Settlement, 309

'N. W. P.' (defined), 31
Nahanda Legend, 339
Naples, 378-380
Narragansett No. 7 (see Gorham)
Naskeag Point (Brooklin), 288
Nasson College for Women (Sanford), 81, 339
National Arsenal, site of (Augusta), 122
National Cemetery (Augusta), 373
National Home for Disabled Volunteer Soldiers (see U.S. Veterans' Administration Facility)
Neal, John, 186
Neal Houses, John (Portland), 186
Needahbeh, Chief, 296
Neighborhood House (Mount Desert), 285
Neptune, Moses, 278-79
Nescambiou, 368
New Auburn, 155
New England Conference of Methodists, 356
'New England Rarities' (book), 210
New Gloucester, 360-61
New Hampshire, 31
New Harbor, 269-70
New Lights (see Shakers)
New Portland, 352
New Sharon, 300
New Somersetshire, 31
New Sweden, 246

470 Index

New Vineyard, 351–52
Newburgh, 353
Newburgh Center, 353
Newcastle, 219–20
Newhall, 342
Newhall, George G., 342
Newport, 298
Newry, 302, 365–66
Newry Mine, 303
Noble, Seth, Rev., 130–31
Nobleboro, 220
Nola, Charles, 279
Nonesuch River, 210–11
Nordica, Lillian, 344–45; birthplace of (Farmington), 344
Normal Schools, legislation for, 80
'Normandie' (ship), 240
Norridgewock, 300, 330
Norse navigators, 28
North Amity, 243
North Anson, 332
North Berwick, 338, 441
North Bridgton, 380
North Castine, 292
North Edgecomb, 264–65
North Harpswell, 257
North Haven, 224, 399
North Jay, 344
North Knox Fairground (Union), 374
North Limington, 384–85
North Lovell, 370
North Lubec, 277
North Lubec Canning Company Plant (Stonington), 400
North Newry, 365
North Searsmont, 371
North Star Camp (Waterboro), 366
'North to the Orient' (book), 399
North Trescott, 277
North Turner, 343
North Whitefield, 373, 436
North Windham, 375
North Yarmouth, 34, 72, 213
North Yarmouth Academy (Yarmouth), 213
Northeast Harbor, 285
Northeastern Boundary Dispute, 121
Northern Maine General Hospital (Eagle Lake), 308
Northport, 225
Norton, Lillian (*see* Nordica, Lillian)
Norumbega Parkway (Bangor), 133
Norway, 362–63
Norway Advertiser-Democrat (newspaper), 362
Notch, The, 303
Nubble Light (York Harbor), 253
Nye, 'Bill' (*see* Nye, Edgar Wilson)
Nye, Edgar Wilson, 98–99

Oak Grove Seminary (Vassalborough), 81, 328
Oak Hill, 209
Oaklands, 326–27
O'Brien, Capt., grave of (Machias), 235
Ocean Park (Old Orchard Beach), 256
Ocean Point, 266
Ogunquit, 205–06
Oilcloth manufacture, 357
Olamon, 295
Old Brick House (Gorham), 341
Old Brick House (Paris), 364

Old City Hall (Bangor), 136
Old Colonial Houses of Topsham (Houlton), 149
Old Courthouse (Castine), 292
Old Devereaux House (Castine), 292
Old Hallowell Academy (Hallowell), 327
Old Houses (Falmouth), 213
Old Iron Works (Pembroke), 238
Old Jail (Newry), 365
Old Johnson House (Belfast), 226
Old Lime Kilns (Rockport), 224
Old Orchard Beach, 256, 405
Old Peterson House (Bath), 216
Old Point (Norridgwock), 300, 330–32
Old Post Office Building (Portland), 181–82
Old Red House (*see* Hunnewell House)
Old Rock Schoolhouse (Bristol), 270
Old Shepley House (Portland), 185
Old Shoppe House (Beddington), 306
Old Stone Jail (Paris), 364
Old Town, 24, 25, 26, 295–96
Old Town Canoe Company Factory (Old Town), 295
Old Windmill (Casco), 377
Opportunity Farm (Gray), 343
Oquossoc, 349
Orient, 243
Orland, 274
Orneville, 315–16
Orono, 26, 296–97
Orono, Joseph, 26
Orr Homestead (Harpswell), 258
Orrington, 228
Orr's Island, 212, 258
Orson, Paul, 296
Ossipee River, 385
Otis House (Belfast), 226
Otter Cliff (Bar Harbor), 284
Owl's Head (Rockland), 223
Oxbow Plantation, 309–10
Oxford, 362
Oxford Paper Co. Mill (Rumford), 301

Paine, John Knowles, 178
Palermo, 372
Palestine Emigration Association, 83–84
Palmyra, 299
Panawamske Island (*see* Indian Island)
Paris, 363–65
Paris Hill, 364
Parker Head, 260
Parks: Acadia National, 282, 284, 440; Bath City, 216; Baxter State, 312; Bear Pond, 344; Belfast City, 225; Coburn, 299; Deering's Oaks, 189; Dix, 228; Fort Allen, 187; Fort Sumner, 187–88; Ganeston, 129; Grotto Cascade, 138; Island, 357; Knox State Arboretum, 222; Lincoln, 176; Narragansett, 341; Norumbega, 133; Stanwood, 300; State, 15, 127; Sunset, 243
Parlin Pond Camps, 334
Parson-Mason House (Castine), 291
Parsonsfield, 385
Parton, Sara Payson (*see* Fern, Fanny)
Partridge hunting, 417
Passamaquoddy Bay, 9, 279
Passamaquoddy Indians, 24, 26, 241–42, *278*; hunting grounds, 230, 241
Passamaquoddy Tidal Power Development

Index

Project, 9, 10, 279; model of (Quoddy Village), 279
'Patent' (ship), 72
Patent of the Plough, 165
Patten, 310
Patten, Gilbert, 321
Peabody House (Houlton), 154
Peacock Tavern (Topsham), 326
Peak's Island, 212, 388
Pearl House (Orr's Island), 258, 392
'Pearl of Orr's Island, The' (novel), 212, 392
Pearse Ennis Art School (Eastport), 280–81
Peary, Robert E., 273, 369
Peirce Memorial (Bangor), 137
Peirce, Waldo, 103
Pejepscots, 140
Pemaquid, 268–69, 270
Pemaquid Point, 270
Pembroke, 238
Pennell Institute (Gray), 343
Penny Collection of Indian Relics (*see* Museum of the Maine Historical Society)
Penobscot, 32, 33, 34, 35, 39, *289*
Penobscot Indians, 24–26, 192, 295–96, 332
Penobscot Monument (Indian Island), 296
Pentagoet (*see* Castine)
Pentagoet Indians, 26
Pepperell House (Kittery), 249–50
Pepperell House, William (Kittery), 250
Pepperell Manufacturing Company Plant (Biddeford), 208
Pepperell, William, 37, 249–50
Pequawket, 384
Pequawket Indians, 303, 384
Perio's Point (Jonesport), 233
Perkins Cove (Cape Neddick), 205
Perkins Mill (Kennebunkport), 254
Perley Pines (Naples), 379
Perry, 238
Pestumokadyik (*see* Passamaquoddies)
Pheasant hunting, 417
Phillips, 345
Phillips Academy (Andover, Mass.), 21, 22
Phillips, William, 338, 339
Phillipstown, 338
Phinney, John, Capt., 341
Phipps Point (Woolwich), 217
Phippsburg, 259–61
Phips, William, Sir, 262; home of (Woolwich), 217
Picture Rocks (*see* Clark's Point)
Pierce Place (Cornish), 367
Pierpole, 300
Pike's Hill (Norway), 363
Pilgrims, 30–31, *118*, 287
Pine, Paper, and Power, 50–62 (*see also* Industry, Commerce)
'Pine Period,' the, 131
Pine Point, 256
Piracy, 173, *234–35*, 290
Piscataqua Plantation, 249
Pittsfield, 321
Pittston, 37, 324, 350
Pittston Farm, 324
Planked trout, 410
Pleasant Lake, 294
Pleasant Point, 278
Plummer House (Scarboro), 210
Plymouth Colony, 118, 234

Plymouth Company, 30, 251
Plymouth Patent, 118, 299
Poisonous Plants, xxiii
Poland, 359, 361–62
Poland, Chief, 375, 378
Poland Spring, 361, 439
Poland Spring House (Poland Spring), 362
Polis, Joseph, 26
Political Parties (*see* by name)
Polk, James K., 123
Pond Cove (South Portland), 211
Pond Cove Village, 211
Pondicherry Mills (Bridgton), 380
Ponds: Cochnewagan, 358; Long, 425; Long (Belgrade Lakes), 351; Massacre, 210; Mattanawcook, 294; Middle Range, 362; Moose, 381; Round, 421; Round (Vinalhaven Island), 398; Saddleback, 430; Sheepscot, 372; Soldier, 308
Popham Beach, 261
Popham Colonists, 52, 55
Popham Colony, 30, 41; site of (Phippsburg), 260
Popham, George, 217, 260–61, 272
Popham, John, 217, 260–61, 272
Poplar Tavern (North Newry), 365
Port Clyde, 272
Port Royal, 29
Portage Lake, 309
Porter, 83, 385
Porter's Landing, 214
Portland, 163–90, 375; commerce, 167–71; communication, 164; cultural interest, 169–70; exploration and settlement, 164–66; great fire, 169; later history, 168–69; Revolution, 166–67
Portland Art Society, 183
Portland City Hall (Portland), 172–76
Portland Country Club (Portland), 212
Portland Hebrew School (Portland), 81
Portland Observatory (Portland), 188
Portland Society of Natural History (Portland), 15, 19
Portland Yacht Club, 438
Portsmouth Conference, 249
Portsmouth Navy Yard (Kittery), 249
Potato Growing (*see* Farming)
Potato warehouses: *Ashland*, 309; *Caribou*, 245–46; *Dyer Brook*, 293; *Houlton*, 154; *Littleton*, 243
Potter, Charles, 313
Pownalborough Courthouse (Dresden), 350
Preble, Edward, Commodore, 177
Preble, William Pitt, 184
Prentiss House (Gorham), 383
Prentiss, Seargent Smith, 383
President's House (Brunswick), 145–46
Presque Isle, 244–45, 441
Presque Isle Fairgrounds (Presque Isle), 245
Princeton, 241–42
Pring, Martin, Capt., 29
Privateering, 397 (*see also* Piracy)
Prohibition Movement, 43–44
'Proprietors of the Kennebec Purchase,' 119
Prospect, 227
Prospect Harbor, 276
Prout's Neck (Scarboro Town), 102, 210, 257
Prout's Neck Bird Sanctuary (Scarboro), 210

Index

Prout's Neck Country Golf Course (Scarboro), 210
Prout's Neck Yacht Clubhouse (Scarboro), 210
Prouty Tavern (Bucksport), 274
Province of Lygonia, 165
Province of Maine, 3, 31, 204
Public Landing (Rockland), 223
Pulpit Rock (Casco), 378
Pulsifer, Harold Trowbridge, 100
Purchase, Thomas, 140
Putnam, George Palmer, 140

Quakers, 74, 328, *355*, 357
Queen Anne's War, 36
Quoddy Village, 279
Quoddy Village Dam, 279

Rabbit hunting, 416, 417
Raccoon hunting, 415–16
Racial elements: Acadians, 74-75; Dutch, 74; English, 75; Finns, 75; French, 74; French Canadians, 75; Germans, 74–75; Icelanders, 75; Irish, 74, 75; Negroes, 75; Norwegians, 75; Scotch, 75; Swedes, 75
Radio Direction Finder Station, 276
Radio Station WCSH (Portland), 84
Ragged Island, 392
Ragged Stream, 422
Raid of 1750, 401
Railroads, xxi
Randolph, 350
Rangeley, 345–46, 348–49
Rangeley Game Preserve, 348
Rangeley Lakes Canoe Trip, 426
Rangeley Lakes Country Club (Rangeley), 349
Rangeley Lakes Region, 408
'Ranger' (ship), 52, 249
Rasle, Sebastian, 33, 80, 82, *331*; memorial to (Norridgewock), 330
Raymond, 376
Raymond Cape (Casco), 377
Raymond Fish Hatchery (Raymond), 376
Readfield, 356
Rearing Pool (Bridgton), 380
Recreation, xxii, 418–38; canoeing, 418–27; hiking and mountain climbing, 427–32; riding, 432–37; yachting, 437–38 (*see also* Sports)
Red Beach, 239
'Red Bridge' (ship), 132
'Red Jacket' (ship), 53
Red Paint People, 20–23, 324; artifacts of, 23; Beothuks, 21; implements of, 22; Red Paint cemeteries, 22
Reed House, David (Benton), 320–21
Reed, Thomas Brackett, 179; birthplace of (Portland), 179; statue of (Portland), 189
Reed, William, 288–89
Reenie, James, 392
Registry of Deeds (Fryeburg), 368
Religion, 82–85; minor sects, 83–84; missionaries, 82; social service organization, 84–85 (*see also* sects by name)
'Remember the Maine' Memorial (Bangor), 137
Republican Party, founding of, 345
Republicans, 36, 38–39
Republicans *vs.* Democrats, 378–79
Revere, Paul, 291

Revolution, *37-38*, 164, 236, 288–89, 346–47
Richards, Laura E., 98, 326
Ricker Classical Institute (Houlton), 154
Ricker, Jabez, 361
Rideout, Milner, 99
Riding (*see* Recreation)
Rigby, Alexander, Col., 165
Ripogenus Dam, 314, 422
Rivers: Allagash, 421; Androscoggin, 302, 386–87; Aroostook, 244, 246; Bear, 365; Kennebec, 117, 118, 120, 217; Little Madawaska, 246; Little Ossipee, 384; Little Wilson, 320; Moose, 425; Penobscot, 5, 295, 310; Pleasant, 320; Saco, 384; Songo, 384; St. Croix, 238–39; St. John, 5; Swift, 301
Robbinston, 238–39
Roberts, Kenneth, 100, 181, 206
Robinson, Edwin Arlington, 99, 326
Rock and Shell Formation (Casco), 377
Rockland, 50, 58, 61, *223–24*
Rockland Breakwater (Rockland), 224
Rockland Community Yacht Club, 223
Rockport, 224–25, 375
Rockwood, 324
Rome, 351
'Roosevelt' (ship), 273
Roosevelt, Franklin D., summer home of (Campobello Island), 278
Round Pond, 270
Round Pond Carry, 420
Royall Garrison House, site of (Falmouth), 213
Ruggles House (Columbia Falls), 232–33
Ruggles, Thomas, Judge, 232
Ruined House (Georgetown), 263
Rum and Water Elms (Albion), 354
Rumford, 301–02, 441
Rural Schools, 81

Sabbathday Lake Village, 360–61
Saco, 208–09, 255–56
Saco-Lowell Company Plant (Biddeford), 208
Saddle Trip Out of Augusta, 435–36
Saddle Trip Out of Bangor, 433–35
Saddleback Mountain Trail, 430
(Saint, *see also* under St.)
'Saint' Aspinquid, 205
Saint Croix Gulf Club (Calais), 239
Saint Luke's Cathedral (Portland), 185
Saint Sauveur Mountain, 285
Salisbury Cove, 282
'Sally' (ship), 264–65
Salmo Sebago (*see* Landlocked salmon)
Salmon Falls, 340
Salmon-fishing Pool (Dennysville), 237
Samoset, 269–70
Sampson, C. A. L., 110
Sandfordites, 84
Sandy Point, 273
Sanford, 338–39
Sanford Mills (Sanford), 339
Sangerville, 317–18
Sapling (*see* Unorganized Township No. 1, Range 7)
Sarampas Falls Camp Site (Eustis), 347
Sargent, Dudley Allen, 148
Sargent Gymnasium (Brunswick), 148
Sargentville, 289
Sayward House (York), 263

Index 473

Scarboro, 210, 256
Scarboro Marshes, 209
'Scarlet Letter, The' (book), 378
Schoodic Mountain, 276
Schoodic Peninsula (Winter Harbor), 276
Schoodic Point (Bar Harbor), 284
School of Fine and Applied Art (Portland), 104, 183–84
Schooner Head (Bar Harbor), 284
Scott, Winfield, Gen., 42, 121
Scottow's Hill, 209
Screw Auger Falls (Newry), 365
Seacoast Mission (Bar Harbor), 85
Seacoast Mission Ship (Jonesport), 234
Seal Harbor, 284
Searles Science Building (Brunswick), 148
Searsmont, 371
Searsport, 227
Seawall, 286
Sebago R.R. Station (Standish), 383
Sebascodegan (see Great Island)
Sebec, 317
Sebomook, 324
Sedgwick, 289
Sedgwick Town Hall (Sedgwick), 289
Settlement of Saint Sauveur, site of (Mount Desert Island), 285
Seven Pennies Shelter, 429
Sewall House (Kittery), 251
Sewall's Bridge (Kittery), 251
Seymour, Richard, Rev., 82
Shakers, 82–83, 360–61
Shell Heaps (Bluehill), 288
Shell Heaps (Damariscotta), 220
Sheridan, Phil, Gen., 121
Sherman, 310
Sherman Station, 310
Shiloh, 214–15
Shiloh Temple (Durham), 84
Ship Harbor (Southwest Harbor), 286
Shipbuilding: contract, 52; early, 51–52; period of steel ships, 53; types of construction, 52–54
Shipping, 60, 63, 132, 166–67 (see also Commerce, Industry, Shipbuilding)
Shirley, 322
Shirley Mills, 322
Shirley, William, Gov., 119
Shoe Industry (see Industry)
Shore Club (Bar Harbor), 283
Sieur de Monts Springs and Park (Bar Harbor), 284
Silver, 11
Simmons, Franklin, 103, 186
Simpson House (South Berwick), 337
Skid Hill (Naples), 379
Skowhegan, 299
Slate Quarrying (see Industry)
Small, Francis, 367
Small's Falls (Madrid), 345
Smith House (Gorham), 341
Smith House (Windham), 342
Smith, John, Capt., 30, 50, 268
Smith, Samuel E., 218–19
Smith, Samuel Francis, 195
Smith, Seba, 95, 379
Smith, Silas G., 340
Smoking Pine (Hallowell), 327
Smyrna, 293

Smyrna Mills, 293
Snow Falls (Paris), 364
Snow, Wilbert, 271
Societies, historical: Androscoggin Historical Society (Auburn), 163; Bangor Historical Society (Bangor), 137; Maine Historical Society (Portland), 182–83; Pejepscot Historical Society (Brunswick), 145
Society for the Preservation of New England Antiquities, 336–37
Society of Christian Endeavor, birthplace of (Portland), 189
Soil, 8–9
Solon, 332–33
Somersetshire (Province of Maine), 31
Somes Sound (Mount Desert), 285
Somesville (see Mount Desert)
Sons of Liberty, 252
Sortwell House (Wiscasset), 218
Sourdnahunk Depot Camp, 314
South Arm, 303–04
South Berwick, 336–38
South Bluehill, 288
South Bristol, 267–68
South Casco, 376–78
South China, 355
South Freeport, 214
South Gouldsboro, 275
South Harpswell, 257
South Hope, 374
South Paris, 363–65
South Portland, 211
South Windham, 342
South Windsor, 373
Southport, 267
Sparhawk House (Kittery), 250
'Spectator Papers' (book), 214
Spinney, Herbert L., home of (Bath), 216
Spite House (Rockport), 224–25
Spofford, Harriet Prescott, 98
Sports: Canoeing: 418–27; Fresh-water fishing: xxii, 407–12; creel limits, 409; open season, 409; Hunting: xxii, 414–18; Game areas: 417–18; Salt-water fishing: xxii, 412–14 (see also Recreation, Winter Sports)
Spouting Horn (St. George), 271–72
Sprague, John Francis, 317
Spring's Tavern (Hiram), 368
Springvale, 339
Squa Pan, 309
Squando, 208
Squaw Mountain Trail, 430
Squirrel Island, 395–96
St. Agatha, 247
St. Croix, 29
St. Croix River, 3, 5
St. David, 247
St. Francis, 248, 422
St. George, 271–72
St. John's River, 3, 5, 8
St. Joseph's Academy (Portland), 189–90
St. Louis School for Boys (Dunstan), 209
St. Pierre et St. Paul Church (Lewiston), 159
Stacyville Plantation, 310
Stair Falls, 424
Standish, 383–84
Standish, Bert L., 321
Standish, Miles, 118
Stanley, Freeland O., 359

474 Index

Stanley Steamer, 359
Staples Inn (Old Orchard Beach), 256
Starrett, Leroy S., 355; birthplace, site of (China), 355
State College of Agriculture and Mechanic Arts (Orono), 296-97
State Fish and Game Department Camp (Beddington), 306
State fish hatcheries: *Caribou*, 246; *East Orland*, 275; *Princeton*, 242; *Unorganized Township, No. 2, Range 6*, 323
State Game Preserve (*see* Ganeston Park)
State Hospital (Augusta), 122
State House (Augusta), 127
State Interdenominational Commission, 84
State name, 3
State of Maine Building (Poland Springs), 362
State Reformatory for Men (South Windham), 342
State Reformatory for Women (Skowhegan), 299
State Street (Portland), 184
State Street Hospital (Portland), 185
Steamship Lines, 73
Stella Maris Home (Biddeford), 255
Stephens, C. A., 96
Stephens High School (Rumford), 301
Stephenson Tavern (Belfast), 227
Steuben, 231
Stevens, Lillian M. N., 317
Stinson Farm House (Woolwick), 262
Stockton Springs, 227, 273
Stone and Allied Industries (*see* Industry)
Stone House (Bath), 216
Stone Quarry (Jay), 344
Stone Store (Sullivan), 231
Stoneham, 370
Stonington, 289, 399
Storer Garrison House, Joseph (Wells), 206
Storer House (Kennebunk), 206
Storer-Mussey House (Portland), 184
Stowe, Harriet Beecher, 97, 145, 148; house of (Brunswick), 145
Strong, 345
Sugar Loaves, 261, 399
Sullivan, 231
Summer Surveying School (East Machias), 237
Surry, 287
Surry Theater (Surry), 287
Swan Island, 401
Swan, James, 401
Sweat Mansion (Portland), 183-84
Sweat Museum (Portland), 104, 183
Swedish immigration, 45
Symphony House (Bangor), 137

Tarantines, 25
Tarkington Art Collection (Kennebunkport), 101, 104
Tarkington, Booth, 100
'Tarranteens' (*see* Tarantines)
Tate, George, 190; house of (Portland), 190
Taylor House (Kennebunk), 207
'Tea Party,' 252
Tefft, Charles E., 136, 137
Telos Lake Dam and Canal, 423
Tenant's Harbor, 271
Textiles (*see* Industry)
Thaxter, Celia, grave of (Kittery), 250

Theater, 105
'Thinks-I-to-Myself' (ship), 132
Thomas, Richard, grave of (Winslow), 329
Thomas, William W., Jr., 45
Thomaston, 222-23
Thoreau, Henry David, 97, 133, 312-13
Thoreau Spring, 429
Thorndike, Israel, 353-54
Thornton Academy (Saco), 209
Thornton Heights (South Portland), 211
Thunder Hole (Bar Harbor), 284
Thuya Lodge (Asticou), 284
Ticonic Falls, 197, 329
Tidal Power Development Project Model (Quoddy Village), 279
Tide Mill (Bath), 259
Tilbury Town (poem), 326
Togus (*see* U.S. Veterans' Administration Facility)
Tomah Stream, 242
Tomhegan, Unorganized Township of, 324
Topsfield, 242
Topsham, 326
Town government, 35, 49
Township No. 1, Range 7, 310
Township No. 3, Range 5, 325
Township C, 303-04
Traffic Regulations, xxi-xxii
'Tragedies of the Wilderness' (book), 401
Trans-Atlantic Radiophone Receiving Station (Houlton), 154
Trans-Atlantic Receiving Station (Houlton), 293
Transportation, 68-73; airports, 73; earliest recorded, 68; postal service, 70; railroad, 71; recent forms of, 73; stagecoach lines, 70-71; Steamboat, 72, 73, 120
Trask, Samuel, 265
Treasure hunting (Jewell Island), 212 (*see also* Kidd, William)
Treat's Island, 277-78
Tremont, 286
Trescott, 277
Triborough Bridge (Stonington), 399
Tripp Lake, 359
Trowbridge, Harold, 100
Troy, 354
True, Eliza S., 95
Tucker Castle (*see* Tucker Mansion)
Tucker Mansion (Wiscasset), 219
Tuna Fishing, 413-14
Turner, 343-44
Turner Center, 343
Twide, Richard, 270
Two Lights, 211
Two Trails, 384
Tyng, Edward, 37
Tyng, William, 37

Underwood Spring (Falmouth Foreside), 213
Union Water-Power Company (Lewiston-Auburn), 157
United Society of Believers in Christ's Second Appearing (*see* Shakers)
United States Arsenal (Augusta), 120
United States Customs and Immigration Station (Arnold Pond), 348
United States Customs Office (Moose River), 335

Index

United States Hatchery and Aquarium (Boothbay Harbor), 267
United States Immigration Station (Jackman Plantation), 334
United States Lighthouse Reservation (Rockland), 223
United States Route 1, 201
United States Veterans' Administration Facility (Augusta), 373
Unity, 354
University of Maine (Orono), 81, 296–97
Unorganized Township No. 1, Range 7, 323
Unorganized Township No. 1, Range 9, 312
Unorganized Township No. 2, Range 6, 323
Unorganized Township No. 2, Range 9, 312
Unorganized Township No. 3, Range 12, 312
Upjohn, Richard, 136, 137
Upper Gloucester, 343
Upton, 366

Vallee, Rudy, 369, 383
Valley House (Blaine), 244
Van Buren, 246–47
Vanceboro, 152
Vanderbilt, Mary S., grave of (Etna), 298
Vannah, Kate (Letitia Katherine), 326
Vassalborough, 328
Vaughan Mansion (Hallowell), 327
Veazie, 297
Veazie Banks vs. Fenno, 297
Veazie House (Bangor), 138
Veazie, Samuel, Gen., 138, 297
Verona, 273
'Village, The' (poem), 127
Vinal, Harold, 100, 398
Vinalhaven, 224, 398
Vinalhaven granite, 398
Vines, Richard, 208
'Virginia' (ship), 52, 59
von Steuben, Baron, 231

Waban Legend, 332
Wadsworth Hall (Hiram), 367–68
Wadsworth, Henry, 177
Wadsworth-Longfellow House (Portland), 182
Wadsworth, Peleg, 367
Waite, 242
Waldo-Hancock Suspension Bridge, 227, 273
Waldo Patent, 31, 220, 222, 371 (see also Muscongus Grant)
Waldo, Samuel, Gen., 31, 74, 220, 222
Waldoboro, 220
Walker Art Galley (Brunswick), 147–48
Walker, John, Capt., 29
Wallagrass, 308
Wallagrass Plantation, 308
Walpole, 267–68
Waltham Watch Company, 139
Wapsaconhagan Stream, 241
War of 1812, *39–40*, 63, 131
Ward, Artemus, 95, 299, *363*; home of (Waterford), 363
Warren, 221–22
Warren, Fiske, 382
Warren Paper Company Mills (Westbrook), 382
Washburn Family, 344
Washburn Homestead (Livermore), 344
Washington Academy (East Machias), 237

Wassataquoik Stream, 424
Wassookeag School (Dexter), 321
Watawasa, Princess, 296
Waterboro, 366
Water Carnival (Kennebunkport), 254
Waterfront (Portland), 181
Water-power legislation, 47
Water Resources, 9
Waterville, as part of Winslow, 192; education and culture, 194–95; foreign elements, 191–92; industry, 191, 194; transportation in, 194; winter sports in, 441
Waterville College (see Colby College)
Waterways, xxi
Watt's Garrison (Georgetown), 262–63
Wawenock Indians, 265
Waymouth, George, Capt., 29, 213, *271, 272*
Wayne, 358
Weary Club (Norway), 362
Webb, Nathan, 185
Webster-Ashburton Treaty, 42
Webster, Daniel, 368–69
Webster Lake Dam, 423
Wedding Cake House (Kennebunk), 207–08
Wells, 205–06
Wesley, 306
West Baldwin, 367
West Enfield, 294–95
West Gorham, 383
West Hampden, 353
West Harpswell, 257
West Outlet, 324
West Paris, 364–65
West Pembroke, 238
West Quoddy Head, 277
West Rockport, 375
Westbrook, 382–83
Westbrook Junior College for Women (Portland), 81–82
Western Promenade (Portland), 189
Western State Normal School (Gorham), 341
Western, Thomas, 119
Westford Hill (Hodgdon), 243
Weston, 243
Weston, Hannah, 234; grave of (Jonesboro), 234
Weston, John Colby, 317
Whaleboats, 393
Wheeler House (Castine), 291
Wheelwright, John, Rev., 205–06
Whidden, James, Capt., 401
Whipping Tree (Alfred), 339
White House (Belfast), 226
White Mountains National Forest, 370
Whitefield, 373–74
Whitefield Academy and Orphan Asylum (Whitefield), 374
Whitefield, George, 36
White's Bridge (Windham), 375
Whiting, 237
Whiting House (Castine), 291
Whitney Brook, 244
Whitney House (Castine), 292
Whitneyville, 234
Whittier, John Greenleaf, 97, 210, 322, 392
Wiggin, Kate Douglas, 98, 338; house of (Buxton), 340; grave of (Buxton), 341
Wilcox House (York), 252
Wild Animals, xxiii (see also Sports)
Willett, Thomas, Capt., 118

'William P. Frye' (ship), 53
Williams, Ben Ames, 100, 371
Williams House, Reuel (Augusta), 122-23
Williams, Paul, 397
Willis, Nathaniel, 95-96, 176
Willis, Nathaniel Parker, 96, 176; birthplace of (Portland), 176
Willoughby, Charles, 128
Willoughby's 'Antiquities' (book), 22
Wilson, J. Howard, 291
Wilson, Thomas, 300
Wilton, 301, 344
Windham, 342, 375-76
Windsor, 120, 373
Winn, 294
Winnecook, 321
Winnegance, 259
Winslow, 328
Winslow, Edward, Gov., 118
Winslow, John, 118, 331
Winter Carnival (Rumford), 302
Winter Harbor, 275-76
Winter, John, 52
Winter Sports: areas, 440-41; dog-sled racing, 439-40; harness racing, 439; iceboats, 439; Winter Carnival (Rumford), 302
Winterport, 228
Winterville Plantation, 309
Winthrop, 357
Winthrop Hall (Brunswick), 146
Wiscasset, 218-19
Witch's Grave (York), 252
Women's suffrage, 396
Wonsqueak Stream, 276
Wood House (Wiscasset), 218

Wood, Madam (*see* Barrel, Sally Sayward)
Woodbridge House (York), 252
Woodcock hunting, 416
Woodland, 241
Woodman, Horace, 208
Woodstock, 365
Woolwich, 217
Woolwich Drawbridge, 262
Worster House (Hallowell), 327
Wreck of the Hesperus (poem), 388
Wrights Lookout (Machiasport), 236
Wyman Dam (Bingham), 333
'Wyoming' (ship), 53

Yachting (*see* Recreation)
Yankee humor, 78
Yarmouth, 213, 393-94
York, 32, 204-05, 251-53
York Beach, 253
York Corner, 204
York Cotton Factory Company, 252
York Country Club (York), 251
York Gaol (York), 252
York Harbor, 253
York Manufacturing Company Plant (Biddeford), 208
York Town Hall (York), 252
Yorkshire, County of, 32
Young Men's Christian Association Camp (Winthrop), 357
Young People's Society of Christian Endeavor, 84
Young Women's Christian Association, International Institute of, 85
Youth's Companion (periodical), 95-96

DATE DUE

DEC 15 78			
GAYLORD			PRINTED IN U.S.A.